❖ *Feminist Legal Theory*

FOUNDATIONS

In the series

Women in the Political Economy,
edited by Ronnie J. Steinberg

Feminist Legal Theory

❖ FOUNDATIONS

Edited by

D. KELLY WEISBERG

TEMPLE UNIVERSITY PRESS

Philadelphia

Temple University Press, Philadelphia 19122
Copyright © 1993 by Temple University. All rights reserved
Published 1993
Printed in the United States of America

The paper used in this publication meets the minimum requirements of American National Standard for Information Sciences—Permanence of Paper for Printed Library Materials, ANSI Z39.48-1984 ⊚

Library of Congress Cataloging-in-Publication Data

Feminist legal theory. Foundations / edited by D. Kelly Weisberg.
    p. cm. — (Women in the political economy)
  Includes bibliographical references.
  ISBN 1-56639-028-1 (cloth). — ISBN 1-56639-029-X (paper)
  1. Sex and law. 2. Women—Legal status, laws, etc. 3. Feminist theory. 4. Feminist criticism. I. Weisberg, D. Kelly.
II. Series.
K349.F46 1993
346.01′34—dc20   92-19135
[342.6134]   CIP

To my children, Aaron and Sarah

CONTENTS

2. THE EQUALITY DEBATE: EQUAL TREATMENT VERSUS SPECIAL TREATMENT

3. NEW APPROACHES TO EQUALITY AND DIFFERENCE

6. FEMINIST LEGAL METHODS

PREFACE

This collection of essays stems from my efforts to organize class materials for a seminar in feminist legal theory. In 1988 when I began that attempt, no collection of reading materials existed. Most of the materials, consisting of law review articles, were scattered in a large number of journals. Many of the articles I wanted to assign to students as readings were extremely lengthy—some numbering fifty or more published pages including several hundred footnotes. I soon realized the enormity of the task of editing the material to a manageable size. In addition, the material needed to be organized around central topic areas into a coherent whole.

This project is the result. It is planned as two volumes: the first volume, *Feminist Legal Theory: Foundations*, exploring theoretical issues in feminist legal theory; the second volume, *Feminist Legal Theory: Applications*, exploring applications of feminist legal theory to specific substantive areas of law (e.g., criminal law, family law, employment law, and the legal profession).

The book is designed for students in law, philosophy, political science, sociology, and women's studies who wish to gain an understanding of this new field of study. It will be useful as well for scholars since it constitutes a convenient source of materials on feminist legal thought. It is also designed for the general reader who wishes to understand the nature of the field and become acquainted with the current debates characterizing it.

The book is a personal and political statement. It was conceived while I was pregnant with my second child; initiated during, and spurred on by, a controversy with my employer over a denied maternity leave; and delayed by innumerable life detours (several relocations including one abroad, two cross-country moves, and the purchase of a new house). During its almost four-year birth process, several events had a profound impact. During the spring of 1991, Professor Mary Joe Frug of New England College of the Law, a teacher and scholar of feminist legal theory, was murdered in Cambridge, Massachusetts. I knew her only for a short time while I was on leave at Boston University. Nonetheless, I was impressed by her contributions to the field and to women law teachers, touched by her warmth, and thankful for her moral support.

The year 1991 also witnessed two events that brought feminist issues to the forefront of public attention: the Clarence Thomas confirmation hearings and the William Kennedy Smith rape trial. Both events were profoundly dissatisfying to many feminists in terms of their handling of feminist concerns. These events highlight the distance we have yet to travel.

A few notes of explanation about details are in order. First, the book emphasizes the school of thought of American feminist legal theory; however, important developments have occurred in other countries, such as the Canadian Charter of Rights with its specific guarantee of equality. Despite the collection's emphasis on contributions by American scholars, it attempts to include some essays representing the points of view of scholars from other English-speaking countries (specifically, England, Canada, and Australia). Second, I selected a cut-off point of 1991 because of the need to reach closure before going to press. Since feminist legal theory is a field witnessing tremendous growth, this means that some recent works on topics relevant to this volume could not be included. Third, some excellent essays had to be left out because there simply was not room for their inclusion.

A further note as to editing and style is in order. I emphasize that the essays in this collection are edited works. If the reader wishes a more in-depth discussion, she is urged to consult the original work. Also, essays were edited with an eye toward substance and readability. Minor and obvious typographical errors have been corrected silently, that is, without the use of "[*sic*]." I edited these essays and thereby greatly shortened them; at the same time I endeavored to retain the essential points and the overall flow of arguments contained therein. Also, given the plethora of footnotes in law review articles, the number of notes had to be substantially reduced. I strove to retain, in particular, those notes containing important bibliographic references and the philosophical insights of the authors. The style of law review articles admits a wealth of information in notes. Regrettably, some of this wealth was lost in the editing process. Finally, the style of the majority of these articles is consistent with the predominant style of law reviews, although minor changes have been made for readability.

Interestingly, at the time the essays in this volume were written, the style manual for legal scholarship (*A Uniform System of Citation*) dictated that only authors' first initials be used to cite the authors of books, and neither initials nor first names be used to designate authors of articles. This practice had the unfortunate result of camouflaging female identity. In response to feminist complaints about this practice, the style manual subsequently was changed (as of the fifteenth edition published in 1991) to permit authors' full names for both books and articles. The articles in this collection, compiled before this change, reflect the earlier accepted usage. Still, the change in policy does reveal the significant feminist influence in legal scholarship in form as well as substance.

ACKNOWLEDGMENTS

MANY PEOPLE contributed to the emergence of this book. First, I would like to thank the many contributors to this volume for sharing their ideas and helping to create this important new field of study. Second, I would like to express my appreciation to Michael Ames, editor-in-chief of Temple University Press—not only for his editorial assistance but also for his foresight in perceiving the need for and value of such a book. In 1988, when the idea for this book was first conceived, many publishers were not receptive. I am also grateful for the substantive suggestions of Ronnie Steinberg, editor of the series Women in the Political Economy for Temple University Press, and especially those of the anonymous referees. Their incisive comments were invaluable in helping shape the final product.

Several students at Boston University and Hastings College of the Law provided research assistance. The work of Jennifer Garrard, Linda Kattwinkel, Alys Masek, and Marilyn Zola is gratefully acknowledged. I want to express appreciation to the students in my feminist legal theory seminar. I also wish to thank Dean Ron Cass of Boston University for providing such generous support for this project, and to the Boston Fem-Crits for providing such a fertile environment in 1990–91.

I am especially grateful to two word processors for their conscientious work on this project. Phyllis Parham at Boston University and Fran Nowve at Hastings College of the Law labored tirelessly to produce the book. Finally, my thanks to my husband George Blumenthal for his encouragement and to my children, Aaron and Sarah, for their patience in sharing my attention.

INTRODUCTION

THIS BOOK is a collection of essays on feminist legal theory. Feminist legal theory is one of the most important movements in legal scholarship today. Legal scholars first began generating a body of what has come to be called feminist legal theory or "feminist jurisprudence" in the early 1970s. The birth of this school of thought has been characterized by a rapidly burgeoning literature, which includes a number of major symposiums in legal periodicals, the creation of several law journals focusing on legal issues affecting women, as well as numerous panels and conferences on feminist legal theory.[1]

In one sense, the concern with the treatment of women by the legal system is not new. Although feminist voices existed centuries before, the "first wave" of organized feminism in the United States occurred in the mid-nineteenth century when feminists united to fight for the vote, for married women's property acts, for custody of their children, and for other legal rights.[2] The enfranchisement of women in 1920 is thought to have marked the end of this wave.

The "second wave" of American feminism was characterized by a reemergence of interest in the legal rights of women during the late 1960s and early 1970s. The rekindling of interest in women's legal rights followed on the heels of the birth of the contemporary women's movement. It was in 1963 that Betty Friedan wrote her best seller, *The Feminine Mystique*, which ignited the women's liberation movement.[3]

Several factors have contributed to the birth of this new school of jurisprudence. Ashe suggests its emergence was attributable to a natural "extension of the engagement of female reflection and speech to one more area of discourse."[4] Following the birth of the women's movement, the past two decades have yielded a large body of writing in the fields of sociology and psychology, philosophy, theology, science, and literary criticism, among others. Women's studies courses proliferated, for example, from twenty in 1969–70 to more than thirty thousand a decade ago.[5] Legal scholars were influenced, then, by the developments in other disciplines.

Kay and Littleton suggest another factor.[6] They cite as a "necessary" condition for the birth of the discipline the large numbers of women who began entering law schools in the late 1960s. They point out that these female law students questioned why the curriculum was silent on issues that mattered deeply to them as women—unequal pay and job opportunities, rape and sexual assault, battering of wives, reproduction. In response to these women's concerns, the law schools initiated in the late 1960s and early 1970s the first courses entitled "Women and the Law."[7] The first shift in nomenclature occurred in the mid-1970s when many of these law school courses were renamed "Sex-Based Discrimination." At about that same time, the first law school texts on sex discrimination appeared.[8] The change of nomenclature was significant. It represented the field's concern with new legal avenues to redress women's unequal status. Legal literature began focusing on the amelioration of the position of women by the utilization of civil rights statutes and the Constitution, especially the proposed Equal Rights Amendment, as well as the equal protection clause of the Fourteenth Amendment. Employment discrimination was a central topic of the day, following enactment of the Equal Pay Act and Title VII of the Civil Rights Act of 1964 prohibiting discrimination in employment on the basis of sex, national origin, or race.[9]

Another factor may be the fertile soil of the 1960s when many feminist legal scholars were in undergraduate or postgraduate education. These women were educated during a period of concern for civil rights characterized by efforts to broaden the legal rights of minorities generally. As Angela Miles writes, in her explanation of the origins of feminist radicals:

> Women activists learned a great deal in the sixties from the youth/student and black movements which revealed the oppression structured into North American society, demonstrated the possibility of mass resistance, gave activists important political skills and taught them the difference between liberal support of another group's struggle and working for one's own liberation.[10]

Just as the first wave of feminism grew out of the nineteenth-century abolitionist movement, the second wave grew out of the concern with the rights of Blacks in the 1960s. The women law students of those years, of course, subsequently became women lawyers. As lawyers, some of these women participated in litigation on behalf of women. Some of these litigators, in turn, became law teachers. Their interest in litigation in turn nourished their scholarship. Some of these women became early theorists in the field of feminist legal theory (e.g., Wendy Williams, Nadine Taub, Elizabeth Schneider).

In fact, much of the initial feminist legal scholarship and feminist legal theory emerged from early feminist litigators' reactions to specific legal problems.[11] Issues pertaining to employment, pregnancy, and battered women, for example, furnished fertile ground for early theoretical discussions. One central debate in feminist legal theory—the equal treatment/special treatment debate (discussed in Part 2)—emerged in relation to the specific issue of employers' treatment of pregnant women in disability schemes. Thus, feminists initially attempted to grapple with fundamental problems involved in their "doing law." Subsequently, some of these litigators, as legal academics, had the opportunity to reflect on and write about fundamental philosophical issues involved in their practice of law. This development has relevance not only as an explanation of the origins of feminist legal theory but also as an explanation of the focus of, and form of argumentation in, early feminist legal scholarship. These specific formative "jurisprudential roots" of litigative efforts also explain why some issues (such as the shortcomings of equality theory) were overlooked initially, until subsequent scholarship brought them into focus.

Menkel-Meadow suggests still another source of origin for feminist legal theory—the critical legal studies (CLS) movement.[12] She points out that some contemporary feminist legal theorists subscribed to the early principles of the critical legal studies movement in the 1970s, including the "basic critique of the inherent logic of the law, the indeterminacy and manipulability of doctrine, the role of law in legitimating particular social relations, the illegitimate hierarchies created by law and legal institutions."[13] But the women at CLS conferences were relegated continually ("ghettoized") to their own sessions. Finally, the organizers of the 1983 CLS conference arranged for a segment of that conference to focus on feminism specifically. In response to that experience, women on each coast began meeting (to form the West Coast and East Coast "Fem-Crits") to discuss issues relevant to feminism and to critical legal studies. Menkel-Meadow notes that their subsequent published feminist critiques of law and legal institutions were similar in many ways to critical legal studies approaches. And, as illustrative examples, she points to, among others, MacKinnon's comparison of sexism to classism and feminism to Marxism, Taub and Schneider's legal analysis of the divisions between the public and private spheres, and Rifkin and Polan's analysis of law as systematic oppression in its creation and support of patriarchy (all essays represented in this volume).[14]

The term "feminist jurisprudence" was first consciously applied to this school of thought in the early 1980s.[15] Courses in the field of sex-based discrimination still existed, but courses with more philosophical underpinnings were now added to the curriculum. Scholars broadened the scope of the course to an exploration of the nature of law and its theoretical foundations.

Feminist legal theorists, despite differences in schools of thought, are united in their basic belief that society is patriarchal—shaped by and dominated by men. Feminist jurisprudence, then, provides an analysis and critique of women's position in patriarchal society and examines the nature and extent of women's subordination. It explores the role of law in maintaining and perpetuating patriarchy. It also examines methods of eliminating patriarchy. Feminist legal theory essentially has two major components. The first is an exploration and critique of theoretical issues about the interaction between law and gender. The second is the application of a feminist analysis and perspective to concrete areas of law: for example, family, work, criminal law, reproductive freedom, pornography, sexual harassment, with an eye toward effectuating law reform.

Feminist legal theory has links to other schools of feminism. An understanding of the nature and underlying assumptions of these other philosophical schools is important in understanding the epistemological strand of feminist legal theory.[16] Several works in this collection explore the link of feminist legal theory to such schools as cultural feminism, liberal feminism, radical feminism, Marxist feminism, and French feminism, to name a few.

The work of feminist legal scholars reflects important differences of opinion. Divisiveness has characterized the present stage of feminism in general[17] and feminist legal theory in particular. Such divisions are apparent even in the nomenclature of the field. Some persons question the use of the title "feminist jurisprudence" as an oxymoron or "conceptual anomaly."[18] In addition, feminists debate the sources of patriarchy, which laws constitute examples of illegitimate patriarchy, as well as the best methods to establish equality for women. Some question whether equality should be the objective.[19] Feminists debate issues concerning pornography and surrogacy. Another debate concerns sex segregation in employment in the context of the *Sears* case.[20] It is a central aim of this volume to highlight the principal debates in feminist legal theory, in particular, debates about similarities and differences, about the meaning of equality and the best manner of achieving it, about gender and race. (A second volume will explore issues of criminal law, pornography, surrogacy, abortion, employment, etc.). It is hoped that this work will contribute thereby to the continued development of the field and to improving the status of women in society.

Notes

1. See, e.g., Feminism in the Law: Theory, Practice, and Criticism, 1989 U. Chi. Legal F.; Women and the Law: Goals for the 1990s, 42 Fla. L. Rev. (1990); Feminist Jurisprudence Symposium, 24 Ga. L. Rev. 759 (1990); Voices of Experience: New Responses to Gender Discourse, 24 Harv. C.R.-C.L. L. Rev. 1 (1989); Women in Legal Education—Pedagogy, Law, Theory and Practice, 38 J. Legal Educ. (1988); Symposium on Feminist Jurisprudence, 25 Tulsa L.J. 657 (1990). Recently created women's law journals include Berkeley Women's Law Journal, Hastings Women's Law Journal, UCLA Women's Law Journal, Wisconsin Women's Law Journal, Yale Journal of Law and Feminism, and the Canadian Journal of Women and the Law. Panels on feminist legal theory have been held at the annual meetings of the Law and Society Association and the Association of American Law Schools. In addition, various law schools have sponsored confer-

ences on feminist legal theory. For example, the University of Wisconsin Law School sponsored the first of several annual conferences on Feminism and Legal Theory in 1985.

2. Several excellent book-length historical accounts of this period exist. On the suffrage movement, see generally E. Flexner, Century of Struggle: The Women's Rights Movement in the United States (Atheneum, 1973); A. Kraditor, The Ideas of the Woman Suffrage Movement 1890–1920 (Anchor, 1971); W. O'Neill, A History of Feminism in America (Quadrangle Books, 1969). On the married woman's property acts, see generally N. Basch, In the Eyes of the Law: Women, Marriage and Property in Nineteenth Century New York (Cornell University Press, 1982); M. Salmon, Women and the Law of Property in Early America (University of North Carolina Press, 1986).

3. B. Friedan, The Feminine Mystique (Dell, 1963). See also G. Steinem, Outrageous Acts and Everyday Rebellions (Holt, Rinehart and Winston, 1983).

4. Ashe, Mind's Opportunity: Birthing a Poststructuralist Feminist Jurisprudence, 38 Syracuse L. Rev. 1129, 1150 (1987).

5. See Boxer, For and About Women: The Theory and Practice of Women's Studies in the United States, 7 Signs 601 (1982).

6. H. Kay and C. Littleton, Feminist Jurisprudence: What Is It? When Did It Start? Who Does It? in H. Kay ed., Sex-Based Discrimination: Text, Cases and Materials 884, 3d ed. (West, 1988).

7. In the introduction to their casebook, Barbara Babcock, Ann E. Freedman, Eleanor Holmes Norton, and Susan C. Ross point out that the first such course was taught in the fall of 1969 at New York University Law School with Susan Ross as one of the initiators. Students at Yale, including Ann Freedman, learned about the N.Y.U. course, taught it themselves in 1970 and 1971, and then prevailed upon the faculty to hire Barbara Babcock to teach the course. She and Ann Freedman then taught the course together at Georgetown in 1971. B. Babcock, A. Freedman, E. Norton, & S. Ross, Sex Discrimination and the Law: Causes and Remedies v (Little, Brown, 1973). Clare Dalton, in her essay in this Part, notes that Ruth Bader Ginsburg and Herma Hill Kay also taught early courses in 1970 and 1971 respectively.

8. Babcock et al., Sex Discrimination and the Law, *supra* note 7; L. Kanowitz, Sex Roles in Law and Society: Cases and Materials (University of New Mexico Press, 1973); K. Davidson & H. Kay, Text, Cases and Materials on Sex-Based Discrimination (West, 1974) (now H. Kay, Cases and Materials on Sex-Based Discrimination, 3d ed. (West, 1988).

9. Civil Rights Act of 1964, tit. VII, 42 U.S.C. §§ 2000e–17 (1982).

10. A. Miles, Feminist Radicalism in the 1980's (Culture Texts, 1985), at 3.

11. Although for some feminist theorists, their role as litigators preceded their academic career, the converse is also true. Some legal academics (Ruth Bader Ginsburg, for example) participated in litigation on behalf of women after entering academia. The interrelationship between feminist litigation and feminist scholarship is discussed in Elizabeth Schneider's essay in Part 5 of this volume. For further discussion of early feminist litigation, see generally Cole, Strategies of Difference: Litigating for Women's Rights in a Man's World, 2 Law & Ineq. J. 33 (1984); Cowan, Women's Rights Through Litigation: An Examination of the

American Civil Liberties Union Women's Rights Project, 1971–1976, 8 Colum. Hum. Rts. L. Rev. 373 (1976); Williams, Notes from a First Generation, 1989 U. Chi. Legal F. 99.

12. Menkel-Meadow, Feminist Legal Theory, Critical Legal Studies, and Legal Education or, 'The Fem Crits Go to Law School,' 38 J. Legal Educ. 61 (1988). On the similarities and differences between feminist legal theory and critical legal studies, see also Rhode, Feminist Critical Theory, 42 Stan. L. Rev. 617 (1990); West, Deconstructing the CLS-Fem Split, 2 Wis. Women's L.J. 85 (1986); and Part 5 this volume.

13. Menkel-Meadow, Feminist Legal Theory, *supra* note 12, at 63.

14. *Id.*, at 64.

15. For early usage of the term, see MacKinnon, Feminism, Marxism, Method and the State: Toward Feminist Jurisprudence, Part 5 this volume (which originally appeared in 1983), and Scales, Towards a Feminist Jurisprudence, 56 Ind. L.J. 35 (1981).

16. For further discussion of the various strands of feminist theory, see J. Donovan, Feminist Theory: The Intellectual Traditions of American Feminism (Frederick Ungar, 1990); A. Jaggar, Feminist Politics and Human Nature (Rowman & Allanheld, 1983).

17. See, e.g., M. Hirsch & E. Keller, Conflicts in Feminism (Routledge, 1990).

18. West, Jurisprudence and Gender, Part 1 this volume; Dalton, Where We Stand, Part 1 this volume.

19. See, e.g., Cain, Feminism and the Limits of Equality, Part 3 this volume, citing the works of Robin West, Ruth Colker, and Drucilla Cornell as steering away from the equality debate and focusing more directly on the question of self-definition.

20. EEOC v. Sears, Roebuck & Co., 628 F. Supp. 1264 (N.D. Ill. 1986), *aff'd*, 839 F.2d 302 (7th Cir. 1988) (holding that women's low representation in high-paying commission sales positions resulted not from discrimination by Sears but rather from women's lack of interest in commission sales).

❖ PART 1

The Elements of
Feminist Legal Theory

❖ *Introduction*

THIS BOOK OPENS with an introductory Part exposing the reader to central ideas of feminist legal theory. The first essay, by Nadine Taub and Elizabeth Schneider, "Perspectives on Women's Subordination and the Role of Law," explores the public–private distinction. The dichotomy between the public and private is central to feminist writing in general and to feminist legal theory as well. In fact, one author has suggested that this dichotomy is "what the feminist movement is about."[1]

Historically, only men had access to the public sphere of work, politics, and civil society. Women were relegated to the private sphere of home and family with its lack of potential for achievement in the public world. The public–private dichotomy is instilled in the public consciousness and informs our visions for the future. Although today women have legal access to the public realm, they remain subordinate to men in society. A prominent theme in feminist literature is the analysis of the public–private distinction to explore why, despite gains in formal equality, women are still denied full participation in society.[2]

Taub and Schneider examine the manner in which law explicitly has excluded women from the public sphere of politics and the economy. They point to the role of law, which by its absence and unwillingness to regulate the domestic sphere, implicitly has ensured constraints that have relegated women to the private sphere. In this manner law plays a powerful role in shaping and maintaining women's subordination.

After exploring these roles of the law, the authors next examine the manner in which law has legitimated sex discrimination by the articulation of ideologies of sexual inequality that justify differential treatment. They trace the development of these ideologies from, first, the early separate spheres doctrine (that women occupied a separate sphere of home and family) of Bradwell v. Illinois,[3] to Muller v. Oregon[4] (grounding the separate spheres ideology in physical fact), to the new ideological approach of the "unequal" equal protection doctrine that permits differential treatment when men and women are not similarly situated. Since pregnancy and socially imposed differences will always prevent women from being

3

similarly situated to men, this approach legitimizes discrimination through the language of equality.

Taub and Schneider conclude by pointing to some progress in the changes in ideological approaches to sexual inequality. Yet they warn of the emergence of a more subtle view of differences that, while holding out "the promise of liberation," in fact "is more dangerous precisely because it appears so reasonable."

Heather Wishik, "To Question Everything," picks up from Taub and Schneider the kinds of challenges women pose to law when asking the "woman question," a methodological technique of exploring feminist concerns. In her essay, Wishik explores the development and scope of feminist jurisprudential inquiry and raises its methodological implications. Wishik begins by describing feminist jurisprudential inquiry as a process of "seeking, describing, and analyzing the 'harms' of patriarchal law." Nevertheless, she emphasizes that feminist legal theory is a form of political practice as well as theory making, and as such it must go beyond mere description to strategize for creation of a nonpatriarchal legal system.

After a brief mention of the links of feminist legal theory to other strands of legal scholarship (which links are explored in more detail by authors in this and subsequent chapters), Wishik traces and criticizes the development of feminist legal inquiry as a form of legal scholarship. The early approach of the field, similar to that of other early feminist scholars, she points out, was the "add and stir" approach that highlights the omission of women. The next step adds a missing dimension by exploring underlying patriarchal assumptions of the law. The third step seeks to solicit critical information on the woman's perspective with an eye toward the addition of this perspective. The final step, moving on to another dimension, conceptualizes a feminist method with which to understand and examine law.

In the conceptualization of feminist method, Wishik frames essential inquiries feminists must pose about the relationship between law and society. Four of these inquiries she identifies and terms "fairly universal" in current feminist jurisprudence. She then reiterates her point that feminist legal theory must envision new alternatives. In an especially provocative part of her article, she questions how we get there from here. She urges constantly keeping an eye toward the kind of world we are trying to create and questioning everything so that we can better create the future we want.

Clare Dalton's "Where We Stand: Observations on the Situation of Feminist Legal Thought" shares several similar observations on feminist legal theory. Like Wishik, Dalton points out aspects of feminist legal theory that are true of feminism in general: its descriptive aspect exploring the nature and extent of women's subordination, analytic aspect (how women continue to be subordinated), and reformative aspect dedicated to change. She also points to the salient feature of feminist legal theory of the interconnection of theory and practice. Dalton then traces the development of feminist legal theory from its roots in the women's movement. She explores its origins in the context of legal education in the late 1970s.

Dalton goes beyond Wishik's concern with feminist methods of inquiry by the introduction of a conceptualization of feminist as "a post-modern project." By this she means that the discipline is one of multiplying challenges to ideas of the Enlightenment—that knowledge can be objective, for example, or that certain ahistorical universal human needs can be identified that justify social and political structures. She then points to positive and negative "obligation" stemming from this conceptualization. She cautions feminist theory against attempting to replace or displace grand male theories by excluding the perspectives of minority or other disadvantaged groups. Another important obligation she discusses concerns feminist legal theory's challenge to essentialism—the idea that there are universal and ahistorical truths about the nature of woman (a point that is taken up in considerably more detail in Part 4). She points to the risks and dangers of this challenge—that in reaction against essentialism, we risk creating new essentialism, that is, asserting new oppressive truths about woman's nature.

Dalton notes difficulties with the term "feminist jurisprudence" as a contradiction in terms. Specifically, she stresses that feminist epistemology is at odds with underlying premises of the Enlightenment and traditional jurisprudence. She urges that we go "beyond" feminist jurisprudence in our challenge to legal institutions and the structure of legal thought and create new scholarship and new visions and mirror new relationships.

Another introduction to feminist legal theory is provided by Leslie Bender in "A Lawyer's Primer on Feminist Theory and Tort." In this "primer" Bender also presents an overview to some of the major components of feminism—its integration of practice and theory and its efforts to describe and expose patriarchy in hopes of constructing a world in which every individual is empowered. Bender's discussion of feminism mentions that there are many feminisms—"[f]eminists do not all think the same way or even about the same kinds of problems." She thereby points to the diversity of viewpoints inherent in feminism in general and feminist legal theory in particular.

Bender, similar to the preceding scholars, recognizes that law is a potent force in perpetuating patriarchy. She urges that feminism and its method of consciousness raising design a legal system that emphasizes legal concerns. Unlike the preceding authors, however, she offers concrete suggestions for the accomplishment of this objective. Specifically, she inquires how tort analysis serves to perpetuate existing power hierarchies and offers suggestions as to how tort law might be improved.[5] In her analysis, Bender emphasizes the "different voice" approach of Carol Gilligan. Gilligan's work has tremendous importance for feminist legal theory and is cited frequently in feminist legal theorists' work. Bender first explains Gilligan's contribution to feminist scholarship with its suggestion that women's moral development reflects a focus on responsibility, contextuality, and caring, as opposed to men's, which relies more on rights and abstract justice. Then, Bender applies Gilligan's theory in her analysis of tort law—specifically the use of the standard of care of "the reasonable man" and the no-duty-to-rescue (a stranger) cases. She concludes by emphasizing that a feminist focus on caring, context, and interconnectedness are central to a new vision of the legal system.

Ann Scales, "The Emergence of Feminist Jurisprudence: An Essay," provides an example of the "epistemological critique" strand of feminist jurisprudence. Her point of departure is a conceptualization of feminism as a critique of objectivity in epistemological, psychological, social, and legal terms. The underlying problem, according to Scales, is the objectification of women—the "tyranny of objectivity." Feminism is premised on the principle that objective reality is a myth and patriarchal myths are projections of the male psyche.

Scales criticizes the Supreme Court's equal protection approach to sex discrimination as a representative of "abstract universality" that makes maleness the norm of what is human—all in the name of neutrality. She then turns to the task of restructuring the legal system. Similar to Bender, Scales also points to the importance of Gilligan's work, although Scales focuses more on the dangers of generalizations drawn from Gilligan's work. Scales is quite critical of the view that a "care-based" and "rights-based" view can be blended. Those who advocate a legal system incorporating rights, rules, relationships, and equity (what Scales terms the "incorporationist" view) suffer from a lack of vision, she chastises, in presuming that inequality is a legal mistake that can be repaired by bringing to light examples of irrationality. "The injustice of sexism is not irrationality; it is domination." Therefore, she concludes the law must embrace a version of equality that focuses on "real" issues, in particular domination, disadvantage, and disempowerment, instead of on issues of differences between the sexes.

Robin West, "Jurisprudence and Gender," constitutes an important piece of scholarship in terms of her analysis of modern legal theory. Her scholarship effectuates a "paradigm shift" in terms of enabling the reader to view fundamental beliefs from a new perspective.[6] Her thesis is that the theoretical underpinning of modern legal theory (in which she includes both liberal legalism and critical legal theory), that human beings are definitionally distinct from one another, is inapplicable to women because it is a masculine conceptualization. In fact, instead of being separate from other human beings, she argues that women are connected to human beings in terms of, for example, their life experiences of pregnancy and breast feeding. She contrasts the idea of the human being as constructed by (non-legal) feminist theory with the idea of the human being as constructed by (masculine) jurisprudence. She then proceeds to explain how this conceptualization presents obstacles for the development of feminist legal theory. She argues that the gap between legal theory's description of human nature and women's true nature presents not only a conceptual obstacle to the emergence of feminist legal theory but also serves as an obstacle to the abolition of patriarchy.

Richard Posner's "Conservative Feminism" presents a viewpoint that is certain to fuel the debates that characterize feminism. His point of departure is that, normally, conservatism is thought to imply a rejection of feminism. Posner admits this to be true; however, he argues that this viewpoint is not true of all conservatives. He describes a branch of feminism that he defines as "conservative feminism"—those who adhere to "the idea that women are entitled to political, legal, social, and economic equality to men, in the framework of a lightly regulated market economy." He argues that this approach, which he favors, has implications for many areas of the law and proceeds to suggest several controversial applications (e.g., in the areas of taxing housewives' imputed earnings, comparable worth, surrogacy, rape, and pornography).[7]

To take one example, Posner's suggestion that housewives' imputed earnings should be taxed is highly debatable. Despite the (in one sense) absurdity of his conclusion, his proposal has roots in the Marxist feminist debate concerning arguments for waged housework. That is, some Marxist feminists argue that women's domestic work is productive work for which the state should pay wages to housewives because capital ultimately profits from women's exploitation.[8] In contrast, other Marxist feminists reason that the provision of wages for housework is neither feasible nor desirable as a liberatory strategy for women.[9] If the former view were adopted and the state were to pay wages for housework, then Posner's radical view has at least some logical basis.

In the course of explicating his thesis, Posner questions the idea of differences between men's and women's thought processes. He also critiques the views of other contributors to Part 1 (Bender and West, for example). He concludes by urging that conservative feminism deserves greater attention for its highlighting of possible indirect effects of policies that ostensibly favor women. Posner's essay appropriately closes this introductory part and provides a transition to the remainder of the collection because it illuminates some of the many controversial issues that currently define feminist legal theory.

Notes

1. C. Pateman, Feminist Critique of the Public/Private Dichotomy, in A. Phillips, ed., Feminism and Equality 103–26 (New York University Press, 1987), at 103.

2. See generally J. Elshtain, Public Man, Private Woman: Women in Social and Political Thought (Princeton University Press, 1981); Z. Eisenstein, The Radical Future of Liberal Feminism (Longman, 1981); Elshtain, Moral Woman and Immoral Man: An Examination of the Public–Private Split and Its Political Ramifications, 4 Politics and Society (1974); Pateman, Feminist Critique of Public/Private Dichotomy, *supra* note 1; Olsen, The Family and the Market: A Study of Ideology and Reform, 96 Harv. L. Rev. 1497 (1983).

3. 83 U.S. (16 Wall.) 130 (1873).

4. 208 U.S. 412 (1908).

5. See also her subsequent work: Bender, Changing the Values in Tort Law, 25 Tulsa L.J. 759 (1990).

6. The term was made famous by T. Kuhn, The Structure of Scientific Revolutions (University of Chicago Press, 1970).

7. See Lacey, Introducing Feminist Jurisprudence: An Analysis of Oklahoma's Seduction Statute, 25 Tulsa L.J. 775, 779 n. 15 (1990) for an interesting discussion of Posner's inconsistency in regard to his treatment of issues affecting women, specifically his difficulty in characterizing economic analysis as resolving the issue of abortion compared to his willingness to view such analysis as capable of resolving other issues in the law.

8. M. Dalla Costa & S. James, Women and the Subversion of the Community, in M. Dalla Costa & S. James, The Power of Women and the Subversion of Community (Falling Wall Press, 1972).

9. See, for example, B. Bergmann, The Economic Emergence of Women (Basic Books, 1986). See also R. Tong, Feminist Thought: A Comprehensive introduction (Westview Press, 1989), especially chap. 2, "Marxist Feminism," for a discussion of the wages-for-housework debate.

❖ Women's Subordination and the Role of Law

Nadine Taub and Elizabeth M. Schneider

THE ANGLO-AMERICAN legal tradition purports to value equality, by which it means, at a minimum, equal application of the law to all persons. Nevertheless, throughout this country's history, women have been denied the most basic rights of citizenship, allowed only limited participation in the marketplace, and otherwise denied access to power, dignity, and respect. Women have instead been largely occupied with providing the personal and household services necessary to sustain family life. . . .

This essay explores two aspects of the law's role in maintaining women in an inferior status. It first considers the way the law has furthered male dominance by explicitly excluding women from the public sphere and by refusing to regulate the domestic sphere to which they are thus confined. It then examines the way the law has legitimized sex discrimination through the articulation of an ideology that justifies differential treatment on the basis of perceived differences between men and women.

The Legal Order and the Public/Private Split

Excluded in the past from the public sphere of marketplace and government, women have been consigned to a private realm to carry on their primary responsibilities, i.e., bearing and rearing children, and providing men with a refuge from the pressures of the capitalist world. This separation of society into the male public sphere and the female private sphere was most pronounced during the nineteenth century. . . .

Men dominate both the public sphere and the private sphere. Male control in the public sphere has often been consolidated explicitly by legal means. The law, however, is in large part absent from the private sphere, and that absence itself has contributed to male dominance and female subservience. . . .

Legal Exclusion from the Public Sphere

The most obvious exclusion of women from public life was the denial of the franchise. . . . This initial exclusion gained even greater significance in the 1820s and 1830s, when the franchise was extended to virtually every white male regardless of property holdings. Even after the Civil War, when black men gained the right to vote, women of all races continued to be denied the ballot. The Nineteenth Amendment, giving women the vote, finally became law in 1920 after what has been described as "a century of struggle."[1]

The amendment's passage, however, did not mean that women were automatically accorded the rights and duties that generally accompanied elector status. For example, the exclusion of women from jury duty was upheld as late as 1961. . . .[2]

Even today, women are excluded from what is viewed as a crucial test of citizenship—armed combat duty.[3] . . .

Women have likewise been excluded from full participation in the economy. Under English common law, not only were they barred from certain professions (such as law), but, once married, they were reduced to legal nonentities unable to sell, sue, or contract without the approval of their husbands or other male relatives.[4]

Although these disabilities were initially rigidified by codification of laws, which began in the 1820s, they were gradually lifted in the middle and latter part of the nineteenth century. Starting in the 1840s, various states passed laws that gave women the right to hold certain property in their own name. Subsequent legislation, enacted over the following half-century, afforded them the right to conduct business and retain their own earnings. The enactments were, however, repeatedly subjected to restrictive judicial interpretations that continued to confirm male dominance in business matters.

Even as women moved into the paid labor force, they were limited in their work opportunities and earning power by the ideological glorification of their domestic role reflected in the law. Women have been consistently excluded from certain occupational choices and denied equal earning power by statute and other governmental action. Such explicit exclusions persist today despite the promise of equal treatment contained in the Fourteenth Amendment and affirmative anti-discrimination legislation enacted in the 1960s and 1970s.[5] For example, in 1977 the Supreme Court found it legal to deny women jobs as guards in maximum-security prisons on the ground that the very presence of women would prompt sexual assaults.[6] In so holding, the Court simply ignored the fact that all guards are subject to assault by virtue of being guards. . . . Post–New Deal social welfare legislation has likewise imposed barriers to women's participation in the public sphere. Reflecting and reinforcing the assumption that men are breadwinners and women are homemakers, Social Security legislation has denied female workers fringe benefits available to male workers.[7] . . .

Legislation denying women the right to determine whether and when they will bear children has also served to exclude women from the public sphere. Beginning in the 1870s, legislative restrictions began to reinforce and supplement existing religious and cultural constraints on birth control. The Comstock Law forbidding obscene material (expressly including contraceptive devices) in the United States mail was invalidated in 1938,[8] while the Supreme Court did not invalidate state restrictions on the marital use of contraceptives until 1965[9] and their distribution to single persons until 1972.[10] Similarly, in the middle and late nineteenth century, most states enacted criminal statutes against abortion, although the procedure, at least in the pre-"quickening" stage, had not been a crime at the common law.[11] While a number of these statutes were liberalized in the 1960s, criminal sanctions remained in force until they were invalidated by the 1973 Supreme Court decisions.[12] Since then, provisions have been upheld that exclude abortion from Medicaid coverage and require the parents of many minors to be notified.[13] And in 1989, the Supreme Court once again signaled to the states that they would uphold restrictions on abortion.[14]

Many nongovernmental practices also help to exclude women from the public sphere. Commercial concerns have refused women credit and work; trade unions and professional associations have excluded women from skilled employment; public accommodations and business clubs have denied women entrance. . . . [I]n distinguishing only between governmental and nongovernmental agencies, and ignoring distinctions based on power, the law has tolerated and tacitly approved discriminatory conduct by a variety of powerful institutions.

The Absence of Law in the Private Sphere

While sex-based exclusionary laws have joined with other institutional and ideological constraints to directly limit women's participation in the public sphere, the legal order has operated more subtly in relation to the private sphere to which women have been relegated. On the one hand, the legal constraints against women retaining their earnings and conveying property—whose remnants endured well into the twentieth century—meant that married women could have legal relations with the outside world only through their husbands. In this sense, the law may be viewed as directing male domination in the private sphere. On the other hand, the law has been conspicuously absent from the private sphere itself. . . . [T]he law generally refuses to interfere in ongoing family relationships. For example, the essence of the marital relation as a legal matter is the exchange of the man's obligation to support the women for her household and sexual services. Yet contract law, which purports to enforce promissory obligations between individuals, is not available during the marriage to enforce either the underlying support obligation or other agreements by the parties to a marriage to matters not involving property. A woman whose husband squanders or gives away assets during the marriage cannot even get an accounting. And while premarital property agreements will be enforced on divorce, courts' enormous discretion in awarding support and distributing property makes it highly unlikely that these decisions will reflect the parties' conduct during the marriage in regard to either the underlying support obligation or other agreements. It is as if in regulating the beginning and the end of a business partnership the law disregarded the events that transpired during the partnership and refused to enforce any agreements between the partners as to how they would behave.

Similarly, tort law, which is generally concerned with injuries inflicted on individuals, has traditionally been held inapplicable to injuries inflicted by one family member on another. Under the doctrines of interspousal and parent-child immunity, courts have consistently refused to allow recoveries for injuries that would be compensable but for the fact that they occurred in the private realm. In the same way, criminal law declined to punish intentional injuries to family members. Common law and statutory definitions of rape in many states continue to carve out a special exception for a husband's forced intercourse with his wife. Wife beating was initially omitted from the definition of criminal assault on the ground that a husband had the right to chastise his wife. Even today, after courts have explicitly rejected the definitional exception and its rationale, judges, prosecutors, and police officers decline to enforce assault laws in the family context. . . .

The state's failure to regulate the domestic sphere is now often justified on the ground that the law should not interfere with emotional relationships involved in the family realm because it is too heavy-handed. Indeed, the recognition of a familial privacy right in the early twentieth century has given this rationale a constitutional dimension. The importance of this concern, however, is undercut by the fact that the same result was previously justified by legal fictions, such as the woman's civil death on marriage. More importantly, the argument misconstrues the point at which the law is invoked. Legal relief is sought when family harmony has already been disrupted. Family members, like business associates, can be expected to forgo legal claims until they are convinced that harmonious relations are no longer possible. Equally important, the argument reflects and reinforces powerfully myths about the nature of family relations. It is not true that women perform personal and household services purely for love. The family is the locus of fundamental economic exchanges, as well as important emotional ties.

Isolating women in a sphere divorced from the legal order contributes directly to their inferior status by denying them the legal relief that they seek to improve their situations and by sanctioning conduct of the men who control their lives. For example, when the police do not respond to a battered woman's call for assistance or when a civil court refuses to evict her husband, the woman is relegated to self-help, while the man who beats her receives the law's tacit encouragement. When the law does not allow for wage attachments or other standard collection devices to be used to enforce orders for child support, it leaves women in desperate financial straits.

But beyond its direct, instrumental impact, the insulation of women's world from the legal order also conveys an important ideological message to the rest of society. . . . [T]he law's absence devalues women and their functions: women simply are not sufficiently important to merit legal regulation. . . . By declining to punish a man for inflicting injuries on his wife, for example, the law implies she is his property and he is free to control her as he sees fit. Women's work is discredited when the law refuses to enforce the man's obligation to support his wife, since it implies she makes no contribution worthy of support. . . . These are important messages, for denying woman's humanity and the value of her traditional work are key ideological components in maintaining woman's subordinate status. . . .

Finally, isolating women in a world where the law refuses to intrude further obscures the discrepancy between women's actual situation and our nominal commitment to equality. Like other collective ideals, the equality norm is expressed predominantly in legal form. Because the law as a whole is removed from women's world, the equality norm is perceived as having very limited application to women. . . .

In short, the law plays a powerful role, though certainly not an exclusive role, in shaping and maintaining women's subordination. The law has operated directly and explicitly to prevent women from attaining self-support and influence in the public sphere, thereby reinforcing their dependence on men. At the same time, its continued absence from the private sphere to which women are relegated not only leaves individual women without formal remedies but also devalues and discredits them as a group. . . .

The Legal Ideology of Sexual Inequality

. . . The law has also perpetuated inequality through the articulation of an ideology that camouflages the fundamental injustice of existing sexual relations. . . . Historically, women's subservient status has been associated with a view of differences between the sexes and differential legal treatment. A succession of Supreme Court decisions has legitimized that subservient status by upholding laws which, on their face, mandate that the sexes be treated differently. This section examines the principal doctrinal bases used by the Court by focusing on three illustrative Supreme Court decisions. . . .

Women's "Separate Sphere": Bradwell v. Illinois

In Bradwell v. Illinois,[15] the Supreme Court upheld the Illinois Supreme Court's decision to refuse Myra Bradwell admission to the Illinois bar because she was a woman. She studied law under her husband's tutelage; raised four children; ran a private school; was involved in civic work; and founded a weekly newspaper, the *Chicago Legal News*, which became an important legal publication. A feminist active in women's suffrage organizations, Myra Bradwell played an important role in obtaining Illinois legislation that removed women's legal disabilities. She took her case to the Supreme Court, arguing that admission to practice law was guaranteed by the privileges and immunities clause of the recently adopted Fourteenth Amendment.

The *Bradwell* litigation took place within the context of a particular conception of sex roles. Although women were in no way the equals of men during the colonial and Revolutionary periods, the nature of their subordination, particularly in the middle classes, changed dramatically between the end of the eighteenth century and the middle of the nineteenth century. The early stages of industrial capitalism involved increasing specialization and the movement of production out of the home, which resulted in heightened sex segregation. Men went out of the house to work; and women's work, influence, and consciousness remained focused at home. . . . [Women] came to occupy [a] "separate sphere," a qualitatively different world centered on home and family. Women's role was by definition incompatible with full participation in society.

"Separate-sphere" ideology clearly delineated the activities open to women. . . . [W]omen's limited participation in paid labor outside the home was most often in work that could be considered an extension of their work within the home. For example, native-born mill girls in the 1820s and 1830s, and immigrant women in the 1840s and 1850s, worked in largely sex-segregated factories manufacturing textiles, clothing, and shoes. Likewise, after a period of time, teaching became a woman's occupation. . . . [T]he law appears to have contributed significantly to the perpetuation of this ideology. Immediately following the Civil War, feminists attempted to have women expressly included in the protections of the Fourteenth and Fifteenth Amendments. The failure of the Fourteenth and Fifteenth Amendments to address the needs of women, and indeed for the first time to write the word "men" into the Constitution, resulted in a long-lasting division in the women's movement. . . . Feminists aligned with the Republican Party stressed black suffrage and saw women suffrage as coming through a constitutional amendment at some future time. The more militant and effective National Woman Suffrage Association favored legal and political efforts to obtain a judicial or congressional declaration that the Wartime Amendments also secured rights for women. Although Myra Bradwell's legal challenge was not known to be part of an organized strategy, her attempt to use the Fourteenth Amendment to challenge state prohibitions on occupational choices legally reflected this tack. By invoking the cult of domesticity as a legal rationale for rejecting this demand, the courts enshrined and reinforced separate-sphere ideology while deferring women's rights.

In rejecting Myra Bradwell's challenge to Illinois' prohibition on occupational choice, the Supreme Court had two options: to construe the new constitutional guarantees narrowly so as to defeat all comers, or to find special reasons for treating women differently. The majority adopted the first approach. . . .

However, Justice Joseph Bradley . . . opted for the second approach. His concurring opinion is the embodiment of the separate-sphere ideology:

> [T]he civil law as well as nature itself, has always recognized a wide difference in the respective spheres and destinies of man and woman. Man is, or should be, woman's protector and defender. The natural and proper timidity and delicacy which belongs to the female sex evidently unfits it for many of the occupations of civil life. . . . The constitution of the family organization, which is founded in the divine ordinance, as well as in the nature of things, indicates the domestic sphere as that which properly belongs to the domain and functions of womanhood. The harmony, not to say identity, of interests and views which belong, or should belong, to the family institution is repugnant to the idea of a woman adopting a distinct and independent career from that of her husband. . . .
>
> It is true that many women are unmarried and not affected by any of the duties, complications, and incapacities arising out of the married state, but these are exceptions to the general rule. The paramount destiny and mission of woman are to fulfill the noble and benign offices of wife and mother. This is the law of the Creator. And the rules of civil society must be adapted to the general constitution of things, and cannot be based upon exceptional cases.[16]

Glorification of women's destiny serves to soften any sense of unfairness in excluding women from the legal profession. Since this "paramount destiny and mission" of women is mandated by "nature," "divine ordinance," and "the law of the Creator," the civil law need not recognize the claims of women who deviate from their proper role. . . .

Women's Physical Differences: Muller v. Oregon

In the nineteenth century, the persisting separate-sphere ideology legitimized and reinforced women's marginal and secondary status in the work force. Working women were suspicious, inferior, and immoral. Those women who joined the work force were predominantly single or widowed, and confined to "women's jobs," serving as a reserve supply of cheap labor. . . .

With industrialization and urbanization in the late nineteenth century came deplorable work conditions for all workers, which prompted unions and social reformers to press for legislation regulating conditions of work, hours, and wages. By the turn of the century, both sex-neutral and sex-based protective laws had been passed and sustained against legal challenge. . . .

Protective-labor legislation was countered legally by conservatives who . . . revived the natural-law notion of freedom of contract and located it in the due process clause of the Fourteenth Amendment. The effort culminated in Lochner v. New York,[17] a decision that, in striking down maximum-hour legislation for bakers by relying on the "common understanding" that baking and most other occupations did not endanger health, cast doubt on the validity of all protective legislation.

Advocates of state "protective" legislation for women could take two routes after *Lochner*: one, to displace the "common understanding" in *Lochner* with scientific evidence that all industrial jobs, when performed more than ten hours a day, were dangerous to a worker's health; or two, by arguing that women's need for special protection justified an exception to *Lochner*. In Muller v. Oregon,[18] the Supreme Court was faced with a challenge to an Oregon statute that prohibited women from working more than ten hours a day in a laundry. The National Consumers' League, which played the major role in the middle- and upper-class reform movement, filed an *amicus* brief, written by Louis Brandeis, Josephine Goldmark, and Florence Kelly,[19] which combined both approaches. The brief portrayed as common knowledge pseudo scientific data regarding physical differences between men and women, emphasizing the "bad effects" of long hours on women workers' health, "female functions," childbearing capacity, and job safety, and on the health and welfare of future generations. Adopting the view urged by the *amici*, the Court upheld the challenged legislation. . . .

Muller expresses a view of women as different from and more limited than men because of their "physical structure" and "natural functions." Although this view of women is every bit as fixed as that expressed in *Bradwell*, it purports to be grounded in physical fact. . . . Women's primary function as mother is now seen as physically incompatible with the demands of equal participation in the work force. . . .

Both social reformers and legal realists regarded the statute's survival and the Supreme Court's recognition of economic and social facts as important victories. However, as organized labor lost interest in protective legislation for men, the primary legal legacy of *Muller* was a view of women that justified excluding women from job opportunities and earning levels available to men. . . .

Unequal Equal Protection: Michael M. v. Sonoma County

Although Supreme Court opinions of the 1960s began to acknowledge some changes in woman's position, it took the rebirth of an active women's movement in the 1960s and the development of a legal arm to obtain a definitive legal determination that sex-based discrimination violated the equal-protection clause of the Fourteenth Amendment. In 1971, the Supreme Court, in Reed v. Reed,[20] for the first time invalidated a statute on the ground that it denied women equal protection. The Court unanimously struck down an Idaho statute preferring males to females in the performance of estate administration, refusing to find generalizations about women's business experience adequate to sustain the preference. . . .

Equal protection rests on the legal principle that people who are similarly situated in fact must be similarly treated by the law. In *Reed* the Court for the first time held that women and men are similarly situated. The Court recognized the social reality, through "judicial notice," that "in this country, presumably due to the greater longevity of women, a large proportion of estates . . . are administered by women." By recognizing a departure from traditional social roles as so obvious as to be able to rely on judicial notice, the Court appeared to presage the erosion of the "differences" ideology.

Over the last ten years, in upholding equal-protection challenges to sex-based legislation, the Supreme Court has repeatedly rejected overgeneralizations based on sex.[21] For example, in Frontiero v. Richardson,[22] the Court upheld an equal-protection challenge to the military's policy of denying dependency benefits to male dependents of female servicewomen. The plurality opinion criticized *Bradwell* as reflective of an attitude of "romantic paternalism" that "in practical effect, put women not on a pedestal but in a cage." Similarly, in Stanton v. Stanton,[23] the Court upheld an equal-protection challenge to a state statute specifying a greater age of majority for males than females with respect to parental obligation for support. In so doing, the Court appeared to understand the effect of stereotypes in perpetuating discrimination and the detrimental impact that differential treatment has on women's situation.

However, the Supreme Court's developing application of equal protection has not lived up to its initial promise. The Court has adopted a lower standard of review for sex-based classifications than for race-based classifications, reflecting its view that race discrimination is a more serious social problem than sex discrimination. The Court has rejected only those stereotypes that it perceives as grossly inaccurate. Indeed, the Court has developed a new and more subtle view of "realistically based differences," which encompasses underlying physical distinctions between the sexes, distinctions created by law, and socially imposed differences in situation, and frequently confuses the three. In these cases, the Court simply reasons that equal protection is not violated because men and women are not "similarly situated."

The paradigmatic physical distinction between the sexes, women's reproductive capacity, has been consistently viewed by courts as a proper basis for differential treatment. The . . . Court does so by refusing to recognize that classifications based on pregnancy involve sex discrimination and by ignoring the similarities between pregnancy and other temporary disabilities. In Geduldig v. Aiello,[24] the Supreme Court rejected an equal-protection challenge to California's disability insurance system, which paid benefits to persons in private employment who were unable to work but excluded from coverage disabilities resulting from pregnancy. . . . This position was effectively reaffirmed in General Electric v. Gilbert,[25] in which the exclusion of pregnancy from General Electric's disability program was upheld in the face of a challenge under Title VII of the Civil Rights Act. . . .

[One] expression of the Court's current ideology of equality is a 1981 Supreme Court case, Michael M. v. Sonoma County,[26] upholding California's statutory rape law, challenged by a seventeen-year-old male, which punished males having sex with a female under eighteen. The thrust of his attack on the statute was that it denied him equal protection since he, not his partner, was criminally liable.

Statutory rape laws have rested historically on the legal fiction that young women are incapable of consent. They exalt female chastity and reflect and reinforce archaic assumptions about the male initiative in sexual relations and the weakness and naïveté of young women. Nevertheless, the Court in *Michael M.* found no violation of equal-protection guarantees and upheld the differential treatment as reasonably related to the goal of eliminating teenage pregnancy. . . .

Justice Potter Stewart's concurring opinion . . . develops the crux of this new ideology of realistically based classifications:

> [W]e have recognized that in certain narrow circumstances men and women are not similarly situated and in these circumstances a gender classification based on clear differences between the sexes is not invidious, and a legislative classification realistically based upon these differences is not unconstitutional. . . .
>
> Applying these principles to the classification enacted by the California legislature, it is readily apparent that [the statute] does not violate the Equal Protection Clause. Young women and men are not similarly situated with respect to the problems and risks associated with intercourse and pregnancy, and the statute is realistically related to the legitimate state purpose of reducing those problems and risks.[27]

Yet, the classification at issue in *Michael M.* had very little to do with biological differences between the sexes. As is seen from the total absence of supportive legislative history, the statute was not designed to address the problem of teenage pregnancy. Moreover, as Justice John Paul Stevens points out, if criminal sanctions are believed to deter the conduct leading to pregnancy, a young woman's greater risk of harm from pregnancy is, if anything, a reason to subject her to sanctions. The statute instead embodies and reinforces the assumption that men are always responsible for initiating sexual intercourse and females must always be protected against their aggression. Nevertheless, the Court's focus on the physical fact of reproductive capacity serves to obscure the social bases of its decision. Indeed, it is striking that the Court entirely fails to treat pregnancy as sex discrimination when discrimination really is in issue, while using it as a rationale in order to justify differential treatment when it is not in issue.

Like *Bradwell* and *Muller*, *Michael M.* affirms that there are differences between the sexes, both the physical difference of childbearing capacity and women's social role, which should result in differential legal treatment. However, because this affirmation comes at the same time as the Court claims to reject "overbroad generalizations unrelated to differences between men and women or which demean [women's] ability or social status," the Court's approval of differential treatment is especially pernicious. The fact of and harms caused by teenage pregnancy are used by the Court to avoid close analysis of the stereotypes involved and careful scrutiny of the pregnancy rationale. The role that the challenged statute plays in reinforcing those harms is never examined. The Court accepts as immutable fact that men and women are not similarly situated, particularly when pregnancy is involved. The Court then appears to favor equal rights for women, but for one small problem—pregnancy.

As an ideological matter, the separation of pregnancy and childbearing capacity, social discrimination, and even legally imposed discrimination from "invidious" discrimination, in which differential treatment is unrelated to "real" differences between men and women, perform an important function of legitimizing discrimination through the language of equality. Although its doctrinal veneer is different, the Court's current approach has the same effect as *Bradwell* and *Muller*. If both pregnancy and socially imposed differences in role always keep men and women from being similarly situated—thereby excluding sex-based differences from the purview of equal protection—then the real substance of sex discrimination can still be ignored. Childbearing capacity is the single greatest basis of differential treatment for women—it is a major source of discrimination in both work and family life, and the critical distinction on which the ideology of both separate spheres and physical differences rests. Yet, by appearing to reject gross generalizations about proper roles of the sexes exemplified by both *Bradwell* and *Muller*, current ideology attempts to maintain credibility by "holding out the promise of liberation."[28] By emphasizing its reliance on a reality that appears more closely tied to physical differences and the hard facts of social disadvantage, e.g., the consequences of teenage pregnancy for young girls, the Court appears sensible and compromising. . . . However, by excluding the core of sex discrimination, the Court is effectively removing women entirely from the reach of equal protection.

This new ideological approach must be viewed, as were *Bradwell* and *Muller*, in its historical context. Although the women's movement provided the triggering change in consciousness, and an understanding of the nature and forms of sex stereotyping on which the sex-discrimination challenges of this period have been based, many of the sex-discrimination cases decided by the Supreme Court have not arisen from feminist struggles and have been presented to the Court by men, not women. As a result, these cases, including *Michael M.*, did not always develop the harm perceived by women for the Court, either as a factual or legal matter. . . .

Although the legal ideology of equality shows some progression from *Bradwell* to *Michael M.*, there is less than might be expected. Certainly the Court's view of women, and the ways in which it sees the sexes, has moved from an overt view of women's separate roles to a more subtle view of limited differences, but this new view is more dangerous precisely because it appears so reasonable. The Court's perception of differences that suffice to justify discrimination has altered somewhat, but it remains equally fixed. The Court continues to validate inequality by legitimizing differential treatment.

Notes

1. E. Flexner, A Century of Struggle, rev. ed. (Harvard University Press, 1975).

2. Hoyt v. Florida, 368 U.S. 57, 61 (1961). In Taylor v. Louisiana, 419 U.S. 522 (1975), a case involving a male rape defendant, the Supreme Court tacitly overruled *Hoyt* but avoided the question of equal protection for women, relying instead on the defendant's Sixth Amendment right to a fair trial.

3. 10 U.S.C. § 6015; 10 U.S.C. § 8549 (Navy and Air Force). The Army and Marine Corps preclude the role of women in combat as a matter of established policy; Rostker v. Goldberg, 453 U.S. Ct. 57 (1981) (upholding the all-male draft registration scheme).

4. There is a dispute as to whether women's actual status during the colonial period corresponded to the position accorded them by law. Initial research suggested that women were able, as a practical matter, to function as managers, traders, artisans, and even attorneys. Thus, despite their exclusion from formal political processes, they were granted a basic and integral, though subservient, role in the community. The same research suggested that women's position declined with the growth of commercial capitalism and specialization. Subsequent research, however, argues that women's crucial economic role failed to translate into power and influence, and that sex roles were far more rigidly defined than had been thought. Cf. M. Ryan, Womanhood in America, 2d ed. (New Viewpoints, 1979), and A. Sachs and J. Hoff Wilson, Sexism and the Law (Free Press, 1978), with M. Beth Norton, Liberty's Daughters: The Revolutionary Experience of American Women (Little, Brown, 1980).

5. The Equal Pay Act of 1963 and Title VII of the Civil Rights Act of 1964 provided civil remedies for employment discrimination, while private discrimination in the housing and credit markets was prohibited in 1974.

6. See Dothard v. Rawlinson, 433 U.S. 321, 336 (1977). See also Phillips v. Martin Marietta Corp., 400 U.S. 542 (1971), suggesting that a company could legally deny jobs to women with preschool children if it could show that such children interfered more with female workers as a group than with male workers as a group.

7. See, e.g., Weinberger v. Wiesenfeld, 420 U.S. 636 (1975); Califano v. Goldfarb, 430 U.S. 199 (1977); Califano v. Westcott, 443 U.S. 76 (1979).

8. United States v. Nicholas, 97 F.2d 510 (2d Cir. 1938); see generally, L. Gordon, Woman's Body, Woman's Right (Penguin, 1977).

9. Griswold v. Connecticut, 381 U.S. 479 (1965).

10. Eisenstadt v. Baird, 405 U.S. 438 (1972).

11. Roe v. Wade, 410 U.S. 113 (1973).

12. *Id.*; Doe v. Bolton, 410 U.S. 179 (1973).

13. Maher v. Roe, 432 U.S. 464 (1977); H.L. v. Matheson, 450 U.S. 398 (1981).

14. Webster v. Reproductive Services, 492 U.S. 490 (1989).

15. 83 U.S. (16 Wall.) 130 (1873).

16. *Id*. at 141–42.

17. 198 U.S. 45 (1905).

18. 208 U.S. 412 (1908).

19. This brief has mistakenly come to be known as the first Brandeis brief, since Louis Brandeis actually filed it, although Josephine Goldmark, Florence Kelly, and other volunteers assembled the data. Barbara A. Babcock et al., Sex Discrimination and the Law: Causes and Remedies (Little, Brown, 1975), at 29.

20. 404 U.S. 71 (1971).

21. Most of these cases have involved assumptions built into government benefit statutes that the male was the breadwinner and the female the dependent at home. See Frontiero v. Richardson, 411 U.S. 677 (1973); Weinberger v. Wiesenfeld, 420 U.S. 636 (1975); Califano v. Goldfarb, 430 U.S. 199 (1977); and Califano v. Westcott, 443 U.S. 76 (1979).

22. 411 U.S. 677 (1973).

23. 421 U.S. 7 (1975).

24. 417 U.S. 484 (1974).

25. 429 U.S. 125 (1976). The Supreme Court's view of pregnancy expressed in *Gilbert* was promptly rejected by Congress. The Pregnancy Discrimination Act, 26 U.S.C. § 3304(a) (12) (1976), was passed by Congress to overturn the *Gilbert* decision. This suggests that the Supreme Court's ideology concerning pregnancy as a permissible basis for differential treatment in employment was not widely accepted. It underscores the tenuousness of relying on Supreme Court opinions as a source of prevailing views on women. . . .

26. 450 U.S. 464 (1981).

27. *Id*. at 477–79.

28. Freeman, Legitimizing Racial Discrimination Through Antidiscrimination Law: A Critical Review of Supreme Court Doctrine, 62 Minn. L. Rev. 1050, 1052 (1978).

❖ To Question Everything: The Inquiries of Feminist Jurisprudence*

HEATHER RUTH WISHIK

WHAT QUESTIONS ARE WE ASKING, we . . . who call our work feminist jurisprudence? . . . As I wonder about this I realize I am using Catharine MacKinnon's suggested definition: "Feminist jurisprudence is an examination of the relationship between law and society from the point of view of all women."[1] . . .

. . . Feminist jurisprudence is a form of feminist theory-making. Feminist theory-making is a form of feminist political activity. Both as theory-making and as political practice, feminist jurisprudence must be self-conscious about its visions and methods. This [essay] is an exploration of the questions we are asking, how these recent questions differ from the conventional questions asked about women and the law, and what methods we may need in the future to formulate our questions well.

Feminist jurisprudence has links to several strands of legal scholarship. It shares with "law and social sciences" scholarship frequent emphasis on the connections between law and society and the ways in which law is non-autonomous. Like law and social sciences scholarship, feminist jurisprudential scholarship also often refers to empirical data. In feminist jurisprudence the data are usually from women's experiences, and they reveal how women use and are affected by law and by law's absence.

Feminist jurisprudence also has links to "critical legal studies" (CLS).[2] It shares with CLS scholarship a focus upon the "politics of law,"[3] that is, upon the ways law legitimates, maintains, and serves the distribution and retention of power in society. Some feminist jurisprudence is also linked to CLS and other critiques of rights theories. These feminist scholars recognize indeterminacy problems in

---

*In the foreword to her collection of essays, Adrienne Rich says that one of feminism's tasks is "[t]o question everything. To remember what it has been forbidden even to mention." A. Rich, On Lies, Secrets, and Silence: Selected Prose, 1966–1978 13 (Norton, 1980).

rights analysis and view rights analysis and "liberal legalism" as patriarchal forms which may serve to mask patriarchal bias in law.[4]

Feminist jurisprudence owes its method . . . to the development of the women's movement and feminist scholarship and theory. The questions posed by the women's movement and by feminist scholars and theorists about gender—its creation, meaning, and implications—are placed in the context of the law by feminist jurisprudential inquiry. As has happened in other disciplines, the asking of such questions leads to a critique of the discipline itself. Thus feminist jurisprudence inevitably raises questions about the methods of jurisprudential inquiry and how these have been or are gender-biased.

Seeing, describing, and analyzing the "harms" of patriarchal law and legal systems is a part of feminist jurisprudential inquiry. . . . The act of seeing patriarchal gender bias as harm contains the implication that a harm-free alternative might be possible. . . . Feminist jurisprudence thus inquires not only into the harms of patriarchal law, but also into the possibility and characteristics of a world without patriarchal law, and of a non-patriarchal legal system.

In [the first] part of this [essay], I explore the development and scope of feminist inquiry in law and in other disciplines and try to situate such inquiry in feminist political practice. In [the second] part a list of questions—a tentative epistemology—for use in feminist jurisprudential inquiry is presented and briefly explained.

Legal Scholarship about Women/Feminist Legal Criticism/Feminist Jurisprudence: The Development of Inquiry and Some Political Ramifications of Method

Legal scholarship about "women and law" has followed the developmental transitions seen in feminist scholarship in general[5] It has included:

1. compensatory scholarship, the "add-women-and-stir" approach to correcting what male legal scholars leave out;
2. criticism of the law and of inquiries about law and society because they exclude women and use patriarchally biased assumptions to further the oppression of women;
3. collection of information about women's experiences of law from the perspective of women;
4. conceptualization of a feminist method with which to understand and examine law. . . .

Compensatory scholarship, the uncovering of heretofore "hidden" female experiences which fit within the categories used by traditionally male modes of scholarship, was an essential beginning of feminist scholarship in many disciplines. Our realization that women are left out or their experience distorted is often the first evidence suggesting that there is something gender specific about the aspect of culture being examined. Yet compensatory scholarship does not question patriarchy's categories, definitions of experience, or assumptions. It simply suggests that there has been an error—the failure to include women. Its solution is to add women.

Reclaiming "lost" women's lives and experiences provides initial insight into the genderedness of culture, but if inquiry stops at such reclaiming, patriarchal assumptions and definitions are legitimized. Feminist jurisprudence must go further by questioning the methods and scope of inquiry, the categories which structure how questions are formed, and the rules which both legitimize sources of information and govern modes of interpretation. We must be cognizant of patriarchal epistemology, and must reconstruct ways of knowing to avoid distortion of female experience. If in the course of our criticism of law and collection of information about women's experiences of law, we fail to ask all the questions about how to know, as well as about what is known, we risk legitimizing patriarchy again, even as we attempt to change it.

Male-vision legal scholarship is to law what law is to patriarchy: each legitimates, by masking and by giving an appearance of neutrality to, the maleness of the institution it serves. Our understanding of this legitimation renders meaningless the idea that any inquiry into law is not political. Feminist jurisprudential inquiry is, methodologically and substantively, inquiry from the point of view of women's experiences. It criticizes and subverts patriarchal assumptions about law, including patriarchal attempts to present law as without a gendered "point of view." To fail to make inquiries about law that are inclusive of the point of view of women's experiences is to support patriarchy.

For example, in his overview of the development of critical legal theory, Robert Gordon says that law is one of the belief systems humans use: "to deal with one of the most threatening aspects of social existence: the danger posed by other people, whose cooperation is indispensable to us . . . , but who may kill us or enslave us. It seems essential to have a system to sort out positive interactions . . . from negative ones. . . ."[6] To say, as if the statement was not open to question, that other people are "one of the most threatening aspects of social existence" because we are at once interdependent and mutually vulnerable, is to assume that people are not only capable of being, but likely to be, aggressive and competitive. This assumption, however, ignores much of culturally female behavior.

If people are expected to be competitive and aggressive or are presumed to be so by nature, then interdependence appears to be dangerous. Safety then requires rules guaranteeing separation from others—that is, a legal system which limits and structures interactions between people. As Carol Gilligan suggests, separation as the motif for safety is a typically Western male motif, one grounded in Western male experience and consistent with continued male domination.[7]

Both the notion that people are dangerous and the idea that personal safety requires protection from that danger are descriptive rather than analytical. They describe the culturally accurate fact that males in patriarchy are frequent "aggressors in sex and in war," and that such frequent male aggression presents danger to everyone, male and female. But to assume such aggression is "human," rather than descriptive of male behavior in patriarchy, legitimates male aggression and the male dominance facilitated by fear of such aggression. Outside patriarchy, fear of "human" aggression and the need for definitions of safety designed to protect against it are not inevitable. Law outside patriarchy would not necessarily serve the function of providing barriers between people in the name of safety.

Feminist jurisprudence, like male-vision critical legal studies, inquires into the politics of law. Yet feminist jurisprudential inquiry focuses particularly on the law's role in perpetuating patriarchal hegemony. Such inquiry is feminist in that it is grounded in women's concrete experiences. These experiences are the source of feminism's validity and its method of analysis. Feminist inquiry involves the understanding and application of the personal as political. Feminism's method is consciousness-raising, "the collective critical reconstruction of the meaning of women's social experience, as women live through it."[8] We who wish to look at law and society from the point of view of all women's experience may help ensure our ability to see from that point of view by collectivising our process of inquiry. This may mean both asking questions which by their scope are careful to be inclusive of *all* women's experience and working collectively with other women in the formulation and exploration of our questions. . . . Just as feminist jurisprudence is political, it is a form of action. The distinctions between theory and practice, thought and action, collapse. Inquiries undertaken from the point of view of all women into the past, present, and imagined future relationships between law and society are not simply academic exercises: they are feminist lawyering tasks. These inquiries are part of feminist legal practice, as well as, in other settings, feminist political action. The questions are questions that must be asked in the course of feminist work for legislative change. . . . To make the inquiry is an act of "revision,"[9] an act of survival.

We risk promoting women's oppression if we attempt only to change the law as it impacts on women's lives and neglect to ask the questions suggested by feminist jurisprudence. Without such inquiries, reforms which may appear positive due to their short-term ability to ameliorate women's oppression may strengthen patriarchy in the long run. Feminist jurisprudential inquiry can help enable women to see such dual effects and to make conscious decisions about whether or which way to proceed.

Andrea Dworkin, for example, has eloquently explicated the simultaneously ameliorating and oppressive effects of current abortion law.[10] Continued use of the privacy doctrine in the name of women's "rights" carries with it risks to women's continued ability to use the law at all to address many aspects of our lives, particularly those having to do with "family."[11] The inquiries of feminist jurisprudence can provide the crucial clarification and understanding necessary to prevent feminists from falling unwittingly into such traps in the future.

In addition, feminist jurisprudence can help us envision the world we wish to create—that is, a world without patriarchy. It can also assist us in focusing our deliberations about the nature of that world. . . .

The Inquiries of Feminist Jurisprudence

The following list of questions might be posed by a feminist inquiry into the relationship between law and society. . . .

1. What Have Been and What Are Now All Women's Experiences of the "Life Situation" Addressed by the Doctrine, Process, or Area of Law Under Examination?

The choice of the phrase "life situation" is deliberate. The inquiry is not about women's experiences of a "problem" as defined by male law, a definition which presumptively distorts women's actual experiences. Rather, feminist inquiry looks to and tries to describe all women's lived experiences, and tries to define "situation" so as to include all women.

For example, if the law defines the problem as the economics of divorce, feminist jurisprudential inquiry might describe the situation as the economics of intimacy and parenthood. By widening the definition of the inquiry we can include unmarried teenage mothers of all races, lesbians, and other unmarried women. This larger scope of inquiry differs from the legal category "economics of divorce" by including all the women left out in an economics of divorce study because they are not, or are not allowed to be, married. . . .

2. What Assumptions, Descriptions, Assertions and/or Definitions of Experience— Male, Female, or Ostensibly Gender Neutral—Does the Law Make in This Area?

The first question, inquiring into women's life situation, addresses the need to collect data about women's actual experience. This second question addresses the need to collect data about the law's assertions regarding women's experience. Legal definitions, assumptions, or assertions—especially those which claim to be either gender specific or gender neutral—reveal what the law is saying about women and how the law operates politically and socially in relation to women's lives.

For example, in H.L. v. Matheson,[12] a case that challenged Utah's parental notice requirement in its abortion law, the statute required that parents of minors seeking abortions be notified of the planned abortion, but it did not require that parents of minors seeking medical prenatal services be notified of the pregnancy and the planned medical services. In justifying Utah's distinction between abortion and pregnancy, Chief Justice Burger asserted that for a pregnant minor, the choice to continue pregnancy does not involve medical decisions as needful of parental involvement as are the medical decisions involved in abortion. "If the pregnant girl elects to carry her child to term, the *medical* decisions to be made entail few—perhaps none—of the potentially grave emotional and psychological consequences of the decision to abort."[13]

The second inquiry, in addition to examining Burger's assertions about young women's experience, would examine other legal assertions about teenage sexuality and parental control. These assertions might include venereal disease treatment laws giving medical providers permission to treat minors without parental notification or consent. Such laws, by implication if not legislative history, acknowledge that many teenagers will not seek medical care related to sexual activity if they must involve their parents.

3. What Is the Area of Mismatch, Distortion, or Denial Created by the Differences Between Women's Life Experiences and the Law's Assumptions or Imposed Structures?

Analyzing the mismatch between the data from women's lives (Inquiry One) and the data from the law's articulated definitions and assumptions about particular life situations (Inquiry Two) helps reveal whose power is being served by the law as it exists, what aspects of women's lives are legally visible, and how women's experience is distorted by law. These are all aspects of understanding the relationship between law and society from the perspective of women's experience.

To examine the mismatch between the life situation and the law's assumptions in the *Matheson* example, we need first look to the young women's "life situation" at issue in *Matheson*. That life situation might be described as sexuality and the risk of pregnancy as experienced by young women who, due to youth, have even less economic and personal autonomy than do many adult women. The life situation information might refute Burger's assumption by suggesting teenage women find the medical decision involved in carrying a child to term—such as amniocentesis, caesarian section, choice of analgesia during labor—at least as complex, difficult, and consequential as the choice to have an early abortion in a particular location with a particular method. The life situation information might also suggest that for teenage women parental notification requirements operate as an effective barrier to their exercise of choice regarding contraception, abortion, and other aspects of their sexuality.

4. What Patriarchal Interests Are Served by the Mismatch?

Having collected the contrasting data, and having described the distortions and inaccuracies in the law's view of women's experience, Inquiry Four attempts to analyze the functional nature of that mismatch, to see how the mismatch serves patriarchy.

There are several sub-inquiries which may be necessary in order to locate the patriarchal interests served by the law's distortions of women's experience:

a. What social, political, economic, and cultural events occurred at or near the time this law or doctrine emerged, and during its development what events marked the moments when the law or doctrine shifted?

b. What ideology or statements of belief surround this area of the law?

c. What past or present women's interests and needs were or are met by this area of law, and what ones were or are not met?

5. What Reforms Have Been Proposed in This Area of Law or Women's Life Situation? How Will These Reform Proposals, if Adopted, Affect Women Both Practically and Ideologically?

Given the resilience and adaptability of patriarchy, we cannot always predict future effects with accuracy. Yet careful inquiry is, nonetheless, an important means of revealing those effects we can anticipate. Given that patriarchy is "metaphysically nearly perfect,"[14] we must probe for the ways in which a proposed reform may be co-opted or oppressive in its longterm outcome.

6. In an Ideal World, What Would This Woman's Life Situation Look Like, and What Relationship, if Any, Would the Law Have to This Future Life Situation?

It is the creation of ourselves as "a sex 'for ourselves'"[15] which is inevitably the core of feminist enterprise. In the act of discovering what we share because of the patriarchal oppression within which all women live, we begin to change our world and ourselves. As Marilyn Frye suggests, it is very important that we attempt this self creation or envisioning. If we fail to do so our political practice is not whole.[16]

7. How Do We Get There from Here?

The first four inquiries are fairly universal in current feminist jurisprudence. . . . They help us to identify how law and existence is gendered by patriarchy. This clarity about the patriarchally determined and dependent aspects of law and existence helps us envision alternatives. The last three questions, however, involve the challenge of inventing, of imagining a world for which we have no givens. . . . There are no precedents except the very minutiae of our lives which the first four inquiries help reveal. Based upon what we know of our lives in patriarchy, we may begin to imagine life outside patriarchy, or without patriarchy.

If we take the time to imagine and to articulate our visions, we will then have descriptions of possible modes of being and of relations between law (if any) and society which will serve to test current reform proposals. We can ask about every proposed change in the law: Does it ameliorate a present problem in women's lives; does it constitute a step toward the end of patriarchy and toward the preferred imagined future; or does the reform ameliorate but also reinforce male dominance?

Even though visions of the preferred future will change over time, the ongoing articulation of them helps clarify our actions. Feminist jurisprudential inquiry is in part an attempt to bring about change. Every such attempt involves assumptions about principles and goals. Our methods must include bringing these assumptions to consciousness, making them available for debate, clarification, and modification. Articulating visions of the future is one way of making explicit our assumptions. Feminists may rightly be afraid of the complexities of such inquiries. The essential and fragile support we find in community with one another may be strained by the revelation of our differences about methods like rights analysis, let alone about visions of the imagined future. Some of the differences which now surface often in our attempts to explain the origins of patriarchy or to advocate for particular legal changes are differences which we will understand better if we try to share our visions of the future, and try to explicate our choices about short-term goals in terms of particular future visions.

What kind of world is it we are trying to create? The analytic frames of patriarchal law are not the spaces within which to create visions of feminist futures. Nothing about existing law should remain immutable in our inquiries, and nothing about existing law should constrain the construction of our visions. Once we have probed the data from law and women's lives and the distance in between, then it seems necessary to skip to an imagined future when all is possible in order to envision what we want. Afterwards we can look at whether and how our desires can be made real through changes in or in spite of existing law. To make the inquiry this large whenever we examine any aspect of law is to help ensure we won't forget to see everything, won't forget to question everything. "Where an old paradigm exists, a new paradigm can come into being. . . . Thus we may have to relearn thinking. We have to learn to tolerate questions . . . we may have to cultivate paradox, welcome contradiction or a troublesome question."[17]

Notes

1. C. MacKinnon, Panel Discussion, Developing Feminist Jurisprudence, at the 14th National Conference on Women and Law, Washington, D.C., April 9, 1983; see also MacKinnon, Feminism, Marxism, Method, and the State: Toward Feminist Jurisprudence, Part 5 this volume. MacKinnon has explained the attempt at common vision: "This feminism seeks to define and pursue women's interest as the fate of all women bound together. It seeks to extract the truth of women's commonalities out of the lie that all women are the same. . . . This politics is struggling for a practice of unity that does not depend upon sameness without dissolving into empty tolerance, including tolerance of all it exists to change

whenever that appears embodied in one of us. A new community begins here. As critique, women's communality describes a fact of male supremacy, of sex "in it-self": no woman escapes the meaning of being a woman within a gendered social system, and sex inequality is not only pervasive but may be universal. . . . For women to become a sex 'for ourselves' moves community to the level of vision." [Footnote was omitted; originally cited at 8 Signs 635, 639–40 n. 8 (1983). *Ed.*]

To look at a life situation from the point of view of *all* women means defining a situation shared by *all* women and including in the experiential data about that situation the experiences of women as they differ by age, race, class, religion, and sexual preference. Feminist jurisprudence must understand and be a practice which includes the understanding that all these factors are variables by which a woman's life situation is specified. Thus teenage sexuality and parental control as a life situation [discussed *infra*] will vary based on the sexual preference of the teenager and of the parents, the economic class of the family, and the religion and race of the family. These variances will include issues as basic as the likelihood that biological parents will even be in the teenager's life to present issues of parental control or whether control agents are more likely to be social welfare workers, foster parents, teachers, or others. Risk of pregnancy has different meanings depending upon the race, class, and sexual preference of the teenager because the occasions giving rise to the risk and the *consequences* of the pregnancy vary drastically. Feminist jurisprudence must include the intertwined and layered specificity of women's lives at every stage of inquiry in order to be accurate.

2. Jaff, Radical Pluralism: A Proposed Theoretical Framework for the Conference on Critical Legal Studies, 72 Geo. L.J. 1143 (1984); Unger, The Critical Legal Studies Movement, 96 Harv. L. Rev. 561 (1983).

3. The phrase comes from the title of a collection of articles from the critical legal studies movement: D. Kairys ed., The Politics of Law: A Progressive Critique (Pantheon, 1982).

4. Olsen, Statutory Rape: A Feminist Critique of Rights Analysis, Part 5 this volume; Klare, Law-Making as Praxis, Telos, Summer 1979, at 123.

5. G. Lerner, The Majority Finds Its Past: Placing Women in History 145–59 (Oxford University Press, 1979); E. Fox Keller, Reflections on Gender and Science (Yale University Press, 1985) at 177; Kelly-Gadol, The Social Relation of the Sexes: Methodological Implications of Women's History, in E. Abel & E. K. Abel eds., The Signs Reader: Women, Gender and Scholarship 11 (University of Chicago Press, 1983); Boxer, For and About Women: The Theory and Practice of Women's Studies in the United States, in N. Keohane, M. Rosaldo, B. Gelpi eds., Feminist Theory: A Critique of Ideology (University of Chicago Press, 1982), at 237.

6. Gordon, New Developments in Legal Theory, in The Politics of Law: A Progressive Critique, *supra* note 3, at 288.

7. C. Gilligan, In a Different Voice 32–33, 40–44 (Harvard University Press, 1982).

8. MacKinnon, Feminism, Marxism, Method, and the State: An Agenda for Theory, Part 5 this volume.

9. "Revision—the act of looking back, of seeing with fresh eyes, of entering an old text from a new critical direction—is for women more than a chapter in

cultural history; it is an act of survival." A. Rich, On Lies, Secrets, and Silence: Selected Prose 1966–1978 (Norton, 1980), at 35.

10. Dworkin suggests that women have a powerful reason to say no to intercourse, a reason some men accept: the risk of pregnancy. According to Dworkin, this reason protects some women from forced sex. When abortion is legal and actually available this risk-of-pregnancy as protection-from-forced-sex disappears. A. Dworkin, Right-Wing Women 71–105 (Putnam, 1983).

11. Privacy doctrine is the body of law evolving from a line of Supreme Court cases beginning with Poe v. Ullman, 367 U.S. 497 U.S. 497 (1961) and Griswold v. Connecticut, 381 U.S. 479 (1965). The doctrine suggests that there are areas of life or activities which the state should not regulate or intrude upon because these areas or activities are "private," and that immunity from state intrusion is part of such constitutionally protected rights as freedom of speech and association, liberty, and due process.

. . . As MacKinnon and others have pointed out, privacy presumes that all who are in the private sphere have sufficient autonomy and power to exercise their individual rights in private, an assumption which too often fails to describe women's reality in the private sphere of family life. MacKinnon, Toward Feminist Jurisprudence, Part 5 this volume. . . . For a critique of ideas of intervention and nonintervention, see generally Olsen, The Myth of State Intervention in the Family, 18 U. Mich. J.L. Ref. 835 (1985).

12. 450 U.S. 398 (1981).

13. *Id.* at 413–14.

14. MacKinnon, Toward Feminist Jurisprudence, Part 5 this volume, at 428.

15. *Id.* [Footnote was omitted; originally cited at 8 Signs 635, 639–40 n. 8 (1983). *Ed.*]

16. M. Frye, The Politics of Reality: Essays in Feminist Theory 52–53 (Crossing Press, 1983). . . .

17. Griffin, The Way of All Ideology, in Feminist Theory: A Critique of Ideology, *supra* note 5, at 289.

❖ *Where We Stand: Observations on the Situation of Feminist Legal Thought*

CLARE DALTON

. . .

TO BE A FEMINIST TODAY, I think it is fair to say, is to believe that we belong to a society, or even civilization, in which women are and have been subordinated by and to men, and that life would be better, certainly for women, possibly for everybody, if that were not the case. Feminism is then the range of committed inquiry and activity dedicated first, to describing women's subordination—exploring its nature and extent; dedicated second, to asking both *how*—through what mechanisms, and *why*—for what complex and interwoven reasons—women continue to occupy that position; and dedicated third to change.

To be engaged in feminist legal thought is to be a feminist who locates both her inquiry, and her activity, in relation to the legal system. The legal system must here be understood broadly, as including the rules that constitute the formal body of law; the discourses in which those rules are situated, and through which they are articulated and elaborated; the institutions by means of which they are constantly subverted and modified in their implementation and administration; the specifically educational institutions through which legal culture is transmitted from generation to generation, and the various actors whose participation, as lawyers, clients, law enforcement officials, judges, jurors, arbitrators, mediators, social workers, legislators, bureaucrats, teachers or students, sustains the enterprise. . . .

Let me begin where feminist legal thinking began, in the courses which appeared in the curriculum in the early seventies under the titles "Women and the Law" or "Sex Discrimination."[1]

. . . First, in directing attention to particular doctrinal areas, the course obscured the way in which the problems of women were present in every area of the curriculum; the way in which their absence from many areas of traditional legal discourse was as significant as their presence in others. Second, the traditional areas of doctrinal coverage themselves imposed particular limitations. . . .

Born in and of the women's movement, and sharing its priorities, the courses were originally designed to track developing legal doctrine that addressed women's unequal treatment in law and in society. They focused on constitutional doctrine, and developing statutory standards, addressing discrimination against women in employment, in education, or as recipients of public benefits. This was a strategy that accepted, for the purpose of argument, the supposedly neutral norms and universal principles of the legal system, like equality, and challenged the arbitrariness with which they were being applied. It taught men how to re-focus their vision, to some extent, and to see women's sameness where before they had seen difference. It was a strategy born of women's exclusion, and designed to secure access for women to the male arenas in which most of society's benefits were handed out.

It was a strategy that brought women important gains. . . . As time went by, however, its limitations became more visible. First, it turned out to have little power in situations where women lacked the ability or the inclination to persuade men that they were "the same." "Women and the Law" courses had traditionally brought within their purview, and within their discrimination analysis, those areas of law encompassing precisely the areas of women's lives in which they seemed most inescapably and concretely unlike men—sexuality and reproduction. But despite heroic feminist efforts, *judicially* developing equality analysis proved un-able to wrap itself around these intractably female issues, leaving the women's movement split on whether to continue to urge equality, or instead to concede difference. Should women, for example, equate pregnancy with prostate trouble, or acknowledge the uniqueness of their childbearing capacity? This conflict and resulting uneasiness began to show up in the courses. . . .

"Feminist Jurisprudence" courses can be seen as one reaction to the prolifera-tion of feminist legal theory produced by the unsettling developments of the late seventies and early eighties. They reflect the urgency of developing new ap-proaches to the problems of women in law and in society, ones that will not foun-der on the rock of "equality," and they celebrate the range and power of the thinking and writing that has responded to this crisis. And yet, [the title] "Femi-nist Jurisprudence" strikes me as . . . expressive of dangers inherent in the project of feminist theory today.

"Feminist Jurisprudence" shares a very particular problem with Jessie Ber-nard's term "Feminist Enlightenment,"[2] which, in its effort to capture the energy and illumination emanating from the intellectual work driven by feminism, risks allying itself with a set of propositions ultimately foreign to feminism. The En-lightenment, after all, was about the Triumph of Reason, the exhilaration of Man's confidence that Truth and Justice were within his grasp. Jurisprudence—the philosophy of law—is, as it has been taught in our law schools, a proto-typically Enlightenment project, having to do precisely with the eternals of truth and justice, dependent precisely on the power and priority of reason. Jurisprudence generates sentiments and aspirations like those expressed in the stone words engraved over the portals of Harvard Law School: "Not under Man, but under God and Law."

The problem was that when the men who ordered those words to be carved looked at God, they saw a man, and a man not unlike themselves. Women have long, if not always, held the suspicion, if not the knowledge, that what passed for point-of-view-lessness was in fact His point of view. A point of view which did not always correspond to hers. Feminist epistemology starts from the premise that what has been presented as "the world" and "the truth" has obscured women's reality, and ignored women's perspective. It contains the explosive suggestion that what have passed as necessary, universal and ahistorical truths have never been more than partial and socio-historically situated versions of truth.[3] It is in this sense, then, that "Feminist Jurisprudence" seems like a contradiction in terms.

Today the Enlightenment project is in trouble all over the place—not only in feminist thought, but in theory more generally—because it rests on those few simple but basic assumptions that many no longer feel able to take for granted: the idea that a "self" can be singular or coherent; the idea that knowledge can be objective (or the real-world-out-there correspond with the world-as-viewed-by-the-subject); the idea that certain minimal universal human needs or rights can be identified that are in no way contingent on the historical particulars of any given society, but for that very reason can be used to justify particular social and political structures. The multiplying challenges to the Enlightenment project in discipline after discipline go generally by the name of post-modernism. Feminism is, I believe, at its most powerful and best as a post-modern project.

Understood as a post-modern project, feminism has both positive and negative obligations. . . . The major negative obligations, I think, are two. First, a feminist narrative or theory should not imagine itself as *replacing* (but only as *displacing*) a male or masculinist one—how could feminists' situated claims to authority become absolute ones? Second, no single feminist narrative or theory should imagine that it can speak univocally for *all* women. We know that grand male theories have traditionally left out of their evidentiary bases and their intellectual formulations the experiences and perspectives not only of women (of all sorts) but also of minority or otherwise disadvantaged groups of men—why should we have different expectations of grand feminist theories?

Living with these limitations is not easy. Sometimes it seems that opposing the grandeur of "Jurisprudence" with anything else than another, perhaps differently gendered, "Jurisprudence" will be an exercise in futility—that proposing the demolition of a historic monument to make way for a variety of makeshift encampments is madness. . . . [I]f feminists can only repeat the territorial battles of the past, if we cannot resist being drawn into the very expansionist warfare we have made it our job to criticize, our medium betrays our message.

This conviction makes me nervous about the kind of legal feminism that most aspires to "Jurisprudence," whether it is based on the core idea of "Woman" as "Mother," drawing usually on the theories of Chodorow,[4] Dinnerstein[5] and Gilligan,[6] or the core idea of "Woman" as "Sexual Subordinate," as represented in the work of Catharine MacKinnon.[7] Feminist theorists must struggle continually against the temptation of asserting new "necessary, universal and ahistorical truths"—about "Woman," or her adversary "Man"—against the temptation, that is, of reincorporating some new form of the Enlightenment project into feminist work. The danger here is that if we incorporate commonly held but unwarranted and essentialist assumptions about the nature of men, women, or their relationships one with another into feminist inquiry, our subjects will be robbed of other features that play important parts in the dynamic the inquiry seeks to understand [such as] [r]ace, class, sexual orientation, religion, ethnicity, gender *identity*, (as opposed to gender attribution), employment status, physical and mental health. . . .

On the other hand, there is an enormous amount that is illuminating in this feminist jurisprudence. It has taught many women new things about themselves as women, empowered them by showing them some of the structures of their disempowerment, offered them new critical tools to apply to the dismantling of those structures, and given them new words to try out in their struggles to communicate with one another, and with the world they would like to change. . . .

At this point I want to point out a complementary danger, which I think feminists have not yet faced as directly. In the work of some of those theorists who react against the kind of new essentialism I have been describing, the voice of gender risks being lost entirely. . . .

Let me identify three quite different ways in which this can happen. One version involves the theorist who, as I have just done, critiques feminist analyses for their essentialism, but who moves on to underscore the differences among and between women, without ever returning to ask whether those differences entirely undercut the "essentialist" claim, or only complicate and modify it. This has happened, I think, in recent reactions to the work of Carol Gilligan, and the ethic of care she identifies as characteristically informing the moral reasoning of her women subjects.[8]

Another version of this dynamic finds support and expression in Lacan's arresting claim that "woman does not exist,"[9] or Luce Irigaray's account of "Ce sexe qui n'est pas un."[10] Taken to the extreme, this is a portrayal of "woman" as so constituted by her oppression that she has no authentic voice in which to speak, no position to urge—the space she inhabits teaches us only about her oppressor, never about herself. Within this framework, the feminist must aspire to root out of herself those attributes woman has been assigned within a patriarchal culture— among which, presumably, would be her ethic of care—and somehow refashion herself, as if she were her own to make.[11]

A third version of the dynamic seems to contain elements of both the prior two. In this version, as in the previous one, the "otherness" of gender, regardless of its particular content, is thought to give the feminist theorist a generic understanding of how dominant groups create "others," enabling her to speak on behalf of other "others" than herself. This feminism of method, to the extent that it orients inquiry towards the differences of handicap, race, religion, and so on, need never focus its gaze on the substance of women's lives. To that extent, it resembles the feminism that critiques feminist essentialism, without asking what is true as well as what is false about those "essential" analyses.[12] Ironically enough, this care for others, to the exclusion of care for oneself, is exactly the behavior that the culture prescribes for women, and that the theorists attacked as essentialist describe as characteristic of women.

Why are feminists drawn away from specific questions about gender oppression and the mechanisms through which it operates? Out of the welter of possibilities let me identify three. One might be anger—an anger that leads us to reject (the existence or the value of) attributes, like caring, or sensitivity to others, that women develop, in significant part, because the important men in their lives insist on being taken care of. Another might be fear—that to acknowledge those attributes is to acknowledge the enemy within; is already to submit, or to be seen as submitting, to male demands that they be exercised, nonreciprocally, in the care and protection of men. In this view, denying the attributes is the only hope of resisting the appeal of their exercise. A third might be denial of a different kind, the kind that allows women, and especially feminists, to hide from ourselves the extent to which we do, in fact, submit to male demands for care and attention, for fear of what would happen if we did not.

Despite the legitimacy of both the anger and the fear that may shape these reactions, I wonder about the consequences, for women, of denying or withholding from themselves aspects of themselves they wish to deny or withhold from those whose claims they regard as illegitimate. There is, after all, a less self-mutilating option for each woman, which is to acknowledge, and even celebrate, those attributes in herself, while struggling to resist illegitimate demands for their exercise, and remaining aware of the extent to which she yields, of the extent to which resistance seems too costly.

For, as helpful as it is to be reminded that "woman," like other "others," is culturally constructed, the *women* whose lives are shaped by that construction, as it intersects with others, do indeed exist. They exist subordinated to men: poor, more than men; physically and sexually abused, more than men; paid less than men; promoted less than men; employed *and* managing a home, more than men; raising the children, more than men; underperforming relative to their male peers, in academic and professional settings; exploited, denigrated and stereotyped in popular cultural imagery, more than men; assigned the cultural function of reflecting men "at twice their natural size."[13] They exist, sometimes colluding in their subordination, sometimes resisting it, using whatever their circumstances offer to piece a life together. And feminists, while continuing to acknowledge, celebrate and support the investigation of all the "differences" that divide and constitute both men and women, need not be embarrassed, and should not be afraid, to describe our work as being *about women*, and to imagine that our work is of a kind in which we have a special competence, and a special stake.

The feminist community within the nation's law schools needs to move on, fortified by the past, beyond the original conception of "Women and the Law," beyond "Feminist Jurisprudence". . . . When the women's movement began, post-modernism was still an alien in America. Now it is everywhere. Its minions live and work in a world of multiple realities, partial explanations, contingent truths, where scrupulous attention to the perspective and fractured nature of your own understanding is your only hope of being able to enlarge it. At the same time, scrupulous attention to the perspective and fractured nature of others' under-standings serves the important function of dislodging theories and facts that claim to be neutral, detached, objective, without bias or taint, without perspective, and (as if that were not already enough) internally flawless, coherent and whole. Post-modernism focuses on the power that legitimates particular understandings and explanations of the world, on the link between power and knowledge, even while it also sees power as diffuse, and legitimation of power as local, plural and imma-nent. It generates new forms of scholarship . . .

> large narratives about changes in social organization and ideology, empiri-cal and social-theoretical analyses of macro-structures and institutions, in-teractionist analyses of the micro-politics of everyday life, critical-her-meneutical and institutional analyses of cultural production, historically and culturally specific sociologies. . . .[14]

. . . Now we can not only research what happens to women in the world shaped by law, law language and legal institutions, but challenge even the struc-ture of legal thought as contingent and in some culturally specific sense "male," implying the need for more radical changes than the ameliorative amendations we have offered in the past. . . . Our theory can be at the same time our practice; at work politically as we work professionally, we can give new meaning to the crucial insight of the women's movement that "the personal is political," "the pri-vate is also public."

I have left until last the question of how legal feminists may expect their work to be received, by the mainstream. In this as in other settings, it is already a disadvantage to be a woman. But to be a woman who teaches and writes as a woman, addressing women's concerns, is to be almost certainly beyond the pale. All post-modernism poses an insistent challenge to the work and identity of main-stream (malestream) academics, undercutting their claims to universality, threat-ening their aspiration to immortality. But academic father-slaying, by sons, while a terrifying prospect for both generations, is at the same time recognized as a generational dynamic, tamed by the cultural institutions in which it plays itself out, and in some sense as permissible as it is inevitable. . . . [W]omen, as mothers, but also as wives and daughters, have been assigned the function of admiring reflection, a task they doubly turn their backs on when they claim women as the subject of their study, and post-modern feminist theory as their intellectual tradition. No cultural model exists which can contain the threat posed by this withdrawal, or curb the fears of those who cease to see their images admiringly reflected in women's work. . . . The distress and disorientation produced by this state of affairs can be diminished, it seems, only by the negotiation between mirror and mirrored of new relationships, and new imageries to instantiate and celebrate them.

Notes

1. The first casebooks in the field were published in 1973 and 1974. L. Kanowitz, Sex Roles in Law and Society: Cases and Materials (University of New Mexico Press, 1973); K. Davidson, R. Bader Ginsburg & H. Kay, Text, Cases and Materials on Sex-Based Discrimination (West, 1974). Ruth Bader Ginsburg first taught a course in sex discrimination in 1970 at Rutgers Law School, Newark campus, then at Harvard in fall 1971, and at Columbia from 1972 to 1979; Herma Hill Kay first taught a course on "Women and the Law" at Boalt Hall in the spring of 1972. Telephone interview with the chambers of Hon. Ruth Bader Ginsburg, March 21, 1988; interview with Herma Hill Kay, at Boalt Hall, March 14, 1988.

2. [Sociologist Jessie Bernard used the term "Feminist Enlightenment" at a lecture at Harvard University in October 1987 to describe two decades of intellectual contributions emerging from the women's movement. Ed.]

3. The original "Women and the Law" project suppressed this core feminist insight, in order to claim the protection arguably offered to all, regardless of gender, under the supposedly neutral and objective system of legal entitlements. It was only as it became clear that this system, administered by men, would never in fact fulfill its expressed commitments that this came to seem an unnecessary and potentially disabling strategy.

4. N. Chodorow, The Reproduction of Mothering (University of California Press, 1978). Chodorow suggests that in a society in which strong cultural norms exist about the proper attributes, roles and behaviors associated with femininity and masculinity, the disproportionate role played by women in the parenting of young children serves to "reproduce" mothering qualities in each succeeding generation of women, while reproducing the antitheses of those qualities in men, who struggle to separate out from mother by becoming everything she is not.

5. D. Dinnerstein, The Mermaid and the Minotaur (Harper & Row, 1976). Dinnerstein, whose book predates Chodorow's, shares Chodorow's perception that the developmental task of separating out from mother, differently experienced by boy and girl children, helps to recreate the cultural differences we commonly see between men and women. More central to her account, however, is the idea that the culturally constructed "mother" role makes successful separation—individuation extremely difficult for children of both genders, leaving men and women allied in a residual (unconscious) hatred and fear of mother, and women more generally. She traces the consequences of these attitudes towards women for adult relationships between men and women, and between men and the planet they inhabit and govern.

6. C. Gilligan, In A Different Voice (Harvard University Press, 1982). Gilligan suggests that there are two very different styles of thinking about moral questions, and the resolution of moral problems. One style, or ethic, stresses autonomy, rights, principles and exclusive solutions; the other stresses connection, contextual and consequentialist thinking and inclusive solutions. The first ethic Gilligan found more prevalent in men, the second in women. Gilligan herself sees the results of her empirical work as confirming the psychoanalytic theory of Nancy Chodorow.

7. C. MacKinnon, Feminism Unmodified (Harvard University Press, 1987). This latest book builds on MacKinnon's earlier work in the areas of both sexual harassment and pornography, as well as her more theoretical contributions to the development of feminist legal theory.

8. . . . For critiques, see, e.g., M. Frug, The Role of Difference in the Study of Women in Law (July 1987, unpublished manuscript) (suggesting that "crude Gilliganism" threatens to discredit women and their cause"); and E. Spelman, Inessential Woman: Problems of Exclusion in Feminist Thought (Beacon Press, 1988).

9. J. Lacan, Encore, le Séminaire XX (Seuil, 1975); J. Lacan, Télévision, *passim* (Seuil, 1974).

10. L. Irigaray, Ce Sexe Qui N'En Est Pas Un (Éditions de Minuit, 1977), translated as This Sex Which Is Not One (C. Porter & C. Burke, trans., Cornell University Press, 1985).

11. As MacKinnon puts it: "Feminism criticizes . . . male totality without an account of our capacity to do so or to imagine or realize a more whole truth. Feminism affirms women's point of view by revealing, criticizing, and explaining its impossibility." C. MacKinnon, Feminism, Marxism, Method, and the State: Toward Feminist Jurisprudence, Part 5 this volume, at 427.

12. The value of using feminist methodology in the service of other oppressed groups is well exemplified in the work of Martha Minow. See, e.g., Minow, The Supreme Court, 1986 Term—Foreword: Justice Engendered, Part 3 this volume (dealing with problems of "difference" in Supreme Court jurisprudence in the contexts of religion, ethnicity, race, and handicapping conditions, as well as gender); and Minow, When Difference Has Its Home: Group Homes for the Mentally Retarded, Equal Protection and Legal Treatment of Difference, Part 3 this volume. My concern is only that feminists not be drawn away from specific attention to or advocacy on behalf of women by these other concerns.

13. The quotation is adapted from V. Woolf, A Room of One's Own 35 (Harcourt, Brace, 1929): "Women have served all these centuries as looking-glasses possessing the magic and delicious power of reflecting the figure of man at twice its natural size." . . .

14. Fraser & Nicholson, Social Criticism without Philosophy: An Encounter between Feminism and Postmodernism, 10 Communication, no. 3 (1988), at 345.

❖ *The Emergence of Feminist Jurisprudence: An Essay*

Ann C. Scales

. . .

We as lawyers have been trained to desire abstract, universal, objective solutions to social ills, in the form of legal rules or doctrine. Much of the history of feminist jurisprudence has reflected that tradition. It has been a debate, in the abstract, about appropriate rules. This essay uses the work of several non-legal authors to illustrate the impossibility of seeing solutions to inequality through that lens of abstraction. This essay concerns feminist efforts to live with, and ultimately to resist, abstraction itself. . . .

Where We've Been

In this country, the engine of the struggle for equality has been Aristotelian: Equality means to treat like persons alike, and unlike persons unlike.[1] Under this model, when legal distinctions are made, the responsible sovereign must point to some difference between subjects which justifies their disparate treatment.[2] That was the model in Reed v. Reed,[3] the first equal protection case decided favorably in the Supreme Court for women . . . [holding] that the state of Idaho could not presumptively deny to women the right to administer estates. With respect to such activities, the Court saw that women and men are "similarly situated." That is, no demonstrable difference between the sexes justified treating them differently.

This is what Professor Catharine MacKinnon has called "the differences approach,"[4] and it worked extraordinarily well . . . until the Court had to face situations where the sexes are not, or do not seem to be, similarly situated—situations involving pregnancy, situations involving the supposed overpowering sexual allure which women present to men [e.g., women as prison guards], and situations

Reprinted by permission of the Yale Law Journal Company and Fred B. Rothman & Company from *The Yale Law Journal*, Vol. 95 (1986), pp. 1373–1403.

involving the historical absence of women [e.g., women's exclusion from the draft]. . . .

Feminist legal scholars have devoted enormous energies to patching the cracks in the differences approach. . . . Which differences between the sexes are or should be relevant for legal purposes? How does one tell what the differences are? Does it matter whether the differences are inherent or the result of upbringing? Is it enough to distinguish between accurate and inaccurate stereotyped differences? Or are there situations where differences are sufficiently "real" and permanent to demand social accommodation?

In response to these questions, feminists have tried to describe for the judiciary a theory of "special rights" for women which will "fit" the discrete, non-stereotypical, "real" differences between the sexes. And here lies our mistake: we have let the debate become narrowed by accepting as correct those questions which seek to arrive at a definitive list of differences. In so doing, we have adopted the vocabulary, as well as the epistemology and political theory, of the law as it is.

When we try to arrive at a definitive list of differences, even in sophisticated ways, we only encourage the law's tendency to act upon a frozen slice of reality. In so doing, we participate in the underlying problem—the objectification of women. Through our conscientious listing, we help to define real gender issues out of existence. Our aim must be to affirm differences as emergent and infinite. We must seek a legal system that works and, at the same, makes differences a cause for celebration, not classification.

. . . Our past reliance on rights/rule structuring has been disappointing, because we have been unable to see the solipsism of the male norm. Our tendency as lawyers to seek comprehensive rules in accordance with that norm is a dangerous learned reflex which defeats feminism's critique of objectification.

The Tyranny of Objectivity

. . .

Underlying the Supreme Court's ruling in Reed v. Reed was a perception that sexism is a distortion of reality. Once the Court made this discovery, it needed to transform its discovery into a legalistic code, to construct an "objective" rule. And here lies the most difficult part of rule-making in our system as it is—phrasing the rule so that people believe that the rule is detached, so that it appears to transcend the results in particular cases.[5]

The philosophical basis of such an approach is "abstract universality."[6] In order to apply a rule neutrally in future cases, one must discern *a priori* what the differences and similarities among groups are. But because there are an infinite number of differences and similarities among groups, one must also discern which differences are relevant. To make this determination, one must first abstract the essential and universal similarities among humans; one must have strict assumptions about human nature as such. Without such an abstraction, there is no way to talk about which differences in treatment are arbitrary and which are justified. Underlying this approach is the correspondence theory of truth: the sovereign's judgments are valid only when they reflect objective facts. Thus, somewhere in the nature of things there must be a list of sex differences that matter and those that do not. Notice, however, that abstract universality by its own terms cannot arrive at such a list. It has no "bridge to the concrete"[7] by which to ascertain the emerging and cultural qualities which constitute difference.

[A]bstract universality . . . made maleness the norm of what is human, and did so . . . all in the name of neutrality. By this . . . system, the "relevant" differences have been and always will be those which keep women in their place. Abstract universality is ideology, pure and simple. It is a conception of the world which takes "the part for the whole, the particular for the universal and essential, or the present for the eternal."[8] With the allegedly anonymous picture of humanity reflecting a picture males have painted of themselves, women are but male subjectivity glorified, objectified, elevated to the status of reality. The values of things "out there" are made to appear as if they were qualities of the things themselves. So goes the process of objectification: the winner is he who makes his world seem necessary.[9]

Feminist analysis begins with the principle that objective reality is a myth. It recognizes that patriarchal myths are projections of the male psyche. The most pernicious of these myths is that the domination of women is a natural right, a mere reflection of the biological family. The patriarchal paradigm of the will of the father informs rationality at every historical stage. . . .

A legal system must attempt to assure fairness. Fairness must have reference to real human predicaments. Abstract universality is a convenient device for some philosophical pursuits, or for any endeavor whose means can stand without ends, but it is particularly unsuited for law. . . . By inquiring into the . . . structure of objectivity, we see that abstract universality explicitly contradicts the ideal of a "government of laws, not men." Our task, therefore, is to construct a system which avoids solipsism, which recognizes that the subjectivity of the law-maker is not the whole of reality.

A Call for Vigilance

It is imperative for jurisprudence to tap the power of the more radical versions of feminism. An effective contemporary feminist critique must be radical in the literal sense. It must go to the root of inequality. Without extraordinary subterranean vigilance, the radical potential of feminism will be undermined. Like other movements that presage revolutionary change, feminism faces a constant threat of deradicalization.

In her popular book, *In a Different Voice*,[10] developmental psychologist Carol

Gilligan observed that little girls and little boys appear to grapple with moral problems differently. Boys tend to make moral decisions in a legalistic way: they presume that the autonomy of individuals is the paramount value, and then employ a rule-like mechanism to decide among the "rights" of those individuals. Gilligan refers to this as the "ethic of rights" or "the ethic of justice." Girls, on the other hand, seem to proceed by the "ethic of care." They have as their goal the preservation of the relationships involved in a given situation. Their reasoning looks like equity: they expand the available universe of facts, rules, and relationships in order to find a unique solution to each unique problem.

Just as Gilligan's work has the potential to inspire us in historic ways, it could also become the *Uncle Tom's Cabin* of our century. Lawyers are tempted to use Gilligan's work in a shallow way, to distill it into a neat formula. . . . Rightly or wrongly, many people feel that such an oversimplified version comports with their experience of the sexes. . . . All in all, Gilligan's work tempts one to suggest that the different voices of women can somehow be grafted onto our right- and rule-based legal system.

One in a non-vigilant mode might be moved to think that we could have a system which in the abstract satisfies all the competing considerations: rules, rights, relationships, and equity. This is what I call the "incorporationist" view.[11] Gilligan asserts that as a matter of personal moral development, the ability to integrate the ethics of care with the ethics of rights signals maturity. I think no one would disagree with such a goal in an emotional realm. Emotional and cognitive maturity have, however, come to mean very different things. In the majority culture, emotional maturity does not count as knowledge. The ad hoc evaluations we must undertake in the emotional realm cannot be acknowledged elsewhere. Such judgments are not "reliable," only "objectivity" is reliable. We should be especially wary when we hear lawyers, addicted to cognitive objectivity as they are, assert that women's voices have a place in the existing system. In the words of James Agee: "Official acceptance is the one unmistakable symptom that salvation is beaten again, and is the one surest sign of fatal misunderstanding, and is the kiss of Judas."[12]

Incorporationism presumes that we can whip the problem of social inequality by adding yet another prong to the already multi-pronged legal tests. . . . Incorporationism suffers from the same lack of vision as the "equal rights/special rights" debate. Both presume that male supremacy is simply a random collection of irrationalities in an otherwise rational coexistence. Both presume that instances of inequality are mere legal mistakes—a series of failures to treat equals as equals which we can fix if we can just spot the irrationality in enough cases. As Professor MacKinnon has demonstrated, however, from such viewpoints we cannot see that male supremacy is a complete social system for the advantage of one sex over another.[13] The injustice of sexism is not irrationality; it is domination. Law must focus on the latter, and that focus cannot be achieved though a formal lens. Binding ourselves to rules would help us only if sexism were a legal error.

A commitment to equality requires that we undertake to investigate the genderization of the world, leaving nothing untouched. The principles of objectivity, abstraction, and personal autonomy are at risk. In our search, we must look for the deeper causes and consequences of Gilligan's findings. Her work is empirical evidence for what feminist theory has already postulated: a male point of view focuses narrowly on autonomy, on the separation between self and others. That disjunction contains the roots of domination. In the terms of feminist theory, male reality manifests itself by negating that which is non-male. The male model defines self, and other important concepts, by opposing the concept to a negativized "other."[14] Male rationality divides the world between all that is good and all that is bad—between objective and subjective, light and shadow, man and woman. For all of these dichotomies . . . , the goodness of the good side is defined by what it is not.

Whereas the male self/other ontology seems to be oppositional, the female version seems to be relational.[15] The female ontology is an alternative theory of differentiation that does not define by negation nor require a "life and death struggle"[16] to identify value in the world. Instead, it perceives relationship as constitutive of the self. It perceives dichotomization as irrational.

Male and female perceptions of value are not shared, and are perhaps not even perceptible to each other. In our current genderized realm, therefore, the "rights-based" and "care-based" ethics cannot be blended. Patriarchal psychology sees value as differently distributed between men and women: men are rational, women are not. Feminist psychology suggests different conceptions of value: women are entirely rational, but society cannot accommodate them because the male standard has defined into oblivion any version of rationality but its own. Paradigmatic male values, like objectivity, are defined as exclusive, identified by their presumed opposites. Those values cannot be content with multiplicity; they create the other and devour it. Objectivity ignores context; reason is the opposite of emotion; rights preclude care. As long as the ruling ideology is a function of this dichotomization, incorporationism threatens to be mere co-optation, a more subtle version of female invisibility.

By trying to make everything too nice, incorporationism represses contradictions. It usurps women's language in order to further define the world in the male image; it thus deprives women of the power of naming.[17] Incorporationism means to give over the world, because it means to say to those in power: "We will use your language and we will let you interpret it." . . .

Feminist Method

. . .

Feminist thinking has evolved dramatically in the last twenty years, from an essentially liberal attack on the absence of women in the public world to a radical vision of the transformation of the world. The demand for "gender neutrality" which served valiantly in the legal struggles of the seventies has inevitably become a critique of neutrality itself, which proceeds by an admittedly non-neutral method. Explanations of our method usually provoke the charge of nominalism, such is the staying power of the ideal of objectivity. Feminist method would appear to be an easy target for that weapon. Feminism does not claim to be objective, because objectivity is the basis for inequality. Feminism is not abstract, because abstraction when institutionalized shields the status quo from critique. Feminism is result-oriented. It is vitally concerned with the oblivion fostered by lawyers' belief that process is what matters.

The next step for theory is therefore to demonstrate that feminist method leads to principled adjudication and a more orderly coexistence. Let us begin by reconsidering Carol Gilligan's results. The little boys' approach divides life into opposing camps. In a moral dilemma, this person or that person shall win, based upon some "essential" difference in their situations. One must be shown to be unworthy and wrong. One must be transformed into the "other."

Perhaps there is something in the paradigm of male infant development which teaches a harsh method of differentiation. Insofar as objectification is taught as the preferred way to see the world, we replicate the emotional substructure of domination. The children are thereby programmed, prepared to fall into the habit of objectification which is at the heart of woman-loathing. As adults, these people may have noble intentions, but it will be too late. At best, they will become incorporationists—people who must co-opt the voices of the powerless, who can't let them speak for themselves because, by definition, "the other" is mute.

Compare the problem-solving method used by the little girls. Their habit of expanding the context, of following the connections among people and events, is descriptive of rationality. When given a situation with which to grapple, the girls do not insist upon uncovering an essence of the problem, but look rather for a solution that is coherent with the rest of experience.

If I am right that the "rights-based" and "care-based" approaches are incompatible, we must make a choice between adjudicative principles. The choice is not, however, between male and female hegemony. The choice is rather between a compulsion to control reality and a commitment to restrain hegemony. Do we want a system that brooks no disagreement or one that invites as many points of view as the varieties of existence require? The values of honesty and pragmatism require us to choose the relational model, because only it describes how we as language-users actually and responsibly perform according to truly meaningful criteria. . . .

Law, like the language which is its medium, is a system of classification. To characterize similarities and differences among situations is a key step in legal judgments. That step, however, is not a mechanistic manipulation of essences. Rather, that step always has a moral crux. . . .

Law needs some theory of differentiation. Feminism, as a theory of differentiation, is particularly well suited to it. Feminism brings law back to its purpose—to decide the moral crux of the matter in real human situations. Law is a complex system of communication; its communicative matrix is intended to give access to the moral crux. Finding the crux depends upon the relation among things, not upon their opposition. . . . It would . . . seem obvious that relational reasoning is law's soul, that law's duty is to enhance, rather than to ignore, the rich diversity of life. Yet this purpose is not obvious; it is obscured by the myth of objectivity which opens up law's destructive potential. Feminism inverts the logical primacy of rule over facts. Feminist method stresses that the mechanisms of law—language, rules, and categories—are all merely means for economy in thought and communication. They make it possible for us to implement justice without reinventing every wheel at every turn. But we must not let means turn into ends. When those mechanisms obscure our vision of the ends of law, they must be revised or ignored. Sometimes we must take the long route in order to get to where we really need to be.

In feminist thought, deciding what differences are relevant for any purpose does not require objectifying and destroying some "other." Feminism rejects "abstract universality" in favor of "concrete universality." The former conjures differences—it elevates some to dispositive principles and defines others out of existence—and makes maleness the norm. The latter reinterprets differences in three crucial ways. First, concrete universalism takes differences to be constitutive of the universal itself. Second, it sees differences as systematically related to each other, and to other relations, such as exploited and exploiter. Third, it regards differences as emergent, as always changing.[18]

In the past, two legal choices appeared to resolve claims of social injustice: law could either ignore differences, thereby risking needless conformity, or it could freeze differences, thereby creating a menu of justifications for inequality. Concrete universality eliminates the need for such a choice. When our priority is to understand differences and to value multiplicity, we need only to discern between occasions of respect and occasions of oppression. Those are judgments we know how to make, even without a four-part test to tell us, for every future circumstance, what constitutes domination. . . . Domination comes in many forms. Its mechanisms are so insidious and so powerful that we could never codify its "essence." The description that uses no formula, but which points to the moral crux of the matter, is exactly what we need.

Psychoanalytic Frameworks

The goal of discerning domination requires that the law recognize the psychological substructures of gender. The legal system recoils from this prescription on the ground that judgments about human development are beyond its ken, that the law's point-of-viewlessness would be sullied by such inquiries. This predictable response, however, is the reason for the psychoanalytic inquiry in the first place. Feminist method discloses that the law has "a personal investment . . . in impersonality." Psychoanalytic theory helps us to understand why the legal system has insisted upon its lack of subjectivity and to analyze the subjectivity that so loudly denies its presence. . . .

Feminist jurisprudence is unique in its demand for an adequate psychology. Feminist jurisprudence goes beyond liberalism in requiring legal decision-makers to reexamine any doctrine that is justified by an ethic of individual autonomy. The liberal humanist goal of protecting the "untrammelled exercise of capacities central to human rationality"[19] not only does not apply to disenabled persons, but often requires the systematic deprivation of the freedom of others.[20] In making the connection between domination and mechanisms of sex-role differentiation, feminism also goes beyond Marxism. The latter sees domination as imposed by external economic and political factors; feminism attends fully to the powerful oppressive forces within us.[21] The social experiences of the sexes are not the same; a social theory without a convincing psychological account of that differentiation cannot remedy gender inequality.

. . . [Freud] did contribute an insight fundamental to feminism: Humans are not wholly rational animals. . . . Our viewpoints are informed by irrational, sometimes morbid patterns. Feminism recognizes within us that which Freud saw as irrational, and asserts, therefore, that when dealing with social inequality there are no neutral principles. . . . But feminism rejects what Dorothy Dinnerstein has shown to be Freud's essentially conservative belief that our defects constitute a fixed condition of the species' existence. Freud's conclusions about us are a contingent rationalization, but his psychoanalytic model is an invaluable description of the process of conscription into socially-determined sex-roles.

In one neo-Freudian account, Dinnerstein describes the process by which infants become dependent upon, and then learn to loathe, women. . . . We are woman-born, and . . . woman-nurtured in our infancy. It is to a woman we turn in our helplessness; it is a woman who gives us our first grief when we discover that she is imperfect and not always available; it is a woman who, by her imperfection and her omnipotence, introduces us to existential angst. Thus, Dinnerstein explains, our social arrangements reflect the necessity of renouncing our first love while at the same time living out our anger at her.[22]

The males of the species have been able to do this by dichotomizing the world, by separating out man from woman, society from nature, enterprise from homeyness, history from love. . . . The enterprise of making history is tinged with residual anger at mother, and can be only a partial consolation for the loss of intimacy. The enterprise becomes a "compulsive concentration on what can be predicted, controlled, manipulated, possessed and preserved, piled up and counted."[23] As should be clear from that description, it is an enterprise reflected, enhanced, and often directed by the legal system.

To this familiar account Dinnerstein adds an analysis of the symbiotic nature of sexual pathology. She argues that both sexes, at least in their stereotypical, genderized roles, have a stake in "keeping history mad."[24] A woman acting in a genderized role—as nurturer, worrier, and lamenter—may have no say in decisions of historical importance, but she does get benefits: she gains the approval of those who are powerful, and, of course, she does not have to take responsibility for making ugly historical decisions. A man acting in a genderized role—as warrior, as history-maker, and as keeper of woman—avoids moral responsibility for his actions and need not admit the ugliness of aggressive behavior. He has women there to ventilate the difficult emotions. Women do the weeping for the world, while the mad megamachine rolls on.

Dinnerstein reveals something crucial about incorporationism: in its simplistic view of the alternative ontologies, incorporationism perpetuates a destructive symbiosis. The rights-based side of things, for all its grand abstraction, describes a pretty grim view of life on the planet. It treats individuals in society as isolated monads, as natural adversaries who must each stake out his own territory and protect it with the sword/shield mechanisms called "rights." This model of aggression is half of what is required for holocaust. False glorification of the "care-based" ethic supplies the other side of the suicidal equation, because a death march requires willing-looking victims. The incorporationist version of the care-based ethic celebrates oblivion. Its Disney-movie appeal diverts attention from the issue of powerlessness, and, indeed, makes a political virtue of it. Masters glorify the contentment of their slaves, empires of their colonies. Here, hegemony strikes again. An incorporationist legal regime would, at best, merely institutionalize a familiar female critique—steady but ineffectual.

Dinnerstein's theory flounders, is itself incorporationist, because she looks at the role of women from a patriarchally sanctioned place. She presupposes the ontology which also served Freud so well: the opposition of self and other, the "either/or 'investment' of libidinal energy."[25] Dinnerstein suggests, for example, that patriarchy is possible because, to infants, male authority is an attractive refuge from female authority. "For this reason he is perceived from the beginning . . . as a more *human* being than the mother, more like an adult version of oneself, less engulfing, less nebulously overwhelming."[26] Dinnerstein argues that, as long as women are responsible for infant care, the need to possess and then reject the "dirty goddess" is an inevitable feature of (male) infant psychology.[27] It seems just as reasonable, however, to view the advent of adult male authority as a set-up. If it's true that daddy looks good compared to mommy, that's a function of the awful way mommy is made to look—irrational, powerless, ingratiating.

> Being on the bottom of a hierarchy is not a pose, it is not a choice, there is nothing safe about it, and it only looks brave and defiant to those for whom its choicelessness and violation and dead-ended chances look romantic and elevated because they are not real.[28]

What the Freudians describe is a life and death struggle in infancy, a necessary choosing of sides resulting in sex roles and arrangements. But that conclusion could represent just another way to avoid facing how power is used and abused. The Oedipus and Electra complexes which "explain" the struggle are just as implausible as they always sounded. . . . Feminism requires the law to question the inevitability of sex differentiation, and to be ever conscious of its role in enforcing female loyalty to men. We must look for that which we have been trained not to see. We must identify the invisible, and take responsibility for the violence built into the genderized world. . . .

Coping with Equality

The problem of inequality of the sexes stands in complex relation to the problem of survival. Inequality in the sexual division of labor assures replication of the model of aggression. Pathological aggression accounts for inequality. . . . [I]f we are serious about survival, we need a radically more serious approach to equality. Law must embrace a version of equality that focuses on the real issues—domination, disadvantage and disempowerment—instead of on the interminable and diseased issue of differences between the sexes. I endorse the definition of equality proposed by Professor MacKinnon . . . "whether the policy or practice in question integrally contributes to the maintenance of an underclass or a deprived position because of gender status."[29] MacKinnon contrasts this to the "differences approach," calling it the "inequality approach." . . .

That is not to say that the proposed standard will be easy to implement. . . . The critics appropriately worry, for example, that classifications designed to address the real problems of women (such as pregnancy legislation) will serve to reinforce stereotypes about women's place.[30] The problem for feminist legal scholars, I think, is that we are unsure how to measure what about stereotyping is at issue in a given case. The notion of stereotyping connotes over-simplification, inattention to individual characteristics, lack of seriousness, and invariance. We use the concept of stereotyping without difficulty when the challenged practice is based upon an untrue generalization. All of the connotations of stereotyping are clearly implicated in negative ways. In such cases, both the differences approach and the inequality approach would prohibit the classification.

The inequality approach focuses upon two other sources of feminist discomfort: first, the need for a reliable approach to generalizations which are largely true (either because of biology or because of highly successful socialization); and second, the need to distinguish between beneficial and burdensome legislation.

Only the inequality approach attempts to reckon with true generalizations. Indeed, in that view, different treatment based upon unique physical characteristics would be "among the *first* to trigger suspicion and scrutiny."[31] In the past, biological differences have been used to show that classifications are not sex-based.[32] Thereby, the reasons for having antidiscrimination laws have been seen as the reasons to allow discrimination.[33] The inequality approach unravels the tautology. It makes no sense to say that equality is guaranteed only when the sexes are already equal. The issue is not freedom to be treated without regard to sex; the issue is freedom from systematic subordination because of sex.

The inequality approach would also reach stereotypes which, though not biologically based, have largely made themselves true through a history of inequality. Consider the situation in Phillips v. Martin Marietta Corp.,[34] where the company hired males with preschool age children, but would not hire women in that category. As a variation, suppose the trial court had found that women with small children did in fact have greater responsibilities, and therefore were, as a group, less well suited for the jobs in question. Such a finding would correspond to the facts of allocation of child-raising responsibility. The only challenge that will work in this scenario is one from an "exceptional" woman candidate for employment— a woman with preschool age children whose job performance will not be impaired by her obligations to them. The policy will be deemed irrational as applied to her.

Compare the inequality approach, which is triggered not by irrationality, but by disadvantage. In our scenario, the inequality approach is superior because it reaches the worse injustice: the fact that women who fit the stereotype are precluded from advancement in our economic system: A challenge adjudicated by that standard would succeed on behalf of the unexceptional as well as the exceptional. Employers (and other employees who have carried a disproportionately lower burden in child-rearing) would then essentially have to compensate for the benefits they have derived from women's double burden. Such payment should include damages, and court-ordered advancement, day care, parents' leave, and reallocation of workers' hours and rewards. This redistribution of historical burdens and benefits may seem a sweeping remedy, but it is the only one which addresses the reality.

With respect to our second problem, the discernment of genuinely beneficial classifications, suppose that the same company offered a hiring preference for women with school age children, and provided some relief from the double burden. The offer undoubtedly "reinforces a stereotype," but what shall we make of the fact that the stereotype is in large part—if only contingently and temporarily—true? But true only because women carry a disproportionate burden of the child-caring responsibility in our society. Especially when women can elect to receive the benefits (as opposed to risking stigmatization by them), what is the objection to such a plan? Disadvantage has a way of replicating and reinforcing itself. To oppose the scheme is to be reduced to relying upon a groundswell of exceptional behaviors within the disadvantaged group itself. Historically, however, disadvantaged groups have been forced to rely upon surrogates to better themselves. That has not required that the groups thus assisted conform for all time to the surrogates' perceptions of them (or even to their own perceptions of themselves).

Beneficial classifications, therefore, seem necessary to the ultimate undoing of stubborn stereotypes. It is true that in our history, stereotypical differences, both real and imagined, have served primarily as convenient, "natural" justifications for imposition of burdens. It does not follow, however, that we cannot use differences progressively. Injustice does not flow directly from recognizing differences; injustice results when those differences are transformed into social and economic deprivation. Our task then, is to exercise our capacity for discernment in more precise ways. Allegedly beneficial classifications, even when they invoke a stereotype, must be measured against what is objectionable in stereotyping. Beneficial classifications, such as the employment preference in our example, will survive under the inequality approach if they do not have those characteristics. Insofar as the employment preference over-simplifies, it is an over-simplification in the service of a profound complexity, as is any well-drafted policy. The preference provides to individuals the opportunity to demonstrate their capacities when the stereotype is set aside. It evinces laudable seriousness toward the problem, especially insofar as the stereotyper takes upon itself some of the burden of the past discrimination. Last, and perhaps most important, it is not invariant. By definition it points to the stereotype for the purpose of undoing it, as an example of how revised present arrangements can relieve centuries of disadvantage. When allegedly beneficial classifications do not have this form, or when once beneficial schemes cease to have it, the inequality approach would prohibit them.

Admittedly, the inequality approach would sometimes require that different standards be used for men and women. If that were not so, however, the approach would not be working. Its emphasis is upon enforced inferiority, not sex-differentiated treatment. When the aim is to discover the reality of domination, the standard to be applied depends upon the context. The inequality approach requires an investigation which must delve as deeply as circumstances demand into whether the challenged policy or practice exploits gender status. To worry in the abstract about which standard should be applied at what time is to replicate the fallacy of the differences approach.

In short, the inequality approach means that we have to think more broadly about what we want "equality" to mean. The traditional bases for differentiation between the sexes are socially created categories, given meaning only by assigned biases. We create the relevant comparisons, and are free to do so de novo in light of social realities. Thus, in the preferential hiring situation, we would say that the right at stake, rather than the right to be treated without regard to sex, is the right not to have one's existence bifurcated because of sex. In the pregnancy situation, it is the right to have one's total health needs taken as seriously as are those of the other sex.

Logic is no obstacle to the implementation of the inequality approach. The obstacles are, rather, perception and commitment. When the fact of judicial manipulation has been so salient in the past, why should we now expect those responsible for implementing the law to be able to see, in any given situation, how women have been disadvantaged? Accustomed as judges are to looking for similarities and differences, they can not or will not make the assessments of deprivation and disempowerment.

My response to this, on optimistic days, is that we are more persuasive than we believe we are. If judges are supposed to accept guidance, we as practitioners and scholars ought to be able to provide it. There has been some progress, however modest. Our duty is to be vigilant in assuring that what happens is real progress, and to guide the courts through our proposed transformation. . . .

At less optimistic moments, candor would compel me to admit that implementation of a feminist approach will ultimately depend upon significant changes in judicial personnel. Given what we have experienced, however, I feel comfortable with such an admission. It is time that feminist lawyers spoke openly about the politics of neutrality, instead of pretending that sexism were a legal mistake. We have, for example, squandered over a decade discussing what legal standard could have prevented the outrage of Geduldig v. Aiello.[35] But let's face it—the problem in that "analysis" (that no discrimination exists if pregnant women and pregnant men are treated the same) is not that the Supreme Court used the wrong legal standard. The problem was much more serious: it was that our highest court cavalierly allowed California to disadvantage women with respect to their reproductive capabilities. Our highest court endorsed a modern version of a centuries-old method of domination.

We must never forget *Geduldig*. Our Supreme Court got away with it because we allowed the question of pregnancy to be sequestered in our own minds from the question of domination. In our search for a liberal resolution, the real issue remained invisible, and our critique came dangerously close to consent. Our objections can no longer be oblique, for then they are lost. Keeping dissent hidden is an ancient tactic which renders the dissent trivial, abnormal, and disconnected from its roots. Due to the distribution of women in society, this has particularly been the case with feminism. Because each new feminist work or insight appears as if from nowhere, "each contemporary feminist theorist [is] attacked or dismissed ad feminam, as if her politics were simply an outburst of personal bitterness or rage."[36] Trust we must have that we can describe the issues; empowered we must be when our trust is violated.

The proposed inequality standard will not take root overnight. Developments in feminist theory take decades to manifest themselves in law. But it will happen; the difficulty of the process must not stop us from demanding that change, or from continuing the tradition that makes it possible.

Feminist Method Revisited

The term "feminist jurisprudence" disturbs people. That is not surprising, given patriarchy's convenient habit of labeling as unreliable any approach that admits to be interested, and particularly given the historic *a priori* invalidation of women's experience. . . .

In the understandable rush to render feminism acceptable in traditional terms, it is sometimes suggested that we ought to advertise our insight as a revival of the Legal Realism of the 1930s. We are surely indebted to the Realists for their convincing demonstration that the law could not be described, as the positivists had hoped, as a scientific enterprise, devoid of moral or political content. The Realists' description of the influence of morality, economics, and politics upon law is the first step in developing an antidote for legal solipsism. In the end, however, the Realists did not revolutionize the law but merely expanded the concept of legal process.[37] The Realists did not press their critique deeply enough; they did not bring home its implications. In the face of their failure, the system has clung even more desperately to objectivity and neutrality. "[T]he effect of the Realists was much like the role that Carlyle pronounced for Matthew Arnold: 'He led them into the wilderness and left them there.' "[38]

Feminism now faces the charge leveled at Realism, that it destroys the citadel of objectivity and leaves nothing to legitimate the law. Our response to this state of affairs begins with an insight not exclusive to feminist thought: the law must finally enter the twentieth century. The business of living and progressing within our disciplines requires that we give up on "objective" verification at various critical moments, such as when we rely upon gravity, or upon the existence of others, or upon the principle of verification itself. Feminism insists upon epistemological and psychological sophistication in law: jurisprudence will forever be stuck in a post-realist battle of subjectivities, with all the discomfort that has represented, until we confront the distinction between knowing subject and known object.

Feminist method is exemplary of that confrontation. . . . [B]ecause we do not separate the observer from the observed, "[f]eminism is the first theory to emerge from those whose interest it affirms."[39] Feminist method proceeds through consciousness raising. The results of consciousness raising cannot be verified by traditional methods, nor need they be. We are therefore operating from within an epistemological framework which denies our power to know. This is an inherently transformative process: it validates the experience of women, the major content of which has been invalidation. . . .

Consciousness raising is a vivid expression of self-creation and responsibility. To Wittgenstein's insight that perceptions have meaning only in the context of experience, feminism would add that perceptions have meaning only in the context of an experience that matters. Consciousness raising means that dramatic eye-witness testimony is being given; it means, more importantly, that women now have the confidence to declare it as such. We have an alternative to relegating our perception to the realm of our own subjective discomfort. Heretofore, the tried and true scientific strategy of treating non-conforming evidence as mistaken worked in the legal system. But when that evidence keeps turning up, when the experience of women becomes recalcitrant, it will be time to treat that evidence as true.

The foundations of the law will not thereby crumble. Though feminism rejects the notion that for a legal system to work, there have to be "objective" rules, we admit that legality has (or should have) certain qualities. There must be something reliable somewhere, there must be indicia of fairness in the system, but neither depends on objectivity. Rather, we need to discard the habit of equating our most noble aspirations with objectivity and neutrality. We need at least to redefine those terms, and probably to use others, to meet our very serious responsibilities.

My admission that feminism is result-oriented does not import the renunciation of all standards. In a system defined by constitutional norms such as equality, we need standards to help us make connections among norms, and to help us see "family resemblances" among instances of domination. Standards, however, are not means without ends: they never have and never can be more than working hypotheses. Just as it would be shocking to find a case that said, "the petitioner wins though she satisfied no criteria," so it must ultimately be wrong to keep finding cases that say, "petitioner loses though the criteria are indefensible." In legal situations, a case is either conformed to a standard or the standard is modified with justification. That justification should not be that "we like the petitioner's facts better"; rather, it is that "on facts such as these, the standard doesn't hold up."

The feminist approach takes justification seriously; it is a more honest and efficient way to achieve legitimacy. The feminist legal standard for equality is altogether principled in requiring commitment to finding the moral crux of matters before the court. The feminist approach will tax us. We will be exhausted by bringing feminist method to bear. Yet we must force law-makers and interpreters to hear that which they have been well trained to ignore. We will have to divest ourselves of our learned reticence, debrief ourselves every day. We will have to trust ourselves to be able to describe life to each other—in our courts, in our legislatures, in our emergence together.

Notes

1. Aristotle, Nichomachean Ethics V(3), at 112–14 (D. Ross trans., 1925).

2. This is what Charles Frankel has called "basic equality." Frankel, Equality of Opportunity, 81 Ethics 191, 194–96 (1971). As Frankel points out, the fact that the sovereign must justify its actions is an advance over Aristotelian formal equality, where any perceived difference produces difference in treatment. "Basic equality" is ultimately unsatisfying, however, because the rule that reasons must exist does not indicate how good those reasons have to be. Id.

3. 404 U.S. 71 (1971).

4. C. MacKinnon, Sexual Harassment of Working Women 101 (Yale University Press, 1979) (emphasis omitted).

5. The quality of transcendence of results has been said to be the primary feature of neutrality in constitutional adjudication. Wechsler, Toward Neutral Principles of Constitutional Law, 73 Harv. L. Rev. 1, 12 (1959).

6. C. Gould, The Woman Question: Philosophy of Liberation and the Liberation of Philosophy, in C. Gould & M. Wartofsky eds., Women and Philosophy: Toward a Theory of Liberation 5–6 (Putnam, 1976).

7. *Id.* at 20.

8. *Id.* at 21.

9. As MacKinnon puts it: "Combining, like any form of power, legitimation with force, male power extends beneath the representation of reality to its construction: it makes women (as it were) and so verifies (makes true) who women "are" in its view, simultaneously confirming its way of being and its vision of truth. . . . Objectivity is the methodological stance of which objectification is the social process. Sexual objectification is the primary process of subjection of women. It unites act with word, construction with expression, perception with enforcement, myth with reality." MacKinnon, Feminism, Marxism, Method, and the State: An Agenda for Theory, Part 5 this volume, at 448–49.

10. C. Gilligan, In a Different Voice (Harvard University Press, 1982).

11. "Incorporationism" is the label I gave to the approach that I supported in 1981. See Scales, Towards a Feminist Jurisprudence, 56 Ind. L.J. 375, 435 (1981). Though not identical to the view that I criticize here, my stance had the same basic flaw—an obsession with what differences between men and women the law could, in the abstract, take into account. Pregnancy and breastfeeding, I thought, had to be accounted for if the law were to take a sufficiently broad view of equality: Equality requires that a woman not be forced to choose between children and career, just as a man need not make that choice. I endorse my former view thus far. I then believed also that *only* pregnancy and breastfeeding could be taken into account, because those were the only two "objectively" determinable differences between the sexes. The law, I believed, needed to steer completely clear of the "subjective" phenomenon of stereotyping. I now see that limitation as unnecessarily reticent and guaranteed to achieve nothing, as many such liberal assumptions are.

12. J. Agee & W. Evans, Let Us Now Praise Famous Men 15 (Houghton Mifflin, 1941).

13. MacKinnon, Sexual Harassment of Working Women, *supra* note 4, at 121.

14. These ideas were first articulated in a feminist context by Simone de Beauvoir. S. de Beauvoir, The Second Sex (H. Parshley trans., Knopf, 1953).

15. The term "self/other ontology" and the distinction between "relational" and "oppositional" ontologies are taken from Whitbeck, A Different Reality: Feminist Ontology, in C. Gould, ed., Beyond Domination: New Perspectives on Women and Philosophy 64 (Rowman and Allanheld, 1984).

16. *Id.* at 69.

17. "Naming" is a critical concept to feminism. When we discover what we really think and express it, we give words and the world new meaning. And when we call each other's names, we affirm a core of our being as women that we are only now *un*learning to *de*value. But this feminist "naming" should not be confused with nominalism nor with a reference theory of meaning. For us "Naming" is a political term. "Naming" means rejecting the Adam myth that the world was made for males to discern; it means reclaiming our own world and our own experiences. Virginia Woolf describes this process in *A Room of One's Own*. V. Woolf, A Room of One's Own 31–38 (Harcourt, Brace, 1957). . . .

18. Gould, The Woman Question, *supra* note 6, at 27.

19. Richards, Free Speech and Obscenity Law: Toward a Moral Theory of the First Amendment, 123 U. Pa. L. Rev. 45, 62 (1974). This liberal humanist rhetoric depends upon the oppositional self/other ontology. As Richards makes clear: "these liberties are fundamental conditions of the integrity and competence of a person in mastering his life and expressing this mastery to others." *Id.* at 82.

20. As MacKinnon says regarding pornography: "To liberals, speech must never be sacrificed for other social goals. But liberalism has never understood that the free speech of men silences the free speech of women." MacKinnon, Not a Moral Issue, 2 Yale L. & Pol'y Rev. 321 (1984), at 337. . . .

21. MacKinnon, Agenda, see Part 5 this volume. . . .

22. D. Dinnerstein, The Mermaid and the Minotaur 33–34, 91– 114 (Harper & Row, 1976).

23. *Id.* at 135.

24. *Id.* at 225–28.

25. Whitbeck, Different Reality, *supra* note 15, at 72.

26. Dinnerstein, Mermaid and Minotaur, *supra* note 22, at 175 (emphasis in original).

27. This analysis leads Dinnerstein to prescribe complete co-responsibility for infant care. *Id.* at 155. Even in those ever numerically diminishing nuclear families where such a solution would be possible, it is simply not enough. As long as differentiation is a violent concept, it seems that with co-responsibility, daddy would also take on that terrible, mystical quality, and we could learn to loathe both parents equally.

28. MacKinnon, Reply to Miller, Acker and Barry, Johnson, West, and Gardiner, 10 Signs 184, 187 (1984).

29. MacKinnon, Sexual Harassment of Working Women, *supra* note 4, at 117. Nearly identical standards could be applied to other historically disadvantaged groups.

30. See Williams, The Equality Crisis: Some Reflections on Culture, Courts, and Feminism, 7 Women's Rts. L. Rep. 175 (1982), at 197–200; Taub, Book Review, 80 Colum. L. Rev. 1682, 1686–93 (1980) (reviewing MacKinnon, Sexual Harassment of Working Women, *supra* note 4).

31. See MacKinnon, *supra* note 4, at 118 (emphasis in original).

32. See, e.g., Michael M. v. Sonoma County Super. Ct., 450 U.S. 464, 476 (1981) (upholding statutory rape law that presumes male is culpable aggressor because "consequences of sexual intercourse and pregnancy fall more heavily on the female than on the male"); Geduldig v. Aiello, 417 U.S. 484, 496 n. 20 (1974) (disability insurance system did not "exclude anyone from benefit eligibility because of gender but merely removes one physical condition—pregnancy—from the list of compensable disabilities").

33. See MacKinnon, Sexual Harassment of Working Women, *supra* note 4, at 227.

34. 400 U.S. 542 (1971) (per curiam) (reversing court of appeals' determination that policy was not sex-based). . . .

35. 417 U.S. 484 (1974). . . .

36. A. Rich, Foreword: On History, Illiteracy, Passivity, Violence, and

Women's Culture, in On Lies, Secrets and Silence: Selected Prose, 1966–1978 (Norton, 1979), at 11. . . .

37. See, e.g., Cohen, Transcendental Nonsense and the Functional Approach, 35 Colum. L. Rev. 809, 812 (1935): "When the vivid fictions and metaphors of traditional jurisprudence are thought of as reasons for decisions, rather than poetical or mnemonic devices for formulating decisions reached on other grounds, then the author, as well as the reader, of the opinion or argument, is apt to forget the social forces which mold the law and the social ideals by which the law is to be judged. Thus it is that the most intelligent judges in America can deal with a concrete practical problem of procedural law and corporate responsibility without any appreciation of the economic, social, and ethical issues which it involves." See also G. Gilmore, The Ages of American Law 87 (Yale University Press, 1977) (arguing that the realist "revolution" may have been merely a palace revolution, not much more than "a changing of the guard.").

38. R. Stevens, Law School: Legal Education in America from the 1950s to the 1980s, at 156 (University of North Carolina Press, 1983).

39. MacKinnon, Agenda, Part 5 this volume, at 450. Because feminism emerges from women themselves, we can largely avoid the old quandary of whether revolutionary consciousness arises from the masses or must be prompted by a revolutionary elite. See M. Barrett, Women's Oppression Today: Problems in Marxist Feminist Analysis 88–98 (Verso, 1980); V. Lenin, What Is to Be Done? 29–53 (International Publishers, 1969). That is not to say that the women's movement has not suffered from elitism. It has, but not due to a theoretical failure; feminism is not plagued with a theory that is "acontextual." See MacKinnon, Agenda, Part 5 this volume.

❖ *A Lawyer's Primer on Feminist Theory and Tort*

Leslie Bender

Feminism is a dirty word. . . . Feminists are portrayed as bra-burners, man-haters, sexists, and castrators. . . . No wonder many women, particularly many career women, struggle to distance themselves from the opprobrium appended to the label. . . . And for every woman that cowers from the word, even more men recoil and raise defenses that cloud their vision and deafen their ears. Although these negative responses make it extremely difficult to understand what feminism is and what promise it holds for all of us, let us try to look with an open curiosity at feminist projects. . . .

The following essay is intended to be both a primer that introduces a few of the major components of feminist theory and an example of how feminist theory might be used to examine a particular area of law. . . . My reflections on negligence law . . . suggest how feminist theory can help us think about the traditional structures of our laws, legal analyses, and legal system.

Introduction to Feminist Methodologies and Terminology

Feminism integrates practice and theory. It is a woman-centered methodology of critically questioning our ideological premises and reimagining the world. . . . We study women's oppression in order to understand what it is, how it happened, the subtle ways it works, and how oppression, exploitation, and exclusion affect different aspects of our lives and thinking. Whatever the focus of our particular work, all feminist efforts are combined in struggle to eradicate women's subordinate status. This is no small task, because male dominance pervades all aspects of

Reprinted from 38 J. Legal Educ. 3 (1988) with permission of the author and by courtesy of the publisher.

our lives—from our knowledge formation to our reproductive control, from our political and social organization to our self-perceptions. Feminism is political, methodological, philosophical, and intent upon social transformation. . . .

There are many feminisms, all with distinctive priorities. Although their strategies for bringing about change may vary, each focuses on women and matters that concern women, particularly women's oppression and its elimination. Some feminists believe that open access to the male world and fair assessment of our accomplishments by its measures will solve the problem. Others believe that the experience of women's subordination will not be resolved without fundamental changes in our institutions and power structures. Many feminists believe that problems of gender cannot be successfully confronted in isolation but must be coordinated with analyses of other kinds of oppression, such as class and race. Still other feminists study differences, understanding that because difference is relational and not an attribute of one person or thing it must not be used to justify hierarchies of power. Feminists do not all think in the same way or even about the same kinds of problems. There are feminists working in all disciplines. There is, however, a coherence to feminism that overrides the differences. My working definition of "feminism" is close to Linda Gordon's: "By feminism I . . . mean an analysis of women's subordination for the purpose of figuring out how to change it."[1] . . .

Much of feminist theory begins by describing, defining, and exposing patriarchy. "Patriarchy" is the feminist term for the ubiquitous phenomenon of male domination and hierarchy.[2] It means that men have had the bulk of the power and have used that power to subordinate women. . . . Their power is not only manifest in the political and economic world; it also governs families and sexual relationships. . . . [I]f you are male, whether or not you are a blatant user of that power, whether you are sexist or a feminist, you benefit from patriarchy just as whites benefit from systemic racism. But the momentary, ostensible benefits are greatly outweighed by the permanent and serious harm to all of us. . . .

In its most blatant forms, we can all recognize patriarchy and sexism. Men created our political system, which in the United States left women disenfranchised until 1920. Our very language uses the word "man" as the generic term for all people. Would men feel included if the generic word for people was "woman"? Would men feel that the "history of woman" was about them? Law contains similar instances of overt sexism in its doctrine. . . .

The role of patriarchy within the construction of substantive law as it affects all women is even more deleterious than its effect upon women practicing law. For centuries a woman lost her legal identity when she married. Until recently rape has been defined and "remedied" from a male perspective, and such experiences as sexual harassment have been excluded from the legal system. Intraspousal and intrafamilial tort immunities shrouded domestic violence against women and children from legal redress. The Supreme Court has even held that discrimination on the basis of pregnancy is not sex discrimination. Because our legal system has developed from an unstated male norm, it has never focussed adequately on harms to women.[3]

[W]omen are not simply passive victims of oppression but are in many ways collaborators. By accepting the implications of male-created imagery, language, thought processes, and power structures, we each day recreate patriarchy. Patriarchy's power persists because we do not challenge it; it is perpetuated generation after generation because too few of us seriously question or study it.

The primary task of feminist scholars is to awaken women and men to the insidious ways in which patriarchy distorts all of our lives. Patriarchy deprives us of the richness of women's voices in public discourse and curtails the range of women's contributions to shaping our world. It takes extraordinary effort to release ourselves from the overpowering ideological yoke of patriarchy. . . .

Unearthing each shard of patriarchy is especially difficult because of the powerful assumptions embedded in our language and logic. Western culture teaches us that the patriarchal description of reality is not biased but neutral; that our knowledge and truths are not subjective, intersubjective, relative, or constructed from narrow perspectives but objective, scientifically based, and universal; that our human nature is autonomous, self-interested, and even aggressively competitive, not interdependent, collective, cooperative, and caring. How do we move beyond traditional ways of knowing, understanding our natures, and theorizing about our social and political structures when we are a product of them? Can we step out of the frame that limits our perceptions?

Feminism and feminist scholarship is an attempt to do just that. Consciousness-raising, a fertile component of feminist methodology designed to accomplish the necessary frame-bursting, is a process of educating and exposing one another to the subtleties and harms of patriarchy. . . .

Academic classrooms and scholarly publications are also important arenas for raising awareness of the ubiquitous features of patriarchy and its impact on women. Feminist scholars are daily participants in consciousness-raising. They raise the consciousnesses of their students, faculty peers, and their academic communities in all disciplines, although their struggle for legitimacy is constant and their acceptance often tenuous and faltering.[4]

To extend feminism's challenges beyond the academy, we must apply the insights of feminism and consciousness-raising to law creation, interpretation, and the training of future lawyers. Law is a potent force in perpetuating patriarchy and controlling social and political organization. . . . If feminism and its consciousness-raising methodology can help us break through our legal system's myths, perhaps we can design transformative social, political, and legal systems that emphasize feminist values and concerns—values and concerns that emerge, for instance, from viewing human nature as interdependent instead of isolated and autonomous, and from attending to contexts and particularity instead of relying on universals and abstractions. . . .

Patriarchy's Power of Naming

Men have had the power of naming our world and giving our words meanings. Naming controls how we group things together, which parts of things are noted and which are ignored, and the perspective from which we understand them. We also learn that "things" that are named somehow count, and that things without names do not merit our attention.

We often accept unquestioningly the male-created language as our own, believing it to be pure and neutral when it is not. Our language is a male language that reinforces male perspectives, interests, and hierarchies of values. Simple examples make this apparent. An important work is "seminal," not "ovular." "Woman" as a word is a derivative of the word "man." The claim that the masculine terms "he" and "man" are generic becomes suspect when we realize that our language does not provide generic feminine terms as well. The most telling example of the male power of naming is the way our sexuality is described and understood [as penetration]. . . .

Part of the problem with having our world named and language created by men is that although men consistently use themselves as norms, they do not do so explicitly. It takes careful sifting to discover where and how the implicit male norm has skewed our understanding. . . .

Negligence Law: The "Reasonable Person" Standard as an Example of Male Naming and the Implicit Male Norm

That implicit male norms have been used to skew legal analysis can be seen in tort negligence law. To assess whether a defendant's conduct is negligent, and hence subject to liability, we ask whether the defendant has a duty to the plaintiff and whether she has met the legally required standard of conduct or care. "Standard of care" is a term of art in the law. It is alternatively described as the care required of a reasonably prudent person under the same or similar circumstances, or of a reasonable person of ordinary prudence, an ordinarily prudent man, or a man of average prudence.[5] Prosser and Keeton explain the standard as some "blend of reason and caution."[6] A "reasonable person" standard is an attempt to establish a universally applicable measure for conduct. This reasonable person is a hypothetical construct, not a real person, and is allegedly objective rather than subjective.

Not surprisingly, the standard was first articulated as a reasonable *man* or *man* of ordinary prudence. Recognizing the original standard's overt sexism,[7] many courts and legal scholars now use a "reasonable person" standard. My concern with the "reasonable person" standard is twofold. Does converting a "reasonable man" to a "reasonable person" in an attempt to eradicate the term's sexism actually exorcise the sexism or instead embed it? My second concern is related. Should our standard of care focus on "reason and caution" or something else?

It was originally believed that the "reasonable man" standard was gender neutral. "Man" was used in the generic sense to mean person or human being. But man is not generic except to other men. Would men regard a "prudent woman" standard as an appropriate measure of their due care? As our social sensitivity to sexism developed, our legal institutions did the "gentlemanly" thing and substituted the neutral word "person" for "man." . . . Although tort law protected itself from allegations of sexism, it did not change its content and character.

This "resolution" of the standard's sexism ignores several important feminist insights. The original phrase "reasonable man" failed in its claim to represent an abstract, universal person. Even if such a creature could be imagined, the "reasonable man" standard was postulated by men, who, because they were the only people who wrote and argued the law, philosophy, and politics at that time, only theorized about themselves. When the standard was written into judicial opinions, treatises, and casebooks, it was written about and by men. The case law and treatises explaining the standard are full of examples explaining how the "reasonable man" is the "man on the Clapham Omnibus" or "the man who takes the magazines at home and in the evening pushes the lawn mower in his shirt sleeves."[8] . . . The legal world that generated the "reasonable man" was predominantly, if not wholly, male.[9] . . . When it was converted to "reasonable person," it still meant "person who is reasonable by my standards" almost exclusively from the perspective of a male judge, lawyer, or law professor, or even a female lawyer trained to be "the same as" a male lawyer.

Changing the word without changing the underlying model does not work. Specifically addressing the "reasonable person" tort standard, Guido Calabresi challenges whether the "reasonable person" is in any way meant to include women or, for that matter, people of non-WASP beliefs or attitudes.[10] Calabresi explains that use of a universal standard is intended to cause those who are "different" from that standard to adopt the dominant ideological stance. Like the notion of America as a melting pot, the reasonable person standard encourages conformism and the suppression of different voices.

Not only does "reasonable person" still mean "reasonable man"—"reason" and "reasonableness" are gendered concepts as well. Gender distinctions have often been reinforced by dualistic attributions of reason and rationality to men, emotion and intuition (or instinct) to women. Much of Western philosophy is built on that distinction. Aristotle . . . regards women as inferior beings whose reasoning capacity is defective.[11] Immanuel Kant observes that women are devoid of characteristics necessary for moral action because they act on feelings, not reason.[12] . . .

Schopenhauer writes that woman "is in every respect backward, lacking in reason and reflection . . . a kind of middle step between the child and the man, who is the true human being. . . . In the last resort, women exist solely for the propagation of the race."[13] We also see evidence of the attitude that woman is unfit for the life of the mind in the Supreme Court's decision in Bradwell v. Illinois.[14] The medical community made similar pronouncements about the unfitness of women for intellectual pursuits.[15] These are but isolated examples of a continuous tendency in our Western culture to define "woman" by an absence of developed rationality or, at best, by an inferior capacity to reason. . . .

We would be hard pressed today to find many people who would openly assert that women cannot be reasonable. Today we are taught to consider women reasonable when they act as men would under the same circumstances, and unreasonable when they act more as they themselves or as other women act. If it is true that somewhere, at some subconscious level, we believe men's behavior is more reasonable and objective than women's, then changing the phrase "reasonable man" to "reasonable person" does not really change the hypothetical character against whom we measure the actors in torts problems. . . . If we are wedded to the idea of an objective measure, would it not be better to measure the conduct of a tortfeasor by the care that would be taken by a "neighbor" or "social acquaintance" or "responsible person with conscious care and concern for another's safety"?

Perhaps we have gone astray in tort-law analysis because we use "reason" and caution as our standard of care, rather than focusing on care and concern. Further study of feminist theory may help to suggest how a feminist ethic can affect our understanding of standards of care in negligence law. . . .

A Feminist Ethic of Caring and Interconnectedness

The concept of an ethic based on care and responsibility informs a great deal of feminist scholarship.[16] Carol Gilligan suggests that women's moral development reflects a focus on responsibility and contextuality, as opposed to men's, which relies more heavily on rights and abstract justice. After studying responses to interview questions in three studies (a college student study, an abortion-decision study, and a rights-and-responsibilities study), Gilligan recognized that there are two thematic approaches to problem solving that generally correlate with gender, although she makes no claims about the origin of the difference. Traditional psychological and moral-development theory recognizes and rewards one approach but undervalues or fails to define the other, the approach Gilligan calls "a different voice." When she asked what characterizes the different methods for resolving and analyzing moral dilemmas, Gilligan found that the "right" answers (according to the traditionally formulated stages of moral development) involve abstract, objective, rule-based decisions supported by notions of individual autonomy, individual rights, the separation of self from others, equality, and fairness. Often the answers provided by women focus on the particular contexts of the problems, relationships, caring (compassion and need), equity, and responsibility. For this different voice "responsibility" means "response to" rather than "obligation for." The first voice understands relationships in terms of hierarchies or "ladders," whereas the "feminine" voice communicates about relationships as "webs of interconnectedness." Gilligan concludes her work as follows:

> My research suggests that men and women may speak different languages that they assume are the same, using similar words to encode disparate experiences of self and social relationships. Because these languages share an overlapping moral vocabulary, they contain a propensity for systematic mistranslation, creating misunderstandings which impede communication and limit the potential for cooperation and care in relationships. At the same time, however, these languages articulate with one another in critical ways. Just as the language of responsibilities provides a weblike imagery of relationships to replace a hierarchical ordering that dissolves with the coming of equality, so the language of rights underlines the importance of including in the network of care not only the other but also the self.
>
> As we have listened for centuries to the voices of men and theories of development that their experience informs, so we have come more recently to notice not only the silence of women but the difficulty in hearing what they say when they speak. Yet in the different voice of women lies the truth of an ethic of care, the tie between relationship and responsibility, and the origins of aggression in the failure of connection. The failure to see the different reality of women's lives and to hear the differences in their voices stems in part from the assumption that there is a single mode of social experience and interpretation. By positing instead two different modes, we arrive at a more complex rendition of human experience which sees the truth of separation and attachment in the lives of women and men and recognizes how these truths are carried by different modes of language and thought.
>
> . . . While an ethic of justice proceeds from the premise of equality— that everyone should be treated the same—an ethic of care rests on the premise of nonviolence—that no one should be hurt.[17]

Gilligan seeks the inclusion of women's "different voice" in our understanding of human development. Others call for the recognition and value of that "different voice" in law.[18] Gilligan's work has had a tremendous impact on feminist scholarship in all disciplines.[19] . . . If we are willing to accept the implications of Gilligan's study, that is, that women have developed different ethical priorities and approaches to experience, then how does a feminist perspective help us think about negligence law?

Negligence Law: A Feminist Ethic of Care and Concern as a Basis for the Standard of Care

Our traditional negligence analysis asks whether the defendant met the requisite standard of care to avoid liability. As I have suggested, if we continue to feel obliged to apply a "universal" standard, we might be better off if we at least expect people to act not as "reasonable persons" but as "responsible neighbors" or with the care and concern of "social acquaintances." But figuring out against whom we should measure our conduct is only a partial solution to the problem. We also need to determine what standard of care to apply and what conduct is negligent or falls below that standard.

In tort law we generally use the phrase "standard of care" to mean "level of caution." How careful should the person have been? What precautions do we expect people to take to avoid accidents? We look to the carefulness a reasonable person would exercise to avoid impairing another's rights or interests. If a defendant did not act carefully, reasonably, or prudently by guarding against foreseeable harm, she would be liable. The idea of care and prudence in this context is translated into reasonableness, which is frequently measured instrumentally in terms of utility or economic efficiency.

When the standard of care is equated with economic efficiency or levels of caution, decisions that assign dollar values to harms to human life and health and then balance those dollars against profit dollars and other evidences of benefit become commonplace. Such cost–benefit and risk–utility analyses turn losses, whether to property or to persons, into commodities in fungible dollar amounts. The standard of care is converted into a floor of unprofitability or inefficiency. People are abstracted from their suffering; they are dehumanized. The risk of their pain and loss becomes a potential debit to be weighed against the benefits or profits to others. The result has little to do with care or even with caution, if caution is understood as concern for safety.

There is another possible understanding of "standard of care" that conforms more closely to Gilligan's "different voice," an alternative perspective rooted in notions of interconnectedness, responsibility, and caring. What would happen if we understood the "reasonableness" of the standard of care to mean "responsibility" and the "standard of care" to mean the "standard of caring" or "consideration of another's safety and interests"? What if, instead of measuring carefulness or caution, we measured concern and responsibility for the well-being of others and their protection from harm? Negligence law could begin with Gilligan's articulation of the feminine voice's ethic of care—a premise that no one should be hurt. We could convert the present standard of "care of a reasonable person under the same or similar circumstances" to a standard of "conscious care and concern of a responsible neighbor or social acquaintance for another under the same or similar circumstances."

The legal standard of care may serve as the minimally acceptable standard of behavior, failing which one becomes liable. But the standard need not be set at the minimum—we do not need to follow Justice Holmes' advice and write laws for the "bad man."[20] Have we gained anything from legally condoning behavior that causes enormous physical and mental distress and yet is economically efficient? The law can be a positive force in encouraging and improving our social relations, rather than reinforcing our divisions, disparities of power, and isolation.

The recognition that we are all interdependent and connected and that we are by nature social beings who must interact with one another should lead us to judge conduct as tortious when it does not evidence responsible care or concern for another's safety, welfare, or health. Tort law should begin with a premise of responsibility rather than rights, of interconnectedness rather than separation, and a priority of safety rather than profit or efficiency. The masculine voice of rights, autonomy, and abstraction has led to a standard that protects efficiency and profit; the feminine voice can design a tort system that encourages behavior that is caring about others' safety and responsive to others' needs or hurts, and that attends to human contexts and consequences.

It is not a simple matter to establish a standard dependent upon caring. Certainly we all care differently for family and friends than we do for strangers. The closer or more intimate the relationship, the greater our duty of care to that person. Tort liability would be greatest for conduct falling below the accepted standard of "care" within families; that is, when family members do not act responsibly for another's safety. Of course we could not possibly have the energy to care about every person as we do our children or lovers. But this tort standard does not require caretaking in the sense of nurturing. It is a conscious concern for the consequences our actions or inactions might have on another's safety or health. We can develop an awareness of the health and safety of others in all our activities without exhausting our ability to care.

There is a considerable distance between the law's current standard of care and a standard that might exceed our capabilities. A standard that would make us duty-bound to act responsibly and assure that our behavior does not harm someone else is not beyond us. The law should not permit us casually to cast aside another's safety, health, or interests because we do not personally know the random person who might be injured. Just as we would not want "strangers" to discount the human consequences of their actions to someone about whom we care, we must recognize that the person we affect by our "carelessness" is interconnected to other people as well—family, friends, colleagues, neighbors, communities.

Through a feminist focus on caring, context, and interconnectedness, we can move beyond measuring appropriate behavior by algebraic formulas to assessing behavior by its promotion of human safety and welfare. This approach will clearly lead to liability for some behaviors for which there was none before. If we do not act responsibly with care and concern for others, then we will be deemed negligent. Just as we can now evaluate behavior as negligent if its utility fails to outweigh its risks of harm, we could evaluate behavior as negligent if its care or concern for another's safety or health fails to outweigh its risks of harm. From a feminist perspective the duty of care required by negligence law might mean "acting responsibly towards others to avoid harm, with a concern about the human consequences of our acts or failure to act." It is tragic that our law has been insightful enough to use the language of care but has understood it as only carefulness or acting with caution. If the law imposed a duty of care and concern towards others' safety, orienting our behavior toward avoiding and preventing harms to others, and making it impossible for us to dismiss the consequences of our acts to people we do not directly know, our tort law would take on new dimensions.

"No Duty" Cases

One of the most difficult areas in which questions of duty and the standard of care arise is the "no duty to rescue" case. The problem is traditionally illustrated by the drowning-stranger hypothetical and the infamous case of Yania v. Bigan.[21] [Does one have] a legal duty to rescue a drowning stranger by throwing her an available lifesaver[?][22] I remember recoiling upon learning that the legal system approved of inaction in the *Yania* case. How could there be no duty to rescue? How could standing by and watching another drown be lawful?

Each year that I teach torts I watch again as a majority of my students initially find this legal "no duty" rule reprehensible. After the rationale is explained and the students become immersed in the "reasoned" analysis, and after they take a distanced, objective posture informed by liberalism's concerns for autonomy and liberty, many come to accept the legal rule that intuitively had seemed so wrong to them. They are taught to reject their emotions, instincts, and ethics, and to view accidents and tragedies abstractly, removed from their social and particularized contexts, and to apply instead rationally derived universal principles and a vision of human nature as atomistic, self-interested, and as free from constraint as possible. They are also taught that there are legally relevant distinctions between acts and omissions.

How would this drowning-stranger hypothetical look from a new legal perspective informed by a feminist ethic based upon notions of caring, responsibility, interconnectedness, and cooperation? If we put abstract reasoning and autonomy aside momentarily, we can see what else matters. In defining duty, what matters is that someone, a human being, a part of us, is drowning and will die without some affirmative action. That seems more urgent, more imperative, more important than any possible infringement of individual autonomy by the imposition of an affirmative duty. If we think about the stranger as a human being for a moment, we may realize that much more is involved than balancing one person's interest in having his life saved and another's interest in not having affirmative duties imposed upon him in the absence of a special relationship,[23] although even then the balance seems to me to weigh in favor of imposing a duty or standard of care that requires action. The drowning stranger is not the only person affected by the lack of care. He is not detached from everyone else. He no doubt has people who care about him—parents, spouse, children, friends, colleagues; groups he participates in—religious, social, athletic, artistic, political, educational, work-related; he may even have people who depend upon him for emotional or financial support. He is interconnected with others. If the stranger drowns, many will be harmed. It is not an isolated event with one person's interests balanced against another's. When our legal system trains us to understand the drowning-stranger story as a limited event between two people, both of whom have interests at least equally worth protecting, and when the social ramifications we credit most are the impositions on personal liberty of action, we take a human situation and translate it into a cold, dehumanized algebraic equation. We forget that we are talking about human death or grave physical harms and their reverberating consequences when we equate the consequences with such things as one person's momentary freedom not to act. . . .

If instead we impose a duty of acting responsibly with the same self-conscious care for the safety of others that we would give our neighbors or people we know, we require the actor to consider the human consequences of her failure to rescue. Even though it is easier to understand the problem if we hone it down to "relevant facts," which may include abstracting the parties into letter symbols (either A and B or P and D) or roles (driver and passenger), why is it that "relevant facts" do not include the web of relationships and connected people affected by a failure to act responsibly with care for that person's safety? Why is it that our legal training forces us to exclude that information when we solve problems and make rules governing social behavior or for compensating some victims of accidents? Why should our autonomy or freedom not to rescue weigh more heavily in law than a stranger's harms and the consequent harms to people with whom she is interconnected?[24]

The "no duty" rule is a consequence of a legal system devoid of care and responsiveness to the safety of others. We certainly could create a duty to aid generated from a legal recognition of our interconnectedness, an elevated sense of the importance of physical health and safety, a rejection of the act/omission dualism, and a strong legal value placed on care and concern for others rather than on economic efficiency or individual liberty. The duty to act with care for another's safety, which under appropriate circumstances would include an affirmative duty to act to protect or prevent harm to another, would be shaped by the particular context. One's ability to aid and one's proximity to the need would be relevant considerations. Whether one met that duty would not be determined by how a reasonable person would have acted under the circumstances but by whether one acted out of a conscious care and concern for the safety, health, and well-being of the victim in the way one would act out of care for a neighbor or friend. If someone is clearly in need of medical help or police protection and your own abilities or limitations make you incapable of providing it, a duty to aid arising from care and concern for another's safety may require you to call for help expeditiously.[25] In circumstances that do not call for rescue, the duty of care would require that one's behavior be governed by a conscious regard for another's safety. This seemingly minor change would transform the core of negligence law to a human, responsive system. Imagine what it could do for areas beyond "no duty to rescue." . . .

. . . Why, for instance, do tort damages recognize financial loss and yet remain reluctant to recognize relational loss, such as loss of the companionship of a child, or intangible harms, such as an increased risk of cancer or loss of a less-than-even chance of survival? Why are tort remedies all translated into money values instead of other forms of compensation? Why do we settle for the ease of monetary payment (particularly insurance premiums) instead of requiring tortfeasors to take fuller and more personally active responsibility for the harms they cause? How does tort analysis serve to perpetuate existing power hierarchies? Feminist critiques challenge the implicit assumptions in the very structure of the analysis we use.

Conclusion

I have presented an overview of some major components of feminist theory and have illustrated how they can be used to critique tort law, focusing in particular on a standard-of-care analysis. The same method can be used to examine many other aspects of negligence and tort law. Feminist themes—a responsibility-oriented ethics, a focus on contextuality and interconnectedness, attention to the power of naming and biases in our language, the inclusion of all voices in the generation of knowledge, an opposition to dualisms, the cry for empowerment of women and an end to our subordination, the critical questioning of all our implicit assumptions, a struggle against hierarchies of power, and an appreciation of difference as a relationship and not an attribute—are critical to a "re-vision" of our tort-law system. Feminist theory helps us understand how tort law has been developed in the language of male orderings, values, power structures, and interests. A proposed revision of tort law would require new categories of analysis, new words, new perspectives, and new values. Our current language ignores many relevant but previously unacknowledged, uncredited "voices" or interests that must be included in the resolution of personal injury problems. These must be named. The hidden patriarchal assumptions must be exposed. We have to eliminate the power structures that perpetuate domination and subordination within tort law. There is a lot of work to be done.

Notes

1. L. Gordon, The Struggle for Reproductive Freedom: Three Stages of Feminism, in Z. Eisenstein, ed., Capitalist Patriarchy and the Case for Socialist Feminism 107n. (Longman, 1979).

2. The connotation feminists give to the word "patriarchy" was introduced into second-wave feminist literature by Kate Millett in K. Millett, Sexual Politics (Doubleday, 1970). For other typical feminist uses of the term, see G. Lerner, The Creation of Patriarchy 238 (Oxford University Press, 1986); A. Rich, Of Woman Born: Motherhood as Experience and Institution 57–58 (Norton, 1976); H.

Eisenstein, Contemporary Feminist Thought 5–14 (G.K. Hall, 1984); Z. Eisenstein, Developing a Theory of Capitalist Patriarchy and Socialist Feminism, in Eisenstein, Capitalist Patriarchy, *supra* note 1, at 5, 16; M. Barrett, Women's Oppression Today: Problems in Marxist Feminist Analysis 10–19 (Verso, 1980); Beechey, On Patriarchy, 3 Feminist Rev. 66 (1979).

3. Male naming and the unstated male norm in the law is the subject of many articles. See, e.g., M. Minow, Supreme Court, 1986 Term: Foreword: Justice Engendered, Part 3 this volume; C. MacKinnon, Feminism Unmodified: Discourses on Life and Law (Harvard University Press, 1987); MacKinnon, Feminism, Marxism, Method and the State: Toward Feminist Jurisprudence, Part 5 this volume; and MacKinnon Feminism, Marxism, Method and the State: An Agenda for Theory, Part 5 this volume; Finley, Transcending Equality Theory: A Way Out of the Maternity and the Workplace Debate, Part 2 this volume; Scales, The Emergence of Feminist Jurisprudence: An Essay, Part 1 herein; Lahey, . . . Until Women Themselves Have Told All They Have to Tell . . ., 23 Osgood Hall L.J. 519, 534–35 (1985), and works cited therein.

4. Our legal community must not . . . fall prey to the pattern of patriarchy that discredits feminist scholarship as "not scholarly" and justifies denial of tenure or academic positions to brilliant feminists. Examples of this in legal academia are disturbing and ever more frequent.

For evidence of problems faced by academic feminists, see, e.g., Aiken, Anderson, Dinnerstein, Lensink & MacCorquodale, Trying Transformations: Curriculum Integration and the Problem of Resistance, 12 Signs 255 (1987); D. Spender ed., Men's Studies Modified: The Impact of Feminism on the Academic Disciplines (Pergamon, 1981); Held, Feminism and Epistemology: Recent Work on the Connection between Gender and Knowledge, 14 Phil. & Pub. Aff. 296, 306 (1985). For a review of the accomplishments of and massive resistance to women's studies in the United States, see Boxer, For and About Women: The Theory and Practice of Women's Studies in the United States, in N. Keohane, M. Rosaldo & B. Gelpi eds., Feminist Theory: A Critique of Ideology 237–71, (University of Chicago Press, 1982). See generally Anthology, Reconstructing the Academy, 12 Signs 203–380 (1987).

5. The Restatement (Second) of Torts § 283 (1965) states: "Unless the actor is a child, the standard of conduct to which he must conform to avoid being negligent is that of a reasonable man under like circumstances." . . .

6. W. Keeton, D. Dobbs, R. Keeton & D. Owen, Prosser and Keeton on the Law of Torts 174, 5th ed. (West, 1984).

7. The standard's sexism became the subject of satirist A. P. Herbert's first case, Fardell v. Potts, in his delightful collection, Uncommon Law. His hypothetical judge in that case illustrates the difficulty of applying "the reasonable man" standard to women:

> [M]y own researches incline me to agree, that in all that mass of authorities which bears upon this branch of the law there is no single mention of a reasonable woman. It was ably insisted before us that such an omission, extending over a century and more of judicial pronouncements, must be something more than a coincidence; that among the innumerable tributes to the reasonable man there might be expected at least some passing reference to a reasonable person of the opposite sex; that no such reference is found, for the simple reason that no such being is contemplated by law;

that legally at least there is no reasonable woman, and that therefore in this case the learned judge should have directed the jury that, while there was evidence on which they might find that the defendant had not come up to the standard required of a reasonable man, her conduct was only what was to be expected of a woman, as such. . . .

It is probably no mere chance that in our legal textbooks the problems relating to married women are usually considered immediately after the pages devoted to idiots and lunatics. Indeed, there is respectable authority for saying that at Common Law this was the status of a woman. . . . It is no bad thing that the law of the land should here and there conform with the known facts of everyday experience. The view that there exists a class of beings, illogical, impulsive, careless, irresponsible, extravagant, prejudiced, and vain, free for the most part from those worthy and repellent excellences which distinguish the Reasonable Man, and devoted to the irrational arts of pleasure and attraction, is one which should be as welcome and as well accepted in our Courts as it is in our drawing-rooms—and even in Parliament. . . . I find that at Common Law a reasonable woman does not exist.

A. P. Herbert, Uncommon Law 1, 5–6, 8th ed. (Methuen, 1969).

8. E.g., Hall v. Brooklands Auto Racing Club, 1 K.B. 205, 224 (1933). See 3 F. Harper, F. James, & O. Gray, The Law of Torts, 2d ed. (Little, Brown, 1986), at § 16.2; James, The Qualities of the Reasonable Man in Negligence Cases, 16 Mo. L. Rev. 1 (1951).

9. It was also a white, educated, and empowered world. It is my heartfelt belief that to rid law of any one of such biases as sexism, classism, and racism without ridding law of the others is inadequate. Sexism, however, provides the best example because it is embedded within the other "isms"—e.g., classism, racism. Sexism invades the black experience, the Latina experience, the working- or upper-class experience. . . . [A]n example from one of my first-year Torts classes . . . illustrates how the "reasonable person" standard fails of its purpose because of different racial and cultural contexts. In a discussion of intentional torts and transferred intent . . . , we turned to a case in which one man (A) had been arguing with another man (B). A third man (C) and his brother were across the street washing their car. As B drove away on his motorcycle, A pulled out a gun and shot at him. A missed B and hit C. The first issue was whether A's intent to shoot B could be transferred to C so that A could be found liable for an intentional tort against C. The discussion was a bit tricky. We had not yet discussed negligence liability, so we tried to steer clear of negligence issues, including contributory negligence. Nonetheless, a black man in my class was having a terrible time dealing with this case. He did not understand how C could be allowed to recover from A when C acted so stupidly (or, in our language, unreasonably). It is common sense, he told the class, to recognize that, if two men are out in the street arguing right across from you and one of them has a gun (or you know that person has a violent temperament), staying out there washing the car is asking to get hurt. His conclusion, without using legal terms of art, was that C, the victim, was at the least contributorily negligent and probably had assumed the risk. His having grown up in a predominantly black Philadelphia ghetto made the story real to him in a way that was unfamiliar to me and to most of his classmates. . . .

10. G. Calabresi, Ideals, Beliefs, Attitudes, and the Law: Private Law Perspectives on a Public Law Problem 26–28 (Syracuse University Press, 1985).

11. Aristotle, Politics 59 (Harvard University Press, 1959). . . .

12. See I. Kant, Observations on the Feeling of the Beautiful and Sublime 76–81 (University of California Press, 1960). . . .

13. C. Gould & M. Wartofsky eds., Women and Philosophy: Toward a Theory of Liberation (Putnam, 1976) at 19, quoting Schopenhauer, "On Women," in E. B. Bax, ed., Selected Essays 338–46 (London, 1900).

14. 83 U.S. (16 Wall.) 130 (1876).

15. In fact, famous doctors and medical school professors, such as Dr. Edward Clarke of Harvard Medical School, wrote and spoke about how women would lose their reproductive capacity if they tried to study beyond puberty. B. Ehrenreich & D. English, For Her Own Good: 150 Years of the Experts' Advice to Women 125–31 (Doubleday, 1979), citing E.H. Clarke, M.D., Sex in Education, or a Fair Chance for the Girls (Boston, 1873; reprint, Ayer, 1972). . . .

16. E.g., C. Gilligan, In a Different Voice: Psychological Theory and Women's Development (Harvard University Press, 1982); N. Noddings, Caring: A Feminist Approach to Ethics and Moral Education (University of California Press, 1984); C. Whitbeck, A Different Reality: Feminist Ontology, in C. Gould ed., Beyond Domination: New Perspectives on Women and Philosophy (Rowman and Allanheld, 1984), at 64–88. . . .

17. Gilligan, In a Different Voice, *supra* note 16, at 173–74.

18. E.g., Karst, Woman's Constitution, 1984 Duke L.J. 447; Sherry, Civic Virtue and the Feminine Voice in Constitutional Adjudication, 72 Va. L. Rev. 543 (1986); Finley, Transcending, Part 2 this volume; Cole, Getting There: Reflections on Trashing from Feminist Jurisprudence and Critical Theory, 8 Harv. Women's L.J. 59 (1985); Menkel-Meadow, Portia in a Different Voice: Speculations on a Women's Lawyering Process, 1 Berkeley Women's L.J. 39 (1985).

19. Gilligan's work is not without its critics in the feminist community. See, e.g., Kerber, Greeno, Maccoby, Luria, Stack & Gilligan, Viewpoint, "On In a Different Voice": An Interdisciplinary Forum, 11 Signs 304–33 (1986); Auerbach, Blum, Smith & Williams, Commentary on Gilligan's "In a Different Voice," 11 Feminist Studies 149 (Spring 1985). One fear is that speaking of an identifiable and different "feminine" voice will revive a biological or sociological determinism that will be used to justify restricting women's options. Gilligan's critics ask whether labeling "feminine" attributes as positive and valuing them will really change the consequences and harms of perpetuating gender-based discrimination. Certainly this is a legitimate concern, one that I partly share, but I feel Gilligan's work is so important that we must benefit from it and at the same time prevent its misuse.

Several critics suggest that the different voice, if added to our current understanding, will lose its transformative potential. See Scales, Part 1 herein; MacKinnon, Feminist Discourse, Moral Values and the Law—A Conversation, 34 Buffalo L. Rev. 11, 20–28 (1985) (remarks of Catharine MacKinnon); MacKinnon, Agenda, Part 5 this volume; MacKinnon, Toward Feminist Jurisprudence, Part 5 this volume; Wishik, To Question Everything: The Inquiries of Feminist Jurisprudence, Part 1 herein. I agree that we cannot just add women's formerly absent voices to the law and stir. (The "add and stir" terminology originated with Charlotte Bunch and early second-wave feminists. C. Bunch, Visions and Revisions: Women and the Power of Change, NWSA Convention, Lawrence, Kansas, June

1979, cited in Boxer, For and About Women, *supra* note 4, at 237, 258 n. 81). We must think the legal system anew without the taint or biases of a jurisprudence created by and for the empowered white male. Jean Grimshaw argues, further, that adding the notion of care to our ethic may exacerbate the oppression of women by "divert[ing] attention from issues of injustice or oppression, or . . . conceal[ing] other objectives which have nothing to do with care." J. Grimshaw, Philosophy and Feminist Thinking 218 (University of Minnesota Press, 1986). Catharine MacKinnon also argues that even if the feminine voice is characterized not by self-interest but by concerns for maintaining relationships and caring for others, and is motivated by attempts to mediate or conciliate disputes rather than engaging in open conflict, it may only be the voice of a people oppressed and subordinated. MacKinnon, Feminist Discourse, *supra* this note, at 25–28, 73–74. Why, MacKinnon asks, should we laud a feminine voice for the values it perpetuates when those values spring from survival instincts of people who are powerless and oppressed?

Even though the feminine voice may have developed from a position of not being empowered, that does not make it less valuable, humane, or important. It may make it even more important, because to rid ourselves of the terrors of patriarchal power—the power to subordinate, demean, silence, or abuse others—we must always speak in the voice and understand from the consciousness of a lack of power over others. It is just this understanding—that our power is in ourselves or in our solidarity with others and not power "over" someone else—that will enable us to reenvision our legal system.

20. Holmes, The Path of the Law, 10 Harv. L. Rev. 457–78 (1890).

21. 397 Pa. 316, 155 A.2d 343 (1959). Yania was a business competitor of Bigan and had gone onto Bigan's land to speak with him. Both men were involved in strip-mining, and Bigan was working at a deep trench partially filled with water. Although the facts are ambiguous, there was testimony that Bigan dared or cajoled Yania to jump into the pit, in which he drowned as Bigan looked on. It is equally possible that Yania jumped into the pit to demonstrate to Bigan his expertise in solving the problem there. In either case, Yania drowned and Yania's widow sued Bigan. She lost. The Pennsylvania Supreme Court refused to impose an affirmative duty on one party to rescue or aid another.

22. The Restatement (Second) of Torts § 314, illustration 1 (1965), uses an equally disconcerting example: "A sees B, a blind man, about to step into the street in front of an approaching automobile. A could prevent B from so doing by a word or touch without delaying his own progress. A does not do so, and B is run over and hurt. A is under no duty to prevent B from stepping into the street and is not liable to B." Although I call this kind of situation the drowning-stranger problem, it could just as poignantly be presented as the blind-stranger problem; indeed, one could substitute any comparable hypothetical. Accord, Buch v. Amory Mfg. Co., 69 N.H. 257, 44 A. 809 (1897)(no duty to trespassing minors; the *Buch* opinion explains that there would be no legal liability for a stranger failing to prevent a two-year-old from crawling on a railroad track in front of an approaching car, even though the stranger may be considered a moral monster).

23. Duties to aid and to protect have been imposed in certain situations, including those involving special relationships. See, e.g., Restatement (Second) of Torts. . . § 314A and § 314B (special duties to aid are imposed on innkeepers, common carriers, invitors, custodians, and employers). . . .

24. A definition of duty that includes a notion of "care" clearly would infringe on the libertarian concerns of theorists such as Richard Epstein, who place individual autonomy and liberty to choose not to act (in duty-to-rescue cases, for example) over human needs for assistance in times of danger. Epstein, A Theory of Strict Liability, 2 J. Legal Stud. 151, 198 (1973). . . .

25. . . . We see hints of the . . . law moving toward creation of [such a duty]. . . . Some states have legislated affirmative duties to aid, e.g., Vermont, Vt. Stat. Ann. tit. 12, § 519 (1973). Many others have enacted Good Samaritan statutes that immunize some aiders from liability for negligence in order to encourage rescue. . . .

❖ *Jurisprudence and Gender*

ROBIN WEST

[V]IRTUALLY ALL MODERN American legal theorists, like most modern moral and political philosophers, either explicitly or implicitly embrace what I will call the "separation thesis" about what it means to be a human being: a "human being," whatever else he is, is physically separate from all other human beings. . . . [T]he separation thesis is hardly confined to the libertarian right. According to Roberto Unger, premier spokesperson for the communitarian left, "[t]o be conscious is to have the experience of being *cut off* from that about which one reflects: it is to be a subject that stands over against its objects. . . . *The subjective awareness of separation . . . defines consciousness.*"[1] The political philosopher Michael Sandel has recently argued that most (not all) modern political theory is committed to the proposition that "[w]hat separates us is in some important sense prior to what connects us— epistemologically prior as well as morally prior. We are distinct individuals first, and *then* we form relationships and engage in co-operative arrangements with others; hence the priority of plurality over unity."[2] The same commitment underlies virtually all of our legal theory. Indeed, Sandel's formulation may be taken as a definitive restatement of the "separation thesis" that underlies modern jurisprudence.

The first purpose of this essay is to put forward the global and critical claim that by virtue of their shared embrace of the separation thesis, all of our modern legal theory—by which I mean "liberal legalism" and "critical legal theory" collectively—is essentially and irretrievably masculine. . . . The second purpose of this paper is to explore and improve upon the feminist jurisprudence we have generated to date, in spite of patriarchy, and in spite of the masculinity of mainstream jurisprudence. . . .

Finally, the conclusion suggests how a humanist jurisprudence might evolve, and how feminist legal theory can contribute to its creation.

---

55 U. Chi. L. Rev. 1 (1988).

Masculine Jurisprudence and Feminist Theory

The . . . split in masculine jurisprudence between legal liberalism and critical legal theory can be described in any number of ways. [One way] is in terms of politics: "liberal legal theorists" align themselves with a liberal political philosophy which entails, among other things, allegiance to the Rule of Law and to Rule of Law virtues, while "critical legal theorists," typically left wing and radical, are skeptical of the Rule of Law and the split between law and politics which the Rule of Law purportedly delineates. . . .

An alternative description of the difference (surely not the only one) is that liberal legal theory and critical legal theory provide two radically divergent phenomenological descriptions of the paradigmatically male experience of the inevitability of separation of the self from the rest of the species, and indeed from the rest of the natural world. Both schools . . . accept the separation thesis; they both view human beings as materially (or physically) separate from each other, and both view this fact as fundamental to the origin of law. But their accounts of the subjective experience of physical separation from the other—an individual other, the natural world, and society—are in nearly diametrical opposition. . . .

I will start with the liberal description of separation. . . . According to liberal legalism, the inevitability of the individual's material separation from the "other," entails, first and foremost, an existential state of highly desirable and much valued freedom: because the individual is *separate* from the other, he is *free* of the other. . . .

This existential condition of freedom in turn entails the liberal's conception of value. Because we are all free and we are each equally free, we should be treated by our government as free, and as equally free. . . . Ronald Dworkin puts the point in this way:

> What does it mean for the government to treat its citizens as equals? *That is . . . the same question as the question of what it means for the government to treat all its citizens as free, or as independent, or with equal dignity. . . .*[3]

Because of the dominance of liberalism in this culture, we might think of autonomy as the "official" liberal value entailed by the physical, material condition of inevitable separation from the other: separation from the other entails my freedom from him, and that in turn entails my political right to autonomy. . . .

Autonomy, freedom, and equality collectively constitute what might be called the "up side" of the subjective experience of separation. . . . However, there's a "down side" to the subjective experience of separation as well. Physical separation from the other entails not just my freedom; it also entails my vulnerability. Every other discrete, separate individual—because he is the "other"—is a source of danger to me and a threat to my autonomy. . . . Our ends might conflict. . . . In an extreme case, you might even try to kill me—you might cause my annihilation. . . .

. . . Hobbes, of course, gave the classic statement of the terrifying vulnerability that stems from our separateness from the other. . . .[4] Bruce Ackerman gives a more modern rendition, but the message is essentially the same. . . .[5]

We can call this liberal legalist phenomenological narrative the "official story" of the subjectivity of separation. According to the official story, we value the freedom that our separateness entails, while we seek to minimize the threat that it poses. We do so, of course, through creating and then respecting the state. . . .

. . . [C]ritical theorists provide a starkly divergent phenomenological description of the subjective experience of separation. . . . Like liberal legalists, critical legal theorists also view the individual as materially separate from the rest of human life. But according to the critical theorist, what that material state of separation existentially entails is not a perpetual celebration of autonomy, but rather, a perpetual longing for community, or attachment, or unification, or *connection*. The separate individual strives to connect with the "other" from whom he is separate. The separate individual lives in a state of perpetual dread not of annihilation by the other, but of the alienation, loneliness, and existential isolation that his material separation from the other imposes upon him. The individual strives through love, work, and government to achieve a unification with the other. . . .

Thus, there is a vast gap, according to critical theory, between the "official value" of liberal legalism—autonomy—and what the individual *truly* subjectively desires, which is to establish a true connection with the other. Similarly, there is a vast gap between the "official harm" of liberal legalism—annihilation by the other—and what the individual *truly* subjectively dreads, which is not annihilation by him, but isolation and alienation from him. . . .

Critical legal theory tells the unofficial story. . . .

Let me now turn to feminist theory. [M]odern feminist theory is as fundamentally divided as legal theory. . . . [W]hile most modern feminists agree that women are different from men and agree on the importance of the difference, feminists differ over which differences between men and women are most vital. According to one group of feminists, sometimes called "cultural feminists," the important difference between men and women is that women raise children and men don't. According to a second group of feminists, now called "radical feminists," the important difference between men and women is that women get fucked and men fuck: "women," definitionally, are "those from whom sex is taken," just as workers, definitionally, are those from whom labor is taken. Another way to put the difference is in political terms. Cultural feminists appear somewhat more "moderate" when compared with the traditional culture: from a mainstream non-feminist perspective, cultural feminists appear to celebrate many of the same feminine traits that the traditional culture has stereotypically celebrated. Radical feminists, again from a mainstream perspective, appear more separatist, and, in contrast with standard political debate, more alarming. They also appear to be more "political" in a sense which perfectly parallels the critical theory–liberal theory split described above: radical feminists appear to be more attuned to power disparities between men and women than are cultural feminists.

I think this traditional characterization is wrong on two counts. First, cultural feminists no less than radical feminists are well aware of women's powerlessness vis-à-vis men, and second, radical feminism, as I will later argue, is as centrally concerned with pregnancy as it is with intercourse. But . . . , instead of arguing against this traditional characterization of the divide between radical and cultural feminism, I want to provide an alternative. . . . Underlying both radical and cultural feminism is a conception of women's existential state that is grounded in women's potential for physical, material connection to human life, just as underlying both liberal and critical legalism is a conception of men's existential state that is grounded in the inevitability of men's physical separation from the species. I will call the shared conception of women's existential lives the "connection thesis." The divisions between radical and cultural feminism stem from divergent accounts of the subjectivity of the potential for connection, just as what divides liberal from critical legal theory are divergent accounts of the subjectivity of the inevitability of separation.

The "connection thesis" is simply this: Women are actually or potentially materially connected to other human life. . . . The potential for material connection with the other defines women's subjective, phenomenological and existential state, just as surely as the inevitability of material separation from the other defines men's existential state. Our potential for material connection engenders pleasures and pains, values and dangers, and attractions and fears which are entirely different from those which follow, for men, from the necessity of separation. Indeed, it is the rediscovery of the multitude of implications from this material difference between men and women which has enlivened (and divided) both cultural and radical feminism in this decade (and it is those discoveries which have distinguished both radical and cultural feminism from liberal feminism). . . . .

. . . [W]hile radical and cultural feminists agree that women's lives are distinctive in their potential for material connection to others, they provide sharply contrasting accounts of the subjective experience of the material and existential state of connection. According to cultural feminist accounts of women's subjectivity, women value intimacy, develop a capacity for nurturance, and an ethic of care for the "other" with which we are connected, just as we learn to dread and fear separation from the other. Radical feminists tell a very different story. According to radical feminism, women's connection with the "other" is above all else invasive and intrusive: women's potential for material "connection" invites invasion into the physical integrity of our bodies, and intrusion into the existential integrity of our lives. Although women may "officially" value the intimacy of connection, we "unofficially" dread the intrusion it inevitably entails, and long for the individuation and independence that deliverance from that state of connection would permit. Paralleling the structure above, I will call these two descriptions feminism's official and unofficial stories of women's subjective experience of physical connection.

In large part due to the phenomenal success of Carol Gilligan's book *In a*

Different Voice, cultural feminism may be the more familiar of these two feminist strands, and for that reason *alone*, I call it feminism's "official story.". . . [C]ultural feminism begins not with a commitment to the "material" version of the connection thesis (as outlined above), but rather, with a commitment to its more observable existential and psychological consequences. [W]omen have a "sense" of existential "connection" to other human life which men do not. . . .

Why are men and women different in this essential way? The cultural feminist explanation for women's heightened sense of connection is that women are more "connected" to life than are men because it is women who are the primary caretakers of young children. A female child develops her sense of identity as "continuous" with her caretaker's, while a young boy develops a sense of identity that is distinguished from his caretaker's. Because of the gender alignment of mothers and female children, young girls "fuse" their growing sense of identity with a sense of sameness with and attachment to the other, while because of the gender distinction between mothers and male children, young boys "fuse" their growing sense of identity with a sense of difference and separation from the other. This turns out to have truly extraordinary and far reaching consequences, for both cognitive and moral development. Nancy Chodorow explains:

> [This means that] [g]irls emerge from this period with a basis for "empathy" built into their primary definition of self in a way that boys do not. . . . [G]irls come to experience themselves as less differentiated than boys, as more continuous with and related to the external object-world and as differently oriented to their inner object-world as well.[6]

Women are therefore capable of a degree of physical as well as psychic *intimacy* with the other which greatly exceeds men's capacity. Carol Gilligan finds that

> The fusion of identity and intimacy . . . [is] clearly articulated . . . in [women's] . . . self-descriptions. In response to the request to describe themselves, . . . women describe a relationship, depicting their identity *in* the connection of future mother, present wife, adopted child, or past lover. Similarly, the standard of moral judgement that informs their assessment of self is a standard of relationship, an ethic of nurturance, responsibility, and care. . . . [In] women's descriptions, identity is defined in a context of relationship and judged by a standard of responsibility and care. Similarly, morality is seen by these women as arising from the experience of connection and conceived as a problem of inclusion rather than one of balancing claims.[7]

. . .

Thus, according to Gilligan . . . , women view themselves as fundamentally connected to, not separate from, the rest of life. This difference permeates virtually every aspect of our lives. According to the vast literature on difference now being developed by cultural feminists, women's cognitive development, literary sensibility, aesthetic taste, and psychological development, no less than our anatomy, are all fundamentally different from men's. . . .

The most significant aspect of our difference, though, is surely the moral difference. According to cultural feminism, women are more nurturant, caring, loving and responsible to others than are men. This capacity for nurturance and care dictates the moral terms in which women, distinctively, construct social relations: women view the morality of actions against a standard of responsibility to others, rather than against a standard of rights and autonomy from others. As Gilligan puts it:

> The moral imperative . . . [for] women is an injunction to care, a responsibility to discern and alleviate the "real and recognizable trouble" of this world. For men, the moral imperative appears rather as an injunction to respect the rights of others and thus to protect from interference the rights to life and self-fulfillment.[8]

Cultural feminists, to their credit, have reidentified these differences as women's strengths, rather than women's weaknesses. Cultural feminism does not simply *identify* women's differences—patriarchy too insists on women's differences—it celebrates them. Women's art, women's craft, women's narrative capacity, women's critical eye, women's ways of knowing, and women's heart, are all, for the cultural feminist, redefined as things to celebrate. . . . Most vital, however, for cultural feminism is the claim that intimacy is not just something women *do*, it is something human beings *ought* to do. Intimacy is a source of value, not a private hobby. It is morality, not habit.

To pursue my structural analogy to masculine legal theory, then, intimacy and the ethic of care constitute the entailed *values* of the existential state of connection with others, just as autonomy and freedom constitute the entailed values of the existential state of separation from others for men. Because women are fundamentally connected to other human life, women value and enjoy intimacy with others (just as because men are fundamentally separate from other human life men value and enjoy autonomy). Because women are connected with the rest of human life, intimacy with the "other" comes naturally. Caring, nurturance, and an ethic of love and responsibility for life is second nature. Autonomy, or freedom from the other constitutes a value for men because it reflects an existential state of being: separate. Intimacy is a value for women because it reflects an existentially connected state of being.

Intimacy, the capacity for nurturance and the ethic of care constitute what we might call the "up side" of the subjective experience of connection. . . . But there's a "down side" to the subjective experience of connection. There's danger, harm, and fear entailed by the state of connection as well as value. Whereas men fear annihilation from the separate other (and consequently have trouble achieving intimacy), women fear separation from the connected other (and consequently have trouble achieving independence). Gilligan makes the point succinctly: "Since masculinity is defined through separation while femininity is defined through attachment, male gender identity is threatened by intimacy while female gender identity is threatened by separation."[9] Separation, then, might be regarded as the official harm of cultural feminism. . . .

. . . It seems quite plausible that women are more physically connected to others in just the way Gilligan describes and for just the reason she expounds. . . . But this psychological and developmental explanation just raises—it does not answer—the background material question: why do women, rather than men, raise, nurture, and cook for children? What is the cause of *this* difference?

Although Gilligan doesn't address the issue, other cultural feminists have, and their explanations converge, I believe, implicitly if not explicitly, on a material, or mixed material–cultural, and not just a cultural answer: women *raise* children— and hence raise girls who are more connected and nurturant, and therefore more likely to be nurturant caretakers themselves—because it is women who bear children. Women are not inclined to abandon an infant they've carried for nine months and then delivered. If so, then women are ultimately more "connected"— psychically, emotionally, and morally—to other human beings because women, as children were raised by women and women raise children because women, uniquely, are physically and materially "connected" to those human beings when the human beings are fetuses and then infants. Women are more empathic to the lives of others because women are physically tied to the lives of others in a way which men are not. Women's moral voice is one of responsibility, duty, and care for others because women's material circumstance is one of responsibility, duty, and care for those who are first physically attached, then physically dependent, and then emotionally interdependent. Women think in terms of the needs of others rather than the rights of others because women materially, and then physically, and then psychically, provide for the needs of others. Lastly, women fear separation from the other rather than annihilation by him, and "count" it as a harm, because women experience the "separating" pain of childbirth and more deeply feel the pain of the maturation and departure of adult children.

Although this material explanation of women's difference now overtly dominates at least some forms of French cultural feminism, it still plays a largely implicit, rather than explicit role in United States cultural feminism, although that status is changing. There are several reasons for the reluctance of American cultural feminists to explicitly embrace a material version of the connection thesis. . . .

The . . . major reason . . . is primarily strategic: American feminists of all stripes are wary of identifying the material fact of pregnancy as the root of moral, aesthetic, and cognitive difference, because, as liberal feminist and law professor Wendy Williams correctly notes, "most of the disadvantages imposed on women, in the workforce and elsewhere, derive from this central reality of the capacity of women to become pregnant *and the real and supposed implications of this reality.*"[10] The response to this "central reality" among American liberal feminists and American feminist lawyers has been to deny or minimize the importance of the pregnancy difference, thus making men and women more "alike," so as to force the legal system to treat men and women similarly.

[T]here is a growing awareness amongst even liberal feminist legal theorists that this strategy has to some extent backfired. It has become increasingly clear that feminists must attack the burdens of pregnancy and its attendant differences, rather than denying the uniqueness of pregnancy . . . .

[T]he "story" of women's relationship with the other as told by cultural feminists contrast in virtually every particular with the story of men's relationship to the other as told by liberals. First, men, according to the Hobbesian account, are by nature equal. "Nature hath made men so equall, in the faculties of body, and mind; as that though there bee found one man sometimes manifestly stronger in body . . . ; yet when all is reckoned together, the difference between man, and man, is not so considerable, as that one man can thereupon claim to himselfe any benefit. . . . [T]he weakest has strength enough to kill the strongest. . . ."[11] Women, by contrast, are not "equal" in strength to the most important "other" they encounter: the fetus and then the newborn child. Rather, the fetus and the woman and later the infant and the mother occupy what might be called a natural, hierarchical web of inequality, not a natural state of equality: whereas men may be "by nature equal" women are "by nature stronger" than those who are most important to them and most dependent upon them. The natural physical equality between self and other on which Hobbes insists is simply untrue of women's natural state. Second, according to Hobbes, "men" are naturally inclined to aggress against those they perceive as the vulnerable other. Again, women are not: infants are dependent upon mothers and vulnerable to them, yet the natural mother does not aggress against her child, she breastfeeds her. And lastly, men respond to the vulnerability of natural equality by developing a morality and a civil state that demand respect for the equality, rights, and freedom of the other. Women do not. Women respond to their natural state of inequality by developing a morality of nurturance that is responsible for the well-being of the dependent, and an ethic of care that responds to the greater needs of the weak. Men respond to the natural state of equality with an ethic of autonomy and rights. Women respond to the natural state of inequality with an ethic of responsibility and care.

We might summarize cultural feminism in this way: women's potential for a material connection to life entails (either directly, as I have argued, or indirectly, through the reproduction of mothering) an experiential and psychological sense of connection with other human life, which in turn entails both women's concept of value, and women's concept of harm. Women's concept of value revolves not around the axis of autonomy, individuality, justice and rights, as does men's, but instead around the axis of intimacy, nurturance, community, responsibility and care. For women, the creation of value, and the living of a good life, therefore depend upon relational, contextual, nurturant, and affective responses to the needs of those who are dependent and weak, while for men the creation of value, and the living of the good life, depend upon the ability to respect the rights of independent co-equals, and the deductive, cognitive ability to infer from those rights rules for safe living. Women's concept of harm revolves not around a fear of annihilation by the other but around a fear of separation and isolation from the human community on which she depends, and which is dependent upon her. If, as I have suggested, cultural feminism is our dominant feminist dogma, then this account of the nature of women's lives constitutes the "official text" of feminism, just as liberal legalism constitutes the official text of legalism.

These two "official stories" sharply contrast. Whereas according to liberal legalism, men value autonomy from the other and fear annihilation by him, women, according to cultural feminism, value intimacy with the other and fear separation from her. Women's sense of connection with others determines our special competencies and special vulnerabilities, just as men's sense of separation from others determines theirs. Women value and have a special competency for intimacy, nurturance, and relational thinking, and a special vulnerability to and fear of isolation, separation from the other, and abandonment, just as men value and have a special competency for autonomy, and a special vulnerability to and fear of annihilation.

Against the cultural feminist backdrop, the story that radical feminists tell of women's invaded, violated lives is "subterranean" in the same sense that, against the backdrop of liberal legalism, the story critical legal theorists tell of men's alienation and isolation from others is subterranean. According to radical feminism, women's connection to others is the source of women's misery, not a source of value worth celebrating. For cultural feminists, women's connectedness to the other . . . is the source, the heart, the root, and the cause of women's different morality, different voice, different "ways of knowing," different genius, different capacity for care, and different ability to nurture. For radical feminists, that same potential for connection—experienced materially in intercourse and pregnancy, but experienced existentially in all spheres of life—is the source of women's debasement, powerlessness, subjugation, and misery. It is the cause of our pain, and the reason for our stunted lives. Invasion and intrusion, rather than intimacy, nurturance and care, is the "unofficial" story of women's subjective experience of connection.

Thus, modern radical feminism is unified among other things by its insistence on the invasive, oppressive, destructive implications of women's material and existential connection to the other. So defined, radical feminism (of modern times) begins not with the eighties critique of heterosexuality, but rather in the late sixties, with Shulamith Firestone's angry and eloquent denunciation of the oppressive consequences for women of the physical condition of pregnancy. Firestone's assessment of the importance and distinctiveness of women's reproductive role parallels Marilyn French's. Both view women's physical connection with nature and with the other as in some sense the "cause" of patriarchy. But their analyses of the chain of causation sharply contrast. For French, women's reproductive role—the paradigmatic experience of physical connection to nature, to life and to the other, and thus the core of women's moral difference—is also the cause of patriarchy, primarily because of men's fear of and contempt for nature. Firestone has a radically different view. Pregnancy is indeed the paradigmatic experience of physical connection, and it is indeed the core of women's difference, but according to Firestone, it is for that reason *alone* the cause of women's oppression. . . .

Pregnancy itself, independent of male contempt, is invasive, dangerous and oppressive; it is an assault on the physical integrity and privacy of the body. For Firestone, the strategic implication of this is both clear and clearly material. The technological separation of reproduction from the female body is the necessary condition for women's liberation.[12]

. . . [I]t's worth recognizing that the original radical feminist case for reproductive freedom did not turn on rights of "privacy" (either of the doctor–patient relationship, or of the marriage, or of the family), or rights to "equal protection," or rights to be free of "discrimination." . . . [T]he original feminist argument for reproductive freedom turned on the definitive radical feminist insight that pregnancy—the invasion of the body by the other to which women are distinctively vulnerable—is an injury and ought to be treated as such. . . .

The radical feminist argument for reproductive freedom appears in legal argument only inadvertently or surreptitiously, but it does on occasion appear. It appeared most recently in the phenomenological descriptions of unwanted pregnancies collated in the *Thornburgh* amicus brief recently filed by the National Abortion Rights Action League (NARAL).[13] The descriptions of pregnancy collated in that peculiarly non-legal document are filled with metaphors of invasion—metaphors, of course, because we lack the vocabulary to name these harms precisely. Those descriptions contrast sharply with the "joy" that cultural feminists celebrate in pregnancy, childbirth, and child-raising. The invasion of the self by the other emerges as a source of oppression, not a source of moral value. . . .

This danger, and the fear of it, is gender-specific. It is a fear which grips women, distinctively, and it is a fear about which men, apparently, know practically nothing. . . .

. . . [W]hat the radical feminists of the eighties find objectionable, invasive, and oppressive about heterosexual intercourse, is precisely what the radical feminists of the sixties found objectionable, invasive, and oppressive about pregnancy and motherhood. . . .

. . . [F]or both Dworkin and Firestone, women's potential for material connection with the other—whether through intercourse or pregnancy—constitutes an invasion upon our physical bodies, an intrusion upon our lives, and consequently an assault upon our existential freedom, whether or not it is also the root of our moral distinctiveness (the claim cultural feminism makes on behalf of pregnancy), or the hope of our liberation (the claim sexual liberationists make on behalf of sex). . . . In their extremes, of course, both unwanted heterosexual intercourse and unwanted pregnancy can be life threatening experiences of physical invasion. An unwanted fetus, no less than an unwanted penis, invades my body, violates my physical boundaries, occupies my body, and can potentially destroy my sense of self. . . . What unifies the radical feminism of the sixties and eighties is the argument that women's potential for material, physical connection with the other constitutes an invasion which is a very real harm causing very real damage, and which society ought to recognize as such.

The material, sporadic violation of a woman's body occasioned by pregnancy and intercourse implies an existential and pervasive violation of her privacy, integrity and life projects. According to radical feminists, women's longings for individuation, physical privacy, and independence go well beyond the desire to avoid the dangers of rape or unwanted pregnancy. Women also long for liberation from the oppression of intimacy (and its attendant values) which both cultural feminism and most women officially, and wrongly, overvalue. Intimacy, in short, is *intrusive*, even when it isn't life threatening (perhaps *especially* when it isn't life threatening). An unwanted pregnancy is disastrous, but even a *wanted* pregnancy and motherhood are intrusive. The child *intrudes*, just as the fetus invades.

Similarly, while unwanted heterosexual intercourse is disastrous, even wanted heterosexual intercourse is intrusive. . . . The deepest unofficial story of radical feminism may be that intimacy—the official value of cultural feminism—is itself oppressive. Women secretly, unofficially, and surreptitiously long for the very individuation that cultural feminism insists women fear: the freedom, the independence, the individuality, the sense of wholeness, the confidence, the self-esteem, and the security of identity which can only come from a life, a history, a path, a voice, a sexuality, a womb, and a body of one's own. . . .

Radical feminism, then, is unified by a particular description of the subjectivity of the material state of connection. According to that description, women dread intrusion and invasion, and long for an independent, individualized, *separate* identity. While women may indeed "officially" value intimacy, what women unofficially crave is physical privacy, physical integrity, and sexual celibacy—in a word, physical exclusivity. In the moral realm, women officially value contextual, relational, caring, moral thinking, but secretly wish that . . . we could pursue our own projects—we loath the intrusion that intimacy entails. In the epistemological and moral realms, while women officially value community . . ., we privately crave solitude, self-regard, self-esteem, linear thinking, legal rights, and principled thought. . . .

Finally, then, we can schematize the contrast between the description of the "human being" that emerges from modern legal theory, and the description of women that emerges from modern feminism:

	The Official Story (liberal legalism and cultural feminism)		The Unofficial Story (critical legalism and radical feminism)	
	Value	*Harm*	*Longing*	*Dread*
Legal Theory (human beings)	Autonomy	Annihilation; Frustration	Attachment; Connection	Alienation
Feminist Theory (women)	Intimacy	Separation	Individuation	Invasion; Intrusion

As the diagram reveals the descriptions of the subjectivity of human existence told by feminist theory and legal theory contrast at every point. . . . First, and most obviously, the "official" descriptions of human beings' subjectivity and women's subjectivity contrast rather than compare. According to liberal theory, human beings respond aggressively to their natural state of relative physical equality. In response to the great dangers posed by their natural aggression, they abide by a sharply anti-naturalist morality of autonomy, rights, and individual spheres of freedom, which is intended to and to some extent does curb their natural aggression. They respect a civil state that enforces those rights against the most egregious breaches. The description of women's subjectivity told by cultural feminism is much the opposite. According to cultural feminism, women inhabit a realm of natural *inequality*. They are physically stronger than the fetus and the infant. Women respond to their natural inequality over the fetus and infant not with aggression, but with nurturance and care. That natural and nurturant response evolves into a naturalist moral ethic of care which is consistent with women's natural response. The substantive moralities consequent to these two stories, then, unsurprisingly, are also diametrically opposed. The autonomy that human beings value and the rights they need as a restriction on their natural hostility to the equal and separate other are in sharp contrast to the intimacy that women value, and the ethic of care that represents not a limitation upon, but an extension of, women's natural nurturant response to the dependent, connected other.

The subterranean descriptions of subjectivity that emerge from the unofficial stories of radical feminism and the critical legalism also contrast rather than compare. According to the critical legalists, human beings respond to their natural state of physical separateness not with aggression, fear and mutual suspicion, as liberalism holds, but with longing. Men suffer from a perpetual dread of isolation and alienation and a fear of rejection, and harbor a craving for community, connection, and association. Women, by contrast, according to radical feminism, respond to their natural state of material connection to the other with a craving for individuation and a loathing for invasion. Just as clearly, the subterranean dread men have of alienation (according to critical legalism) contrasts sharply with the subterranean dread that women have of invasion and intrusion (according to radical feminism). . . .

. . . [T]he individuation prized by radical feminism is not the same as the autonomy liberalism heralds, although it may be a precondition of it. The "autonomy" praised by liberalism is one's right to pursue one's own ends. "Individuation," as understood by radical feminism, is the right *to be* the sort of creature who might have and then pursue one's "own" ends. Women's longing for individuation is a longing for a transcendent state of individuated being against that which is internally contrary, given, fundamental, and first. Autonomy is something which is natural to men's existential state and which the state might protect. Individuation, by contrast, is the material precondition of autonomy. Individuation is what you need to be before you can even begin to think about what you need to be free.

These, then, are the differences between the "human beings" assumed by legal theory and women, as their lives are now being articulated by feminist theory. . . . The human being assumed or constituted by legal theory precludes the woman described by feminism. . . .

Feminist Jurisprudence

By the claim that modern jurisprudence is "masculine," I mean two things. First, I mean that the values, the dangers, and what I have called the "fundamental contradiction" that characterize women's lives are not reflected at any level whatsoever in contracts, torts, constitutional law, or any other field of legal doctrine. The values that flow from women's material potential for physical connection are not recognized as values by the Rule of Law, and the dangers attendant to that state are not recognized as dangers by the Rule of Law.

First, the Rule of Law does not value intimacy—its official value is autonomy. The material consequence of this theoretical undervaluation of women's values in the material world is that women are economically *impoverished*. The value women place on intimacy reflects our existential and material circumstance; women will act on that value whether it is compensated or not. But it is not. Nurturant, intimate labor is neither valued by liberal legalism nor compensated by the market economy. It is not compensated in the home and it is not compensated in the workplace—wherever intimacy is, there is no compensation. Similarly, separation of the individual from his or her family, community, or children is not understood to be a harm, and we are not protected against it. The Rule of Law generally and legal doctrine in its particularity are coherent reactions to the existential dilemma that follows from the liberal's description of the male experience of material separation from the other: the Rule of Law acknowledges the danger of annihilation and the Rule of Law protects the value of autonomy. Just as assuredly, the Rule of Law is *not* a coherent reaction to the existential dilemma that follows from the material state of being connected to others, and the values and dangers attendant to that condition. It neither recognizes nor values intimacy, and neither recognizes nor protects against separation.

Nor does the Rule of Law recognize, in any way whatsoever, muted or unmuted, occasionally or persistently, overtly or covertly, the contradiction which characterizes women's, but not men's, lives; while we value the intimacy we find so natural, we are endangered by the invasion and dread the intrusion in our lives which intimacy entails, and we long for individuation and independence. Neither sexual nor fetal invasion of the self by the other is recognized as a harm worth bothering with. Sexual invasion through rape is understood to be a harm, and is criminalized as such, only when it involves some other harm; today, when it is accompanied by violence that appears in a form men understand (meaning a plausible threat of annihilation); in earlier times, when it was understood as theft of another man's property. But marital rape, date rape, acquaintance rape, simple rape, unaggravated rape, or as Susan Estrich wants to say "real rape"[14] are either not criminalized, or if they are, they are not punished—to do so would force a recognition of the concrete, experiential harm to identity formation that sexual invasion accomplishes.

Similarly, fetal invasion is not understood to be harmful, and therefore the claim that I ought to be able to protect myself against it is heard as nonsensical. The argument that the right to abortion mirrors the right of self defense falls on deaf ears for a reason; the analogy is indeed flawed. The right of self defense is the right to protect the body's security against annihilation liberally understood, not invasion. But the danger an unwanted fetus poses is not to the body's security at all, but rather to the body's integrity. Similarly, the woman's fear is not that she will die, but that she will cease to be or never become a self. The danger of unwanted pregnancy is the danger of invasion by the other, not of annihilation by the other. In sum, the Rule of Law does not recognize the danger of invasion, nor does it recognize the individual's need for, much less entitlement to, individuation and independence from the intrusion which heterosexual penetration and fetal invasion entails. The material consequence of this lack of recognition in the real world is that women are *objectified*—regarded as creatures who can't be harmed.

The second thing I mean to imply by the phrase "masculine jurisprudence" is that both liberal and critical legal theory, which is about the relation between law and life, is about men and not women. The reason for this lack of parallelism, of course, is hardly benign neglect. Rather, the distinctive values women hold, the distinctive dangers from which we suffer, and the distinctive contradictions that characterize our inner lives are not reflected in legal theory because legal theory (whatever else it's about) is about actual, real life, enacted, legislated, adjudicated law, and women have, from law's inception, lacked the power to make law protect, value, or seriously regard our experience. Jurisprudence is "masculine" because jurisprudence is about the relationship between human beings and the laws we actually have, and the laws we actually have are "masculine" both in terms of their intended beneficiary and in authorship. Women are absent from jurisprudence because women *as human beings* are absent from the law's protection: jurisprudence does not recognize us because law does not protect us. The implication for this should be obvious. We will not have a genuinely ungendered jurisprudence (a jurisprudence "unmodified" so to speak) until we have legal doctrine that takes women's lives as seriously as it takes men's. We don't have such legal doctrine. The virtual abolition of patriarchy is the necessary political condition for the creation of non-masculine feminist jurisprudence.

It does not follow, however, that there is no such thing as feminist legal theory. Rather, I believe what is now inaccurately called "feminist jurisprudence" consists of two discrete projects. The first project is the unmasking and critiquing of the patriarchy behind purportedly ungendered law and theory, or, put differently, the uncovering of what we might call "patriarchal jurisprudence" from under the protective covering of "jurisprudence." The primary purpose of the critique of patriarchal jurisprudence is to show that jurisprudence and legal doctrine protect and define men, not women. Its second purpose is to show how women—that is, people who value intimacy, fear separation, dread invasion, and crave individuation—have fared under a legal system which fails to value intimacy, fails to protect against separation, refuses to define invasion as a harm, and refuses to acknowledge the aspirations of women for individuation and physical privacy.

The second project in which feminist legal theorists engage might be called "reconstructive jurisprudence." The last twenty years have seen a substantial amount of feminist law reform, primarily in the areas of rape, sexual harassment, reproductive freedom, and pregnancy rights in the workplace. For strategic reasons, these reforms have often been won by characterizing women's injuries as analogous to, if not identical with, injuries men suffer (sexual harassment as a form of "discrimination"; rape as a crime of "violence"), or by characterizing women's longing as analogous to, if not identical with, men's official values (reproductive freedom—which ought to be grounded in a right to individuation—conceived instead as a "right to privacy," which is derivative of the autonomy right). This misconceptualization may have once been a necessary price, but it is a high price, and, as these victories accumulate, an increasingly unnecessary one. Reconstructive feminist jurisprudence should set itself the task of rearticulating these new rights in such a way as to reveal, rather than conceal their origin in women's distinctive existential and material state of being. The remainder of this article offers a . . . criticism of the feminist jurisprudence we have generated to date. . . . I then suggest further lines of inquiry.

The Critique of Patriarchal Jurisprudence

Structurally, the feminist attempt to describe and critique patriarchal jurisprudence by necessity tracks the methodological divisions in masculine jurisprudence, so I need to make one further diversion. Masculine jurisprudence is divided internally by a methodological issue which is as definitive and foundational as the substantive issues that divide liberal from critical legalism. Some legal theorists practice what might be called a "narrative" and "phenomenological" jurisprudential method, (hereinafter, simply narrative) and some practice what might be called an "interpretivist" method. Narrative and interpretive methodology have adherents in both liberal and critical legal literature. Thus, if we look at both substance and method, (instead of just substance) there are not two, but four major jurisprudential traditions in legal scholarship. Liberal legalism can be either interpretive or narrative, as can critical legal theory. Put differently, a narrative methodology can be either critical or liberal, as can interpretivism.

"Narrative legal theory," whether it be liberal or critical, moves methodologically from a description of justice, the state of nature, or of the "human being" which aims for some degree of generality if not universality, and then tells either a narrative *story* about how human beings thus described come to agree on the Rule of Law, or, alternatively, a phenomenological *description* of how it *feels* to be a person within a legal regime. . . . Interpretive theorists begin with an interpretation of law, or of a body of legal doctrine, or of the idea of law itself, and derive from that interpretation an account of justice. . . .

Putting together substance and method, we can generate a . . . matrix, with representative participants. . . .

	Narrative	*Interpretive*
Liberal	Hobbes Ackerman Rawls	Blackstone R. Dworkin
Critical	"Phenomenology Project" (rights) Unger, Gabel	D. Kennedy "Deconstruction Project"

THE NARRATIVE AND PHENOMENOLOGICAL CRITIQUE

By "the critique of patriarchal jurisprudence" I mean four distinct projects, which parallel the matrix given here. First, *narrative* critical jurisprudence aims to provide, in a Hobbesian (or Ungerian) manner, the material, internal, phenomenological, subjective story of women's experience of the emergence and present reality of the Rule of Law. That story goes something like this. Prior to the advent of the "Rule of Law," we might hypothesize, women bore, breast fed, nurtured, and protected children. Women did the nurturant work. As described above, women lived in a "natural web of hierarchy": they were profoundly unequal to the infants they raised. While men responded to their condition of natural equality with mutual aggression, women responded to their condition of natural inequality with nurturance and an ethic of care. Women were at the same time profoundly unequal to men. Prior to the Rule of Law, women, and only women, were vulnerable to sexual invasion. As Catharine MacKinnon suggests, on the only "first day that matters," and this day occurred long before the signing of the social contract, men established sexual power over women.[15] Thus, inequality vis-à-vis both children and men, an ethic of care for the weak, and sexual vulnerability to the male, was women's natural state, while equality, mutual fear, and suspicion was men's.

Then, on day two, came the Rule of Law. According to the Hobbesian story, the Rule of Law significantly improved the quality of men's lives: men's lives became longer, less nasty, less brutish (even if somewhat more alienated), and more productive. But not so for women: the same Rule of Law left women's natural lives intact, worsened her material condition, and reified her sexual vulnerability into a male right of access. The Rule of Law changed the conditions that uniquely pertained to women in the state of nature, but the change was for the worse: after the Rule of Law, women are still uniquely capable of intimacy, but newly unrecognized for their nurturant activity in a world that values autonomy and compensates individuated labor. Similarly, women remain uniquely vulnerable to invasion, but newly unprotected against that injury in a world that protects against other injuries. The narrative and phenomenological task for the critique of patriarchal jurisprudence is to tell the story and phenomenology of the human community's commitment to the Rule of Law from women's point of view. We need to show what the exclusion of women from law's protection has meant to both women and law, and we need to show what it means for the Rule of Law to exclude women and women's values.

The way to do this—the only way to do this—is to tell true stories of women's lives. The Hobbesian "story" of deliverance from the state of nature to the Rule of Law, as both liberal and radical legal scholars are fond of pointing out, does not purport to be history. But that doesn't make it fantasy. The Hobbesian story of the state of nature (and the critical story of alienation as well) is a synthesis of umpteen thousands of personal, subjective, everyday, male experiences. *Images* are generated from that synthesis, and those images, sometimes articulate, sometimes not, of what is means to be a human being then become the starting point of legal theory. Thus, for example, the Hobbesian, liberal picture of the "human being" as someone who treasures autonomy and fears annihilation from the other comes from men's primary experiences, presumably, of school yard fights, armed combat, sports, games, work, big brothers, and fathers. Similarly, the critical picture of the human being as someone who longs for attachment and dreads alienation comes from the male child's memory of his mother, from rejection experiences painfully culled from his adolescence, and from the adult male's continuing inability to introspect, converse, or commune with the natural world, including the natural world of others. When Peter Gabel says "Let me start by making a descriptive assertion [about human beings] . . . which seems to me . . . [to be] self-evidently true"[16] and then what follows is a descriptive statement which is self-evidently untrue of women, he is not simply "mistaken," he is mistaken in a particular (male) way and for a particular (male) reason. When Hobbes, Ackerman, Dworkin, Rawls, and the rest of the liberal tradition describe the natural human predicament as one of natural equality and mutual antagonism, and describe human beings as inevitably separate and mutually self-interested, thus definitionally excluding pregnant women and breast-feeding mothers from the species, they also are mistaken in a particular way and for a particular reason. Gabel has confused his male experience of separation and alienation with "human" experience, and liberals have confused their male experiences of natural equality, mutual suspicion, fear of annihilation, and pervasive, through-and-through selfishness with "human" experience, and they have done so because women have not made clear that our day-to-day, lived experience—of intimacy, bonding, separation, sexual invasion, nurturance, and intrusion—is incommensurable with men's. . . . [M]en's narrative story and phenomenological description of law is not women's story and phenomenology of law. We need to dislodge legal theorists' confidence that they speak for women, and we need to fill the gap that will develop when we succeed in doing so.

Put phenomenologically, instead of narratively, feminist legal theorists need to show through stories the value of intimacy—not just to women, but to the community—and the damage done—again, not just to women, but to the community—by the law's refusal to reflect that value. . . . We not only need to show that these values are missing from public life and not rewarded in private life, but we also need to show how our community would improve if they were valued. We need to show (as Suzanna Sherry,[17] Lynne Henderson,[18] Martha Minow,[19] and others have begun to do) that a community and a judiciary that relies on nurturant, caring, loving, empathic values rather than exclusively on the rule of reason will not melt into a murky quagmire, or sharpen into the dreaded spector of totalitarianism.

On a more local level, we need to show that a law school which employs, protects, and even *compensates* for these competencies will be a better law school. We need to show (as Martha Fineman has done in the area of custody decisions[20]) that a legal and economic system which values, protects, and rewards nurturant labor in private life will make for a better community. We need to show that community, nurturance, responsibility, and the ethic of care are values at least as worthy of protection as autonomy, self-reliance, and individualism. We must do that, in part, by showing how those values have affected and enriched our own lives. Similarly, we need to show—and again, I think we need to do it with stories—how the refusal of the legal system to protect those values has weakened this community, as it has impoverished our lives.

From a radical point of view, we also need to explain, through stories, how physical invasion and intrusion harm women, and how they harm women distinctively. We need to explain, as Susan Estrich, Lynne Henderson, and Diana Russell have begun to do, the danger and the harm of rape that is not seen as rape: invasive marital intercourse and invasive intercourse with "dates."[21] We need to explain how it feels to live entirely outside the protection of rape law: how it feels to be a wife in a state which defines rape as the "nonconsensual sexual intercourse by a man with a woman not his wife"; how it feels to be the person that another person has a legal right to invade without your consent. We need to provide stories rich enough to show that this harm is not the harm of annihilation protected by the Rule of Law, although it may accompany it. We need to show that the harm of invasive intercourse is real even when it does not look like the kind of violence protected by the Rule of Law. We need to show that invasive intercourse is a danger even when it cannot be analogized in any way whatsoever to male experience.

Similarly, we need to explain, as the National Abortion Rights Action League has begun to do, the harms and dangers of invasive pregnancy. We need to explain that this harm has nothing to do with invading the privacy of the doctor–patient relationship, or the privacy of the family, or the privacy of the marriage; but that rather, it has to do with invading the physical boundaries of the body and the psychic boundaries of a life. Finally, we need to provide phenomenological accounts of those ameliorative institutions, ideologies and psychic constructs that purport to make the invasiveness and intrusiveness of our lives tolerable. . . . With the exception of MacKinnon and Dworkin's work on pornography, we haven't done much of this sort of jurisprudence, and we need to do a lot more.

THE INTERPRETIVE CRITIQUE

The purpose of the interpretive critique of patriarchal jurisprudence complements that of the narrative critique. As the narrative critique explores the Rule of Law from women's point of view, the interpretive critique aims to explore women from the point of view of the Rule of Law. The interpretive critique shows how patriarchal doctrine constructs, defines, and delimits women, just as interpretive masculine jurisprudence, both liberal and critical, aims to provide accounts of how doctrine constructs, defines, and delimits the human being. For although women—people who value intimacy and are harmed by invasion—have not been accorded the protection of the Rule of Law, we have hardly been ignored. Women are not constructed as human within this sytem, but we are nevertheless constructed as something else: as valueless, as objects, as children, or as invisible. The interpretive critique should aim to articulate what that something else might be. The interpretive critique is a lot like shining a light on darkness, or proving a negative—it involves looking at what lies between the images of legalism, instead of looking directly at legalism. The interpretive critique must deconstruct the images that authoritatively diminish women, sometimes down to nothing.

On the cultural side of the substantive divide, this means showing how legalism devalues women, by not valuing what women value. To name just a few examples, Martha Fineman has tried to show who and what a "mother" is understood to be in a legal system where nurturant labor is neither recognized nor valued in custody disputes.[22] Other interpretive cultural feminists have tried to show what it means, objectively, not to be paid for housework, for child-raising, and for relational work in the workplace. On the radical side, this means showing what it means to be objectified. Again, to take just a few examples, Andrea Dworkin has begun to show who the "woman" is defined to be by the pornographer, and Catharine MacKinnon has begun to show how the First Amendment has defined the pornographer's definition of the woman.[23] Susan Estrich, Diana Russell, and others have begun to show what a "wife" *is* in a legal system which defines rape as the nonconsensual intercourse by a man with a woman *not his wife*.[24] We need, I think, to do more of this: most notably, we need to understand how laws criminalizing abortion construct "motherhood" and how Roe v. Wade[25]— which constructs the right to abortion as the product of a need to balance medicinal privacy rights of doctors and patients against the right to life of a fetus—constructs the female. Henderson has done some of this work. The matrix I foresee, with a sample of representative participants, looks like this:

Critique of Patriarchal Jurisprudence

	Cultural Feminism	*Radical Feminism*
Interpretive Jurisprudence	Sherry and Henderson (on judging) Fineman (motherhood) Dalton (midwives)	MacKinnon (First Amend) A. Dworkin (porn) Estrich (rape)
Narrative Jurisprudence	Littleton Fineman	*Deconstruction Projects* NARAL (abortion) MacKinnon (sex harass) Estrich (rape) *Phenomenological Projects* (of romance, porn etc.)

Reconstructive Jurisprudence

The goal of reconstructive feminist jurisprudence is to render feminist reform rational. We must change the fact that, from a mainstream point of view, arguments for feminist legal reform efforts are (or appear to be) invariably irrational. The moral questions feminist reforms pose are always incommensurable with dominant moral and legal categories. Let me put it this way: given present moral categories, women's issues are crazy issues. Arguments for reproductive freedom, for example, are a little insane: pro-choice advocates can't explain the difference between reproductive freedom and infanticide; or how this right can possibly be grounded in the Constitution; or how it is that women can claim to be "nurturant" and at the same time show blatant disregard for the rights and feelings of fetuses. In fact, my sense, drawn from anecdotal evidence only, is that the abortion issue is increasingly used in ethics as well as constitutional law classrooms to exemplify the "irrationality" of individual moral commitment. Rape reform efforts that aim to expand the scope of the defined harm are also perceived, I believe, as insane. Why would anyone possibly object to non-violent sex? Isn't sex always pleasurable? Feminist pornography initiatives are viewed as irrational, and the surrogate motherhood issue is no better. There's an air of irrationality around each of these issues.

That air of irrationality is partly real and partly feigned. The reason for the air of irrationality around particular, substantive feminist legal reform efforts, I believe, is that feminist legal reforms are by necessity advocated in a form that masks rather than reflects women's true subjective nature. This is hardly surprising: language, of course, constrains our descriptive options. But whether or not surprising, the damage is alarming, and we need to understand its root. Arguments for reproductive freedom, for example, are irrational because the categories in which such arguments must be cast are reflective of men's, not women's, nature. This culture thinks about harm, and violence, and therefore self defense, in a particular way, namely a Hobbesian way, and a Hobbesian conception of physical harm cannot possibly capture the gender-specific subjective harm that constitutes the experience of unwanted pregnancy. From a subjective, female point of view, an abortion is an act of self defense (not the exercise of a "right of privacy"), but from the point of view of masculine subjectivity, an abortion can't possibly be an act of self defense: the fetus is not one of Hobbes' "relatively equal" natural men against whom we have a right to protect ourselves. The fetus is unequal and above all else dependent. That dependency and inequality is the essence of fetus-hood, so to speak. Self-defense doctrine with its Hobbesian background and overlay simply doesn't apply to such dependent and unequal "aggressors," indeed, the notion of aggression itself does not apply to such creatures.

Rape reform efforts to criminalize simple rape are also irrational, as Susan Estrich has discovered, and for the same reason: subjectively, "simple rapes" are harms, but from the point of view of masculine subjectivity, non-violent acts that don't threaten annihilation or frustration of projects can't possibly be "harmful." In both cases, we have tried to explain feminist reform efforts through the use of analogies that don't work and arguments that are strained. The result in both cases is internally inconsistent, poorly reasoned, weak, and ultimately vulnerable legal doctrine.

"Reconstructive feminist jurisprudence," I believe, should try to explain or reconstruct the reforms necessary to the safety and improvement of women's lives in direct language that is true to our own experience and our own subjective lives. The dangers of mandatory pregnancy, for example, are invasion of the body by the fetus and the intrusion into the mother's existence following childbirth. The right to abort is the right to defend against a particular bodily and existential invasion. The harm the unwanted fetus does is not the harm of annihilation, nor anything like it: it is not an assault, or a battery, or a breached contract, or an act of negligence. A fetus is not an equal in the state of nature, and the harm a fetus can do is not in any way analogous to that harm. It is, however, a harm. The fetus is an "other," and it is perfectly sensible to seek a liberal sounding "right" of protection against the harm the fetus does.

We need, though, to be more accurate in our description of the harm. Unwanted intercourse is "harmful" because it is invasive, not because it is (necessarily) violent. For that reason alone, the harm of intercourse is descriptively incommensurate with liberal concepts of harm. But it is not incommensurate with women's lives. The goal of reconstructive feminist jurisprudence should be to provide descriptions of the "human being" underlying feminist legal reforms that will be true to the conditions of women's lives. Our jurisprudential constructs—liberalism and critical theory—might then change as well to account for true descriptions of women's subjectivity.

Conclusion: Toward a Jurisprudence Unmodified

The "separation thesis," I have argued, is drastically untrue of women. What's worth noting by way of conclusion is that it is not entirely true of men either. First, it is not true materially. Men are connected to another human life prior to the cutting of the umbilical cord. Furthermore, men are somewhat connected to women during intercourse, and men have openings that can be sexually penetrated. Nor is the separation thesis necessarily true of men existentially. As Suzanna Sherry has shown, the existence of the entire classical republican tradition belies the claim that masculine biology mandates liberal values. More generally, as Dinnerstein, Chodorow, French, and Gilligan all insist, material biology does not *mandate* existential value: men *can* connect to other human life. Men can nurture life. Men can mother. Obviously, men can care, and love, and support, and affirm life. Just as obviously, however, most men don't. One reason that they don't, of course, is male privilege. Another reason, though, may be the blinders of our masculinist utopian visionary. Surely one of the most important insights of feminism has been that biology is indeed destiny when we are unaware of the extent to which biology is narrowing our fate, but that *biology is destiny only to the extent of our ignorance.* As we become increasingly aware, we become increasingly free. As we become increasingly free, we, rather than biology, become the authors of our fate. Surely this is true both of men and women.

On the flip side, the "connection thesis" is also not entirely true of women, either materially or existentially. Not all women become pregnant, and not all women are sexually penetrated. Women can go through life unconnected to other human life. Women can also go through life fundamentally unconcerned with other human life. Obviously, as the liberal feminist movement firmly established, many women can and do individuate, speak the truth, develop integrity, pursue personal projects, embody freedom, and attain an atomistic liberal individuality. Just as obviously, most women don't. Most women are indeed forced into motherhood and heterosexuality. One reason for this is utopian blinders: women's lack of awareness of existential choice in the face of what are felt to be biological imperatives. But that is surely not the main reason. The primary reason for the stunted nature of women's lives is male power.

Perhaps the greatest obstacle to the creation of a feminist jurisprudence is that feminist jurisprudence must simultaneously confront both political and conceptual barriers to women's freedom. The political barrier is surely the most pressing. Feminists must first and foremost counter a profound power imbalance, and the way to do that is through law and politics. But jurisprudence—like law—is persistently utopian and conceptual as well as apologist and political: jurisprudence represents a constant and at least at times a sincere attempt to articulate a guiding utopian vision of human association. Feminist jurisprudence must respond to these utopian images, correct them, improve upon them, and participate in them as utopian images, not just as apologies for patriarchy. Feminism must envision a post-patriarchal world, for without such a vision we have little direction. We must use that vision to construct our present goals, and we should, I believe, interpret our present victories against the backdrop of that vision. That vision is not necessarily androgynous; surely in a utopian world the presence of differences between people will be cause only for celebration. In a utopian world, all forms of life will be recognized, respected, and honored. A perfect legal system will protect against harms sustained by all forms of life, and will recognize life affirming values generated by all forms of being. Feminist jurisprudence must aim to bring this about and, to do so, it must aim to transform the images as well as the power. Masculine jurisprudence must become humanist jurisprudence, and humanist jurisprudence must become a jurisprudence unmodified.

Notes

1. R. Mangabeira Unger, Knowledge and Politics 200 (Free Press, 1975) (citation omitted) (emphasis added).

2. M. Sandel, Liberalism and the Limits of Justice 133 (Cambridge University Press, 1982).

3. R. Dworkin, A Matter of Principle 191 (Harvard University Press, 1985) (capitalization omitted) (emphasis added).

4. T. Hobbes, Leviathan 183–84 (C. B. Macpherson ed., Penguin, 1968).

5. B. Ackerman, Social Justice in the Liberal State 3 (Yale University Press, 1980). . . .

6. N. Chodorow, The Reproduction of Mothering 167 (University of California Press, 1978).

7. C. Gilligan, In a Different Voice 159–60 (Harvard University Press, 1982).

8. *Id.* at 160.

9. *Id.* at 8.

10. Discrimination on the Basis of Pregnancy, 1977, Hearings on S.995 Before the Subcommittee on Labor of the Senate Committee on Human Resources, 95th Cong., 1st sess. 123 (1977) (remarks of Professor Wendy Williams) (emphasis added).

11. Hobbes, Leviathan, *supra* note 4, at 183.

12. S. Firestone, The Dialectic of Sex: The Case for Feminist Revolution (Bantam 1971); M. French, Beyond Power: Women, Men and Morals (J. Cape, 1975).

13. Amicus Brief for the National Abortion Rights Action League et al.,

Thornburgh v. American College of Obstetricians and Gynecologists [476 U.S. 747 (1986)]. . . .

14. S. Estrich, Real Rape (Harvard University Press, 1987).

15. C. MacKinnon, Feminism Unmodified 40 (Harvard University Press, 1987).

16. Gabel, The Phenomenology of Rights-Consciousness and the Pact of the Withdrawn Selves, 62 Tex. L. Rev. 1563, 1566 (1984).

17. Sherry, Civic Virtue and the Feminine Voice in Constitutional Adjudication, 72 Va. L. Rev. 543, 584 (1986); Suzanna Sherry, The Gender of Judges, 4 Law & Ineq. J. 159 (1986).

18. Henderson, Legality and Empathy. 85 Mich. L. Rev. 1574 (1987).

19. Minow, Foreword: Justice Engendered, Part 3 this volume.

20. Fineman and Opie, The Uses of Social Science Data in Legal Policymaking: Custody Determination at Divorce, 1987 Wisc. L. Rev. 107; Fineman, A Reply to David Chambers, 1987 Wisc. L. Rev. 165; Fineman, Dominant Discourse, Professional Language and Legal Change in Child Custody Decisionmaking, 101 Harv. L. Rev. 727 (1988).

21. Estrich, Real Rape, *supra*, note 14; Henderson, Review Essay: What Makes Rape a Crime?, 3 Berkeley Women's L.J. 193 (1987–88); D. Russell, Rape in Marriage (Macmillan, 1982).

22. M. Fineman, Dominant Discourse: The Professional Appropriation of Child Custody Decision-Making, Institute For Legal Studies, Working Papers Series 2 (April 1987).

23. MacKinnon, Feminism Unmodified, *supra* note 15, at 206–13.

24. Estrich, Real Rape, *supra* note 14; Russell, Rape in Marriage, *supra* note 21.

25. 410 U.S. 113 (1973).

❖ *Conservative Feminism*

Richard A. Posner

My title may seem an oxymoron: Does not conservatism imply the rejection of feminism? Some brands of conservatism do; many social and religious conservatives believe that a woman's place is in the home. No one harboring such a belief would be likely to describe himself or herself as a feminist. But conservatives who consider themselves libertarians—conservatives in the classical liberal tradition of Adam Smith, John Stuart Mill (a distinguished feminist), Herbert Spencer (another pioneering feminist), and Milton Friedman—do not believe that law or government should prescribe a particular role for women or discourage them from exercising free choice regarding occupation, marriage, and style of life. . . . Nor do they have much faith in the power of government to put things right. The libertarian, noting that the history of legislation and common law with respect to women has indeed been one of oppression and discrimination, is not optimistic that the law can be flipped over and become an engine of liberation. The libertarian also notes that women are so large and diverse a part of the population and their welfare is so entwined with men—particularly their sons, husbands, fathers, and brothers—that it is hard to imagine what kind of legislation or legal rules could be devised that would benefit women as a group, unless society as a whole benefited.

So what is "conservative feminism"? It is, I suggest, the idea that women are entitled to political, legal, social, and economic equality to men, in the framework of a lightly regulated market economy. It is the libertarian approach to issues of feminist jurisprudence, provided that "libertarian" is understood to refer to a strong commitment to markets rather than to some natural-rights or other philosophical underpinning of such a commitment. The implications of such an approach are not limited to narrowly "economic" issues. . . . The implications extend, as we shall see, to the headiest heights of jurisprudential speculation, where the question whether women have a fundamentally different outlook on law from

1989 U. Chi. Legal F. 191.

men is being debated. My discussion is in three parts: employment, the family and sex, and the nature of law.

Employment

There should be no legal barriers to the employment of women. Laws that forbade women to work in dangerous occupations, or to work as long hours as men, were for the most part either paternalistic or designed to reduce competition faced by male workers. This was eventually recognized, and the laws have been repealed; but a subtler barrier to female employment remains. I refer to the fact that housewives' imputed earnings are not taxed. This may seem an esoteric and impractical—if not downright provocative—topic with which to began an examination of feminist jurisprudence; but we shall see that it illustrates the limitations of more familiar forms of feminist jurisprudence and social thought.

It is plain that housewives do useful work, in the sense of work for which families pay—as by forgoing the income that the housewife could earn in the market.[1] A lower-bound estimate of its value is, indeed, the amount housewives would earn in a world without income taxes if they entered the market. (It is a lower bound because a given woman might be more productive in the household than in the market.) Because the housewife's "earnings" in the home are not taxed, however, women will stay at home even when they would be worth more in the market. For example, suppose the value of a housewife's work is $40,000 a year; her earnings in the market (net of all expenses associated with market work—commuting costs, etc.) would be $50,000; and she would be in the 28 percent income-tax bracket if she did enter the market. Then her after-tax income would be lower in the market than at home, and she will stay home even though she is worth more in the market.[2]

Although this distortion could be eliminated or at least reduced by taxing housewives' imputed earnings, the measurement problems would be formidable, to say the least. Otherwise there would be no economic explanation for failing to tax all significant nonpecuniary goods, notably leisure. Even if there were no formidable problems of measurement, however, a tax on nonpecuniary income would be greatly resented because few taxpayers would understand its rationale. It would seem like a tax on motherhood—and would seem so precisely because other forms of nonpecuniary income are not taxed. . . .

An alternative to taxing housewives' imputed earnings would be exempting working wives' income from income tax up to an amount equal to some estimate of the average value of the earnings from housework. But there would still be a problem of measurement. And the exemption would operate as a subsidy to marriage and thereby distort the choice of women whether (or when) to marry. The most feasible approach might be to allow an income-tax deduction for the costs of household help, on the ground—which is entirely realistic—that these costs actually are business expenses. Notice, however, that this approach might have distributive effects somewhat similar to those of a housewives' tax, because by lowering the tax revenues collected from working women the deduction would require an increase (with no offsetting deduction) in the tax burden borne by households with a housewife.

Whatever the solution, the distortion caused by the failure to tax housewives' real (though nonpecuniary) earnings is an important question for research. Why then is it not a question in which feminists are interested? Perhaps because economic analysis is thought to cut against women's interests. Or perhaps because the proposal of a tax on housewives' imputed earnings is thought to imply increasing the tax burden on women—indeed to invite comparison to a proposal to tax slaves on the ground that they produced real though nonpecuniary income. The comparison is superficial. To isolate the effect of a tax reform designed to reduce the misallocative effects of the existing system of taxation, the analyst must assume that the overall tax burden is not to be increased; that any new tax will be offset by a reduction in an existing tax. (I employed this assumption in discussing the distributive effect of an income-tax deduction for the cost of household help.) Suppose a housewives' tax would be offset by a reduction in the federal income-tax rate. Then taxes paid by working women and their husbands would fall; so would taxes paid by the husbands of housewives. The effect on husbands' income is relevant even if we do not care anything about men's welfare. Because much consumption within the household is joint, each spouse benefits from the income earned by the other, and an increase in husbands' income will therefore benefit wives as well. For both reasons (the fall in the taxes paid by working women and the fall in the taxes paid by working husbands), there is no ground for supposing that a tax on housewives' imputed income would increase the tax burden borne by women. It would, however, eliminate tax incentives from the decision whether to work within or outside the home. In doing so it would have the incidental but relevant effect of making men more comfortable with the idea of their wives' working outside the home. But the most important point is that the economic or libertarian perspective (these are not identical, of course, but they are connected) shows that things are not always as they seem; legislation superficially inimical to women's interests may actually serve those interests—and vice versa as we shall see. Feminists who are not libertarians may not like the vocabulary, methods, and assumptions of economics, but if they refuse to consider the economic consequences of policies affecting women they may end up hurting rather than helping women.

The concept of housewives' imputed earnings has implications that go beyond taxation. One concerns the assessment of damages in tort cases and turns out to be a clearly "pro-woman" implication or corollary of the idea of a housewives' tax. If a housewife is disabled, how should her lost "earnings" be evaluated? My analysis of a housewives' tax implies that a *minimum* estimate of a disabled housewife's lost earnings is the wage she would have commanded in the market (summed over the estimated period of disability and then discounted to present value at the appropriate interest rate), for if those earnings were less, she would switch from household to market employment. This method of estimation would probably yield higher estimates than the "replacement cost" method, which is the one most courts use at present and is flawed by the tendency to ignore the quality dimension of the housewife's services. . . .

Where the libertarian is apt to part company with the liberal or radical feminist in the field of employment is over the question whether employers should be forced to subsidize female employees, as by being compelled to offer maternity leave or pregnancy benefits, or to disregard women's greater longevity than men when fixing pension benefits. To the extent that women workers incur higher medical expenses than men (mainly but not entirely due to pregnancy), or live longer in retirement on a company pension, they cost the employer more than male workers do. So the employer should not be required to pay the same wage *and* provide the same package of fringe benefits. (Of course, to the extent that women impose lower costs—for example, women appear to be more careful about safety than men, and therefore less likely to be injured on the job—they are entitled to a correspondingly higher wage or more extensive fringe benefits.) This is not to suggest—which would be absurd—that women are blameworthy for getting pregnant or for living longer than men. It is to suggest merely that they may be more costly workers and that, if so, the disparity in cost should be reflected in their net compensation. If this disparity is not reflected, then male workers are being discriminated against in the same sense in which women would be discriminated against if they received a lower wage than equally productive (and no less costly) male workers. What is sauce for the goose should be sauce for the gander. More than symmetry is involved; we shall see in a moment that laws designed to improve the welfare of women may boomerang, partly though not wholly because of the economic interdependence of men and women.

I anticipate three objections to my analysis. The first is that in speaking of employers subsidizing women I am taking as an arbitrary benchmark the costs and performance of male workers. I am not. Consider an employer who is female in a hypothetical female-dominated society and whose entire labor force is also female, so that for her the benchmark in setting terms of employment is female. A man applies for a job. He asks for a higher wage on the ground that experience shows that the average male employee's medical costs are lower than the average female employee's medical costs. If the employer refuses to pay him the higher wage, then, assuming that this worker is just as good as the employer's average female worker, the employer is discriminating against him. This would answer the second objection—that nature should not be allowed to determine social outcomes. I agree that natural law does not compel the conclusion that women should be penalized in the marketplace or anywhere else for living longer or for incurring greater medical costs on average than men. But neither is there any reason why men should be penalized for not living as long as women by being forced to pay for women's longer years of retirement. The matter should be left to the market.

The third objection to my analysis is that, in suggesting that the employer be allowed to make cost-justified differentiations based on sex, I am necessarily implying that he should be permitted to treat employees as members of groups whose average characteristics the particular employee may not share, rather than as individuals. That is true. Some women die before some men, just as some women are taller than some men. The difference is that while it is obvious on inspection whether a given woman is taller than a given man—and therefore it would be absurd for an employer to implement a (let us assume valid) minimum-height requirement of 5 feet 8 inches by refusing to accept job applications from women, it is not obvious which women employees will not live as long as which men employees or will not take as much leave or incur as high medical expenses. Any cost-based differentiation in these areas must be based on probabilistic considerations, of which sex may be the most powerful in the sense of having the greatest predictive power. The average differences between men and women are not invidious, and many cut in favor of women—they are safer drivers, and they live longer, and in a free insurance market would therefore be able to buy liability insurance and life insurance at lower rates than men. Women would not be stigmatized if the market were allowed to register these differences.

It is not even clear, moreover, that women benefit, on balance from laws that forbid employers to take into account the extra costs that female employees can impose. Such laws discourage employers from hiring, promoting, and retaining women, and there are many ways in which they can discriminate in these respects without committing detectable violations of the employment-discrimination laws.[3]

There is an additional point. Most women are married—and many who are not currently married are divorced or widowed and continue to derive a benefit from their husband's earnings. The consumption of a married woman is, as I have noted, a function of her husband's income as well as of her own (in the divorce and widowhood cases as well, for the reason just noted). Therefore a reduction in men's incomes as a result of laws that interfere with profit-maximizing and cost-minimizing decisions by employers will reduce women's welfare as much as men's. Moreover, women who are not married are less likely to have children than women who are married; and where employer benefits are child-related—such as pregnancy benefits and maternity leave—their effect is not merely to transfer wealth from men to women but from women to women. The effect could be dramatic. Compare the situation of a married woman with many children and an unmarried woman with no children. Generous pregnancy benefits and a generous policy on maternity leave will raise the economic welfare of the married woman. Her and her husband's wages will be lower, because all wages will fall in order to finance the benefit, but the reduction will probably be smaller than the benefits to her—in part because the unmarried female worker will experience the same reduction in wages but with no offsetting benefit. Feminists who support rules requiring employers to grant pregnancy benefits and maternity leave may therefore, and I assume unknowingly, be discouraging women from remaining single or childless. Feminists of all persuasions would think it outrageous if the government required fertile woman to have children, yet many feminists support an oblique form of such a policy—a subsidy to motherhood. They do this, I suspect, because they have not considered the economic consequences of proposals that *appear* to help women.

The principle of equal pay for equal work makes perfectly good economic sense,[4] provided that equal work is understood, consistently with the previous discussion, to mean equal in cost to the employer as well as in benefit to the employer (productivity). It does not follow, however, that women are bound to have the same average wage rate as men even if there is no difference in medical or other costs or those differences are offset by other factors. Whether, despite being just as "good" as men, women will have the same average wage rate depends critically on whether they are willing to make the same commitment to the labor force as men do. A woman who takes several years out of the work force to stay home with her young children cannot expect to have the same average wage as a man who works continuously. Since her expected working life is shorter, she will invest less in her human capital (earning capacity), and part of a wage is a return to that investment.

Feminists who are not libertarians may retort that the propensity of women rather than men to take leave from work to raise their children is itself a subtle consequence of sex discrimination, "sex role socialization," or related factors. Whether it is nature or culture that is responsible for the fact that on average male self-esteem is more involved in career than female self-esteem is a profoundly difficult question on which I can claim no expertise; but certainly it would be rash to reject nature out of hand. It is possible that women are more devoted to children than men are and more talented at child rearing and that these differences reflect a genuine comparative advantage possessed by women as a result of millions of years of evolution, rather than just "brainwashing" by men and male-dominated women. The human infant requires prolonged nurture, and there may well have been efficiency advantages, under the exceedingly primitive conditions that obtained throughout all but the most recent history of the human race, to a sexual division of labor in which one spouse specializes in nurture and the other in hunting and in protection from enemies. To an unknown extent, that division may be "hard-wired" into our brains.

Even if these speculations are correct, they are correct about the average woman versus the average man rather than about every woman and every man. Within each there is a distribution of attitudes toward children. And the two distributions intersect. Many women are less devoted to children and less skillful at raising children than many men. The point of intersection is undoubtedly influenced by cultural factors that are changeable, as well as by biological factors that may be changeable if at all only at great cost. But whether biological or cultural factors predominate in the observed differences between the job commitments of men and women may be peripheral to the questions of policy that involved in the debate over the male–female earnings gap. It is a mistake to suppose that biological differences are always more refractory than cultural ones. Genetic vision defects can be corrected by glasses more easily than social customs can be changed by government. But the point cuts in both directions. The fact—if it is a fact—that the predominant role of women in child rearing is culturally contingent rather than biologically determined does not imply that it can easily be changed by governmental intervention or that we should greet governmental regulation of the family structure with open arms. The idea that government should try to alter the decisions of married couples on how to allocate time to raising children is a strange mixture of the Utopian and the repulsive. The division of labor within marriage is something to be sorted out privately rather than made a subject of public intervention. Liberal and radical feminists can if they want urge women to stay in the labor force and have no children or fewer children, or persuade their husbands to assume a greater role in child rearing. Others can urge the contrary. The ultimate decision is best left to private choice (Parallel arguments can be made—and often are made by feminists—against laws that forbid abortion or that subsidize marriage and childbearing.)

This analysis argues against publicly financed day-care centers for children of working women (other than those who are very poor), beyond the obvious libertarian argument that if the families of working mothers are willing and able to pay for day care, the market will provide the service more efficiently than the government—and if they are not willing, on what ground should taxpayers be forced to pay for this service? A comprehensive public system of day-care centers, on the Swedish model, would require a substantial increase in taxation. This increase would significantly, perhaps dramatically, reduce the disposable income of all households, but the crunch would be particularly severe in households with a nonworking wife. Although, as I have said, the work that housewives do is valuable, it is not pecuniary, and a household could encounter liquidity problems if one wage earner's income had to bear the full brunt of taxation. So, the day-care program would drive women out of the home. Besides the liquidity effect, a taxpayer-supported day-care program would distort the woman's choice between home and market by driving a wedge between the social cost of day care and the private cost (zero, if the subsidy paid the household's full cost of day care). Again we find feminists supporting a form of public intervention that would interfere with free choices by women. Admittedly, the distortion just noted might offset the distortion noted earlier that is created by the failure to tax housewives' real but nonpecuniary income from household production. And the taxing of housewives' income, a project with plausible economic support, would create the same liquidity problem as taxation designed to support universal day care.

Another ambitious feminist proposal that is economically questionable is "comparable worth,"[5] at least when extended from government employment (which may well embody departures from competitive wage-setting that are due to sex discrimination since government is subject to, at best, weak competitive constraints) to the private sector. The idea behind comparable worth is that occupations traditionally dominated by women, such as nursing, are underpaid relative to occupations traditionally dominated by men, such as driving a truck. The problem is that while it is relatively easy to determine when men and women are being paid differently for the same work—at least where they are performing standardized chores in which productivity varies little among workers—it is next to impossible to determine when the wage differential among occupations is greater than is necessary to compensate for differences in skills, working conditions, etc. The best evidence is a queue of workers seeking entry into higher-paid occupation and a shortage of workers in the lower-paid occupation. But the very nature of this evidence is also a clue to the self-correcting character of "comparable worth" problems. If one occupation is overpaid relative to another, workers will flow from the second to the first, causing wages to rise in the second and fall in the first until comparable worth is restored. Comparable worth is the equilibrium, and disequilibrium is self-correcting provided there are not artificial barriers to entry. (This is a clue to why the argument for comparable worth is stronger when applied to public employment.) If women are not excluded from higher-paid occupations or (what is the same thing) confined to lower-paid occupations, a difference that exceeds the equilibrium pay difference between occupations that will draw them into the higher-paid occupation and comparable worth will be achieved automatically, without any need for public intervention beyond, perhaps, prohibitions against the exclusion of women from occupations—and that is already prohibited by Title VII.

All this may be too sunny and certainly is in tension with the evidence that at least *some* of the male–female earnings gap is due to discrimination, although as I said earlier, the gap is narrowing. It might be better to attack the remaining discrimination directly, difficult though that is, rather than settle for a "separate but equal" solution, as comparable worth has been described.[6] The costs of achieving comparable worth in the private sector could be considerable, since it will reduce the efficiency with which labor is utilized; private employers, even those not entirely free from discriminatory tendencies, will make more efficient employment decisions than, for example, the bureaucrats in the Department of Labor. And comparable worth may not succeed in redistributing wealth in favor of women. Its effect is to attract into the "women's" fields both men who formerly worked in the "men's" fields and the (few) women who worked there, resulting in more workers—many of them men—bidding for fewer jobs (since employers will respond to a rise in the cost of labor by hiring fewer workers). Women displaced from the now better-paid "women's" fields will compete with women in fields not covered by comparable worth, resulting in lower wages for the women in those fields. And to the extent that men are hurt, the women married to those men are hurt too, since, as noted earlier, to the extent that consumption in the household is joint, each spouse benefits from the other's income.

The Family and Sex

The questions become even more difficult when we switch focus from employment to the family and sex, where such issues as abortion, surrogate motherhood, rape (including "date rape" and marital rape), incest, battered wives, divorce, and pornography fill the horizon. The libertarian perspective provides a unified, though in some places a highly controversial and in other places an indeterminate, approach to these issues. From that perspective the focus is, once again, on freedom of contract.[7] People should be able to cut their own deals, in matters of sex and the family as well as in more conventionally economic arenas, subject to a duty not to impose uncompensated costs on third parties. When transaction costs are high, the law should try to impose the deal that the parties would have struck if negotiation had been feasible.

This approach works well with such issues as divorce and surrogate motherhood, less well with rape, incest, and pornography, and poorly with abortion. When marriage is viewed as a contract, divorce becomes the name for contract termination, and the question becomes one of the proper remedy. The closest analogy to marriage in the sphere of contracts is partnership, and the rule in partnership law is that upon dissolution each partner takes back the assets that he had contributed to the partnership. Until recently, the law had failed to value the wife's contributions adequately. For example, in the common case when the wife had put her husband through medical school or law school, the courts failed to recognize that she was part owner of the degree her husband had obtained and of the earning power conferred by that degree, and thus tended to award less alimony (which in this analysis is installment "repatriation" of the wife's share of the nonliquid assets of the marriage) than was economically efficient. This inequity is gradually being corrected.

Surrogate motherhood is, from the woman's standpoint, the nine-month rental of her reproductive capacity to another family. Why there is a movement afoot—supported by many though not all feminists—to forbid women to obtain a monetary return on this valuable, uniquely female asset puzzles me. The movement is paternalistic (pun intended), indeed patronizing, because it denies the capacity of the surrogates to make advantageous contracts. It treats women as children, men (the father) as wily, deceitful, and manipulative; it reinforces the stereotype of women as being dominated by emotion rather than reason; and it reminds us of the time when married women were not legally competent to make contracts. The surrogates (even those—who are, I believe, the majority—who have borne children before) are not credited with sufficient foresight or emotional maturity to charge a price that will compensate them not only for the risk and expense of the pregnancy but for the emotional wrench experienced at giving up the newborn baby. There are, of course, women who lack the requisite foresight and emotional maturity, just as there are men who lack the requisite foresight and emotional maturity to make rational decisions to engage in such characteristically male voluntary activities as high-stakes gambling, illegal trafficking in drugs, military combat, and dangerous sports. The saga of "Baby M"[8] has distorted public and professional thinking on surrogate motherhood. One is not surprised that some surrogate mothers experience deep regret when it comes time to surrender the newly born baby; but a sensible decision on whether to forbid contracts of surrogate motherhood—that is, whether to deem adult women incompetent to enter into binding contracts of a particular type—requires consideration not only of these women but also of the surrogates who complete the performance of their contractual undertaking without incident, of the father and adoptive mother, and of the children. As far as I am able to discover,[9] the vast majority of surrogates are satisfied with the arrangement, as are, of course the fathers and the adoptive mothers. It is too soon to tell whether surrogate motherhood will harm the children, but the likelihood seems small. The only practical difference between surrogate motherhood and adoption is that the price is somewhat higher under the former arrangement—$10,000 on average versus about $3,000 (some adoption agencies, however, charge as much as $15,000)—although the comparison is somewhat academic since very few healthy white infants are available from adoption agencies any more, and, whether rightly or wrongly, those are the children that most people want to adopt. How the price difference might cause psychological injury to the surrogate children is beyond me.

I might react differently if persuaded that many surrogate mothers are desperate women, driven by extreme poverty to engage in a form of sale that causes them deep emotional distress. I might say in such a case that society should do something to relieve their poverty and desperation beyond merely permitting them to sell their only marketable asset. But I have not seen the evidence that would persuade me of this—and I have been looking for it.

It might seem that from the surrogate mother's standpoint the best of all possible worlds would be a rule that permitted her to take money in exchange for agreeing to bear a child for another couple but entitled her to change her mind, when the baby was born, about giving it up. But the price she would receive for the rental of her reproductive capacity would be lower under such a regime. The couple would be getting considerably less for their money, since if the surrogate mother decided to keep the child they would have lost many months in their quest for a child. A final consideration is that if contracts of surrogate motherhood are forbidden, married men who are desperately eager for a child may decide to abandon their wives.

Rape and pornography present easier issues in principle than in practice. Rape parallels theft in being a coerced taking in a setting of low transaction costs.

Persons who want sex (violent or otherwise) should be required to "bargain" for it. This is not to say that sex is characteristically commercial or that legalizing prostitution is the answer to the problem of rape. It is to say that personal relationships, like commercial ones, can be presumed to be welfare-enhancing only when they are consensual, involving commitments (implicit or explicit) of mutual pleasure, emotional support, marriage, children, etc. Just as someone who covets my compact-disc player should be required to bargain for it with me rather than allowed to purloin it, so men should not be permitted to impose themselves on unwilling women. The difficult problem in rape, as in incest, child abuse, and wife-battering, is that criminal activity which occurs in private, and which may leave few or no physical traces, poses difficult evidentiary problems for courts.

Pornography parallels pollution in being the result of a voluntary activity (the sale of pornography to the consumers of pornography, the sale of the factory's product to the consumers of that product) that may have uncompensated third-party effects, such as inciting its consumers to rape. The rape and pornography examples are convergent for those who believe that pornography encourages its consumers to commit rape by teaching that women enjoy forcible subordination to men.

The practical problems arise from the evidentiary difficulties that I have just alluded to that complicate rape cases (mainly but not limited to difficulties connected with the defense of consent), uncertainty about the existence or magnitude of the effects of pornography on third parties (pornography may have little or no effect on the incidence of sex crimes—may be, indeed, at least for some consumers of pornography, a substitute for rape), and difficulty in distinguishing pornography from socially valuable forms of expression concerning sex. About these problems I have nothing new to say,[10] but I do want to comment on the suggestion that using misrepresentation to obtain consent to sexual intercourse should be declared a form of rape, though perhaps punished less seriously than forcible rape.[11] The evidentiary problems would be serious, but I am interested in another point: the implicit modeling of sexual relations on the economic market. Obtaining money by fraud or false pretenses is a crime; thus, the suggestion goes, obtaining sex by fraud or false pretenses should also be a crime. Many feminists are hostile to capitalism in general and to prostitution in particular. They may not realize that to imply that the criminal law of fraud provides an appropriate model for the law of rape is to embrace the economic model of social interaction in a particularly uncompromising form.

I now turn to an issue about which the libertarian has, I believe, nothing to say except that the issue resists fruitful analysis in libertarian or economic analysis. That is the issue of abortion. At first glance there might appear to be a simple libertarian solution: The mother should be entitled to abort the fetus at any stage of pregnancy and for whatever reason, provided she is willing to pay the cost of the abortion. The only condition would be that she must get the father's permission if, but only if, the implicit or explicit contract between her and the father made the fetus a joint "asset" of its parents rather than the mother's asset only. Assuming either that the father does consent or that he is not required to consent because he has no contractual interest in the fetus, abortion would appear to be a voluntary transaction with no third-party effects. But this analysis ignores the effect on the fetus itself. *If* the fetus is deemed a member of society, with the consequence that its welfare counts in the social calculus along with that of the mother and father, then it is not obvious that abortion is value-maximizing on the average, unless perhaps the fetus has some terrible deformity that might permit us to say with some confidence that if it could be consulted in the matter it would say that it would rather not be born—in other words, unless the fetus would incur a net disutility, both expected and realized, from living. Of course, even a healthy fetus might "prefer" to be born to more mature parents (abortion when used as a device for family planning affects the timing but not necessarily the number of children that a woman has); but it would be a different fetus that would be born later.

The decision whom to count as a member of society (foreigners? animals?) for purposes of determining whether his or her or its welfare shall count in the design of social institutions is a moral question about which libertarians (in the sense in which I am using the word) and economists have nothing to say. Nor is the status of the fetus the only moral issue; so is the freedom of the woman who finds herself involuntarily or accidentally pregnant. The libertarian can point out that regardless of how the moral issues are resolved, laws forbidding abortion are unlikely to be any more effective than other laws penalizing victimless crimes (the fetus is not an articulate victim and its family can't be counted on to bring its "killers" to justice). And abortion laws are undoubtedly a severe curtailment of women's liberty, and one having no counterpart in laws affecting men. But as the moral issue both depends critically on the status to be assigned the fetus and is central to the controversy over abortion, economic or libertarian analysis will not resolve the controversy.

Do Women and Men Think Differently about Law?

The discerning reader will have noticed in the discussion up to now three stages of feminist thought. In the first, which corresponds to the first stage in the civil rights movement, women seek simply to be relieved from legal disabilities that limit their range of choice compared to that of men. (Abortion is a complicated instance of the simple point.) In the second stage, which corresponds to the second, "affirmative action" stage in the civil rights movement—the stage this movement is in now—women seek affirmative benefits in order to remove a residue of past discrimination. Comparable worth is best understood in this light. In both stages it is assumed that women are identical to men in every respect to which public policy might be relevant. In the third stage, which has no counterpart in the civil rights movement, women are admitted to be different (on average) from men in certain policy-relevant respects such as longevity and pregnancy but it is argued that these differences should not be allowed to influence employers; nature should not dictate, or even justify, social outcomes. Desexed annuity tables, subsidized day care, and compulsory disability benefits for pregnancy are all products of this third stage. But while conceding physical differences between men and women, third-stage feminists do not argue (and indeed would be inclined to deny) that women *think* differently from men. Such an argument would undermine their position. It is one thing to say that differences between the male and female reproductive systems, or differences in physical strength or longevity, or the different roles of men and women in nurturing infants—all differences that we share with other primates—should not affect marketplace compensation, and quite another to say that women and men should receive the same compensation even if there are profound and permanent mental and psychological differences between the sexes. Yet fourth-stage feminists, heavily represented in contemporary feminist jurisprudence, appear to claim precisely this.[12]. . .

This stage owes much to the work of Carol Gilligan, a psychologist who in an influential book[13] distinguished between an "ethic of rights" that she regarded as distinctively masculine and an "ethic of care" that she regarded as distinctively feminine. . . .

The ethic of rights sketched by Gilligan corresponds rather closely to the formalistic style of law, and the ethic of care to the more contextual, personal, and discretionary style. Maybe it's true that women tend to prefer a less formalistic style of law than men. Although in twenty years of teaching law to students of both sexes and seven years of being a judge assisted by law clerks of both sexes I have not noticed any such difference, this may be due to the self-selection of female students who apply to elite law schools, to the socialization that they undergo in law school, or to my own lack of sensitivity. If there is such a difference, we can expect that as women come to play a larger and larger role in the legal profession and the judiciary, the character of our law will change; we will see fewer rules and more standards, less talk about logic and more about practical reason, and less anxiety about maintaining law's determinacy, objectivity, and impersonality.

I myself, male though I am, would welcome such a change; for although women may on average be less formalistic than men (I am skeptical that this is so, but it is possible), there are many men who dislike formalism and I am one of them. . . . [A]t its formalist extreme law is monstrous, inhuman, socially irrelevant, and thoroughly bogus. . . . Law properly is a mixture of rules and discretion, law and equity, rule and standard, positive laws and ethical principles (corresponding to natural law), logic and practical reason, lay judges and professional judges, objectivity and subjectivity. And the "feminine" pole should be the last thing that any member of an oppressed group—if that is how the modern American woman should be described—wants to see dominant legal thought: As Shylock rightly feared, in arguing for a literal interpretation of his bond with Antonio, discretion in a legal system is apt to be exercised against the pariah. It is hard to say whether women would be on balance better or worse off if the legal system were more empathetic than it is, but it does not appear that women fare particularly well under the discretionary system of qadi justice in traditional Moslem law.

In this connection it should be noted that the men who reject formalism are not feminist jurisprudes in any useful sense. They are (in the Anglo-American sphere) legal realists, or pragmatists, or instrumentalists, or skeptics—which is to say that they possess outlooks on law that long predate the entry of women in significant numbers into positions of influence in the legal profession. I question whether there is a distinctively feminine outlook on law, as distinct from an outlook that men and women share, though perhaps in different proportions.

I therefore disagree with Suzanna Sherry's argument that "a feminine jurisprudence, evident, for example, in the decisions of Justice O'Connor, might thus be quite unlike any other contemporary jurisprudence."[14] What Sherry actually finds in her examination of Justice O'Connor's opinions are a dislike of "bright line" rules and a sensitivity to community interests (this is how Sherry explains the fact that O'Connor is a "law and order" conservative in criminal cases). Sherry would have found the same things if she had read the opinions of Justice Tom Clark or any number of other conservative jurists.

I have the same reaction to the suggestion by Frank Michelman, made in the course of a minute examination of one opinion of Justice O'Connor's, that her use in that case of a "balancing test" may reflect a distinctively feminine outlook.[15] Many is the male jurist who has been drawn to balancing tests; indeed, such attraction is one of the defining characteristics of the pragmatic, instrumental, or "realist" style of judging. I challenge Sherry and Michelman to pick out Justice O'Connor's opinions in a blindfold test; I find nothing distinctively feminine in the style or content of her opinions.

Leslie Bender suggests that a feminist tort law would replace the "reasonable man" with the "caring neighbor."[16] This suggestion misunderstands the significance of the "reasonable man" (or, as it is now more often and more appropriately referred to, the "reasonable person") rule in tort law. Its significance lies in preventing tortfeasors (or victims of torts) from arguing that while the average person could have avoided the accident, the actual party in the case could not have done so, because he had a below-average capacity to take care. I do not understand Bender to be quarreling with this result. Her point rather is that in deciding how much care is optimal, we should suppose that potential injurers are not completely strangers to their potential victims but are mildly altruistic toward them (a caring neighbor is more altruistic than a stranger but less so than a close relative). However, people are what they are; most neighbors are not caring, and most accident victims are not neighbors. Human nature will not be altered by holding injurers liable to having failed to take the care that a caring neighbor would have taken. The only effect of adopting Bender's proposal would be to shift negligence liability in the direction of strict liability. Her "caring neighbor" is an unnecessary step in the analysis. Bender might as well argue directly for strict liability on the ground that it is the more altruistic regime than negligence.

Is it? Strict liability is sometimes defended on the ground that it provides more compensation to more accident victims. This is a partial analysis. Strict liability can also result in higher prices, and the burden may be borne by consumers. The net distributive impact is unclear. If these complications are ignored, maybe a feminine outlook on law could be expected to stress compensation—obviously Bender associates altruism with women. On the other hand, strict liability is more rule-like, less standard-like, less contextualist, less sensitive to the particulars of the individual accident, than negligence is; in that respect it is the more masculine standard. Maybe Gilligan's ethic of care cannot be made the basis for a coherent feminist jurisprudence. And if it can be, the result may not be anything distinct from old-fashioned American legal realism, provided we understand that altruism is a feature of some but not all versions of legal realism. Both Holmes and Cardozo were realists, but only Cardozo was a liberal (in the modern, not classical, sense). Plenty of male jurists have worn their hearts on their sleeves.

A recent article by Robin West articulates a slightly different version of feminist jurisprudence.[17] She begins by describing a formalistic conception of law that she calls "legal liberalism" (critics of liberalism like to assume that liberalism depends on a formalistic approach to law); and she stresses the importance that the legal liberal ascribes to individual liberty as a value served by law and the legal liberal's dread of having his individuality submerged in the community. The radical males of the critical legal studies movement, she goes on to explain, relabel individuality as alienation and turn it from an object of longing to one of dread; and relabeling annihilation as connection, they perform a similar inversion of the liberal's dread. Women, however, differ fundamentally from men in that their basic experience is not of individuality but of connection because of pregnancy and breast-feeding, because women are raised primarily by the parent of the same sex as theirs, and because women are penetrated, rather than penetrating, in sexual intercourse. The liberal feminist, who is basically satisfied with this order of things, replaces the liberal legalist's value of autonomy with the value of intimacy and the liberal legalist's dread of annihilation with a dread of separation. The radical feminist, however, longs for individuality (unlike the male radical) and dreads not alienation but invasion, intrusion.

Here we may pause and consider whether any of this is true. That is a large subject, to which I cannot begin to do justice here. My tentative view is that there are only two significant (both probably innate) differences, on average (as always a very important qualification), between men and women, in addition to the obvious differences in primary and secondary sexual characteristics. First, women tend to be less aggressive than men. Second, they tend to be more devoted to their children. As Gilligan puts it in a recent article, "stereotypes of males as aggressive and females as nurturant, however distorting and however limited, have some empirical claim. The overwhelmingly male composition of the prison population and the extent to which women take care of young children cannot readily be dismissed as irrelevant to theories of morality or excluded from accounts of moral development. If there are no sex differences in empathy or moral reasoning, why are there sex differences in moral and immoral behavior?"[18] These differences could explain the greater attachment that the average man appears to have to the job market than the average woman.

But what, if any, implications these differences have for the law—beyond the trivial conjecture that women are less likely to be excessively combative in litigation or to be willing to work the absurd hours that are demanded of partners and associates at some law firms—are obscure. Nor are these the differences that interest West. But her idea that "connectedness" is the defining characteristic of the female experience, and her attribution of this characteristic to the female role in reproduction and child rearing, are neither well supported by empirical evidence nor, on the whole, especially plausible. Most women do not appear to lack a sense of themselves as individuals; nor is that sense diminished by pregnancy and breast-feeding. The point about penetration is particularly unconvincing; it would make as much sense to describe the female as ingesting as it does to describe the male as penetrating.

The fact that girls are raised primarily by the parent of the same sex, and boys primarily by the parent of the opposite sex, is a somewhat more plausible, though speculative, ground for thinking that boys may grow up to be more individualistic than girls.[19] So if men assume a greater role in child rearing, the male and female outlooks may become more convergent. I expect they will become more convergent anyway, as more and more women participate in the labor force.

However the large questions are answered, it seems that West's ambitions for feminist jurisprudence are, at least in the article under discussion, relatively modest ones. She doesn't aspire to make law feminist, either in Gilligan's or Sherry's or Bender's sense, or in West's own version of Gilligan's thesis. Mainly she wants the law to become more protective of women's interests by recognizing the vulnerabilities that the woman's sense of connectedness creates. West wants lawyers, judges, and legislators to understand women's distinctive experience, just as blacks or Jews or Asians or Mormons want the law to be sensitive to their own experience. A libertarian can hardly quarrel with this aspiration—provided that West has identified what is indeed distinctive in women's experience. But the implications for jurisprudence are limited. Beyond that, it appears that West wants the legal system to be more empathetic to all marginal groups, and again there can be no quarrel with this desire. But the polarity between empathetic, equitable, discretionary, situation-specific justice, on the one hand, and the "rule of law" virtues of neutrality and "ruled-ness," on the other, is far older than feminist jurisprudence.

Conservative feminism takes a more cautious stance on issues of concern to women than radical or liberal feminism (I mean "liberal" in the modern sense, for the libertarian considers himself or herself the true, the classical, "liberal"). But I believe that it has much to offer women—if only a warning to consider carefully the indirect effects of policies ostensibly favoring women—and that it deserves a greater voice in the feminist chorus.

Notes

1. One estimate is that a full-time housewife contributes, on average, 40 percent of the full (that is, pecuniary plus nonpecuniary) income of the household. Calculated from Gronau, Home Production—A Forgotten Industry, 62 Rev. Econ. & Stat. 408 (1980). But the reader should be warned of the variety of estimates of housewives' imputed earnings, and of the lurking methodological problems. . . .

2. I ignore the complications arising from the fact that many women who work full-time also do considerable housework.

3. Suits for employment discrimination are not a terribly effective remedy. They are rarely worth bringing even when the prospects for winning are good, because, in general, the successful plaintiff can obtain only back pay and reinstatement, not common law damages, and because the filing of an employment discrimination suit identifies the plaintiff as a "troublemaker," thereby making him or her unattractive to future employers. (Many women, I have been told, regard filing a sex-discrimination suit as tantamount to committing professional suicide.) In addition, most discrimination cases are difficult to win, because the plaintiff, unless irrationally willing to invest resources in investigation and proof that are disproportionate to the modest stakes in most such cases, will be hard-pressed to establish the counterfactual proposition essential to victory: for example, that she would not have been fired if she had been male. I am speaking here primarily of disparate-treatment (intentional discrimination) rather than disparate-impact litigation, but the latter will not eliminate most forms of sex discrimination.

4. This is not to say that a law *requiring* such equality on the part of private employers (an important qualification, as will shortly became apparent) makes perfectly good economic sense. Such laws are costly to administer, can backfire, and are of dubious efficacy. It might make more sense to allow market forces, which penalize irrational discrimination (see G. Becker, The Economics of Discrimination, 2d ed., chap. 2 [The University of Chicago Press, 1971]; R. Posner, Economic Analysis of Law, 3d ed., chap. 27 [Little, Brown, 1986]), to take care of irrational discrimination against women in employment, such as discrimination based on an erroneous assessment of the costs and qualities of women as workers or on a refusal (perhaps motivated by hostility to women) to act on a correct assessment. I am not such a Pollyanna as to think that market forces will eliminate all discrimination against women, but if they eliminate most of it, eliminating the rest may not be worth the cost of the legal remedies.

A difficult case is sexual harassment in the workplace. Although market forces militate against such harassment, they may not be completely effective (for reasons I discuss in my book Law and Literature: A Misunderstood Relation 190–91 [Harvard University Press, 1988]); this is suggested by the fact that such harassment is found even in firms operating in highly competitive markets. Yet it is not "efficient," merely because it has survival qualities. It is a market abuse, like embezzlement or commercial bribery—or, for that matter, rape, which sexual harassment resembles. So a law against sexual harassment, as Title VII of the Civil Rights Act of 1964, 42 U.S.C § 2000e (1964), has been interpreted to be, is consistent with libertarian principles—more so, oddly enough, than the basic prohibition against discrimination in hiring, firing, promotion, and wages. Discrimination may in some cases serve the employer's interests and even be socially efficient. See Posner, Economic Analysis of Law, *supra* note 4, at 624; Phelps, The Statistical Theory of Racism and Sexism, 62 Am. Econ. Rev. 659 (1972). Sexual harassment is much less likely to have any redeeming social value. See Posner, Law and Literature, *supra* this note, at 190–91.

5. For discussion and references, see Posner, Economic Analysis of Law, *supra* note 4, at 314; Fischel and Lazear, Comparable Worth and Discrimination in Labor Markets, 53 U. Chi. L. Rev. 891 (1986); Weiler, The Wages of Sex: The Uses and Limits of Comparable Worth, 99 Harv. L. Rev. 1728 (1986).

6. See Greenwood, The Institutional Inadequacy of the Market in Determining Comparable Worth: Implications for Value Theory, 18 J. Econ. Issues 457, 463 (1984).

7. And here it is timely to remember that until this century the limitations on the contractual rights of married women, and on the right of divorce, were so substantial that it was possible for a sober observer to state: "The law of the status of women is the last vestige of slavery." N. St. John Green, Married Women, in his Essays and Notes on the Law of Tort and Crime 31, 48 (George Banta, 1933) (first published in 1871). Yet as is now widely recognized, "no fault" divorce is not the answer. More men than women desire divorces. Therefore, allowing either spouse to divorce at will deprives women of substantial bargaining power: Since their consent to granting their husband a divorce is no longer required, they can't condition that consent on the husband's agreeing to pay reasonable alimony and child support. "The major economic result of the divorce law revolution is the systematic impoverishment of divorced women and their children." L. Weitzman, The Divorce Revolution: The Unexpected Social and Economic Consequences for Women and Children in America xiv (Free Press, 1985). This finding is a warning to feminists about the unintended consequences of public policies.

8. See Matter of Baby M, 109 N.J. 396, 537 A.2d 1227 (1988).

9. See Posner, The Ethics and Economics of Enforcing Contracts of Surrogate Motherhood, 5 J. Contemp. Health L. & Policy 21, 25 (1989).

10. I discuss the feminist challenge to pornography briefly in Posner, Law and Literature, *supra* note 4, at 334–37.

11. See S. Estrich, Real Rape 103 (Harvard University Press, 1987).

12. For illustrations, see Bender, A Lawyer's Primer on Feminist Theory and Tort, Part 1 herein; Kornhauser, The Rhetoric of the Anti-Progressive Income Tax Movement, 86 Mich. L. Rev. 465 (1987); Sherry, Civic Virtue and the Feminine Voice in Constitutional Adjudication, 72 Va. L. Rev. 543 (1986); West, Jurisprudence and Gender, Part 1 herein.

13. C. Gilligan, In a Different Voice: Psychological Theory and Women's Development (Harvard University Press, 1982). In a similar vein, see also M. Be-

lenky et al., Women's Ways of Knowing: The Development of Self, Voices, and Mind, chap. 6 (Basic Books, 1986). Gilligan's findings have been questioned. See Friedman, Robinson & Friedman, Sex Differences in Moral Judgments? A Test of Gilligan's Theory, 11 Psych. Women Q. 37 (1987), and references cited therein. Empirical support for Gilligan's theory is presented in Ford and Lowery, Gender Differences in Moral Reasoning: A Comparison of the Use of Justice and Care Orientations, 50 J. Personality & Soc. Psych. 777 (1986); Rothbart, Hanley & Marc Albert, Gender Differences in Moral Reasoning, 15 Sex Roles 645 (1986).

14. Sherry, 72 Va. L. Rev., *supra* note 12, at 543.

15. See Michelman, The Supreme Court 1985 Term—Foreword: Traces of Self-Government, 100 Harv. L. Rev. 4, 17 n. 68, 32–36 (1986).

16. See Bender, Part 1 herein.

17. See West, Part 1 herein.

18. C. Gilligan & G. Wiggins, The Origins of Morality in Early Childhood Relationships, in J. Kagan & S. Lamb eds., The Emergence of Morality in Young Children 277, 278–79 (University of Chicago Press, 1987). . . .

19. See Lorber et al., On "The Reproduction of Mothering": A Methodological Debate, 6 Signs 482 (1981).

❖ PART 2

The Equality Debate:
Equal Treatment versus
Special Treatment

❖ *Introduction*

EQUALITY IS A fundamental concept of our legal system. The debate over the meaning of equality has been central to the development of both feminism and feminist legal theory. The notion of equality has taken on a different meaning in different historical periods and according to different philosophical traditions. As British feminist Juliet Mitchell wrote early in the contemporary women's movement: "A history of the concept of equality would run in tracks very similar to a history of feminism."[1] Mitchell traces with broad brush strokes the evolution of the concept of equality for feminism. She points out that seventeenth-century feminists' equality arguments concentrated on equating woman's power of reason to man's. Any deficiency in this regard, these feminists argued, resulted from woman's lack of opportunity for improving her mind. Seventeenth-century feminists' concerns, then, focused on equal rights to educational and social opportunities.

Eighteenth-century feminists continued this focus, although, according to Mitchell, they adopted a different perspective.[2] Feminists of this period, such as Mary Wollstonecraft, who wrote "A Vindication of the Rights of Women" in 1792, emphasized the damage done to women and to society by conditioning women into inferior social beings. In contrast to the earlier generation of feminists, "it was the hurtfulness, not the uselessness, of the oppression of women that was uppermost in the writers' minds."[3] By the nineteenth century, the notion of equality had changed from a feminist struggle about a philosophical notion to an organized political movement for the attainment of equal rights.[4]

Twentieth-century feminists continue to debate the meaning of equality and the optimum method of achieving it. Those in the tradition of liberal feminists offer one perspective, radical feminists another. For example, Betty Friedan, a founder of the National Organization for Women (NOW), in her early feminist work calls for bringing women into the mainstream of American society in an equal partnership with men.[5] Her notion of equality is one of equal access to educational and economic institutions.[6] In contrast, Shulamith Firestone, another leader of the contemporary feminist movement and one who represents the radi-

121

cal feminist perspective, argues that women's reproductive capacities have marked them as a subordinate class. In order for women to achieve full equality, they must be freed from the demands of forced reproduction and motherhood. Firestone argues that the tranformation of culture from patriarchy to equality will take place through the agency of technology.

The equality debate has reached feminist legal theory. Its emergence was perhaps inevitable as a stage of scholarship. According to Martha Minow,[7] one can identify three stages of feminist scholarship. The first stage of feminist scholarship articulated women's claims to be granted the same rights and privileges as men. "The problem writers identified centered on the exclusion of women from the rights and prerogatives granted to at least some men. The goals in this first stage included securing rights to vote and to hold the same jobs as men."[8] The second stage of feminist scholarship included writers who advocated respect and accommodation for women's historical and contemporary differences.

> For those writing in this second stage, the problem needing redress was the undervaluation or disregard for women's historical and persistent interests, traits and needs. Examples of second-stage goals include obtaining pregnancy and maternity leaves from paid employment, pursuing comparable worth to revalue traditional women's work, and elaborating special rights for women to respond to rape, battery of women by men, and self-determination about whether to conceive or bear a child.[9]

Writers in the third stage reject the preoccupation with women's similarities to and differences from men. The essays in Part 2 reflect first- and second-stage feminist scholarship in their discussion of the development of the concept of equality. Essays in Part 3 reflect third-stage scholarship with their focus on the limitations of equality analysis.

As discussed in the introduction to Part 1 of this collection, one explanation for the development of feminist legal scholarship is that much of early feminist legal theory emerged from feminist litigators' reactions to specific legal problems—employment discrimination, for example. These formative roots contributed to the focus of, and form of argumentation in, early feminist legal scholarship. This also explains the initial inattention to the shortcomings of equality theory by early feminist theorists. Subsequent scholarship was necessary to bring them to focus.

The debate in this Part over the meaning of equality in feminist legal theory is premised on an understanding of equality as rooted in the classic liberal tradition. The ideology of equality is based on the principle that all persons are equal and have equal rights under the law. Women, therefore, should be treated the same as men, that is, should be granted the same rights. During the early stage of feminist legal thought in the 1970s, feminists approached gender equality as signifying that women should be treated similarly to men with respect to characteristics they share. Yet women are not biologically the same as men: they have the capacity to, and do, become pregnant. The argument for equal rights falters when one confronts this biological difference. In the subsequent stage, feminist theorists grappled with how to accommodate pregnancy within equality analysis. In the context of litigation over pregnancy-specific disability benefits, the question became, If equality means treating women like men, how should pregnancy be treated? How should this difference, this unique characteristic, be taken into account in efforts to achieve equality between the sexes? This Part thus explores issues of sameness and difference in the context of the meaning of equality.

The meaning of equality in the United States has been influenced by the evolution of equal protection doctrine. Equality is guaranteed by the Constitution. Enshrined in the Fourteenth Amendment is the promise that no state shall "deny to any person within its jurisdiction the equal protection of the laws." Unlike the Canadian Charter of Rights and Freedoms, for example, with its specific guarantee (against "discrimination based on race, national or ethnic origin, colour, religion, sex, age or mental or physical disability"), our Constitution contains a broadly worded clause. The meaning of our broad guarantee was influenced by an article authored by two law professors in 1949.[10] These scholars phrased the question as whether a complainant was "similarly situated with respect to the purpose of the law" to other individuals. The idea of comparison, then, was integral to their perspective of equal protection. This comparison approach has become the jurisprudential model for equal protection analysis.

The Supreme Court first applied constitutional equal protection analysis to the context of pregnancy in Geduldig v. Aiello.[11] The Court held that a state disability insurance program's pregnancy-based classification did not violate equal protection. Refusing to characterize the classification as gender based, the Court described the classification as one between "pregnant women and non-pregnant persons." Thus, pregnancy discrimination did not involve "discrimination based upon gender as such." Two years later, in General Electric Co. v. Gilbert,[12] the Court used *Geduldig*'s reasoning to uphold a similar disability plan under Title VII's prohibition of sex discrimination in employment. Once again, the Court reaffirmed the view that pregnancy-based discrimination is not sex discrimination. The Court's opinions provoked a spate of feminist criticism. In response, Congress passed the Pregnancy Discrimination Act (PDA), amending Title VII explicitly to prohibit discrimination on the basis of pregnancy, childbirth, and related medical conditions.[13]

The PDA's definition of pregnancy discrimination as sex discrimination prevents employers from treating pregnant workers less favorably than other disabled workers. Nevertheless, it might also be interpreted to prevent *more* favorable treatment of pregnant workers (since it only mandated women so affected be treated "the same" as others similarly affected). Some states adopted a more generous approach than Congress. A number of states enacted legislation that gave women benefits not available to other workers. Two such statutes were challenged as preempted by the PDA (Miller-Wohl Co. v. Commissioner of Labor & Industry[14] and California Federal Savings & Loan Association v. Guerra).[15] These cases both addressed the fundamental question, How should the law treat pregnancy in order to treat women and men equally?

This question split feminist theorists into two camps. One camp, labeling itself "equal treatment," argued that gender equality requires identical treatment of the sexes without regard to pregnancy. Instead of a unique condition justifying special treatment, equal treatment advocates view pregnancy as one of many physical conditions that affect an employee's ability to work. Pregnant women should be treated no differently from similarly situated workers with other disabilities.

The other camp, known as "special treatment," rejects equal treatment's formal equality model in favor of an equal opportunity model. These theorists argue that the way to ensure equal opportunity for women in the workplace is through positive pregnancy-specific benefits that ensure that pregnant women are not disadvantaged because of biological difference. This Part begins with two essays that present the opposing sides of the debate: Wendy Williams defends equal treatment, whereas Linda Krieger and Patricia Cooney advocate the position of special treatment (they term it "positive action.")

Williams, "Equality's Riddle: Pregnancy and the Equal Treatment/Special Treatment Debate," begins her defense of equal treatment by grounding its approach to pregnancy within the doctrinal framework of the gender equality analysis advanced successfully by feminist litigators since the early 1970s. She offers a valuable historical perspective by tracking the history of pregnancy litigation through five stages, beginning with the era of protective legislation, which forced women out of the workforce when they became pregnant, and ending with our current "crossroads."

Williams next offers a critique of the special treatment position. She concludes that the remaining problems faced by pregnant workers illustrate not a flaw in equal treatment theory, but rather the limitations of relying on litigation to achieve social change. Positive legislation based on the equal treatment model, which would guarantee adequate disability and parental benefits for all workers, is necessary to promote ultimate equality of women in the workplace. Equal treatment's vision of realigning sex roles in the family and the workplace, she urges, should not be sold short by settling for more expedient special treatment solutions.[16]

Krieger and Cooney, in "The Miller-Wohl Controversy: Equal Treatment, Positive Action and the Meaning of Women's Equality," present the opposing side of the debate.[17] Krieger and Cooney utilize the *Miller-Wohl* case (in which Montana's Maternity Leave Act providing affirmative job security to pregnant workers was challenged under the PDA) to illustrate the limitations of the equal treatment approach.

Krieger and Cooney examine the models of equality underlying the equal treatment versus special treatment sides of the debate. They explain that the liberal model of equality rests on assumptions that promote the formal appearance of equality over equality of effect. While the liberal model works well in situations where women approximate the male norm, this model must be supplemented, they assert, with a different theory that promotes equality within heterogeneous groups. Krieger and Cooney propose that the "bivalent model," as modified by the "incorporationist approach," provides such a theory. The bivalent/incorporationist model changes the male norm by modifying institutions to accommodate women. Unlike other approaches, it is analytically equipped, they argue, to achieve equality of effect.

In conclusion, Krieger and Cooney examine different views of social change (metaphysical vs. materialist dialectical) that are implicit in the equal treatment and special treatment approaches. They conclude that the materialist dialectic view better responds to the concrete, material reality of women's problems in the workforce.

In response to the equal treatment versus special treatment debate, Herma Kay, "Equality and Difference: The Case of Pregnancy," suggests a third approach, "episodic analysis," for dealing with pregnancy within an equality framework.[18] Episodic analysis limits different treatment to the discrete episode of pregnancy. It treats biological sex differences as legally significant only when they are being utilized for reproductive purposes. In contrast to equal treatment's analogy of pregnancy to disability, episodic analysis focuses on the workplace consequences of the exercise of reproductive behavior for men and women. Men's abilities to work are not impaired as a result of the exercise of their reproductive behavior. The principle of equal opportunity, therefore, dictates the affirmative accommodation of pregnant workers to prevent employment disadvantages that their reproductively active male co-workers do not encounter.

Kay's episodic analysis offers a useful compromise position in the equal treatment/special treatment debate. By limiting different treatment to the discrete episode of pregnancy, episodic analysis (similar to equal treatment) separates pregnancy from childrearing. Both approaches require that childrearing leave be made available to both parents. Thus, episodic analysis furthers equal treatment's strategic aim of restructuring workplace policies to eliminate their reinforcement of traditional stereotypical roles. Yet episodic analysis supports special treatment's contention that the best manner in which to enable women to compete on an equal basis with men in the workplace is to ensure that pregnancy will not disadvantage them. Professor Kay's work introduces an alternative to the either-or conceptualization of the equal treatment/special treatment debate and proposes a means of reconciling the opposing views.

The final essay in this Part, Lucinda Finley's "Transcending Equality Theory: A Way Out of the Maternity and Workplace Debate," adds another voice to the equality debate. Finley also critiques the legal doctrinal framework of equality analysis using the special treatment/equal treatment debate as a context. She identifies several problems with the framework of equality analysis. The first problem, she points out, is its indeterminacy: how to identify relevant differences. A second problem with equality analysis is its acceptance of our culture's ideal of homogeneity. Equality analysis is also limited by our cultural ideal of isolated autonomy, which values self-sufficiency, and our legal individualistic definition of rights, based on noninterference. It fails to question the devaluation of interdependence, caring and responsibility perpetuated by separate spheres ideology, reflected in the workplace and our legal system.

To transcend these limitations, Finley proposes that the "language of equality" must be shed. Finley's analysis goes beyond that of the preceding authors, providing a more radical "way out of" the maternity debate. Williams, Krieger and Cooney, as well as Kay, all attempt to square their views of the appropriate legal treatment of pregnancy within the traditional doctrinal framework of equality analysis. In contrast, Finley advocates transformation of traditional legal discourse that will result, in turn, in the transformation in society.

Finley's essay comports with the goal of many feminists[19] not merely to criticize existing practices but to propose transformative devices to improve women's status. Finley's essay also serves as a transition to Part 3, which continues the critique of the meaning of equality and proposes new approaches to equality and difference.

Notes

1. J. Mitchell, Women and Equality, in A. Phillips ed., Feminism and Equality 31 (New York University Press, 1987). The essay appeared originally in 1976. For other discussions of Mitchell's views, see generally J. Mitchell, Woman's Estate (Penguin, 1971); and J. Mitchell, Women: The Longest Revolution (Virago, 1984).

2. Josephine Donovan also points to historical factors influencing the views of eighteenth-century feminists. She cites their roots in the intellectual world of Enlightenment liberalism. "These eighteenth-century feminists were responding to the tide of revolutionary fervor that was sweeping the Western world. Theories developed during the so-called Enlightenment or Age of Reason were being put into practice: the idea, for example, that people have certain inalienable or 'natural' rights upon which governments may not intrude was at the philosophical heart of both the American Declaration of Independence (1776) and the French Declaration of the Rights of Man (1789). Feminists hoped to assure that women be considered entitled to the same natural rights as men." J. Donovan, Feminist Theory: The Intellectual Traditions of American Feminism 1 (Frederick Ungar, 1985).

3. Although this theme was present in seventeenth-century feminist writings, it was more pronounced in the eighteenth century because societal changes had occurred that concretized social definitions of sexual differences of "masculinity" and "femininity". Femininity became more sharply defined as economic and emotional dependence. Mitchell, Women and Equality, *supra* note 1, at 35.

4. *Id.* at 37.

5. B. Friedan, The Feminine Mystique 384 (Norton, 1975).

6. Ironically, Friedan later disavowed this model of equality. In her book *The Second Stage* (Summit, 1986) (addressed to professional rather than working-class women), Friedan argues that women have become focused on their careers to the detriment of their roles as wives and mothers. She criticizes her earlier call for equality as antifamily and as overemphasizing female autonomy. See generally Zillah R. Eisenstein's critique of Friedan's revisionist form of liberal feminism in Z. Eisenstein, Feminism and Sexual Equality: Crisis in Liberal America 189–208 (Monthly Review Press, 1984).

7. Minow, Introduction: Finding Our Paradoxes, Affirming Our Beyond, 24 Harv. C.R.–C.L. L. Rev. 1, 2–3 (1989), citing M. J. Frug, Feminist Histories (1987)(unpublished manuscript).

8. Minow, Paradoxes, *supra* note 7, at 2.

9. *Id.*

10. Tussman & tenBroek, The Equal Protection of the Laws, 37 Calif. L. Rev. 341 (1949).

11. 417 U.S. 484 (1974).

12. 429 U.S. 125 (1976).

13. 42 U.S.C. § 2000e(k) (1982).

14. 479 U.S. 1050 (1987), vacating 214 Mont. 238, 692 P.2d 1243 (1984).

15. 479 U.S. 272 (1987).

16. See also Williams's subsequent writing on this topic. Taub & Williams, Will Equality Require More than Assimilation, Accommodation or Separation from the Existing Social Structure?, 37 Rutgers L. Rev. 825 (1985); Williams, Notes from a First Generation, 1989 U. Chi. Legal F. 99.

17. See also Krieger, Through a Glass Darkly: Paradigms of Equality and the Search for a Woman's Jurisprudence, Hypatia 2 (1987).

18. For another alternative to the two discussed above, see Law, Rethinking Sex and the Constitution, 132 U. Pa. L. Rev. 955 (1984), proposing a principle that would recognize "limited differences" defined by the biological differences pertaining to reproduction.

19. The distinction in approach is also illustrated by Gerda Lerner's categorization of "women's rights feminism" as opposed to "woman's emancipation feminism." The former include individuals and groups who define their goal as entrance into institutions on an equal basis; the latter include those emancipationists who want that and more—the transformation of patriarchy. Lerner, Politics and Culture in Women's History: A Symposium, 6 Feminist Stud. 51 (1980).

❖ Equality's Riddle: Pregnancy and the Equal Treatment/Special Treatment Debate

Wendy W. Williams

THE LEGAL BATTLE for gender equality gave birth, in the early 1970s, to a riddle. Faced with the pervasive and profound effect of employer responses to women's reproductive function on their status and opportunity in the paid workforce, feminist litigators asked how laws or rules based on a capacity unique to women—the capacity to become pregnant and give birth—could be susceptible to challenge under any equality doctrine the courts of this country might realistically be persuaded to employ. In response to that question, the proponents of gender equality developed a theory which has been used with moderate success in scores of cases challenging pregnancy rules under Title VII and, for a time, under the equal protection clause as well. Most of these cases have arisen in the employment context; courts have been asked to compare an employer's treatment of pregnancy to its treatment of other physical conditions with similar workplace consequences. The approach has been, in the words of the 1978 Pregnancy Discrimination Act (PDA), to require that "women affected by pregnancy, childbirth or related medical conditions . . . be treated the same for all employment related purposes . . . as other persons not so affected but similar in their ability to work."[1]

Today, commentators have raised questions about the wisdom and propriety of this "equal treatment" approach to pregnancy rules and laws. In Professor Ann Scales's version of the critique, she states her basic assumption as follows:

> The only differences between the sexes which apparently cannot be ignored are *in utero* pregnancy, and breastfeeding, the one function in the childrearing process which only women can perform. In observing that these are the capabilities which *really* differentiate women from men, it is crucial that we overcome any aversion to describing these functions as "unique." Uniqueness is a "trap" only in terms of an analysis, such as that generated in Geduldig v. Aiello, which assumes that maleness is the norm. "Unique" does not mean uniquely handicapped.[2]

---

13 N.Y.U. Rev. L. & Soc. Change 325 (1984/85).

Linda Krieger and Patricia Cooney, in their extension of the Scales's position, add:

> It is likely that to both the Supreme Court and the American public, the distinctions between the condition of pregnancy, of a potential child developing within a woman's body, and any medical condition faced by a man, would leap out with much greater force and vigor than the similarities. The liberal [equal treatment] model, however, relies completely on the acceptance of the analogy. It fails to focus on the effect of the very *real* sex difference of pregnancy on the relative positions of men and women in society and on the goal of assuring equality of opportunity and effect within a heterogeneous "society of equals."[3]

Thus, at least superficially, the dispute centers on whether pregnancy should be viewed as comparable to other physical conditions or as unique and special. On a deeper level, the dispute is about whether pregnancy "naturally" makes women unequal and thus requires special legislative accommodation to it in order to equalize the sexes, or whether pregnancy can or should be visualized as one human experience which in many contexts, most notably the workplace, creates needs and problems similar to those arising from causes other than pregnancy, and which can be handled adequately on the same basis as are other physical conditions of employees. On the deepest level, the debate may reflect a demand by special treatment advocates that the law recognize and honor a separate identity which women themselves consider special and important and, on the equal treatment side, a commitment to a vision of the human condition which seeks to uncover commonalty rather than difference.

The critics believe that the "equal treatment model" precludes recognition of pregnancy's uniqueness, and thus creates for women a Procrustean bed—pregnancy will be treated as if it were comparable to male conditions when it is not, thus forcing pregnant women into a workplace structure designed for men. Such a result, they believe, denies women's special experience and does not adequately respond to the realities of women's lives.

The proponents of the equal treatment model are also concerned with ensuring that workplace pregnancy rules do not create structural barriers to the full participation of women in the workforce. Unlike the critics, however, they are prepared to view pregnancy as just one of the physical conditions that affect workplace participation for men and women. From their perspective, the objective is to readjust the general rules for dealing with illness and disability to ensure that the rules can fairly account for the whole of workplace disabilities that confront employed people. Pregnancy creates not "special" needs, but rather exemplifies typical basic needs. If these particular typical needs are not met, then pregnant workers simply become part of a larger class of male and female workers, for whom the basic fringe benefit structure is inadequate. The solution, in that view, is to solve the underlying problem of inadequate fringe benefits rather than to respond with measures designed especially for pregnant workers.

The case that brought these conflicting views into sharp focus is Miller-Wohl and Company, Inc. v. Commissioner of Labor and Industry,[4] a case in which an employer sought invalidation of a Montana law that made it illegal for an employer to terminate a woman's employment because of pregnancy or to refuse to grant her a reasonable leave to absence . . . .

. . . [F]or the first time in the decade that pregnancy cases had been brought before the federal courts, a case involved a challenge to a provision that singled out pregnancy for favorable rather than unfavorable treatment. The feminist legal community split over whether the Montana law guaranteeing pregnant women a "reasonable" leave of absence should be defended and if so, on what theory. . . .

I purpose to further the debate by offering a rationale for the "equal treatment" approach to pregnancy . . . [and exploring] the larger implications of the "equal treatment" model as compared to the "special treatment" model for resolving the pregnancy dilemma.

The General Doctrinal Framework and How Pregnancy Fits within It

The legal theories concerning pregnancy have always been part of a larger theoretical framework advanced by feminist litigators since the early 1970s. . . . In its gross contours, that framework is the same whether one is considering the meaning of equality under a statutory prohibition on sex discrimination, such as that contained in Title VII of the Civil Rights Act, or under the constitutional prohibition of the equal protection clause. . . . Differences in detail result from the different origins, language and purposes of the different sources of the equality guarantees. As will become apparent, the framework has won more acceptance under Title VII than under the equal protection clause. . . .

The General Doctrinal Framework

The first proposition essential to this analysis is that sex-based generalizations are generally impermissible whether derived from physical differences such as size and strength, from cultural role assignments such as breadwinner or homemaker, or from some combination of innate and ascribed characteristics, such as the greater longevity of the average woman compared to the average man. . . . The basis for this proposition is a belief that a dual system of rights inevitably produces gender hierarchy and, more fundamentally, treats women and men as statistical abstractions rather than as persons with individual capacities, inclinations and aspirations—at enormous cost to women and not insubstantial cost to men.

The second essential proposition is that laws and rules which do not overtly classify on the basis of sex, but which have a disproportionately negative effect upon one sex, warrant, under appropriate circumstances, placing a burden of justification upon the party defending the law or rule in court. . . .

The goal of the feminist legal movement that began in the early seventies . . . has been to break down the legal barriers that restricted each sex to its predefined role and created a hierarchy based on gender. . . . The first proposition (sex classifications are generally impermissible) facilitates the elimination of legislation that overtly classifies by sex. The second proposition (perpetrators of rules with a disparate effect must justify them) provides a doctrinal tool with which to begin to squeeze the male tilt out of a purportedly neutral legal structure and thus substitute genuine for merely formal gender neutrality.

How Pregnancy Fits within the Framework

How does pregnancy fit into this general framework? The short answer is that the general framework applies, with minor alteration, to laws or rules based on physical characteristics unique to one sex. The proponents contend that classifications based on such characteristics, of which pregnancy is the central example, are sex-based. Under the equal protection clause, the consequence of that conclusion would be that the intermediate standard of review applicable to gender-based classifications would apply to pregnancy classifications. . . . Under Title VII, the consequence of characterizing pregnancy classifications as sex-based is that pregnancy-based employer rules constitute unlawful sex discrimination unless the employer can establish that its pregnancy rule is, in the words of the statute, a "bona fide occupational qualification reasonably necessary to the normal operation of that particular business or enterprise." This interpretation of Title VII was . . . finally imposed by Congress through the amendment known as the Pregnancy Discrimination Act, a 1978 amendment to Title VII. . . .

The approach in [these] legal contexts assumes that for some purposes, sex-unique physical characteristics and capacities are comparable to other characteristics and capacities. Where the purposes of the legislation render them comparable, classifications which single them out for unfavorable treatment would be invalid. Where they are not comparable, such classifications would be upheld. Under this approach, all the classifications would be scrutinized by the courts, and the burden . . . would be on the party defending the classification to justify its existence.

The companion principle—that neutral laws and rules which have a disproportionately negative effect upon one sex, may warrant shifting the burden of justification to the party defending the law or rule—would apply to "neutral" rules whose disproportionate effects on one sex were due to pregnancy. That principle was recognized for Title VII purposes in the original EEOC guidelines on pregnancy and reiterated in the post–Pregnancy Discrimination Act guidelines. Because of the Supreme Court's insistence in equal protection cases on the existence of an intent to discriminate, narrowly defined, the theory is not available in sex discrimination cases brought under the Fourteenth Amendment. . . .

A History of the Pregnancy Litigation

. . . The treatment of pregnancy and maternity under the law developed in stages that went something like this.

Stage One: 1870–1970

From the beginnings of our Republic until well into the twentieth century, the legal rights and duties of men and women were pervasively and significantly different from each other. The legal distinctions flowed from the central premise that men and women were destined for separate social roles because of innate differences between them, most centrally women's reproductive function. Whether manifested by the late eighteenth and early nineteenth century merging of the legal identity of wife into husband (with the accompanying loss of civil and political rights) or by the twentieth century protective labor legislation for women (limiting the hours they could work, putting a floor on their hourly wages, prohibiting night work and excluding them from certain "hazardous" occupations), women's "maternal function" formed the basis of a dual system of law. The system treated women differently than men under the claim that it sought to accommodate to and provide for women's special needs. Muller v. Oregon stated it explicitly: "Though limitations upon personal and contractual rights may be removed by legislation, there is that in her disposition and habits of life which will operate against full assertion of those rights. She will still be where some legislation to protect her seems necessary to secure a *real equality of right*."[5]

In addition to the general "protective" labor laws designed to equalize women in their separate sphere, there were, beginning in the 1940s, a very few provisions dealing specifically with pregnancy. In the early 1940s, the Women's Bureau of the U.S. Department of Labor recommended that pregnant women not work for six weeks before and two months after delivery.[6] Some states adopted laws prohibiting employers from employing women for a period of time before and after childbirth to protect the health of women and their offspring during that vulnerable time. Where leaves were not accompanied by a guarantee of job security or wage replacement, they "protected" pregnant women right out of their jobs, as the Women's Bureau conceded. At the same time, the unemployment insurance laws of many states rendered otherwise eligible women workers ineligible for unemployment insurance if they were pregnant or had recently given birth. Women unemployed because of state laws or employer policies of mandatory unpaid leave thus were precluded from the resources available to other unemployed workers. Four states, including California, created disability insurance programs to provide partial wage replacement to temporarily disabled workers, but those programs either excluded pregnancy-related disabilities altogether or provided restricted benefits. The absence of legislation concerning pregnancy and employment meant that the issue was left to employers (and, where there were unions, to collective bargaining).

By 1960, the dawn of the decade that would usher in Title VII, many employers simply fired women who became pregnant. Others provided unpaid maternity leaves of absence, frequently accompanied by loss of seniority and accrued benefits. Few provided job security, much less allowed paid sick leave and vacation time to be used for maternity leave. Payment of disability benefits for childbirth was, at best, restricted, and employer-sponsored medical insurance provided, at most, limited coverage of pregnancy-related medical treatment and hospitalization.

Pervasively, pregnancy was treated less favorably than other physical conditions that affected workplace performance. The pattern of rules telegraphed the underlying assumption: a woman's pregnancy signaled her disengagement from the workplace. Implicit was not only a factual but a normative judgment: when wage-earning women became pregnant they did, and should, go home.

Stage Two: 1970–1976

By 1970, women were in the workforce in unprecedented numbers. Moreover, an increasing number of them were staying after the birth of children. Pregnancy rules which left women unemployed and without income also affected escalating numbers of women. Not surprisingly the magnitude of change finally drew attention to the institutional disadvantages long experienced by women who sought to maintain their attachment to the workforce after childbirth.

In 1968, a task force of President Johnson's Citizens Advisory Council on the Status of Women recommended "a general system" of protection of wage earners against temporary wage loss because of disability and urged that pregnancy-related disability be included within such a program. By 1970, the Council itself issued a policy statement urging that pregnancy be treated under an equality model—neither worse nor better than other physical conditions that affect one's ability to work. In 1971, Elizabeth Duncan Koontz, then head of the Women's Bureau of the Department of Labor, . . . point[ed] out that Title VII, state human relations laws, and the Fourteenth Amendment were weapons for challenging disadvantageous employer pregnancy rules. She asserted optimistically that "it seems certain that the courts, after full consideration, will adopt the obvious conclusion that pregnancy is a temporary disability and that women are entitled to the same autonomy and economic benefits in dealing with it that employees have in dealing with other temporary disabilities."[7]

Suits were filed under Title VII and the equal protection clause on the theory that treating pregnancy disabilities differently and less favorably than other disabilities discriminates on the basis of sex. In 1972 the EEOC [Equal Employment Opportunity Commission] issued guidelines heavily influenced by the Citizens Advisory Council's equality concept. Courts began to reject the arguments of employer and government defendants that pregnancy was unique—"sui generis"— and to grant women plaintiffs the employment benefits available to others experiencing temporary work disability.

In 1974, however, the United States Supreme Court eliminated the equal protection clause as a vehicle for an "equal treatment" attack on legislation singling out pregnancy for special treatment. The state statute challenged in Geduldig v. Aiello[8] created a state disability fund, providing temporary, partial wage replacement to private sector workers who became physically unable to work. The statute was liberally interpreted to cover every conceivable work disability, including, according to the record in the case, disability arising from cosmetic surgery, hair transplants, skiing accidents and prostatectomies. It excluded only one type of work disability from coverage—those "arising out of or in connection with" pregnancy.

The plaintiffs in *Geduldig* argued first, that discrimination based on pregnancy is sex discrimination and thus warranted application of the more activist standard of review then applicable in sex discrimination cases. Several reasons were given for this conclusion. The reproductive organs associated with pregnancy, they said, are definitional characteristics—the sexes are sorted on their presence or absence. Moreover, the reasons for holding sex-based legislation to the higher standard of justification, they asserted, applied with equal force to pregnancy—namely that stereotypes and generalizations about women who become pregnant result in laws and rules which relegate them to an inferior legal status and deny them benefits and opportunities without regard to their individual capacities. Finally, they argued that California's disability program discriminated on the basis of sex because it provided total coverage for men and only partial coverage for women.

Second, plaintiffs asserted that under the standard of review applicable in sex discrimination cases, California's statutory exclusion of pregnancy-related disabilities failed to pass constitutional muster. Women who sought partial wage replacement for such disabilities were denied equal protection by the program's exclusion of their particular disability, because their relationship to the program's purposes was similar to that of those granted benefits for other disabilities.

Justice Stewart, on behalf of a majority of the Court, rejected the first argument, stating that the case did not involve discrimination based on gender as such: "The California insurance program does not exclude anyone from benefit eligibility because of gender but merely removes one physical condition—pregnancy—from the list of compensable disabilities."[9] Translated, this means that the statute bases the exclusion on pregnancy, not on sex itself (a point made evident, the Court noted, by the fact that the persons covered by the program—disabled nonpregnant persons—included women). This mechanical parsing was apparently reasoning enough for the Court. The majority opinion contained no discussion of the plaintiffs' policy arguments for including pregnancy classifications in the universe of classifications considered to be based upon sex.

The conclusion that discrimination on the basis of pregnancy was not sex discrimination freed the Court from the obligation to engage in the more activist review it reserves for sex discrimination cases. Indulging the strong presumption of constitutionality appropriate to rational basis review, it concluded that a legislature legitimately could exclude a costly disability from an otherwise comprehensive program. . . . The state did not, presumably because it could not, argue that pregnancy disabilities would have constituted the most expensive category of disabilities, nor did the Court explain why it was rational to pick pregnancy disabilities rather than some other costly type of disability for exclusion.

Perhaps the answer lies in its hint that pregnancy disabilities are intrinsically different from other disabilities: "normal pregnancy," it said in a footnote, is an objectively "identifiable physical condition with unique characteristics."[10] Its failure to specify the "unique characteristics" which distinguished pregnancy-related disabilities from all others covered by the California program and encompassed within its particular purposes is unfortunate. Forced to articulate such differences, the Court either would have exposed its failure to rise above preconceptions and stereotypes about pregnant women or else it would have presented policy conclusions which future courts, commentators and legislators could debate and evaluate. Justice Stewart managed at one stroke to assert that pregnancy is unrelated to gender—is sex neutral—and to imply that pregnancy's unique features make it readily distinguishable from other disabilities and hence properly excludable from the comprehensive disability program, all without exposing the particular facts and policy judgments that lead him to that conclusion.

Justice Brennan, joined in dissent by Justices Marshall and Douglas, adopted the plaintiffs' position in its entirely. Women disabled by pregnancy-related causes were comparable to other disabled workers for purposes of the California program:

> Disabilities caused by pregnancy . . ., however, like other physically disabling conditions covered by the Code, require medical care, often include hospitalization, anesthesia and surgical procedures, and may involve genuine risk to life. Moreover, the economic effects caused by pregnancy-related disabilities are functionally indistinguishable from the effects caused by any other disability: wages are lost due to a physical inability to work, and medical expenses are incurred for the delivery of the child and for postpartum care.[11]

Moreover, the exclusion of pregnancy-related disabilities constituted sex discrimination:

> In my view, by singling out for less favorable treatment a gender-linked disability peculiar to women, the State has created a double standard for

disability compensation: a limitation is imposed upon the disabilities for which women workers may recover, while men receive full compensation for all disabilities suffered, including those that affect only or primarily their sex, such as prostatectomies, circumcision, hemophilia, and gout. In effect, one set of rules is applied to females and another to males. Such dissimilar treatment of men and women, on the basis of physical characteristics inextricably linked to one sex, inevitably constitutes sex discrimination.[12]

To grasp the full significance of *Geduldig*, it is necessary to consider other cases decided by the Supreme Court. . . . The case decided just before *Geduldig* was Cleveland Board of Education v. LaFleur,[13] in which women challenged an unfavorable pregnancy rule and won in the Supreme Court, but on a legal theory different from that rejected in *Geduldig*.

The plaintiffs in *LaFleur* were public school teachers placed on mandatory unpaid maternity leaves under school board rules requiring pregnant teachers to commence a leave in the fourth or fifth month of pregnancy and precluding their return to work for specified periods after childbirth. Such rules were typical in public schools throughout the country.

The Court held that the mandatory maternity leave rules impinged on the teachers' "freedom of personal choice in matters of marriage and family life." It quoted Eisenstadt v. Baird, a 1972 case invalidating a law which prohibited the provision of birth control devices to unmarried persons, for the proposition that there is a right to be free from unwarranted governmental intrusion into matters so fundamentally affecting a person as the decision whether to bear or beget a child."[14] Thus, when the Court struck down the pregnancy policies in *LaFleur*, it invoked not the sex discrimination cases decided under the equal protection clause, but rather, the reproductive choice cases, such as *Eisenstadt* and Roe v. Wade.

. . . [T]he lower court opinions in the two cases consolidated as Cleveland Board of Education v. LaFleur . . . had decided the validity of the school board rules not on due process grounds—not as cases involving the fundamental right to choose whether to bear or beget children—but rather as equal protection cases, and both addressed the question whether pregnancy discrimination was sex discrimination. . . .

Thus, when the cases reached the Supreme Court, the issue was neatly framed by the irreconcilable views of the two lower courts: should discrimination against pregnant women be treated as sex discrimination and judged under the Court's new and tougher standard of review in sex discrimination cases brought under the equal protection clause? Or should the Court . . . hold that pregnancy is *sui generis* and not amenable to analysis as sex discrimination? The majority opinion of the Supreme Court in *LaFleur* did neither. It did not even mention, much less appear to resolve, the lower court dispute.

. . . At the time *LaFleur* was decided, the Court had already set for oral argument . . . Geduldig v. Aiello, which raised for a second time that term the question whether the Court would view discrimination on the basis of pregnancy as sex discrimination. Thus, the Court knew as it decided *LaFleur* that its next pregnancy case would permit it to speak again on the constitutionality of state pregnancy regulations and, if it chose, to resolve the debate that surfaced in the Fourth and Seventh Circuit opinions. In *LaFleur* the Court, presented with two possible doctrinal approaches to pregnancy, chose to apply the due process rather than the equal protection analysis. That it had also rejected the latter became explicit when *Geduldig* was decided. . . .

The doctrinal distinction between due process and equal protection analysis of pregnancy issues represented by *LaFleur* and *Geduldig* is in a sense a reiteration of the special treatment/equal treatment dichotomy. To oversimplify, the due process approach is not troubled by and, indeed, invokes a form of special treatment analysis. The liberty interest at stake, defined as the right to choose whether to bear or beget a child without undue state interference, is recognized as "fundamental" precisely because of the central and unique importance to the individual of reproductive choice. The characterization of pregnancy discrimination as sex discrimination, by contrast, requires the comparative analysis of the equal protection mode. Its emphasis is on what is not unique about the reproductive process of women.

The practical consequences of the Court's choice can be illustrated by looking at the facts of the *LaFleur* case from both perspectives. Under the due process/fundamental rights doctrine, the Court asks whether the employer pregnancy rule burdens the exercise of a women's freedom to choose whether or not to bear a child, and, if so, whether the burden is justified. The Court in *LaFleur* had no trouble saying that a rule requiring a women to take an unpaid leave in the middle of her pregnancy constituted a "heavy burden" and was not adequately justified.

But suppose the leave policy were less extreme. Suppose, for example, that the rule or law provided that a woman must take a leave six weeks before her due date and could not return for six weeks after childbirth, as did the laws of several states until recently. The Court might well conclude that a six-week-before-six-week-after rule did not burden the pregnant woman's procreative choice or that even if it did, it did not do so unreasonably. Indeed the *LaFleur* majority took pains to say that it was not passing on the constitutionality of a maternity leave regulation requiring termination of employment "at some firm date during the last few weeks of pregnancy." Justice Powell, concurring, suggested that "in light of the Court's language . . . a four-week pre-birth period would be acceptable." In reaching these conclusions, the Justices would, as they did in *LaFleur*, look solely at the characteristics of pregnancy itself in the context of an educational institution.

The sex equality approach would require a different analysis. In assessing the validity of the six-week-before-six-week-after-childbirth rule, the Court would engage in a comparative analysis. How does the school district deal with other work absences due to physical incapacity? Perhaps more on target, how does it deal with other potentially disabling conditions? If a school district in general permitted an employee with a potentially disabling physical condition or elective surgery to work until there were medical indications to the contrary, then the pregnant woman would be entitled to work until it became medically appropriate for her to cease.

The equality analysis thus shifts the focus, providing by reference to the employees' general rules governing disability a tangible benchmark for measuring the appropriateness of the pregnancy rule. In contrast to the due process analysis which entails only a look at the internal logic of the pregnancy rule, the equality analysis does not automatically place a woman in a separate class when she becomes pregnant. Rather, she is a person like any other person who may be forced to leave work due to a physical condition. Moreover, the influence of sex role assumptions, stereotyped expectations and normative judgments about pregnancy is explicitly examined as part of the sex discrimination analysis. To the extent that these factors infect legislation, it is constitutionally doomed.

Thus, when the Supreme Court chose, in *LaFleur* and *Geduldig*, to view pregnancy as a special case, it made a decision to permit government to single out pregnant women for regulatory purposes, subject only to the limitation that a rule may not impose too great a burden on the choice to bear a child. This is not to say that the reproductive choice cases are somehow unimportant or misguided in their approach to reproductive issues. A woman's ability to control, to time, to prevent conception is no less than the ability to control her own destiny. A society bent on keeping women in their traditional role would first seek to deny them reproductive choice. The doctrine developed in the reproductive choice cases has, as a practical matter, a crucial bearing on women's status. The doctrine in the due process cases, however, is not explicitly sensitive to or focused on women's equality. It is a doctrine that concerns itself not with the status of persons, but rather with the freedom of persons to make certain choices without "undue" state interference. Due process and equal protection doctrines produce distinctly different constraints and consequences. Because the two doctrines focus on different aspects of the reproductive phenomenon—the one on protecting the liberty to make certain reproductive choices free of state intervention, the other on whether the state has treated the sexes evenhandedly—the Court could (and feminists thought should) have made both applicable to the pregnancy problem. In certain contexts, such as those in *LaFleur* and *Geduldig*, the equal protection approach speaks more relevantly to the position in which pregnant women find themselves, and in all contexts in which pregnancy is regulated, a concern for the equality as well as the liberty implications of the regulation is warranted. . . .

. . . *LaFleur* was from the start a peculiar case. The Court, without explaining why, applied a substantially less rigorous standard than the compelling state interest standard announced in *Roe* to the facts of that case. The Court may have viewed the mandatory leave rule as so obviously irrational that it did not feel the need to apply the higher standard, or it may have had some other reason. Its logic remains unexplained. At any rate, Title VII was extended to cover public employment shortly after the *LaFleur* plaintiffs fell victim to the school board policies, and similar cases have since been brought under the statute rather than the Fourteenth Amendment. Plaintiffs have correctly perceived, for the reasons outlined above, that Title VII's equality analysis provides the stronger tool.

Thus, by 1976, the end of Stage Two, the dimensions of constitutional analysis of pregnancy legislation were established. The battle to bring pregnancy within the "equal treatment" model through the equal protection clause had been lost. . . . The Supreme Court, however, had not yet ruled on the question of pregnancy under Title VII.

Stage Three: 1976–1978

In General Electric Company v. Gilbert,[15] . . . the Supreme Court dropped the other shoe. Relying heavily on Geduldig v. Aiello, it interpreted Title VII as it had the equal protection clause: it held that discrimination on the basis of pregnancy was not sex discrimination. *Gilbert,* on its facts, was very similar to *Geduldig.* It involved a private employer's disability insurance plan almost identical to the California state plan both in its general scope and in its exclusion of pregnancy-related disabilities. Justice Rehnquist began his analysis on behalf of the majority by invoking *Geduldig*'s conclusion that discrimination on the basis of pregnancy, a unique physical characteristic, is not gender discrimination "as such." Thus, rules concerning it are "neutral," not sex-based. As Justice Stewart had done in *Geduldig,* Rehnquist went on to assert that the pregnancy rule, like the one in *Geduldig,* was not a "pretext" for sex discrimination either. But, in contrast to the equal protection clause relied upon in *Geduldig,* Title VII doctrine provides a third theory of violation, and it is with respect to that third theory that Rehnquist made a unique contribution to the law on pregnancy and equality.

Under Title VII, rules that are "neutral" but have disproportionate sex-based effect may also violate the Act. However, the particular "neutral" General Electric pregnancy disability rule, said Justice Rehnquist, could not even be viewed as having a discriminatory *effect* on women. Men and women, he said, are both covered by the disability program. Moreover, they are covered for the disabilities common to both sexes. Pregnancy disabilities are therefore an "*additional* risk, unique to women."[16] Failure to compensate women for them does not upset the basic sex equality of the program. In a footnote, he drove home the point: Title VII does not require "that 'greater economic benefit[s]' . . . be paid to one sex or the other because of their differing roles in the 'scheme of human existence.'" This conclusion makes breathtakingly explicit the underlying philosophy of the majority of the justices in *Geduldig* and *Gilbert.* Pregnancy, for Rehnquist, is an "extra," an add-on to the basic male model for humanity. Equality does not contemplate handing out benefits for extras—indeed, to do so would be to grant special benefits to women, possibly discriminating against men. The fact that men were compensated under the program for disabilities unique to their sex troubled his analysis not at all.

Justice Brennan, in his dissent in *Geduldig*, almost grasped the essence of the problem when he observed that "the State has created a double standard for disability compensation; a limitation is imposed upon the disabilities for which women workers may recover, while men receive full compensation for all disabilities suffered, including those that affect only or primarily their sex. . . ." What eluded even Justice Brennan was that the statute did not create a "double" standard. Rather, it made man the standard (whatever disabilities men suffer will be compensated) and measured women against that standard (as long as she is compensated for anything he is compensated for, she is treated equally).

For Rehnquist, as long as women are treated in the same way as men in the areas where they are like men—in the disability program this would mean coverage for things like heart attacks, broken bones, appendicitis—that's equality. To the extent the Court will consider the equities with respect to childbearing capacity, it will consider them only in the category where they belong—extra, separate, different. A family, marital or reproductive right—yes, in appropriate circumstances. A public matter of equality and equal protection of women—no.

A subsequent Title VII case, Nashville Gas Company v. Satty,[17] provides an important footnote to the majority's attitude. The relevant portion of *Satty* involved a challenge to a company policy under which women returning from maternity leave were stripped of all their pre-leave seniority. Pursuant to this policy, when Nora Satty returned to work, she found her seniority abolished. . . .

Justice Rehnquist again wrote for the Court. This time, however, the plaintiff prevailed. In *Gilbert*, Rehnquist explained, women sought an extra benefit; they wanted disability benefits for a disability in addition to those which men could suffer. *Satty*, by contrast, involved a burden imposed on women to which men were not subjected: forfeiture of seniority. This, he concluded, violated Title VII. Why loss of income during a pregnancy disability leave was not a burden while loss of seniority upon return to work was a burden remains something of a mystery. . . .

The explanation must lie in Rehnquist's basic conception of pregnancy as extra and extension of benefits accordingly a special privilege. For him, *Satty* was distinguishable from *Gilbert* because the *Satty* plaintiff sought no benefits based on the pregnancy itself. She had earned the seniority prior to her pregnancy leave and was deprived of that seniority upon her return when she was no longer pregnant. She just wanted to keep after pregnancy what she earned before pregnancy intervened. A rule stripping women of benefits they earned as "normal" workers when they again returned to the "normal" (non-pregnant, malelike) status would, for Rehnquist, implicate equality concerns, while women's ascension into the no-man's land of pregnancy would not.

Stage Four: 1978–Present [1984–1985, Ed.]

In reaction to *Gilbert* and *Satty*, Congress in 1978 passed the Pregnancy Discrimination Act (PDA) as an amendment to Title VII, quite plainly requiring that pregnancy be treated under the equality model. The PDA, an amendment to the definitions section of Title VII, provides that employment discrimination on the basis of pregnancy, childbirth and related medical conditions is sex discrimination for purposes of that Act.

The second sentence illustrates how the Act is to be interpreted: "[w]omen affected by pregnancy, childbirth or related medical conditions shall be treated the same for all employment-related purposes, including receipt of benefits under fringe benefit programs, as other persons not so affected but similar in their ability or inability to work.". . . Pregnancy is to be understood as a physical event comparable to other physical events which befall workers. A physically fit pregnant worker cannot be laid off when other fit workers are not (the *LaFleur* result) nor can physically disabled pregnant workers be treated differently than other disabled workers (overriding the *Gilbert* result). The requirement that women affected by pregnancy be treated the same for all employment-related purposes as others similar in their work ability underscores the intent of the Pregnancy Discrimination Act to bring pregnancy rules within the general non-discrimination requirements of Title VII. It is apparent from this language that Congress intended that pregnant workers are to be treated no worse—nor any better—than other "similar" workers.

In its first interpretation of the PDA [Newport News Shipbuilding and Dry Dock Co. v. Equal Employment Opportunity Commission, 462 U.S. 669 (1983)], the Supreme Court expressed its understanding that Congress meant to eradicate both the holding of *Gilbert* and the principle on which that holding was based. . . .

With *Newport News*, *Gilbert*'s conceptual framework is definitively interred. Pregnancy-based rules prima facie violate Title VII. The burden is on the employer to show that its rule comes within Title VII's BFOQ [bona fide occupational qualification] exception. The more complicated inquiries required by *Gilbert* and *Satty*—whether the pregnancy rule is a pretext for sex discrimination, and whether it has a disproportionate effect on women not justified by business necessity—are now irrelevant. The equal treatment approach, despite its rocky progress in the Supreme Court, has transformed employer pregnancy policies.

. . . Employer policies requiring terminations and mandatory leaves are plainly illegal and have been nearly eliminated.[18] Women are entitled to work until disabled and to return on the same basis as other temporarily disabled employees. Women disabled by pregnancy are entitled to claim paid sick leave, personal leave, disability benefits and medical and hospitalization benefits on the same basis as other workers. The "unjust denial of economic benefits and arbitrary restrictions on employment" that caused hardship for low income workers and thus particularly concerned Elizabeth Koontz, Director of the Women's Bureau, in 1971, is now largely remedied.

Serious problems remain, however. . . . [For example,] although substitution of the disability model for the old maternity leave approach to pregnancy has generated a substantial increase in monetary benefits to pregnant employees when they become incapacitated, it may also have encouraged employers to restrict leaves to the disability period. Mandatory maternity leaves often included a time period after childbirth, unrelated to physical incapacity of the women, during which a mother could spend time away from the job with her newborn. Although unpaid, and often not optional for the employee, it met an important need of employees, too frequently unrecognized by employers today, to spend the early months of a child's life at home.

Finally, there remains the reality that Title VII guarantees to the pregnant worker only the benefits already extended by the employer to others. When Elizabeth Koontz surveyed the status of pregnant workers in 1971 and recommended that pregnant workers be included in preexisting benefits schemes, she noted that forty percent of working men and women had no protection from unemployment due to disability. "A long range goal," she said, "is the achievement of protection against loss of income for temporary disabilities. . . . This goal could be secured through the enactment of additional state temporary disability insurance laws or through a federal law [creating a temporary disability insurance system as a part of a federal-state unemployment insurance program]."[19]

To date, her long range goal has not been realized, and the gap she noted then has not been bridged by employers. In the meantime, perhaps not surprisingly, a few states[20] have passed legislation aimed at the partial alleviation of this gap and have provided a right to unpaid leave and reinstatement—but only for employees who become pregnant. These are the provisions that have engendered the recent debate about the appropriate legal treatment of pregnancy. . . .

The Equal Treatment/Special Treatment Debate

We now reach Stage Five, a crossroads. The questions raised by Scales, Krieger and Cooney require an answer. Has the . . . experiment with an equal treatment approach to pregnancy been a failure? Is the approach fatally flawed, or perhaps a temporary tactic for which there is no longer any need? If so, is there a workable alternative which avoids the scylla of "equal treatment" but also the charybdis of *Geduldig* and *Gilbert*?

I continue to believe that the course upon which feminist litigators set out at the beginning of the 1970s—the "equal treatment" approach to pregnancy—is the one best able to reduce structural barriers to full workforce participation of women, produce just results for individuals, and support a more egalitarian social structure. Though not without problems, this approach is rooted in a theory and produces results superior to the others. . . .

In Defense of "Equal Treatment"

For equal treatment advocates, the approach is part of a larger strategy to get the law out of the business of reinforcing traditional, sex-based family roles and to alter the workplace so as to keep it in step with the increased participation by women.

The workplace pregnancy rules evident at the beginning of the 1970s were not simply a random collection of malevolent or irrational impediments for wage earning women. They were not a byproduct of ignorance or inadvertence. Rather, they formed a coherent structure which reflected women's predominant pattern of workforce behavior and reified a particular set of values and objectives about women, work and family.

At the core was an ideology defining men's "natural" function as family bread-winners and women's "natural" function as childbearers and rearers. A woman worker's pregnancy was a signal (as her marriage had been decades earlier) of her impending assumption of her primary role. Workplace rules accordingly treated her as terminating her workplace participation. If she defied the presumption and sought to continue her workforce attachment, she met with numerous obstacles. If she avoided outright termination, then she faced mandatory leaves that had nothing to do with her desire or capacity to work. She was not guaranteed the right to return, she was denied sick leave or disability, she lost seniority, and she became ineligible for unemployment insurance. Moreover, her medical coverage for expenses associated with pregnancy was reduced or nonexistent. All of this underscored for her a lesson that pregnancy is not a workplace but a family issue. Employer and state would not recognize her as a worker again until the pregnancy and the infancy of her child were behind her.

Today's feminists from the outset rejected the separate spheres ideology which assigned men to the workplace and women to the home. The crucial functions of the traditional family arrangement—financial support, housework and childrearing— should not, they asserted, be assigned by sex. To the extent that laws and rules force the traditional preassignment and inhibit choice, they should be replaced by laws and rules that make no assumptions about the sex of the family childrearer or wage earner, but simply address those functions directly. Moreover, the workplace should be restructured to respond to the reality that all adult members of a household in which there are children are frequently in the workforce and that co-breadwinner parents might choose or need to share childrearing functions. Equally importantly, a significant number of families today contain only one parent, who must perform both wage earning and childrearing functions.

Accommodation to parental needs and obligations should penetrate to the core of the workplace rather than remain a peripheral "women's issue." Treating parenthood as a non-issue structurally marginalizes women as workforce participants.[21] Women's increasingly pervasive workforce attachment means that pregnancy should no longer be treated as a private problem of marginal workers best handled by the old exclusionary methods. Justice Rehnquist notwithstanding, it will not do to treat women as "real" workers entitled to the full panoply of benefits only until they become pregnant.

Today the workplace remains unacceptably tailored to the old sex-based allocation of childrearing duties. The basic structures still assume that the "real" workers are men whose "personal lives" do not and should not create obstacles to long, uninterrupted hours of work over an adult lifetime. The majority of women are still in a secondary, segregated, marginal workforce, engaged in the dual careers of worker and mother, in jobs where turnover is assumed and provides minimum disruption.

The "equal treatment" model is designed to discourage employers and the state from creating or maintaining rules that force people to structure their family relationships upon traditional sex-based lines and from refusing to respond to pregnancy as within the normal range of events which temporarily affect workers.[22]

Maternity leave, when available, was traditionally an unpaid leave for a woman beginning during pregnancy and extending some months after childbirth. It was typically a package that included not only pregnancy but also infant care, on the assumption that the woman who became pregnant would inevitably be the primary caretaker of the child. The "equal treatment" model separates pregnancy and childrearing and insists that each be independently analyzed.[23]

The separation has important implications. When the childrearing function is considered separately from pregnancy, it becomes apparent that parents of either sex might undertake that responsibility. To grant childrearing leave to mothers only would be, under this analysis, to discriminate against fathers. Employers who provide leaves for childrearing must therefore substitute "parental" for "maternal" leaves. This separation of early childrearing from pregnancy thus serves the objective of prohibiting workplace rules that discourage families from opting for an egalitarian or nontraditional assignment of parental roles and from ordering their lives in a way that best meets their economic and personal needs. Further, it explicitly rejects stereotypes about motherhood and fatherhood, undermining the view that holds the mother naturally and inevitably responsible, and the father exempt from responsibility, for the nurturing of young children. Finally, it may reduce the vulnerability of working single mothers by making childrearing obligations something that the employer must expect that any parent, male or female, may experience.

The separation of childbearing and childrearing also promotes reanalysis of pregnancy in the workplace context. Much of the disadvantageous treatment of pregnant wage earners by employers was based not on the pregnancy itself but on predictions concerning the future behavior of the pregnant woman when her child was born or on views about what her behavior should be. When shorn of its implications about future behavior by the separation of childbearing and child-rearing, pregnancy can be analyzed as a purely physical event. As such, it is susceptible to a functional analysis which compares the way it affects the pregnant worker to how other physical conditions affect other workers. Under a functional analysis, it becomes possible to argue that pregnancy, when not disabling, should not be a basis for termination or forced leave any more than any other nondisabling condition should be, and that when pregnancy does become disabling, the benefits appropriate for other workers should be extended to pregnant workers as well.

The contention that the "equal treatment" approach does not work because the need to "compare exclusively female characteristics to cross-sex analogues often results in reliance on strained analogies which are unconvincing to courts"[24] seems absolutely wrong when one analyzes the circumstances in which the analogy is made or looks at what the lower federal courts have been doing for over ten years on the pregnancy issue. The comparative approach provided a potent tool, with which the courts outlawed within a few years time the most detrimental of the employment pregnancy rules, and continues today to provide important protections.

The question is not *whether* pregnancy is different (it is, of course—it has its own specific physical manifestations, course of development, risks, and a different, usually desirable and certainly life altering outcome), but *how* it is different. Men and women, blacks and whites are different. If they were not, they would not exist as categories. The focus in the pregnancy debate, as with men and women or blacks and whites, should be on whether the differences should be deemed relevant in the context of particular employment rules. For purposes of eating peas, a knife is not functionally the same as a fork; but if both utensils are silver, the difference is irrelevant to a thief. Similarly, when a woman goes into labor, the measures appropriate for someone having a heart attack won't help; but if both childbirth and a heart attack cause an inability to work and income loss, it makes sense to encompass both within a disability program designed to cushion the economic effects of temporary inability to work.

The workplace rules governing pregnancy have been singularly burdensome and unfair to women. Pregnancy's centrality to human reproduction, and hence to women's traditional role, has made it the basis for rules which express and reinforce old ideologies about women's proper place. The tangible, physical nature and high visibility of pregnancy have made such rules seem natural and appropriate, but upon close examination, the rules are often only tenuously related to their purposes and are premised on the very "old notions" about women that the Supreme Court has ruled will not justify sex-based legislation. As the plaintiffs argued in Geduldig v. Aiello:

Placed in historical context, it should be apparent that discrimination on the basis of pregnancy, a "unique" characteristic, is not separable from previous sex discrimination, but rather part of a continuum of discrimination. For practical purposes there is no difference between refusing to permit women to become lawyers because of their physical and emotional differences from men and refusing women certain jobs on the more narrow ground that they might become pregnant or firing them because they are pregnant. The issue for courts is not whether pregnancy is, in the abstract, sui generis, but whether the legal treatment of pregnancy in various contexts is justified or invidious.[25]

Katharine Bartlett's conclusion . . . is relevant here: "Paradoxically, the uniqueness of pregnancy is probably the most important reason why it warrants special protection, for pregnancy's unique identifiability facilitates drafting laws and regulations based on exactly those generalizations, stereotypes and assumptions that constitutional doctrine in the area of sex discrimination was intended to curb."[26]

There may indeed be instances where special pregnancy rules are neither over- nor underinclusive and are free of sex role stereotypes. In the abstract, at least, one could posit that rules singling out pregnancy, because of its functional implications, may, to a greater degree than male–female distinctions in general, be justified. While, in the employment context, examples are scarce, where they exist, they would appropriately fall within the bona fide occupational qualification exception to Title VII and would be permitted.

When we get past the simplistic assertion that pregnancy is different and cannot be compared to anything else, is there anything left of objections to "equal treatment"? The answer to that question is clearly yes. Exploration of "what is left" requires a more detailed exposition of the critics' views.

Professor Ann Scales's search for a principle for resolving the pregnancy cases begins with a basic contention with which equal treatment proponents wholeheartedly agree:

[T]rue equality requires not just women in men's jobs and operating men's institutions, but also that those institutions be replaced by others broad enough to accommodate the full range of human activities. To demand only the chance to compete is to embrace the status quo in a way that tends to sanction oppressive arrangements—for example, the necessity of choosing between children and career. Moreover, to ask only for equal opportunities to compete is to obscure the fact that the restrictions presently imposed on individual women are functions of class characteristics. The emphasis comes to be on the exceptional woman, on the one who has overcome the obstacles of womanhood, and future change is hindered by throwing the blame for circumstances of class onto individual capabilities.[27]

Likewise Scales's goal of incorporating women into the public world, fully taking into account the legal and economic aspects of childbearing, seems to me to be precisely the right one. Equal treatment proponents would certainly agree with her that "of central concern are proposals which facilitate continuity between the experience of childbearing and working," that "at a minimum, the mandate of the PDA must be vigorously enforced, ensuring that disability, sick leave and medical benefits available to other workers through employment are not arbitrarily withheld from pregnant workers," also that "more can be done." The "more" Scales contemplates consists of legislative proposals, which consistent with her "incorporationist" vision, provide across-the-board protections for workers which also meet the needs of pregnant employees.

Where Scales goes astray is in her analysis of where the courts went wrong. She sees clearly that the Supreme Court in *Gilbert* and *Geduldig* adopts a stance that excludes women's unique capacity from a range of employment benefit schemes. Thus pregnancy, rather than being "incorporat[ed] . . . into the social continuum," and thereby "reflecting the reality of women's lives," continues to be excluded. The doctrine developed in those cases thus preserves a male model for the workplace, refusing to accept and account for those unique qualities of women that differentiate them from men.

Having delineated the Court's position with impeccable accuracy, Scales advances a solution, and it is here that her analysis drops the skein. Looking at the *Geduldig–Gilbert* outcome, she concludes that it is the attempt to analogize pregnancy to any other condition or enterprise that is the problem. To do so, she thinks, permits maleness to be the norm. But the Court preserved the male model by *failing* to take seriously the similarity in the position of pregnant disabled workers and other disabled workers. It preserved the discontinuity between motherhood and workforce participation by failing to understand that the stake of pregnant workers in such benefits was like other workers' stakes—and thus failed to require that women be integrated fully into the basic system of worker protections. . . .

Scales fails to see that her incorporationist vision—a vision of the inclusion and proper accounting for pregnancy in the public sphere—is best served by the equal treatment approach. It is precisely that vision that gave birth to the equal treatment model in the first place. The model was proposed in the context of an exclusionary workplace, and it was urged to promote the "normalization" of pregnancy. In the litigation context, the model was the basis for insisting on the incorporation of pregnancy into existing benefit schemes. The litigators sought incorporation not by insisting that pregnancy was "the same" as other physical events but that the position of the pregnant worker was analogous to the position of other workers. The approach was based on the notion that the pregnant woman is entitled to respect and dignity as a worker and that the stake a woman shares with other workers in job security and economic viability does not suddenly evaporate when she becomes pregnant. It sought to overcome the definition of the prototypical worker as male and to promote an integrated—and androgynous—prototype.

Nonetheless, if the equal treatment approach were limited to the integration of pregnancy into the pattern of existing provisions for job security and economic benefits, Ann Scales would have good reason to protest that the incorporationist vision cannot fully be implemented through that approach. An existing system of protections and benefits, she might point out, is structured to respond to the needs and characteristics of the typical male worker. Even if such protections and benefits are extended to women workers (and this might be especially true for those who become pregnant), they will not necessarily deliver equivalent advantages to women. Schemes set up on a male model are likely to be misconfigured from a woman's perspective. To grasp this point one need only envision what workplace rules would look like if the entire workforce were composed of women of childbearing years. The present scheme of things is thus unlikely to account for the needs and characteristics of women workers to the same extent that it accounts for the needs and characteristics of men.

But the "equal treatment" feminists do not contend only that women who are pregnant must be treated the same as other workers in analogous situations. They also assert that apparently neutral rules that have a disproportionate effect on women, whether because of pregnancy or some other class-based characteristic, may violate Title VII.

The disparate effects theory is fundamentally "incorporationist" in the Scales's sense. It permits, in effect, a challenge to "neutral" rules based on a male prototype. It goes beyond assessment of discrimination against individuals to identify the group effects of particular rules. When those effects are substantial, this approach imposes a burden upon the employer to justify its rule or policy. Where the rule or policy cannot meet the standard of justification, it is invalidated— not just for the group upon whom it places a disproportionate burden, but for all affected workers. The employer is left to pursue its objectives in some way that avoids the untoward effects. In short, its replacement rule must be truly, not simply formally, neutral. The tendency of the disparate effects theory is thus to require employers' policies to account for the needs and characteristics of both sexes.

Krieger and Cooney share Scales's basic concern that a legal doctrine which demands only that individual women be treated as well as similarly situated men permits the continuation of "male defined" structures and practices that have a negative effect upon working women as a class. Despite considerable attention devoted to what they see as shortcomings in the basic nondiscrimination principle, these lawyers recognize its utility. What they propose is not a substitute for it but a supplement to it. Their supplemental principle—presented, oddly enough, as if feminist litigators, particularly those involved in the *Miller-Wohl* controversy, reject it—is none other than Title VII's disparate effects theory. In fact, their perception that the doctrine is a necessary companion to the basic nondiscrimination principle is universally accepted among feminist litigators precisely because it is attuned to the differential effect of laws and rules on the sexes. What is not universally accepted is Krieger and Cooney's interpretation of the principle.

Unlike Scales's vision of inclusion, which encompasses disability and health insurance for all, Krieger and Cooney enlist Scales's reasoning and the disparate effects doctrine to support legislation that singles out pregnant women for special protection. They reason that such legislation is a fundamental prerequisite for women's equality in the workplace. A law which requires the employer to give pregnant women "reasonable leave" of absence, but requires no leaves for other employees, they contend, "places women on an *equal* footing with men and permits males and females to compete *equally* in the labor market." It does not "provide women with an additional benefit denied to men; it merely prevents women from having to suffer an additional burden which no male would ever have to bear."

In so conceptualizing the pregnancy issue, Krieger and Cooney reveal a kinship with the majorities in *Geduldig* and *Gilbert*. In *Geduldig*, the Court concluded that women "received insurance protection equivalent to that provided all other participating employees," although pregnancy disabilities were excluded from an otherwise comprehensive program. The Court implicitly visualized pregnancy-related disabilities as disabilities in addition to those men might suffer. In *Gilbert*, the Court went even further, denying that the exclusion of pregnancy disabilities from the program had a class-based *effect* on women. It did this by explicitly labeling pregnancy as an "extra" condition of women, compensation of which constituted a benefit beyond that which men could obtain.

Thus both Krieger and Cooney and the Court majority in *Geduldig* and *Gilbert* define women as men plus pregnancy. Once within the male-oriented definition, the fight is over the proper response to the "reality" upon which they essentially agree. Krieger and Cooney view pregnancy as creating for women a burden in addition to those suffered by men. They contend that an equality principle should, because of the extra burden, approve special laws that make up the difference. The Court's majority reached the opposite conclusion, viewing as discrimination the extension of disability benefits to pregnant women. Moreover, it squarely rejected the notion that equality means making up for "women's more burdensome role in the scheme of human existence."[28]

Krieger and Cooney's view leads them to assert that pregnancy is a difference which must be "accommodated," in the manner that Title VII requires employer accommodation to religious practices, or federal regulations require accommodation to employee handicaps. However, the Supreme Court has interpreted accommodation requirements very narrowly. It has little sympathy for provisions which make employers go out of their way for the atypical worker. This result seems predictable. Special "favors" for such workers are viewed as an imposition unconnected to the employer's business needs and interests. In contrast, provisions for the "typical" worker are more easily seen as necessary or desirable responses to the nature of the workforce which may increase employee loyalty and productivity. Moreover, the special treatment approach for women will always embroil its proponents in a debate about whether they are getting more or not enough. Finally, such provisions are a double-edged sword for their beneficiaries because they impose upon employers special costs and obligations in connection with pregnant workers, rendering them less desirable employees and creating an incentive to discriminate against them. By contrast, the equal treatment approach, premised squarely on an androgynous rather than a male prototype and reaching for an incorporationist rather than accommodationist vision, seeks to avoid these consequences by requiring a fundamental reorganization of the way the presence of pregnant working women in the workplace is understood. The vision is not, as is Krieger and Cooney's, a workplace based on a male definition of employee, with special accommodation to women's differences from men, but rather a redefinition of what a typical employee is that encompasses both sexes.

Not only is Krieger and Cooney's underlying conceptualization of the pregnancy problem different from that of the equal treatment feminists, but the interpretation of Title VII through which Krieger and Cooney seek to effectuate their accommodationist view is unsound. They urge that "accommodation" is to be achieved through an interpretation of the disparate effects doctrine that permits special pregnancy rules or laws to be upheld where they were instituted to overcome the adverse impact of workplace structures on women. However, disparate effects doctrine has not traditionally been, and should not be, put to such a use. Its purpose is to force the evaluation of neutral rules that are shown to have a disproportionate effect. The remedy when such an effect is shown is neither the construction of a dual system in which the rule continues in effect for one group but not the other, nor the formulation of special rules for the adversely affected classes. Instead, the remedy is reformulation or elimination of the rule for everyone. . . .

So, too, in the case of pregnancy. The replacement for a rule or policy that disproportionately affects women because of pregnancy is not a sex- (or pregnancy-) based rule, but a revised rule that, in Scales's terminology, fairly "incorporates" pregnancy into the general scheme of worker protections. That this was Congress's intent when it passed the Pregnancy Discrimination Act is explicit in the language of the Act itself. . . .

Andrew Weissman goes even further than Kreiger and Cooney. He contends that the PDA should be interpreted to provide that employers who have no disability plan at all violate Title VII by failing to create special rules for pregnancy disabilities. Congress, he thinks, intended that pregnancy be accorded *different* treatment in order to "rectif[y] the natural asymmetry of the sexes."[29] He urges that women, like the handicapped, need special accommodation in order to participate in the workforce on an equal basis; failure of the employer to provide special provisions violates the PDA. As with Krieger and Cooney, his vision implicitly accepts men as the norm and seeks to make special provision for women insofar as they are not like men.

The equal treatment feminists reject the fundamental assumption that men should be treated as the prototype. An androgynous prototype requires sex neutral schemes that take into account the normal range of human characteristics—including pregnancy. Weissman's approach, like that of Krieger and Cooney, constitutes a fine tuning of the old order. More than the provision of identical services may seem necessary when services are geared to the male norm. But inherent in such an approach is the continued definition of women as "other." Dual standards have always been the law's response to the sexes. The equal treatment feminists seek a more radical transformation. . . .

Equal Treatment Beyond the Courts

The . . . dispute illuminates . . . the limits of reliance on courts for fundamental social change. . . . An anti-discrimination provision is a device for telling legislatures, governments and designated others what they may not do, thus setting parameters within which they must operate. It does not, and cannot, do the basic job of readjusting the social order. Fundamentally, courts are not the place to seek such important changes. . . . Title VII, or—even if *Geduldig* were overruled—the equal protection clause, cannot produce fundamental change. For that, we must seek solutions outside the courtroom.

Curiously, Krieger and Cooney characterize the dispute about the proper treatment of pregnancy as a debate about whether there should be "equal treatment" or "positive action." These terms mix apples and oranges, conflating two quite distinct contrasting pairs. First, there is the difference between a non-discrimination law (i.e., an employer may not discriminate in the provision of disability leaves) and a law which grants particular substantive entitlements (i.e., employers must provide reasonable disability leaves to employees). Second, there is the difference between a law based on an equal treatment model (i.e., employers must provide reasonable disability leaves to employees) and one based on a special treatment model (i.e., employers must provide reasonable disability leaves to pregnant employees). Krieger and Cooney's criticisms of equal treatment arise out of, and are distorted by, their consideration of the limits of equal treatment doctrine solely under a non-discrimination provision. If pregnant workers and others are treated equally badly by the employer, and if the employer's rule does not disproportionately harm women, then a non-discrimination law like Title VII is not violated. The remedy in such a situation may indeed be "positive action," but Krieger and Cooney fail to grasp that a statute or policy creating "positive" rights can be based on either an "equal treatment" or a "special treatment" model. Because of this they miss a fundamental point of agreement between special treatment and equal treatment advocates. All parties to the debate agree that "positive action" is needed. The question is what form it should take. . . .

. . . [I]t is possible to identify some essential features of a leave system toward which we might realistically aspire and work. In this country positive legislation based on the equality model would have the following features. First and most fundamental, it would focus on parental rather than maternal responsibilities. It would recognize that there is a period of time when a woman is physically unable to work because of pregnancy-related disability. During this period of time she will, like other disabled workers, have her job protected and be eligible for wage replacement benefits. The system should further recognize the social advantage of parental childrearing for parent and child in the early months of the baby's life. Thus, it will require that a reasonable parental leave be allowed a new parent to engage in early childrearing. Such legislation might also create an entitlement on the part of nonparents to take leave to tend sick family members.

The twin goals of disability leaves and parenting leaves can be pursued in a number of ways. Five states now have disability insurance programs that cover pregnancy-related disabilities on the same basis as other disabilities. Other states should consider such a program. . . . While no state today requires employers to provide parental leaves, such legislation has been proposed. . . . Some employers are instituting such leaves and some unions are seeking them through collective bargaining. A number of groups have made parental leave a research or advocacy priority.

Most significantly, a bill recently introduced in the House of Representatives will, if passed, require that employers provide unpaid leaves with job security for persons temporarily disabled from working and for parents of either sex upon the birth of a child. . . . [The Family and Medical Leave Act is currently being considered by Congress. It would require employers of 50 or more persons to provide unpaid leave, job security, and health benefits to employees who take leave to care for a newborn or newly adopted child or a seriously ill child or parent. *Ed.*]

Conclusion

The dispute among feminists about whether women and men are essentially similar or dissimilar as to their stake in the workplace is as old as feminism itself. Assumptions about similarities and differences yield different theories of what will break down gender hierarchy and promote equality between women and men. The vigorous dispute among those feminists who supported and those who attacked protective labor legislation earlier in this century has been replaced by the debate over whether the fact of pregnancy should be given "equal treatment" or "special treatment" in workplace policies to promote the ultimate equality of women. I have contended here that the "equal treatment"[30] approach to pregnant wage workers, both as a litigative and legislative matter, is demonstrably the better approach.

There is one sense in which I feel the attraction of "special treatment." Visions of equality are one thing; ability to realize a particular vision at a particular historical moment and place is another. It has always been easier to wrench from the jaws of the political system special provisions for women in the name of motherhood than general provisions aimed at the realignment of sex roles in the family and restructuring of the workplace. Urgent problems cry out for immediate solutions. Half the proverbial loaf . . . sometimes seems better than none.

If this were some other time and place, perhaps expediency would suggest that the benefits of special treatment rules . . . outweigh the cost. For the moment, however, Elizabeth Koontz's 1971 vision remains within the realm of possibility. Much of what she suggested has come to pass. The enormous pressure created by the changed demography of the workforce as well as initiatives by public and private groups indicates that major change is indeed possible. To settle for special treatment now would be to sell equality short.

Notes

1. 42 U.S.C. § 2000e(k) (1983).
2. Scales, Towards a Feminist Jurisprudence, 56 Ind. L.J. 375, 435 (1981).
3. Krieger & Cooney, The Miller-Wohl Controversy: Equal Treatment, Positive Action and the Meaning of Women's Equality, Part 3 herein, at 164.
4. [Miller-Wohl filed an action in federal district court for a declaratory judgment maintaining that the MMLA was unconstitutional and in conflict with Title VII. After the district court upheld the act on constitutional as well as statutory grounds, Miller-Wohl appealed. Rather than decide the case on the merits, the appellate court dismissed the case on the basis that the Iowa court did not have subject matter jurisdiction. 515 F. Supp. 1264 (D. Mont. 1981), vacated, 685 F.2d 1088 (9th Cir. 1982). After similar issues were presented to the Supreme Court in terms of California legislation, the *Miller-Wohl* judgment was remanded (479 U.S. 1050 [1987]) for further consideration in light of California Federal Savings and Loan Association v. Guerra, 479 U.S. 272 (1987). *Ed.*]
5. 208 U.S. 412, 422 (1908) (emphasis added).
6. Women's Bureau, Maternity Protection of Employed Women 7 (1952) (Bull. No. 240).
7. Koontz, Childbirth and Child Rearing Leave: Job-Related Benefits, 17 N.Y.L. Forum 480, 501 (1971). In her conclusion she states:

> The prompt removal of inequities in existing systems is a high-priority goal, as many low-income women workers are suffering great hardship through unjust denial of economic benefits and arbitrary restrictions on employment. With median earnings of white women working year-round, full-time at a little over five thousand dollars per year and black women at four thousand dollars per year, it is clear that most women workers cannot afford any unnecessary loss of wages or loss of coverage of medical bills.
>
> Groups concerned with human rights should make full use of the courts and human relations agencies to challenge employers' special requirements regarding length of absence for childbirth, exclusion of childbirth from health insurance and temporary disability insurance coverage,

special disqualifications for pregnancy in unemployment insurance laws, and the exclusion of pregnancy from state temporary disability insurance laws.

A long-range goal is the achievement of protection against loss of income for temporary disabilities for the forty percent of working men and women who now have no protection. This goal could be secured through the enactment of additional state temporary disability insurance laws or through a federal law, such as that suggested by the Task Force on Social Insurance and Taxes in 1968.

With respect to child rearing leave, it might be best to experiment with a variety of approaches before seeking legislation. The women's caucuses of the professional organizations are actively seeking adoption by universities of this type of leave, and perhaps unions would give it high priority. *Id.* at 502. . . .

8. 417 U.S. 484 (1974).

9. *Id.* at 496 n. 20.

10. *Id.* at 496 n. 10.

11. *Id.* at 500–01.

12. *Id.*

13. 414 U.S. 632 (1974).

14. *Id.* at 640.

15. 429 U.S. 125 (1976).

16. *Id.* at 139 (emphasis in original).

17. 434 U.S. 136 (1977).

18. Terminations still occur, no longer on the basis of an overt policy of terminating pregnant women, but in other guises. . . .

19. Koontz, Childbirth and Child Rearing Leave, *supra* note 7, at 502.

20. Cal. Gov't Code § 12945(b)(2) (West 1980); Conn. Gen. Stat. Ann. § 46 a-60(7) (West Supp. 1984); Mont. Code Ann. § 49-2-310 (1)-(2)(1983).

21. See Frug, Securing Job Equality for Women: Labor Market Hostility to Working Women, 59 B.U.L. Rev. 55, 94–103 (1979) My own experience . . . suggests that pregnancy is a minor obstacle to full workforce integration of women compared to the ongoing responsibilities of parenthood. . . . Parents (almost always mothers) suppress aspirations, curtail work-related activities, change jobs, become part-time employees—all to provide children with the care that they believe is necessary or desirable. Men infrequently make such sacrifices. *Id.*

22. Some will object that pregnancy is voluntary and its consequences therefore appropriately visited exclusively upon the employee. Individual pregnancies may be and often are voluntary in the sense that the individual woman made a conscious choice to become pregnant. But, as a social matter, pregnancy is not meaningfully voluntary any more than eating or sleeping is voluntary. All are basic functions of the human animal necessary to survival. In a workforce composed of men and women, it is as appropriate to expect employers to provide for pregnancy-related absence as it is to expect them to provide time off to employees to eat and sleep. There is considerable wisdom in the comment, whose source I no longer recall, that "if pregnancy is voluntary, it's a very good thing that women volunteer." Without such "volunteers," there would be no labor force at all.

23. In her pathbreaking legal article on the "equal treatment" model, . . . Elizabeth Duncan Koontz, Director of the Woman's Bureau of the United States

Department of Labor, suggested that the term "childbirth leave" be substituted for the ambiguous term "maternity leave" and that a separate concept, "childrearing" leave, available to both sexes, be developed, stating: "The conceptual framework of childbearing and childrearing fits both present and future reality better than a conceptual framework that assumes that childbearing and childrearing are both solely the responsibility of women. The young women feminists insist, quite logically, that assumption by men of a full share in the rearing of children would contribute to the welfare of the whole family." Koontz, Childbirth and Child Rearing Leave, *supra* note 7, at 481.

24. Krieger & Cooney, Miller-Wohl Controversy, *supra* note 3, at 538.

25. Brief for Appellees, at 37–38.

26. Bartlett, Pregnancy and the Constitution: The Uniqueness Trap, 62 Calif. L. Rev. 1532, 1536 (1974). "Special protection," in context, refers to the heightened scrutiny applied in sex discrimination cases brought under the equal protection clause. It does not mean laws making special provisions for pregnant women.

27. Scales, Towards a Feminist Jurisprudence, *supra* note 2, at 427.

28. 429 U.S. at 139 n.17 (referring to *Gilbert*, 373 F. Supp. at 383).

29. Note, Sexual Equality Under the Pregnancy Discrimination Act, 83 Colum. L. Rev. 690, 717 (1983). . . .

30. "Equal treatment" appears in quotation marks because the label means one thing to Krieger & Cooney, . . . and another, . . . to the opponents of special pregnancy legislation of the Montana and California types. After all is said and done, we probably need a new label.

❖ The Miller-Wohl Controversy: Equal Treatment, Positive Action and the Meaning of Women's Equality

Linda J. Krieger and Patricia N. Cooney

In the summer of 1979, Tamara Buley was hired as a sales clerk by the Miller-Wohl company in Great Falls, Montana. Shortly after she started working Ms. Buley discovered that she was pregnant, and in the weeks that followed, missed a few days of work because of morning sickness. Pursuant to Miller-Wohl's policy of denying any sick leave to employees during their first year with the company, Tamara Buley was fired. She felt that she had been fired because of her pregnancy. Knowing this to be illegal, she filed a discrimination complaint with the Montana Human Rights Commission.

Had Tamara Buley lived in most states, she would almost certainly have lost her case against Miller-Wohl because federal and most state sex discrimination laws provide no affirmative job protection at all to pregnant workers. Federal and most state laws require only that pregnancy-related disabilities be treated no worse than other types of disabilities. There was no evidence in Ms. Buley's case suggesting that Miller-Wohl applied its no-leave policy unevenly.

But because Tamara Buley lived in Montana she succeeded in her complaint against Miller-Wohl. Montana, like Connecticut and California,[1] goes further than the federal government and other states and provides affirmative job security to women workers who are temporarily disabled by pregnancy-related medical conditions. So in Tamara Buley's case, the Montana Commissioner found that Miller-Wohl had violated the Montana Maternity Leave Act (MMLA) by firing Ms. Buley rather than granting her an unpaid disability leave.

Miller-Wohl sparked a serious controversy, one might even say a crisis, in feminist legal community over the meaning of equality for women. Rather than rallying to the Montana statute's defense when Miller-Wohl challenged it in federal court,[2] feminist attorneys split over the statute's validity. For the most part, those attorneys who were instrumental in drafting, lobbying for, and passing Title VII's Pregnancy Discrimination Amendment (PDA) took the position that equality is

---

13 Golden Gate U. L. Rev. 513 (1983).

synonymous with equal treatment, and that any law, such as the MMLA, which deviates from the equal treatment principle is both contrary to Title VII and ultimately dangerous for women. Pregnancy-related disabilities, they contended, can be treated neither better nor worse than non-pregnancy-related medical conditions.

In opposition to this equal treatment view, other feminists, including the authors of this essay, supported the positive action approach of the MMLA. We contended that in some situations, including those presented by pregnancy-related disabilities, equal treatment of the sexes actually results in inequality for women. In these situations, positive action to change the institutions in which women work is essential in achieving women's equality because those institutions are, for the most part, designed with a male prototype in mind. . . .

The *Miller-Wohl* controversy . . . has brought into painfully sharp focus the absence of a consensus among feminists as to the meaning of the term "equality." At an even deeper level, it has unearthed two very different conceptions of the nature and process of social change and their impact on the formulation of political and legal strategies within the women's movement. . . .

[This essay] will examine the legal issues raised by the *Miller-Wohl* case by contrasting the equal treatment approach of the Pregnancy Discrimination Amendment with the positive action or reasonable accommodation approach of the MMLA. Such an examination leads to two conclusions. The first is that the PDA's equal treatment approach is by itself inadequate to assure employment opportunity for women who, because of their role as childbearers, confront employment obstacles not faced by men. The second is that laws such as the MMLA, which recognize and take affirmative steps to equalize this inherent sex difference, can be legally supported without indirectly justifying either less favorable treatment of women in other contexts, or under- and over-inclusive "protective" legislation. . . . [The essay] will demonstrate [that] the liberal model of equality which underlies the equal treatment approach is structurally inadequate to effectuate equality between the sexes. . . .

Equal Treatment versus Positive Action: The Need for Affirmative Job Protection and the Legal Issues Raised by *Miller-Wohl*

The only federal statute which bears significantly on the issue of pregnancy and sex-based employment discrimination is the Pregnancy Discrimination Amendment (PDA) to Title VII of the Civil Rights Act of 1964. . . . It requires only that pregnancy be treated *the same* as other conditions affecting, or not affecting, an employee's ability to work or entitlement to fringe benefits. The PDA does not require that employers grant pregnant workers any affirmative accommodation such as sick leave if they experience pregnancy-related medical complications, or a leave for normal childbirth. Only less favorable treatment of pregnancy as compared to other conditions is prohibited.

. . . This limitation has serious implications for women workers in the United States. More than eighty percent of the female workforce in the United States are in their prime childbearing years, ages fifteen through forty-four. Ninety-three percent of women in this age group are likely to have at least one child during those years.[3] Consequently, more than four out of five female workers in the United States' labor force are likely to become pregnant at some point in their working lives. The House Report recommending passage of the PDA noted the pregnancy and childbirth do result in some time period during which a woman is medically unable to work. For ninety-five percent of women this period is six weeks or less.[4]

In light of these statistics, it is clear that a no-leave policy like Miller-Wohl's is tantamount to a policy of dismissal for pregnancy. But under the equal treatment approach of the PDA, a woman who is terminated for missing work due to pregnancy or childbirth has no legal remedy unless she can prove that a specific and "similarly situated" co-worker was permitted to take a comparable length leave for a non-pregnancy-related reason, and that there was no legitimate nondiscriminatory reason for the difference in treatment.

The essential importance of some affirmative protection for women temporarily disabled by pregnancy-related medical conditions is widely recognized and accommodated by other industrialized nations. In fact, the United States stands alone among all other major industrialized countries, capitalist or socialist, in its failure to guarantee women temporarily disabled due to pregnancy job-protected leave and a cash benefit to replace wages. Among these countries, which include Canada, England, Denmark, Finland, France, West Germany, East Germany, Israel, Norway and Sweden, the minimum leave provided is twelve weeks, while the average is five months. These provisions have their historical basis in the International Labor Organization's Convention on Maternity Protection for Working Women, originally enacted in 1919. When first adopted, the ILO Conventions provided pregnant workers six weeks leave prior to their due date and prohibited them from working in the six weeks following delivery. During the mother's absence from work, she could receive wage replacement benefits funded by a public mandatory insurance system. In 1952, the Convention was amended to extend leave periods, raise cash benefit levels, and to guarantee job security and paid nursing breaks on the mother's return to work. As even those who most staunchly opposed statutes such as the MMLA will admit, the ILO approach provides women with vastly greater assistance in reconciling their dual roles as workers and childbearers than does the "impoverished" PDA. . . .

This problem is exacerbated by two facts characterizing women's status in the American labor market. First, women workers, especially working class women, tend to be segregated into a relatively small number of female dominated occupations. Second, women tend to occupy positions in the "secondary labor market" which is characterized by the absence of union representation, provisions for job security, or fringe benefits. . . .

The fact that men and women tend to be segregated into different occupations makes it more difficult for female employees who are denied pregnancy-related leaves to find a suitable "similarly situated" male employee for comparison purposes. If an employer hires males and females into different types of jobs, there may be differences between those jobs which defeat a disparate treatment claim. This was precisely what happened in the *Miller-Wohl* case. . . .

Women's status as occupants of the secondary labor market has also contributed to the lack of employment protections relating to pregnancy. Women tend to work in unorganized sections of the American labor force. . . . In addition to being unorganized, jobs in the secondary labor market are often designated "temporary" or "part-time" and may be excluded from employer fringe benefit programs, thus precluding a disparate treatment challenge to denial of pregnancy-related benefits which might be possible were women covered by such plans. . . . [Thus,] [t]he PDA's equal treatment approach simply does not meet the real needs of a vast proportion of this country's women workers. . . .

Legal Issues Raised by **Miller-Wohl***:*
The Problem of Federal Preemption

The gravamen of Miller-Wohl's attack on the MMLA was that the literal language of the PDA requires that women affected by pregnancy, childbirth, or related medical conditions be treated *the same* for all employment-related purposes as other persons not so affected, but similar in their ability or inability to work. Because the MMLA as applied to Miller-Wohl's "no leave" policy requires that pregnancy-related conditions be treated more favorably than other disabilities, it conflicts with, and is consequently preempted by, Title VII.

This preemption argument can be adequately countered. Although the MMLA goes further than Title VII in protecting women from discrimination based on pregnancy, the two statutes do not conflict. Congress was aware of and implicitly approved the MMLA when it added the PDA to Title VII in 1978.[5] . . .

In addition to there being no evidence of congressional intent to preempt, it is also apparent that Title VII, the PDA, and the MMLA were enacted to serve the same legislative goals. Title VII was enacted in 1964 to prohibit employment discrimination on the basis of race, sex, color, national origin, and religion. That purpose was further refined in 1978 by the passage of the Pregnancy Discrimination Amendment. Congress' intent in enacting this amendment was "to insure that working women are protected against all forms of employment discrimination based on sex".[6] . . . The legislative history of the MMLA demonstrates that Montana first determined that denial of pregnancy-related disability leaves to women workers constituted sex-based employment discrimination, and then acted to form a remedy to rectify that discrimination.[7] As such, it is clear that Montana lawmakers intended to create equality of opportunity by guaranteeing reasonable leave and job protection to pregnant workers. . . .

The MMLA is also consistent with Title VII in that it in effect recognizes that no-leave policies have an adverse impact on women and therefore constitute sex-based discrimination. . . .

Positive Action Laws and the
Problem of Protective Legislation

In addition to the contention that the MMLA was preempted by the literal language of the PDA, Miller-Wohl argued that the Montana law was a state protective law which, because it provided women with a benefit denied to men, ran afoul of Title VII. The protective legislation issue provoked heated debate within the feminist legal community. Equal treatment proponents argued that the Montana statute is indistinguishable from laws which until very recently "protected" women out of their jobs. Supporting such a statute, they argued, could lend implicit justification to future "protective" laws which would do more harm than good. Advocates of the MMLA's positive action approach, on the other hand, argued that the Montana law can be sufficiently distinguished from the "protective" legislation so recently invalidated.

State protective legislation can take two forms. In its restrictive form, protective legislation limits the employment opportunities of women by excluding them from certain job functions or working conditions, or by denying them entire categories of employment altogether. This type of protective legislation was held to violate Title VII. . . . Clearly, the MMLA is not a restrictive state protective law; it in no way limits the employment opportunities of women. Rather, by assuring that women, who alone can become pregnant, will not lose their jobs as a result of pregnancy-related disabilities, the MMLA promotes equality of opportunity and puts women on an equal footing with men.

[T]here is a second, "beneficial" type of protective legislation which may also violate Title VII. . . . "[B]eneficial" protective legislation will run afoul of Title VII when it requires different treatment of men and women based on stereotypic assumptions about, or normative differences between, the sexes, resulting in under- and over-inclusive classifications.

It is this under- and over-inclusiveness of statutes which classify on the basis of sex or race that brings them into conflict with commonly held notions of equality embodied in the equal protection clause, as well as Title VII. But the Montana law providing for pregnancy-related disability leave is not, and cannot possibly be, under- or over-inclusive. No man will ever *need* a pregnancy-related leave, so the statute is not under-inclusive. No pregnant woman who does not choose or need to go on leave for a pregnancy-related disability is forced to do so by the statute. Therefore it cannot be said to be over-inclusive. . . .

. . . Laws which grant such benefits to women but not to men based on the chauvinistic assumption that women are weaker and thus need these benefits more than men, violate Title VII because they further limit the employment opportunities of women. But the problem treated by the MMLA and the policies underlying the solution it provides are wholly different. Montana's law places women on an *equal* footing with men and permits males and females to compete *equally* in the labor market. The MMLA does not provide women with an additional benefit denied to men; it merely prevents women from having to suffer an additional burden which no male would ever have to bear. . . .

Through a Glass Darkly: Paradigms of Equality and the Challenge of Miller-Wohl

If the *Miller-Wohl* debate has done nothing else, it has revealed a lack of consensus as to, and perhaps a clear understanding of, what is meant by the term sexual equality. . . . With respect to the women's movements of the early and mid-twentieth century, the cry for equality has been a protest against the way things have been, i.e., against disparate treatment of women because of their sex, and not as a description of a unified or clearly envisioned social goal. [P]erhaps the most significant . . . effect of the *Miller-Wohl* debate is to afford feminist legal theorists an opportunity to examine diverse notions of the meaning of sexual equality and to use the term not as a protest against what society is now, but as a vehicle for thinking about what we want society to become.

. . . [V]arious models or paradigms of sexual equality . . . have emerged during the past two decades. . . . Professor Ann Scales identifies and describes four such models which she terms the liberal view, the assimilationist view, the bivalent view, and the incorporationist view.[8] Each of these views has emerged at some point during the *Miller-Wohl* debate. In fact, the controversy could accurately be described as a conflict between adherents of the liberal and incorporationist views. A thorough and critical understanding of these models—of their origins, strengths, and weaknesses—can help chart a course through the present crisis in feminist legal theory.

This section examines these four models in the context of the *Miller-Wohl* debate and asks the following questions: What are their underlying assumptions or theoretical origins and how do these limit their utility? Which groups in society are they best calculated to benefit and whose problems do they leave unaddressed? What are their dangers in the context of today's political and legal climate and how can we adequately guard against these dangers? By . . . asking these . . . questions, two conclusions emerge. The first is that the equal treatment approach to equality cannot, in and of itself, effectuate equality between the sexes. Its analytical assumptions and structural limitations have prevented it from solving the equality problems presented by inherent differences between men and women in the areas of pregnancy and childbirth. The second conclusion is that the equal treatment or "liberal" view of equality must be expanded to permit, indeed to require, positive action accounting for inherent sex differences, and facilitating equality of effect.

The Liberal Model of Equality

The liberal view of equality is primarily concerned with the elimination of laws or social practices which treat women differently than men specifically because of their sex. The historical foundations of the liberal model can be seen in the writings of John Stuart Mill, who in the nineteenth century advocated against laws and social practices which specifically denied women equal civil rights in the areas of property, suffrage, marriage and employment. . . . The liberal view of equality is the theoretical model being advanced by the "equal treatment" proponents in the *Miller-Wohl* debate and has, in fact, been the prevalent ideology of the women's movement of the 1960s and 1970s.

The liberal model of sexual equality is based on two fundamental assumptions. The first is that there are no "real" differences between the sexes; that is, no differences that cannot be dismissed as illusory sex-stereotypes or the normative results of sex-stereotyped socialization, or which cannot be effectively compared to and treated the same as some cross-sex analogous condition. The second is that once all vestiges of disparate treatment are removed, men and women, by virtue of their inherent similarity, will achieve equal status through individual freedom of choice and equal competition in the social and economic marketplace. The dangers and limitations of the liberal view stem from these two basic assumptions.

These assumptions render the model structurally incapable of defining sexual equality in the context of sex-specific conditions such as pregnancy and childbearing, which are non-normative and which are at most only marginally amenable to cross-sex analogy. The liberal view's need to compare exclusively female characteristics to cross-sex analogues often results in reliance on strained analogies which are unconvincing to courts and consequently rejected, leaving courts without a standard for effectuating equality. In addition, it is foreseeable that courts' *acceptance* of the cross-sex comparisons approach could lead to disastrous results in certain abortion cases. Perhaps the most serious flaw in the liberal approach is that by virtue of its second assumption, it accepts maleness as the norm and permits a denial of equality of effect to women who are either unwilling or unable to assimilate to that norm.

THE RELIANCE ON COMPARABLES AND THE PROBLEM OF THE STRAINED ANALOGY

The liberal model works best when "normative" sex differences are used as the basis for sex-based classifications or private decisions regulated by sex discrimination laws.[9] In such contexts, the liberal view, which has gained substantial judicial acceptance in the last decade, establishes that normative differences cannot justify discriminatory classification. It is the characteristics of similarly situated individuals, and not of the groups to which they belong, which must govern classification or selection.

There are, however, some sex differences which are not normative but rather inherent, or exclusive to one sex. The most obvious examples include the capacity to become pregnant and the conditions of pregnancy and childbirth, which characterize women, but not men. When faced with a law or practice in these contexts which is challenged as "unequal," the liberal equal treatment approach must rely on analogy. Without some male characteristic to analogize to the female trait, the model breaks down due to its complete reliance on comparisons of "similarly situated" men and women.

Herein lies the model's first flaw: it relies on courts' willingness to accept imperfectly fitting, often strained analogies, which they have at various times in the past refused to accept. It was this flaw in the comparisons approach that resulted in the plaintiffs' defeat in Geduldig v. Aiello.[10] The plaintiffs' theory in *Geduldig* relied on analogizing pregnancy to medical conditions confronted by men. They argued that pregnancy should be treated the same as prostatectomy, which like pregnancy is exclusive to one sex, or like cosmetic surgery, since both are voluntary, or like a heart attack, since both are expensive. The Supreme Court, however, chose to emphasize the distinctions between pregnancy and these other medical conditions and rejected the analogy, thus stripping the liberal model of its analytical effectiveness.

A corollary problem inherent in the liberal view's reliance on like treatment of groups deemed to be "similarly situated" was revealed in *Geduldig*. Once the Court rejected the preferred analogies and determined that "pregnant women and non-pregnant persons" were not similarly situated, nothing in the liberal model required that they treat pregnant women in a manner that resulted in equality of effect. This results from the fact that the liberal view is a formalistic model; it is only equal treatment that is required, regardless of any inequality of effect that such treatment occasions. . . .

Another manifestation of the limitations of this approach is seen in its inability to serve as a theoretical foundation for the proposition that a woman's right to abortion is an issue of sexual equality. In Roe v. Wade,[11] the Court established a limited constitutional right to abortion, but it did not do so on the grounds that denial of that right violated a woman's right to equal protection of the laws. In fact, Justice Blackmun did not analyze abortion as an issue of sexual equality at all, but rather based the majority opinion on the "penumbral," and significantly qualified, right to privacy implicitly contained in the Bill of Rights. Although various commentators have urged that Roe v. Wade should have been based on an equal protection theory[12] following the liberal model, it is not surprising that the Supreme Court declined to do so. In the abortion, as well as the pregnancy context, the comparisons approach is analytically problematic.

The capacity to become pregnant is unique to women; it is an inherent, not a normative sex difference. Therefore, in order to apply the liberal view's essential principle of like treatment of similarly situated individuals, the proponent would have to rely, as in *Geduldig*, on analogizing pregnancy to some condition unique to men. The argument would go something like this: It is true that only women can become pregnant and desire to have an abortion. But there are many analogous medical conditions that men alone may have for which they may want corrective surgery, such as a vasectomy or a hair transplant. Thus the principle of equal treatment requires that women be able to choose to have an abortion on the same basis that men can choose to have a vasectomy, a hair transplant, or any medical procedure.

As in the pregnancy-related disability context then, the liberal model must rely on the acceptance of the analogy between pregnancy and medical conditions faced by men, on the proposition that abortion and vasectomy are actually the same. To condition a woman's right to abortion on the acceptability of such an analogy would be a grave tactical error. It is likely that to both the Supreme Court and the American public, the distinctions between the condition of pregnancy, of a potential child developing within a woman's body, and any medical condition faced by a man, would leap out with much greater force and vigor than the similarities. The liberal model, however, relies completely on the acceptance of the analogy. It fails to focus on the effect of the very *real* sex difference of pregnancy on the relative positions of men and women in society and on the goal of assuring equality of opportunity and effect within a heterogeneous "society of equals." This is the same flaw, stemming from the formalistic nature of the liberal view, that led to the plaintiffs' downfall in Geduldig v. Aiello.

Given that the liberal view has been offered to the courts by feminist litigators and legal theorists as virtually the exclusive paradigm in sex discrimination law, it is not surprising that it is on the issues of pregnancy and abortion, where cross-sex analogies are weak, that women have made the least progress in the courts. Neither is it hard to understand why after reading Roe v. Wade or Geduldig v. Aiello, the feminist is left with the distinct impression that somehow in the midst of all this complex if not contorted analysis, the Court has missed the point. The liberal model of sexual equality is only as strong as the analogy upon which it relies. If feminist litigators continue to rely exclusively on that model, we are not apt to make substantial progress in obtaining functional equality for women in the areas of pregnancy and abortion. We need a supplemental construct which does not rely on homogeneity between the sexes.

In its failure to come to grips with the meaning of equality in the context of inherent sex differences not susceptible of cross-sex analogy, the liberal view also declines the opportunity to define clearly the distinction between a sex difference which can justify differential treatment and one which cannot. The absence of such a standard has two consequences. The first is that a large degree of uncontrollable subjectivity as to whether a sex-based classification is "substantially related to the achievement of an important government objective" is introduced into the legal analysis in equal protection cases. The second consequence is that the liberal view's insistence that differences can never justify differential treatment could lead to results in the abortion context that the vast majority of women, feminist and non-feminist alike, would find completely unacceptable.

. . . Throughout the *Miller-Wohl* debate, equal treatment proponents have stressed that any acknowledgment that pregnancy is in some way a unique condition potentially warranting special treatment of some kind is extremely dangerous and must be avoided. [A] *failure* to acknowledge that pregnancy is in some ways a unique condition deserving special treatment may also lead to disastrous results. The equal treatment approach inherent in the liberal model focuses excessively on an attempt to "nullify" sex differences. It does not articulate standards for the proper equality-effectuating implications of those differences. It is in the areas of pregnancy and childbirth, where differences between men and women are the most marked, that this structural limitation causes troubling results.

. . . [T]he primary defect in the liberal feminist's concept of equality is that it accepts an inherent assumption that men are the norm. Women are permitted to compete with men under the same rules and within the same institutions, but those institutions were designed in accordance with normative male values, priorities and characteristics. The liberal model, in and of itself, does nothing to require that those rules or structures be changed to accommodate the normative or inherent needs, values or priorities of women.

The result of this is that any individual or group of women that in fact differs from the male norm will be correspondingly disadvantaged in the competitive marketplace and will find no remedy under the liberal view. Thus, the model works relatively well for women who are willing and able to conform to the male norm. . . .

However, the model works significantly less well for women who deviate substantially from the male norm, specifically working class and single mothers. The failure of the liberal model in addressing these women's difficulties in balancing their dual role cannot be over-emphasized. . . .

The liberal view's appeal to the political elite is strong because it accepts and reflects the unarticulated postulates of American equality theory: the assumptions of homogeneity and interchangeability within a society of equals, and the individualistic theory of rights. . . . [However,] [l]iberal American political theory, upon which jurisprudential constructs of equality have in large part been based, has been unable to develop a theory of nonhierarchial pluralism which accommodates differences within the society of equals.

Likewise, the liberal view is superficially persuasive because it views equality as an individual right, and, like the mainstream political theory on which it is based, elevates equality of treatment over equality of effect. However, a close examination of the reasons for the liberal model's persuasive value reveals that those very characteristics accounting for its appeal are also the source of its inability to solve many of the most pressing race and sex equality problems of our time.

EQUALITY AND THE ASSUMPTION OF HOMOGENEITY

The fact that homogeneity was a prerequisite for admission to the American "society of equals" can be observed in written expressions of colonial and revolutionary era political theory. . . . [D]uring the colonial and revolutionary era . . . homogeneity was a necessary condition of equality. Black slaves, Indians, Chinese, and women were observed as being distinct from and thus innately incapable of assimilating into the homogeneous Anglo-Saxon male core. Their exclusion from the society of equals was consequently not only justified, but logically necessary. Equality was predicated on homogeneity. . . .

The liberal view's insistence on a strict equal treatment approach to pregnancy reflects the same implicit acceptance that assimilation is a prerequisite to equality. . . . Its ardent deemphasis of even those "real" differences between the sexes that pregnancy epitomizes is, in effect, an effort to say: "See, we are really just like you and (consequently) we have a right to be your equals."

Before accepting the liberal view because of its high persuasive value, the principles which make it so appealing should be critically examined. The assumption of homogeneity, although deeply rooted in our national ideology, has operated to deny equality to groups that would not or could not assimilate. . . .

THE EQUAL TREATMENT MODEL AND THE
INDIVIDUALISTIC THEORY OF RIGHTS

In addition to the homogeneity assumption and assimilationist imperatives discussed above, a second and related factor accounting for the appeal of the liberal view is that it accepts the same individualistic theory of rights which underlies majority American equal protection jurisprudence. This individualism principle strengthens the "persuasive value" of the equal treatment theory. But it is also the source of that construct's inability to provide solutions to many of the current issues regarding equality between the sexes and the races.

The individualistic theory of rights stems from the Enlightenment era reductionist philosophy of John Locke and Thomas Hobbes.[13] The individualism principle dissociates the individual person from any context of family, religion, or class and invests in him *as an individual*, certain "natural" or "inalienable" rights. In the context of equality theory, Lockean reductionism posits that each individual has a right to be treated as other similarly situated individuals, or that each has the right to equal access to a particular opportunity, resource or burden. Equal treatment is the touchstone of the individualistic theory of rights. Its influence on American jurisprudence can hardly be over-emphasized. In addition to the direct influence on jurisprudential concepts of equality, the individualism principle has an indirect, more subtle effect on the way we conceptualize what is "equal," and what is not, and encourages a broad interpretation of the notion of "similarly situated persons." This tendency can be seen in the *Miller-Wohl* debate in the controverted issue of whether or not a man who is nauseous with a hangover and misses work is "similarly situated" with a woman who has morning sickness. The equal treatment proponents focus on the point of view of the individual man and the individual woman in defining similar situation. Conversely, the positive action advocates focus on the potentially disparate effect of a no-leave policy on men as a group and women as a group. The equal treatment view's adherence to an individualistic approach to equality enhances its "persuasive value," in the minds of those inculcated with the theoretical precepts of Anglo-American law.

Before concluding however that the equal treatment model is the better or the only model to support, the problematic "underside" of individualistic jurisprudence should be examined. Such an examination reveals that the same individualistic theory of rights which makes the equal treatment mode so "persuasive" in the context of the *Miller-Wohl* debate is also responsible for the Supreme Court's decision in Regents of the University of California v. Bakke,[14] which invalidated the University of California at Davis Medical School's affirmative action plan.

It is easy, after reading the *Bakke* decision, to be left with the feeling that somehow, the Supreme Court missed a very important point—that somehow the "equality" effectuated by the elimination of affirmative action admissions programs is neither "equal" nor "just.". . . The Court's treatment of the *Bakke* case, and the entire concept of "reverse discrimination" reveal a fundamental flaw in the individualistic theory of rights. The individualistic view exalts equality of treatment over equality of effect and, as a result, is unable to ameliorate the material conditions of inequality characterizing our society.

In his book *Taking Rights Seriously*,[15] Ronald Dworkin points out that the concept of equality can be viewed in two very different ways. The first is to view the right to equality as a right to equal treatment. The second is to view equality as the right to treatment as an equal, which focuses on equality of effect rather than equality of treatment. Dworkin distinguishes these two concepts with the following illustration.

Assume a person has two children, and one is dying of a disease which is making the other merely uncomfortable. In such a situation, if the parent has but one remaining dose of a drug, she does not divide it in half and treat the two children "equally." She gives the remaining dose to the dying child, hoping to keep them both alive.

This illustration demonstrates two points. The first is that the right to treatment as an equal is morally fundamental and the right to equal treatment derivative. The second is that, in some circumstances, the right to treatment as an equal entails a right to equal treatment, but sometimes it does not. Equality can be seen as an individual right to equal treatment or as a social policy promoting equality of effect—a distinction that American jurisprudence and political theory has virtually ignored.

In the context of the affirmative action controversy, the individualistic model conceptualizes equality as a personal right rather than as a social policy; it exalts equality of treatment over equality of effect. Mr. Bakke gets into medical school, but blacks remain proportionally excluded from the medical profession. The appearance of equality embodied in uncompromised equal treatment takes precedence over the goal of equality of effect as a social reality. . . .

The strict equal treatment position being advanced in the *Miller-Wohl* debate falls into the same "individualism trap" that resulted in the Court's *Bakke* decision. . . . The result of the individualistic analysis in each case is the same: the appearance of equality that equal treatment provides takes precedence over equality of effect.

The individualistic conception of rights is not worthy of feminists' exclusive support. As Fiss reminds us, it contains "structural limitations that prevent it from adequately resolving or even addressing certain central claims of equality being advanced. For these claims, the antidiscrimination principle either provides no framework of analysis or, even worse, provides the wrong one."[16] . . . In addition to the homogeneity and individualism assumptions discussed above, there is a third, similarly related, factor which both accounts for the liberal model's appeal, and proves to be the source of its limitations.

The individualism principle discussed above, when linked with the ideal of equality, combines to form the construct of interchangeability. The interchangeability principle posits that individual members of different groups are inherently no different from one another by virtue of their group identity. Given the necessary training and experience, a constituent of one racial, ethnic or sexual group could take the place of another. It would thus be a violation of an individual's right to equality to treat him or her differently from members of another group, even if the two groups manifest normative differences.

At various points in American political history, the dominant group has opposed the extension of equal rights to a subordinate group by attacking the assumption of interchangeability. So, for example, the case against equality of civil rights for women was largely based on the argument that women were inherently "different" from men. Women were not seen to be interchangeable with men, and were deemed inadmissible into the "society of equals."

It is no surprise then that feminists advocating equality for women would have attacked this noninterchangeability assumption justifying their opponents' position. It has been a primary goal of the women's movement since the 1960s—to refute the argument that women are inherently distinct from the male core. The liberal view advanced by these women and their male supporters *accepts* the interchangeability prerequisite and attempts to establish that women fulfill it. Liberal feminism accepts the predominant cultural and political ideology, and for that reason has "high persuasive value."

Given that American equality theory is based on an assumption of interchangeability, it is also not surprising that feminists' most successful legal forays have involved rectifying cases of sexual inequality in situations where the sexes are not inherently different. In such cases the courts, once presented with sufficient sociological evidence of interchangeability, have been able to base their decision on a well-established construct of equality that leaves the homogeneity, individualism and interchangeability principles intact. But in the context of pregnancy and abortion, the courts, unable to find these three constructs present, have been noticeably less successful in dealing with equality issues. Neither mainstream American political theory nor American jurisprudence has yet developed a construct of equality that actually facilitates equality of effect in the context of functional heterogeneity between the sexes.

The fundamental mistake being made by the strict "equal treatment" proponents is that they make no attempt to supplement the interchangeability/homogeneity theory of equality that has permitted so many injustices in the legal and political history of our society. The liberal view works well in many situations and should not be discarded. But unless the goal of feminist jurisprudence is only to obtain a "piece of the pie" for women who approximate the male norm, the liberal model of equality must be complemented by another theory which will assure equality of effect within a heterogeneous group. Elizabeth Wolgast's model provides such a construct.

The Bivalent View

In her provocative book, *Equality and the Rights of Women*,[17] Elizabeth Wolgast proposes a paradigm of sexual equality which she refers to as the "bivalent" view. This view differs considerably from the liberal model. Wolgast rejects the two primary tenets of the liberal feminist view: that sex differences are "illusory," and that equal treatment of the sexes will result in functional equality. Rather, she asserts that the differences between men and women are substantial, and that sexual equality will result only if society deals with sex differences respectfully and fairly by developing accommodating institutions which permit equality of effect. In short, Wolgast acknowledges that the conditions of the sexes, at least in some respects, are asymmetrical or heterogeneous, and sets out to devise a conception of equality that takes this asymmetry into account, something which the liberal model is structurally unable to do.

The essence of Wolgast's theory is that there are two types of rights: "equal" rights and "special" rights. In explicating the differences between these two types of rights, Wolgast uses the following illustration. Within our society, every individual is deemed to have an "equal" right of access to public buildings. That this right is an "equal right" means that with respect to that right, any one person is interchangeable with any other. The right adheres to every individual. But, a disabled person who uses a wheelchair will be unable to exercise this "equal" right unless a ramp is provided. He or she is not being affirmatively discriminated against or denied equal treatment. But the effect of no ramp is a denial of the equal right. In such a circumstance, equality is effectuated only if the disabled person is granted a "special" right to a ramp.[18]

Wolgast's illustration demonstrates that the failure to provide a "special" right to a group whose members are disadvantaged because they deviate from the norm has the effect of denying them an "equal" right to which they are entitled. In such a situation, to accord members of the institutionally disadvantaged group equal treatment denies them equality. This harkens back to Dworkin's illustration involving the two sick children: The "equal" right to continued life can be effectuated only if the dying child has a "special" right to receive the one remaining dose of medication. . . .

One can see that Wolgast's model reconciles the fact of heterogeneity with the theoretical construct of interchangeability underlying traditional egalitarian thinking. Her view acknowledges the fact that institutions such as employment policies, building access, etc. were designed in accordance with normative standards to which some groups within society do not conform. By affording those individuals a special right accommodating their difference, institutions are modified so that the principle of interchangeability is restored. So long as the building has a ramp, the walker and a wheelchair user can be substituted one for the other.

Wolgast's bivalent view of rights provides a cogent and convincing justification for laws such as the MMLA, a justification which is consistent with statutory and case law regarding reasonable accommodation of religion and physical disability. Every individual has a right to equal employment opportunity. However, men and women are not interchangeable with respect to physical conditions which may affect their need to be absent from work. In addition to all the medical disabilities that members of either sex may face, or those sex-specific disabilities for which there exists some cross-sex analogue, women have the capacity to, and do, become pregnant. As a result, they are subjected to an additional disability that no man will confront. Thus, in the context of an employer with a no-sick leave policy such as Miller-Wohl's, men and women will not have equal employment opportunity. Women will be disadvantaged. In order to effectuate equality of opportunity, the MMLA provides women with a "special right" to a reasonable unpaid leave. . . . The MMLA is nothing more than a reasonable accommodation statute, such as those statutes feminists generally support in the context of discrimination against the disabled or against members of religious minorities.

Wolgast's bivalent model can contribute substantially to efforts to effectuate women's equality. Its most significant analytical asset is that it eliminates the assimilationist imperative implicit in the liberal view. Under Wolgast's model, women do not have to be proven homogeneous with men in order to gain admission to the "society of equals." On the contrary, the bivalent view provides for changes in societal institutions to accommodate differences. It does not require that women assimilate into institutions built with a white male norm in mind, which often leaves women swimming up a swiftly moving stream.

Wolgast offers a model of sexual equality which can deal with issues such as pregnancy or abortion. Consider for example how the issue of a woman's right to abortion could be established by an application of the bivalent model of equality. Anglo-American jurisprudence implicitly recognizes that individual members of society are invested with a right to bodily integrity. . . . This right is an "equal" right, possessed by every individual. With respect to this right, every member of society, black, white, male or female should be interchangeable. But women and men are different from one another. Women have the capacity to become pregnant, while men do not. Unless women are accorded the special right to abortion, they will in effect be denied access to the equal right to bodily integrity. Seen in this way, laws prohibiting abortion clearly abrogate women's right to equality on the basis of sex. The bivalent model has the capacity to effectuate equality in the context of functional heterogeneity, and for this reason can provide a constructive companion to the more traditional "anti-discrimination" principle.

However, the bivalent view leaves unaddressed a very troubling issue. Any theory that permits the conferral of special rights based on differences between groups must logically permit the imposition of special burdens based on differences as well. This concern is expressed by equal treatment adherents because permitting special "positive" treatment of pregnancy opens the door to special "negative" treatment as well.

Wolgast recognizes that this is a problem inherent in the bivalent view:

> The problem of women's rights has this two-sided form. In regard to some rights we want to say that sex is an important difference and ought to have a bearing on rights. With respect to others we want to say that it is unimportant and, like race, ought to be entirely ignored. Is there a single principle by which the two kinds of rights can be sorted?[19]

After an intriguing review of a variety of modern equal protection cases, Wolgast concludes that no such principle can be found. From the point of view of the feminist legal strategist, this is a serious flaw in the bivalent model. For as Scales points out, absent such a limiting principle, the bivalent approach to equal protection cases could be a constitutional disaster. "Without a rule limiting which differences between the sexes can be taken into account and a requirement that in all other circumstances men and women be treated as equals, its proponents have their feet planted on the slippery slope of judicial stereotyping."[20]

Nothing in the bivalent view prohibits the use of normative differences to trigger the conferral of special rights resulting in over- and under-inclusive sex-based classifications. . . .

In permitting normative differences to be used to trigger special rights, the bivalent view could lead to the reinforcement of societal norms and attitudes having their basis in stereotypical sex roles. . . . This absence of a limiting principle permits over- and under-inclusive classifications which violate the disparate treatment principle so fundamental to our society's conception of equality. . . .

A Limiting Principle for the Bivalent View: The Incorporationist Approach

In "Towards a Feminist Jurisprudence," Scales proposes a limiting principle which, when combined with Wolgast's bivalent model, results in what Scales terms an "incorporationist" approach. This approach posits that women should be regarded as having rights different from men only with respect to sex-specific conditions which are completely unique to women, namely pregnancy and breast-feeding. Under the incorporationist view, normative differences between the sexes cannot serve as the basis for the conferral of special rights or burdens.

This is an extremely important and constructive modification of the bivalent approach, which, while limiting it, leaves the bivalent model's conceptual advantages intact. In requiring that the differences triggering special rights be inherent as opposed to normative, the incorporationist approach would . . . eliminate the possibility of over- and under-inclusive classifications which offend prevailing conceptions of equality. It also guards against the conferral of special rights or burdens based on stereotypic assumptions about the differences between the sexes which could perpetuate limiting, stereotypic sex roles. Yet at the same time, the incorporationist model recognizes the existence of some inherent sex differences, and in permitting their accommodation, equalizes the relative positions of men and women in a culture whose institutions were designed with a male norm in mind. As Scales points out, the currently dominant liberal view tends to minimize the process of childbearing in an unrealistic way that operates to women's detriment. The incorporation of childbearing into social institutions, as is permitted by the bivalent and incorporationist views, "has the advantage of reflecting the realities of women's lives."[21]

The assumptions underlying the liberal and incorporationist views are very different. Under the liberal view, sex differences, including inherent sex differences such as pregnancy and childbearing, are minimized. No provision is made for their accommodation by societal institutions. The result is that to avoid being disadvantaged in a society modeled to suit a male prototype, women must conform to a male norm. In contrast, the incorporationist view requires, or at least permits, the modification of those institutions to accommodate differences and to equalize the "competitive" position of the sexes. The incorporationist model embodies a transformational approach to respectful accommodation of differences, whereas the liberal view leaves the male norm and the assimilationist imperative intact.

Should the *Miller-Wohl* case be reincarnated in another guise, it will offer feminist litigators an opportunity to present a version of the incorporationist view as a new model for sexual equality. The liberal comparisons approach to equality is in many instances useful, but alone it has not, and cannot, adequately address a number of the most pressing equality issues confronting women today. An additional construct, one which can effectuate equality in the context of inherent sex differences, must be developed and presented to the courts.

Conflicting Paradigms of Change: Metaphysical versus Dialectical Materialist Analysis of the Pregnancy Disability Issue

The previous section explored how the equal treatment and positive action positions in the *Miller-Wohl* debate reflect profoundly different conceptions about the meaning of equality. Stepping forward one more step into the anatomy of the

Miller-Wohl controversy, one can observe even more fundamental conceptual differences between adherents of the two opposing views. The strict equal treatment approach is based on a metaphysical conception of the nature and process of social change, in contrast to the dialectical and materialistic conception underlying positive action arguments. The metaphysical analytic origins of the equal treatment approach, like its reliance on a liberal model of equality, limit its ability to address and solve major equality problems confronting women in American society. This limitation can be remedied only by a more materialist, dialectic approach to the formulation of legal strategies. To analyze the *Miller-Wohl* debate in this context, it is first necessary to understand what is meant by the terms "metaphysical" and "dialectical materialist" thinking.

Metaphysical thinking has three outstanding characteristics. First, it entails thinking about things in the abstract rather than in the material temporal context in which they are found. Second, it entails thinking about things in light of preconceived formulae or theories, defining them as either "this" or "that," entailing an "either-or" dichotomy which remains constant over time. And third, it views the process of development as one of continuous, unidirectional movement towards an ultimate ideal. If these three characteristics are examined in the context of the *Miller-Wohl* debate, the metaphysical ideology underlying opposition to positive action statutes such as the MMLA can clearly be seen.

The very essence of metaphysics is to think about things in an abstract way, in light of some theory or scheme of existence, isolated from the concrete, material circumstances in which the "thing" is found to exist. . . .

The equal treatment proponents in the *Miller-Wohl* debate are thinking metaphysically. They approach the question of whether to support statutes such as the MMLA by asking whether or not the statute conforms to a particular legal construct, i.e., the equal treatment principle. They focus the debate on legal theoretical levels, rather than starting with an analysis of the concrete material problems of women in the workforce. As a result of this theoretical orientation, equal treatment proponents are willing, albeit regretfully, to accept the fact that the PDA's equal treatment approach is actually inadequate to address the problems of women workers with respect to their role as childbearers. The metaphysical thinker is programmed to accept the fact that the model does not ameliorate these material problems. This is a necessary and accepted result of metaphysically oriented political strategy-making.

The second characteristic of metaphysical thinking is that it seeks to fix the nature, properties and potentialities of everything it considers once and for all. A thing is either "this" or "that," and once so designated, remains in the same designation accompanied by the same value judgment across temporal contexts. Consequently, metaphysical thinking views things in terms of set antitheses. It opposes things of one sort to things of another sort, and everything must fit into one or the other exclusive categories or formulae, where it remains over time.

This conception characterizes the arguments raised by equal treatment proponents as well. They seek to "fix" the nature of the MMLA within one of two mutually exclusive designations. According to this view, a statute provides for either "equal treatment" (read "equality") or "special treatment" (read "inequality"). All equal treatment provisions are inherently the same and seen as "good for women." All "special treatment" statutes are inherently the same and seen as "bad for women," thus dangerous, and not to be supported.

It is a result of metaphysical thinking that the "equal treatment" proponent sees no distinction between the MMLA and "protectionist" statutes excluding women from various professions, even though the former expands employment opportunities for women while the latter restricts them. The equal treatment advocate classifies the MMLA with other "protectionist" legislation of the late nineteenth and early twentieth centuries, and, seeing both as examples of "differential treatment," labels them "dangerous" and promoting of "inequality," regardless of their immediate, concrete effect on existing, material social conditions.

The arguments in favor of a strict equal treatment approach to pregnancy also reflect a metaphysical conception of the process of social change and development by which evolution is seen as a continuous, unidirectional, although variably paced progress towards the realization of an absolute, abstract ideal. The social activist governed by a metaphysical conception of change attempts to propagate an ideal view of society and seeks to implement changes which bring the observed into ever-increasing theoretical conformity with the abstracted ideal. Metaphysical thinking, in its concentration on this idea, often pays little attention to the distinction between reformist and transformational change, or to an analysis of which is more or less likely to be effectuated at a particular time and within particular material social conditions. The ideal must be increasingly approximated with each step, and no change which is seen as ideologically contradictory with the ideal is deemed "progressive."

This ideology is reflected in many equal treatment arguments, most notably in the position that because we ultimately want to see *all* disabilities accommodated by employers, it is not only inadequate, but also "counter-progressive" to support a statute that covers only pregnancy-related ills. To take the partial step, the argument goes, acts as a sort of political "steam valve" that *inhibits* rather than advances progress towards the social goal. At the same time, the partial step is claimed to cause divisions and animosities between men and women which also hinder progress. Thus, the metaphysical cry is always for immediate conformity with the ideal, with relatively little regard for the material social or political conditions of the times in which the issue is joined.

The metaphysically based "steam-valve" view of partial reform is not borne out by experience. Consider, for example, the course of the ILO Conventions. When first enacted in 1919, and as amended in 1952, the Conventions had some serious flaws. Specifically, they provided certain childrearing related benefits to mothers and not to fathers; they contained over- and under-inclusive sex biases. In Europe now, however, there is a movement towards new conventions which provide childrearing related benefits to both working parents. In the social and political context of 1919 and the 1950s, the Convention was a progressive step, even with its sex-biased provisions. In accordance with changing attitudes about sex roles, modifications are being made to improve the old scheme. The sex-biased provisions of the first ILO scheme did *not* prevent this transformation from occurring. The net result will soon be that European countries will have a positive, comprehensive social scheme for accommodating the needs of working parents, while America will have the PDA.

The effect of metaphysical thinking on the participants of the *Miller-Wohl* debate is understandable. Anglo-American law, like Anglo-American political philosophy, is a metaphysical system of thought. As lawyers, we have been thoroughly trained in its precepts. Legal analysis embodies all three of the characteristics discussed above. First, lawyers are often criticized by laypeople because they approach problems abstractly, theoretically, without primary consideration for the material conditions of the "real world." Second, the process of legal analysis involves categorizing events into preconceived theoretical constructs, designating them into sets of opposing formulae, where, once designated, they remain over time and across varying material circumstances. Third, the law envisions progress as being continuous and definitely noncontradictory. The very foundation of legal thinking is the concept of precedent and of theoretical consistency with precedent. Contradiction is abhorrent to the law.

Legal analysis must be a central consideration in the process of deciding what to do about statutes such as the MMLA. An assessment of the legal implications and potential consequences of any given strategy is crucial. However, legal analysis should not be the only one considered. Feminist legal theorists must be aware of the nonconscious assumptions and practical implications of the metaphysical world view that underpins legal analysis, and must consider alternative ideological constructs and their applications. To do otherwise subordinates the interests of our constituents to the goal of consistency with the precepts of Anglo-American jurisprudence.

The metaphysical system is not the only method of analysis available in deciding what to do about the pregnancy disability dilemma. The process can be examined dialectically and materially as well. In contrast to metaphysics, a dialectical way of thinking is rooted in the observation that, in processes taking place in society, as in the natural world, things come into being, change, and pass out of being, not as separate, individual units, but in essential relation and interconnection.[22] In contrast to the dualism of metaphysics, nothing can be understood separately, as an abstract unit, but only in light of its relation and interconnection with its material/temporal context and with ongoing processes of change and development.

This ideological foundation results in a sharp divergence from the three characteristics of metaphysical thinking discussed above. First, the dialectical materialist method teaches that strategy decisions should be made not according to theoretical abstractions, but in light of the material circumstances of each particular temporal and social context. Applied to the *Miller-Wohl* controversy, the most important question to be asked is: "What are the material needs of working women, and what strategy can best meet those needs now?" The fact that given the choice between the PDA and the ILO Conventions, working women would choose the latter takes on greater significance under dialectical materialist analysis than under the metaphysical approach.

Second, dialectical materialist thinking does not classify things in "either-or" dichotomies remaining consistent over time and across social and political contexts. Rather, dialectics urges that no one position or strategy can be characterized as "progressive" or "reactionary," "helpful" or "dangerous," outside of its relation to the whole and to the time and place in which it arises. Internal contradictions are inherent in all things and phenomena—all have positive and negative sides, a past and a future. The process of change takes place not continuously or unidirectionally, but "dialectically." As the material context interacts with the properties of any particular thing, that "thing" rises, then manifests contradictions, then is replaced by something else in a synthetic, transformational process.

To illustrate the differences between metaphysical and dialectical thinking in this regard, it is instructive to examine the divergent views the equal treatment and positive action proponents hold of the "protective legislation" issue. One of the equal treatment advocates' most emotionally powerful arguments is that the MMLA is "just like" the protective legislation of the late nineteenth and early twentieth centuries. Although enacted to protect women, equal treatment adherents claim such legislation limited women's employment opportunities. The metaphysically thinking equal treatment proponent concludes from the course of protective legislation that such legislation, and any other that fits into the "special treatment" construct was, is, and always will be detrimental to women. Consequently, no "special treatment" legislation should be supported, regardless of temporal or historical context.

Dialectical thinking leads to a quite different analysis of the protective legislation issue. It recognizes that, when first proposed and enacted, much of protective legislation, such as that limiting working hours and providing minimum salaries, was a very progressive reform given the material conditions in which it arose. In many cases it ameliorated the crushing exploitation to which women workers of that era were subjected, an exploitation largely unmitigated by the male-dominated labor unions. It is also reasonable to assume, although further research into this issue would be needed to conclude, that the enactment of wages and hours legislation for women and children facilitated the eventual extension of such benefits to men as well.

But, counters the metaphysical thinker, protective legislation, whatever benefit it might have provided at one time, ended up being used to the detriment of women. Consequently, it was a mistake to enact it in the early twentieth century, and anything based on a similar "special treatment" model should be eschewed now.

The dialectical thinker comes to a very different conclusion about the eventual harmful use of some "protective" statutes and its implications for present and future strategies. The dialectician observes that, unavoidably, as the material conditions of American society changed between the late 1800s and early 1900s and the 1950s, the same legislation which was "progressive" became "reactionary." As it interacted with the process of change, the contradictions inherent in protective legislation became apparent, just as they do in all things, and a transformation took place in the form of extension of benefits to men and the injunctions against disparate treatment. . . .

Metaphysical thinking attempts to freeze this process of ascendance, contradiction and transformation and jump all of a piece into an idealized future. It looks at a detached piece of the course of protective legislation (the contradictions phase) and consequently categorizes any legislation based on a special treatment model as "bad" and equal treatment statutes as "good," regardless of their social or temporal contexts. The dialectical interpretation is quite different. It suggests that, viewed over the course of time, protective legislation or any "special treatment" legislation is inherently neither progressive nor regressive; it has no nature as one or the other independent of its relation to the entire ever-changing social context in which it exists.

To judge the value of positive action laws regarding pregnancy and childbirth, feminist legal theorists should not think abstractly, but should look at the material circumstances confronting women now. Any strategy which is successfully implemented will, without doubt, eventually be revealed to contain contradictions which manifest themselves as disadvantages. The once progressive strategy will become regressive and require transformation—a transformation which both history and science teach will take place. It may not take place without effort, but it will take place. The error inherent in the metaphysical thinking of equal treatment advocates is that it seeks to bypass this process of change and therefore in the attempt will inhibit it. Positive action statutes such as the MMLA can facilitate substantive, rather than merely formalistic, equality between men and women. Such statutes deserve the support of the feminist legal community.

Conclusion

The *Miller-Wohl* case brought into uncomfortable focus the limitations of the equal treatment theory which feminist attorneys have advocated and relied upon for many years. With these limitations apparent, we have a difficult choice to make. We can continue to rely exclusively on, and attempt to strengthen, the equal treatment approach, but in the process leave unremedied equality problems not solved by equal treatment analysis. Or, we can begin to develop a supplemental construct which can better effectuate equality in the face of heterogeneity, but face the potential dangers and uncertainties such an endeavor will entail.

There are no easy answers to the problems presented by the *Miller-Wohl* debate. At times it seems to present a web of unsolvable dilemmas and irresolvable contradictions. But our most serious mistake would be to ignore the opportunities that those dilemmas and contradictions represent for expanding feminist jurisprudence. . . .

Notes

1. Mont. Rev. Codes Ann. § 39-7-203 (1981); Conn. Gen. Stat. Ann. § 46a-60 (West 1982); Cal. Gov't Code § 12945 (West 1980).

2. Miller-Wohl filed a declaratory judgment action in federal district court, maintaining that the MMLA, which it admitted having violated, was unconstitutional and in conflict with Title VII. The district court upheld the validity of the MMLA as to both the constitutional and statutory challenges. 515 F. Supp. 1264, 1266 (D. Mont. 1981). Miller-Wohl appealed the district court's decision to the Ninth Circuit. The Ninth Circuit did not decide the case on the merits. Rather, following the argument raised by *amici curiae* California Department of Fair Employment and Housing, Employment Law Center, and Equal Rights Advocates, Inc., the court held that the district court did not have subject matter jurisdiction over the case and ordered it dismissed. Miller-Wohl Co. v. Commissioner of Labor & Indust., 685 F.2d 1088 (9th Cir. 1982). [Similar issues were presented to the Supreme Court subsequently in the case of California Federal Savings and Loan Association v. Guerra, 479 U.S. 272 (1987). The *Miller-Wohl* judgment was vacated and the case remanded for further consideration in light of *Cal. Fed.*, 479 U.S. 1050 (1987). *Ed.*]

3. Kamerman, Maternity and Parental Benefits and Leaves: An International Review 8 (1980), *cited in* Brief of Amici Curiae at 23, Miller-Wohl Co. v. Commissioner of Labor & Indus., 685 F.2d 1088 (9th Cir. 1982).

4. H.R. Rep. No. 948, 95th Cong., 2d sess. 5, *reprinted in* 1978 U.S. Code Cong. & Ad. News 4749, 4753. The House Report states: "[T]estimony before the Committee indicates that in 95 percent of the cases, the time lost from work due to pregnancy is 6 weeks or less, so barring any medical complications, this period would be the normal time a pregnant woman would be covered."

5. The House Committee Report includes the finding that "[t]he following six States, as well as the District of Columbia, specifically include pregnancy in their Fair Employment Practices laws: Alaska, Connecticut, Maryland, Minnesota, Oregon, and Montana." H.R. Rep. No. 948, *supra* note 4, at 11, *reprinted in* 1978 U.S. Code Cong. & Ad. News 475. Montana's law was also alluded to in the Senate debate by Senator Williams, a sponsor of the Pregnancy Discrimination Amendment. 123 Cong. Rec. 29,648 (1977). Approval of such laws was reiterated throughout the legislative reports. See, e.g., S. Rep. No. 331, 95th Cong., 1st sess. 3 (1977). . . .

6. S. Rep. No. 331, 95th Cong., 1st sess. 3 (1977). Discriminatory employment practices based on pregnancy have always been at the core of the problems faced by working women, and it is clear from legislative history that Congress intended to forbid these discriminatory practices. While congressional concern

was focused particularly on the issue of temporary disability insurance benefits for pregnancy, Congress explicitly stated its broader goals: "Although recent attention has been focused on the coverage of disability benefits programs, the consequences of other discriminatory employment policies on pregnant women and women in general has historically had a persistent and harmful effect upon their careers. Women are still subject to the stereotype that all women are marginal workers. Until a woman passes the child-bearing age, she is viewed by employers as potentially pregnant. Therefore, the elimination of discrimination based on pregnancy in these employment practices in addition to disability and medical benefits will go a long way toward providing equal employment opportunities for women, the goal of Title VII of the Civil Rights Act of 1964." H.R. Rep. No. 948, *supra* note 4, at 6–7, *reprinted in* U.S. Code Cong. & Ad. News 4754–55.

7. See Minutes of the Meeting, Labor and Employment Relations Committee, Mont. State Sen., February 3 and 5, 1975; Montana Legislative Council Equality of the Sexes, Interim Study by The Subcommittee on Judiciary, 1974 Leg. Sess. Montana.

8. Scales, Towards a Feminist Jurisprudence, 56 Ind. L.J. 375 (1980–81).

9. A "normative" sex difference refers to a statistical variance in the extent to which males, on the average, and females, on the average, exhibit a certain aptitude, interest, or characteristic, such as physical strength.

10. Geduldig v. Aiello, 417 U.S. 484 (1974), reh'g, Aiello v. Hansen, 359 F. Supp. 792 (N.D. Cal. 1973) (exclusion of pregnancy-related disabilities from a state administered disability insurance plan did not constitute a denial of equal protection of the laws to women.) . . .

11. 410 U.S. 113 (1973).

12. See, e.g., Regan, Rewriting Roe v. Wade, 77 Mich. L. Rev. 1569 (1979).

13. See T. Hobbes, The Citizen (Appleton-Century-Crofts, 1949); Laslett, Introduction to J. Locke, Two Treatises of Government (Cambridge University Press, 1960).

14. 438 U.S. 265 (1978).

15. R. Dworkin, Taking Rights Seriously (Harvard University Press, 1978).

16. O. Fiss, Groups and the Equal Protection Clause, in, M. Cohen, T. Nagel & T. Scanlon eds., Equality and Preferential Treatment 84–154 (Princeton University Press, 1976).

17. E. Wolgast, Equality and the Rights of Women (Cornell University Press, 1980).

18. *Id.* at 51.

19. *Id.* at 78.

20. Scales, Towards a Feminist Jurisprudence, *supra* note 8, at 433.

21. *Id.* at 436.

22. See M. Cornforth, Materialism and the Dialectical Method (International Publishers, 1977).

❖ Equality and Difference: The Case of Pregnancy

HERMA HILL KAY

WOMEN AND MEN in the United States are entitled to the equal protection of the laws, and to freedom from discrimination in employment because of sex. Beginning in the 1970s, the United States Supreme Court has applied the laws that guarantee these rights so as to enable both women and men to gain access to positions and privileges formerly dominated by the other sex. The resulting exchange of power between the sexes reflected in Supreme Court litigation has not been equal, nor has the process of exchange been completed. Men, who hold and historically have held most of the power in American society, have been called upon to concede their exclusive authority in the economically dominant public sphere, while women have been asked to relinquish their priority in the less highly valued private sphere. . . .

In ruling upon the legal aspects of this exchange of power, the Supreme Court has attempted to use an assimilationist model of equality drawn from earlier cases challenging race discrimination. I have argued that a model of cross-sex assimilation is useful in those many situations in which women and men share the relevant characteristics that are compared for purposes of measurement.[1] In those few situations where the biological reproductive differences that define the sexes are directly involved, however, I have concluded that the assimilationist model is not useful in achieving legal equality between women and men, and that a different model must be developed. This paper represents a beginning effort to develop an alternative model for thinking about the reproductive difference that has been used to justify the existence of a separate sphere for women: pregnancy. . . .

Equality and Difference

An Episodic Analysis of Biological Reproductive Sex Differences

The philosophical claim that all men—or all women—are equal is commonly challenged by the existence of such inequalities as those of intelligence, ability, merit, physical condition, wealth, status, or power. Some philosophers have chosen to respond to challenges of this sort by invoking a generalized ideal of equality that transcends inequalities stemming from the specific differences of the human condition, such as equality of respect owed to all humans,[2] equality of opportunity,[3] or equality of consideration of interests.[4] Others have sought to justify some forms of social and economic inequalities within a theory of justice.[5] With rare exceptions, these philosophical discussions of equality have been phrased in terms of equality among men, with the term "man" being used in its generic sense to include "woman." When the specific question is raised about what equality between women and men might mean, the debate focuses on a particular set of differences: the biological differences that define the two classes of male and female. The question then becomes: Given that biological reproductive sex differences exist and may be expected to persist, how can it be argued that men and women are equal?

At least two approaches to this question have been taken. The significance of biological reproductive sex differences can be minimized, or it can be exalted. The first approach holds that, although differences of this sort may be acknowledged, no public consequence should turn on whether a person is male or female.[6] Equality between men and women is achieved by removing sex as a consideration of consequence; that is, by making the sexes morally, if not physically, indistinguishable. A second approach identifies biological reproductive sex differences as the basis of sexual identity and uses that identity, in turn, as the foundation for social differences that establish separate sex roles for women and men.[7] This approach would abandon egalitarian models in favor of a bivalent concept of the interests of women and men, to create a sort of "separate but equal" social model for the sexes. Adherents of the first position generally support a vision of the good society in which cross-sex assimilation is the norm and difference is limited as narrowly as possible. Those holding to the second position may support a range of social arrangements, from traditional ones in which women and men occupy separate spheres,[8] to more modern views of an androgynous society in which the spheres converge, preserving the best characteristics of both sexes.[9]

I wish to propose a third, alternative, approach: that we take account of biological reproductive sex differences and treat them as legally significant only when they are being utilized for reproductive purposes. I suggest that biological reproductive sex differences should be recognized as a functional attribute, rather than an inherent characteristic, of sexual identity, and as one that may or may not be exercised. A woman may be distinguished from a man by her capacity for pregnancy, childbirth, and lactation: but she may choose never to utilize that capacity. Is she any less female? A man has the unique capacity to produce and ejaculate sperm. But if he fathers no children, he is still a man. Infertile women and men retain their sexual identity, if not their distinguishing sexual capacity. In our society salient distinctions are based on sexuality rather than reproductive behavior. Women and men do not exercise their different biological reproductive capacities when they conform to social norms of appropriate interaction, nor do they necessarily do so when they engage in sexual intercourse. Those differences appear only when the reproductive function is manifested through a pregnancy that resulted from the reproductive behavior of both sexes.[10]

This way of looking at reproductive behavior permits us to examine biological reproductive differences in a new light. It becomes clearer that reproductive behavior is episodic and temporary. Male reproductive behavior is quite brief in duration; that of females occupies approximately nine months, but its cycle is complete following childbirth. Men and women who are parents are not functionally distinguishable by sex in their capacity to care for the newborn infant, except where breast-feeding is utilized as the method of choice for providing nourishment. Some have argued that a cultural preference for females over males in the role of primary nurturing parent produces psychological differences based on sex in children that in turn reinforce existing social patterns of male domination, and have proposed that the recurrent cycle be broken by having males join females in caring for children.[11] Such arguments rest on the assumption that no innate biological traits prevent men from forming primary bonds with infants.

The relevance of this episodic analysis of biological reproductive sex differences for a theoretical model of equality between women and men is that it recognizes that those differences exist, but regards them as inconsequential except during the specific occasions on which they are utilized. Upon those occasions, as the result of the union between sperm and egg, pregnant women experience a complex of needs that are different from those of men and, indeed, of non-pregnant women. Pregnant women may be advised to follow a certain diet, to abstain from ingesting particular substances, to avoid identified toxic environments, and to engage in or refrain from specified conduct in order to maximize their chances of delivering a healthy child. And, as a consequence of their changing physical condition, pregnant women may be temporarily disabled from work.

The necessary result of a woman's reproductive behavior is that, for a limited time and in ways that may vary widely among pregnant women, her condition will be different from that of other persons of both sexes. Is she therefore unequal to those persons? In particular, is she unequal to a man who has also engaged in reproductive conduct?

I think it is clear that if a woman who is not pregnant is assumed to be equal to a man on some such measure as, say, equality of respect or equality of consideration of interests, her reproductive behavior does not remove or detract in any way from her claim to that sort of equality. A woman may, however, unlike a man who engages in reproductive behavior, be placed at a temporary disadvantage with respect to equality of opportunity. In order to bear a child, she may be temporarily disabled from pursuing her own self-interests. If she becomes pregnant more than once, she may face recurrent disadvantages. It appears unjust to place the consequential disadvantages of reproductive conduct only upon women. This unjust result need not follow, however, for a philosophical basis exists for alleviating the temporary disadvantages of pregnancy within a framework of equality.

Philosophers recognize that, just as the concept of equality requires that equals be treated equally, so it requires that unequals be treated differently.[12] To treat persons who are different alike is to treat them unequally. The concept of formal equality, however, contains no independent justification for making unequals equal. A different concept, that of equality of opportunity, offers a theoretical basis for making unequals equal in the limited sense of removing barriers which prevent individuals from performing according to their abilities. The notion is that the perceived inequality does not stem from an innate difference in ability, but rather from a condition or circumstance that prevents certain uses or developments of that ability. As applied to reproductive behavior, the suggestion would be that women in general are not different from men in innate ability. During the temporary episode of a woman's pregnancy, however, she may become unable to utilize her abilities in the same way she had done prior to her reproductive conduct. Since a man's abilities are not similarly impaired as a result of his reproductive behavior, equality of opportunity implies that the woman should not be disadvantaged as a result of that sex-specific variation.

As applied to the employment context, the concept of equality of opportunity takes on the following form. Let us postulate two workers, one female, the other male, who respectively engage in reproductive conduct. Assume as well that prior to this activity, both were roughly equal in their ability to perform their similar jobs. The consequence of their having engaged in reproductive behavior will be vastly different. The man's ability to perform on the job will be largely unaffected. The woman's ability to work, measured against her prior performance, may vary with the physical and emotional changes she experiences during pregnancy. At times, her ability to work may be unaffected by the pregnancy; at other times, she may be temporarily incapacitated by it. Ultimately, she may require medical care to recover from miscarriage, or to complete her pregnancy by delivery, or to terminate it earlier by induced abortion. In order to maintain the woman's equality of opportunity during her pregnancy, we should modify as far as reasonably possible those aspects of her work where her job performance is adversely affected by the pregnancy. Unless we do so, she will experience employment disadvantages resulting from her reproductive activity that are not encountered by her male co-worker.

. . . Here, note a possible objection: the cost of compliance. Cost, however, is a function of social value. As the enactment of Title VII demonstrates, our society has made equality between women and men in the workplace a high priority. At the same time, it has accorded to individual decisions concerning procreation the status of a constitutionally-protected fundamental right. Men do not experience a conflict between their right to engage in reproductive conduct and their right to be free of discrimination based on sex at work. Women, however, have experienced such a conflict, and will continue to do so unless pregnant workers are safeguarded from the loss of employment opportunities during pregnancy. The social value of accommodating reproduction and employment opportunities so that women remain free to engage in both activities on an equal basis with men justifies the additional cost of enabling working women to cope with the differential physical and emotional changes associated with pregnancy. . . .

Episodic Analysis and the "Equal Treatment/Special Treatment" Debate

The episodic analysis as applied to pregnancy may serve as a basis for harmonizing some of the views of the opposing participants in the so-called equal treatment/special treatment debate. For example, episodic analysis highlights how narrowly the dispute is limited. In her excellent defense of the "equal treatment" model, Wendy Williams identifies two propositions as essential to the theoretical framework within which that model was developed. They are, first, "that sex-based generalizations are generally impermissible whether derived from physical differences such as size and strength, from cultural role assignments such as breadwinner or homemaker, or from some combination of innate and ascribed characteristics, such as the greater longevity of the average woman compared to the average man";[13] and second, "that laws and rules which do not overtly classify on the basis of sex, but which have a disproportionately negative effect upon one sex, warrant, under appropriate circumstances, placing a burden of justification upon the party defending the law or rule in court."[14] Neither of these propositions is in conflict with the episodic analysis of biological reproductive sex differences offered in this paper. I agree with Williams that, taken together, these two propositions form the basis of a legal doctrine of equality between women and men that has served both sexes well in breaking down "the legal barriers that restricted each sex to its predefined role and created a hierarchy based on gender."[15] As I have shown elsewhere, this assimilationist view of equality has worked well as a tool against both race discrimination and sex discrimination, where the two groups being compared are not different in any relevant way.

Episodic analysis departs from the "equal treatment" model, however, at the point where Williams claims that her "general framework applies, with minor alteration, to laws or rules based on physical characteristics unique to one sex."[16] In my view, biological reproductive sex differences are not comparable to other traits or characteristics that are shared by both sexes, and cannot adequately be analyzed within a framework that turns on differential treatment of two comparable groups. Instead, episodic analysis recognizes that biological reproductive sex differences exist, but confines their legal significance to the brief period during which they are utilized. I take it that Williams and I agree that women and men should be deemed equals prior to the time either engages in reproductive behavior. At the moment of conception, sperm and egg play equally important roles. Following childbirth, we both would place equal responsibility for childrearing on men and women who are parents. But, unlike Williams, I insist that during the episode of pregnancy itself the woman's body functions in a unique way. We must recognize that unique function in order to prevent penalizing the woman who exercises it. If confined in this way, the recognition of pregnancy as "unique"[17] will enable the law to treat women differently than men during a limited period when their needs may be greater than those of men as a way of ensuring that women will be equal to men with respect to their overall employment opportunities.

The narrow difference between my approach and that taken by Williams is also emphasized by another consideration. One of the major arguments of proponents of the equal treatment model has been strategic, rather than theoretical. It is that ultimately women will be more successful in escaping traditional stereotypical roles if they refrain from seeking special treatment for the uniquely female condition of pregnancy and rely primarily on demands for benefits that can be pressed in common with all workers. Thus, Williams points out that the equal treatment model "separates pregnancy and childrearing and insists that each be independently analyzed,"[18] so that the workplace can be restructured to accommodate parenting as the joint responsibility of working fathers and mothers.

As I have noted above, my analysis, like that of Williams, makes clear that the woman's reproductive cycle ends with childbirth. In those cases where two parents are available to care for the child, episodic analysis carries no implications for how they should assign between themselves the ensuing stage of childrearing. My analysis envisions a bright line between pregnancy and child care that requires the provision of any available childrearing leave to both parents. More fundamentally, episodic analysis is consistent with a model of equality that acknowledges the reproductive conduct of both men and women, while allowing a woman's pregnancy to be recognized and provided for on its own terms.[19] It is thus consistent with the view of proponents of the "special treatment" approach that the best way to enable women to compete on an equal basis with men is to assure them that pregnancy will not hinder their achievements.

Williams has questioned the fairness of a differential approach to pregnancy, using the *Miller-Wohl* case as a vehicle. She asks: "[o]n what basis can we fairly assert, for example, that the pregnant woman fired by Miller-Wohl deserved to keep her job when any other worker who got sick for any other reason did not?"[20] The short answer to this question is that no male worker who had exercised his reproductive capacity lost his job as a result. Episodic analysis supports that brief response, and also provides a more complete justification. The point at which that longer justification begins, however, is not when Miller-Wohl was thinking of firing Tamara Buley, but rather when she was thinking of going to work. Planned pregnancy, unlike other medical conditions, is an episode that is intended to culminate in the birth of a child. A woman who plans both to work and to have children must take account of how she will manage her pregnancy at work. If she knows that her employer has in place a program that will accommodate her pregnancy-related needs, she will be able to enter the workforce without fear of encountering obstacles to her decision to bear a child. Such employer programs will encourage women to enter and remain in the job market by mitigating the disadvantages to women caused by pregnancy. Not being fired, of course, is an important part of such a program of accommodation. An employer disability policy that limits the amount of sick leave to very short periods, or that has long probationary periods, cannot provide the necessary assurance to women that they will not be penalized at work if they become pregnant. Such provisions are, therefore, inadequate for pregnant workers, although they may be justifiable—even if undesirable—when applied to fortuitous sickness or injury suffered by other workers. Although employers and their insurers can predict statistically how many workers will be injured or disabled while at work, individual workers themselves normally do not plan for such disabling events. Therefore, they are not deterred from entering the workforce by the anticipation of such risks.

Ruth Bader Ginsburg put the point nicely, although I do not claim that she shares my views on this specific issue. Commenting on some of the pregnancy cases decided prior to the enactment of the PDA, she observed:

> The likelihood that childbirth will occur nowadays normally twice in a working woman's life, and the cost generated by insurance coverage for pregnancy-related physical disability no doubt influenced the Court's decisions—its meandering course and its current position that discrimination based on pregnancy is unlawful "sometimes." If Congress is genuinely committed to eradication of sex-based discrimination and promotion of equal opportunity for women, it will respond to the uneven pattern of adjudication by providing firm legislative direction assuring job security, health insurance coverage, and income maintenance for childbearing women. Women will remain more restricted than men in their options so long as this problem is brushed under the rug by the nation's lawmakers.[21]

I do not believe that enactment of the PDA, unless it is interpreted to permit employers to provide coverage for pregnant workers regardless of whether other workers are covered for other conditions, has responded satisfactorily to Ginsburg's argument. Such an interpretation would be consistent with the Congressional goal of ending discrimination against working women because of their pregnancy. If such an approach is adopted, feminists on both sides of the "equal treatment/special treatment" debate will be free to pursue our common goal of eradicating the pervasive prejudice against working mothers.

Conclusion

The biological fact that only women have the capacity to become pregnant has been used historically to define women as different from men along social, psychological, and emotional dimensions. Those asserted differences, in turn, have served to justify the legal, political, and economic exclusion of women from men's public world. Even now, when the barriers that separate women and men in the work force are breaking down, the uniqueness of pregnancy remains an obstacle to equal opportunity for women.

The nadir of this isolation of pregnancy was reached in modern times by the Supreme Court's distinction in *Geduldig* [Geduldig v. Aiello, 417 U.S. 484 (1974)] between pregnant women and non-pregnant persons, an overly broad characterization properly condemned as artificial and demeaning. Yet the Court's flawed perception of the relevant comparison groups contained an element of factual truth, albeit one from which the Court drew the wrong conclusion. Episodic analysis allows us to reclaim the accurate biological fact of sexual reproductive difference, and to draw the appropriate legal conclusion that difference requires. The Court's false conclusion was that pregnant persons are not women. That conclusion led to the improper legal result that women were protected against sex discrimination only when they are like men—that is, when they are not pregnant. Episodic analysis reveals the right conclusion: that both men and women engage in reproductive conduct, and that women are pregnant persons only for brief and self-contained periods. That insight can give rise to the proper legal result that women continue to be women even when pregnant, and should be provided with legal redress against discrimination based either on their sex or their pregnancy. On both legal and philosophical grounds, the temporary inequality that stems from the condition of pregnancy can and should be accommodated within a framework of equal opportunity for both sexes.

Notes

1. See Kay, Models of Equality, 1985 U. Ill. L. Rev. 39, 77–78 (1985). The Court's use of an assimilationist model is limited by its failure to apply that model free of stereotypical notions about the proper roles of women and men. . . .

2. See B. Williams, The Idea of Equality, in Problems of the Self 230, 234–39 (Cambridge University Press, 1973) (discussing and refining Kant's view of the respect owed to each man as a rational moral agent). Nancy Hauserman has used the concept of equality of respect to defend equality between men and women. See Hauserman, Sexual Equality: An Essay on the Importance of Recognizing Difference, 7 ALSA Forum 251 (Special Double Issue on Women and Law, 1983).

3. See Frankel, Equality of Opportunity, 81 Ethics 191 (1971). Compare Simon, The Liberal Conception of Equal Opportunity and Its Egalitarian Critics, in M. Darrough & R. Blank eds., Biological Differences and Social Equality (Green-

wood, 1983), at 95–98, with Schaar, Equality of Opportunity, and Beyond, in Nomos IX: Equality 228, 233–36 (1967).

4. See Benn, Egalitarianism and the Equal Consideration of Interests, in Nomos IX: Equality 61 (1967).

5. See, e.g., J. Rawls, A Theory of Justice 60 (Harvard University Press, 1971) (justifying certain social and economic inequalities provided that they are arranged so that they are both "(a) reasonably expected to be to everyone's advantage, and (b) attached to positions and offices open to all"). See, for an application of Rawls's difference principle to sexual justice, J. Radcliffe Richards, The Sceptical Feminist 90–120 (Routledge, Chapman & Hall, 1980).

6. This position is defended by Alison Jaggar and Richard Wasserstrom. See Wasserstrom, Racism, Sexism, and Preferential Treatment: An Approach to the Topics, 24 UCLA L. Rev. 581, 605–15 (1977); Jaggar, On Sexual Equality, 84 Ethics 275 (1974).

7. This position is defended by Elizabeth Wolgast. See E. Wolgast, Equality and the Rights of Women 25–30, 103–37 (Cornell University Press, 1980). Reviewers have criticized Wolgast for her failure to distinguish adequately between childbearing, a function that can be performed only by women, and childrearing, which can be carried out by either parent. See, e.g., Pierce, Book Review, 93 Phil. Rev. 93 (1984); Keohane, Review Essay, 93 Ethics 102, 108–11 (1982); Beggs, Recent Publications, 17 Harv. C.R.-C.L. L. Rev. 287, 288–89 (1982).

8. See, e.g., De Marco, Men and Women, Their Difference and Its Importance, 56 Thought 449 (1981); Browne, Biology, Equality, and the Law: The Legal Significance of Biological Sex Differences, 38 Sw. L.J. 617 (1984).

9. See, e.g., Rossi, Gender and Parenthood, 49 Am. Soc. Rev. 1 (1984).

10. Some pregnancies are the planned-for result of heterosexual intercourse, artificial insemination, or in vitro fertilization. Others are the presumably unanticipated consequence of recreational heterosexual intercourse. Still others are the product of rape or incest. Whether the pregnancy is desired by both participants, unanticipated, or even unwanted by one or both, does not affect the analysis presented in this paper. . . .

11. See generally N. Chodorow, The Reproduction of Mothering: Psychoanalysis and the Sociology of Gender (University of California Press, 1978); D. Dinnerstein, The Mermaid and the Minotaur: Sexual Arrangements and Human Malaise (Harper & Row, 1976).

12. The point seems to have been made originally by Aristotle. See Nichomachean Ethics V(3), 1113a-13b (W. Ross trans., 1925). . . .

13. Williams, Equality's Riddle: Pregnancy and the Equal Treatment/Special Treatment Debate, Part 2 herein, at 130.

14. *Id.* at 131.

15. *Id.*

16. *Id.*

17. Katharine Bartlett accurately identified the danger to working women posed by treating pregnancy as a unique condition without carefully scrutinizing the stereotypical assumptions that often accompany such a characterization: "With childbearing came the duties of childraising and taking care of the home, and the skill and habit which resulted from practice-fed stereotypes that women prefer to stay at home and have children; that they make better parents than their hus-

bands; that they don't want to do real work anyway." Bartlett, Pregnancy and the Constitution: The Uniqueness Trap, 62 Calif. L. Rev. 1532, 1533 (1974). . . .

18. Williams, Equality's Riddle, Part 2 herein, at 144.

19. The episodic analysis of pregnancy does not extend without qualification to a woman's capacity to lactate. Lactation is a biological sex difference associated with reproduction which becomes functional following delivery. Lactation makes possible the choice of breastfeeding as one method of providing nutrition to the child, and it has valuable health consequences for the mother as well. . . .

Unlike pregnancy, however, breastfeeding is not an unavoidable consequence of reproductive conduct. After childbirth, in two-parent families, either parent can feed the child. Single mothers may be able to call on friends or relatives for help if necessary. Mothers can express milk and refrigerate it for use within 24 hours or freeze it for longer periods, if appropriate. . . .

It follows that the constitutional arguments advanced in support of preventing disadvantages to women resulting from pregnancy . . . do not apply with the same force to breastfeeding mothers. On the other hand, lactation is similar to pregnancy in that it is a sex-specific trait, and it is stimulated by childbirth. One court has held that breastfeeding is a constitutionally protected liberty. See Dike v. School Bd. of Orange County, Fla., 650 F.2d 783, 785–87 (5th Cir. 1981). For Title VII purposes, the logic that equates discrimination based on pregnancy with discrimination based on sex may be sufficiently strong to extend to lactation. If so, an employer could not fire, or refuse to hire or promote, a breastfeeding woman. If an employer allowed flextime policies, parents could use those policies for childcare purposes, including breastfeeding. A state statute that mandated extra time off for breastfeeding only for working mothers, however, would probably be preempted by Title VII.

20. Williams, The Equality Crisis: Some Reflections on Culture, Courts, and Feminism, 7 Women's Rts. L. Rep. 175, 196 (1982).

21. Ginsburg, Some Thoughts on Benign Classification in the Context of Sex, 10 Conn. L. Rev. 813, 826–27 (1978).

❖ Transcending Equality Theory: A Way Out of the Maternity and the Workplace Debate

LUCINDA M. FINLEY

THE FACT THAT WOMEN bear children and men do not has been the major impediment to women becoming fully integrated into the public world of the workplace. . . . Assumptions and stereotypes about the physical and emotional effects of pregnancy and motherhood, about the appropriate role of women in society stemming from the physical fact of childbearing, and about the perceived response of women to childbearing, have contributed more than any other factor to the discriminatory treatment of women in the workplace and to the maintenance of the ideology of separate spheres.

The characterization of the separate spheres has become less a description of everyday life than one of a persistent ideology. The public–private dichotomy is entrenched in and fostered by our legal system. In the context of pregnancy and the workplace, this is illustrated by the judicial tolerance of excluding pregnancy from disability or other benefit plans, by the fact that women still can be legally fired from certain jobs when they become pregnant, by the difficulty pregnant women or new mothers have in some states in obtaining unemployment compensation, and by the general lack of adequate pregnancy and maternity leave and benefit policies in this country.[1] The result is that many women are forced out of the workplace and into the home when they give birth, are denied economic opportunities because of their childbearing role, or are forced back into the workplace sooner than sound child development policy would dictate in order to preserve job rights. This situation reinforces the notion that the home and the workplace are incompatible worlds, that women and men must choose between them, and that women's needs, interests, or perspectives must inevitably give way to the male-defined needs and interests of the workplace.

Our legal system also reinforces the ideology of separate spheres through its use of a doctrinal framework—equality or antidiscrimination—which founders on the differences presented by pregnancy and maternity. This doctrinal framework is incapable of challenging the underlying structures of institutions and the way in which these structures perpetuate barriers to the integration of home lives and work lives for both men and women. It leaves unquestioned the notion that life patterns and values that are stereotypically male are the norm, such as the idea that competitiveness and focus on work to the exclusion of other concerns is necessary to the productive functioning of the workplace. It leaves unexamined the assumption that it would cost too much, in terms of money or productivity, for an employer to make it possible for workers of both sexes to better integrate family responsibilities with job commitments.

Most feminists agree that one of the crucial issues to be addressed in order to eliminate the economic and social subordination of women is how to make the workplace more accommodating to pregnancy and parenting needs. Although legislation has overturned the most egregious example of judicial blindness to the link between workplace pregnancy policies and the subordinate economic status of women,[2] many examples of the persistence of stereotypes about the special vulnerability of pregnant women and their suitability for certain jobs can still be found in judicial decisions and in employer policies. Despite agreement on the ultimate goal, feminists are deeply divided over how best to eliminate the biases that pregnant women face in retaining either their jobs or a reasonable degree of economic security while pregnant and during their babies' early months. This division, which has become known as the special treatment/equal treatment debate, focuses on state laws requiring employers to provide reasonable maternity leave even if they do not generally provide illness or disability leave.

My purpose in this essay is not to join the special/equal treatment debate, because . . . I think that in significant respects the arguments of each side are both correct and flawed. Rather, the debate is used principally to critique the usefulness of equality analysis as a transformative device for challenging the social and economic subordination of women. . . .

The Equal Treatment/Special Treatment Debate and a Critique of Equality Analysis

The ideal of equality—that similarly situated individuals should be treated alike—is basic to our political and legal system. By appealing to equality and the doctrine of antidiscrimination, women have been able to make great strides toward the goal of improving their social status and power. Equality theory has been particularly useful for gaining access to traditionally male prerogatives within the public sphere. It works well and should continue to be the guide when the goal is assimilation of women into male institutions. Assimilation, however, too often means the creation of "a world in which persons of both genders are encouraged to act as men currently do and in which current 'female behavior' will gradually wither away."[3] This conception of the ideal world that underlies equality jurisprudence is precisely why it is limited and problematic in the pregnancy context. . . . Pregnancy is essential to the human race, and it is an area in which women cannot and should not act like men. . . . Where gender distinctions arise from biological facts, or where they have culturally existed, women are not similarly situated to men. Existing institutional structures therefore have distinct implications for women and men. Given this reality, equality doctrine is not going to advance women very far. The doctrine inherently assumes that the goal is assimilation to an existing standard without questioning the desirability of that standard and thus it limits the debate to what policies will best achieve the assimilation.

The Special Treatment/Equal Treatment Debate Summarized

The special treatment/equal treatment debate reflects the limiting focus of equality analysis. Each side agrees that women should have the right not to be penalized as workers for being childbearers and for having principal childrearing responsibility.[4] The split comes over how to realize that right and about what constitutes a penalty: is it not being treated as men are, or is it not being treated as a woman? The answer, however, is that it can be both, depending on the situation, and what one considers male-like or "equal" treatment, and on what form the female-like or "special" treatment will take.

Essentially, the debate is between two strands of traditional liberal equality theory—formal versus substantive equality, or equal opportunity versus equal outcomes. By formal equality I mean the doctrinal model that would treat likes alike. The rule requires us first, to identify relevant similarities and then, to treat two similar individuals the same. By substantive equality I mean the doctrinal model which acknowledges that parceling out goods such as workplace benefits according to egalitarian distributive principles may not result in people's positions actually coming out equal in the end. To make the competition equal, people may need varying underlying substantive entitlements. Individual needs and positions may have to be taken into account in any particular situation in order to achieve equality of outcome.

In many respects, each side of the debate accepts the notion that the public world of the workplace and the private world of the home are separate spheres. They both see the problem as the relegation of women to the private sphere through barriers erected in the public sphere. The goal, then, is to make women more equal in the workplace sphere. Both agree that one way to achieve this goal is to support legislative initiatives to make parenting leaves available to men and women.

Equal treatment proponents emphasize that a woman's "specialness"—her childbearing function—historically has led to paternalistic protective legislation which has forced women back into the home. They argue that women cannot have it both ways by asserting that they should be treated just like men in some situations yet claiming the right to be treated better than men in others. They reject the notion that pregnancy "naturally makes women unequal," (i.e., unlike men) and contend instead that "pregnancy can or should be visualized as one human experience which in many contexts, most notably the workplace, creates needs and problems similar to those arising from causes other than pregnancy, and which can be handled adequately on the same basis as are other physical conditions of employees."[5] The focus is not on whether pregnancy itself is just the same as other conditions, but on the effects of pregnancy on a worker. These effects can be the same as the effects of other conditions. According to this view, the flaw in the Supreme Court's analysis in *Geduldig* and *Gilbert* was its failure to recognize the basic similarities between the effects of pregnancy and other disabling conditions. Consequently, the language of the Pregnancy Discrimination Act, which was promoted by equal treatment proponents, declares that "women affected by pregnancy, childbirth or related medical conditions shall be treated the same for all employment-related purposes . . . as other persons not so affected but similar in their ability or inability to work. . . ."

This approach of comparing women to men is defended as preferable because it highlights commonalities in human experiences. In de-emphasizing the uniqueness of pregnancy, the assumption that pregnancy is just a woman's problem can be overcome. The formal equality model of treating likes alike is also justified as the more objective and value-neutral approach. Thus, it is argued, it poses less danger of judges or employers letting their biases and stereotypes about women guide their decisions.

When employers have inadequate sickness and disability policies, equal treatment proponents contend that women should be just as vulnerable as male workers to job loss. After all, the individualized matching approach requires that pregnant workers be treated neither better nor worse than other "similarly situated" workers. The proper response to inadequate leave policies, in the view of equal treatment proponents, is to fight laws that require only maternity leave, and to lobby for laws that extend adequate illness, disability, and parenting leaves to all workers.

On the "special treatment" side of the debate are those who would treat pregnancy in the workplace as something warranting its own specially tailored policies apart from sickness and disability plans. Special treatment advocates consequently support, as legitimate under Title VII, state laws that require employers to provide maternity leave to those who want or need it. Those who hold this view contend that, given the deep and often unconscious way in which assumptions about pregnancy are so central to our accepted system of gender hierarchy, it is unlikely that a majority of the Supreme Court and the American public will ever view pregnancy as being the same as other conditions, either in its significance or its effects. Many special treatment proponents assert that pregnancy is indeed distinct from any other human condition, and that it is neither necessary, desirable, nor possible to eliminate this biologically rooted sex difference. Consequently, according to special treatment advocates, we need two kinds of rights: equal rights and special rights. Special rights are rights based on human differences, taking them into account so that the ultimate outcome between different individuals can be the same.[6] Those who support special treatment for pregnant women insist that a so-called neutral policy, or one that assumes that no group or individual is starting out with special needs or special disadvantages, can, in fact, have differential group effects. Thus, the special treatment argument often relies on the disparate impact strand of antidiscrimination theory. It also draws from group-based, rather than individualized, models of antidiscrimination theory. Since women as a group have traditionally been discriminated against in the workplace because of their childbearing capacity, positive action in the form of special rights that affirmatively take childbearing into account is necessary to break down the disparities. A no-leave policy, or a policy that provides so little time off that virtually any pregnant woman will require more than she is entitled to and will thus lose her job because of her pregnancy, has a negative, disparate effect on women as a group.

Special treatment proponents are concerned because the equal treatment model can do nothing positive for women in a workplace that offers inadequate leave policies; it is only as good as the male model with which it can be compared. The fundamental objection to the equal treatment approach is that it inevitably accepts the male norms of the workplace. Special treatment advocates point out that the aversion displayed by equal treatment proponents to talking about pregnancy as unique, and their consequent insistence that women really are just like men, are rooted in an acknowledgment that male is the standard against which we all should be measured. Uniqueness is a trap for women only under an analysis that assumes maleness is the norm. The way out of the trap, according to special treatment proponents, is to challenge the male standard by insisting on the incorporation of women into the workplace with due regard for their special capacities and needs.

Special treatment advocates insist that it is acceptable to move incrementally toward the goal of equality in the workplace. They think it is foolhardy to fight against legislation that women badly need in order to accommodate childbearing and working, just because the vision of an ideal society compels us to recognize that men and nonpregnant women also need certain workplace protections that they currently do not have. Those who urge equal treatment warn that the incremental approach was previously used against women during the era of protective legislation, and that we must therefore work to achieve the entire ideal set of legal protections for men and women at the same time.

There is an insoluble quality to this debate. . . . Both sides of the debate appeal to aspects of the doctrinal framework of equality analysis, yet that very framework provides no objectively principled, apolitical basis for making a general choice between the sometimes competing visions of equality of opportunity and equality of outcome.

The Special Treatment/Equal Treatment Debate as a Device for Critiquing Equality Analysis

The limitations of equality analysis as a transformative device for challenging the economic and social subordination of women and attendant limitations on male roles stem from its inability to come to terms in any acceptable, unproblematic manner with the reality of human variety. We are all different, and distinctions of gender are one type of difference that is unlikely ever to disappear.

THE INDETERMINACY OF EQUALITY ANALYSIS

The first problem with the analysis of traditional equality theory is its indeterminacy—the theory of equality and the legal analysis that implements the theory cannot tell us how to define or identify what is a relevant difference and what is a relevant similarity in any given situation. Equality analysis, along with much of our system of legal reasoning, rests on a process of classifying by analogy. We are taught that to arrive at the right answer we must divide things into groups of "similars," and then we must treat everything within each group "similarly." But who is to say what is a difference or similarity, in the abstract or in the particular? Every person, thing, or condition will always have some qualities that are similar, and some that are different from everything else, even when there is agreement on the category of classification.

For example, the equal treatment proponents are correct when they point out that pregnancy is similar to other conditions in its effect on people's ability or inability to work. But how similar? Pregnancy may require lengthier leave times, and leave may be needed for unique reasons different from other noncatastrophic physical happenings. Thus, special treatment proponents and the Supreme Court majority are, to a degree, correct when they point out that pregnancy is unique. So, the question that currently, and historically, has so torn feminists concerns the legal implications of this simultaneous condition of being alike, yet not alike.[7]

Equality analysis simply cannot provide the answer. Only basic political and moral judgments about ultimate social aims can suggest a basis for choosing among possible similarities and dissimilarities. Even when the discourse moves to this value-laden level, it is not possible to guarantee completely satisfactory solutions free of perverse effects that can undermine whatever ultimate goal is at stake. These perverse effects are intrinsic to being both the same and different simultaneously, because as women choose to focus on certain similarities that we think will reduce gender hierarchy, the nagging differences will not disappear from view.

The equal treatment–special treatment debate illustrates this tension between sameness and difference. Undeniably, the equal treatment view embodied in the Pregnancy Discrimination Act has accomplished a great deal for pregnant workers, because the problem too often had been that employers were not treating women workers as well as men workers. The Act served as an impetus for numerous employers to include pregnancy in their sickness and disability plans. At the same time, however, the focus on male–female comparisons caused some employers to cut back on maternity provisions, such as the availability of lengthier leaves than were offered for most other disabilities.[8] These generous policies were probably more responsive than sick leave periods to the actual physical and emotional needs of pregnant workers, their children, and other family members.

On the other hand, the special treatment approach, while perhaps leading to the desirable outcome of longer maternity leaves than are now routinely available in this country, is a double-edged sword. As long as there are similarities to be perceived between the effects of pregnancy and other conditions, women may be regarded as receiving an undeserved benefit. This may produce resentment among fellow employees, cause employers to avoid hiring women because of fears that they will be more expensive workers to carry, and further entrench the unhelpful stereotype that women are frail and in need of paternalistic protection. Avoiding this danger in the refuge of the equal treatment approach does not solve the problem, because many of the employers with the least adequate illness, disability, or maternity policies are in small businesses or the service and retail sectors where a majority of working women are found. Here, the comparative focus of the PDA founders because there are few or no men for comparative purposes. Nevertheless, equal treatment advocates fear that the additional costs of employing pregnant women that can flow from special treatment will lead employers to shy away from hiring anyone they think is likely to become pregnant. However, the supposedly neutral solution proposed by equal treatment advocates could have the same adverse impact on pregnant women as special treatment due to cost factors. If a company increases its allowed disability leave time to encompass time for maternity, or makes parenting leaves available to workers of both sexes, far more women than men will avail themselves of the benefit. Thus, it will still be more expensive to employ women, in the sense that women may take more time off from work.

The competing strands within equality theory of equal outcome versus equal opportunity give the entire analytic framework an internally contradictory quality. Thus, the doctrinal framework itself does not provide a basis for choosing between the strands in any particular situation. Two important lessons from history are that women have not been treated the same as men, and that women have lost their jobs and benefits due to pregnancy. So, choosing the equal treatment approach undermines the equal opportunity value, and choosing that value undermines the equal treatment ideal.

This realization demonstrates that equality analysis is neither objective nor value neutral. The outcome of the analysis which asks whether someone is different or the same, or similarly or differentially situated, depends entirely on the characteristic or factor selected for emphasis. This selection is a highly political, value-laden choice, determined by one's world view and perspective. The supposedly objective strictures of equality analysis did not screen out from the factors of decision the world view apparently held by a male majority of the Supreme Court that women do and should disengage from the workplace and its attendant benefits when they become pregnant. Thus, the "neutral" command to treat likes alike has not constrained the use of judicial power to perpetuate the subordination of women.

EQUALITY ANALYSIS AND HOMOGENEITY: THE MALE NORM

A second feature of equality analysis more troubling than its indeterminacy is the way it views differences among people. A fundamental, but too often unquestioned, assumption of our cultural and political tradition is the ideal of homogeneity. When the historical content of the homogeneous ideal is examined, it becomes apparent that it is hardly an objective, inclusive ideal. The defenders of the American ideal of homogeneous equality wrote in sweeping terms about the commonalities among American citizens, yet their descriptions bore a striking resemblance to the world of the white, Anglo-Saxon Protestant male. The American melting pot has been a cauldron into which we have put black, brown, red, yellow, and white men and women, in the hope that we will come up with white men. The ideal of homogeneity has legitimated much invidious discrimination throughout our history. The ideal blinds us both to the fact and to the value of our diversity. Consequently, it marginalizes, disempowers, and renders invisible those such as women, who have seemed most unlikely to ever melt into the white male model of homogeneity.

The ideal of homogeneous assimilation has been a motivating force behind our legal system's definition of equality as the similar treatment of those who are similar. The search for categories of similarity means that there must be a standard against which similarities are to be measured, and the choice of the standard will determine the nature of the outcome of the comparison. But, there is something inherent in the concept of a *standard* for assessment that views the standard as the norm, and everything that is dissimilar from the standard as the deviate "other." "Different" and "other" consequently have pejorative connotations in our tradition of equality jurisprudence.

The idea that to be "different" is undesirable leads to the "difference dilemma."[9] Our tradition of equality has too often meant prejudice toward those whom the dominant group has labeled as different. Thus, to be considered different can mean being stigmatized or penalized. "Difference" is stigmatizing because the assimilationist ideal underlying our society's conception of equality presumes sameness. Thus, the recognition of difference threatens our conception of equality, and the proclamation or identification of difference can serve as a justification for existing inequities.[10] On the other hand, to hide the fact of difference from the prevailing norm means being treated according to a "faulty neutrality," or a standard that, because it was not created with the difference in mind, advances the dominant group to the detriment of those who are not, in fact, like it.

The special treatment/equal treatment debate reflects each side of the difference dilemma. The equal treatment position, by emphasizing sameness, is designed to avoid further instances of discrimination in the male dominated and defined workplace because of ways in which women are different from men. The special treatment position recognizes the disadvantage of this emphasis on sameness, which is to recreate and entrench instances of discrimination that occur because the standards of the workplace have not been determined according to the needs and perspectives of women. To be treated as if you were the same as a norm from which you actually differ in significant ways is just as discriminatory as being penalized directly for your difference.

The very idea of a norm implies that whatever is considered "normal" can take on a quality of objective reality, so that it is no longer possible to see that the standard of measurement reflects simply one group of qualities out of the infinite variety of human experience. The qualities chosen as the standard for measurement for legal equality analysis have been determined by those who have had the power to define or to imprint their view of what is real, important, and normal, on others. In our society, that power has always been held by white men. . . . Men have then defined and structured institutions, such as the family and the workplace, according to their own situation and needs. The way in which the structure of institutions then affects people's lives becomes understood as a natural consequence of differences, rather than as attributable to the directions that may be imposed on us by structural inequities. For example, the notion of the home and work as disconnected, incompatible separate spheres, with the private sphere occupied almost exclusively by women and the other by men, has been viewed as a natural, biologically based dichotomy. The way in which each institution has been socially constructed to bind its occupants to it has only infrequently been subjected to critical analysis.

The role of men in defining the standard of normalcy and in assigning significance to female differences, means that the whole premise of our equality jurisprudence is whatever is male is the norm. Thus, the questions asked are whether women are like men, or when, and on what terms, women should be allowed into the male world where, if they can act just like men, they can succeed. The equal treatment/special treatment debate reflects this focus on a male-defined norm. The formal equality approach tells us specifically to treat women the same as men, so that women can have the same opportunities men have had to compete in the male-valued work world, and so that women can escape the female populated, and male-devalued, home world. . . . In this way a focus on equal treatment accepts the idea that work and family are dichotomous spheres, and asks primarily that women be allowed out of one world and into another.

There seems no way out of the male norm for the equal treatment position, since its insistence on comparisons runs up against the problem that in the legal system men are the referent against which all comparisons are made. . . . Categories such as childrearing, sexuality, and the consequences of pregnancy, which have been drilled into us as biologically determined differences, will remain particularly resistant to being put into the male-focused sameness classification.

The special treatment view does not entirely escape the male norm, either. In many respects the options given to women by equality analysis "of either being the same as men or being different from men are just two ways of having men as your standard."[11] Something like maternity leave is a "special" right only because it is not something men need. It is not a "male" right. With male as the reference point, the label "special," or "for women" takes on a pejorative cast because of the history of glorifying that which is male and devaluing the experiences and qualities of women.

Simply by focusing on women as women (as unlike men) and calling attention to their unmale needs, the special rights strategy may reinforce the stereotype of pregnancy as a woman's problem. This focus on pregnancy diverts attention from the ways in which other aspects of the workplace besides disability have been defined by men with men in mind. This can reinforce the disparity of roles, and the relegation of women to the confining institution of motherhood and the separate realm of the home. The special treatment approach may help perpetuate the separate spheres ideology, both because it can be interpreted as accepting that women, as childbearers, are and will always be the primary childrearers, and because it leaves unchallenged workplace values in areas besides childbearing that stem from the separate spheres. The special treatment approach thus has a tendency to define the problem as figuring out what female needs must be accommodated by, or incorporated into, the male workplace so that women will be better able to compete with men according to the existing value structures.

These tensions in the equal treatment/special treatment debate are a direct result of the male norm in equality theory. After all, the special rights view contradicts the equal treatment view only if we take as the limit of possibilities those rights and expectations already created by and for the dominant group. When we stop accepting men's needs as determining all desirable "rights" for both women and men and thus as constituting the standard for equality analysis, we will cease being so concerned about whether maternity leave is a "special right" because it is not male oriented.

The focus of equality analysis on comparisons with the male norm makes it well-suited for perpetuating existing distributions of power. Because those in power are the ones making the attribution of difference, they will see themselves as normal and everyone else as the undesirable other. One need only make a cursory examination of the pregnancy cases, and the assumptions that continue to permeate the law, to grasp this point. Indeed, equality analysis has sometimes been used to legitimate discrimination rather than successfully to eradicate it.

If the effort to eliminate gender hierarchy is to bear fruit, the male norm must constantly be questioned. We must redefine the standards against which humans are evaluated to be more inclusive of the full range of human experience and perspective. We must examine the ways in which institutions such as the workplace and the family have been structured with the male norm in mind. Because equality analysis cannot give us the tools to perform these tasks, we must transcend it and try to think about these problems in other ways. Both equal treatment and special treatment proponents are trapped in a circular debate over what is a relevant sameness and what is a relevant difference, and energy is being devoted to fighting this battle up to the Supreme Court, rather than to working together to achieve meaningful change. Instead, feminists should address, in political terms that openly acknowledge the values at stake, what they really want and what women need—structures that recognize that our family lives and work lives are importantly interconnected and will always affect each other, and devices for legal decisionmaking that do not always require hierarchical value to be assigned to various human conditions or experiences.

EQUALITY ANALYSIS AND RESPONSIBILITY

Equality analysis is also limited because it is only as useful a tool for changing the status quo as the conceptions of human rights[12] and human nature that underlie it. Our legal system has tended to view the person who holds rights, including the right to either equality of opportunity or equality of outcome, as an isolated, self-sufficient, autonomous actor. This conception of the self has little room in it for recognizing and embracing interconnectedness with and responsibility to others. The relationship between this view of human nature and equality doctrine is that in building on a conception of isolated autonomy, the ideal of equality searches for an irreducible and universal aspect of humanity. This requires a focus on sameness and a desire to obliterate differences. Sameness means generality; it means removing individuals from their context and connection, so that they are like all others in being nothing more than their self-contained and autonomous essences.[13] Difference, on the other hand, can be troublesome precisely because it requires thought about connections and context. Autonomy, which is held out as the ideal for decontextualized human beings, is defined as the realization of self-fulfillment guided by the ultimate authority of self-judgment without interference from others.

This underlying view of human nature has produced a negative, highly individualistic definition of rights. The critique of rights analysis has been thoroughly developed elsewhere, including from a feminist perspective. I need only recount it here briefly. The conception of abstract individualism leads to a definition of freedom as noninterference from other individuals. Rights are seen as necessary to protect our glorious isolation—to provide just the measure of security from others that is necessary to guarantee freedom from others and from the state. Of course, one can never tell in the abstract just what the necessary measure of freedom is—hence, there exists what has been called the "fundamental contradiction" of liberalism, the conflict between our need for freedom and our need for security. The rights that we have are largely negative and inward looking, in the sense that they are designed to keep us apart in our isolated selves by proscribing certain activity and setting out protected zones of noninterference. We mostly have rights "against," rather than affirmative conceptions of rights "for," or rights "to."

The inadequacies of these underlying visions of human nature and rights for describing human reality are readily apparent. The most fleeting contemplation of reproductive biology demonstrates that individual self-sufficiency is neither possible nor desirable. At the species level, we are biologically interdependent. To a large extent, many of us, as individuals, are also emotionally interdependent. Our conceptions of self worth more often come from our attachments to other human beings, from the knowledge that others care about us, need us, like us, or respect us, than from an unanchored, decontextualized, intrinsic sense of self worth. Moreover, the conception of autonomy as self-definition is challenged by the recognition that our desires and values are often socially constructed. The theory of equality that operates on abstract individuals suffers from a glaring flaw—real human beings have a determinate race, age, and sex. Thus, when considering what equality is to mean for women, we cannot be blind to the fact that the law operates on gendered subjects.

Thus, our conception of rights and equality ignores the many human needs apart from disconnection and noninterference. The notable absence of values of interconnectedness and care in our system of rights, and the tendency of equality analysis to overlook context in its search for essential similarities, suggest that these analytic approaches may only reflect the male aspect of human experience. It is the male aspect of human experience because men are generally removed from bodily concerns such as preparing food for the table and assuring clean clothes in the drawer, and have been removed from human experiences that can foster a sense of interconnectedness, such as birth and childrearing. Thus, it is much easier for men to conceive of themselves as disconnected, autonomous beings.

The limits of our reform imaginations are usually defined by the search to extend more rights to people. As long as the concept of rights remains based on the value of noninterference, so that affirmative rights such as the right to reasonable maternity leave are a distrusted anomaly in our legal system, we can travel only so far in restructuring institutions. Since equality analysis is fundamentally designed to do no more than extend equal rights to individuals, it too suffers from the limited transformative potential of our current conceptions of rights.

The drawback of limited horizons is reflected in the tendency of equality analysis to divert attention from and to obscure the deeper nature of the problem leading to the plea for equal rights.[14] This has occurred at two levels. First, the search for categories of sameness and difference fails to appreciate the full context of the social conditions that provoke an equality claim. The pregnancy cases are notable for their absence of attention to context. The judges reviewing airlines' grounding policies have rarely put the issue in the context of the initial refusal to hire married women, the former policy of firing pregnant women, and the final response of removing them from flight duty. The judges reviewing exclusionary policies in the chemical industry have often failed to place that issue in the context of formerly all male, high paying jobs that had grudgingly been opened up to women, coupled with the biases of science that tend to assume that all reproductive risks visit women rather than men. When the Supreme Court reviewed the exclusion of pregnancy from disability plans, it did not broaden the inquiry of what "uniqueness" implied for the plans' fiscal integrity to encompass the decades of blatantly hostile, stereotyped, and penalizing treatment of pregnant women in the workplace. It is easy to come away from these cases that talk about the validity of differential treatment with a gloomy sense that the courts fundamentally missed the point.

There is yet a deeper level, however, that has been obscured by equality analysis. The context in which gender hierarchy problems arise includes the need to question why we value some kinds of human activity as "work" and not others of equal societal value, and why some kinds of "work" are considered appropriate for one sex rather than the other. It is also necessary to question why we view those who are engaged in the remunerative kinds of work as abstract individuals with little responsibility to each other and with totally separate lives "outside" work. A central aspect of the problem that eludes equality analysis is the maintenance of separate spheres of work and home, and the devaluation of the home sphere and values associated with it in the work world. Consequently, the values of interdependence, care, and responsibility that are characteristic of the home sphere are absent from the public sphere of the workplace and the legal system.

Suggestions for Transcending Equality Analysis

The effort to fit all our approaches to gender problems into the current framework of equality may obscure the deeper context of the issues and may curtail our thinking about the means for addressing underlying issues such as the implications of the ideology of separate spheres. Although it is possible to infuse the word "equality" with a conception that is more sensitive to the bias embedded in structures and values than the comparative approach, at present it may be easier to make advances toward the goal of meaningful change in social structures and attitudes if we try not to think about problems such as accommodating pregnancy as "equality" problems, but instead look at them in a new light. I certainly have no objection to the ideal of equality, and think that the principle should be maintained in those situations where the traditionally disempowered are seeking access to the privileges of the powerful, without seeking to change the existing value structures of those privileges. Nevertheless, the current conception of the ideal articulated by the equality doctrine has taken on a meaning that keeps referring us to a male norm. The word has come to equate difference with stigma, and to exalt similarity as the ideal. In the process, the idea of "equality" overlooks the socially constructed nature of difference. The inherited language of equality does not easily convey the meanings of those who urge a broader definition of "equality."[15] The language seduces us into the circularity of the special treatment/equal treatment debate. Thus, we need to acknowledge that the borrowed language[16] is no longer well suited to expressing many of the problems women must address, now that women have advanced in ever increasing numbers into previously male domains and privileges.[17] Once our society's conceptions of sameness and difference, male and female, have undergone some change, it may be profitable to start talking about "equality" again.

To move beyond the confines that equality analysis places on our imagination, it is necessary first to restate the social problem symbolized by inadequate pregnancy and parenting leave policies in the American workplace. The problem to be addressed through legal and institutional change is not simply, as equality analysis suggests, one of the failure to treat women similarly to men in the public sphere, or the failure to make some accommodating adjustments in the public sphere so that women can have the same opportunities or outcomes within that sphere as men. The problem is that the spheres of work and family have been viewed as separate in a way that has excluded the values, needs, and perspectives of one from recognition in the other. This dichotomy of values has limited the ability of both women and men to become fully realized interdependent human beings, because it has tolerated the assumption by employers and the rest of society that workers can be dealt with as disembodied from the entire context of their lives.

It has been assumed that women naturally are more suited for the home sphere. Consequently, they have been forced to primarily occupy that sphere, because of inhospitable structures and values of the work sphere and the tendency of our legal tradition of equality jurisprudence to view both the underlying structures and the divisions as normal. The separation has rendered working women's lives into a stressful, exhausting juggling act that leaves them little time or energy for feeling fulfilled and expanded by their dual roles and their relationships within each role. We do not conceive of work roles and home roles as integrated, mutually reinforcing experiences, but rather see them in competition with each other. The benefits to be gained from working are not seen as enhancing a woman's contributions to her roles as wife, lover, friend, or mother. The benefits from these latter roles of being sensitive to others' needs and of receiving the personal validation that comes from relationships are not seen as enhancing a woman's contributions to the work world.

The situation for men is similar in its detrimental effects. Men have been assumed naturally to occupy the public work world. Consequently, that world has been structured without regard to the needs and values of the family world, such as a recognition of the importance of human interdependence and solidarity. The structures and values of the work world are built around the conception of atomized individuals, where freedom, such as freedom of contract, is viewed as a very individual matter that can be pursued outside of social context, and competition against others, rather than solidarity *with* others, is the ethic. These views have kept men as much out of the family world and out of touch with values of support and connection as they have kept women out of the work world. For men, too often it has not even been a matter of juggling, but of being forced to accept that the need to work reduces the kind of commitment one can make to family. This is as limiting for men as the opposite is for women, because our work and family, or our lack of them, are crucially interrelated defining aspects of our lives, our self-conceptions, and thus our prospects for fulfillment as members of the human community.

If we are going to have any success in tackling the problem of gender hierarchy and transforming the situations of both men and women, we need to focus not so much on traditional conceptions of equality, but on the values at stake in current structures and role conceptions. We need to focus on the falsity of the public–private dichotomy and the need to integrate the values and structures of both the public and home worlds accordingly. It is necessary to challenge openly certain assumptions about men and women that flow from the dichotomy, such as the definition of career commitment that allows work demands to crowd out other needs and the related assumptions that the career commitments of women are reduced by their family responsibilities or by their desire to give time to both worlds,[18] and that men do not care as much as women about their families or human attachments.

To move toward this goal, and to transcend the limitations of equality analysis, we need to enlarge our legal discourse in two ways. First, it is necessary to devise a new approach to differences that sees them as relational and thus accepts them in a nonhierarchical, nonpejorative way. The approach must abandon total assimilation as an ideal and must strive to make the law sensitive to the way in which the perspective of the more powerful, the legal decision maker, can lead to attributions of difference. Second, we must supplement existing notions of rights as zones of noninterference, because interference is not the only paradigm of human interaction. Human interaction can also mean support, enrichment, and the establishment of sustaining bonds of community. But, we must also struggle with the issue of how to draw lines between policies that respond to values of interconnection, and the need of people to maintain a zone to themselves, in order to avoid the problem of forced community.

The difficulty of enlarging the meanings of the words and the conceptions of human nature underlying existing theories of equality and rights while using their language should not be underestimated. To solve these dilemmas and to work out completely how the law should respond to differences or view human needs is an enterprise larger than the scope of this essay. Indeed, problems such as the difference dilemma and the tension between the human need for interconnectedness and the need for individual space are perennial philosophical questions. Suggesting new ways to start thinking about these problems, however, will correct an imbalance in the ways the law at present conceptualizes them. Equality analysis currently approaches the problem of differences either by pretending they do not exist, or by stigmatizing those who are different; rights analysis is tilted much too far towards the solitary end of the individual–community continuum. Once the rethinking has begun, we can turn back to maternity policies in the workplace and suggest the kinds of policies and justifications for them that would flow from a new conception of differences and interconnection. . . .

Notes

1. For a description of maternity policies in the United States and an analysis of their inadequacy, see S. Kamerman & A. Kahn, Maternity Policies and Working Women (Columbia University Press, 1983); see also Catalyst, Preliminary Report on a Nationwide Survey of Maternity/Parental Leaves, Perspective no. 17 (June 1984) (survey of leave policies of top Fortune 500 corporations); S. Hewlett, A Lesser Life: The Myth of Women's Liberation in America (Morrow, 1986) (describing effects of absence of maternity leave policies).

2. The Pregnancy Discrimination Act of 1978, 42 U.S.C. § 2000e(k) (1982), overruled the Supreme Court's decision in General Electric Co. v. Gilbert, 429 U.S. 125 (1976), that the exclusion of normal pregnancy and associated illnesses from a company's disability benefit plan was not sex-based discrimination.

3. Note, Toward a Redefinition of Sexual Equality, 95 Harv. L. Rev. 487, 487–88 (1981).

4. The preeminent academic spokeswoman for the equal treatment view is Professor Wendy Williams. See Williams, Equality's Crisis, The Equality Crisis: Some Reflections on Culture, Courts, and Feminism, 7 Women's Rts. L. Rptr. 175 (1982); Williams, Equality's Riddle: Pregnancy and the Equal Treatment/Special Treatment Debate, Part 2 herein. The special treatment, or special rights, view is set forth in E. Wolgast, Equality and the Rights of Women (Cornell University Press, 1980) (proposes what has become known as bivalent approach, under which a variety of differences between the sexes, both biological and socially constructed, are taken into account under a regime of special rights); Krieger & Cooney, The Miller-Wohl Controversy: Equal Treatment, Positive Action and the Meaning of Women's Equality, Part 2 this volume; Scales, Towards a New Feminist Jurisprudence, 56 Ind. L.J. 375 (1981), at 435 (pregnancy and breastfeeding are true biological gender differences which must be incorporated into equality jurisprudence to make it more encompassing of female experience; the thrust of her position is to alter our conceptions of equality rather than to work within the given framework of equality doctrine). . . .

5. Williams, Equality's Riddle, Part 2 herein, at 129.

6. The classic example of a special right is the requirement that buildings be equipped with wheelchair ramps so that both those who can walk and those who cannot *can* realize their equal right to have access to public buildings. Wolgast, Equality and the Rights of Women, *supra* note 4, at 51.

7. The historian Ellen DuBois has noted the similarity of the current debate over maternity leave to the debate over protective wage and hour laws that occurred in the early part of this century, which she characterizes as a debate between "egalitarian-feminism," which stresses that women are just like men and

thus should have the rights accorded to men, and "domestic-feminism," which stresses the special and different interests and needs of women and the consequent way in which men's rights and needs cannot necessarily define what women want and need. DuBois, Feminist Discourse, Moral Values, and the Law—A Conversation, 34 Buffalo L. Rev. 11, 64–68 (1985). . . .

8. Kamerman & Kahn, Maternity Policies, *supra* note 1, at 111, 118. The approach of comparing pregnancy with disabilities has exacerbated the gap between policies in this country and in others. The disabilities approach has been one of the reasons why the United States lags so far behind the rest of the industrialized world in its maternity and parenting policies. *Id.* at 144–46. Concern for parent–child development has rarely been a motivating concern of labor policies and their design in the United States. *Id.* at 145.

9. See Minow, Learning to Live With the Dilemma of Difference: Bilingual and Special Education, 48 Law & Contemp. Probs. 157, 159 (1985).

10. This is why some feminists have reacted so strongly to the work of Carol Gilligan, which explores differences in the moral orientations of men and women. . . . [S]ee, e.g., Kerber, Greeno, Maccoby, Luria, Stack & Gilligan, On "In a Different Voice": An Interdisciplinary Forum, 11 Signs 304 (1986).

11. DuBois, Feminist Discourse, *supra* note 7, at 21 (remarks of C. MacKinnon). MacKinnon relates this constant use of male as the reference point to hierarchy and the powerlessness of women. She argues that "[m]en are set up as a standard for women by saying either: 'You can be the same as men, and *then* you will be equal,' or 'You can be different from men, and then you will be *women.*'" *Id.*

12. Given that equality is closely linked with rights, Professor Peter Westen has advanced the idea that "equality" is an empty concept, because in his view all debates phrased in equality terms in essence boil down to debates about rights. Westen, The Empty Idea of Equality, 95 Harv. L. Rev. 537 (1982). While I agree that equality analysis is inextricably tied to, and limited by, existing concepts of rights, and that talking in terms of equality can obscure underlying issues of rights or needs, . . . I do not conclude from these observations that equality is an idea without content. Much of my preceding discussion is intended to illustrate that the comparison orientation of equality analysis does have content. The search for similarities and differences limits one's view of the problem and thus has an impact on the issue under examination. Moreover, the idea of a norm, or a standard of measurement, that underlies equality analysis, gives content to the idea of equality—it comes to mean assimilation to the characteristics defined by those with the power to define the norm. Professor Westen illustrates his view by suggesting that the . . . Equal Rights Amendment would have had the same import if it had simply been the Rights Amendment, declaring that "[r]ights under the law shall not be denied . . . on account of sex." *Id.* at 594. This latter formulation, however, might have freed our thinking from the strictures of comparing women to men and enabled us to talk more openly about what rights women as women, rather than as not men, might need in our society.

13. I am indebted to Clare Dalton for this analysis. See C. Dalton, Remarks on Personhood, delivered at Association of American Law Schools panel, January 5, 1985 (unpublished manuscript). . . .

14. Fran Olsen has pointed out that it is necessary to challenge the social conditions that make rights seem necessary. Olsen, Statutory Rape: A Feminist Critique of Rights Analysis, Part 5 this volume.

15. Professor Chris Littleton . . . admitted that her proposal to move beyond the assimilation model by questioning the social conditions that make certain differences operate as handicaps would constitute a complete redefinition of "equality." Note, Toward A Redefinition of Sexual Equality, 95 Harv. L. Rev. 487 (1981), at 507–08. She also admitted that "[a] coherent redefinition of the meaning of sexual equality may not be possible at the moment. . . . *Id.* at 507. What I fear is that by trying to fit a redefinition into the existing terminology, one becomes vulnerable to the objection that the proposed redefinition is not what "equality" as pronounced in the existing antidiscrimination doctrine means. . . .

16. I call the equality doctrine a borrowed language because litigators in the first sex discrimination cases looked to the race discrimination doctrine developed during the heyday of the civil rights movement. See Karst, Woman's Constitution, 1984 Duke L.J. 447, 470.

17. . . . Although women are now faced with issues for which the current model of equality may not be suited to accomplish necessary social change, that does not mean that the principle of equality should be completely abandoned. Rather, it is necessary to analyze the ultimate goal—mere access to male prerogatives, or a more profound change in values, structures, and policies—and equality analysis should be used only when, despite its limitations, it is tailored to the goal.

18. It would seem that a woman who requests scheduling accommodations from her employer is actually demonstrating her sincere job commitment. She is showing that she has given mature thought to her numerous responsibilities and has realized that to continue giving top-level performance to the job she must make adjustments in when she will be available to work. A woman who did not have a strong career commitment might not seek to remain in a demanding job. Employers should not blindly accept the stereotypes about career commitment that make it acceptable for a man to talk about his family in the office, but make it politically dangerous for a woman to show similar concern. Rather, they should realize that human beings of both sexes can be dedicated to their families and careers at the same time, but that doing so requires some adjustments in both worlds.

❖ PART 3

New Approaches to Equality and Difference

❖ *Introduction*

FEMINIST SCHOLARS and litigators in the 1970s agreed that one general abstract standard of equality should be applied to women. This abstract standard of equality, based on the Aristotelian notion, guaranteed that likes would be treated alike and unlikes would be treated unalike. That is, women similarly situated to men should be accorded the same entitlements as men. This standard of equality faltered in the face of situations such as pregnancy, in which women are not like men. The answer for some feminists was that perhaps treating women differently was the more appropriate route to equality. The essays in Part 2 give a flavor of the impassioned debate over the sameness versus difference approach to equality.

Subsequent to the sameness–difference debate, many feminist scholars have become increasingly critical of this approach to equality. For example, some feminists suggested that poststructuralism be used to transcend the sameness–difference debate. Poststructuralism is a school of influential French thinkers (Lacan, Derrida, and Foucault among them) who have been concerned with the same issues of difference and differentiation that plague feminist legal theory. These French thinkers explore these concerns as issues of knowledge and power. One feminist legal theorist, Marie Ashe, urged using poststructuralism to exit from the impasse of the sameness–difference debate.[1] Additional feminist scholars have joined in this suggestion. For example, Joan Scott argues against the oppositional pairing of the either-or dilemma that the debate presents, and suggests a redefinition of equality.[2]

> The solution of the "difference dilemma" comes neither from ignoring nor embracing difference as it is normatively constituted. Instead, it seems to me that the critical feminist position must always involve two moves. The first is the systematic criticism of the operations of categorical difference, the exposure of the kinds of exclusions and inclusions—the hierachies—it constructs, and a refusal of their ultimate "truth." A refusal, however, not in the name of an equality that implies sameness or identity, but rather (and this is the second move) in the name of an equality that rests on dif-

ferences—differences that confound, disrupt and render ambiguous the meaning of any fixed binary opposition. . . .[3]

Similarly, Zillah Eisenstein in her book *The Female Body and the Law*[4] advocates the need to abandon the notion of sexual dichotomy in favor of a plurality of differences. She also suggests a method of ending the debate: through integration of each side's insights rather than the triumph of one position at the expense of the other.[5]

The authors of the essays in Part 3 all share a perspective that is critical of the traditional approach to equality. Thus they join the long-standing feminist debate over the appropriate goal of feminism and the best methods of achieving that goal.

Professor Mary Becker in "Prince Charming: Abstract Equality," begins this Part by challenging the assumption that one general standard of equality should be applied by judges. Utilizing several legal cases to illustrate her point, she demonstrates a variety of problems with the doctrine of "formal equality," or treating like cases alike, including its subjectivity, false promise of neutrality, and assumption that it is possible to ignore a person's sex. Moreover, Becker notes, formal equality has proven dangerous to women. It has harmed women by eliminating traditional sex-based rules that formerly protected women.

The limitations of current equality doctrine lead Becker to conclude that feminists should not search for another general standard of equality. Instead, she advocates that feminists should work for legislative change that is likely to be more effective in improving the lives of women.

Christine Littleton, in "Reconstructing Sexual Equality," also offers a critique of equality theory. She points to a different limitation of equality theory: its "phallocentrism." She proposes that equality analysis be reconstructed to overcome its ensnarement in the male-dominated perspective. To that end, she conceptualizes a new model of equality: "equality as acceptance." Whereas Becker proposes abandoning the judicial approach and the constitutional standard, Littleton proposes an alternative theoretical model of equality.

Littleton begins by categorizing feminist models of equality into two groups: symmetrical and asymmetrical. She uses the terminology of "symmetry" and "asymmetry" to describe the two directions in feminist legal thought usually identified as "equal treatment" and "special treatment." Under symmetrical models, she subsumes assimilation and androgynous approaches.

Equality as acceptance differs from other asymmetrical models by focusing, not on sources of differences, but on their consequences. Under her model, differences between human beings, whether biological or cultural, would not make a difference in equality. To illustrate how the acceptance model would operate, Littleton proposes using "gender complements." Equality as acceptance matches a female-gendered difference to its male complement and treats them equally in terms of compensation, status, and opportunity for promotion into decision-making positions. For example, to make difference costless, mothers would be paid the same wages and benefits as soldiers.

Littleton acknowledges that matching gender complements to equalize them has its shortcomings. It might reinforce harmful stereotypes, for example. Nevertheless, she suggests that phallocentric meanings of value will change as women achieve equal decision-making opportunities. Despite the limitations of her acceptance model, she suggests that it will provide a methodology for facilitating inquiry into gender difference, as well as "reclaiming equality across difference."

Diana Majury's essay, "Strategizing in Equality," shares an important similarity with Becker's. Similar to Becker, Majury concludes that feminists should abandon the search for one general abstract equality formula. Unlike Becker, however, she does not advocate abandoning the language of equality in the context of litigation. Instead, she argues that equality formulas should be utilized as strategies for redressing women's experiences of sexism. Hence her "equality as strategy" approach could be viewed as a companion litigative approach to Becker's "piecemeal legislative" approach.

Majury begins her essay by focusing on the feminist critique of equality. She notes that the major shortcomings of equality are its lack of precision, its open-endedness and indeterminacy. Majury observes that proponents of the various equality models, influenced by common law's reverence for consistency, assume that one single model of equality should be adopted. She sees this pursuit of one equality formula as the "trap" of the equality debate for several reasons. First, even if one feminist equality formula could be agreed on, it is politically naive to assume that this would be accepted as the prevailing approach to equality by our patriarchal legal system. Second, experience teaches us that no single equality model would work exclusively in women's interests: once a theory is successful in assisting women, decision makers reformulate it to limit women's options and impede their progress.

For these reasons, Majury urges against the adoption of one equality formula, pointing to the flexibility that the indeterminacy of equality offers. Rather than pursue one formula, Majury proposes that feminists utilize an inequality-based strategy to eliminate forms of women's oppression by focusing on specific and concrete manifestations of inequalities. While this strategy would abandon equality as a goal, it would not abandon the advantages of equality-based discourse. It would utilize equality's indeterminacy to respond to women's experiences of inequality and employ equality rhetoric to counter domination and subordination. Pursuing "equality as strategy" will enable feminists to develop women-centered equality arguments to counter male-based arguments that have used equality provisions to further men's interests at the expense of women's.

Majury's approach of equality as strategy would begin not by referring to definitions, legal models, or frameworks of equality, but by identifying women's specific needs and problems and determining the desired solution. The second step would be to devise an appropriate means to achieve that solution. If a legal method is desirable, feminists would assess models of equality as potential strategies by looking at how they have been used by decision makers. Strategies and results would be evaluated not in terms of their impact on a particular model of equality, but in terms of their effects on disadvantaged groups. If a given equality formula would operate against women's interests, it would be rejected. Thus, instead of allowing one equality formula to dictate solutions, equality as strategy allows more responsive and creative solutions to women's problems.

Finally, Majury asserts that feminist advocates must see their various theories and strategies not as mutually exclusive, but rather as mutually supportive. Thus, her equality as strategy approach cannot stand alone; its effectiveness depends on simultaneous pursuits of other reform and revolutionary strategies.

Catharine MacKinnon, one of the foremost feminist legal theorists, explores issues of equality and difference in her "Difference and Dominance: On Sex Discrimination." She first explored these issues in an earlier book *Sexual Harassment of Working Women: A Case of Sex Discrimination* (1979). Similar to Becker and Majury, MacKinnon proposes abandoning the prevailing standard of equality as a route to improve women's status. And, similar to Littleton, MacKinnon proposes an alternative formula. Yet MacKinnon's formulation goes far beyond Littleton's. MacKinnon presents her "dominance approach" as a universal replacement with a broad theoretical foundation of its own, one that provides a new theory of the state. (The latter issue is explored in Part 5 in other MacKinnon essays.)

The first half of MacKinnon's essay here is a critique of dominant sex equality theory for treating equality questions and gender questions as issues of sameness and difference. She identifies two "alternate paths to equality." What Littleton terms the "symmetrical" and "asymmetrical" models of equality (or the equal treatment and special treatment models), MacKinnon calls the "sameness and differences branches of the difference approach to sex discrimination." The sameness standard's definition of sexual equality as gender neutrality, MacKinnon notes, results in equality only when women are not distinguishable from men. In instances when there is no male standard (i.e., pregnancy), it becomes sex discrimination to give women what only women need; and it is not discrimination to treat women differently by denying to women what only women need. In contrast, men's differences from women are already affirmatively compensated in society before men even enter the courtroom. Thus, argues MacKinnon, the sameness standard misses the fact of social inequality (e.g., women's poverty, financial dependence, motherhood, and sexual accessibility) imposed by male supremacy.

The differences branch is not significantly better in MacKinnon's view. The law's embracing differences (imposed on women by male supremacy), MacKinnon believes, merely affirms the qualities of powerlessness assigned to women and perpetuates the damage of sexism. Thus the traditional approaches, according to MacKinnon, are incapable of achieving sexual equality.

In response to the problem, MacKinnon proposes an alternative to the traditional approach. She terms it the "dominance approach." This approach treats gender equality issues as questions of the distribution of power, of male supremacy and female subordination. The dominance approach would treat as issues of sex discrimination many issues that are not so regarded by the law, for example, the abuse of women in rape, battering, prostitution, and pornography, and the sexual abuse of children.

The difference and dominance approaches endorse different views of law as an agent of social change, according to MacKinnon. The difference approach treats the status quo as its standard and accepts the arrangements of male supremacy. The difference approach sees any attempt to change social reality as a moral dilemma that requires a separate judgment of how things ought to be. In contrast, the dominance approach sees social inequalities from the standpoint of the subordination of women to men. It does not require a separate question of what ought to be. Instead, it asserts that, as with race, no amount of group difference justifies treating women as subhuman. The dominance approach demands equal power for women in social life. This is the objective, for MacKinnon, of equality law.

Ruth Colker's essay, "The Anti-Subordination Principle," reveals several parallels with MacKinnon. Both theorists' point of departure is a desire to remove the discussion of equality from the equal treatment/special treatment debate. Both theorists recognize that the objective of the law should be to eliminate differences in power and control. But whereas MacKinnon speaks of the dominant approach as being more effective than traditional equality analysis in addressing women's status, Colker substitutes the term "the anti-subordination principle." The anti-subordination principle, similar to MacKinnon's dominance approach, seeks a perspective that emerges from women's and Blacks' own understandings of their condition.

Colker argues that the principle of antisubordination, rather than antidifferentiation, should underlie equal protection doctrine. The dominant antidifferentiation principle assumes that all racial and sexual differentiations are equally invidious. A classic individual rights analysis, it lacks a historical perspective to distinguish between different kinds of racial and sexual differentiations. That is, rules that exclude whites are as bad as rules that exclude Blacks. In contrast, the antisubordination principle encompasses a group-based perspective that perceives society as a racial patriarchy; it recognizes historical power hierarchies that make rules excluding Blacks more invidious than rules excluding whites. The antidifferentiation principle values the abstract concepts of color-blindness and sex-blindness; it sees the evil as differentiation itself. In contrast, the antisubordination principle seeks a perspective that emerges from women's and Blacks' own understandings of their condition; the evil is not differentiation, but lack of power and control.

The antidifferentiation principle is evidenced by the two ways to establish a prima facie case of discrimination under existing equal protection doctrine. By focusing completely on the perspective of the person in power, the intent requirement is a pure articulation of antidifferentiation. Disparate impact comes closer to antisubordination, but it still cannot distinguish more invidious forms of differentiation. In contrast, a pure antisubordination perspective views discrimination as a societal mechanism that results in Blacks and women having less power. The intent of the actor does not matter; instead, the effects on those acted on are important. The issue becomes how the action contributes to the subordination of Blacks, women, or both. Under existing constitutional and statutory standards of review (reflecting the antidifferentiation approach), levels of scrutiny reflect less tolerance of race differentiations than sex differentiations. Once lower courts find discrimination, defenses are limited to economic arguments justifying differentiation. In contrast, pure antisubordination would apply one standard of scrutiny to race and sex classifications, permitting differentiation only if it redresses subordination. Further, the inquiry in the latter case would always be from the perspective of women, Blacks, or both, even if they are not parties to the suit.

Whereas MacKinnon has been criticized for her failure to operationalize her theory, Colker applies her new principle. She uses three hypotheticals to illustrate how the antidifferentiation principle has enabled law to ignore important issues that the antisubordination principle would highlight. She focuses on the following situations: (1) single Black mothers, (2) pretty secretaries, and (3) gender-segregated baseball teams. In the first situation, a women's public interest organization primarily employs Black women as clericals and secretaries. The organization decides to address the problem of the absenteeism of its employees by making available special leave and insurance programs only to Black women with family responsibilities. In the second situation, a law firm hires only pretty women to be secretaries. And in the third hypothetical, a community establishes segregated baseball teams. A young Black male excluded from playing on the girls' league team desires to become a member. Colker analyzes whether these cases violate existing law (reflecting the antidifferentiation principle) as well as under her proposed antisubordination principle.

Based on her analysis of the foregoing situations, Colker concludes that the antisubordination principle is more responsive to the subordination of Blacks and women. While existing law assumes that all problems should be phrased in sex-neutral and race-neutral language, antisubordination recognizes the importance of letting subordinated groups decide whether they want race- or sex-specific solutions. Thus, it would give equal protection doctrine the flexibility to use differentiations to redress subordination. Colker's essay is significant for its contribution of illustrating how an improved formulation of the equality standard would address issues that heretofore the law has ignored.

In her essay "Feminism and the Limits of Equality," Patricia Cain joins the ranks of other theorists here who conclude that the feminist search for one equality theory should be abandoned. Her discussion moves away from the practicalities of judicial application to evaluating feminist legal theory once again on an abstract level.

Cain categorizes feminist theories into four schools of thought to illustrate disagreements over the meaning of equality and accompanying different perceptions of "woman." She explores underlying assumptions of the schools of thought of liberal feminism, radical feminism, cultural feminism, and postmodern feminism. For example, the first school of thought, liberal feminism, sees "woman" defined by patriarchy as one confined to the private sphere. Liberal feminists argue that women are as rational as men. Thus, according to liberal feminists, equality signifies equal opportunity with men so that women may exercise their individual rights to make rational, self-interested choices. This assimilationist view of equality has been criticized by the proponents of other feminist approaches for forcing women from one male-constructed category (private home sphere) to another unchanged male-constructed category (public work sphere).

In contrast to liberal feminists' equality arguments based on individual rights and on the similarities of women to men, radical feminists advocate class-based equality theories that focus on differences between women and men. Radical feminist theories, including Littleton's equality as acceptance theory and MacKinnon's dominance theory, endorse affirmative measures to counter inequalities built into the socially constructed definition of "woman" as man's sexual object. Similarly, proponents of the third school, cultural feminists, like radical feminists, focus on women's differences from men. Unlike radical feminists, however, they view women's differences as positive. Theorists of this school, including Carol Gilligan and Robin West, argue that the category "woman" has been not so much misdefined by men as undervalued. These theorists use equality rhetoric to argue for changes to support female values of caring and relational connectedness. While some cultural feminists share radical feminists' thesis that the category "woman" is a total social construction, others believe that beneath the current socially defined woman-identified values lies a natural essential "woman."

The fourth school of thought, postmodern feminism,[6] admits that gender categories as well as equality doctrines are social constructs that, as products of patriarchy, are in need of feminist reconstruction. But, postmodernists reject the search for one new truth to replace the old. They believe that the essential woman does not exist and join some liberal theorists in criticizing the tendency in radical and cultural feminism toward "essentialism" (the reliance on a single concept of "woman" abstracted from the experience of white heterosexual women). Postmodernists see "woman" as so overly determined that she is an absence, not a presence. Thus, they do not focus on the category "woman"; instead, they focus on the situated realities of women, plural. Instead of employing abstract universal theory, postmodernists favor practical solutions to women's concrete situations.

Following Cain's analysis of the different schools of feminist thought, she proposes a different objective for feminism than equality. Her goal for feminist legal theorists is the development of legal theories that will support the process of self-definition. She calls on feminists to refocus the debate from equality theories to conversations about women's self-definition. Thereby, she echoes the call of Majury, Colker, and others to look at women's individual situations. According to Cain, these alternative legal theories that support the feminist goal of self-defini-tion should acknowledge the importance of feminist method by embracing the values of consciousness raising; they should support the telling of individual truths while protecting women's connectedness.

Cain's analysis of the views of the different feminist schools of thought about equality and the nature of woman offers a valuable effort, similar to West's essay in Part 1, by which readers may understand the diverse feminist theories and theorists. Finally, Cain's emphasis on women's diversity provides an important transition to the final focus of this section, that is, rethinking approaches to differ-ence.

Martha Minow, one of the preeminent difference theorists, addresses differ-ence theory here in two essays: "Justice Engendered" and "When Difference Has Its Home." Her first essay moves the section's focus away from the surface debate about equality to deeper underlying issues. This essay provides an excellent intro-duction to the discussion on difference by describing unstated assumptions un-derlying legal theories of difference.

In "Justice Engendered," Minow describes three versions of what she terms "the dilemma of difference" faced by judges and lawmakers who must determine which differences between people should matter. The dilemma of difference oc-curs when one claims equality based on rights grounded in difference and poses an obstacle to social and legal change. These versions include the following: First, difference can be re-created either by noticing it or by ignoring it. Second, neu-trality poses a riddle: does remaining neutral mean maintaining the status quo by ignoring difference or making difference matter by accommodating it? And third, should legal officials grant broad discretion to accommodate difference or construct formal rules to constrain discretion that thereby makes difference sig-nificant?

These dilemmas appear unsolvable because of several unstated assumptions, which Minow then identifies, about the nature of difference. Minow argues that these assumptions frustrate legislative and constitutional commitments to chang-ing the treatment of differences in regard to race, gender, ethnicity, and hand-icap, for example. Once the assumptions underlying the difference dilemmas are articulated, the dilemmas can be understood not as unsolvable problems about neutrality but struggles over which versions of reality the legal system should em-brace. Minow concludes that justice will become "engendered" when judges, law-makers, and legal theorists recognize that there is no single, superior perspective for judging questions of difference and admit the limits of their own partiality.

Minow's "When Difference Has Its Home" develops the author's theme fur-ther. In this essay, Minow isolates and contrasts three approaches to difference analysis, thereby illustrating sharp divisions about the meaning of difference in equal protection doctrine. These include (1) the "abnormal persons" approach, which views differences as basic, immutable traits; (2) the "rights analysis" approach, which regards legal rights as applying to everyone; and (3) the "social relations" approach, which assumes that assertions of difference are statements of relationships, not natural, immutable traits.

Minow prefers the social relations approach, which contributes to the understanding that difference is not fixed but is socially constructed. This approach, she argues, would improve the traditional approach to equality theory. Analyses preoccupied with treating likes alike and unlikes differently could be replaced with analyses of the manner in which institutions (including legal institutions) construct and utilize differences to justify and enforce exclusions with an eye toward transforming such practices. Minow's conclusion favoring the "social relations" approach (or, at least the "rights analysis" approach modified by social relations insights) suggests new possibilities for a feminist approach to the question of equality and legal treatment of difference.

Minow's work is not without its critics. For example, her views have been criticized for a lack of attention to the effects of power and for an undue optimism that judges will take into account the perspectives of the disadvantaged.[7] Despite these arguable shortcomings, Minow's work marks an important and essential first step in understanding difference. We must first understand the nature and sources of difference before being able to formulate the best response to the problem of inequality. Moreover, Minow's work makes another important contribution. It illustrates that feminist legal theory can advance feminist analysis in new contexts. Thus, feminist legal theory can offer valuable insights to legal issues of difference, for example, that involve not only gender but other disadvantages as well.

Notes

1. Ashe, Mind's Opportunity: Birthing a Poststructuralist Feminist Jurisprudence, 38 Syracuse L. Rev. 1129 (1987).

2. Scott, Deconstructing Equality-Versus-Difference: Or, The Uses of Poststructuralist Theory for Feminism, 14 Feminist Studies 33 (Spring 1988).

3. *Id.* at 48.

4. Z. Eisenstein, The Female Body and the Law (University of California Press, 1988).

5. See also Williams, Feminism and Post-Structuralism (Book Review, The Female Body and the Law), 88 Mich. L. Rev. 1776 (1990).

6. Much has been written recently on postmodernism and feminism. See, e.g., L. Nicholson ed., Feminism/Postmodernism (Routledge, 1990); Frug, A Postmodern Feminist Legal Manifesto (An Unfinished Draft), 105 Harv. L. Rev. 1045 (1992); Minow, Incomplete Correspondence: An Unsent Letter to Mary Joe Frug,

105 Harv. L. Rev. 1096 (1992); Patterson, Postmodernism/Feminism/Law, 77 Cornell Law Review 254 (1992).

7. Hutchinson, Inessentially Speaking (Is There Politics After Postmodernism?) (Book Review, Making All the Difference), 89 Mich. L. Rev. 1545, 1558, 1566 (1991). This is a review of Minow's book that elaborates on the theories she expresses here. See M. Minow, Making All the Difference: Inclusion, Exclusion, and American Law (Cornell University Press, 1990).

❖ *Prince Charming: Abstract Equality*

Mary E. Becker

MOST LAWYERS, SCHOLARS, AND JUDGES interested in changing the relative status of women and men assume that there is an appropriate general or abstract standard of equality which should be applied by judges. The debate centers on what standard is most appropriate and how to apply it. Throughout the seventies, most participants agreed that formal equality was the most appropriate general standard,[1] though the more flexible disparate impact standard should perhaps be available in some employment cases. Today, these are the two dominant legal standards. The standard of formal equality is applied in constitutional cases under the Equal Protection Clause of the Fourteenth Amendment. And in Title VII cases, involving discrimination in employment, formal equality is augmented by disparate impact, which is available in some cases.

In the eighties, feminists became increasingly critical of these two legal standards. Within the feminist community, a consensus seems to be developing that formal equality is inadequate. Some feminists have proposed alternatives.[2]

This debate has, however, assumed a questionable proposition: that a single general standard of equality should be adopted and applied. Rather than attempt to find one abstract standard to solve women's problems, we should identify objectionable aspects of particular situations and argue for particular changes in the appropriate forum, which will often be the legislature. Any general, or abstract, approach is unlikely to effect much real change without seriously risking worsening the situation of many women, especially ordinary mothers and wives. [C]ases . . . serve to illustrate these points: California Federal Savings & Loan Ass'n v. Guerra,[3] [and] Johnson v. Transportation Agency.[4] . . .

1987 Sup. Ct. Rev. 201. © 1988 by The University of Chicago. All rights reserved.

Contemporary Legal Standards of Equality

I begin with *Guerra* and *Johnson*. In *Guerra,* the question was the legality of a California statute requiring employers to give workers disabled by childbirth (but not workers otherwise disabled) up to four months unpaid leave. The case arose when Lillian Garland sought to resume working as a receptionist after taking a two-month leave following the birth of her daughter. Her employer told her that her old job had been filled and that there were no similar positions available. Garland was unable to find another job immediately, and because of her unemployment, she lost her apartment and eventually custody of her daughter. When Garland sought to enforce her statutory right before the California Department of Fair Employment and Housing, her former employer, Cal. Fed., brought an action in federal district court seeking a declaration that the California statute was inconsistent with and preempted by Title VII.

The feminist community divided sharply on whether employers should be required to give unpaid leave to workers disabled by pregnancy. NOW, the ACLU's Women's Rights Project, and a number of other feminist organizations (hereinafter NOW et al.), argued against permitting states to require disability leaves only for pregnancy.[5] Other feminist groups argued that such statutes should be permissible despite their violation of formal equality.[6] The Supreme Court agreed, and ruled that the California statute guaranteeing jobs only to women disabled by pregnancy was permissible despite Title VII's ban on sex and pregnancy discrimination.

In *Johnson,* the question was the legality of an affirmative action plan for women in promotions to a position previously held only by men. The Santa Clara County Transit District Board of Supervisors adopted an Affirmative Action Plan for the County Transportation Agency in December 1978. The Plan authorized the agency to consider sex as one factor in deciding which of several qualified applicants to promote to traditionally male job classifications. A year later, in December of 1979, the Agency announced a road-dispatcher opening. Dispatchers assign road crews, equipment, materials, and maintain records of road maintenance jobs. Twelve employees applied for this promotion, including Paul Johnson and Diane Joyce. Joyce was the first woman ever to be a road maintenance worker. She was the only woman in a force of 110 road maintenance workers at the time of the promotion, and the promotion requirements included at least four years of dispatch or road maintenance work. No woman had previously been road dispatcher, a skilled craft position, nor had any woman ever held any of the 238 skilled craft positions at the Agency. Joyce and six men were certified as eligible for promotion after an interview by a two-person board. This board scored applicants on their interview performance. Johnson received a seventy-five; Joyce a seventy-three. (A score over seventy was required to be deemed eligible for the promotion.)

Thereafter, three Agency supervisors conducted a second interview. One of these supervisors had been Joyce's supervisor when she began work as a road maintenance worker. He had issued her coveralls (routinely issued to the men) only after she had ruined her clothes on several occasions, complained several times, and finally filed a grievance. Another member of this panel described Joyce as a "rebel-rousing [*sic*], skirt-wearing person." This member scheduled the interview (apparently deliberately) so as to conflict with Joyce's disaster-preparedness class. The three-man panel recommended that Johnson be given the promotion.

James Graebner, the Director of the Agency, was authorized to make the final selection of the new road dispatcher from among those eligible. Graebner, consistent with the recommendation of the Agency's Affirmative Action Coordinator, promoted Joyce. Women's groups unanimously argued that this affirmative action was permissible under Title VII, and the Supreme Court agreed. . . .

. . . These cases illustrate a number of problems with formal equality. First, . . . the question of who is similarly situated is hardly susceptible to answer by objective, value-free analysis. There is, for example, a sense in which disabled pregnant workers are similar to other workers disabled for similar periods. From another perspective, it seems strange to consider women and men similarly situated with respect to pregnancy-related disabilities since only women are physically disabled by the onset of parenthood. Which perspective seems appropriate depends on the particular issue and on one's perspective and values. As this example illustrates, formal equality is not capable of discerning discrimination against pregnant people. This, in itself, is a major failing.

As another example of the subjectivity inherent in identifying those similarly situated, consider *Johnson*. Giving Joyce an edge over Johnson at the end of the promotion process is affirmative action only if Johnson and Joyce were similarly situated. If they were not similarly situated, it would not violate formal equality to treat them differently. The notion that they might have been similarly situated is fanciful. Their prior employment experiences were not similar even when they had identical titles. For Joyce, work as the only female road maintenance worker would have involved a constant struggle, including dealing with hazing and harassment. Johnson was one of the boys. It is, however, likely that many male decision makers would neither see what Joyce went through nor appreciate that her unique experiences might be qualifications for promotion. They would be more likely to consider Johnson better qualified because as road dispatcher, Joyce will probably continue to have problems operating in a male world.

To date, standards have not been developed to identify the appropriate perspective from which to decide whether groups or individuals are similarly situated. Typically, judges simply note, in a conclusory fashion, that A and B are (or are not) similarly situated, as though the point was obvious and noncontroversial. In the absence of appropriate standards, women are not likely to be served well by a formal equality standard applied by predominantly male judges on the basis of their subjective values and perspectives.

Second, under formal equality, women who are perceived to be like men are entitled to be treated like men. This "nondiscrimination" rule is not neutral with respect to sex; it is androcentric.[7] Women cannot use formal equality to challenge workplace rules and practices which fit well with men's life-styles, needs, and experiences but less well with women's. Formal equality is not violated by workplace rules under which—as happened in *Guerra*—a new mother loses her job and custody of her daughter because she was the parent who was pregnant. Similarly, when the next Lillian Garland returns to work at Cal. Fed. following her statutorily guaranteed pregnancy leave, her employer can ignore that she is primarily responsible for the care of her daughter. Such results are not sex-neutral. As Mackinnon puts it, "day one of taking gender into account" was the day the job was structured with the expectation that its occupant would have no child care responsibilities.[8] . . .

A third major problem is that formal equality is based on a counterfactual assumption; because of this assumption formal equality will, in practice, actually mean inequality. Formal equality assumes that it is possible to ignore an individual's sex. Both common sense and empirical data suggest that we cannot and do not ignore sex in dealing with an individual. Moreover, the empirical data indicate that the routine, unconscious differential treatment of individual women and men tends to dampen ratings of women's competence and potential relative to the ratings of men.[9] To the extent that we cannot treat similarly situated women and men the same, formal equality can mask real, though perhaps unconscious, discrimination.

Johnson illustrates this point, The promotion interviews were conducted entirely by men, who had never promoted a woman to that position before, nor any similar position. [One] interviewer had been her first supervisor as a road maintenance worker, the one who issued her work coveralls only after she filed a grievance. Those interviews cannot have been precisely equal opportunities for both Joyce and Johnson. In the absence of the affirmative action plan challenged in *Johnson*, it is most unlikely that Joyce would have had a promotion opportunity equal to Johnson's. Yet, after a two-day trial, the district court found that the Agency had never discriminated on the basis of sex.

A two-day trial could not possibly have afforded a factual basis for concluding that an employer with 238 skilled craft workers and no woman ever in such a position (and one woman out of 110 road maintenance workers) had never discriminated on the basis of sex. Even after the passage of Title VII, women were routinely and overtly excluded from skilled craft positions by both unions and employers. Yet the incredible finding—that the Agency had never discriminated on the basis of sex in hiring skilled craftsmen (as the workers were doubtless originally described)—was not overruled by either reviewing court. . . .

[W]omen's exclusion was apparently invisible to all the judges deciding *Johnson*. Justice Scalia relied heavily on the district court's finding that the Santa Clara Transportation Agency had never discriminated on the basis of sex and apparently believed it. None of the Justices dismissed the finding as incredible and necessarily lacking a factual basis after a two-day trial. Judges can say no woman was ever discriminated against, but saying it cannot make it true.

Justice Scalia would probably respond that even if road maintenance and skilled craft positions had always been open to women, and even if the agency had advertised for women, it is likely that there would never have been a woman actually interested in either position prior to Joyce. This point brings out another problem with formal equality as a solution to sexual inequality. Systemic discrimination against women is often so effective that no woman will apply for a traditionally male job. Perhaps some women do prefer lower-paying women's jobs. But some may think that the job is only nominally open to them. Others may dread the harassment likely to be experienced in breaking into male jobs, especially blue-collar ones; there is no effective remedy for such harassment. Perhaps women have been socialized not to consider rough outdoor jobs but could be interested with a little encouragement. Formal equality ignores all these problems. As long as the job is open to women, so that there is no discrimination by this decision maker today, formal equality is satisfied. . . .

[F]ormal equality . . . cannot be expected to transform society by equalizing the status of women and men. In the context of employment, it only opens men's jobs to women on the terms and conditions worked out for men. Further, under formal equality, it is likely that the differences in treatment of women and men will often be invisible to the extent that the differences consist of preferential treatment of men. More specifically, it is likely that a man will appear better qualified when there is no relevant difference between a woman and a man or when the woman is marginally better qualified. And it is likely that a woman's unique qualifications (because of her experiences as a woman) will not be visible, let alone regarded as qualifications. . . .

[Another] problem with formal equality is not simply that it is incapable of radically changing society or of ensuring that similarly situated women and men are treated similarly. Formal equality has actually hurt many women. . . .

Despite the failure of the ERA campaign, formal equality has been implemented wholly or partially, directly and indirectly, through legislation and judicial changes in many ways. Because of this trend, women have lost many of the traditional sex-based rules which gave them some measure of financial security and protection. For example, consider the effect on women of the shift from the traditional maternal preference in child custody disputes. During the sixties judges assumed that it was in the best interest of a child of tender years to give custody to its mother. Many jurisdictions have either eliminated this presumption or replaced it with a presumption in favor of joint custody, thus giving a bargaining chip to fathers in negotiations with mothers. Because mothers seem to want custody much more than fathers, the result of giving this bargaining chip to fathers is that mothers who desperately want custody offer economic concessions to settle the custody issue rather than submit it to a judge.[10]

The gender-neutral custody rules adopted to date have not effected any radical restructuring of parenting roles. Instead, these rules may have contributed to the further economic impoverishment of divorced women and their children. The poverty of divorced women and their children (relative to men[11]) is not, of course, entirely attributable to the move away from the maternal presumption. There are no estimates of the effect of movement away from the maternal preference on the post-divorce economic status of women and children. The point is only that notions of formal equality have had a negative economic effect on a group that is not in a good position to bear the cost of social change.

In calculating child or spousal support at the time of divorce, which will typically be paid (if it is paid) by the father to the custodial mother, judges today often assume that the ex-homemaker will find a good-paying job. After all, Title VII and the Equal Pay Act ban wage discrimination; women and men are equal. But full-time female workers continue to earn substantially less than full-time male workers, and a woman who has no recent wage-work experience is likely to have difficulty finding even a decent woman's job. If she is the custodian of small children, as is typically the case when there are small children at the time of the divorce, she cannot enter the workforce unless she either neglects her children or earns a great deal so that she is able to pay for child care. Here, too, treating women and men as though they are equal when, in fact, they are not has worsened the post-divorce economic position of women and children, especially those women (and their children) who are most in need because they are least like men.

Traditionally, during marriage, husbands had a duty to support their wives (and not vice versa). That duty has never been directly enforceable by wives during marriage,[12] but wives' creditors were sometimes able to enforce the duty.[13] In recent cases, in pursuit of formal equality, some judges have imposed a duty on all women to support their husbands, a duty enforceable by creditors.[14] As a result, a widow who has been a homemaker all her life may find, after her husband's expensive final illness, that she is personally liable for his hospital expenses. Ordinary wives are, however, less likely than their husbands to be economically capable of supporting their spouses, especially at age sixty-five or over when the husband dies. Again, treating women and men as though they are similarly situated when they are not hurts many women. . . .

A number of the decisions hailed as giant steps for women have hurt rather than helped many women by banning sex-based legislative classifications. And some of the Supreme Court cases striking explicitly sex-based classifications as impermissible forms of discrimination seem shockingly irrelevant to discrimination in the real world. Orr v. Orr[15] and Otis v. Otis[16] illustrate these points.

In *Orr* the Supreme Court held that state statutes could not constitutionally provide for alimony to be paid by some husbands to some wives. . . . .

Statutes imposing alimony obligations only on some husbands are hardly the linchpin of systemic discrimination on the basis of sex. Far more important, by any measure, are sex-neutral statutes giving employment preferences to veterans and statutes, rules, and practices which result in the ex-husband's receiving the lion's share of the financial security (including old-age security) accumulated during the ordinary marriage. Yet of these policies, formal equality captures only the relatively trivial case of alimony imposed only on men. Such statutes are less than ideal; they reinforce notions that women are dependents because they are women. But they are not of much importance in the systemic subordination of women.

More importantly, Orr v. Orr has hurt ordinary mothers and wives. During the last twenty-five years, there has been a decrease in alimony awarded even to full-time long-term homemakers. It is likely that Orr v. Orr (and the notion of formal equality which both produced it and was reinforced by it) have contributed to this decline. In Orr v. Orr, the Court could imagine only two reasons for awarding alimony: a needy recipient and as compensation for discrimination in marriage. The Court never explains what it means by the latter, rather nebulous, concept. The other reason is need. Need is not, in itself, a very compelling reason for post-divorce payments to an ex-spouse. Far more compelling reasons are ignored entirely by the Court.

Consider Otis v. Otis, which was decided a year after *Orr* by the Supreme Court of Minnesota. The Otis marriage had lasted over twenty years. The trial judge ordered the husband (who earned over $120,000 a year as a vice-president of Control Data) to pay his ex-wife alimony for four years (at an average rate of $1,500 per month). Ms. Otis quit her job as an executive secretary when her son was born "in order to fulfill the expected, role of wife and hostess for a rising and successful business executive." She played an important role in her husband's career. For example, before his last promotion, she, too, was interviewed. When the board of directors met in Greece for a week in 1977, she was the official hostess. She had wanted to return to work a number of years previously, but her husband said he was "'not going to have any wife of mine pound a typewriter.'" When she was awarded only short-term alimony, she was forty-five years old and had been out of the workplace for approximately twenty years. The Supreme Court of Minnesota upheld the award of the trial court because, it explained, post-divorce transfer payments are based on need and Ms. Otis should be able to "rehabilitate" herself within four years.

Ms. Otis's need—in and of itself—is the weakest imaginable reason for awarding her post-divorce transfer payments. Her current need reflects her investment in her husband's career, an investment from which he will continue to profit. Her need reflects the reliance loss she sustained by not working in order to raise their son and further her husband's career (and in order to avoid embarrassing him by typing). Having relied so substantially for so long, she cannot now, at forty-five, recover what she would have had had she put her own career first. Her needs should be met because a reasonable term of their arrangement, with its traditional division of labor, is that in exchange for her reliance in engaging exclusively in non-wage domestic production and reproduction and contributing to his career rather than her own, she would receive a reasonable share of the profit brought in by her husband's career and a reasonable share of the financial security accumulated for their old age.[17] . . .

Orr v. Orr is not, of course, solely responsible for cases like Otis v. Otis. Orr v. Orr reflects and reinforces notions of formal equality which have eliminated the notion that ex-wives should receive alimony because they are women. Judges, like the Justices in Orr v. Orr, have been unable to think of any very good alternative reasons for awarding anyone alimony. Many, probably most judges, like the Justices in Orr v. Orr, have been unable to come up with anything more compelling than simple need. As a result, alimony (even when awarded) tends to be for relatively short periods of time (typically two to four years) and designed only to allow the ex-wife to become self-supporting. In the past, alimony was more often awarded permanently, that is, until the ex-wife remarried or either spouse died.[18] This change has not been good for most women, especially women who, like Ms. Orr, were homemakers for twenty years or more. Many women would have been better off if feminists had argued for needed economic rights and greater economic security for women (in recognition of their domestic production and reproduction) rather than for strict formal equality in family law matters. . . .

In the end, there are two distinct kinds of problems associated with formal equality. One is that formal equality cannot be the basis for implementing the kinds of changes that must be made if the status of women and men is to be equalized. The other is that the limited changes effected by formal equality will often hurt many women, especially ordinary mothers and wives.

Formal equality is dangerous for women in a way in which it is not dangerous for other minority groups. Few, if any, traditional racially explicit classifications ever had either the purpose or overall effect of benefiting a racial minority. There is, for example, no racial analogy to the maternal preference standard in custody disputes, no traditional racial classification which, despite its reinforcement of a stereotype, also gave a racial minority a better bargaining position in negotiations with nonminorities than would race-neutral rules. Because the legal system has protected women better than it has protected other minorities (though not, of course, as well as it has protected men), formal equality is dangerous for women in a unique way. . . .

An Impossible Dream?

We use equality to refer to a number of things, including both (i) the situation in an ideal (nonsexist) world and (ii) a legal standard to be applied by judges (based either in the Constitution or in a statute such as Title VII). Hopefully, (ii) should be a means to get from this world to the ideal world imagined in (i).

We cannot, today, know what an "ideal" world with equality between the sexes would look like, let alone how best to get there. This is another difference between race and sex. With race, we can at least imagine a world in which Blacks and whites are equal. We can imagine a world in which race is no more important than eye color. We cannot so easily imagine a world in which women and men are equal or in which sex would matter no more than eye color. Most of us would not want to live in a world in which sex was no more important or relevant than eye color. Perhaps equality could occur in a world in which sex still matters, but in different ways from the ways in which it matters in this world. Few of us can imagine what that world might look like.

For those, including myself, who think that whatever it might look like, a reasonably ideal world would look rather different from this one, formal equality must be rejected. Formal equality is not capable of producing enough change in the status quo, and is likely to impose significant costs on those women most in need of change because they are most unlike men.

Perhaps formal equality's proponents regard harm to some women (especially ordinary mothers and wives) as a justifiable cost of effecting social change. If the economic position of ordinary women (especially after divorce, an ever present danger today) becomes tenuous enough, fewer women will be willing to fulfill traditional roles or (as is often the case) attempt to combine traditional roles and some (often limited) wage work. As a result of greater insecurity, more women will work, even while their children are small, will regard their own jobs as important as their husbands', and will refuse to be primarily responsible for either child care or other domestic duties. Also, if their chances of having post-divorce custody are no greater than their husbands', they will invest less in their children during marriage, thus equalizing fathers' and mothers' investments in raising children.

There are, however, a number of problems with such justifications for formal equality. First, formal equality tends to help most exceptional professional women, with the costs borne by another group. The elite who lead the feminist movement should be reluctant to press for change they consider desirable by imposing its costs on other women.

Second, it is likely that a majority of women would consider this "solution" unacceptable. It is, for example, unlikely that most women would want to be only as involved with children as their husbands. Perhaps this is the result of their socialization, and a form of false consciousness about their own best interests. We should, however, be reluctant to use false consciousness as the basis for ignoring women's desires. One important aspect of women's subordination has been that others have defined who women are and what they want. Feminists have generally stressed the importance of listening to what women say rather than dictating what women should say and feel.

Most women might prefer other means to other ends. True, one way of effecting change is to make traditional roles (even when combined with limited employment) too risky. But one could, instead, improve the position of ordinary women by making women's traditional roles less risky, empowering women by making them less dependent on men. Is "our" goal a world in which there is more respect for and reward of those traits, skills, and contributions traditionally associated with women? Or should we try to discourage these traits, skills, and contributions so that women will be more like men? Feminists today are deeply divided on these issues. . . . Formal equality should be rejected because it takes one particular approach to a number of complicated questions about which women disagree vehemently.

Third, our young people continue to have different expectations about their futures—and different futures—depending on their sex. As long as we continue producing girls and boys with different expectations, it is fundamentally unfair to treat women, once they are grown, as though they were like men in order to foster change. Change could be more effectively and fairly fostered by changing socialization than by making motherhood, child care, and domestic work riskier through implementation of strict formal equality.

Fourth, if—as feminists have suggested—women tend (more than men) to define themselves in terms of others, it may be very unrealistic to think that women will respond to increased insecurity by taking steps in their own individual self-interest despite harms to the interests of those closest to them. Yet increased risks associated with traditional roles will effect an appropriate level of change only if women act in their individual self-interest.

Fifth, making traditional roles more costly as a means of effecting change assumes that women will assess correctly the risk associated with traditional roles given the probability of divorce. Although some women, especially remarried women, seem to take the risk of another divorce into account in making decisions about wage work versus full- or part-time homemaking, many women (especially women who have never been divorced) seem irrationally confident that divorce will not happen to them.

For all these reasons, as well as the reasons stated earlier, formal equality should not be regarded as the solution to women's problems and should not be too rigidly applied in challenges to sex-based classifications. To date, we have not developed any workable and satisfactory general alternative to formal equality, any alternative which judges would be willing to use and which would effect significant change. The remaining question is whether we should continue to seek another general standard for equality, or substitute therefore, as a solution to women's problems.

It is not feasible to prove an abstract negative: that we cannot possibly imagine a workable satisfactory general standard of equality (or substitute therefore) to replace formal equality and to be applied by judges. That may, however, be the case. I suspect it is, at least for the foreseeable future. Any standard capable of effecting real change would have to be based on a notion of both the desired end and of the appropriate means. If we do not know what equality means, we cannot know where we are going nor how to get there. How, then, can we give judges a standard of equality that will ensure our arrival? Women are not a homogenous group with widely shared beliefs on these issues. Instead, women are a large group of very different people with vastly different interests and concerns. I suspect that for the foreseeable future, any abstract standard capable of effecting real change would implement one subgroup's notion of equality with the risk that other subgroups would bear most of the cost.

Current Standards, Institutional Concerns, and Change

The Constitutional Standard

Even if we could imagine a satisfactory general standard capable of effecting real change, we should be hesitant about adopting it as a constitutional standard to be enforced by judges, at least for the foreseeable future. Judges are, and are likely to remain for the foreseeable future, mostly older, relatively conservative males. They are powerful members of the established order. One cannot realistically expect them to use a general abstract standard to implement much real change in the relative status of women and men. More importantly, as the experience with formal equality suggests, one must worry that an abstract standard will be implemented in ways that will hurt women. Harmful decisions are then enshrined as part of constitutional law and difficult to change.

A flexible constitutional standard, allowing a fair amount of leeway to legislatures rather than a rigid one like formal equality is, of course, dangerous. Under a flexible standard, a legislature may enact legislation which expressly discriminates between women and men in a way detrimental to women, and the Constitution would afford no reliable basis for striking the statute. But formal equality illustrates that using an abstract standard to overrule legislation creating distinctions between women and men is also dangerous. Under such a standard, courts can replace standards distinguishing between women and men with sex-neutral standards which worsen the position of many women (especially ordinary mothers and wives), because women and men are not similarly situated.

The current constitutional standard, although it has gone a ways toward formal equality, is still fairly flexible. I would suggest that it has gone too far already; we should not push for further movement toward either strict formal equality for sex-based classifications (analogous to the standard for racial classifications) or for any alternative general standard as a constitutional matter.

I do not mean to suggest that feminists should be content with the current constitutional standard. That standard is seriously flawed, and it may be possible to fashion concrete refinements which make it more effective while retaining some flexibility. We should not, however, expect even a refined constitutional standard to solve all, or even many, of women's problems.

For example, MacKinnon suggests one possible refinement to the current constitutional standard. Women might be better off were the current constitutional standard modified so that, instead of permitting express distinctions between women and men based on reasonable differences, express distinctions would be permitted only when they would pass muster under MacKinnon's inequality standard. Judges would decide whether a distinction between women and men was part of the system subordinating women.[19] One could not expect to see any radical restructuring of society with a standard which would only examine express classifications to see if they contribute to the subordination of women. This refinement might, nevertheless, be better than the current standard; it might be less dangerous to entrust the question of whether an express classification contributes to the subordination of women to judges than for judges to continue to uphold express distinctions based on sex whenever supported by a difference perceived as relevant. Thus, for example, were *Johnson* (the affirmative action case) a constitutional challenge to an affirmative action plan designed to increase the number of women in traditionally male jobs, a court could use a refined equal protection standard to uphold it, because such a plan is much more likely to empower women than it is to contribute to their subordination; the alternative to affirmative action is not sex-neutral treatment but invisible discrimination in favor of men. . . .

Change through the Political Process

Since it is unlikely that we will be able to imagine one abstract standard capable of providing an effective means for resolving all such problems, much change in the legal system must occur (if it is to occur at all) as a result of legislative change, often piecemeal legislative change. This "solution" will not, however, be easy.

A responsive political process would seem an ideal forum for resolving women's conflicting visions of equality and how to get there. There are other advantages to legislative forums. One can make all kinds of arguments. Effective arguments need not be traditional arguments. Disparate impact arguments can be effective in this setting and need a label no more esoteric than the simple word "fairness." A legislature can choose which of many policies to modify, to effect a desired change. Unlike a court, a legislature can choose the appropriate "defendant." Specific legislative reform—such as changing the social security system so that homemakers receive credits in their own accounts for their contributions (based, perhaps, on their husbands' wages)—is often the only way to effect needed changes. Only a legislature will do the kind of detailed tinkering necessary to implement many of the changes needed if the legal system is to be as responsive to women's needs as it is to men's. Many needed changes simply cannot and will not be ordered by a court pursuant to an abstract standard of equality. A final advantage of the legislative forum is that legislatures can experiment with various approaches more easily than courts. It may not always be apparent whether a certain change would be desirable or not. Or a change, desirable at one time, may become obsolete or undesirable at another. It is easier for legislatures than for courts to take different approaches at different times.

Unfortunately, it is not going to be easy to change the status of women through the legislative process, for two major reasons. The first is that the political process itself is not responsive to women, in part because women are not a homogeneous group. A number of factors make it difficult for women to operate as a cohesive political force: women are geographically dispersed; women are members of different classes; women identify with male interests because of relationships that are often only temporary; women are still raised to consider the home (rather than the public arena) their special sphere of interest; women still do not enter politics in proportion to their numbers in the population; women tend (more than men) to define themselves in terms of the interests of others (their husbands and children), and may therefore be less likely than other groups to push for their own interests in the legislative arena; women tend to have less time and money (than men) to spend lobbying; legislatures are still predominantly male enclaves and not, one imagines, much easier for individual women to break into, or to effect change within, than the all-male road maintenance gang on which Joyce worked. In addition, many issues of special concern to women are state-law issues, and many state legislatures are very conservative, even hostile, to "women's lib," a label likely to taint any change designed to equalize the status of women and men.

The second major problem is that even when women succeed in effecting legislative change, the new laws will be more or less general and will typically require judicial implementation. Judges may fail fully to implement the desired change. To some extent, this problem can be avoided by careful drafting and detailed legislative history. But, to be effective, the groups interested in change must continue to monitor the situation after the desired legislation is enacted and, when necessary, begin another round of lobbying for additional legislative reform.

Legislative change, especially piecemeal legislative change, is not a miraculous solution. If, however, for the foreseeable future, it is the only solution to many of women's problems with the current legal structure, surely it is better to face squarely that fact and attempt to implement piecemeal legislative change than to continue to strive to implement some vague and abstract standard of equality which will effect too little good and too much harm.

Conclusion

To date, we have not discovered any abstract standard of equality (or substitute therefore) with the potential for real change. Formal equality (with and without limited exceptions when there are biological differences)—the leading contender as the general standard—can effect only limited change. It cannot, for example, ensure that jobs are structured so that female workers and male workers are equally able to combine wage work and parenthood. Nor can it ensure that social security, unemployment compensation, and other safety nets are structured so as to provide for women's financial security as well as they provide for men's. Moreover, women, especially ordinary mothers and wives, have been harmed by the changes effected to date by the movement toward formal equality. Further movement in that direction could bring additional harm. Any other satisfactory and workable general standard to be applied by judges is as yet unimagined and likely to be so for the foreseeable future.

Women do not share a single vision of equality or one view of how to get there from here. Women are not a homogeneous group with homogeneous values, concerns, and interests. Were the legislative process more responsive to women, it would be a good forum for women to resolve their conflicting interests and visions of equality. Unfortunately, it is unresponsive, and certainly far from ideal. Nevertheless, piecemeal legislative change, especially in the area of economic rights, is likely to be more effective in improving the lives of many women than is the development of any abstract standard of equality.

Notes

1. See, e.g., Ginsburg, Sexual Equality under the Fourteenth and Equal Rights Amendments, 1979 Wash. U.L.Q. 161; Ginsburg, Gender and the Constitution, 44 U. Cin. L. Rev. 1 (1975); Ginsburg, Sex and Unequal Protection: Men and Women as Victims, 11 J. Fam. L. 347 (1971); Cole, Strategies of Difference: Litigating for Women's Rights in a Man's World, 2 Law & Ineq. J. 33 (1984); Brown, Emerson, Falk, & Freedman, The Equal Rights Amendment: A Constitutional Basis for Equal Rights for Women, 80 Yale L.J. 871 (1971).

2. See C. MacKinnon, Sexual Harassment of Working Women (Yale University Press, 1979); Littleton, Rethinking Sexual Equality, 75 Calif. L. Rev. 201 (1987); Scales, The Emergence of a Feminist Jurisprudence: An Essay, Part 1 this volume; Kay, Models of Equality [1985] Univ. Ill. L. Rev. 39; Kay, Equality and Difference: The Case of Pregnancy, Part 2 this volume; Law, Rethinking Sex and the Constitution, 132 U. Penn. L. Rev. 95 (1984). See also E. Wolgast, Equality and the Rights of Women (Cornell University Press, 1980) (suggesting some ways in which the standard of equality might be improved but not suggesting any one developed equality standard); Note, 95 Harv. L. Rev. 487 (1981) (similar); Freedman, Sex Equality, Sex Differences, and the Supreme Court, 92 Yale L.J. 913 (1983) (similar).

3. 479 U.S. 272 (1987).

4. 480 U.S. 616 (1987).

5. See Brief, Amici Curiae of the National Organization for Women (and six other signatories); Brief of the American Civil Liberties Union (and four other signatories). Both briefs argued that the Supreme Court should extend the statutory benefit to all workers disabled for four months or less.

6. See, e.g., Brief, Amici Curiae of Coalition for Reproductive Equality in Workplace; Betty Friedan; International Ladies' Garment Worker's Union, AFL-CIO; 9 to 5; National Association of Working Women; Planned Parenthood Federation of America, Inc., California School Employees Association; American Fed-

eration of State, County and Municipal Employees, District Council 36; California Federation of Teachers; Coalition of Labor Union Women, Los Angeles Chapter (and thirty other signatories).

7. For discussions of the chimera of neutrality, see McConnell, Neutrality under the Religion Clauses, 81 Nw. U.L. Rev. 146 (1986); Minow, The Supreme Court 1986 Term—Foreword: Justice Engendered, Part 3 herein; Sunstein, *Lochner*'s Legacy, 87 Colum. L. Rev. 873 (1987).

8. C. MacKinnon, Feminism Unmodified 37 (Harvard University Press, 1987).

9. See, e.g., W. McArthur, Social Judgment Biases in Comparable Worth Analysis, in H. Hartmann ed., Comparable Worth: New Directions for Research 53, 55–64 (National Academy Press, 1985); Gerdes & Garber, Sex Bias in Hiring: Effects of Job Demands and Applicant Competence, 9 Sex Roles 307 (1983); Francesco & Hakel, Gender and Sex as Determinates of Hireability of Applicants of Gender-Typed Jobs, 5 Psychol. Women Q. 747 (1981); Plake, Murphy-Berman, Derscheid, Gerber, Miller, Speth, & Tomes, Access Decisions by Personnel Directors: Subtle Forms of Sex Bias in Hiring, 11 Psychol. Women Q. 225 (1987); Francesco, Gender and Sex as Detriments of Hireability of Applicants for Genders-Typed [sic] Jobs, 5 Psychol. Women Q. 747 (1981).

10. See J. Schulmann & V. Pitt, Second Thoughts on Joint Child Custody: Analysis of Legislation and Its Implications for Women and Children, in J. Folberg, ed., Joint Custody and Shared Parenting 209 (Bureau of National Affairs, 1984); Scott & Derdeyn, Rethinking Joint Custody, 45 Ohio St. L.J. 455, 478 and n. 106 (1981); Pearson & Ring, Judicial Decision-Making in Contested Custody Cases, 21 J. Fam. L. 703, 719 (1982); Neely, The Primary Caretaker Parent Rule: Child Custody and the Dynamics of Greed, 3 Yale L. & Pol'y Rev. 168 (1984).

11. See L. Weitzman, The Divorce Revolution, xii (Free Press, 1987); Espenshade, The Economic Consequences of Divorce, J. Marriage & Fam. 615 (August 1979); Women's Research and Education Institute, Congressional Caucus for Women, The American Woman, 1987: A Report in Depth 78–82 (Norton, 1987) (citing surveys).

12. See, e.g., McGuire v. McGuire, 157 Neb. 226, 59 N.W.2d 336 (1953).

13. See, e.g., Sharpe Furniture, Inc. v. Buckstaff, 99 Wis.2d 114, 299 N.W.2d 219 (1980).

14. See, e.g., Jersey Shore Medical Center v. Estate of Baum, 84 N.J.2d 137, 417 A.2d 1003 (1980) (rule to be applied in future cases).

15. 440 U.S. 268 (1979).

16. 299 N.W.2d 114 (Minn. 1980).

17. In *Otis*, the court divided approximately equally the property accumulated during the marriage except that it also awarded Mr. Otis all of his vested pension plan. The court does not attach any specific value to that plan.

18. If alimony is basically a form of expectation–reliance (contract) damages for the needy traditional wife when a marriage breaks up, it should not necessarily terminate entirely with her remarriage. Thus, I do not mean to suggest that traditional rules could not be improved upon.

19. Granted, it is not always easy to distinguish benefits (empowerment) from burdens (disempowerment), and women may be hurt if burdens are judged bene-

fits. In addition, as has been noted repeatedly here, often a policy helps some women and hurts others. On the other hand, as the affirmative action cases illustrate well, it is not always impossible to judge that it is likely that a certain policy benefits more women than it hurts. This standard might work out to be much like that proposed by Sherry, Selective Judicial Activism in the Equal Protection Context: Democracy, Distrust, and Deconstruction, 73 Georgetown L.J. 89 (1984) (only disfavored classes should be able to bring equal protection challenges).

❖ *Feminism and the Limits of Equality*

Patricia A. Cain

Feminist legal theorists, at least in this country, seem to be obsessed with the concept of equality. Given the pre-eminence of the equal protection clause in twentieth century constitutional litigation, this obsession is not surprising. . . .

Despite its possibilities, the meaning of equality as a constitutional norm has remained limited to the concept of formal equality. This limitation persists despite extensive feminist attempts to reconceptualize the meaning of equality. Feminists have not been able to agree among themselves on a uniform core definition for equality. . . .

In this essay, I will consider four schools of feminist thought: liberal, radical, cultural and postmodern. My initial purpose is to highlight and explain the disagreements over the meanings of equality that have occurred among feminist legal scholars influenced by these four schools of thought. I believe these disagreements reflect real differences of opinion about how "woman" is currently defined by male power and how she should be defined by feminists. . . .

. . . [I] will conclude with some thoughts about the future. Specifically, I will propose that feminists in law concentrate on alternative legal arguments—that is, arguments based not on equality, but on other concepts that are better-tailored to accomplishment of the feminist goal of self-definition. . . .

Schools of Feminist Thought: Perspectives on "Woman" and "Equality"

Liberal Feminism

Liberal feminism is rooted in the belief that women, as well as men, are rights-bearing, autonomous human beings. Rationality, individual choice, equal rights and equal opportunity are central concepts for liberal political theory. Liberal

24 Ga. L. Rev. 803 (1990).

feminism, building on these concepts, argues that women are just as rational as men and that women should have equal opportunity with men to exercise their right to make rational, self-interested choices. Early liberal feminists include Mary Wollstonecraft (1759–1799) and Harriet Taylor.

Today, liberal feminism is often associated with Betty Friedan and other founders of the National Organization of Women. Within the legal academy, it is a term associated with Ruth Bader Ginsburg, Herma Hill Kay, Wendy Williams and Nadine Taub. Liberal feminism is viewed as the dominant theory behind much of the post-Reed v. Reed constitutional litigation brought on behalf of women. This litigation was spearheaded by Ruth Bader Ginsburg, who was then a Professor of Law at Rutgers and subsequently at Columbia University. . . .

Liberal feminists have been criticized by more radical feminists for being concerned only with equal pay in the public sphere. Litigators, like Ruth Bader Ginsburg, have been charged as being short-sighted because they adopted an assimilationist theory of equality that would benefit women only if they acted like men.[1]

Let me spell out the critique a bit further. Remember that equality theory, as applied to gender, has been conceptually limited by the "similarly situated" requirement. If members of the dominant gender (men) enjoy rights that members of the nondominant gender (women) want, then the only way for women to obtain these rights under existing equal protection doctrine is to argue that, as to the right in question, women are similarly situated to men. If men are being paid X dollars for performing a job in the public sphere, then women should be entitled to the same pay for performing the same job. The equality argument is that women are workers just like men. It is this argument of similarity that makes it possible to expand women's rights. Radical feminists complain, however, that to argue on the basis of women's similarity to men merely assimilates women into an unchanged male sphere. In a sense, the result is to make women into men.

The liberal feminist response to this is that early feminist litigation was concerned with breaking down male-created categories. The point was not to make women into men, but to expand the possibilities for female life-experience by freeing women from the limitations of the male-constructed category "woman." "Woman" was to be freed from the private domestic sphere, if she so chose.

The radical feminist rejoinder is: Yes, but on whose terms? The workplace remains male-constructed. The category "worker" is male-constructed. To force women from one male-constructed category to another is not a real victory, especially if the newly constructed female worker adopts the existing patriarchal view of the world.

Wherever one comes out on this particular debate between liberal and radical feminists, it is important to understand both sides. Both sides agree that women should not be limited by male-constructed categories. Their disagreement is over which categories are most worthy of challenge. At this level, the disagreement is political and instrumental. The disagreement becomes substantive, however, when we shift the focus to the question of what should take the place of the male-constructed category "woman." Radical feminists fear that arguments couched in equal protection terms alleging the similarity between women and men may ultimately be harmful because such arguments endorse entrenched patriarchal values. The new category "woman" that emerges from such arguments is still male-constructed. This concern is valid. But if radical feminists think that liberal feminist legal scholars do not share this concern, they are mistaken.

As Wendy Williams, a liberal feminist, has recently explained, the problem with the presently constructed sex categories, male and female, is that they are defined as "discontinuous complementary poles." Furthermore, the problem with antidiscrimination law is that it

> requires that we be female or male . . . before it will extend its protection.
> . . . Thus discontinuity and complementarity are the prerequisites to remedies under the antidiscrimination laws: A person must *be* one sex, maintain the appearance (in clothing and effect) of that sex, and prefer sex with the "opposite" sex. If a person has complied with the requirement that he or she be properly "sexed," the law will then provide partial protection against penalties for being of a sex.[2]

Williams does not embrace the law's definition of "woman" when she argues that a woman (as defined by the law) is the victim of sex discrimination. Yet, as much as she may be troubled by the law's construction of "woman," she is willing to use that construction to prevent even narrower definitions from limiting the possibilities of real women in the world today.

Radical Feminism

Radical feminism is not easily defined because it takes many forms. For my purposes, it will be sufficient to contrast radical feminist thought with liberal feminist thought. First, whereas liberal feminists emphasize the individual (men and women as individual human beings), radical feminists focus on women as a class, typically as a class that is dominated by another class known as men. Second, whereas liberal feminist equality arguments are based primarily on the similarities between men and women, radical feminists tend to build arguments that focus on the differences between men and women. These differences, argue radical feminists, have been constructed in such a way as to contribute to women's inequality.

Radical feminists in the legal academy include Catharine MacKinnon and Christine Littleton. Littleton has argued for a reconstructed concept of sexual equality which would recognize woman's difference from man. She calls her model "equality as acceptance." To "accept" woman's difference, society must do something more than merely accommodate the difference. I interpret Littleton's "equality as acceptance" thesis to require the centralization of "woman" (her identity, her specificity, her difference from man) in normative debates about how the world ought to be structured. Consider the current dilemma over pregnancy in the workplace. If women had participated equally in designing the workplace from the beginning, employers would not be asked to make accommodations for pregnancy. Instead, the workplace would have been structured so that pregnant workers were not viewed as different from the norm. To move from the male-modeled workplace that currently exists to one that fully accepts women will require some fundamental changes in the model itself. We will have achieved "equality as acceptance" only when woman's difference from man is costless.

Catharine MacKinnon argues that because men have defined women as different, equality arguments cannot succeed.

> Put another way, gender is socially constructed as difference epistemologically; sex discrimination law bounds gender equality by difference doctrinally. A built-in tension exists between this concept of equality, which presupposes sameness, and this concept of sex, which presupposes difference. Sex equality thus becomes a contradiction in terms, something of an oxymoron, which may suggest why we are having such a difficult time getting it.[3]

Recognizing that women as a class are different from men as the two sexes have been socially constructed, MacKinnon would abandon liberal equality arguments. In MacKinnon's view, "an equality question is a question of the distribution of power." The most important difference between women and men is the difference in power. Men dominate women. Men take from women. Furthermore, men have been in control for so long that legal discourse completely ignores the reality of women's lives. Thus, equality theory, as a legal discourse, has focused on public sphere issues like pregnancy in the workplace—issues of import in male lives—rather than focusing on those long-silenced parts of female experience such as rape and other forms of sexual assault.

Using the rhetoric of domination and sexual subordination instead of equality, radical feminists in the MacKinnon camp argue for changes in laws that will end the inequality in power. Sex equality, in this view, affirmatively requires protecting women from such things as sexual harassment, rape and battering by men. An extension of this theory is used to justify a ban on pornography because pornography is thought to contribute to women's sexual subordination.

Some liberal feminists question parts of the radical feminist agenda on grounds that special protections for women often lead to inequality. The most serious disagreement between liberal and radical feminists is over pornography. Radical feminists, especially MacKinnon, support laws that will suppress pornography. Pornography, in their view, is male-created, and defines "woman" as a sexual object. Liberal feminists agree that most pornography is male-created and that male-created pornography defines "woman" as a sexual object. But, argue liberal feminists, to allow the state to ban pornography is to give the state power to define acceptable sex. Since the current state is a creature of male power, there is no reason to believe the state will define acceptable sex in a way that is consistent with an individual woman's own definition of her sexual self. In the pornography debate, the radical feminists' reliance on equality theory as a class-based theory (pornography contributes to women's inequality) clashes with the liberal feminists' commitment to individual liberty.

Some liberal feminists[4] (as well as postmodern feminists) also challenge the radical feminists' emphasis on "woman" as a class. They argue that radical feminists fail to take account of the many differences among women, focusing only on how all women are different from men. To focus on "woman" as a unitary category is to define her in some essential way, to claim that all women are alike in some essential way.

Radical feminists respond to this challenge by denying the existence of a female essence. Radical feminists embrace totally the claim that women are socially constructed. They do not believe that by deconstructing her we will find some underlying true essence. Rather they believe that by challenging the male construction of the category "woman," we can begin to construct our own category. We may not be able to free ourselves from socially constructed categories, but a woman-defined "woman" is at least an improvement over the present state of affairs.

Cultural Feminism

Cultural feminists,[5] like radical feminists, focus on woman's difference from man. Cultural feminists, however, unlike their radical sisters, embrace woman's difference. Carol Gilligan, for example, argues that women, because of their different life experiences, speak in a "different voice" from their male counterparts. Gilligan identifies the female voice with caring and relationships. Woman's moral vision encompasses this different voice. Woman's difference is good.

Feminists in the Gilligan camp are interested in changing institutions to give equal weight to woman's moral voice. They argue that the category "woman" has not been so much misdefined by men, as it has been ignored and undervalued. Yes, women are nurturing. Yes, women value personal relationships. These attributes are to be valued. Using equality rhetoric, cultural feminists argue for material changes in present conditions that would support woman-valued relationships.

Martha Fineman, for example, has argued for a concept of equality that recognizes and values the special relationship between mother and child.[6] Similarly, Robin West has charged that all modern legal theory is "masculine" because it is based on a view of human beings as primarily distinct and unconnected to each other. A properly constructed feminist jurisprudence would reflect the reality of women's lives—their essential connectedness.[7] I have defined cultural feminism to include feminists who ascribe fully to the social construction thesis. In such cases, the only difference between radical and cultural feminists is that radical feminists have chosen to emphasize in their theory a negative aspect of "woman"—her sexual objectification—whereas, cultural feminists emphasize a positive aspect—her special bond to others. Because their emphasis is different, radical and cultural feminists may contribute differently to the project of self-definition.

Some cultural feminists, however, can be understood to support the concept that "woman," although currently constructed in a certain way, has a discoverable natural essence. Whether viewed as natural or socially constructed, woman's capacity for caring and connection has provided substance for an interesting debate between radical feminist MacKinnon and cultural feminist Gilligan. Gilligan's work encourages us to value woman's view of herself and the world around her. MacKinnon, however, is suspicious of this "different voice." This voice, after all, has been constructed in response to the patriarchy. For those who subscribe to the social construction thesis, the voice is just another voice of the patriarchy. Alternatively, if there is such a thing as a natural or authentic "woman," how can we know that this is her voice? MacKinnon argues that until women cease to be victims of subordination they cannot speak for themselves.

This argument has a certain Catch-22 effect. Woman-identified values, such as caring and connection to others, are suspect because they are values that women have created in response to the patriarchy. We value caring because that is what our oppressors have caused us to value (because we define ourselves in relation to our oppressors, we aren't really engaging in self-definition). But if all women are victims of the patriarchy, how can any woman ever claim knowledge of what is truly in woman's best interest? How can we know that any equality arguments will further the best interests of women?

There must be some way to free ourselves sufficiently from the patriarchy to engage in the project of self-definition. Feminist theorists outside the field of law have argued in favor of separatism at least as an interim step in creating a woman-defined "woman." But legal theorists have been obsessed with equality, a concept which is inconsistent with separatism.

Postmodern Feminism

Postmodern feminists eschew the idea of unitary truth, of objective reality. They readily admit that categories, especially gender categories, are merely social constructs. Equality, too, is a social construct. It is true that these constructs, as products of the patriarchy, are in need of a feminist reconstruction. But postmodern feminism tells us to beware of searching for a new truth to replace the old. There simply is no such thing as the essential "woman." There is no such thing as the woman's point of view. There is no single theory of equality that will work for the benefit of all women. Indeed, there is probably no single change or goal that is in the best interest of all women.

Some would argue that the concept "postmodern feminism" is an oxymoron. It is a phrase that combines two concepts—postmodernism and feminism—that cannot logically coexist. For if postmodernism views the category "woman" as being so multifarious that it denies unitariness, how can it ever ascribe to be feminist, since feminism is a theory that focuses on the unitary category "woman"?

My own answer to this supposed conundrum is that postmodern feminism does not focus on the category "woman." Rather, it focuses on the situated realities of women, plural. Postmodern feminists question earlier feminist attempts to redefine the category "woman." Any definition, even one articulated by feminists, is limiting and serves to "tie the individual to her identity as a woman."[8] Furthermore, feminists who support any single definition of "woman" are viewed by postmodernists as tending toward essentialism.

One need not embrace postmodernism completely to criticize the tendency toward essentialism found in radical and cultural feminist writings. Wendy Williams, usually viewed as a liberal feminist, has raised concerns about the homogeneity of certain feminists concepts of "woman." Similarly, Angela Harris has argued that the meta-theories of gender constructed by Catharine MacKinnon and Robin West rely on a concept of "woman" that has been abstracted from the experience of white women.[9] I have made a similar claim that the "woman" constructed by these theorists also appears to be heterosexual. If feminists are fighting for maximum liberation, then equality arguments and theories aimed primarily at white heterosexual women will not accomplish this task.

At the same time, postmodern thought poses a certain dilemma. Any theory requires some degree of abstraction and generalization. Thus, if feminists embrace the particular situated realities of all individual women, plural, we will find it difficult to build a theory, singular, to combat oppression. As to the category "woman," postmodernism suggests that it is a fiction, a non-determinable identity. Linda Alcoff complains that whereas feminist definitions of "woman" tend toward essentialism, postmodernism tends toward nominalism.

I am reluctant to classify any feminist theorists within the legal academy as purely postmodern, although a number of such scholars do incorporate postmodern themes in their writing. For example, strains of postmodern thought can be found in the critical feminist legal scholarship of Frances Olsen[10] and Deborah Rhode.[11] Both Katharine Bartlett and Martha Minow have focused on the importance of multiple perspectives in the construction of reality.[12] Margaret Jane Radin, in writing about feminism and pragmatism, echoes the postmodern feminist's rejection of abstract universal theory in favor of practical solutions to concrete situations.[13]

Within the legal academy, the feminist theorist most closely aligned with postmodern feminism is Drucilla Cornell. Building on the work of deconstructionist Jacques Derrida and the psychoanalytic theories of Jacques Lacan and Julia Kristeva, Cornell shows us how we might reconstruct "woman" without resorting to essentialism or unitary concepts. She names her brand of feminism "ethical feminism" and contrasts it with liberal and radical feminism.[14] Rather than derive what "woman" ought to be from the reality of what is, Cornell encourages us to create, with the help of allegory and myth, an "imaginative universal," a mythology of the feminine in which all women can find themselves. This appeal to myth carries with it a call for collective imagining, informed by women's realities, but not limited by them. Cornell's "ethical feminism" offers us the possibility of building a shared concept of "woman" that is always more than we are individually, and thus is never limiting.

The Future

I have identified the four schools of feminist thought, or feminisms. There are, of course, other ways to categorize these feminisms. Whatever the categorization, the boundaries are never as fixed as the labels make them seem. And some feminists slip in and out of the various categories.[15] I chose to draw the lines as I drew them to emphasize one aspect of the various feminisms: how they see the category "woman" as she is presently constructed by male society. Liberal feminists, according to my taxonomy, see "woman" defined primarily as someone confined to the private sphere. Radical feminists see her as man's sexual object. Cultural feminists see her as caring and connected to others. Finally, postmodern feminists see her as so overly determined that she is an absence, not a presence.

These different perspectives reflect a variety of woman's experience. Since feminist theory is built from the real life experience of real women, our theories will necessarily be varied if they are to capture the breadth of that experience. Our theories are built to address the harms that we see. But our theories must not divide us. They must not prevent us from seeing the harms that others see. . . .

I began this essay with the observation that feminist legal theorists have spent too much time debating equality and not enough time debating the meaning of self-definition for women. The equality debate has at times assumed *sub silentio* varying definitions of what "woman is" and what "woman *should be*." The equality debate has also assumed *sub silentio*, at a minimum, that "woman" *is* and, perhaps further that "woman" *should be*, a working definition or category for law.

I propose that, in the future, feminist legal theorists be more explicit about their understanding of what "woman is" and what "woman should be." I believe this conversation about the meaning of "woman" is, at least for the moment, much more important to feminist theory than the development of any sort of abstract equality theory. To have the conversation is to engage in the process of self-definition. We must have the conversation before we can conclude whether "woman," however defined, is a category that ought to continue.

Some feminist legal theorists have already steered away from the equality debate and focused more directly on the question of self-definition. Robin West, in particular, has focused directly on the meaning of "self" for feminist theorists, warning us to beware of postmodernism's rejection of essentialism.[16] Ruth Colker's recent work grapples with the meaning of authentic existence for women.[17] And Drucilla Cornell encourages us to continue the search for the feminine employing myth as a necessary part of the process. I believe this discussion of the meaning of self and questioning of who defines whom is a useful development for the future of feminist legal theory.

The challenge I pose to feminist legal theorists is a challenge to develop legal theories that will support the process of self-definition—theories that will support the conversation. By focusing on the process of self-definition, I mean to suggest that we more fully acknowledge the importance of feminist method in building our substantive theories.

I have suggested that consciousness raising is the cornerstone of feminist method. Consciousness raising is about giving voice to the unknown in women's experience. Consciousness raising makes available stories that are personal and private. Consciousness raising brings new understanding by making known the unknown. Legal theories to support consciousness raising would include not only theories that protect speech, but theories that encourage the right kind of listening, a listening that privileges (temporarily) the previously silenced. . . .

. . . Feminist theorists have made valuable contributions to law by adding a female perspective to legal discussions. But feminist theorists should not privilege one perspective over another. Our contributions are especially valuable, not because we speak from a female perspective, but because we speak from a previously silenced perspective. . . .

. . . [W]e should fashion feminist legal theorists with a view to uncovering the silences. At the same time, these theories should reflect our obligations to listen and to participate positively in the construction of another's self-identity. Our theorists must not rely on definitions that limit another's self-conception. We must be principled in our interactions with one another, yet we must also be always open to the truth of the other's story.

Feminist method, as I conceive it, is about being in the world in a way that embraces both our separateness and our connectedness with others. Similarly, self-definition is not solely an individual enterprise grounded in our separation from each other, nor solely a group project impervious to individual realities. Thus, we need to build feminist legal theories that support the telling of our individual truths, as well as theories that protect the space we share with others as we construct our identities. I believe it is time to recapture from the patriarchy such principles as individual autonomy, privacy, free speech, intimacy and association.

I agree with the postmodern insight that there is no single, unitary definition of "woman." Indeed, it is precisely because there is no single definition of "woman" that our conversations about the meaning of "woman" become so important. I propose that we put substantive theories (such as equality) to one side until we have continued our conversations further. . . .

Notes

1. Some feminists additionally criticize this early equality litigation because it included cases like Craig v. Boren, 429 U.S. 190 (1976), in which men successfully argued for rights held by women: in *Craig*, the right to buy 3.2% beer. See Ratterman, Liberating Feminist Jurisprudence, in Off Our Backs 12 (1990). Such criticisms seem misplaced to me. First of all, Ginsburg did not initiate the litigation in Craig v. Boren and did not view it as a central part of her litigation strategy. Furthermore, all these cases were used by feminist litigators to educate the Justices about the danger of sexual stereotyping in general. See Ginsburg & Flagg, Some Reflections on the Feminist Legal Thought of the 1970s, 1989 U. Chi. Legal F. 9, 17.

2. Williams, Notes from a First Generation, 1989 U. Chi. Legal F. 99, 105–06 n. 16.

3. C. MacKinnon, Feminism Unmodified 32–33 (Harvard University Press, 1987).

4. E.g., Williams, First Generation, *supra* note 2, at 107–08.

5. Although I am carving out cultural feminists as a separate category from radical feminists, the categories are not so easily divided as my taxonomy may suggest. Cultural feminism, as I use the phrase, is often described as relational feminism; that is, feminists who focus on women's relationships. Although I cite to both Martha Fineman and Robin West as examples of legal theorists who are cultural feminists, there are significant differences between these two. Fineman, for example, is clear that women's relationships are socially constructed. They are part of what is and law ought to protect these relationships because failure to do so causes real harm to existing women. Whether these relationships ought to be preserved in their current form is a separate question. West's views, by contrast, tend toward biological determinism. Women's relationships occur because of woman's nature. For West, woman's nature is not only what is, but forms the basis for what ought to be. Thus, according to West, we ought to build legal theories to protect these relationships because these relationships are good. . . .

6. Fineman, Dominant Discourse, Professional Language and Legal Change in Child Custody Decisionmaking, 101 Harv. L. Rev. 727 (1988); Fineman, Implementing Equality: Ideology, Contradiction, and Social Change; A Study of Rhetoric and Results in the Regulation of the Consequences of Divorce, 1983 Wis. L. Rev. 789.

7. West, Jurisprudence and Gender, Part 1 this volume.

8. Alcoff, Cultural Feminism Versus Post-Structuralism: The Identity Crisis in Feminist Theory, 13 Signs 405 (1988).

9. Harris, Race and Essentialism in Feminist Legal Theory, Part 4 this volume.

10. See, e.g., F. Olsen, The Sex of Law, in David Kairys ed., The Politics of Law, 453, 458 (Pantheon, 1990); Olsen, Feminist Theory in Grand Style (Book Review), 89 Colum. L. Rev. 1147, 1169–77 (1989) (reviewing C. MacKinnon, Feminism Unmodified) (explaining, with approval, feminist objections to grand theory, yet defending MacKinnon's grand theory as politically useful); Olsen, The Family and the Market: A Study of Ideology and Legal Reform, 96 Harv. L. Rev.

1497 (1983) (challenging dichotomous thinking and embracing androgyny as a goal that allows for multiplicity and diffusiveness).

11. See, e.g., D. Rhode, Introduction: Theoretical Perspectives on Sexual Difference, in D. Rhode ed., Theoretical Perspectives on Sexual Difference 1, 7–9 (Yale University Press, 1990); Rhode, Feminist Critical Theories, 42 Stan. L. Rev. 617 (1990).

12. See Bartlett, Feminist Legal Methods, Part 6 this volume; Minow, Beyond Universality, 1989 U. Chi. Legal F. 115; Martha Minow, Foreword: Justice Engendered, Part 3 herein.

13. "If feminists largely share the pragmatist commitment that truth is hammered out piecemeal in the crucible of life and our situatedness, they also share the pragmatist understanding that truth is provisional and ever-changing." Radin, The Pragmatist and the Feminist, 63 S. Cal. L. Rev. 1699 (1990).

14. Cornell, The Doubly-Prized World: Myth, Allegory and the Feminine, 75 Cornell L. Rev. 644 (1990).

15. Martha Fineman, for example, tells me she identifies herself more as a socialist feminist than a cultural feminist. Wendy Williams, although identified with liberal feminism, nonetheless embraces the social construction thesis of radical feminism.

16. See West, Feminism, Critical Social Theory and Law, 1989 U. Chi. Legal F. 59.

17. See, e.g., Colker, Feminism, Theology, and Abortion: Toward Love, Compassion, and Wisdom, 77 Calif. L. Rev. 1011 (1989); Colker, Feminism, Sexuality, and Self: A Preliminary Inquiry into the Politics of Authenticity (Book Review), 68 B.U. L. Rev. 217 (1988) (reviewing C. MacKinnon, Feminism Unmodified).

❖ *Reconstructing Sexual Equality*

CHRISTINE A. LITTLETON

Introduction: The Project

. . .

FEMINIST CRITIQUE HAS illuminated the "male-dominated" or "phallocentric"[1] nature of every social institution it has examined, including law. . . .

Although one more criticism of men's domination of the public discourse on equality might not be amiss, that is not the focus of this [essay]. Rather, the focus here is on a more insidious and complex form of male domination, which I term "phallocentrism.". . . "[T]o be a man" does not simply mean to possess biologically male traits, but also to take on, or at least aspire to, the *culturally* male. Similarly, social institutions within a male-dominated culture can be identified as "male" in the sense that they are constructed from the perspective of the culturally male. By use of the term "phallocentrism" I hope to capture this perspective—not the perspective of biological males, but the perspective to which the culture urges them to aspire, and by which the culture justifies their dominance. . . .

Equality, belonging both to law and to language, provides its own case study of phallocentrism. Using feminist methodology's primary questions—"What has been women's concrete experience?" and "What has been left out?"—feminist critique has examined the phallocentrism of equality as both a concept and a form of legal analysis. As a concept, equality suffers from a "mathematical fallacy"—that is, the view that only things that are the same can ever be equal. In legal analysis, courts routinely find women's "difference" a sufficient justification for inequality, constructing at the same time a specious "sameness" when applying phallocentric standards "equally" to men and women's different reproductive biology or economic position to yield (not surprisingly) unequal results for women.

Reprinted from Calif. L. Rev. (1987), Vol. 75, No. 4, pp. 1279–1337, by permission. © 1987 by California Law Review, Inc.

This feminist critique of equality has cast doubt on the merits of another feminist enterprise—the as yet only partially successful attempt by feminist lawyers to have sex accepted as similar to, and coextensive with, race under constitutional and statutory guarantees of equality. "Equality," which has historically been the rallying cry of every subordinated group in American society, can no longer be embraced unambivalently by feminists.

Equality is enmeshed in, and ensnared by, the very gender system feminists are resisting. But I believe it is capable of having meaning beyond that system. To the extent that it is a social construct, equality can be deconstructed and, at least theoretically, reconstructed as a means of challenging, rather than legitimating, social institutions created from the phallocentric perspective.[2] . . .

This [essay] attempts a speculative reconstruction of sexual equality. . . . My proposal is easy to state, somewhat harder to fill with content, and even harder to implement. It is simply this: *The difference between human beings, whether perceived or real, and whether biologically or socially based, should not be permitted to make a difference in the lived-out equality of those persons.* I call this the model of "equality as acceptance." To achieve this form of sexual equality, male and female "differences" must be costless relative to each other. Equal acceptance cannot be achieved by forcing women (or the rare man) individually to bear the costs of culturally female behavior, such as childrearing, while leaving those (mostly men and some women) who engage in culturally male behavior . . . to reap its rewards. . . .

Development of Feminist Legal Theory

. . .

Legal Equality

Legal concern with sexual equality is very recent. It developed primarily in response to powerful analogies between the situation of racial minorities, especially Blacks as a class, and the situation of women. Those analogies were and are highly problematic, both theoretically and historically, but they supported the claim that women must necessarily be included within the equality-of-persons norm embedded in the political and social framework of this society, and specifically articulated in the equal protection clause of the Fourteenth Amendment. . . .

Feminist Responses

Feminist legal theory has been primarily reactive, responding to the development of legal racial equality theory. The form of response, however, has varied. One response has been to attempt to equate legal treatment of sex with that of race and deny that there are in fact any significant natural differences between women and men; in other words, to consider the two sexes symmetrically located with regard to *any* issue, norm, or rule. This response, which I term the "symmetrical" approach, classifies asymmetries as illusions, "overbroad generalizations," or temporary glitches that will disappear with a little behavior modification. A competing response rejects this analogy, accepting that women and men are or may be "different," and that women and men are often asymmetrically located in society. This response, which I term the "asymmetrical" approach, rejects the notion that all gender differences are likely to disappear, or even that they should.

SYMMETRICAL MODELS OF SEXUAL EQUALITY

Feminist theorists frequently take the symmetrical approach to sexual equality, not as an ideal, but as the only way to avoid returning to separate spheres ideology. For example, in her highly compelling defense of symmetry in the law, Wendy Williams warns that "we can't have it both ways, we need to think carefully about which way we want to have it."[3]

There are two models of the symmetrical vision—referred to here as "assimilation" and "androgyny." Assimilation, the model most often accepted by the courts, is based on the notion that women, given the chance, really are or could be just like men. Therefore, the argument runs, the law should require social institutions to treat women as they already treat men—requiring, for example, that the professions admit women to the extent they are "qualified," but also insisting that women who enter time-demanding professions such as the practice of law sacrifice relationships (especially with their children) to the same extent that male lawyers have been forced to do.

Androgyny, the second symmetrical model, also posits that women and men are, or at least could be, very much like each other, but argues that equality requires institutions to pick some golden mean between the two and treat both sexes as androgynous persons would be treated.[4] However, given that all of our institutions, work habits, and pay scales were formulated without the benefit of substantial numbers of androgynous persons, androgynous symmetry is difficult to conceptualize, and might require very substantial restructuring of many public and private institutions. In order to be truly androgynous within a symmetrical framework, social institutions must find a single norm that works equally well for all gendered characteristics. Part of my discomfort with androgynous models is that they depend on "meeting in the middle," while I distrust the ability of any person, and especially any court, to value women enough to find the "middle." Moreover, the problems involved in determining such a norm for even one institution are staggering. At what height should a conveyor belt be set in order to satisfy a symmetrical androgynous ideal? . . .

ASYMMETRICAL MODELS OF SEXUAL EQUALITY

Asymmetrical approaches to sexual equality take the position that difference should not be ignored or eradicated. Rather, they argue that any sexually equal society must somehow deal with difference, problematic as that may be. Asymmetrical approaches include "special rights," "accommodation," "acceptance," and "empowerment."

The special rights model affirms that women and men are different, and asserts that cultural differences, such as childrearing roles, are rooted in biological ones, such as reproduction. Therefore, it states, society must take account of these differences and ensure that women are not punished for them. This approach, sometimes referred to as a "bivalent" model,[5] is closest to the "special treatment" pole of the asymmetrical/symmetrical equality debate. Elizabeth Wolgast, a major proponent of special rights, argues that women cannot be men's "equals" because equality by definition requires sameness.[6] Instead of equality, she suggests seeking justice, claiming special rights for women based on their special needs.[7]

The second asymmetrical model, accommodation, agrees that differential treatment of biological differences (such as pregnancy, and perhaps breastfeeding) is necessary, but argues that cultural or hard-to-classify differences (such as career interests and skills) should be treated under all equal treatment or androgynous model. Examples of accommodation models include Sylvia Law's approach to issues of reproductive biology and Herma Hill Kay's "episodic" approach to the condition of pregnancy.[8] These approaches could also be characterized as "symmetry, with concessions to asymmetry where necessary." The accommodationists limit the asymmetry in their models to biological differences because, like Williams, they fear a return to separate spheres ideology should asymmetrical theory go too far.

My own attempt to grapple with difference, which I call an "acceptance" model, is essentially asymmetrical. While not endorsing the notion that cultural differences between the sexes are biologically determined, it does recognize and attempt to deal with both biological and social differences. Acceptance does not view sex differences as problematic per se, but rather focuses on the ways in which differences are permitted to justify inequality. It asserts that eliminating the unequal consequences of sex differences is more important than debating whether such differences are "real," or even trying to eliminate them altogether.

Unlike the accommodationists, who would limit asymmetrical analysis to purely biological differences, my proposal also requires equal acceptance of cultural differences. The reasons for this are twofold. First, the distinction between biological and cultural, while useful analytically, is itself culturally based. Second, the inequality experienced by women is often presented as a necessary consequence of cultural rather than of biological difference. If for instance, women do in fact "choose" to become nurses rather than real estate appraisers, it is not because of any biological imperative. Yet, regardless of the reasons for the choice, they certainly do not choose to be paid less. It is the *consequences* of gendered difference, and not its sources, that equal acceptance addresses. . . .

The focus of equality as acceptance, therefore, is not on the question of whether *women* are different, but rather on the question of how the social fact of gender asymmetry can be dealt with so as to create some symmetry in the lived-out experience of all members of the community. . . . [According to] this view, the function of equality is to make gender differences, perceived or actual, costless relative to each other, so that anyone may follow a male, female, or androgynous lifestyle according to their natural inclination or choice without being punished for following a female lifestyle or rewarded for following a male one.

As an illustration of this approach, consider what many conceive to be the paradigm difference between men and women—pregnancy. No one disputes that only women become pregnant, but symmetrical theorists analogize pregnancy to other events, in order to preserve the unitary approach of symmetrical theory. Such attempts to minimize difference have the ironic result of obscuring more fundamental similarities.

In California Federal Savings & Loan Association v. Guerra (*Cal. Fed.*), Lillian Garland, a receptionist at California Federal, tried to return to her job after the birth of her child. The bank refused to reinstate her, and she sued under the California Fair Employment and Housing Act (FEHA). . . . The bank in turn sued in federal court, claiming that the FEHA was preempted by Title VII of the Civil Rights Act of 1964, as amended by the Pregnancy Discrimination Act (PDA). . . .

In addition to narrow questions of statutory interpretation, *Cal. Fed.* raised more fundamental questions about the meaning of equal employment opportunity for women. Citing the dangers of separate spheres ideology raised by "protectionist" legislation, the national ACLU filed an amicus brief arguing that the California law should be struck down, and that the remedy should provide for job-protected leave for all temporarily disabled employees, whatever the source of their disability. California feminist groups, such as Equal Rights Advocates, filed on the other side of the debate, arguing that the California law guaranteed equality of opportunity, and was thus consistent with federal law and policy.

Missing in these arguments, however, was any recognition that working men and women shared a more fundamental right than the right to basic disability leave benefits or job protection. The Coalition for Reproductive Equality in the Workplace (CREW) advanced the position that working women and men share a right to procreative choice in addition to an interest in disability leave. In order to ensure equal exercise of procreative rights, it argued, an employer must provide leave adequate to the effects of pregnancy.

> The California statute eliminates barriers to equality in both procreation and employment faced by women who cannot afford to lose their jobs when they decide to become parents. Male employees who become fathers and female employees who become mothers are thus enabled to combine procreation and employment to the same extent.[9]

This form of acceptance, unlike those that analogize pregnancy to disability, emphasizes the basic commonality of procreation as a human endeavor involving both women and men. By recognizing pregnancy as "different" from other causes of disability, it supports efforts to equalize the position of working women and men with respect to this fundamental right.

The foregoing asymmetrical models, including my own, share the notion that, regardless of their differences, women and men must be treated as full members of society. Each model acknowledges that women may need treatment different than that accorded to men in order to effectuate their membership in important spheres of social life; all would allow at least some such claims, although on very different bases, and probably in very different circumstances.[10]

A final asymmetrical approach, "empowerment," rejects difference altogether as a relevant subject of inquiry.[11] In its strongest form, empowerment claims that the subordination of women to men has itself constructed the sexes, and their differences. For example, Catharine MacKinnon argues:

> [I]t makes a lot of sense that women might have a somewhat distinctive perspective on social life. We may or may not speak in a different voice—I think that the voice that we have been said to speak in is in fact in large part the "feminine" voice, the voice of the victim speaking without consciousness. But when we understand that women are *forced* into this situation of inequality, it makes a lot of sense that we should want to negotiate, since we lose conflicts. It makes a lot of sense that we should want to urge values of care, because it is what we have been valued for. We have had little choice but to be valued this way.[12]

A somewhat weaker version of the claim is that we simply do not and cannot know whether there are any important differences between the sexes that have not been created by the dynamic of domination and subordination. In either event, the argument runs, we should forget about the question of differences and focus directly on subordination and domination. If a law, practice, or policy contributes to the subordination of women or their domination by men, it violates equality. If it empowers women or contributes to the breakdown of male domination, it enhances equality.[13]

The reconceptualization of equality as antidomination, like the model of equality as acceptance, attempts to respond directly to the concrete and lived-out experience of women. Like other asymmetrical models, it allows different treatment of women and men when necessary to effectuate its overall goal of ending women's subordination. However, it differs substantially from the acceptance model in its rejection of the membership, belonging, and participatory aspects of equality.

THE DIFFERENCE THAT DIFFERENCE MAKES

Each of the several models of equality discussed above, if adopted, would have a quite different impact on the structure of society. If this society wholeheartedly embraced the symmetrical approach of assimilation—the point of view that "women are just like men"—little would need to be changed in our economic or political institutions except to get rid of lingering traces of irrational prejudice, such as an occasional employer's preference for male employees. In contrast, if society adopted the androgyny model, which views both women and men as bent out of shape by current sex roles and requires both to conform to an androgynous model, it would have to alter radically its methods of resource distribution. In the employment context, this might mean wholesale revamping of methods for determining the "best person for the job." Thus, while assimilation would merely require law firms to hire women who have managed to get the same credentials as the men they have traditionally hired, androgyny might insist that the firm hire only those persons with credentials that would be possessed by someone neither "socially male" nor "socially female."

If society adopted an asymmetrical approach such as the accommodation model, no radical restructuring would be necessary. Government would need only insist that women be given what they need to resemble men, such as time off to have babies and the freedom to return to work on the same rung of the ladder as their male counterparts. If, however, society adopted the model of equality as acceptance, which seeks to make difference costless, it might additionally insist that women and men who opt for socially female occupations, such as childrearing, be compensated at a rate similar to those women and men who opt for socially male occupations, such as legal practice. Alternatively, such occupations might be restructured to make them equally accessible to those whose behavior is culturally coded "male" or "female."

The different models also have different potential to challenge the phallocentrism of social institutions. No part of the spectrum of currently available feminist legal theory is completely immune to the feminist critique of society as phallocentric. We cannot outrun our history, and that history demonstrates that the terms of social discourse have been set by men who, actively or passively, have ignored women's voices—until even the possibility of women having a voice has become questionable. Nevertheless, the models do differ with respect to the level at which the phallocentrism of the culture reappears.

Under the assimilationist approach, for example, women merit equal treatment only so far as they can demonstrate that they are similar to men. The assimilation model is thus fatally phallocentric. To the extent that women cannot or will not conform to socially male forms of behavior, they are left out in the cold. To the extent they do or can conform, they do not achieve equality *as women*, but as social males.

Similarly, empowerment and androgyny (an asymmetrical and a symmetrical approach, respectively) both rely on central concepts whose current meaning is phallocentrically biased. If "power" and 'neutrality" (along with "equality") were not themselves gendered concepts, the empowerment and androgyny approaches would be less problematic. But our culture conceives of power as power used by men, and creates androgynous models "tilted" toward the male. As Carrie Men-

kel-Meadow put it, the trouble with marble cake is that it never has enough choco-
late; the problem with androgyny is that it never has enough womanness.[14] Similarly, empowering women without dealing with difference, like assimilation, too
easily becomes simply sharing male power more broadly. . . .

Equality as acceptance is not immune from phallocentrism in several of its
component concepts. However, these concepts are not necesarily entailed by the
theory and may be replaced with less biased concepts as they reveal themselves
through the process of equalization. For example, in discussing employment-related applications of the model, I use the measures already existing in that
sphere—money, status, and access to decisionmaking. These measures of value
are obviously suspect. Nevertheless, my use of them is contingent. Acceptance
requires only that culturally coded "male" and "female" complements be equally
valued; it does not dictate the coin in which such value should be measured. By
including access to decisionmaking as part of the measure, however, the theory
holds out the possibility that future measures of value will be created by women
and men *together*. Thus, acceptance strives to create the preconditions necessary
for sexually integrated debate about a more appropriate value system.

The various models of equality arise out of common feminist goals and enter-
prises: trying to imagine what a sexually equal society would look like, given that
none of us has ever seen one; and trying to figure out ways of getting there, given
that the obstacles to sexual equality are so many and so strong.

The perception among feminist legal thinkers that the stakes in the symmetrical vs. asymmetrical debate are high is correct. Difference indeed makes a difference. Yet, the frantic nature of the debate about difference between the sexes
makes the divergent views within feminist legal thought appear as a deadly danger rather than an exciting opportunity. The label "divisive" gets slapped on before the discussion even gets underway.

We need to recognize difference among women as diversity rather than division, and difference between women and men as opportunity rather than danger. . . .

Making Difference Costless

[A]lthough I do not claim to offer a blueprint for specific application, I will attempt . . . to lay out the foundation for the house that a reconstructed sexual
equality may someday build.

Differently Gendered Complements

The problem of identifying gendered complements lies along two axes of difference. One axis measures the "source" of differences, ranging from the clearly
biological to the clearly social (with a great deal of controversy in between). The

other measures the degree of overlap between the sexes, and runs from more-or-less differences on one end to yes-or-no differences on the other.

For gender differences that are more-or-less, there is a significant degree of overlap between the sexes. Height is one of these. Not all women would have been disaffirmed by the too-high podium that was "built for a man,"* and not all men would have been affirmed by it. But more women than men in this society would have had the feminist lawyer's experience. Additionally, differences of the more-or-less variety are easier to deny, since there is always some woman over six feet or some man under five, and a great number of both in between. These differences are also easier to "match," because shorter and taller are both measures of the same concededly shared human characteristic of height.

For yes-or-no gender differences, there is no overlap at all. The primary example of this is, of course, pregnancy. No man can become pregnant, and most women can. However, women who have never had the capacity for pregnancy are not thereby made either biologically or socially male, even when the dominant culture has tended to view them as "not women." Thus, although it is useful for purposes of analysis to separate yes-or-no differences from more-or-less ones, they represent two poles of the same spectrum.

Disparate treatment analysis under Title VII allows individuals who are exceptions to the "rule" of their biological sex to be socially classed with the other sex. Thus, tall women must be treated the same as tall men, and short men the same as short women. As the podium example demonstrates, phallocentrism in such cases usually involves setting the norm by reference to the center of the male bell curve. When the norm is set by reference to the female bell curve, the same analysis applies; men who can type must be allowed into socially female secretarial positions. . . .

Disparate impact analysis . . . allows socially female women to bring equality claims if the job qualification containing the gendered norm is irrelevant to the applicant's ability to perform the job. No showing of direct intent to discriminate is required. Under disparate impact doctrine, then, a woman can establish discrimination by demonstrating that women as a class are more severely affected than men by a facially neutral employment practice such as a height requirement. The employer can, however, justify the discriminatory impact by demonstrating that the practice is "job related" or necessary to the employer's business. Moreover, the relevance of the practice is tested solely by reference to the way the job is already structured. Thus, even disparate impact analysis—as currently practiced—does not allow for challenges to male bias in the structure of businesses, occupations, or jobs.

---

*[In an omitted section, Littleton recounts the story of a feminist lawyer walking up to a podium to deliver a speech. The podium was so high that she could not reach the microphone. While modifications were made, she pointedly noted, "Built for a man!" The author remarks that accommodation is a step platform for the woman to stand on. Acceptance is a podium whose height is adjustable. *Ed.*]

Equality as acceptance would support challenges to government and employer policies and practices that use male norms even when such norms are considered job-related, necessary to the business, or "substantially related to an important governmental interest." Unlike the more radical version of the model of androgyny referred to above, however, acceptance would not necessarily require the *elimination* of such norms. Acceptance could instead be achieved by inventing complementary structures containing female norms. For example, assume an employer successfully defends its 5'9" minimum height requirement as necessary to the job of sorting widgets as they pass on a conveyor belt. Equality as acceptance could be achieved by restructuring the job itself—in this case, by changing the height of the conveyor belt or by adding a second belt. Alternatively, the employer could defend the requirement by demonstrating that equal job opportunities exist in the plant for applicants shorter than 5'9". Acceptance would thus permit de facto sex segregation in the workplace, but *only* if the predominantly male and predominantly female jobs have equal pay, status, and opportunity for promotion into decisionmaking positions.

Yes-or-no differences do not yield so readily to matching. This has helped focus the "equal treatment/special treatment" debate on pregnancy—specifically, on the question of whether requiring employers to grant pregnancy leaves for women violates the equal rights of men, who can never take advantage of such leaves. If pregnancy were a more-or-less difference, such as disabling heart trouble or childcare responsibility, it would be easy for the current legal system to answer this question. Since it is a yes-or-no difference, however, the legal system runs in circles: the Supreme Court in Geduldig v. Aiello said pregnancy is different, so women can be punished for it; the federal district court in *Cal. Fed.* said pregnancy is not different, so women should not benefit from it; the Supreme Court, affirming the Ninth Circuit in *Cal. Fed.* said pregnancy is different, so men are not hurt by taking account of it.

I think that the appropriate unit of analysis in yes-or-no cases is *interaction* of the sexes rather than comparison. Even with rapidly developing reproductive technology, it is still necessary for some part of a woman to interact with some part of a man to produce a pregnancy. In that interaction, the gendered complements are pregnancy for the woman and fewer sperm cells for the man. Since pregnancy almost always results in some period of disability for the woman, making the sex difference costless with respect to the workplace requires that money, status, and opportunity for advancement flow equally to the womb-donating woman and the sperm-donating man (himself an equal contributor to the procreative act).[15]

Both average height and pregnancy lie near the biological pole of the source axis; these differences are clearly biological. Their existence and degree of overlap are less problematic as an empirical matter than differences lying closer to the cultural pole. The clearly cultural differences, on the other hand, are more problematic, primarily because they are even more likely than biological differences to give rise to stereotypes that harm women. Arguments for ignoring difference are also more plausible with reference to the cultural axis. Because these differences are acquired, they can presumably be done away with, if not for us then for our children or grandchildren.[16] This combination of danger and plausibility has led several sex equality theorists to place themselves toward the middle of the symmetrical vs. asymmetrical debate. I am, however, either brave or foolhardy enough to believe that even cultural differences can be made accessible to equality analysis.

Cultural differences of the more-or-less variety can be dealt with along the same general lines as biological differences that overlap. Under acceptance, marital dissolution decrees, for example, could value the contributions of the non-earner spouse (usually, but not always, the woman), take into account services in the home performed after divorce, and treat realistically the expenses necessarily incurred by the custodial parent. These measures would go further toward reducing the potentially devastating economic impact of divorce for women than current experiments, such as presumptions in favor of joint custody.

Cultural differences of the yes-or-no variety are easier to identify than those of the more-or-less, but harder to deal with. Fortunately, there are relatively few of them (far fewer than there were a few decades ago). The most visible is employment in the armed services. Women are excluded from draft registration, and female volunteers are excluded from combat positions.[17]

Just as gendered complements in the "biological" realm come from our current perceptions of biology, so must gendered complements in the "cultural" realm come from our current perceptions of culture. The traditional gender divide sets up "warrior" in its cultural sense directly opposite "mother" in its cultural sense. The "cult of motherhood" resembles the "glory of battle" in a number of ways. Both occupations involve a lot of unpleasant work, along with a real sense of commitment to a cause beyond oneself that is culturally gussied up and glamorized culturally to cover up the unpleasantness involved. Both involve danger and possible death. And, of course, the rationale most frequently given for women's exclusion from combat is their capacity for motherhood.

Making this gender difference less costly could mean requiring the government to pay mothers the same low wages and generous benefits as most soldiers. It could also mean encouraging the use of motherhood as an unofficial prerequisite for governmental office. As a paying occupation with continuing status perks, many more men might be induced to stay home and raise their children. Alternatively, but less likely, making difference costless could mean ceasing to pay combat troops.

For example, in Personnel Administrator v. Feeney [442 U.S. 256 (1979)], the Supreme Court upheld Massachusetts' lifetime veteran's preference against an equal protection challenge, reasoning that Massachusetts had not intended that preference to lock women into lower-level and dead-end civil service positions, regardless of this obvious effect. Under an equality as acceptance model, a state's failure to provide equal preference for the gendered female complement to military service would be evidence of intentional discrimination. Thus, even without additional constitutional or statutory enactment, a change in the Court's underlying model of equality could alter the result in actual cases.

Matching gendered complements in order to equalize across cultural differences may sound like marching directly into the valley of the stereotypes. Those who consider Carol Gilligan's discovery of "a different voice" sexist are not likely to find this appealing. Nevertheless, allow me to make two disclaimers. First, almost all cultural differences are, or could easily be, "more or less." Lots of biological men exhibit socially female characteristics (for which they are all too often punished); at least as many biological women exhibit socially male ones (for which they are often rewarded, although they are simultaneously punished for not having the biological form to match); and many more women and men fall in the middle, exhibiting no readily identifiable "male" or "female" behavior patterns. Second, what is objectionable about stereotypes is not that they are *never* true, but rather that they are not *always* true. Demonstrating that not every woman with children is primarily responsible for their care may help those women who do not have such responsibility to compete for certain jobs, but it does little to help those women struggling to hold down two jobs, only one of which is paid.

Disclaimers aside, what is relevant for this exercise is not the accuracy or inaccuracy of any set of gendered complements, but rather how the complements reward or punish those who are perceived to fall on one side or the other. Studies of sex-segregated workplaces tend to show that there is a high correlation between employer perceptions of gender differences and the segregation patterns themselves. These perceived gender differences, such as lifting strength and small-muscle dexterity, are of the more-or-less type, and tend to fall toward the middle of the "source" axis. Requiring individual testing alleviates segregation to some extent, but it only helps those women who do not fit the female stereotype (at the expense, of course, of those men who do not fit the male stereotype). However, the main problem with sex segregation is that promotion patterns and pay scales are determined by entry-level job classifications. Thus, those women who do fit the female stereotype (of, say, low lifting strength and high small-muscle dexterity) are stuck. They are not harmed by the "female" job classification as such; they are harmed by the disparity in pay and opportunity for promotion that goes along with it. And the disparity in promotion opportunities continues the cycle of overvaluation of "male" characteristics and undervaluation of "female" ones, because employers will continue to select those biological men and women who are socially male.

If, alternatively, both "male" and "female" entry-level positions paid the same and offered the same promotion opportunities, individual testing would not matter so much. Indeed, assuming proportionate numbers of openings, applicants might well self-select into the classification that better utilizes their particular strengths and minimizes their particular weaknesses. If so, the segregation pattern would gradually break down unless employers actively and, legally speaking, "intentionally" sought to maintain it. Moreover, even if self-selection by individual skills did not occur, a better sex mix at the management level would eventually have a significant impact throughout the firm.

As Frances Olsen sets forth in "The Sex of Law," we tend to think in dichotomies, and those dichotomies are both sexualized (with one side masculine and the other feminine) and hierarchicized (with one side in each pair superior).[18] She argues that the sexualization and hierarchicization should be attacked simultaneously, to the end of deconstructing the dichotomies themselves. While I do not disagree with this goal, I do think Olsen's strategy is impractical. Dichotomies that purport to describe gender differences are, I think, only likely to fall apart once they no longer accurately describe differences in pay scales, hiring patterns, or promotion ladders. Additionally, since we presently think in these dichotomies, we may as well use them to help us in our struggle to discard them.

The rigidity of sexualized dichotomies does appear to be gradually breaking down in many areas. . . . With regard to the practical problem of implementation, however, the true breakdown of any particular male–female dichotomy is not a problem, but a benefit. It puts us one step closer toward eliminating them entirely. . . .

[M]ajor lines of further inquiry and analysis remain largely unexplored. . . . We need to engage in more sophisticated inquiry into gender difference, and a model of equality as acceptance facilitates, but does not accomplish, that inquiry.

Equality as acceptance provides a methodology for assuring that sexual differences do not take on the unnecessary consequence of sexual inequality. In order to apply that methodology, we must open inquiry into the identification, use, and meaning of such differences. Through a model of equal acceptance, the legal system, which has historically been a conduit through which perceived difference between both sexes has rationalized concrete disadvantage to one, may finally become an arena for reclaiming equality across difference. . . .

Notes

1. . . ."Phallocentric" or "phallologocentric" are terms coined by the French feminists of the "politique et psychoanalyse" school, which tends to view social institutions as created from the male viewpoint—i.e., as epistemologically "male." See E. Marks & I. de Courtivron eds., New French Feminisms: An Anthology 5, 36 (Schocken, 1980); L. Irigaray, This Sex Which Is Not One 163 (C. Porter trans., Cornell University Press, 1982). . . .

2. "Deconstruction" in Critical Legal Studies circles denotes a method of analyzing legal materials. Using the internal contradictions within legal texts and between the texts and their referents, the analyst can demonstrate either intellectual incoherence, see, e.g., Dalton, An Essay in the Deconstruction of Contract Doctrine, 94 Yale L.J. 997 (1985) (discussing indeterminacy of contract rules), or

political bias, see, e.g., Klare, Judicial Deradicalization of the Wagner Act and the Origins of Modern Legal Consciousness, 1937–1941, 62 Minn. L. Rev. 265 (1978) (discussing the judicial impact upon organized labor and its consequences). For a cogent critique of Critical Legal Studies' use of deconstruction, see Brosnan, Serious But Not Critical, 60 S. Cal. L. Rev. 259, 374–88 (1987).

Some CLS scholars avoid attempts to move beyond deconstruction into reconstruction because of the danger of incorporating pre-critical elements. This caution is not without reason. See, e.g., Peller, The Politics of Reconstruction (Book Review), 98 Harv. L. Rev. 863 (1985) (reviewing B. Ackerman, Reconstructing American Law) (criticizing Ackerman's recapitulation of conservative ideology). Yet reconstruction is crucial for less powerful groups such as women and Blacks, who are not in a position to abandon hard-won rights for the ephemeral promise of direct political struggle. See, e.g., Crenshaw, Race, Reform, and Retrenchment, 101 Harv. L. Rev. 1331 (1988) (advocating civil rights struggle that avoids demobilizing effects of abstract rights rhetoric by rooting such struggle in the concrete experience of Blacks).

3. Williams, The Equality Crisis: Some Reflections on Culture, Courts and Feminism, 7 Women's Rts. L. Rep. 175, at 196. . . .

4. For example, Wendy Williams describes the "equal treatment" response to the pregnancy in the workplace dilemma as androgynous because it promotes the "normalization" of pregnancy. Williams, Equality's Riddle: Pregnancy and the Equal Treatment/Special Treatment Debate, Part 2 this volume. By treating disability arising from pregnancy just like disability arising from illness and injury, the equal treatment model "incorporat[es] pregnancy into the existing benefit schemes." *Id.* But it is the existence of male-oriented benefit schemes that makes treating pregnancy like a hernia look like "normalizing" it. And, of course, if the "existing benefit schemes" are paltry or insufficient, then women share the burden of illness and injury while carrying the whole burden of procreation. Escaping from the male norm is not as easy as it looks.

5. See Scales, Towards a Feminist Jurisprudence, 56 Ind. L.J. 375 (1981), at 430–34; see also E. Wolgast, Equality and the Rights of Women 61–63 (Cornell University Press, 1980).

6. Wolgast, Equality and Rights of Women, *supra* note 5, at 122 ("Consider, if both men and women are taught about the delivery of a baby, and both are taught to 'participate' in it, their roles will still be sex-differentiated. And similarly, there will be some sex-differentiation in parenthood.")

7. "The rights needed by women in different life forms will differ. The wife and homemaker will need some special provisions for her old age; the career woman will not need these, but will need equal rights with respect to work. The woman who pursues a part-time career will need both kinds of rights less urgently; the woman whose career begins late will have a special set of needs again; while the divorced mother's needs are probably the greatest of all." *Id.* at 157. Wolgast's argument relies on an analogy to the condition of disabled persons rather than the analogy to Blacks. It thus also fails to ground the claims of women as a class in our own situation and, ironically, reintroduces notions of similarity.

8. Law, Rethinking Sex and the Constitution, 132 U. Pa. L. Rev. 955, 1007–13 (1984) (calling for equal treatment in all areas *except* reproduction, where an analysis based on an empowerment approach . . . should be adopted); Kay, Equal-

ity and Difference: The Case of Pregnancy, Part 2 this volume (sex differences should be ignored, *except* during the time a female is actually pregnant).

9. Brief for the Coalition for Reproductive Equality in the Workplace (CREW) as amicus curiae, *Cal. Fed.*, 479 U.S. 272 (1987) (No. 85-494). Littleton was the attorney of record for CREW, and the principal author of the CREW amicus brief.

10. For example, Herma Hill Kay argues that differential treatment must be strictly limited to pregnancy, breastfeeding, menstruation, and rape. Kay, Models of Equality, 1985 U. Ill. L. Rev. 39, 81 (1985).

11. This model has been articulated most fully by Catharine MacKinnon, and draws heavily on the work of radical feminist theorists such as Andrea Dworkin. . . .

12. DuBois, Dunlap, Gilligan, MacKinnon & Menkel-Meadow, Feminist Discourse, Moral Values and Law—A Conversation, 34 Buffalo L. Rev. 11 (1985), at 27 (emphasis added.)

13. This formulation has enabled MacKinnon to view sexual harassment . . . and pornography . . . as violations of women's civil rights.

14. A. Allen, C. Littleton & C. Menkel-Meadow, Law in a Different Voice, 15th National Conference on Women and the Law, Address by C. Menkel-Meadow (March 31, 1984).

15. Equality as acceptance does not itself dictate whether this acceptance should be accomplished by (1) female and male workers sharing the disadvantage that the workplace now visits on women alone—perhaps through requiring male employees to take on without extra pay some portion of the work of the absent female employees; (2) eliminating the disadvantage to women through some form of pregnancy leave rights; or (3) reshaping the structure itself so that no disadvantage arises at all—through more radical time shifting, time-sharing work schedules or through elimination of the workplace–home dichotomy. While equality as acceptance would support arguments for all three, option (2) is probably the most viable currently.

16. Why bother with making these differences costless relative to each other if we can get rid of them altogether? My response is similar to that given to androgyny as an equality model: getting rid of difference in a system of male dominance means getting rid of *women's* differences. For example, "equality" in private law firm practice seems to mean that both women and men who take parenting leave fail to make partner; "equality" in academia seems to mean that both women and men whose research field is women's studies are not considered "serious" scholars. Cf. Lynn v. Regents of the Univ. of Calif., 656 F.2d 1337 (9th Cir. 1981) (university's disdain for women's studies is evidence of sex discrimination), *cert. denied*, 459 U.S. 823 (1982). Similarly, my female students are consistently counseled to wear gray or navy blue "power suits" to job interviews (often with little string or silk "ties").

Until such time as "getting rid of sex differences" has some chance of operating equally, it is an empty (perhaps deadening) promise for women. Moreover, it does not seem particularly unfair for women to demand a little equality now, for ourselves, without waiting for our grandchildren to "grow up free." Nor does it seem unjustified for women to be accepted as equal members of this society in spite of our cultural skewing—after all, men are skewed too, albeit differently. Of course, there is the obligatory fallback position that the opportunity for "social transvestitism" I envision as a result of this strategy will actually hasten the day that sex differences cease to operate for most people. However, societies are not built by or for people who may never exist, nor even for the purpose of creating such people.

17. Feminists are as deeply divided in their responses to this issue as they are with regard to separate pregnancy leave. On the one hand, the current institution of combat is the apotheosis of phallocentrism, a nonstop program of hierarchy, barely controlled aggression, and alienation. . . . Perhaps we should be grateful to be excluded and spend our energy working to get the men excluded, too. On the other hand, it is combat experience that sends soldiers up the military promotion ladder, increases their pay and benefits, and apparently fits them for high public office. . . .

Are women reluctant to engage in defense, or are they merely reluctant to engage in the glorification of brutality and apparent hysteria that combat training seemingly entails? I agree with Dru Cornell's prediction that if it were not so expensive for men to opt out of this particular warrior role, more of them would do so. D. Cornell, Equality and Gender Difference: Toward a Critical Theory of Equality 72 (1983)(unpublished manuscript). If fewer men were willing to engage in the warrior role, we as a society might be forced, in order to attract enough men and women, to experiment with different visions of the role—to move from warrior to defender, for example.

18. F. Olsen, The Sex of Law, in D. Kairys ed., The Politics of Law 453, rev. ed. (Pantheon, 1990).

❖ *Strategizing in Equality*

Diana Majury

Feminist lawyers, legal scholars and activists are currently engaged in a major debate about the usefulness of framing legal arguments in terms of equality. For those who consider that equality is a concept that can be used to further women's interests, the debate is over what theory or model of equality can most effectively be presented and pursued in legal forums.

Although acknowledged to encompass a wide range of diverse issues, the legal equality debate in the United States centers on the question of maternity leave for women in the paid labor force. The maternity leave discussion has fostered important analysis and provided access to a fuller understanding of the complexity of the issues involved. However, because so much of the discussion has been in the form of a debate, the discussion has been both limited and limiting, as well as frequently counter-productive. The focus is more on justifying one's own position while exposing the shortcomings of the arguments of those "on the other side" than on the problem of the inadequacies of the protection of pregnant women in the paid labor force and what to do about them. . . .

In this essay, I wish to add my voice to the equality debates by proposing what I describe as an inequality-based strategy.[1] . . .

Rather than describing equality as a goal, I refer to equality as a strategy, which can be used to address women's current inequalities. Equality as a goal is somewhat of an oxymoron—if women and men were treated "equally"—then equality would have no meaning; there would be nothing or no-one with whom to be "equal." I do not share the vision of equality as some abstract ideal that is to be imposed on society to solve the problems of women and other oppressed groups. To me, the focus and emphasis presently placed on equality are misdirected; the focus should instead be on inequality. Equality is more effectively seen as a means that can be used to address the inequalities that women in our society experience.[2] Equality is given meaning and substance only by the inequalities which give rise to

---

3 Wis. Women's L.J. 169 (1987).

the need for a guarantee of equality. Equality does not define inequality; inequality defines equality.

Why Equality?

I see myself participating in very much the same project on equality that Alison Jaggar describes with respect to feminism:

> My goal is not the discovery of a Platonic ideal form of [equality] and exposure of rival theories as pretenders. Instead, I want to contribute to formulating a conception of [equality] that is more adequate [I would say more effective *at this time*] than previous conceptions in that it will help women to achieve the fullest possible liberation. . . . [L]iberation is not some finally achievable situation; instead it is the process of eliminating forms of oppression as long as these continue to arise.[3]

There are a number of reasons why equality might be useful strategy to employ in the process of "eliminating forms of oppression" against women. One of the major advantages of equality as a concept is that it allows for a focus on inequality, on the specific and concrete manifestations of women's oppression. . . .

For some critics of equality the lack of precision and open-endedness of equality are its major shortcomings. For some, this indeterminacy is sufficient to render equality a useless concept.[4] In response to this criticism many legal writers, among them many feminists, are trying to develop some kind of equality formula. Such a formula would delineate the meaning of equality and eradicate any uncertainty as to its application or effect. To me, the indeterminacy of equality offers greater promise and provides more fertile ground for exploration and argumentation than any equality formula. An open-ended approach allows "equality theory" to respond to the different circumstances and factors which combine to make a specific woman's situation inequal or to perpetuate women's inequalities more generally.

Equality is a useful tool because it enables women to speak in a language which is counter to domination and subordination. This does not mean that equality rhetoric cannot be, and is not, also used as a tool of legitimation to maintain the status quo and to reinforce and perpetuate the subjugation of women. But, at the same time, equality can be used to open up a discourse within which these injustices can be exposed and confronted.

Pragmatically, at least in Canada, women have no choice but to address equality-based arguments; at the very least, we have to be ready to respond to arguments framed in terms of equality. Equality is, at present, too much a part of the dominant discourse in Canada to be ignored.[5] The entrenchment of equality rights in the *Canadian Charter of Rights and Freedoms*[6] should put an end to, or perhaps foreclose, any discussion of whether or not Canadian women should advocate or support an equality-based approach to issues. Although women in Canada could still reject equality and decide not to invoke or rely upon the Charter equality provisions, this would be a "high risk" strategy. Whether we like it or not, by virtue of its "entrenchment" in the Charter, equality has gained a level of prominence which makes it difficult for Canadian women simply to opt out of the equality discourse.

The Charter equality provisions are being used in a large number and variety of cases. In many cases, equality arguments have been successfully employed directly against women. In others, equality arguments have been used to further men's interests at the expense of women's interests. In a number of cases where other Charter rights have been used against women, women have defended themselves by relying on the Charter equality provisions.[7] These situations demonstrate the need for women in Canada to focus on how best to use the equality provisions to address the inequalities which women suffer and how best to protect women against the use of the equality provisions to entrench and perpetuate existing inequalities. As feminists legal advocates, we need to prepare ourselves to be able to counter male-based equality arguments with women-centered equality arguments.

Trapped in Equality

It is only recently that I have begun to approach equality as a strategy and to appreciate the flexibility which the indeterminacy of equality offers. A few years ago, I was very much struggling to determine to which "side" of the equality debate I subscribed and how the different models of equality might apply to the specific issues I was anxious to address. I was, at that time, working on a project which was set up to review Ontario and federal legislation and government policy to assess their compliance with the Charter equality provisions. In order to carry out this assessment the project participants had to look at a great variety and range of women's issues.

I felt completely overwhelmed by the task of fitting these diverse and varied problems into an existing equality analysis so that the Charter could be used to address them. I desperately needed a definition or theory of equality which could make sense to these issues when taken as a whole. I sought a unified and coherent understanding of equality which would enable lawyers and advocates to argue consistently and effectively for an equality which furthered women's interests.

None of the existing equality models seemed adequate to address all, or even most, of the situations of women's inequalities that we were examining.[8] Yet proponents of the various equality models seemed to agree (some explicitly, some implicitly) that one must adopt a single model of equality and use it exclusively. Within the common law legal system, consistency is considered to be of paramount importance. Given this reverence for consistency, it is generally considered unthinkable to go into court to argue that equality means one thing in one fact situation and something different (often inappropriately characterized as contradictory) in another.

I was caught in the prototypical dilemma which characterizes the feminist equality debates. Any attempt to specify and respond to the many varied inequalities to which women are subjected elicits accusations that one is reproducing and perpetuating those inequalities. . . .

Conversely, to premise legislation on the understanding that women and men can, or should, or will be, treated equitably under a gender neutral, androgynous approach is to be accused of ignoring the very real conditions of inequality under which most women live. For example, including pregnancy under general disability leave or promoting the [gender neutral] nurturing leave . . . denies the substantial extra burdens which pregnancy, child-bearing and child care place on women in this society—burdens which are in no way shared equally by men. There are debates about what an "ideal" world might look like with respect to child care, but there is little disagreement that, at present, the vast majority of child care is done by women.

I took, and still do take, these criticisms of the different feminist equality models very seriously. The criticisms raise very real concerns that need to be considered in any equality strategy. But taking all of the criticisms seriously leaves one without a theory of equality. Accepting the need for a single, comprehensive approach to equality, and at the same time noting the inadequacy of any one approach to address all of women's inequalities, and the potential for any formula to be used against women, there seemed no way out of the equality/inequality box in which I saw women trapped.

This was a profoundly depressing realization. Yet, as is often the case, as I was reaching the depths of despair with equality, I was developing an analysis which would assist me to work my way out of this paralyzing pessimism. The recognition that there is no perfect equality formula was very liberating. I no longer felt so restrained and hesitant in my approach to the issues on which I wanted to work.

I realized that the pursuit of an equality formula was itself the trap. I saw that I had allowed myself to be constrained and silenced by the abstract concept of equality. I had felt that we had to get the application of the Charter equality provisions "right" and that, if somehow we couldn't or didn't, we would have failed. I had accepted that the potential offered by the Charter equality provisions could never be brought to fruition until the inconsistencies and contradictions were eliminated from the feminist analysis of equality. I feared that, without a "model of equality," feminist advocates could easily be dismissed as muddle-headed and inconsistent, unclear as to what we really want.

In my pursuit of an equality formula, I had not ignored the existence of liberal and other models of equality. I had understood that no feminist approach would be adopted immediately as "the" meaning of equality and displace the dominant liberal concept. However, it was my expectation that, once developed, the feminist model of equality would compete with these other models, and hopefully, eventually gain acceptance as the prevailing approach to equality. Thus articulated, the unrealistic optimism of my expectations is painfully clear. Even were it possible to develop "the" feminist equality theory—or even a feminist equality model—the expectation that a feminist theory could gain ascendency, either on its own "merits" or through feminist advocacy, seems naive, at the least. To argue in terms of competing theories and "merits" ignores the power dynamics and vested interests, the psychological and cultural systems, and the social institutions through which women's oppression is maintained and reinforced. In ignoring these factors, I myself fell victim to the liberal equality myth, the "anyone can make it" American dream.

Further, "the" feminist equality theory project is not only impractical on political grounds, it is also impossible on practical grounds. No feminist theory of equality capable of application within the existing legal system could, in operation, retain its integrity and function effectively to eliminate women's subordination. The recurring feminist experience is that once any "theory" developed to assist women in the legal arena starts to become effective in that arena (that is it starts to be adopted in some form by decision-makers), the theory is reformulated and redirected by those decision-makers so as to limit its potential and contain women's self-determination. While some improvements for women are made, such gains are usually limited and are almost always accompanied by a counter-vailing loss.[9] By the time that feminist advocates have refined an approach or a strategy into a "theory," it has generally reached its maximum utility for women. At that point, the theory is very likely to be co-opted into liberal service and used to limit women's options or to impede their progress.

The equality strategy in which I see myself engaged is substantially different from the feminist sexual equality model that I initially pursued with such desperate intensity. I no longer seek in equality a concept capable of generating a theory which can provide answers and direction to the difficult legal questions which face women.[10] The notion that it is possible to develop an equality theory which, when applied, would always benefit women without ever operating to our detriment, places far too great a burden on equality as well as on feminists working in the legal equality field. Because of sexism, stereotypes and myths, and the varied, multiple and compound inequalities to which women are subject, no single model of equality could possibly work exclusively in women's interests. In an unequal society, equality will always be a double-edged instrument: a tool which can be used to assist women in some circumstances, or some women, or a woman; but also a weapon which can be used to restrict women, to punish them for failure to conform to the male standard, or to take away women's "advantages."

The recognition that the best we could do was to try to use the equality guarantees to make some limited improvements for some women in some circumstances enabled me to start looking for ways to apply the Charter to do just that. Instead of looking for an external solution—called "equality"—that could be imposed on a situation to rectify an existing inequality, I realized that the solution had to be developed from the problem itself and that "equality," as a concept, had nothing to contribute to this process.

Equality as Strategy

To pursue equality as a strategy, I have had to turn away from definitions of equality, legal models and frameworks. Instead I have begun to look at the specific needs and problems that women experience and the inequalities that women suffer in order to develop ways of addressing these issues in an equality context. The strategy is to argue from the particularized inequality as the means to get it recognized as such—heard, seen and felt as inequality. In this undertaking, none of the existing equality models are of any help. As abstract constructs, these models do not and cannot address the realities of women's lives. An equality framework does not assist one in identifying problems nor in figuring out how to respond to them. In fact, the imposition of an equality model can tend to obscure or distort the realities of women's lives and the inequalities as they are experienced by women.[11] Once the problem is identified and the desired solution determined, an equality-based approach might be helpful as a tool to work toward the desired result, but an "equality" analysis as such provides no insight into the problem.

My concern when a lot of time and energy are spent talking and theorizing about equality is that equality becomes vested with a life and meaning of its own, divorced from the particularized experiences of inequality it is intended to address. Equality then becomes a formulaic solution to be imposed on situations of inequality with little or no consideration for the particularities of that situation. In this process, people tend to become wedded to their own equality formula, thereby losing their ability to respond to changing circumstances.

An equality strategy involves two very separate undertakings. First, one has to isolate the problem, the specific inequality to be addressed and determine the desired solution. Second, one has to devise an appropriate way to achieve that solution. Many equality theorists seem to have collapsed these two undertakings into one and in so doing have lost sight of the original problem. Isolating the problem is usually a fairly clear task, although the problem itself is often complex. Determining the desired solution is usually more difficult. . . .

The second undertaking in the equality as strategy approach is to identify the method(s) that can be employed toward the desired solution. The legal process is, of course, only one possible method: it can be rejected as inappropriate in the circumstances; it can be adopted as the exclusive strategy or as the strategy of first instance; or it can be used in conjunction with other methods. Having decided to use the legal system, reliance upon an equality guarantee is only one of a number of possible legal approaches. In making the choice for or against using an equality guarantee it is inappropriate to allow pre-existing equality formulae to foreclose or constrain one's decision. It is, however, important, in assessing equality as a strategy, to consider the prominence of such equality formulas and their acceptance by decision-makers. One must be prepared to argue against the application of an equality formula where such a formula would operate to women's detriment. It would be a mistake, however, to reject equality arguments altogether. Given the current ambiguity about the legal meaning of equality, it would be shortsighted at this time to concede equality to the equal treatment proponents or to those who argue for a limited acknowledgement of women's difference. These approaches are too easily turned against women.

In this undertaking, it is critically important that feminists not evaluate strategies and desired results in terms of their impact on a particular model of equality. This is not to say that the potential effect of a particular strategy should not be part of the evaluation process. An assessment of the anticipated "costs" of a particular strategy, and upon whom the burden of those costs might principally fall, is a critical part of the evaluation of any strategy. Strategies and results need to be evaluated in terms of their effect upon women and other disadvantaged groups, not in relation to some abstract theory of equality. Solutions should not be adjusted to fit a narrow concept of equality. Reliance upon an equality guarantee should not be rejected as a strategy simply because the desired solution does not seem to fit into an accepted model of equality.

Feminist equality discussions would be better focused on specific issues rather than on the abstract polar notions of "equal treatment" and "special treatment." In contrast, equality strategy seeks to expand the meanings and understandings of equality to address the inequalities to which women are subjected. Given the prominence and lip-service currently paid to equality discourse in Canadian legal forums, women would be foolish to abandon "equality" to those who seek to use it against women. Rather, we should use the indeterminacy of equality to argue on women's behalf in a variety of different circumstances.

The equality project, as I have outlined it, requires that the identification of the problem and the determination of the solution be seen as distinct and separate from implementation. Notions of "equality" should not dictate the solution. The role of legal advocates should be to create and develop implementation strategies, that is, to determine how to pursue the desired solution most effectively.

An Equality Process

I became involved in equality strategizing in Canada through my work with the statute audit project, a review of federal and Ontario legislation and policy conducted in order to document non-compliance with the sex equality guarantees of the Charter. . . .[12] We conducted the project in the absence of a specific model of equality to inform or direct us. We did this, not based on any preference for an unstructured, open-ended approach, but because we were unable, as a group, to choose or develop a model of equality. Ironically, in retrospect I think we approached "equality" in the most appropriate and productive manner. We started from what we knew—the inequalities as women experience them—and strove to present those inequalities in an equality context. We sought either to direct our analysis toward a particular solution or, if we did not yet have a specific solution to propose, to present the analysis so that women's inequalities would be recognized as such. Without an equality model to impose on the problems we were addressing, we were able to be more responsive and creative. In the absence of a commitment to a particular meaning of equality, we were open to any equality-based argument which might assist in redressing the specific problem under review. Rather than allow the law to define the issues for us, we started with women's experiences of inequality and worked from there.

The statute audit participants were divided into seven groups—criminal, education, employment, family, health, immigration and poverty. Each group was to ascertain the problems women experience in that area and to develop an analysis of those problems as equality issues. We desperately wanted to have a theory or model of equality that would provide us with the analysis of the issues and lead us to the appropriate solution. But we had not developed such a theory and we were unable to find one with which we were all comfortable. At the time, I attributed our inability to agree upon a theory of equality to the time constraints under which we were operating and to our lack of familiarity with the equality discourse. I now see that the inability to adopt a theory did not stem from the shortcomings of the audit participants but from the equality theories themselves.

In the absence of an equality formula, each group was asked to generate its own model, based upon its analysis of the issues. We hoped that at the end an appropriate model of equality would emerge fully formed from the collective thinking of all the participants. Of course, no such phantom emerged and we are still without an equality formula. In contrast to my earlier feelings of anxiety and incompleteness, I now feel relieved and challenged by the absence of such a formula.

I learned a number of important things from the statute audit project. First, through my work with the statute audit project, I came to see equality and equality work as a process and not as an end in itself. The project reaffirmed for me the importance, not only of what we do, but of how we do it. . . .

The second lesson I learned from the project is how difficult it is to articulate women's experience within an equality context, despite the fact that women know and experience a multitude of issues as inequalities. Women's narratives generally do not speak in terms of equality. We clearly impose something upon those narratives when we try to put them into a legal equality framework. We need to be sure that we do not lose the meaning and power of the narrative, of the experience, in the equality process.

Finally, I came to recognize that it was not an accident that no model of equality emerged from our analysis. No consistent and precise model of equality can be applied to the inconsistencies and contradictions which make up women's inequal-ities. Attempts to squeeze and cajole women's experiences into some pre-deter-mined equality model deny the complexity and depth of the inequalities which women suffer, and fail to respond to the realities of women's lives. In our over-whelming desire to see and have "equality," we have ignored the inequalities.

Conclusion

Instead of a theory of equality which can be applied in the legal process to further women's dreams of equality, feminists need to develop some equality-based tools which might assist feminist advocates in their work on specific issues. This is the limited use to which I think equality discourse can be put for women within the existing legal system.

Equality's primary value to women is the forum it provides for the raising of issues and presenting of arguments on behalf of women. I now see equality as the packaging through which one attempts to sell a particular end result with respect to a particular issue, rather than itself the end result. The choice of equality as the package is, to a large extent, pragmatic. In the discourse which currently domi-nates the legal and political forums in Canada, equality is, for the moment, highly marketable.

At least on the abstract level, current support of sexual equality is motivated in part by the perceived need for logical consistency. This ideological commitment, in conjunction with the perception that women (and other "minority" groups) are increasingly powerful political forces, make equality arguments something to which liberal decision-makers are forced to listen and respond. Because of the prominence which equality has played within feminist discourse, this, in and of itself, is a significant victory for women.

The current debate is taking place almost exclusively on the terrain of the meaning of equality. In this context, I argue that it is in women's interest to refuse to subscribe to, or commit themselves to, any single meaning of equality. Feminist advocates need to learn to use the equality discourse on behalf of women in as many and in as diverse situations as the term can bear. The needs and experi-ences of women will dictate the meaning of equality in each particular context. It is these needs and experiences which should be brought into the open and pro-moted, not some reified ideal of equality.

I have proposed a strategy for using Canada's new equality provisions on be-half of women, a strategy which I regard as particularly well suited to the legal process and which will take advantage of the prominence which equality discourse has gained within that forum. However, similar to the problems which inhere in advocating a single meaning for equality, reliance upon a single strategy is dan-gerously limited. Feminists have tended to accept the revolution versus reform dichotomy and the rigid and mutually exclusive choices that such dichotomized thinking requires.[13] In contrast, the strategy which I have outlined cannot stand alone. Its effectiveness is, in large measure, dependent upon the simultaneous pursuit of other more "revolutionary" and other more "reform" strategies.

It is vital that women continue to theorize about the meaning of equality and question equality as a goal for women; that women continue to expose and denounce their oppression; that feminists continue to question women's participation in the legal process and raise the specter of co-optation; that women continue to struggle to be heard within the male discourse and struggle to create a women's discourse. Far from being seen as mutually exclusive these strategies must be recognized as mutually supportive. Possibly in this way, through feminist process and methodology, women will be able to operationalize equality; we will not be merely defining it through legal analysis and theory making.

Notes

1. I find myself in somewhat of a terminological quandary in my attempts to describe my approach to equality. Although my approach has a methodology, it is not itself a methodology. My approach is a tool, but not just a tool. It is informed by a theory, but is not a theory. I have settled for the word "strategy" because it is an active, process-based word. However, I do not feel that this word adequately reflects what it is that I am struggling to do.

2. The "inequalities which women in our society experience," are the disadvantages, risks and deprivations which women suffer because they are women. The focus on inequality does not eliminate the problem of comparison, nor the use of "the male" as a basis for that comparison. It does, however, shift the comparison to questions of power and powerlessness, advantage and disadvantage. An inequality-based approach asks how to redress the power imbalance which inheres in a specific inequality rather than whether or not it is appropriate to treat women the same as men in specific circumstances. Equality focuses on men; inequality focuses on women.

3. A. Jaggar, Feminist Politics and Human Nature 5–6 (Rowman and Allanheld, 1983).

4. See, for example, Westen, The Empty Idea of Equality, 95 Harv. L. Rev. 537 (1982).

5. The prominence which equality has gained in the dominant (liberal) discourse in Canada is due, at least in part, to the efforts of the Canadian women who organized and lobbied for the inclusion of strong equality rights provisions in the Charter of Rights and Freedoms. The fact that Canadian women were successful in their lobbying efforts for the inclusion of three equality provisions in the Charter (S.15(1), S.15(2) and S.28) may be an indication that the notion of formal equality has reached the limits of its utility for women and that it is time for us to develop a more woman-centered understanding of equality. It might be that we attain our victories only at the point when what we win will no longer be of use to us.

6. The Constitution Act, 1982 (en. by the Canada Act, 1982 (U.K.), C.11, Schedule B).

§ 15(1) Every individual is equal before and under the law and has the right to the equal protection and equal benefit of the law without discrimination and, in particular, without discrimination based on race, national or ethnic origin, colour, religion, sex, age or mental or physical disability.

(2) Subsection (1) does not preclude any law, program or activity that has as its object the amelioration of conditions of disadvantaged individuals or groups including those that are disadvantaged because of race, national or ethnic origin, colour, religion, sex, age or mental or physical disability.

§ 28 Notwithstanding anything in this Charter, the rights and freedoms referred to in it are guaranteed equally to male and female persons.

7. For example, there have been a number of cases in Canada in which an accused rapist has argued that he has the constitutional right to cross-examine the rape victim on her prior sexual history. A women's organization has intervened and argued that to allow such a cross-examination would contravene the victim's guaranteed rights to equality.

8. The range of issues included, for example, custody and support, pregnancy leave, boys-only sports teams, social assistance, sexual assault, the testing and regulation of women's health products, housing and women-only professional associations.

9. Crocker, The Meaning of Equality for Battered Women Who Kill Men in Self-Defense, 8 Harv. Women's L.J. 121 (1983) provides a good illustration of this point in her discussion of the "battered wife syndrome" which was originally introduced into court to support battered women's claims to self-defense and has now become a new stereotype used against any battered woman who does not conform to it.

The current move by the Ontario government to introduce access enforcement legislation to "counter-balance" the new child support enforcement legislation in the child custody area is a classic example of the undermining of an apparent benefit to women.

10. In fact, many of the legal questions facing women are being made more difficult by the perceived need for a theory of equality and the desire to comply with some predetermined understanding of equality. For example, maternity leave should not be a troubling question; the need is clear. The propriety of women in combat is not an immediate question. However, women's access to careers in the armed services is a pressing concern. These two issues, like many others, have become difficult and contentious questions when placed in the equality context. This formulation is backward—the theory should not dictate the issues but should flow from the issues. It is a truism of feminism that women's experience should be the starting place for any women-centered undertaking.

11. It seems to me, for example, a distortion to characterize the problem of women losing their jobs because of pregnancy as a problem with disability benefits. This is not to downplay the seriousness of inadequate disability benefits nor to say that the solution to the absence of maternity benefits *might* not be improved

disability benefits. But the problem is not the rules regarding disability benefits, it is an unwillingness to accommodate pregnancy within the paid labor force.

12. The project involved almost 100 lawyers, community workers, students, academics and feminist activists.

13. This is the same mode of thinking, frequently described as "male," which posits as dichotomy between "special treatment" and "equality." Women who accept this dichotomy are forced into the box of choosing between the two. This type of thinking and the reform-versus-revolution dichotomy have been critiqued by numerous feminist and other scholars.

❖ Difference and Dominance: On Sex Discrimination

CATHARINE A. MACKINNON

WHAT IS A GENDER QUESTION a question of? What is an inequality question a question of? . . . I think it speaks to the way gender has structured thought and perception that mainstream legal and moral theory tacitly gives the same answer to . . . both: these are questions of sameness and difference. The mainstream doctrine of the law of sex discrimination that results is, in my view, largely responsible for the fact that sex equality law has been so utterly ineffective at getting women what we need and are socially prevented from having on the basis of a condition of birth: a chance at productive lives of reasonable physical security, self-expression, individuation, and minimal respect and dignity. Here I expose the sameness/difference theory of sex equality, briefly show how it dominates sex discrimination law and policy and underlies its discontents, and propose an alternative that might do something. . . .

According to the approach to sex equality that has dominated politics, law, and social perception, equality is an equivalence, not a distinction, and sex is a distinction. The legal mandate of equal treatment—which is both a systemic norm and a specific legal doctrine—becomes a matter of treating likes alike and unlikes unlike; and the sexes are defined as such by their mutual unlikeness. Put another way, gender is socially constructed as difference epistemologically; sex discrimination law bounds gender equality by difference doctrinally. A built-in tension exists between this concept of equality, which presupposes sameness, and this concept of sex, which presupposes difference. Sex equality thus becomes a contradiction in terms, something of an oxymoron, which may suggest why we are having such a difficult time getting it.

Upon further scrutiny, two alternate paths to equality for women emerge within this dominant approach, paths that roughly follow the lines of this tension. The leading one is: be the same as men. This path is termed gender neutrality doctrinally and the single standard philosophically. It is testimony to how substance gets itself up as form in law that this rule is considered formal equality. Because this approach mirrors the ideology of the social world, it is considered abstract, meaning transparent of substance; also for this reason it is considered not only to be *the* standard, but *a* standard at all. It is so far the leading rule that the words "equal to" are code for, equivalent to, the words "the same as"—referent for both unspecified.

To women who want equality yet find that you are different, the doctrine provides an alternate route: be different from men. This equal recognition of difference is termed the special benefit rule or special protection rule legally, the double standard philosophically. It is in rather bad odor. Like pregnancy, which always calls it up, it is something of a doctrinal embarrassment. Considered an exception to true equality and not really a rule of law at all, this is the one place where the law of sex discrimination admits it is recognizing something substantive. Together with the Bona Fide Occupational Qualification (BFOQ), the unique physical characteristic exception under ERA policy, compensatory legislation, and sex-conscious relief in particular litigation, affirmative action is thought to live here.[1]

The philosophy underlying the difference approach is that sex *is* a difference, a division, a distinction, beneath which lies a stratum of human commonality, sameness. The moral thrust of the sameness branch of the doctrine is to make normative rules conform to this empirical reality by granting women access to what men have access to: to the extent that women are no different than men, we deserve what they have. The differences branch, which is generally seen as patronizing but necessary to avoid absurdity, exists to value or compensate women for what we are or have become distinctively as women (by which is meant, unlike men) under existing conditions.

My concern is not with which of these paths to sex equality is preferable in the long run or more appropriate to any particular issue, although most discourse on sex discrimination revolves about these questions as if that were all there is. My point is logically prior: to treat issues of sex equality as issues of sameness and difference *is to take a particular approach*. I call this the difference approach because it is obsessed with the sex difference. The main theme in the fugue is "we're the same, we're the same, we're the same." The counterpoint theme (in a higher register) is "but we're different, but we're different, but we're different." Its underlying story is: on the first day, difference was; on the second day, a division was created upon it; on the third day, irrational instances of dominance arose. Division may be rational or irrational. Dominance seems or is justified. Difference *is*.

There is a politics to this. Concealed is the substantive way in which man has become the measure of all things. Under the sameness standard, women are measured according to our correspondence with man, our equality judged by our proximity to his measure. Under the difference standard, we are measured according to our lack of correspondence with him, our womanhood judged by our distance from his measure. Gender neutrality is thus simply the male standard, and the special protection rule is simply the female standard, but do not be deceived: masculinity, or maleness, is the referent for both. Think about it like those anatomy models in medical school. A male body is the human body; all those extra things women have are studied in ob/gyn. . . . Approaching sex discrimination in this way—as if sex questions are difference questions and equality questions are sameness questions—provides two ways for the law to hold women to a male standard and call that sex equality. . . .

[T]he strongest doctrinal expression of [the] sameness idea would prohibit taking gender into account in any way. Its guiding impulse is: we're as good as you. Anything you can do, we can do. Just get out of the way. I have to confess a sincere affection for this approach. It has gotten women some access to employment and education, the public pursuits, including academic, professional, and blue-collar work; the military; and more than nominal access to athletics. . . .

The issue of including women in the military draft[2] has presented the sameness answer to the sex equality question in all its simple dignity and complex equivocality. As a citizen, I should have to risk being killed just like you. The consequences of my resistance to this risk should count like yours. The undercurrent is: what's the matter, don't you want me to learn to kill . . . just like you? Sometimes I see this as a dialogue between women in the afterlife. The feminist says to the soldier, "we fought for your equality." The soldier says the feminist, "oh, no, *we* fought for *your* equality."

Feminists have this nasty habit of counting bodies and refusing not to notice their gender. As applied, the sameness standard has mostly gotten men the benefit of those few things women have historically had—for all the good they did us. Almost every sex discrimination case that has been won at the Supreme Court level has been brought by a man.[3] Under the rule of gender neutrality, the law of custody and divorce has been transformed, giving men an equal chance at custody of children and at alimony. Men often look like better "parents" under gender-neutral rules like level of income and presence of nuclear family, because men make more money and (as they say) initiate the building of family units. In effect, they get preferred because society advantages them before they get into court, and law is prohibited from taking that preference into account because that would mean taking gender into account. The group realities that make women more in need of alimony are not permitted to matter, because only individual factors, gender-neutrally considered, may matter. So the fact that women will live their lives, as individuals, as members of the group women, with women's chances in a sex-discriminatory society, may not count, or else it is sex discrimination. The equality principle in this guise mobilizes the idea that the way to get things for women is to get them for men. Men have gotten them. Have women? We still have not got equal pay, or equal work, far less equal pay for equal work. . . .

Here is why. . . . [V]irtually every quality that distinguishes men from women is already affirmatively compensated in this society. Men's physiology defines most sports,[4] their needs define auto and health insurance coverage, their socially designed biographies define workplace expectations and successful career patterns, their perspectives and concerns define quality in scholarship, their experiences and obsessions define merit, their objectification of life defines art, their military service defines citizenship, their presence defines family, their inability to get along with each other—their wars and rulerships—defines history, their image defines god, and their genitals define sex. For each of their differences from women, what amounts to an affirmative action plan is in effect, otherwise known as the structure and values of American society. But whenever women are, by this standard, "different" from men and insist on not having it held against us, whenever a difference is used to keep us second class and we refuse to smile about it, equality law has a paradigm trauma and it's crisis time for the doctrine.

What this doctrine has apparently meant by sex inequality is not what happens to us. The law of sex discrimination that has resulted seems to be looking only for those ways women are kept down that have *not* wrapped themselves up as a difference—whether original, imposed, or imagined. Start with original: what to do to about the fact that women actually have an ability men still lack, gestating children in utero. Pregnancy therefore is a difference. Difference doctrine says it is sex discrimination to give women what we need, because only women need it. It is not sex discrimination not to give women what we need because then only women will not get what we need.[5] Move into imposed: what to do about the fact that most women are segregated into low-paying jobs where there are no men. Suspecting that the structure of the marketplace will be entirely subverted if comparable worth is put into effect, difference doctrine says that because there is no man to set a standard from which women's treatment is a deviation, there is no sex discrimination here, only sex difference. Never mind that there is no man to compare with because no man would do that job if he had a choice, and of course he has because he is a man, so he won't.[6]

Now move into the so-called subtle reaches of the imposed category, the de facto area. Most jobs in fact require that the person, gender neutral, who is qualified for them will be someone who is not the primary caretaker of a preschool child. Pointing out that this raises a concern of sex in a society in which women are expected to care for the children is taken as day one of taking gender into account in the structuring of jobs. To do that would violate the rule against not noticing situated differences based on gender, so it never emerges that day one of taking gender into account was the day the job was structured with the expectation that its occupant would have no child care responsibilities. Imaginary sex differences—such as between male and female applicants to administer estates or between males aging and dying and females aging and dying[7]—I will concede, the doctrine can handle.

. . . What the sameness standard fails to notice is that men's differences from women are equal to women's differences from men. There is an *equality* there. Yet the sexes are not socially equal. The difference approach misses the fact that hierarchy of power produces real as well as fantasied differences, differences that are also inequalities. What is missing in the difference approach is what Aristotle missed in his empiricist notion that equality means treating likes alike and unlikes unlike, and nobody has questioned it since. Why should you have to be the same as a man to get what a man gets simply because he is one? Why does maleness provide an original entitlement, not questioned on the basis of *its* gender, so that it is women—women who want to make a case of unequal treatment in a world men have made in their image (this is really the part Aristotle missed)—who have to show in effect that they are men in every relevant respect, unfortunately mistaken for women on the basis of an accident of birth? . . .

The special benefits side of the difference approach has not compensated for the differential of being second class. The special benefits rule is the only place in mainstream equality doctrine where you get to identify as a woman and not have that mean giving up all claim to equal treatment—but it comes close. Under its double standard, women who stand to inherit something when their husbands die have gotten the exclusion of a small percentage of the inheritance tax, to the tune of Justice Douglas waxing eloquent about the difficulties of all women's economic situation.[8] If we're going to be stigmatized as different, it would be nice if the compensation would fit the disparity. . . . Women have also gotten excluded from contact jobs in male-only prisons because we might get raped, the Court taking the viewpoint of the reasonable rapist on women's employment opportunities.[9] We also get protected out of jobs because of our fertility. The reason is that the job has health hazards, and somebody who might be a real person some day and therefore could sue—that is, a fetus—might be hurt if women, who apparently are not real persons and therefore can't sue either for the hazard to our health or for the lost employment opportunity, are given jobs that subject our bodies to possible harm.[10] Excluding women is always an option if equality feels in tension with the pursuit itself. They never seem to think of excluding men. . . .

The double standard of these rules doesn't give women the dignity of the single standard; it also does not (as the differences standard does) suppress the gender of its referent, which is, of course, the female gender. I must also confess some affection for this standard. The work of Carol Gilligan on gender differences in moral reasoning[11] gives it a lot of dignity, more than it has ever had, more, frankly, than I thought it ever could have. But she achieves for moral reasoning what the special protection rule achieves in law: the affirmative rather than the negative valuation of that which has accurately distinguished women from men, by making it seem as though those attributes, with their consequences, really are somehow ours, rather than what male supremacy has attributed to us for its own use. For women to affirm difference, when difference means dominance, as it does with gender, means to affirm the qualities and characteristics of powerlessness.

Women have done good things, and it is a good thing to affirm them. . . . Women have a history all right, but it is a history both of what was and of what was not allowed to be. So I am critical of affirming what we have been, which necessarily is what we have been permitted, as if it is women's, ours, possessive. As if equality, in spite of everything, already ineluctably exists.

I am getting hard on this and am about to get harder on it. I do not think that the way women reason morally is morality "in a different voice." I think it is morality in a higher register, in the feminine voice. Women value care because men have valued us according to the care we give them, and we could probably use some. Women think in relational terms because our existence is defined in relation to men. Further, when you are powerless, you don't just speak differently. A lot, you don't speak. Your speech is not just differently articulated, it is silenced. Eliminated, gone. You aren't just deprived of a language with which to articulate your distinctiveness, although you are; you are deprived of a life out of which articulation might come. Not being heard is not just a function of lack of recognition, not just that no one knows how to listen to you, although it is that; it is also silence of the deep kind, the silence of being prevented from having anything to say. Sometimes it is permanent. All I am saying is that the damage of sexism is real, and reifying that into differences is an insult to our possibilities.

So long as these issues are framed this way, demands for equality will always appear to be asking to have it both ways: the same when we are the same, different when we are different. But this is the way men have it: equal and different too. They have it the same as women when they are the same and want it, and different from women when they are different and want to be, which usually they do. Equal and different too would only be parity. But under male supremacy, while being told we get it both ways, both the specialness of the pedestal and an even chance at the race, the ability to be a woman and a person, too, few women get much benefit of either. . . .

There is an alternative approach, one that threads its way through existing law and expresses, I think, the reason equality law exists in the first place. It provides a second answer, a dissident answer in law and philosophy, to both the equality question and the gender question. In this approach, an equality question is a question of the distribution of power. Gender is also a question of power, specifically of male supremacy and female subordination. The question of equality, from the standpoint of what it is going to take to get it, is at root a question of hierarchy, which—as power succeeds in constructing social perception and social reality—derivatively becomes a categorical distinction, a difference. Here, on the first day that matters, dominance was achieved, probably by force. By the second day, division along the same lines had to be relatively firmly in place. On the third day, if not sooner, differences were demarcated, together with social systems to exaggerate them in perception and in fact, *because* the systematically differential delivery of benefits and deprivations required making no mistake about who was who. Comparatively speaking, man has been resting ever since. Gender might not even code as difference, might not mean distinction epistemologically, were it not for its consequences for social power.

I call this the dominance approach, and it is the ground I have been standing on in criticizing mainstream law. The goal of this dissident approach is not to make legal categories trace and trap the way things are. It is not to make rules that fit reality. It is critical of reality. Its task is not to formulate abstract standards that will produce determinate outcomes in particular cases. Its project is more substantive, more jurisprudential than formulaic, which is why it is difficult for the mainstream discourse to dignify it as an approach to doctrine or to imagine it as a rule of law at all. It proposes to expose that which women have had little choice but to be confined to, in order to change it.

The dominance approach centers on the most sex-differential abuses of women as a gender, abuses that sex equality law in its difference garb could not confront. It is based on a reality about which little of a systematic nature was known before 1970, a reality that calls for a new conception of the problem of sex inequality. This new information includes not only the extent and intractability of sex segregation into poverty, which has been known before, but the range of issues termed violence against women, which has not been. It combines women's material desperation, through being relegated to categories of jobs that pay nil, with the massive amount of rape and attempted rape—44 percent of all women— about which virtually nothing is done;[12] the sexual assault of children—38 percent of girls and 10 percent of boys—which is apparently endemic to the patriarchal family;[13] the battery of women that is systematic in one quarter to one third of our homes;[14] prostitution, women's fundamental economic condition, what we do when all else fails, and for many women in this country, all else fails often; and pornography, an industry that traffics in female flesh, making sex inequality into sex to the tune of eight billion dollars a year in profits largely to organized crime.

These experiences have been silenced out of the difference definition of sex equality largely because they happen almost exclusively to women. Understand: for this reason, they are considered *not* to raise sex equality issues. Because this treatment is done almost uniquely to women, it is implicitly treated as a difference, the sex difference, when in fact it is the socially situated subjection of women. The whole point of women's social relegation to inferiority as a gender is that for the most part these things aren't done to men. Men are not paid half of what women are paid for doing the same work on the basis of their equal difference. . . . When they are hit, a person has been assaulted. When they are sexually violated, it is not simply tolerated or found entertaining or defended as the necessary structure of the family, the price of civilization, or a constitutional right.

Does this differential describe the sex difference? Maybe so. It does describe the systematic relegation of an entire group of people to a condition of inferiority and attribute it to their nature. If this differential were biological, maybe biological intervention would have to be considered. If it were evolutionary, perhaps men would have to evolve differently. Because I think it is political, I think its politics construct the deep structure of society. Men who do not rape women have nothing wrong with their hormones. Men who are made sick by pornography and do not eroticize their revulsion are not underevolved. This social status in which we can be used and abused and trivialized and humiliated and bought and sold and passed around and patted on the head and put in place and told to smile so that we look as though we're enjoying it all is not what some of us have in mind as sex equality.

This second approach—which is not abstract, which is at odds with socially imposed reality and therefore does not look like a standard according to the standard for standards—became the implicit model for racial justice applied by the courts during the sixties. It has since eroded with the erosion of judicial commitment to racial equality. It was based on the realization that the condition of Blacks in particular was not fundamentally a matter of rational or irrational differentiation on the basis of race but was fundamentally a matter of white supremacy, under which racial differences became invidious as a consequence. To consider gender in this way, observe again that men are as different from women as women are from men, but socially the sexes are not equally powerful. To be on the top of a hierarchy is certainly different from being on the bottom, but that is an obfuscatingly neutralized way of putting it, as a hierarchy is a great deal more than that. If gender were merely a question of difference, sex inequality would be a problem of mere sexism, of mistaken differentiation, of inaccurate categorization of individuals. This is what the difference approach thinks it is and is therefore sensitive to. But if gender is an inequality first, constructed as a socially relevant differentiation in order to keep that inequality in place, then sex inequality questions are questions of systematic dominance, of male supremacy, which is not at all abstract and is anything but a mistake.

If differentiation into classifications, in itself, is discrimination, as it is in difference doctrine, the use of law to change group-based social inequalities becomes problematic, even contradictory. This is because the group whose situation is to be changed must necessarily be legally identified and delineated, yet to do so is considered in fundamental tension with the guarantee against legally sanctioned inequality. If differentiation is discrimination, affirmative action, and any legal change in social inequality, is discrimination—but the existing social differentiations which constitute the inequality are not? This is only to say that, in the view that equates differentiation with discrimination, changing an unequal status quo is discrimination, but allowing it to exist is not.

Looking at the difference approach and the dominance approach from each other's point of view clarifies some otherwise confusing tensions in sex equality debates. From the point of view of the dominance approach, it becomes clear that the difference approach adopts the point of view of male supremacy on the status of the sexes. Simply by treating the status quo as "the standard," it invisibly and uncritically accepts the arrangements under male supremacy. In this sense, the difference approach is masculinist, although it can be expressed in a female voice. The dominance approach, in that it sees the inequalities of the social world from the standpoint of the subordination of women to men, is feminist.

If you look through the lens of the difference approach at the world as the dominance approach imagines it—that is, if you try to see real inequality through a lens that has difficulty seeing an inequality as an inequality if it also appears as a difference—you see demands for change in the distribution of power as demands for special protection. This is because the only tools that the difference paradigm offers to comprehend disparity equate the recognition of a gender line with an admission of lack of entitlement to equality under law. Since equality questions are primarily confronted in this approach as matters of empirical fit—that is, as matters of accurately shaping legal rules (implicitly modeled on the standard men set) to the way the world is (also implicitly modeled on the standard men set)— any existing differences must be negated to merit equal treatment. For ethnicity as well as for gender, it is basic to mainstream discrimination doctrine to preclude any true diversity among equals or true equality within diversity.

To the difference approach, it further follows that any attempt to change the way the world actually is looks like a moral question requiring a separate judgment of how things ought to be. This approach imagines asking the following disinterested question that can be answered neutrally as to groups: against the weight of empirical difference, should we treat some as the equals of others, even when they may not be entitled to it because they are not up to standard? Because this construction of the problem is part of what the dominance approach unmasks, it does not arise with the dominance approach, which therefore does not see its own foundations as moral. If sex inequalities are approached as matters of imposed status, which are in need of change if a legal mandate of equality means anything at all, the question whether women should be treated unequally means simply whether women should be treated as less. When it is exposed as a naked power question, there is no separable question of what ought to be. The only real question is what is and is not a gender question. Once no amount of difference justifies treating women as subhuman, eliminating that is what equality law is for. In this shift of paradigms, equality propositions become no longer propositions of good and evil, but of power and powerlessness, no more disinterested in their origins or neutral in their arrival at conclusions than are the problems they address.

There came a time in Black people's movement for equality in this country when slavery stopped being a question of how it could be justified and became a question of how it could be ended. Racial disparities surely existed, or racism would have been harmless, but at that point—a point not yet reached for issues of sex—no amount of group difference mattered anymore. This is the same point at which a group's characteristics, including empirical attributes, become constitutive of the fully human, rather than being defined as exceptions to or as distinct from the fully human. To one-sidedly measure one group's differences against a standard set by the other incarnates partial standards. The moment when one's particular qualities become part of the standard by which humanity is measured is a millennial moment.

To summarize the argument: seeing sex equality questions as matters of reasonable or unreasonable classification is part of the way male dominance is expressed in law. If you follow my shift in perspective from gender as difference to gender as dominance, gender changes from a distinction that is presumptively valid to a detriment that is presumptively suspect. The difference approach tries to map reality; the dominance approach tries to challenge and change it. In the dominance approach, sex discrimination stops being a question of morality and starts being a question of politics.

You can tell if sameness is your standard for equality if my critique of hierarchy looks like a request for special protection in disguise. It's not. It envisions a change that would make possible a simple equal chance for the first time. To define the reality of sex as difference and the warrant of equality as sameness is wrong on both counts. Sex, in nature, is not a bipolarity; it is a continuum. In society it is made into a bipolarity. Once this is done, to require that one be the same as those who set the standard—those which one is already socially defined as different from—simply means that sex equality is conceptually designed never to be achieved. Those who most need equal treatment will be the least similar, socially, to those whose situation sets the standard as against which one's entitlement to be equally treated is measured. Doctrinally speaking, the deepest problems of sex inequality will not find women "similarly situated" to men. Far less will practices of sex inequality require that acts be intentionally discriminatory. All that is required is that the status quo be maintained. As a strategy for maintaining social power first structure reality unequally, then require that entitlement to alter it be grounded on a lack of distinction in situation; first structure perception so that different equals inferior, then require that discrimination be activated by evil minds who *know* they are treating equals as less.

I say, give women equal power in social life. Let what we say matter, then we will discourse on questions of morality. Take your foot off our necks, then we will hear in what tongue women speak. So long as sex equality is limited by sex difference, whether you like it or don't like it, whether you value it or seek to negate it, whether you stake it out as grounds for feminism or occupy it as the terrain of misogyny, women will be born, degraded, and die. We would settle for that equal protection of the laws under which one would be born, live, and die, in a country where protection is not a dirty word and equality is not a special privilege.

Notes

1. The Bona Fide Occupational Qualification (BFOQ) exception to Title VII of the Civil Rights Act of 1964, 42 U.S.C. §2000 e-(2)(e), permits sex to be a job qualification when it is a valid one. . . .

2. Rostker v. Goldberg, 453 U.S. 57 (1981). See also Lori S. Kornblum, Women Warriors in a Men's World: The Combat Exclusion, 2 Law & Ineq. J. 353 (1984).

3. David Cole, Strategies of Difference: Litigating for Women's Rights in a Man's World, 2 Law & Ineq. J. 34 n. (4) (1984) (collecting cases).

4. A particularly pungent example comes from a case in which the plaintiff sought to compete in boxing matches with men, since there were no matches sponsored by the defendant among women. A major reason that preventing the woman from competing was found not to violate her equality rights was that the "safety rules and precautions [were] developed, designed, and tested in the context of all-male competition." Lafler v. Athletic Board of Control, 536 F. Supp. 104, 107 (W.D. Mich. 1982). As the court put it: "In this case, the real differences between the male and female anatomy are relevant in considering whether men and women may be treated differently with regard to their participating in boxing. The plaintiff *admits* that she wears a protective covering for her breasts while boxing. Such a protective covering . . . would violate Rule Six, Article 9 of the Amateur Boxing Federation rules currently in effect. The same rule *requires* contestants to wear a protective cup, a rule obviously designed for the unique anatomical characteristics of men." *Id.* at 106 (emphasis added). The rule is based on the male anatomy, therefore not a justification for the discrimination but an example of it. This is not considered in the opinion, nor does the judge discuss whether women might benefit from genital protection, and men from chest guards, as in some other sports.

5. This is a reference to the issues raised by several recent cases which consider whether states' attempts to compensate pregnancy leaves and to secure jobs on women's return constitute sex discrimination. . . .

6. Most women work at jobs mostly women do, and most of those jobs are paid less than jobs that mostly men do. . . . To the point that men may not meet the male standard themselves, one court found that a union did not fairly represent its women in the following terms: "As to the yard and driver jobs, defendants suggest not only enormous intellectual requirements, but that the physical demands of those jobs are so great as to be beyond the capacity of any female. Again, it is noted that plaintiffs' capacity to perform those jobs was never tested, despite innumerable requests therefor. It is also noted that defendants have never suggested *which* of the innumerable qualifications they list for these jobs (for the first time) the plaintiffs might fail to meet. The court, however, will accept without listing here the extraordinary catalogue of feats which defendants argue must be performed in the yard, and as a driver. That well may be. However, one learns from this record that one cannot be too weak, too sick, too old and infirm, or too ignorant to perform these jobs, *so long as one is a man*. The plaintiffs appear to the layperson's eye to be far more physically fit than many of the drivers who moved into the yard, over the years, according to the testimony of defense witnesses. . . . In short, they were all at least as fit as the men with serious physical deficits and disabilities who held yard jobs." Jones v. Cassens Transport, 617 F. Supp. 869, 892 (1985)(emphasis in original).

7. Reed v. Reed, 404 U.S. 71 (1971) held that a statute barring women from administering estates is sex discrimination. If few women were taught to read and write, as used to be the case, the gender difference would not be imaginary in this

sense, yet the social situation would be even more sex discriminatory than it is now. Compare City of Los Angeles v. Manhart, 434 U.S. 815 (1978), which held that requiring women to make larger contributions to their retirement plan was sex discrimination, in spite of the allegedly proven sex difference that women on the average outlive men.

8. Kahn v. Shevin, 416 U.S. 351, 353 (1974).

9. Dothard v. Rawlinson, 433 U.S. 321 (1977). . . .

10. Doerr v. B.F. Goodrich, 484 F.Supp. 320 (N.D. Ohio 1979). Wendy Webster Williams, Firing the Woman to Protect the Fetus: The Reconciliation of Fetal Protection with Employment Opportunity Goals Under Title VII, 69 Georgetown L.J. 641 (1981). See also Hayes v. Shelby Memorial Hospital, 546 F.Supp. 259 (N.D. Ala. 1982); Wright v. Olin Corp., 697 F.2d 1172 (4th Cir. 1982). [But compare United Auto Workers v. Johnson Controls, Inc., 111 S.Ct. 1196 (1991) (fetal protection policy is facially discriminatory and violates Title VII, as employer did not establish that sex was a Bona Fide Occupational Qualification.) *Ed.*]

11. Carol Gilligan, In a Different Voice (Harvard University Press, 1982).

12. Diana Russell and Nancy Howell, The Prevalence of Rape in the United States Revisited, 8 Signs: Journal of Women in Culture and Society 689 (1983)(44 percent of women in 930 households were victims of rape or attempted rape at some time in their lives).

13. Diana Russell, The Incidence and Prevalence of Intrafamilial and Extrafamilial Sexual Abuse of Female Children, 7 Child Abuse & Neglect: The International Journal 133 (1983).

14. R. Emerson Dobash and Russell Dobash, Violence against Wives: A Case against the Patriarchy (Free Press, 1979); Bruno v. Codd, 90 Misc. 2d 1047, 396 N.Y.S. 2d 974 (Sup. Ct. 1977), *rev'd*, 64 A.D.2d 582, 407 N.Y.S. 2d 165 (1st Dep't 1978), *aff'd* 47 N.Y. 2d 582, 393 N.E.2d 976, 419 N.Y.S. 2d 901 (1979).

❖ *The Anti-Subordination Principle: Applications*

R**UTH** C**OLKER**

L**AW'S RECOGNITION OF** the subordination of blacks and women[1]—through slavery, disenfranchisement, segregation and a general denial of full citizenship—provided the impetus for the development of modern equal protection doctrine. The principle underlying equal protection doctrine, however, is not purely the principle of anti-subordination. Instead, it is often the principle of anti-differentiation. The anti-differentiation principle seeks a color blind and sex blind society where racial and sexual differentiations do not exist. The anti-subordination principle, in contrast, is not hostile to racial and sexual differentiations unless they perpetuate the subordination of women or blacks. I argue that the principle of anti-subordination rather than the principle of anti-differentiation should underlie the equal protection framework because the principle of anti-subordination can be more effective and flexible in responding to the problem of subordination. I try to explain how the anti-subordination principle should resolve equal protection problems.

This discussion is important for many reasons. First, it might influence courts that are already concerned about the problem of subordination. Some courts may desire to remedy subordination more effectively but do not have a framework to do so. By devising a workable framework, some courts may be assisted in this task. Second, this discussion is useful in our attempts to create legislation. Although existing constitutional and statutory nondiscrimination doctrine may not embody the anti-subordination principle, new legislation could embody that perspective. Finally, it is useful as an organizing tactic to understand how various solutions to institutional problems may redress subordination. Because the existing dialogue is usually phrased in terms of the anti-differentiation principle, we often do not think enough about the anti-subordination principle.[2]

Too often we proceed pragmatically without recognizing the full range of consequences of our actions. A solid theoretical framework could check us against

---

3 Wis. Women's L.J. 59 (1987).

creating unintended consequences in our haste to respond to a problem pragmatically.

Several basic assumptions have influenced both the context and structure of this article. . . . [T]his essay is premised on a desire to get the discussion of equal protection doctrine out of the language of the equal treatment/special treatment debate. . . .

[T]his essay is premised [also] on a commitment to doing comparative race and sex work. Much of feminist jurisprudence looks at sex discrimination in a vacuum. Thus, we lose sight of the big picture. By trying to explore race and sex issues together, we can get a much better handle on legal theory and the solution to practical problems.

Finally, this essay assumes that theory is only useful to the extent that it can respond to practical problems. Thus, this essay is shaped around a discussion of hypotheticals. If we can find ways to integrate theory and practice, we will emerge much stronger in both arenas. . . .

Theoretical and Doctrinal Discussion

First, this section will define the principles of anti-differentiation and anti-subordination, and then show how they are used under existing equal protection doctrine.[3]

Definitions

The principle of anti-differentiation is premised on the assumption that racial and sexual differentiations are invidious. . . . Under this perspective, a rule that excludes whites is equally as bad as a rule that excludes blacks. The evil is the differentiation rather than who is acted upon.

In contrast, the principle of anti-subordination is premised on the assumption that society is a racial patriarchy.[4] The problem with this hierarchy is that the people at the bottom, e.g., women and blacks, do not have sufficient power to control or value their own lives. The evil is therefore the lack of power and control, not differentiations. The evil is denying women and blacks fullness as human beings by seeing them as objects to be acted upon rather than subjects entitled to control of their own lives. The anti-subordination principle is a group-based perspective grounded in an understanding of the way certain groups have been historically treated unequally. Under this perspective, it is more invidious to have a rule that excludes blacks than to have a rule that excludes whites, because whites, as a class, have not faced subordination. Under this perspective, it is possible to have a doctrinal discussion that focuses on the historical role of society in perpetuating subordination.

. . . The important point is that we seek a perspective that emerges from blacks' and women's understandings of their condition rather than an abstract concept of color blindness and sex blindness which is equally applicable to whites and blacks, men and women.

Equal Protection Doctrine

Existing equal protection doctrine involves a two-step process. The first step is the prima facie case and the second step is the defense. At step one the plaintiff says that she was discriminated against. At step two the defendant tries to justify the alleged discrimination.

PRIMA FACIE CASE

Two ways exist to establish a prima facie case: intent or impact.

Intent. Under the intentional discrimination method of proof, the plaintiff shows that the actor intended to differentiate on the basis of race or sex. Evidence of this intention is the language used in the rule itself or in the motivations of the actor. . . .

The intent requirement is a pure articulation of the anti-differentiation perspective. . . . It analyzes discrimination from the perspective of the actor—what the actor said and what the actor intended. It does not consider what the actions mean to the person acted upon. Hence, it is an individual-based perspective from the perspective of the person in power or control.

Impact. The disparate impact method of proof is limited to some statutory cases; it is not available in constitutional cases. Under this method of proof, the plaintiff shows that the effect of the defendant's actions was to limit the plaintiff's opportunities. One looks at what actually happened rather than at the intended effect. . . .

Some disparate impact cases may look like cases of intentional discrimination, especially when they contain a strong element of foreseeability. However, disparate impact cases are not concerned about intent; they are satisfied with evidence of impact. Impact is not a proxy for intent; it is a separate area of concern.

The disparate impact method of proof has a stronger anti-subordination underpinning than the intent method of proof. It analyzes discrimination more from the perspective of the person acted upon. It is also more group-based in considering the implications of an institution's actions. Nevertheless, it is not a perfect articulation of the anti-subordination perspective because it lacks the normative principle that it is worse for an institution to exclude blacks or women from opportunities than to exclude whites or men. It also has a limited definition of impact that does not capture all the ways that women and blacks face discrimination.

Anti-Subordination Perspective. An anti-subordination perspective views discrimination as a societal mechanism that results in blacks and women having less power and control than whites and men. The intention of the actor does not matter; how the actions feel to those acted upon does matter. The issue is how the action contributes to or perpetuates the existing subordination of blacks and women. Evidence of impact may suggest subordination, especially if one adds normative principles that recognize that impact on blacks and women is probably only a proxy for subordination. The impact is not the harm itself. This will become more evident when we examine the hypotheticals.

STANDARD OF REVIEW

Existing Framework. Courts have two ways to review these cases. In constitutional cases, if race discrimination is alleged, the courts use strict scrutiny to analyze the defendant's justifications. By contrast, if sex discrimination is alleged, the courts use intermediate scrutiny. The scrutiny that is used in statutory cases is not called strict or intermediate, but it also differs in race and sex cases [e.g. Title VII's BFOQ exception is available for sex discrimination cases but not race discrimination cases *Ed.*]. The statutes require the courts to be more intolerant of racial differentiations than sexual differentiations.

The anti-differentiation principle is used less rigidly in the sex context but this less rigid principle is not an anti-subordination principle. It reflects the fact that the courts and Congress are less concerned about sex discrimination than race discrimination, and are therefore willing to carve out more exceptions to preserve certain gender-role stereotypes. For example, the principle of nondiscrimination does not mean that women should be drafted into military service, that beauty pageants should be abolished, that college dormitories should be coeducational or that women should be prison guards. Nevertheless, one exception to the principle of anti-differentiation does exist that corresponds to the principle of anti-subordination. That is the principle of recognizing the need for affirmative action. In some cases, the courts will permit racial or sexual differentiations for the purpose of redressing prior discrimination. . . .

Nevertheless, this principle is very limited. The courts will only permit temporary affirmative action measures that are designed to redress a recent history of discrimination in a particular workplace. This principle will not permit broad-based attempts to redress societal subordination.

Anti-Subordination Perspective. From an anti-subordination perspective, differentiation can only be justified if it redresses subordination. An anti-subordination perspective would retain the rigidity of strict scrutiny in all cases except those in which the facially differentiating rule could be justified as redressing subordination. In such a case, the framework would adopt some of the flexibility of intermediate scrutiny to permit this justification.

The inquiry at this stage would still be from the perspective of the women or blacks who are allegedly being assisted even though it is the defendant who is seeking to justify the differentiating rule. Thus, one would want to know whether women or blacks thought that the differentiating rule served to redress subordination. Under existing law, women and blacks often have no role in making this determination. For example, if a law school decided to use affirmative action in admissions to recruit more black students, white applicants for admissions might challenge the policy. The plaintiffs would be white students and the defendant would be the educational institution. No one would necessarily ask the black students for input about the admissions policy.[5] Under an anti-subordination perspective, it would be crucial to have input from existing and potential black students because they would be the only group qualified to say whether the policy redressed subordination.[6] (It could be a poorly designed policy that stigmatized blacks and was ineffective in helping them successfully complete law school once admitted.)

Hypotheticals

Now that we have examined the major theoretical principles underlying equal protection doctrine, we should try to apply the anti-subordination principle. This section will use a series of hypotheticals to apply the proposed framework.

Single Black Mothers

Single black mothers have historically had few financial resources to raise children. They also have had many obstacles to earning a good living and getting good health care. They usually live far from the workplace in areas with poor transportation. Health care in our society is usually employment based, and often not family based for low paid workers, so that black women have had difficulty affording health care for themselves and their families. Because the labor force is both race and sex segregated, the women often work in job categories in which most of the employees are black women.

HYPOTHETICAL

A women's public interest organization predominantly employs black women to do clerical and secretarial tasks. In addition, it employs white women to do professional work. No one in the workplace is well paid, but the professional employees do make more money than the nonprofessional employees. The nonprofessional employees are paid on an hourly basis and the professional employees are salaried.

The organization notices over the years that black women either do not stay at the job very long or are fired because of poor attendance. It decides to study the problem further to see if structural barriers exist which are limiting the black women from performing effectively. The employer presently insures each employee, provides the employee with the option of purchasing family health insurance for an additional ninety dollars per family member, and provides all employees with two weeks of leave time each year, which can be used for sick leave or vacation. If an hourly employee arrives late to work or leaves early, then that time is deducted from the employee's available leave.[7] The organization decides that one solution would be to double the amount of leave available to black women with family responsibilities and to purchase health insurance for these women's entire families. Because the organization does not have much money, it accomplishes this change by not giving professional employees a pay raise and by not replacing several employees who have left recently (both professional and nonprofessional).

Do these changes violate equal protection doctrine?

ANALYSIS UNDER EXISTING LAW

Under existing law, the employer would have to be concerned about an employment discrimination challenge from white women, white men or black men without family responsibilities—all of whom are being provided less leave time than the black women with family responsibilities. The most difficult challenge would be from persons who would argue that they also have family responsibilities and should receive increased leave time as well as health insurance. Existing legal doctrine would prefer the employer to use neutral criteria, such as family responsibilities and salary, rather than race and sex-specific criteria.

The problem with the approach of existing law is that it downplays the importance of the race and sex variables. It assumes that all problems can be and should be defined in race and sex-neutral language.[8] That assumption undercuts the recognition that we live in a racist and sexist society. It is not true that a white female employee with family responsibilities encounters the identical barriers at the workplace as a black female employee with family responsibilities. It may be useful to affirm the differences between black and white women with family responsibilities in order to call society's attention to the special problems faced by black women. The counter to this argument, however, is that poor white women and black women may have more in common than they have differences. From an organizing perspective it may not be wise to accentuate those differences.

The decision whether to emphasize the similarities or differences between poor white and black women is probably best resolved pragmatically. Existing law, however, does not even leave that option open.

ANALYSIS UNDER ANTI-SUBORDINATION PRINCIPLE

The anti-subordination principle would begin by asking what black women want, and how they feel about the changes in the workplace. Do black women feel that the old leave policy and health insurance policy served to perpetuate their subordination? How did the old policy affect them? Did it make them perform Herculean tasks to get to work on time so that they would not miss more work than allowed? Did it make them unable to provide decent health care to their family members, thereby helping to perpetuate the subordination of their family members? Did the old policy put any strain on white men, white women, or black women without family responsibilities?

If the black women feel subordinated by the old policy, then the question would be directed to how they feel about the new policy. Does it help them redress their subordination or does it stigmatize them at the workplace? Do they want to affirm their differences from other persons at the workplace or would they feel more comfortable if the new policy were also available to some other category of workers? Are they facing new instances of subordination as a result of this new policy, e.g., as a result of old employees not being replaced? Do they feel that they have gained power and control through the new policy? Were they able to participate in the formulation of the policy?

Pretty Secretaries

Secretaries historically have been hired based on their appearance as well as their secretarial skills. These appearance requirements usually conform to appearance norms for white Anglo-Saxon, middle-class women. Black women, Hispanic women, Asian women, Jewish women, fat women, tall women, lesbians, muscular women, old women, and differently-abled women generally do not fit these norms.

HYPOTHETICAL

A law firm hires only women to be secretaries. These women are considered pretty under traditional norms for women, as defined above.

Is there an equal protection problem?

ANALYSIS UNDER EXISTING LAW

Under existing law, the women who were not hired would not be able to bring a claim of discrimination because only women were hired. A man who could not be hired as a secretary or meet the definition of pretty for women might be able to bring a challenge. If no black women are hired under this policy, then a black woman might be able to bring a race discrimination claim. The race claim, however, would be difficult to prove under existing law because the criteria are probably so subtle that they would be difficult to identify. In addition, it is possible that the employer might occasionally hire a black woman who had the traditional features of whites.

The problem with using a man as a plaintiff is that it does not attack the gendered and racial definitions of womanhood that are embodied in the rule. It pretends that any woman could meet this definition and no man could, as if the rule was only a sex-based rule rather than also a gender-based and race-based rule. Moreover, the present analysis obscures the fact that women are forced to make their livings as sexual objects. The problem is not simply that women have fewer options in their choice of appearance; the problem is that women are always forced to make their appearance choices on male terms.[9]

ANALYSIS UNDER ANTI-SUBORDINATION PRINCIPLE

The anti-subordination principle would ask whether this prettiness requirement perpetuates the subordination of women and blacks. It perpetuates the subordination of blacks and women by giving them few options for appearance and by making them conform to a white male standard. Having only one option, which is defined by white men, for sex-role or racial characteristics is a part of the subordination of women and blacks.

Little League

Athletic opportunities have historically been segregated on the basis of sex and race.[10] Little League has traditionally been popular for white boys. The experiences that boys have in Little League are often important in terms of networking and the development of leadership abilities. Some communities have now started Little League for girls which often involves softball rather than baseball, and a less competitive atmosphere. For instance, everyone gets to play. Little League is almost entirely a white, middle-class, suburban phenomenon, because it needs lots of outdoor space and equipment. Basketball is more commonly a black, working-class, urban phenomenon because it uses comparatively little space and equipment. Both sports are dominated by boys and men.

HYPOTHETICAL

The city has created girls' and boys' Little Leagues. The teams in the girls' league play everybody and do not cut anyone from the roster. The teams in the boys' league only play the best players and cut players from the roster. Most of the players in the league are white. Black boys in the city are more likely to play basketball. Black girls are unlikely to participate in organized sports. Jason Doe, a black boy, wants to play on a team in the girls' league.[11] Does his exclusion from the girls' league violate equal protection?

ANALYSIS UNDER EXISTING LAW

Under existing law, the boy would have a strong claim of sex discrimination. The rule excluding boys from the girls' league is sex-specific. The girls' and boys' leagues are also different in their composition and in their rules, so he is missing certain opportunities. Existing law would treat his claim of discrimination no differently than it would treat a claim of discrimination by a girl who wanted to play in the boys' league.

The problem with the approach is that it only asks what the effect is on the boy. It does not consider how the girls feel about the existing rules. It also does not consider how blacks in the community feel about putting resources into play activities for white children.

ANALYSIS UNDER ANTI-SUBORDINATION PRINCIPLE

The anti-subordination perspective would not be able to comprehend the idea of a boy having a claim of discrimination in athletic opportunity, because boys have traditionally had overwhelmingly more athletic opportunities than girls.

From an anti-subordination perspective one would ask whether the girls who played Little League believed that the exclusion of boys from the girls' league perpetuated the subordination of girls. Another issue would be how the girls feel about the rules that are being used for their team. A third issue would be whether the structure of Little League is subordinating to Jason as a black person. Are the rules in both leagues "white" rules? What rules would the black community prefer? In addition, do blacks in that community (or the adjacent city) believe that Little League contributes to their subordination?

Do the girls who play Little League feel that their team is stigmatized because it excludes boys? Would they be more able to achieve their athletic potential with boys present? Would any kind of boy be acceptable or do they want to have criteria for the boys they will play with? How many boys are they willing to play with? Do the girls want to maintain a policy of using everybody and not "cutting" anyone from the team? Did they have a role in creating the league's rules or did the adults assume that girls would want them? How do the girls feel about being excluded from the boys' league? How do they feel about the rules that are used on the boys' league? Would they prefer to play in the boys' league if it had different rules? Would they like to reverse the existing rules—have the boys' league not cut and have the girls' league make cuts—if they are to be partially or fully integrated?

Would blacks in the community prefer that the city fund basketball rather than Little League? Or, because of segregated housing and political boundaries, do blacks have no voice in the way the white community uses its resources? Why don't black girls participate in organized sports in the city? Would they like to play baseball or basketball? Would black boys be more willing to play Little League if the rules were modified? What changes to these sports would be necessary for black girls or black boys to be interested in participating? Or would they prefer the city to fund another kind of activity instead?

Conclusion

Each hypothetical helps us develop the contours of an anti-subordination principle that considers equal protection claims from the perspective of the groups of people who are subordinated. The first hypothetical shows the importance of letting groups that are subordinated decide whether they want race- or sex-specific solutions. Rather than have a blanket rule against differentiations, equal protection doctrine needs to have the flexibility to consider the use of differentiations to redress subordination.

The first hypothetical, however, also shows that it may be difficult to resolve whether to use explicit race or sex differentiations. These differentiations may acclaim the unique experiences of black people and women but may also hide the similarity of their experiences with other working-class people.

The second hypothetical shows the importance of considering gender impact as well as sex-based impact in resolving the implications of a policy. Because we live in a society in which jobs are segregated on the basis of both race and sex, it is important for women and blacks within predominantly female and black job categories to be able to raise claims of equal protection violations. Any rules that limit their ability to break out of stereotypes for their race or sex must also constitute equal protection claims.

The final hypothetical shows the importance of questioning how gender-based and race-based rules came to be created even though males and females and whites and blacks seem to be going along with them without complaint. Because we live in a society in which gender-based and race-based norms are prevalent, we should not assume that those norms exist without coercion. Any signs of gender-based or race-based norms need to be examined closely.

In utilizing an anti-differentiation perspective, the law has ignored issues which the anti-subordination perspective raises. We need to begin to raise these issues and to discuss them seriously.

Notes

1. By referring to the subordination of blacks and women throughout this essay, I do not mean to suggest that these are the only groups that have faced subordination. However, I do mean to suggest that they are the groups that law has most recognized as having faced subordination. For example, heightened judicial scrutiny does not exist for distinctions on the basis of handicap, age, wealth or sexual preference. . . .

By referring to the subordination of blacks and of women together, I do not mean to suggest that their subordination or the recognition of their subordination has been identical. Nevertheless, this essay proceeds from an emphasis on the similarities of that subordination rather than the differences.

2. Catharine MacKinnon has attempted to embody an anti-subordination perspective in the Anti-Pornography Ordinance that she co-authored with Andrea Dworkin. . . . MacKinnon has also presented the legal theory against sexual harassment from both an anti-differentiation and anti-subordination perspective. See C. MacKinnon, Sexual Harassment of Working Women (Yale University Press, 1979). The influence that MacKinnon's sexual harassment book has had on the development of that legal theory suggests that theoretical discussions can influence interpretation of existing legislation as well as new legislation. Although the MacKinnon-Dworkin Anti-Pornography Ordinance has not been implemented, its perspective has influenced the general perspective on the issue. (Several years ago, no one discussed this issue in terms of women's civil rights.) Hence, even an unsuccessful attempt to pass an ordinance with an anti-subordination perspective may influence our understanding of an issue.

3. By the phrase "equal protection doctrine" this essay refers to both constitutional claims of discrimination brought under the Fourteenth Amendment and

statutory claims brought under various federal civil rights statutes. . . . Admittedly, this is not a conventional use of these terms.

4. I thank Barbara Omolade for this phrase. It is the best term I have heard to describe both racial and sexual hierarchies.

5. Derek Bell has made this point strongly in reference to the *Bakke* litigation: Minority interests were not represented on either side of the counsel table as the *Bakke* case wound its way through the courts. . . .

> If minority groups had been represented directly in the *Bakke* case, they would have brought a sorely needed realism to litigation that has been treated more like a law school exam or an exercise in moral philosophy than a matter of paramount importance to black citizens still striving for real citizenship after all these years. Evidence of past and present racial discrimination in the California public school system almost certainly would have been introduced. Minority groups were also prepared to argue that the Davis medical school itself had discriminated against minority applicants in the past—when the school opened in 1968, for example, no blacks or Chicanos were admitted, and only two blacks and Chicanos were admitted in 1969. If the case had been remanded for a full trial, impressive evidence would have been introduced indicating that the Medical College Admission Test (MCAT) is not a valid indicator of minority performance in medical school, and that Davis therefore was justified in attempting to compensate for the test's antiminority bias. A record of proof of this character would have made a much stronger case for minority admissions, and might well have resulted in a decision far more favorable to minority admissions than the one the Regents obtained. Of course, such a record would have transformed the litigation from an expedition through an uncharted constitutional frontier into a difficult but entirely predictable trip along routes well traveled by civil rights litigators over the last three or four decades.

Bell, *Bakke*, Minority Admissions and the Usual Price of Racial Remedies, 67 Cal. L. Rev. 3, 4–7 (1979).

6. Vicki Schultz [Professor, University of Wisconsin School of Law. *Ed.*] has suggested that this requirement could be implemented in at least two ways. First, the law could embody a consultation requirement, e.g., no employer could argue that its differentiation was an attempt to redress subordination unless it first showed that it had consulted members of the subordinated group and had listened to their needs or desires in good faith. Second, a procedural requirement could exist that subordinated groups be joined as indispensable parties in litigation affecting their interests. . . .

Although I like both of these suggestions, I also recognize that they suffer from serious problems. Those of us who have abided by local consultation rules for resolving discovery problems know how rarely those rules are used in good faith. . . . The second solution seems preferable but it raises the larger problem that we cannot expect women or minorities to speak with one voice. Many of the examples discussed in this essay have split the feminist and black civil rights communities. . . . The court would then have the difficult task of determining who best represented the community. Finally, we have the problem of false consciousness. What do we do about blacks or women who purport to be in favor of subordinating policies or actions? Unfortunately, I have no answer. Moreover, I recognize that traditional, male judges may not be a good vehicle for resolving the issue of authentic female or black voice. . . .

7. This hypothetical was based, in part, on my experience in working at the Civil Rights Division of the United States Department of Justice. Virtually all the secretaries were black women and virtually all the attorneys were white (men or women). Many of the secretaries had childcare responsibilities. Although many of the male attorneys had children, few of them had primary and sole responsibility for those children. The secretaries usually used nearly all of their sick leave hours to care for children and were penalized if they were late to work, whereas the attorneys had much more flexibility with their schedules. . . .

8. This argument forces me to disagree with Wendy Williams's parental leave solution to this hypothetical. See proposed Parental and Medical Leave Act, H.R. 4300 (99th Cong., 1st sess. 1986). This bill would entitle employees to parental leave in cases involving the birth, adoption or serious health condition of a son of daughter, and temporary medical leave in cases involving inability to work because of a serious health condition, with protection of the employees' employment and benefit rights. . . . The major problem with this bill is that it assumes that all people are equally deserving of its benefits. It assumes that white men who take leave to care for a child face the same obstacles as black women who take leave to care for a child. Nowhere in the hearings on the bill did people even mention the racial factors of poverty that make this bill more important for black women than white men. . . . I don't like the idea of solving a problem with race and sex-neutral language when we have not sufficiently defined the problem with race and sex-specific language.

I am also bothered that family-oriented language was substituted for race and sex-specific language. Every time family-oriented language is used, the societal benefits that accrue to the traditional heterosexually oriented family are reinforced. Lesbians who co-parent, black women who care for the children of friends and relatives, etc., are rarely included in such family-oriented language. . . . The important point is that family-oriented language is not inherently more neutral than sex-specific language. It simply singles out a new group to favor (the heterosexual family) rather than a race and sex-specific group (black women). . . .

9. For an excellent discussion of this phenomenon, see MacKinnon, Sexual Harassment of Working Women, *supra* note 2, at 23. According to MacKinnon: "The point is that it is the very qualities which men find sexually attractive in the women they harass that are the real qualifications for the jobs for which they hire them. . . . It is this good-girl sexiness (in the case of black women, well-contained, bad-girl sexiness) that qualifies a woman for her job that leaves her open to sexual harassment at any time and to the accusation that she invited it."

10. I discuss the gender and race-based segregation of athletics in my article, Rank-Order Physical Abilities Selection Devices for Traditionally Male Occupations as Gender-Based Employment Discrimination, 19 U.C. Davis L. Rev. 761, 767–72 (1986). This article argues that stereotypes about women's physical abilities extend from the athletic fields to the employment setting. It is important to

remember that limitations on blacks' and women's athletic opportunities do not end on the playing field. . . .

11. This hypothetical is taken from one that Chris Littleton gave. . . . It is based on a California case.

❖ *The Supreme Court 1986 Term, Foreword: Justice Engendered*

Martha Minow

Introduction

What's the Difference?[1]

THE USE OF ANESTHESIA in surgery spread quickly once discovered. Yet the nine-teenth-century doctors who adopted anesthesia selected which patients needed it and which deserved it. Both the medical literature and actual medical practices distinguished people's need for pain-killers based on race, gender, ethnicity, age, temperament, personal habits, and economic class. . . . How might we, today, evaluate these examples of discrimination? What differences between people should matter, and for what purposes? . . .

The Problem and the Argument

Each Term, the Supreme Court and the nation confront problems of differ-ence in this heterogeneous society. . . . [I]ssues [arise] about the permissible legal meanings of difference in the lives of individuals, minority groups, and majority groups in cases involving gender, race, ethnicity, religion, and handicap.

Uniting these questions is the dilemma of difference. The dilemma of differ-ence has three versions. The first version is the dilemma that we may recreate difference either by noticing it or by ignoring it. Decisions about employment, benefits, and treatment in society should not turn on an individual's race, gender, religion, or membership in any other group about which some have deprecating or hostile attitudes. Yet refusing to acknowledge these differences may make them continue to matter in a world constructed with some groups, but not others, in mind. If women's biological differences from men justify special benefits for women in the workplace, are women thereby helped or hurt? Are negative stereo-types reinforced, and does that matter? Focusing on differences poses the risk of

---

recreating them. Especially when used by decisionmakers who award benefits and distribute burdens, traits of difference can carry meanings uncontrolled and unwelcomed by those to whom they are assigned. Yet denying those differences undermines the value they may have to those who cherish them as part of their own identity.

The second version of the dilemma is the riddle of neutrality. If the public schools must remain neutral toward religion, do they do so by balancing the teaching of evolution with the teaching of scientific arguments about divine creation—or does this accommodation of a religious view depart from the requisite neutrality? Governmental neutrality may freeze in place the past consequences of differences. Yet any departure from neutrality in governmental standards uses governmental power to make those differences matter and thus symbolically reinforces them.

The third version of the dilemma is the choice between broad discretion, which permits individualized decisions, and formal rules that specify categorical decisions for the dispensing of public—or private—power. If the criminal justice system must not take the race of defendants or victims into account, is this goal achieved by granting discretion to prosecutors and jurors, who can then make individualized decisions but may also introduce racial concerns, or should judges impose formal rules specifying conditions under which racial concerns must be made explicit to guard against them? By granting discretion to officials or to private decisionmakers, legislators and judges disengage themselves from directly endorsing the use of differences in decisions; yet this grant of discretion also allows those decisionmakers to give significance to differences. Formal rules constrain public or private discretion, but their very specificity may make differences significant.

I believe these dilemmas arise out of powerful unstated assumptions. . . .

Behind and Beyond the Dilemma

. . .

The dilemma of difference appears unresolvable. The risk of non-neutrality—the risk of discrimination—accompanies efforts both to ignore and to recognize difference in equal treatment and special treatment; in color- or gender-blindness and in affirmative action; in governmental neutrality and in governmental preferences; and in decisionmakers' discretion and in formal constraints on discretion. Yet the dilemma is not as intractable as it seems. What makes it seem so difficult are unstated assumptions about the nature of difference. Once articulated and examined, these assumptions can take their proper place among other choices about how to treat difference. I will explore here the assumptions underlying the dilemma of difference, assumptions that usually go without saying.

The Five Unstated Assumptions

ASSUMPTION #1: DIFFERENCE IS INTRINSIC, NOT RELATIONAL

. . .

Can and should the questions about who is different be resolved by a process of discovering intrinsic differences? Is difference an objective, verifiable matter rather than something constructed by social attitudes? . . .

The difference inquiry functions by pigeonholing people into sharply distinguished categories based on selected facts and features. Categorization helps people cope with complexity and understand each other. The legal analyst tends to treat the difference question as one of discovery rather than of choice. The judge asks: "Into what category does a given person or feature belong?" The categories then determine the significance of the persons or features situated within them. . . .

Legal analysis of difference, and its focus on categorization, bears much similarity to legal analysis in general. Legal analysis, cast in a judicial mode, typically addresses whether a given situation "fits" in a category defined by a legal rule or instead belongs outside of it. Many questions presented to the Supreme Court, for example, take the form, "Is this a that?" A leading expositor of the nature of legal reasoning explains the three steps involved: "similarity is seen between cases; next the rule of law inherent in the first case is announced; then the rule of law is made applicable to the second case. . . . The finding of similarity or difference is the key step in the legal process."[2] Again, as critics have noted for nearly a century, these patterns of legal analysis imply that legal reasoning yields results of its own accord, beyond human control.[3]

For both legal difference and difference in general, a difference "discovered" is more aptly a statement of relationship, expressing one person's deviation from an unstated norm assumed by the other.[4] But where do these criteria for comparison come from, and why do they seem so natural that they escape debate? Especially when legal analysis overlaps with social analysis of difference, the criteria for comparison may express perceptions and prejudices of those with the power to define and name others.[5]

In some cases, members of the [Supreme] Court have acknowledged that differences are not intrinsic but socially constructed, which implies in turn that the criteria for comparison are not "real" but humanly chosen.[6] . . . [For example,] the Court . . . acknowledged the socially and historically contingent construction of difference in *Shaare Tefila** and *Saint Francis.*** The Court reasoned that objec-

---

*Shaare Tefila Congregation v. Cobb, 481 U.S. 615 (1987), involved a claim by members of a Jewish congregation whose synagogue was defaced that a federal guarantee against interference with property rights on racial grounds had been violated.

**Saint Francis College v. Al-Khazraji, 483 U.S. 1011 (1987), involved a claim of racial discrimination brought by a teacher from Iraq who failed to secure tenure from his employer.

tive, scientific sources could not resolve whether Arabs and Jews represent distinct races for the purposes of civil rights statutes. In essence, the Court acknowledged that racial identity is socially constrained and yet, oddly, the Justices turned to middle and late nineteenth-century notions of racial identity, prevalent when the remedial statutes were adopted, rather than examining contemporary assumptions and current prejudices.

In both *Shaare Tefila* and *Saint Francis*, members of minority groups sought to obtain protection by reinvoking the categories that had been used to denigrate them. As the cases thus illustrate, groups that seek to challenge socially assigned stigmas and stereotypes run into this dilemma: "How do you protest a socially imposed categorization, except by organizing around the category?" Although some people have resisted and challenged the meanings assigned to them, recipients of labels are often unable to control the many layers of negative association those labels carry. The web of negative associations assigned to the outsider complicates any effort to resist the denigration implied by difference.

What *Shaare Tefila* and *Saint Francis College* neglect to state is that attributions of difference reflect choices by those in power about what characteristics should matter. . . .

Assumption #2: The Unstated Norm

> . . .
>
> Anyone who deviates from the official norm whatever that is, anyone who fails to bear a likeness to the Standard Product, is simply not viewed as fully human, and then becomes at best invisible, at worst a threat to the national security.
>
> —*Giles Gunn*[7]

To treat someone as different means to accord them treatment that is different from treatment of someone else; to describe someone as "the same" implies "the same as" someone else. When differences are discussed without explicit reference to the person or trait on the other side of the comparison, an unstated norm remains. Usually, this default reference point is so powerful and well-established that it need not be specified. . . .

When women argue for rights, the implicit reference point used in discussions of sameness and difference is the privilege accorded some males. This reference point can present powerful arguments for overcoming the exclusion of women from activities and opportunities available to men. For example, reform efforts on behalf of women during both the nineteenth and the twentieth centuries asserted women's fundamental similarities to privileged, white men as a tactic for securing equal treatment. . . .

A prominent "difference" assigned to women, by implicit comparison with men, is pregnancy, especially as experienced by women working for pay outside their homes. The Supreme Court's treatment of issues concerning pregnancy and the workplace highlights the power of the unstated male norm in analyses of problems of difference. In 1975, the Court accepted the similarity of women to the male norm in striking down a Utah statute that disqualified a women from receiving unemployment compensation for a specified period surrounding child-birth, even if her reasons for leaving work were unrelated to the pregnancy.[8] Although the capacity to become pregnant is a difference between women and men, this fact alone did not justify treating women and men differently on matters unrelated to pregnancy. Using men as the norm, the Court reasoned that any women who can perform like a man can be treated like a man. A woman could not be denied unemployment compensation for different reasons than a man would.

What, however, is equal treatment for the woman who is correctly identified within the group of pregnant persons, not simply stereotyped as such, and who is different from nonpregnant persons in ways that are relevant to the workplace? The Court first grappled with these issues in two cases that posed the question of whether discrimination on the basis of pregnancy amounted to discrimination on the basis of sex. In both instances, the Court answered negatively, arguing that pregnancy marks a division between the groups of pregnant and nonpregnant persons and that women fall into both categories.[9] Congress responded by enacting the Pregnancy Discrimination Act (PDA), which amended Title VII to include discrimination on the basis of pregnancy within the range of impermissible sex discrimination. Yet even under these new statutory terms, the power of the unstated male norm persists in debates over the definition of discrimination.

In *Cal. Fed.*,[10] the Court debated whether the PDA forbids differentiation based on pregnancy, even if the differentiation benefits rather than injures the person who becomes pregnant. The case presented a choice between "equal treatment" and "special treatment." Thus framed, this question treated men as the norm and presumed a workplace designed for men (or nonpregnant persons). Any effort to remake the workplace to accommodate pregnancy would be "special treatment." This approach supports a ban against such accommodation, which leaves in place the male norm and treats women and pregnancy as different.

The majority in *Cal. Fed.* understood this problem and construed the PDA to permit employers to remove barriers in the workplace that disadvantaged pregnant people compared with others. The majority shifted from a narrow workplace comparison to a broader comparison of men and women in their full familial roles. The Court found no conflict between the PDA and the challenged state law (requiring reinstatement of women following maternity leaves) because "California's pregnancy disability leave statute allows women, as well as men, to have families without losing their jobs."[11] The majority's second rationale explicitly used women's experience as the benchmark and called for treating men equally. Using the minimum benefits for women as the starting point, the Court held that the state law and the federal law were compatible because employers could comply with both by providing to men reinstatement benefits comparable to those available to women following leaves for pregnancy. The dissenters, on the other hand, countered by emphasizing that the PDA's commitment to equal treatment bans preferential treatment on the basis of pregnancy. The dissenters persisted in using the male norm as the measure for equal treatment in the workplace.

By contrast, the Court in *Wimberly*[12] used just such an implicit male standard in concluding that the federal law against discriminating on the basis of pregnancy in unemployment compensation provides no check against states that refuse to provide compensation for a broad range of situations, including pregnancy. In a work world designed without pregnancy in mind, requiring women to be treated like men means that there is no discrimination when women, as well as men, receive no benefits for unemployment due to pregnancy. At a doctrinal level, the Court's holding that a state need not provide unemployment compensation to a women who left her job because of pregnancy rested on the conclusion that the state treated pregnant women the same as all other persons who left for reasons unconnected with work. There was no discrimination when pregnancy was not singled out for detrimental treatment. . . .

Wimberly is not an illogical ruling; a plausible theory of equality would call for a comparison between pregnant persons and other similarly situated persons. But what, exactly, is a situation similar to pregnancy? Unlike in *Cal. Fed.*, where the Court used a statute prohibiting pregnancy discrimination to establish the pregnant person as the point of comparison, the Court in *Wimberly* laid a neutral non-discrimination demand on top of a workplace world and a state statute modeled without pregnancy in mind. Missing altogether was the equality norm that combined the work and family worlds and called for no difference in the abilities of men and women to work and have a family.[13] By allowing employers to ignore the difference of pregnancy, the Court keeps in place the assumption that equal treatment is measured by a male norm. . . .

Similar, unstated reference points appear in many other contexts. . . . Unstated reference points lie hidden in legal discourse, which is full of the language of abstract universalism. Legal language seeks universal applicability, regardless of the particular traits of an individual. Yet abstract universalism often "takes the part for the whole, the particular for the universal and essential, the present for the eternal."[14] Making explicit the unstated points of reference is the first step in addressing this problem; the next is challenging the presumed neutrality of the observer who in fact sees from an unacknowledged perspective.

ASSUMPTION #3: THE OBSERVER CAN SEE WITHOUT A PERSPECTIVE

> Inevitably, "seeing" entails a form of subjectivity, an act of imagination, a way of looking that is necessarily in part determined by some private perspective. Its results are never simple "facts," amenable to "objective" judgments, but facts or

pictures that are dependent on the internal visions that generate them.

—*Evelyn Fox Keller*[15]

I will never be in a man's place, a man will never be in mine. Whatever the possible identifications, one will never exactly occupy the place of the other—they are irreducible the one to the other.

—*Luce Irigaray*[16]

If differences are intrinsic, then anyone can see them; if there is an objective reality, then any impartial observer can make judgments unaffected and untainted by his or her own perspective or experience. Once rules are selected, regardless of disputes over the rules themselves, a distinct aspiration is that they will be applied even-handedly. This aspiration to impartiality, however, is just that—an aspiration rather than a description—because it may suppress the inevitability of the existence of a perspective and thus make it harder for the observer, or anyone else, to challenge the absence of objectivity.

What interests us, given who we are and where we stand, affects our ability to perceive. Philosophers such as A. J. Ayer and W. V. Quine note that although we can alter the theory we use to frame our perceptions of the world, we cannot see the world unclouded by preconceptions. The impact of the observer's perspective may be crudely oppressive. Yet, we continue to believe in neutrality.

For example, in Johnson v. Transportation Agency,[17] in which the Court upheld an affirmative action plan for women, the press reported that the employer promoted a woman less qualified than a man, even though their scores differed by merely two points after a first interview. Paul Johnson, the male applicant, earned the second highest score (with another applicant), whereas Diane Joyce, the female applicant, had the next highest score. A second interview was conducted by three agency supervisors, two of whom had either harassed or made sexist comments to Joyce. Based on all the evidence and the recommendation of the affirmative action office, the employer promoted Joyce. To treat this as a case of a less qualified woman getting the job over a more qualified man perpetuates the mythology of neutral observers. The Court itself criticized this myth, noting that for unexceptional middle-level craft positions, final selection decisions are inevitably subjective, once a pool of fully qualified candidates is assembled.

Recently, Justice O'Connor has been the most explicit about the myth of a single perspective. She has advanced in the establishment clause context the idea of multiple perceptions of reality, noting the difference between the perspective of decisionmakers and the perspectives of those affected by governmental decisions dealing with religious difference. . . .[18] Justice O'Connor . . . suggests the powerful possibility of multiple meanings and perceptions of reality, influenced by the positions of listeners and speakers. This possibility has been widely pursued by sociologists, anthropologists, literary theorists, and philosophers.[19]

Justice O'Connor's more significant contribution may lie in her hint . . . that insights about one area of difference may be relevant and instructive to other areas of difference. Those who understand invidious messages about race or sex might thus borrow those understandings. . . . We learn by importing understandings from one context to another. Thus, in her awareness of the potential analogies across differences, and in her sensitivity to contrasting perspectives, Justice O'Connor effectively challenges the often unstated assumption that the observer can be free from a perspective. . . .

Justice Scalia's opinion manifests, rather than exposes, the impact of the observer's perspective on the observed. He provides a generous and sympathetic view of Johnson, the male plaintiff, while demonstrating no comparable understanding of Joyce, the woman promoted ahead of him. In his description of the facts, Justice Scalia offered more details about Johnson's desires and efforts to advance his career and in effect tried to convey Johnson's point of view that the promotion of Joyce represented discrimination against Johnson. Unlike the majority, Justice Scalia gave no description of Joyce's career aspirations and her efforts to fulfill them, and thus betrayed a critical lack of sympathy for those most injured by societal discrimination in the past. Most curious is his apparent inability to imagine that Joyce and other women working in relatively unskilled jobs are, even more so than Johnson, people "*least* likely to have profited from societal discrimination in the past."[20] Operating under the apparent assumption that people fall into one of two groups—women and blacks, on the one hand, or white, unorganized, unaffluent, and unknown persons, on the other[21]—Justice Scalia neglects the women who have been politically powerless and need the protection of the Court. Although Justice Scalia's opinion reveals that the Court may be blind to the way it protects professional jobs from the affirmative action it prescribes for nonprofessionals, he remains apparently unaware of the other effects his own perspective has on his ability to sympathize with some persons, but not others.

Judges often see difference in relation to some unstated norm or point of comparison and fail to acknowledge their own perspective and its influence on the assignment of difference. . . .

ASSUMPTION #4: THE IRRELEVANCE OF OTHER PERSPECTIVES

> We have seen the blindness and deadness to each other which are our natural inheritance. . . .
>
> —*William James*[22]

> Jurisprudence will forever be stuck in a post-realist battle of subjectivities, with all the discomfort that has represented, until we confront the distinction between knowing subject and known object.
>
> —*Ann Scales*[23]

Glimpsing contrasting perspectives helps resolve problems of difference. Several of the Justices have tried, on different occasions, to glimpse the point of view of a minority group or a person quite different from themselves; some have articulated eloquently the difficulty or even impossibility of knowing another's perspective, and have developed legal positions that take into account this difficulty. Others have rejected as irrelevant or relatively unimportant the experience of "different" people and have denied their own partiality, often by using stereotypes as though they were real.[24]

Justice Powell's majority opinion in McCleskey v. Kemp,[25] for example, ignored its own partial perspective in upholding the death penalty against a black defendant, despite strong statistical evidence of racial discrimination in capital sentencing generally. The petitioner, explained Justice Powell, failed to show that the decisionmakers in *his* case acted with a discriminatory purpose. This formulation takes seriously the vantage point of decisionmakers like the reviewing court and the jury, but not the perspective of the criminal defendant. From the black defendant's point of view, however, proof of the intent of the individual jury is much less important than the disproportionate risk of the death penalty.

The rarity of glimpses of such minority perspectives is underscored by their power when taken seriously. For example, consider Justice Brennan's dissent in *McCleskey*. Perhaps knowing that neither he nor many of his readers could fully grasp the defendant's perspective, Justice Brennan in his dissent tried to look through the eyes of the defense attorney who is asked by the black defendant about the chances of a death sentence. Adopting that viewpoint, Justice Brennan concluded that "counsel would feel bound to tell McCleskey that defendants charged with killing white victims in Georgia are 4.3 times as likely to be sentenced to death as defendants charged with killing blacks." . . .[26] Yet a judicial stance that treats its own perspective as unproblematic makes other perspectives invisible and puts them beyond discussion.

In the context of religious freedoms, by contrast, several of the Justices, regardless of their own religious views, have demonstrated an acute awareness of the perspective of religious persons or groups, contrasted with that of a secular employer or the government. [For example,] [i]n Hobbie v. Unemployment Appeals Commission,[27] Justice Brennan . . . announced that when a state denies an important benefit "because of conduct mandated by religious belief, thereby putting substantial pressure on an adherent to modify his behavior and to violate his beliefs, a burden upon religion exists."[28] Here is an effort to look at the experience of the religious adherent, even under a rule that appears neutral and non-discriminatory. Similarly, Justice White, in *Presiding Bishop*,[29] proposed taking the perspective of a religious organization to evaluate the impact of a governmental regulation affecting its secular activities. . . .

Thus, some Justices, on some occasions, have tried to see beyond the dominant perspective and reach an alternative construction of reality. In many other instances, however, the Justices presume that the perspective they adopt is either universal or superior to others. A perspective may go unstated because it is so powerful and pervasive that it may be presumed without defense; it may also go unstated because it is so unknown to those in charge that they do not recognize it as a perspective. . . .

ASSUMPTION #5: THE STATUS QUO IS NATURAL, UNCOERCED, AND GOOD

> To settle for the constitutionalization of the status quo is to bequeath a petrified forest.
>
> —*Aviam Soifer*[30]

Connected with many of the other assumptions is the idea that critical features of the status quo—general social and economic arrangements—are natural and desirable. From this assumption follow three propositions: first, the goal of governmental neutrality demands the status quo because existing societal arrangements are assumed to be neutral. Second, governmental actions that change the status quo have a different status than omissions, or failures to act, that maintain the status quo. Third, prevailing social and political arrangements are not forced on anyone. Individuals are free to make choices and to assume responsibility for those choices. These propositions are rarely stated, both because they are deeply entrenched and because they view the status quo as good, natural, and freely chosen. At times, however, the Justices have engaged in debate that exposes the status quo assumption. . . .

Judges operating under the assumption that the world is neutral do not find discrimination unless it is specifically proven. In McCleskey v. Kemp, for example, the Court refused to find discrimination in the case before it, despite strong statistical evidence that the race of the victim and of the defendant often determines who receives the death penalty. Similarly, in *Johnson*, Justice Scalia explained historical disparities as nondiscriminatory. He described the job category of road dispatcher, a job sought by a woman in that case, as traditionally segregated not due to systematic exclusion by the employer, but because of the long-standing social attitudes held, among others, by women themselves that it was not desirable work.[31] Surprisingly, Justice Scalia then acknowledged that some people "believe that the social attitudes which cause women themselves to avoid certain jobs and to favor others are as nefarious as conscious, exclusionary discrimination." He rejected societal attitudes, however, as an insufficient justification for the expansive judicial action approved by the Court. Nonetheless, his opinion acknowledged the questionable status of the assumption that existing social arrangements are natural, chosen and good. . . .

For the most part, unstated assumptions work in subtle and complex ways. Assumptions fill the basic human need to simplify and to make our world familiar and unsurprising. Yet, by their very simplification, assumptions exclude contrasting views. Moreover, they contribute to the dilemma of difference by frustrating legislative and constitutional commitments to change the treatment of differences in race, gender, ethnicity, religion, and handicap. Before justice can be done, judges need to hear and understand contrasting points of view about the treatment of difference.

Perspectives on Perspectives

The difference dilemma seems paralyzing if framed by the unstated assumptions described [above]. Those assumptions so entrench one point of view as natural and orderly that any conscious decision to notice or to ignore difference breaks the illusion of a legal world free of perspective. The assumptions make it seem that departures from unstated norms violate commitments to neutrality. Yet adhering to the unstated norms undermines commitments to neutrality—and to equality. Is it possible to proceed differently, putting these assumptions into question? . . .

. . . Even moral and legal theorists who argue for taking the perspective of excluded or less powerful groups and individuals have been vulnerable to the power of the unstated assumptions.[32] Theorists and reformers assert that members of many groups have been wrongly labeled as different, that their perspectives have been ignored, and that the status quo can and should be changed. Yet they often repeat in new contexts new versions of the old assumptions they set out to challenge. As current debates among feminists demonstrate, dedication to the interests of a disempowered group is not itself sufficient to eradicate the unstated assumptions.

Leading feminists have contributed incisive critiques of the unstated assumptions behind political theory, law, bureaucracy, science, and social science. Their work exposes the dominance in field after field of conceptions of human nature that take a male as the reference point and treat women as "other," "different," "deviant," "exceptional," or baffling.[33] Feminist work has thus named the power of naming and has challenged both the use of male measures and the assumption that women fail by them. . . .

. . . [F]or more than a century, feminists have claimed that distinctive aspects of women's experiences and perspectives offer the resources for constructing more empathic, more creative, and in general, better theories, laws, and social practices.

Yet by urging the corrective of the women's perspective, or even a feminist standpoint, feminists have jeopardized our own challenge to simplification, essentialism, and stereotyping. Women fall into every category of race, religion, class, and ethnicity, and vary in sexual orientation, handicapping conditions, and other sources of assigned difference. Claims to speak from women's point of view, or to use women as a reference point, threaten to obscure this multiplicity and install a particular view to stand for the views of all. Some, for example, have expressly argued that sexism is more fundamental than racism.[34] This claim is disturbing because it suggests that feminists fail to take account not only of forms of oppression or domination beyond sexism but also of women's own varied experiences. As Elizabeth V. Spelman persuasively argues, any account of gender relation that "obscur[es] the workings of race and class is likely to involve—whether intentionally or not—obscuring the workings of racism and classism."[35]

In a thoughtful paper on this danger, Nancy Fraser and Linda Nicholson conclude that "since women's oppression is not homogeneous in content, and since it is not determined by one root, underlying cause, there is no one 'feminist method,' no 'feminist epistemology.'"[36]

These critiques are internal; these are feminists admonishing feminists. . . . Yet why, when it comes to our own arguments and activities, do some feminists forget the very insights we advance about the power of unstated reference points and points of view, the privileged position of the status quo, and the pretense that a particular is the universal? I suggest that our own insights elude us for three reasons: we are attracted to simplifying categories; all of us have an unconscious attachment to stereotypes; and the contests over power and versions of reality take place under rules that themselves are difficult to challenge.

Full acknowledgment of all people's differences threatens to overwhelm us. Cognitively, we need simplifying categories, and the unifying category of "woman" helps to organize experience, even at the cost of denying some of it. Ideas that defy neat categories are difficult to hold on to, even if the idea itself is about the tyranny of categories. We especially attach ourselves to categories like male/female because of our own psychological development in a culture that has made gender matter.

Moreover, feminists are not free from the stereotypes that occupy thought throughout the culture. White feminists may well carry stereotypes about people of color, and similar stereotypes may divide women with different religions, political persuasions, abilities and disabilities, and sexual preferences. Some stereotypes may be passed on through cultural lessons. Stereotypes provide clues to who has the power to define agendas and priorities within feminist communities. Ignoring differences among women may permit relatively privileged women to claim identification with all discrimination against women, while also claiming special authority to speak for women unlike themselves.

Finally, the version of reality that has for the most part prevailed in the entire culture gives us internal scripts about how to argue and, indeed, how to know. The dominant culture has established certain criteria for theories, for legal arguments, for scientific proofs—that is, for authoritative discourse. Thus, the very ground rules for disputing which version of reality should prevail belong to the world view that has been dominant in the past. . . .

The difference dilemmas, disrobed, are not insoluble problems about neutrality and discretion, but are instead serious struggles over which versions of reality judges should embrace. Taking minority perspectives seriously calls for a process of dialogue in which the listener actually tries to reach beyond the assumption of one reality, one version of the truth. There is no neutrality, no escape from choice. But it is possible to develop better abilities to name and grasp competing perspectives, and to make more knowing choices thereafter. [E]fforts along these lines are central to the challenge of engendering justice.

Engendering Justice

. . .

If we want to preserve justice, we need to develop a practice for more knowing judgments about problems of difference. We must stop seeking to get close to the "truth" and instead seek to get close to other people's truths. The question is, how do we do this? [W]e must persuade others as much as they must persuade us about the reality we should construct. Justice can be impartial only if judges acknowledge their own partiality. Justice depends on the possibility of conflicts among the values and perspectives that justice pursues. Courts, and especially the Supreme Court, provide a place for the contest over realities that govern us—if we open ourselves to the chance that a reality other than our own may matter. Justice can be engendered when we overcome our pretended indifference to difference and instead people our world with individuals who surprise one another about difference. . . .

It is a paradox. Only by admitting our partiality can we strive for impartiality. Impartiality is the guise partiality takes to seal bias against exposure. . . . The idea of impartiality implies human access to a view beyond human experience, a "God's eye" point of view. Not only do humans lack this inhuman perspective, but humans who claim it are untruthful, trying to exercise power to cut off conversation and debate. . . . If we treat other points of view as irritants in the way of our own vision, we are still hanging on to faulty certainty. Even if we admit the limits of our view, while treating those limits as gaps and leaving the rest in place, we preserve the pretense that our view is sufficiently rooted in reality to resist any real change prompted by another.

Acknowledging partiality may cure the pretense of impartiality. But unless we have less capacity to step outside our own skins than I think we do, we then have a choice of which partial view to advance or accept. Whose partial view should resolve conflicts over how to treat assertions of difference, whether assigned or claimed? Preferring the standpoint of an historically denigrated group can reveal truths obscured by the dominant view, but it can also reconfirm the underlying conceptual scheme of the dominant view by focusing on it. Similarly, the perspective of those who are labeled "different" may offer an important challenge to the view of those who imposed the label, but it is a corrective lens, another partial view, not absolute truth. We then fight over whether to prefer it. "Standpoint theories" may also deny the multiple experiences of members of the denigrated group and create a new claim of essentialism. . . .

The solution is not to adopt and cling to some new standpoint, but instead to strive to become and remain open to perspectives and claims that challenge our own. . . .

It takes practice to make a habit of glimpsing the perspectives of others. A pessimistic view suggests that we can never glimpse another's world, because our self-absorption limits our own self-knowledge. A more hopeful view maintains that through emotional maturity we can learn to identify with others, even those we have treated as different from ourselves. This goal demands a continual process of taking stock of the barriers we erect out of self-interest.

Two exercises can help those who judge to glimpse the perspectives of others and to avoid a false impartiality. The first is to explore our own stereotypes, our own attitudes toward people we treat as different—and, indeed, our own categories for organizing the world. . . . It is a process that even we who see ourselves as victims of oppression need to undertake, for devices of oppression are buried within us. We must also examine and retool our methods of classification and consider how they save us from questioning our instincts, ourselves, and our existing social arrangements. Putting ourselves in the place of those who look different can push us to challenge our ignorance and fears and to investigate our usual categories for making sense of the world. . . .

The second exercise is to search out differences and celebrate them, constructing new bases for connection. We can pursue the possibilities of difference behind seeming commonalities and seek out commonalities across difference, thereby confronting the ready association of sameness with equality and difference with inferiority. One route is to emphasize our common humanity, despite our different traits. Another tack is to disentangle difference from the allocation of benefits and burdens in society—a tack that may well require looking at difference to alter how people use it. The Court's effort to assure equality for women and men in the conjunction of work and family life in *Cal. Fed.* represents such an effort to disentangle institutional arrangements from the difference they create. A third approach is to cherish difference and welcome anomaly. Still another is to understand that which initially seems strange and to learn about sense and reason from this exercise—just as philosophers, anthropologists, and psychologists have urged us to take seriously the self-conceptions and perceptions of others. In the process of trying to understand how another person understands, we may even remake our categories of understanding. Other persons may not even define "self" the same way we do, and glimpsing their "self-concepts" thus challenges us to step beyond our operating assumptions. A further skill to practice is to recognize commonality in difference itself: in the relationships within which we construct difference and connect and distinguish ourselves from one another.

These exercises in taking the perspective of the other will deepen and broaden anyone's perspective. For judges, who debate the use of the coercive forces of the law in relation to issues of difference, these exercises are critical. Judges can and should act as representatives, standing in for others and symbolizing society itself.

Judicial acts of representation must also be responsive to the demands of the people they govern, in order to secure apparent legitimacy and, ultimately, to remain effective.

. . . Justice is engendered when judges admit the limitations of their own viewpoints, when judges reach beyond those limits by trying to see from contrasting perspectives, and when people seek to exercise power to nurture differences, not to assign and control them. Rather than securing an illusory universality and objectivity, law is a medium through which particular people can engage in the continuous work of making justice. The law "is part of a distinctive manner of imagining the real."[37] Legal decisions engrave upon our culture the stories we tell to and about ourselves, the meanings that constitute the traditions we invent. Searching for words to describe realities too multiple and complex to be contained by their language, litigants and judges struggle over what will be revealed and what will be concealed in the inevitable partiality of human judgment. Through deliberate attention to our own partiality, we can begin to acknowledge the dangers of pretended impartiality. By taking difference into account, we can overcome our pretended indifference to difference, and people our worlds with those who can surprise and enrich one another. As we make audible, in official arenas, the struggles over which version of reality will secure power, we disrupt the silence of one perspective, imposed as if universal. Admitting the partiality of the perspective that temporarily gains official endorsement may embolden resistance to announced rules. But only by admitting that rules are resistible—and by justifying to the governed their calls for adherence—can justice by done in a democracy. "[I]t is only through the variety of relations constructed by the plurality of beings that truth can be known and community constructed."[38] Then we constitute ourselves as members of conflicting communities with enough reciprocal regard to talk across differences. We engender mutual regard for pain we know and pain we do not understand.

Notes

1. Note how this phrase is both an insistent inquiry into difference and a casual shrug about why a difference does not matter. In an episode of the television show "All in the Family," Edith Bunker asks whether her husband would like the laces of his bowling shoes laced under or over the holes. Her husband, Archie, says, "What's the difference?" Edith begins to explain, but Archie explodes because he meant to say, "Who cares?" Thus the phrase "What's the difference?" engenders two meanings that are mutually exclusive: the literal meaning asks for the concept (difference), whose existence is denied by the figurative meaning. See de Man, The Epistemology of Metaphor, 5 Critical Inquiry 13 (1978).

2. E. Levi, An Introduction to Legal Reasoning 2 (University of Chicago Press, 1972). . . .

3. See G. Gilmore, The Ages of American Law (Yale University Press, 1977) (discussing Cardozo and uncertainty); Cohen, Field Theory and Judicial Logic, 59

Yale L.J. 238, 244–49 (1950); Singer, Legal Realism Now: Review of Laura Kalman, Legal Realism at Yale: 1917–1960, 76 Cal. L. Rev. 465 (1988); Singer, The Player and the Cards: Nihilism and Legal Theory, 94 Yale L.J. 1 (1984).

4. See A. Jaggar, Feminist Politics and Human Nature 362 (Rowman and Allanheld, 1983) (arguing that difference is a function of relationships and power). . . .

5. See H. Eisenstein, Introduction, in H. Eisenstein & A. Jardine eds., The Future of Difference xxii–xxiii (G. K. Hall, 1980) ("The defining of difference has traditionally been linked to the exercise of power, to those who have been in a position to say who is 'different,' and should therefore be subordinate."); Scales, The Emergence of Feminist Jurisprudence: An Essay, Part 1 this volume (noting that feminism "sees differences as systematically related to each other, and to other relations, such as exploited and exploiter").

6. Thus, recognition that difference is socially constructed refutes the premise that difference is intrinsic in two ways: first, by noting how nothing is "different" except in relationship to something else; and second, by noting that the traits identified for comparison and the meanings of those traits are themselves socially selected.

7. G. Gunn, The Interpretation of Otherness: Literature, Religion, and the American Imagination 177 (Oxford University Press, 1979).

8. . . . Turner v. Department of Employment Sec., 423 U.S. 44 (1975) (per curiam). . . .

9. See General Electric Co. v. Gilbert, 429 U.S. 125 (1976) (Title VII); Geduldig v. Aiello, 417 U.S. 484 (1974) (equal protection).

10. California Federal Savings & Loan Ass'n v. Guerra, 479 U.S. 272 (1987). . . .

11. 479 U.S. at 289. . . .

12. Wimberly v. Labor & Industrial Relations Comm'n, 479 U.S. 511 (1987).

13. See Frug, Securing Job Equality for Women: Labor Market Hostility to Working Mothers, 59 B.U. L. Rev. 55 (1979); Law, Rethinking Sex and the Constitution, 132 U. Pa. L. Rev. 955, 967–68, 1003–36 (1984); Olsen, The Family and the Market: A Study of Ideology and Legal Reform, 96 Harv. L. Rev. 1497, 1544–45, 1560–61 (1983). In a society that has made the public world the domain of men and the private world the domain of women, the only cure for sex discrimination is to merge the two realms, as the *Cal. Fed.* Court did. . . .

14. C. Gould, The Woman Question: Philosophy of Liberation and the Liberation of Philosophy, in C. Gould & M. Wartofsky eds., Women and Philosophy: Toward a Theory of Liberation 21 (Putnam, 1976).

15. E. Keller, A Feeling for the Organism: The Life and Work of Barbara McClintock 150 (W. H. Freeman, 1983).

16. L. Irigaray, Ethique de la Différence Sexuelle 19–20 (1984), *quoted in* Heath, Male Feminism, in A. Jardine & P. Smith eds., Men in Feminism I, 30 (Methuen, 1987).

17. 480 U.S. 616 (1987).

18. See Lynch v. Donnelly, 465 U.S. 668 (1984).

19. See, generally P. Berger & T. Luckmann, The Social Construction of Reality (Doubleday, 1966) (sociology); J. Culler, On Deconstruction (Cornell University Press, 1982) (literary interpretation); C. Geertz, Local Knowledge: Further Essays in Interpretive Anthropology (Basic Books, 1983) (anthropology); P. Rabinow &

W. Sullivan, The Interpretive Turn: Emergence of an Approach, in P. Rabinow & W. Sullivan eds., Interpretive Social Science I, 4–8 (University of California Press, 1979) (philosophy of social science).

20. 480 U.S. at 676 (Scalia, J., dissenting) (emphasis in original).

21. See *id.* at 677 ("The irony is that these individuals [the Johnsons of the country]—predominantly unknown, affluent, unorganized—suffer this injustice at the hands of a Court fond of thinking itself the champion of the politically impotent.").

22. W. James, What Makes a Life Significant, in On Some of Life's Ideals (H. Holt, 1912), at 49, 81.

23. Scales, Part 1 this volume, at 53.

24. Stereotyped thinking is one form of the failure to imagine the perspective of another. Those who rely on stereotypes ignore the importance of this alternative perspective, obscuring the individuality of the person the stereotype describes. Social psychologists who study stereotyping and stigmatizing attitudes point to the needs that these techniques of denigration serve for both individuals and social groups who have the power to label others. See K. Erikson, Wayward Puritans 4–15, 69–81, 114, 196–99 (Wiley, 1966) (noting that Puritans used attributions of deviance to sustain community identity and boundaries); S. Gilman, Difference and Pathology: Stereotypes of Sexuality, Race and Madness 12, 25–35 (Cornell University Press, 1985), at 12, 18–23 (arguing that stereotyping deals with anxieties and desires for control). In assigning the label of difference, the group confirms not only its identity, but also its superiority, and displaces doubts and anxieties onto the person now called "different." See *id.* at 20. . . .

25. 481 U.S. 279 (1987).

26. 481 U.S. at 321 (Brennan, J., dissenting).

27. 480 U.S. 136 (1987). . . .

28. *Id.* at 141 (quoting Thomas v. Review Bd., 450 U.S. 707, 717–18 (1981)).

29. Corporation of the Presiding Bishop of Jesus Christ of the Latter Day Saints v. Amos, 483 U.S. 327 (1987). . . .

30. Soifer, Complacency and Constitutional Law, 42 Ohio St. L.J. 383, 409 (1981).

31. A similar problem arose in EEOC v. Sears, Roebuck & Co., 628 F. Supp. 1264 (N.D. Ill. 1986). The issue presented was whether the absence of women from jobs as commission salespersons grew from women's own choices and preferences or from societal discrimination. The legal framework, a disparate treatment theory, seemed to force the issue into either/or questions: either women's workforce participation was due to their own choices or to forces beyond their control; either women's absence from certain jobs was due to employers' discrimination or not. Choices by working women and decisions by their employers were undoubtedly both influenced by larger patterns of economic prosperity and depression and shifting social attitudes about appropriate roles for women—and these larger patterns become real in people's lives when internalized and experienced as individual choice. For a cogent discussion of the underlying problem, see K. Ferguson, Feminist Case against Bureaucracy 177 (Temple University Press, 1984).

32. See, e.g., J. Rawls, A Theory of Justice 75 (Harvard University Press, 1971). Admirable in its effort to acknowledge the influence of position on belief, Rawls's difference principle nonetheless implicitly assumes a single and universal

perspective from which all expectations can be discerned. Indeed, Rawls's operational premise—that the norms he elaborates are like ones anyone would pick, if placed behind a veil of ignorance about what position, gender, race, or other traits he or she ultimately would have—imposes this single, universal perspective. . . . Thus, Rawls' difference principle is insufficiently sensitive to the possibility of competing perspectives, and the difficulties facing anyone in a higher social position trying to know the perspective of those they call "different."

Similar problems arise with Ronald Dworkin's theory of treating another as an equal. See R. Dworkin, Taking Rights Seriously (Harvard University Press, 1978). Dworkin's approach risks imposing one's view of the person, submerging contrasting perspectives about what constitutes equal regard, who determines when a difference is relevant, and from what point of view.

John Ely . . . atributes the need for judicial concern with minorities to defects in the majoritarian political process. See J. Ely, Democracy and Distrust (Harvard University Press, 1980). This approach goes some distance toward recognizing that dominant groups effectively exclude minority points of view, but Ely does not consider the risk that judicial solicitude for these neglected perspectives may exacerbate the problem by presuming an unstated norm or by assuming that the minority perspective coincides with the dominant one.

Perhaps building from similar criticisms of the relationship between privilege and knowledge, Roberto Unger proposes continual processes for redistributing power so that no one group can remain in command of political or economic resources for long. See Unger, The Critical Legal Studies Movement, 96 Harv. L. Rev. 561, 596–97 (1983). Elsewhere, he has called for smashing contexts and perpetual revolution. . . . Yet these proposals may not appeal to the supposed beneficiaries, who may believe that they need more order to guard against oppression. . . .

33. See, e.g., S. de Beauvoir, The Second Sex 161 (H. Parshley trans., Knopf, 1974); C. Gilligan, In a Different Voice (Harvard University Press, 1982) (psychology); N. Hartsock, Money, Sex, and Power: Toward A Feminist Historical Materialism (Longman, 1983) (political theory); Jaggar, Feminist Politics, *supra* note 4 (feminist theory); E. Keller, Reflections on Gender and Science (Yale University Press, 1985) (science); J. Miller, Toward a New Psychology of Women (Beacon, 1976) (psychology); E. Showalter, The New Feminist Criticism: Essays On Women, Literature and Theory (Pantheon, 1985) (literature); S. Okin, Women in Western Political Thought (Princeton University Press, 1979) (political theory); A. Scott, Making the Invisible Woman Visible (University of Illinois Press, 1984) (history); M. Rosaldo & L. Lamphere eds., Woman, Culture and Society (Stanford University Press, 1974) (anthropology); MacKinnon, Feminism, Marxism, Method, and the State: An Agenda for Theory, Part 5 this volume; (feminist theory); MacKinnon, Feminism, Marxism, Method, and the State: Toward Feminist Jurisprudence, Part 5 this volume; (feminist theory).

34. See C. MacKinnon, Feminism Unmodified 166–68 (Harvard University Press, 1987); Thomas, Sexism and Racism: Some Conceptual Differences, 90 Ethics 239, 243–50 (1980); Wasserstrom, Racism, Sexism and Preferential Treatment: An Approach to the Topics, 24 UCLA L. Rev. 581, 587–91 (1977).

35. E. Spelman, Inessential Woman: Problems of Exclusion in Feminist Thought, chap. 5 (Beacon, 1988); cf. Bartlett, Book Review: Catharine MacKin-

non, Feminism Unmodified, 75 Cal. L. Rev. 1559 (1987) (attacking notion that a single unifying theme of "power" explains the history and current status of women).

36. Fraser & Nicholson, Social Criticism Without Philosophy: An Encounter Between Feminism and Postmodernism, 10 Communication No. 3, at 345 (1988). Fraser and Nicholson nonetheless conclude that feminism can continue to mean something: a commitment to actual diversity and a complex, multi-layered feminist solidarity. Cf. S. Harding, The Science Question in Feminism 194 (Cornell University Press, 1986) ("By giving up the goal of telling 'one true story,' we embrace instead the permanent partiality of feminist inquiry.").

37. Geertz, Local Knowledge, *supra* note 19, at 184.

38. Hartsock, Money, Sex, and Power, *supra* note 31, at 254 (describing the view of Hannah Arendt).

❖ When Difference Has Its Home: Group Homes for the Mentally Retarded, Equal Protection and Legal Treatment of Difference

MARTHA MINOW

> Only when difference has its home, when the need for belonging in all its murderous intensity has been assuaged, can our common identity begin to find its voice.
>
> —*Michael Ignatieff*[1]

Introduction

How SHOULD THE LAW treat people whom the law labels as [different]? . . .

Discussions of such matters can become abstract very quickly. To ground this discussion, I will . . . examine a 1985 Supreme Court case considering the rights of the mentally retarded.[2] . . .

The chief purpose in this article is to demonstrate how categorical approaches—attributing difference to "different people"—undermine commitments to equality. . . .

In City of Cleburne v. Cleburne Living Center [CLC], the Supreme Court considered the constitutionality of a city's refusal to grant a group of mentally retarded people a permit to build a residential group home. The plaintiffs, applicants for the group home, challenged the city's action on the grounds that it discriminated against the mentally retarded, and argued that mental retardation should be treated as a "quasi-suspect" classification for the purpose of equal protection analysis.

Justice White, writing for the Supreme Court's majority, declined to treat the mentally retarded as a quasi-suspect class. Instead, the majority opinion concluded that under equal protection analysis, legislative categories based on mental retardation need only be rationally related to a legitimate end. . . .

. . . The Court reasoned that the city had no rational basis to believe that the proposed home posed a special threat to the city's legitimate interests in protect-

22 Harv. C.R.–C.L.L. Rev. 111 (1987). Reprinted by permission of the author and Harvard Civil Rights–Civil Liberties Law Review. Copyright © 1987 by the President and Fellows of Harvard College.

ing safety, restricting density, and the like, when the city did not require a special permit for apartments, dormitories, private clubs, fraternity and sorority houses, nursing homes for convalescents or the aged (who are not "insane, feeble-minded or alcoholics or drug addicts"), or other multiple dwellings.[3] The Court thus invalidated the ordinance permit requirement as applied to the CLC applicants. But the Court left in place the regulatory scheme that could require other groups of mentally retarded people to apply for a special permit to maintain a home in the specified residential zones. . . .

. . . Behind the argument lies a clash of world-views. . . . I will call these the "abnormal persons" approach, the "rights analysis" approach, and the "social relations" approach. [T]his section will define and explore these approaches [and] locate these approaches within the history of legal thought.

The "Abnormal Persons" Approach

One version of the debate in *Cleburne* looks backward to a legal theory that society is composed of two classes of persons, normal and abnormal, and that different legal treatments follow from the assignment of individuals to one or the other class. Under this approach, which owes its origins in part to feudal notions of fixed status relations, that assignment rests on asserted facts about the person's basic or immutable nature, and most importantly, on those facts concerning the person's mental competence and capacity. Those with normal competence and capacity can enjoy rights and can be held responsible for their acts; those with abnormal competence and capacity can be subjected to legal restraints on their autonomy and rights, and can be submitted to legal protections to guard themselves and others from the effects of their incapacities. . . .

A further feature of this approach is that although abnormal persons themselves have many variations among them, these variations dim in contrast to their similarities when compared with normal persons. . . .

In *Cleburne*, all the opinions manifest some aspects of this view. Mainly, the opinions treat the mentally retarded as one class of people who share more with each other then with the rest of the community. This, of course, presumes that the characteristic of mental retardation is a more important measure of similarity than, say, eye color or age. . . . The majority expressly embraces the conception that because differences based on mental competence are real, natural, and immutable, governmental action based on this difference is not suspicious but instead legitimate.

The Rights Analysis Approach

A contrasting approach applies to the mentally incompetent the rights apparatus utilized during eras of legal reform. Drawing primarily from the desegregation and civil liberties litigation strategies of the 1950s to the 1970s, groups of mentally handicapped individuals and their professional advocates have developed a rights analysis to challenge mental competence classifications.

Rights analysis begins with the view that legal rights apply to everyone: the facts of personhood and membership in the polity entitle each individual to rights against the state and rights to be treated by the state in the same way as others are treated.

Rights historically have been denied to certain groups for reasons that can no longer be defended. Political and scientific innovations have rejected many old ideas about differences that used to justify denials of rights. Even though there persists an idea that some differences are true and natural, that notion is coupled here with a skepticism about the accuracy of particular assumptions and classifications, especially where there has been a history of prejudice and cruel treatment. This view animates the thought of those who seek the same legal rights enjoyed by "normal" people for those historically labeled abnormal and mentally incompetent. . . .

. . . In [one] respect[], rights analysis contains a central instability. It starts with the idea that everyone enjoys the same rights, but proceeds with the possibility that some special rights may be necessary either to remove the effects of past exclusion or deprivation of rights, or to address some special characteristics of certain groups. This approach, then, uses differences to justify special rights—in contrast to a rights theory that emphasizes "sameness." . . .

. . . Yet, unlike the "abnormal persons" approach, rights analysis acknowledges that historical attributions of difference have been in error at times, and to guard against error in the future it prescribes a constitutional rights analysis for those labeled mentally incompetent.

Rights analysis itself offers no answer to the question it poses: when are historic attributions of difference acceptable, and when are they false? Nor does it specify when a violation of rights is remedied by treating the retarded like nonretarded persons, and when such a violation justifies a new kind of special treatment. Instead, rights analysis calls for a careful judicial inquiry into these issues, and thus reposes confidence in the perceptions of the judiciary about similarities that transcend as well as differences that endure.

In many ways, all three opinions in *Cleburne* subscribe to this form of rights analysis. . . . Yet the opinions in the case also demonstrate divergent views about when rights analysis should reject differential treatment and when it should approve it—the very problem left unresolved by this approach. . . .

The Social Relations Approach

A DEFINITION

Undoubtedly the least familiar and most difficult to define of the three approaches to difference, the social relations approach is the youngest and the least embedded in language and practice.[4] Nonetheless, the following elements can be identified. Unlike rights analysis, but bearing some resemblance to the "abnormal persons" approach, the social relations approach assumes that there is a basic connectedness between people, instead of assuming that autonomy is the prior and essential dimension of personhood. Yet, like rights analysis, and unlike the view of abnormal persons, the social relations approach is dubious of the method of social organization that constructs human relationships in terms of immutable categories, fixed statuses, and inherited or ascribed traits.

Indeed, even more fundamentally than rights analysis, the social relations approach challenges the categories and differences used to define and describe people on a group basis. Such suspicion stems not only from an awareness of historical errors in the attribution of difference, but also from a view that attribution itself hides the power of those who classify as well as those defined as different. A focus on social relations casts suspicion on the very claim to knowledge manifested by the labeling of any group as different, because that claim disguises the act of power by which the namers simultaneously assign names and deny their relationships with, and power over, the named. Relationships of power are often so unequal as to allow the namers to altogether ignore the perspective of the less powerful. The social relations approach embraces the belief that knowledge is rooted in specific perspectives, and that "prevailing views" or "consensus approaches" express the perspectives of those in positions to enforce their points of view in the structure and governance of society.

If one assumes that people are related to each other, then assertions of differences are actually statements of relationships, since they express a comparison between the one doing the asserting and the one about whom the assertion is made. Acts of comparison, then, express and distribute power. Differences do not reside in any one person. Instead, differences are comparisons drawn by some to locate themselves in relation to others.

This approach, then, emphasizes the social relations of groups and how these relationships between people construct and express power and knowledge. Categories and attributions of difference can perpetuate or increase disparities of power between different groups. Attributions of difference should be sustained only if they do not express or confirm the distribution of power in ways that harm the less powerful and benefit the more powerful.

Undertaking such an analysis is a deeply problematic task for a court, which itself is in a position of power. . . . Rights analysis treats as unproblematic the perspective of those looking into the bases for a challenged difference, even though the perspective of those doing the looking may itself construct the relationships behind the attributed difference. The social relations approach, in contrast, calls for the development of new strategies to expose the very problematic nature of a court's relationship to the question of difference.

One judicial strategy for analysis under this approach tries to take the perspective of the group which those in power have defined as different. There are two ways in which this strategy is problematic. First, no one can ever really take the perspective of another; at best, one can only try to imagine that perspective. . . . The strategy of taking the perspective of another is problematic, though, for a second reason. This strategy attributes a unitary kind of difference to the "different" group, at the risk of obscuring the range of differences within that very group. A focus by male judges on the perspective of women, for example, could obscure the variety of perspectives among women, and could thereby reinforce, rather than challenge, the attribution by men of a particular conception of difference to women. Still the very effort to imagine another perspective could sensitize the court to the possibility of a variety of perspectives. Once a judge recognizes that he does not possess the only truth, he may be more ready to acknowledge that there are even more than two truths, or two points of view.

A second judicial strategy taking the social relations approach explores the social meanings that exclusion and isolation carry in a community. The strategy builds on a premise of ongoing relationships, and considers the relationship between the namer and the named that is manifested in categories and labels and that is lived in daily experiences. . . .

SOCIAL RELATIONS IN *CLEBURNE*

Although the majority's opinion in *Cleburne* barely hints of either of the judicial social relations strategies, Justice Stevens' opinion at a few points tries to take the perspective of mentally retarded persons burdened by the zoning ordinance requirement of a special permit for their group home. Justice Marshall's opinion adopts both this strategy and the focus on ongoing relationships, including relationships between the namer and the named. An exploration of the social relations ideas in these opinions suggests the relative merits of this approach.

In a remarkable flourish, Justice Stevens concluded his opinion by stating, "I cannot believe that a rational member of this disadvantaged class could ever approve of the discriminatory application of the city's ordinance in this case."[5] The phrase is remarkable because it deems significant how the class burdened by the governmental classification views the treatment. . . .

. . . In the opinion by Justice Marshall, a focus on the relationships between the powerful and the less-powerful shapes an assessment of the meanings that exclusion and isolation carry. Thus, his opinion analyzes the historical experience of the mentally retarded by focusing on the meaning of segregating and excluding mentally retarded people from the rest of the community. . . . To Justice Marshall, the history of isolation is "most important." . . . [T]he opinion identifies a chief root of prejudice: separation among groups exaggerates difference.

. . . The opinions by both Justices Stevens and Marshall manifest strategies that advance the social relations approach. Neither opinion, however, fully embraces this view. Justice Stevens' analysis primarily stresses his oft-advanced single standard for equal protection analysis, and it is a standard that implies that the Court can simply ask, across contexts, about the class harmed by the legislation, the public purpose of the law, and the nature of the class that justifies the disparate treatment. By emphasizing a single standard, the opinion appears predominantly to use rights analysis, and yet by presuming that real differences exist between groups of people, the opinion also draws on assumptions about abnormal persons. Justice Stevens for the most part treats as unproblematic the Court's own relationship to the necessary knowledge about classifications and harms, and thereby fails to recognize the relationship between knowledge and power. Justice Marshall's opinion also straddles approaches, especially in its use of evolutionary rights notions, and its discussion of false stereotypes—as if any stereotypes are true.

An opinion fully embracing the social relations approach would adopt new locutions. For example, it would not assign difference to a group and its members but instead locate it as a comparison drawn between groups. It would pay close attention to who exactly names the difference, and it would consider whether a more powerful group uses the assignment of meaning to difference in order to express and consolidate power. Similarly, the relationships between people, including the Court and those affected by the Court's decision, would be discussed overtly; the opinion would thus have an obligation to disclose their own involvement and responsibility in the assertions they made.

The three approaches to legal treatment of difference help to identify the lines of disagreement among the Supreme Court Justices in contemporary cases. Yet, beneath the debates over the proper fit between ends and means of legislative action and the proper level of scrutiny for reviewing legislative classifications lies a sharp division about the meaning of difference. . . . The "abnormal persons" view makes differential treatment seem natural, unavoidable, and unproblematic; the "social relations" view makes differential treatment a problem of social choice and meaning, a problem for which all onlookers are responsible. The "rights analysis" approach, perhaps the dominant framework of contemporary analysis, shares some elements with the other approaches, and yet cannot itself resolve the tension between them. What can? Which approach is better and why? . . .

Three Approaches in Relationship

. . .

How, then, to evaluate the three approaches to legal problems of difference? . . .

. . . This question is hard to answer because each view implies contrasting fundamental assumptions about not only what to value, but how to evaluate—even how to know. Here is a brief reprise of the competing views that sober the would-be evaluator:

—the steady certainty of the "abnormal persons" view treats difference as "out there" in a reality that can be discovered, in a universe of facts whose discovery also confirms their propriety;

—the crusading intensity of the rights analysis approach casts suspicion on attributions of differences if they land upon minority groups whom majorities historically have disfavored; and yet assigned difference can stand if the suspicion uncovers (note the language of discovery again) real differences, genuinely related to justifiable purposes for differential treatment;

—the social relations approach challenges the usually unstated point of view of the one who "sees" differences as a human construction of the relation between viewer and viewed, and thus as an expression of the relation between power and knowledge; issues about the "truth" or "falsity" of differences fade before concern over the meanings and uses of those differences; and differences that yield social distance and exclusion are likely to be condemned as self-serving expressions of the more powerful.

The very nature of truth is contested by the views, and so by which view of truth may I judge them? Without resolving this question, I will proceed with two efforts in response to it. . . .

Mutual Critique

With different but related histories, the three approaches to legal problems of difference become more meaningful when considered in relation to one another. Especially since the social relations approach can be understood as a synthesis of and response to the other approaches, an examination of the relationships among the approaches should amplify the perspective of this essay.

The approach that assumes that there are "abnormal persons" seems both manipulable and self-sealing, static and arbitrary. In relation to rights analysis, the "abnormal persons" approach often appears to deny rights and even an inquiry into the possible violation of rights, and it risks obscuring abuses committed in the name of care or protection for dependent people. This approach treats as unproblematic the sources of knowledge about differences between people, and it offers no vantage point of critique for current practices beyond an inquiry into whether those practices depart from the inherited scheme. Yet, founded in conceptions of social status and social order, the "abnormal persons" approach perceives society as assuming and reinforcing patterns of human relationships that matter, as opposed to rights analysis which envisions autonomous and disconnected individuals. The social relations approach shares this concern for human relations, but the "abnormal persons" approach appears more certain, knowable and reliable, insofar as it imposes a more static, hierarchical set of relations that reinforce existing distributions of power.

Rights analysis, as applied to the problems of difference examined in this essay, faces a dilemma in attempting to justify both equal and special treatment. While it enables some previously dependent persons to assert their independence and be recognized as similar to others, as in the deinstitutionalization movement, it has difficulty in formulating a basis for assisting those who remain dependent, as well as those who can achieve independence only through the aid of others. Celebrating independence, rights analysis has little to say about dependency.

Rights analysis affords a vantage point from which the "abnormal persons" approach may be criticized for its validation of a social order that imposes hierarchical and fixed statuses, as well as for its assertions of immutable differences between people. Yet at the same time, rights analysis obscures social relations, obligations between groups and connections between people. It treats each individual as a separate unit, related only to the state, rather than as a member of a group or a participant in a network of social bonds. On the other hand, unlike the social relations approach, rights analysis affords some apparently foundational claim for criticizing those differences it exposes as unfounded. Rights analysis invokes similarities between people as a basis for claims to equality, but, by corollary, permits differences to justify unequal treatment. Contrasted with the view of social relations, it assumes the existence of reliable empirical sources of knowledge about the differences between people, and it presumes that such real differences can be discerned—or dissolved—upon scrutiny, without concern about the way in which the observer constructs what is "real."

The approach of social relations, like the "abnormal persons" view, includes within its analysis the networks of relationships. Unlike the "abnormal persons" view, the social relations theory challenges fixed statuses and attributed differences. And unlike rights analysis, the social relations approach eschews the appearance of objectivity and legitimacy. Instead, it asserts that those who enforce difference and assign rights themselves have perspectives, and that their power to enforce their perspectives is what makes those perspectives "true." By stressing the unavoidability of perspective, the social relations approach makes all claims of knowledge vulnerable to the same charge: "but that's just your view." Indeed, the social relations theory makes problematic the very use of judicial power to declare some attributions of difference unacceptable, for that declaration constructs and strengthens the power differential between the court and those subjected to its decisions.

Undermining the claims of knowledge about difference, the approach of social relations undermines all positions, including its own. This quality may frighten people into abandoning this approach, whether they admit it or not. Some may simply claim that they know what is good and needed by others, rather than learn to challenge their first impressions by struggling to take the perspective of another. The social relations approach makes it difficult to express the common perception that people really are different—risking perhaps more insidious expressions of such perceptions.

These contrasts suggest a deep tension between faith in an authoritative basis from which to know the world and from which to approve and condemn practices, and the conviction that there is no foundation for knowledge apart from what human beings construct. The first position is perpetually vulnerable to charges that power and position influence perceptions and judgments; the second seems perpetually unstable, for it implies that there is not even a certain vantage point from which to identify the relations between knowledge and power. Yet rather than understanding the tension between these views as a defect in the social relations approach, I would venture that this tension identifies the issues which the approach highlights and addresses. In this sense, the social relations approach identifies a set of considerations for an ongoing dialogue accompanying our choices about social life.

Conclusion: A Case for Social Relations— and Its Ongoing Relations to Other Views

It is obvious by now that I am sympathetic towards the social relations view. Thinking about social relations offers:

1. Ways to challenge the complacency about fixed and assigned hierarchical statuses associated with a view that some people are simply abnormal—a view that has justified exclusion and denigration of racial minorities, women, and mentally disabled people.
2. Ways to challenge the pretense of identity and sameness that animates rights analysis, a pretense that can undermine special programs aiming to assist mentally disabled people to function and flourish in a world not designed with them in mind.
3. Ways to integrate into law notions about the social dimensions of knowledge and the interpersonal dimensions of individual identity that have replaced earlier ideas about objectivity and autonomy in science, psychology, and other fields.
4. Ways to highlight as human choices, rather than as acts of discovery, how we treat people, including those who seem or who are labeled "different."
5. Ways to direct legal inquiry into the social and historical patterns of power and exclusion in which a given problem arises, and thus, ways to direct legal decision-makers to address the practical meanings of their decisions for the people affected.
6. Ways to make the perspective of "different people" critical to decisions concerning difference; this could help erase the labels that separate, isolate and hide "different people" and bring them closer to the experience and imagination of those who judge them.
7. Ways to emphasize the responsibility of those in power for the decisions they make, especially in terms of the relationships they have with those affected by those decisions.

Working toward these directions through the social relations approach means embracing beliefs that society is a human invention and that those entrusted with societal power can and should exercise that power to recognize and deepen the shared humanity of others.

The social relations approach, as I have described it, is far from fully developed, and, in its own terms, could never yield general principles that would generate determinate answers in specific applications. It is more a point of view than a body of norms, but beyond it is a normative commitment to engage in a self-critical process, to accept responsibility for choices that give various kinds of significance to particular human traits, and to refrain from assigning social meanings to those traits that deny relationships between people.

Using "differences" like physical and mental disabilities as points of departure, the following suggestions proceed with a social relations approach to generate alternatives to treating "differences" as given and as residing in the "different" persons:

1. We frequently view a student's deafness as *her* difference, and then debate whether she deserves either a sign-language interpreter in the mainstream classroom, no special assistance, or instruction in a classroom for deaf students. Taking the student's relationships with other classmates as the point of departure, however, the "problem" becomes one for the whole class, which is as deprived of communicating fully with the student as she is deprived of communicating fully with them. A program to teach all the students sign-language is a step that would affirm the social relations approach.

2. We often treat pregnancy as a disability, especially for purposes of defining an employee's eligibility for insurance or leave benefits related to the job. When we do so, however, we turn pregnancy into something negative, an interference with "normal" activity, and a problem for the individual woman who becomes pregnant. An alternative approach would treat pregnancy as the mode of species reproduction in which all persons, not just the pregnant person, have an interest, and from this vantage point, programs like work-leaves and adjusted work hours would be services for everyone, and not programs that reiterate stereotypes about women's "differences."

3. We could redesign our buildings and physical environment to ease access for people bound to wheelchairs, so that their disability does not necessitate certain exclusion. Similarly, perhaps we can make aspects of our social infrastructure less disabling for people with mental disabilities. Contracts, banking practices, and other routine legal and financial transactions could be simplified, enabling people with mental disabilities to conduct their own affairs and participate in communal economic and social life.

In each of these examples, the conventional approach that treats disability as a real difference, residing in the "different person," can be challenged by a view that emphasizes the meaning of differences as features of people's relationships with one another. Moreover, analytic approaches preoccupied with treating like alike and unlike differently can be replaced by an analysis of the ways in which institutions construct and utilize differences to justify and enforce exclusions— and the ways that such institutional practices can be changed. Controversy is bound to ensue concerning the meanings of differences, the possible changes in institutional practices, and the groups that are empowered or disempowered by certain practices, but the social relations approach suggests that such controversy is more useful than supposedly empiricist debates over what is or is not a "real difference." At the least, controversy will confront people with their relationships and interconnectedness with those who seem alien, and confront those in positions of power with the meanings their exercises of power have in the lives of those affected.

. . . The hope of the social relations approach is that by talking about these things the people behind the labels may become vivid to those who would exclude them; and notions of difference will no longer end, but instead begin an inquiry about how to live.

I cannot, however, pretend that mere adoption of the language of the social relations approach would change the way people think and act, much less actually recognize and deepen the shared humanity of others. Language and rules matter in the formation of social meaning, and help construct what people think, believe, and choose, but language and rules do not dictate results nor do they necessarily change the people who use them. Moreover, the social relations approach invites heightened humility about how little anyone can know about another. Such humility could yield quite unpredictable results. Humility could be used to justify differential treatment of people historically treated as different or to justify eliminating such differential treatment—with no guarantee in either case that anyone is better off. Thus, the same doubts about claims of what is a "real difference" could well be leveled against claims about what attributions of difference disempower others and how. In its defense, the social relations approach guides an expressly normative debate over these questions of power rather than hiding it behind allegedly objective and empiricist questions about the discovery of difference.

Perhaps most disturbing about the social relations approach, from my vantage point, is the loss of certainty it implies. Especially in an era when law reform on behalf of minority groups and social welfare programs in general suffer major political assaults, it seems foolhardy to abandon, much less undermine, the sharpness of rights claims. Perhaps due to its origins, rights analysis enables a devastating, if rhetorical, exposure of and challenge to hierarchies of power. As social policies turn to the politics of selfishness, exclusion, and denial of public responsibility for social problems, those who have the weakest toeholds in the dominant social structure become most vulnerable to poverty and degradation. For people who still are members of groups traditionally labeled as "different," these risks are compounded by new forms of parentalism announced on their behalf. Claims to act on behalf of another have been used so often to justify exclusions, deprivations, and attributions of difference that stigmatize rather than valorize or accept. Here the power of rights analysis seems especially appealing. It affords a purchase on the slippery matters of human relationships by commanding a searching inquiry from an allegedly certain point of view. And its equation of sameness with equality offers a spiritual commitment with a kind of positivist certainty: because we can measure characteristics of similarity and difference, we can tailor legal treatment to match.

Yet the internal instabilities of rights analysis, the mounting political reaction to its past successes, and the theoretical assault posed by newer theories of knowledge and meaning, make rights analysis vulnerable to critics on the right and the left, and to critics concerned with both practice and theory. There may be ways at once to strengthen and to embolden rights analysis with the kinds of probing inquiries offered by the social relations approach. Investigations into historical attributions of differences undertaken through rights analysis could be more vigorously armed with understandings of the social construction of differences. Lawyers and judges could devise their inquiries to connect majorities and minorities in diagnosis and remedy, and to highlight the responsibilities of those in power, at least in terms of past injurious meanings of difference. Rights analysis could come to emphasize as the prerequisite "sameness" the shared "right" to be included and to participate in society—on terms that may vary for each individual, but that may also entail special rights to make inclusion and participation possible.

The social relations approach offers at least these three challenges to rights analysis which may strengthen rights analysis from the vantage point of social relations: Can we construct a kind of rights analysis that emphasizes the relations among the judges and the judged, and calls for the judges to take the perspective of another while coming to know that they can never really know that other perspective? Can rights analysis survive the challenge to its claims of knowable differences and to its reinforcement of autonomous individualism posed by the epistemological and ethical turns of the social relations approach? And, may we discover who we are by finding our boundaries and surpassing them?

Notes

1. M. Ignatieff, The Needs of Strangers 131 (Viking, 1985).
2. City of Cleburne v. Cleburne Living Center, 473 U.S. 432. . . .
3. *Id.* at 447.
4. The social relations approach can be understood in a Hegelian dialectical fashion: the feudal, hierarchical qualities of the "abnormal persons" view yielded its antithesis—a rights analysis premised upon autonomous individualism and essential sameness among persons. This new approach synthesizes the two earlier views by recapturing the social connectedness of the notion of abnormal persons while also preserving the freedom from outwardly imposed categorization advanced by rights analysis.
5. Cleburne, 473 U.S. at 455. . . .

❖ PART 4

The Debate over Essentialism:
Gender and Race

❖ *Introduction*

QUESTIONS OVER the definition of woman are at the heart of feminist theory. For example, are there certain attributes which characterize women? How are women similar to and different from men? What is significant about such similarities and differences? Are women's differences from men rooted in biology, or are they socially constructed? A number of writers currently are shifting the focus of feminist theory from the sameness–difference debate. They are part of a movement attacking essentialism in feminism.[1]

The notion of a "feminine identity" has become increasingly suspect to feminist theorists. For example, the issue of identity is central to the school of French feminism. Over the past twenty years, French feminists such as Julia Kristeva, Hélène Cixous, and Luce Irigaray have grappled with issues of identity and subjectivity. Much of the work of these feminists has been in response to Jacques Lacan, who challenges the notion of the individual as a whole or unified subject.[2]

This Part continues the exploration on issues of woman's identity. It focuses on issues of self-definition in yet another important debate in feminist legal theory: essentialism versus antiessentialism. Thus, it explores the sameness–differences controversy not in the context of equality, as in the preceding two Parts, but in the context of woman's self-definition.

Essentialism constitutes the view that all women are alike, sharing a common "essence" or certain "essential" traits that differentiate them from men. Essentialism is characterized by central assumptions: first, the meaning of gender identity and the experience of sexism are similar for all women; and, second, any differences between women are less significant than the traits women share in common.

For example, one of the best-known modern subscribers to this perspective is Carol Gilligan, who in her book[3] describes women and men as possessing distinct and mutually exclusive traits. Men, she claims, are more likely to justify moral decisions by the application of abstract rules, emphasizing rights. Women, in contrast, tend to construe moral dilemmas as breaches in relationships, emphasizing the importance of connection. Whereas men are autonomous and self-interested, women are selfless, compassionate, and caring. Gender alone, then, according to Gilligan, is determinative of an individual's perspective on moral issues.

Essentialism has long-standing philosophical roots. In one of the foremost critiques of the role of essentialism in feminist theory, Elizabeth Spelman[4] traces the development of the essentialist perspective. She reminds us that both Plato and Aristotle espoused certain beliefs about women's essential nature. Even feminists such as Simone de Beauvoir also fall prey to this shortsightedness, Spelman points out. Spelman's antiessentialist work persuasively argues that essentialism results in negative consequences for feminists and for feminist thought.

Antiessentialism highlights criticisms of the essentialist perspective. For example, the women's movement (both contemporary and historical) has been the target of the antiessentialist critique for its exclusion of Black women.[5] The primary antiessentialist critique is that feminists have taken the experiences of white middle-class women to be representative of the experiences of all women. In so doing, it may be argued, they obscure women's diversity; reinforce the privilege of white middle-class women; result in other women being labeled as "different," deviant, and lacking; distort feminism in the same way as masculine privilege has done; contribute to feminism being exclusionary in its concerns; and, ultimately, forestall the possibility of social change. Antiessentialism captures a paradox at the heart of feminism: any attempt to talk about all women in terms of what women have in common undermines attempts to assess the significance of women's differences.

The essentialist versus antiessentialist controversy is central not only to feminism but also to feminist legal thought. Feminist legal theorists increasingly are thinking about issues of race and gender.[6] Feminist legal scholars have been up-braided for their tendency toward essentialism, and for ignoring the importance of a variety of determinative variables in explaining women's experience. Particular feminist legal theorists have been criticized for their essentialist views.[7] The authors in this Part all join the critique of essentialism in feminist legal theory and bring their voices to bear on this topic in different ways.

Martha Minow's "Feminist Reason: Getting It and Losing It," provides an excellent introduction to the problem of essentialism in feminist legal thought.[8] Minow's point of departure is that feminism has confronted assumptions of universality embodying the male norm by demanding that distinctive aspects of women's experiences be recognized in developing theory, laws, and social practices. Minow argues that, in so doing, feminist theorists have projected the experiences of some women as representative of all and ignored differences stemming from, for example, race, class, religion, ethnicity, sexual preference, and disabilities. Thus, feminists run the risk of promoting a universal female norm analogous to the male norm exposed by the feminist critique.

Minow's essay advocates that feminists recall feminist insights into the power of the unstated norm, the privileged position of the status quo, and the pretense of asserting that a particular is the universal. Minow explores several reasons these insights are often overlooked. She then examines Supreme Court decisions regarding pregnancy leave and the workplace to illustrate one particular feminist insight, that is, the power of the unstated male norm. In California Federal Savings and Loan v. Guerra, 479 U.S. 272 (1987), for example, she finds guidance for an exit from the universalist dilemma. Instead of accepting the dominant unstated male norm with its underlying assumption that existing social arrangements are natural and necessary, the Court considered versions of reality at odds with dominant social arrangements. Minow concludes that feminists can avoid imposing a new female universal norm by demanding this same reconsideration of different points of view.

Angela Harris, in "Race and Essentialism in Feminist Legal Theory," expands the Part's discussion of essentialism with a critique of essentialism in the work of several feminist legal theorists. In particular, Harris uses a racial critique to challenge essentialism in the work of Catharine MacKinnon and Robin West.

Next, Harris continues a theme touched on by Minow. She discusses the reasons essentialism prevails in feminist theory. Harris's antidote to essentialism is "multiple consciousness," a concept that recognizes that "people are not oppressed only or primarily on the basis of gender, but on the bases of race, class, sexual orientation, and other categories in inextricable webs." She concludes her essay with suggestions by which Black women's experiences can contribute to subverting essentialism and, thereby, energizing legal theory.

Patricia Cain's "Feminist Jurisprudence: Grounding the Theories" provides another voice that answers Minow's call for feminists' consideration of different points of view. In the process Cain joins Harris's critique of certain feminist theorists (e.g., West, MacKinnon) for their essentialist tendencies. But Cain adds a distinct point of view—critiquing essentialism in feminist legal theory from a lesbian perspective. Her essay challenges feminist theorists to understand heterosexuality as a patriarchal institution and not simply as the naturally dominant form of sexuality.

Marlee Kline's essay, "Race, Racism, and Feminist Legal Theory," returns to the specific issue of race. She offers a broader perspective than Harris by focusing on the interaction between law and gender in several different racial contexts as well as in several different legal contexts. Her essay also adds a Canadian perspective in critiquing essentialism in legal theory.

Kimberle Crenshaw's final essay in this Part, "Demarginalizing the Intersection of Race and Sex," returns to concerns relevant, specifically, to Black women.[9] Crenshaw adds a critique of antidiscrimination doctrine and antiracist politics for their exclusion of Black women. She argues that legal doctrine, legal theory, and politics all have perpetuated what she terms "single-axis analysis," which treats gender and race as mutually exclusive categories. Her essay provides an answer to the dilemma posed by essentialism. Her strategy of "demarginalizing the intersection" (or embracing the intersection of race and gender issues) goes beyond mere recognition of the problem of essentialism and poses a means of breaking free of gender hierarchy. She urges that reformers must "embrace the intersection" of race and gender, by putting those individuals who are currently marginalized, the multiply disadvantaged, at the center of reform attempts. By developing strategies and theories to restructure the world to accommodate the multiply disadvantaged, she points out, benefits to all will follow.

Notes

1. Joan Williams cites an article by historian Nancy Hewitt as signaling "a major reorientation" among American feminists to the issue of essentialism. Williams, Feminism and Post-Structuralism (Book Review, The Female Body and the Law), 88 Mich. L. Rev. 1776, 1777, citing Hewitt, Beyond the Search for Sisterhood: American Women's History in the 1980s, 10 Soc. His. 299 (1985). Hewitt's article was soon followed by Z. Eisenstein, The Female Body and the Law (University of California Press, 1988) and E. Spelman, Inessential Woman: Problems of Exclusion in Feminist Thought (Beacon, 1988) both of which also attacked essentialism in feminist theory. See also de Lauretis, Upping the Anti [sic] in M. Hirsch & E. Keller eds., Feminist Theory, Conflicts in Feminism (Routledge, 1990).

2. See generally E. Marks & I. de Courtivron eds., New French Feminisms (University of Massachusetts Press, 1982); J. Lacan, God and the Jouissance of the Woman, in J. Mitchell and J. Rose eds., Feminine Sexuality (Norton, 1982).

3. C. Gilligan, In a Different Voice: Psychological Theory and Women's Development (Harvard University Press, 1982).

4. E. Spelman, Inessential Woman, *supra* note 1.

5. See especially P. Giddings, When and Where I Enter: The Impact of Black Women on Race and Sex in America (Morrow, 1984), and D. Rhode, Justice and Gender 60–62 (Harvard University Press, 1989) (and sources cited at 341 n. 22).

6. See, e.g., recent symposia devoted to this topic: Black Women Law Professors: Building a Community at the Intersection of Race and Gender, a Symposium, 6 Berkeley Women's L.J. (1990–91); Frontiers of Legal Thought: Gender, Race, and Culture in the Law, 1991 Duke L.J.

7. In addition to the critiques in this Part, see Cornell, The Doubly-Prized World: Myth, Allegory and the Feminine, 75 Cornell L. Rev. 644, 649–650 (1990) and Williams, Deconstructing Gender, 87 Mich. L. Rev. 797, 800 (1989) (both criticizing Robin West for her essentialism).

8. See also M. Minow, Making All the Difference: Inclusion, Exclusion, and American Law (Cornell University Press, 1990).

9. For additional recent discussions of Black women and feminist legal theory, see Austin, Sapphire Bound!, 1989 Wis. L. Rev. 539; Scales-Trent, Black Women and the Constitution: Finding Our Place, Asserting Our Rights, 24 Harv. C.R.-C.L.L. Rev. 9 (1989); and Scales-Trent, Commonalities: On Being Black and White, Different and the Same, 2 Yale J.L. & Feminism 305 (1990). These works are also part of another developing body of jurisprudence, sometimes referred to as "critical race theory," which encompasses the work of legal scholars of color who explore the role of racism in law. For a comparison of essentialism in feminist legal theory and critical race theory, see Williams, Dissolving the Sameness/Difference Debate: A Post-Modern Path Beyond Essentialism in Feminist and Critical Race Theory, 1991 Duke L.J. 296.

❖ *Feminist Reason:*
Getting It and Losing It

Martha Minow

> As white women ignore their built-in privilege of whiteness and
> define [woman] in terms of their own experience alone, then
> women of Color become "other," the outsider whose experience
> and tradition is too "alien" to comprehend.
>
> —*Audre Lorde*[1]

Judges and lawyers in the contemporary legal system in the United States . . .
treat their own points of reference as natural and necessary. Judges' preoccupation with neutrality, for example, especially notable in constitutional and statutory
equality jurisprudence, upholds existing institutional arrangements while shield-
ing them from open competition with alternatives. . . .

Feminists have shown how such assertions of neutrality hide from view the use
of a male norm for measuring claims of discrimination. Adopting such feminist
critiques can deepen the meaning of equality under law. I advocate developing
similar feminist critiques in contexts beyond gender, such as religion, ethnicity,
race, handicap, sexual preference, socioeconomic class, and age. Yet attempts to
advance feminist analyses in new contexts come up against unstated assumptions
about other traits—assumptions embedded in prevailing feminist arguments. In
critiques of the "male" point of view and in celebrations of the "female," feminists
run the risk of treating particular experiences as universal and ignoring differences of racial, class, religious, ethnic, national, and other situated experiences.

Thus, feminist analyses have often presumed that a white, middle-class, heterosexual, Christian, and able-bodied person is the norm behind "women's" experience. Anything else must be specified, pointed out. This set of assumptions recreates the problem feminists seek to address—the adoption of unstated reference
points that hide from view a preferred position and shield it from challenge by other
plausible alternatives. These assumptions also reveal the common tendency to treat
differences as essential, rather than socially constructed, and to treat one's own perspective as truth, rather than as one of many possible points of view.

---

38 J. Legal Educ. 47 (1988).

Feminism has contributed to the campaign that challenges the convergence between knowledge and power. Feminists question assertions of knowledge that owe their effectiveness to the power wielded by those making the assertions. Some feminists, however, assert as reality claims that hide the power of those doing the claiming. This essay thus pursues the perpetual critique initiated by feminist work while also searching, as feminists do, for practical justice, not just more theory.

Insights

Feminists have contributed incisive critiques of the unstated assumptions behind political theory, law, bureaucracy, science, and social science that presuppose the universality of a particular reference point or standpoint.[2] In field after field of human thought, feminist work exposes the dominance of conceptions of human nature that take men as the reference point and treat women as "other," "different," "deviant," or "exceptional." Male psychology, feminist theorists argue, is the source in a male-dominated society of conceptions of rational thought that favor abstraction over particularity and mind over body. Similarly, the assumption of autonomous individualism behind American law, economic and political theory, and bureaucratic practices rests on a picture of public and independent man rather than private—and often dependent, or interconnected—woman. The norms and the dynamics of the natural world—the way its biological, evolutionary, and even chemical and physical properties are explained—embody unstated male reference points.

Feminist work confronts the power of naming and challenges both the use of male measures and the assumption that women fail by them. If, at times, feminists appear contradictory, arguing both for the right of women to be included and treated like men and for the right to have special treatment (which valorizes women's differences), feminists have an explanation. The inconsistency lies in a world and set of symbolic constructs that have simultaneously used men as the norm and denigrated any departure from the norm. Thus, feminism demands the dual strategy of challenging the assumptions that women are too different from the unstated male norm to enjoy male privileges and that women's differences actually justify denial of privileges or benefits. For over a century now, feminists have claimed that distinctive aspects of women's experiences and perspectives offer resources for constructing more representative, more empathic, more creative, and, in general, better theories, laws, and social practices.

New Claims, Old Risks

As many feminist theorists are beginning to recognize, our critique runs the great risk of creating a new standpoint that is equally in danger of projecting the experience of some as though it were universal.[3] By urging the corrective of women's perspective, or even a feminist standpoint, feminists may jeopardize our challenge to simplifications, essentialism, and stereotypes.

Many feminists acknowledge that women fall into every category of race, religion, class, and ethnicity, and vary in sexual preference, handicapping conditions, and other sources of assigned difference. Any claim to speak from women's point of view, or to use women as a reference point, threatens to obscure this multiplicity by representing a particular view as the view of all.[4] Some have expressly argued that sexism is more fundamental than racism.[5] This claim is disturbing because it suggests not just that feminists may fail to take account of other forms of oppression or domination beyond sexism but that they may fail to take account of women's own experiences in all their variety. Elizabeth V. Spelman persuasively argues that we ought to be "skeptical about any account of gender relations which fails to mention race and class or consider the possible effects of race and class differences on gender: for in a world in which there is racism and classicism, obscuring the workings of race and class are likely to involve—whether intentionally or not—obscuring the workings of racism and classism."[6] Focusing on the same danger, Nancy Fraser and Linda Nicholson conclude that there is neither one "feminist method" nor one feminist epistemology, "since women's oppression is not homogenous in content, and since it is not determined by one root, underlying cause."[7] Audre Lorde puts it powerfully: "Some problems we share as women, some we do not. You fear your children will grow up to join the patriarchy and testify against you, we fear our children will be dragged from a car and shot down the street, and you will turn your backs upon the reasons they are dying."[8]

Why Do We Make the Mistake We Identify in Others?

Such critiques of feminism are internal, voiced by feminists, admonishing feminists. In a sense, the method of consciousness-raising—personal reporting of experience in communal settings to explore what has not been said—enables a practice of self-criticism among feminists even about feminism itself. Yet why, when it comes to our own arguments and activities, do feminists forget the very insights that animate feminist initiatives, insights about the power of unstated reference points and points of view, the privileged position of the status quo, and the pretense that a particular is the universal?

Perhaps our own insights elude us because of our attraction to simplifying categories, our own psychodynamic development, our unconscious attachment to stereotypes, and our participation in a culture in which contests over power include contests over what version of reality prevails. We are afraid of being overwhelmed, which is what full acknowledgment of all people's differences may portend. Cognitively, we need simplifying categories, and the unifying category of "woman" helps to organize experience, even at the cost of denying some of it.

Ideas that defy neat categories are difficult to hold on to, even though the idea itself is about the tyranny of categories. We especially attach ourselves to such categories as male/female because of our own psychological development in a culture that has made gender matter, and our own early constructions of personal identity forged in relationship to parents who made gender matter.

Feminist activities themselves also reveal relationships between knowledge and power. Feminists are no more free than others from the stereotypes in cultural thought. White feminists may well carry unconscious stereotypes about people of color, and similar stereotypes may divide women of different religions, political persuasions, abilities and disabilities, and sexual preferences. Some stereotypes may be an unconscious cultural inheritance, but they also may be clues to who has power to define agendas and priorities within feminist communities.[9] Ignoring differences among women may permit the relatively more privileged women to claim identification with all discrimination against women while also claiming special authority to speak for women unlike themselves.

Finally, we share the version of reality that has for the most part prevailed in the entire culture. Not only does this instill conceptions of difference and stereotypic thinking, it also gives us internal scripts about how to argue, and indeed, how to know. The dominant culture has established certain criteria for theories, for legal arguments, for scientific proofs—for authoritative discourse. These established criteria are the governing rules. If we want to be heard—indeed, if we want to make a difference in existing arenas of power—we must acknowledge and adapt to them, even though they confine what we have to say or implicate us in the patterns we claim to resist.

The Example of Pregnancy

The Supreme Court's treatment of issues concerning pregnancy and the workplace highlights the power of the unstated male norm in analyses of problems of difference. . . . [See cases discussed Part 2 this volume. *Ed.*] The Court considered, both as a statutory and a constitutional question, whether discrimination in health insurance plans on the basis of pregnancy amounted to discrimination on the basis of sex. In both instances, the Court answered negatively because pregnancy marks a division between the groups of pregnant and nonpregnant persons, and women fall in both categories. Only from a point of view that treats pregnancy as a strange occasion, rather than a present, bodily potential, would its relationship to female experience be made so tenuous; and only from a vantage point that treats men as the norm would the exclusion of pregnancy from health insurance coverage seem unproblematic and free from forbidden gender discrimination.

With judicial decisions such as these, litigators working for women's rights have discovered that unless we fit our claims into existing doctrines, we are unlikely to be understood, much less to succeed. Yet trying to fit women's experiences into categories forged with men in mind reinstates gender differences by treating the male standard as unproblematic. Feminist attacks on the problem face a double risk. Either we reinvest unstated male norms with legitimacy by trying to extend them to women, or we criticize those norms and posit a new, female norm that may be insensitive to the variety of women's experiences. . . . Reformers approaching the issues of pregnancy and the workplace and seeking both litigation and legislation to establish women's right to pregnancy benefits and leaves may merely carve a new norm that produces new exclusions.

Political and legal reactions to past victories pose the real danger that legal decisions may grow worse for women and minority men. We are more likely than ever to attempt to frame conventional arguments that can succeed in the courts and legislatures, both of which enshrine convention. Arguments that women are just like men—and deserve to be treated like men—reappear when legal and political authorities reject arguments that mainstream institutions should be revamped to include women's experiences.

When formerly excluded groups such as women want to be recognized or represented in mainstream, established institutions, our own efforts at reform become most vulnerable to the version of reality that has in the past excluded us.[10] We risk becoming tokens, and taking our meanings and identities from those who have let us in. . . .

[T]he critic faces the special dilemma of how to claim authority while rejecting its usual forms of subduing and vanquishing others. Feminists, no less than anyone else, and perhaps more than people who have felt at home in the prevailing conceptions of reality, want something to hang on to, some sense of the validity of our own perceptions and experience, some certainty—not more experiences of doubt. Yet, each form of certainty hazards a new arrogance, projecting oneself, one's own experience, or one's own kind as the model for all.

Thus, feminists make the mistake we identify in others—the tendency to treat our own perspective as the single truth—because we share the cultural assumptions about what counts as knowledge, what prevails as a claim, and what kinds of intellectual order we need to make sense of the world. Like the systems of politics, law, and empiricism feminists criticize for enthroning an unstated male norm, feminist critiques tend to establish a new norm that also seeks to fix experience and deny its multiplicity.

A Pointed Effort to See Points of View

No new principle or rule can solve the problem: challenging the hidden privileging of one perspective privileges another in its place. Instead we need a stance, one that helps us accept complexity but not passivity. As people who judge others and who face the judgments of others, we should challenge any ready assignment of "difference" that seems to allocate benefits or burdens, as though the results were natural rather than chosen. This means doubting words and concepts that we take for granted, and looking to the consequences when we do use them. A useful strategy is to pay attention to competing perspectives on a given problem, and to challenge unstated points of view that hide their assumptions from open competition with others. In sum, we need to pay attention to what we give up as well as what we embrace.

Rather than create a new female norm for use in claiming equality, I suggest that we contest the ready association of sameness with equality and difference with inferiority. Similarly, we could take challenges to differential treatment as occasions to assess not difference but treatment, not individual and group traits but social arrangements that make those traits seem to matter.

Again, let us take pregnancy and the workplace as an example. Although tortured in its framework and controverted in its results, the Supreme Court's 1987 decision in California Federal Savings and Loan Association v. Guerra,[11] represents an effort to remake an apparent issue of neutrality toward gender differences in the workplace into an issue of neutrality toward gender differences in the conjunction between work and family. In so doing, the Court—and the legislatures whose enactments the Court construed—converted the difference question into a challenge to prevailing social arrangements that had made a gender difference significant. . . .

. . . [T]he suit questioned whether the federal ban against discrimination on the basis of pregnancy allows treating pregnant workers like other workers, or instead allows special treatment. Thus framed, the problem treats men as the norm and presumes a workplace designed for men or for people who never become pregnant. Any effort to remake the workplace to accommodate pregnancy would be "special treatment" and would not be neutral with regard to the workplace. Yet a ban against such accommodation, focused on pregnancy, leaves in place the male norm that makes women and pregnancy seem "different."

The majority for the Court understood this and construed the statute to permit employers to permit barriers in the workplace that had disadvantaged pregnant people compared with others. Most important, Justice Marshall's opinion for the Court shifted from the comparison between men and women in the workplace to a comparison of men and women in the conjunction of their workplace and family lives. "By 'taking pregnancy into account,' California's pregnancy disability leave statute allows women, as well as men, to have families without losing jobs."[12]

The majority's second rationale—that the state and federal laws are compatible because employers may comply with both by providing comparable reinstatement benefits to men and women following leaves for reasons such as pregnancy—uses women's experience as the benchmark.[13] The Court called for equal treatment of men and women and permitted the state's elected representatives to determine the minimum threshold level for such treatment. By allowing this legislative alteration of the employers' obligation to workers, the Court unmasked the employers' effort to rely on the federal law for what is was—an attempt to implant the male norm as the reference for workplace equality. Although the task of asserting the permissible significance of gender-linked characteristics remains, the Court successfully resisted the role of reinstating social arrangements that had made gender difference at the workplace significant. . . .

What the Court did in *Cal. Fed.* . . .[was to take] seriously versions of reality at odds with the structure of social arrangements: the perspectives of pregnant women . . . whose needs are not embedded in the rules of employers and the laws governing unemployment benefits. At the same time, the Court [allowed] legislative initiative with an important limitation. Existing social arrangements are no more privileged or immune from challenge than any competing arrangement when confronting allegations of burdens based on a personal or group difference.

Discussing legal disputes in terms of how existing social arrangements appear in light of competing minority and majority perspectives would have the advantage of exposing initial answers to the same scrutiny. An explicit inquiry into these matters would help guard against the risk that new answers might reestablish a preference for one point of view disguised as the necessary and natural arrangement. . . .

Feminist insights into the power of unstated norms demand just this perpetual reconsideration of the point of view buried within social arrangements and in critiques of them, the point of view that makes some differences matter and others irrelevant. Otherwise, outsiders who become insiders simply define new groups as "other." Taking the point of view of people labeled "different" is one way to move beyond current difficulties in treating differences as real and consequential. Generating vivid details about points of view excluded from or marginalized by particular institutions is another. Seeking out and promoting participation by voices typically unheard are also critical if equality jurisprudence is to mean more than enshrining the point of view of those sitting on the bench. The concerted and persistent search for excluded points of view and the acceptance of their challenges are equally critical to feminist theory and practice. Otherwise, feminists will join the ranks of reformers who have failed to do more than impose their own point of view. . . .

Notes

1. A. Lorde, Age, Race, Class, and Sex: Women Redefining Difference, in Sister Outsider: Essays and Speeches, 114, 117 (Crossing Press, 1984).

2. See, e.g., S. de Beauvoir, The Second Sex (H. Parshley trans., Knopf, 1953); C. Gilligan, In a Different Voice: Psychological Theory and Women's Development (Harvard University Press, 1982); K. Ferguson, The Feminist Case Against Bureaucracy (Temple University Press, 1984); N. Hartsock, Money, Sex,

and Power: Toward a Feminist Historical Materialism (Longman, 1983, 1985); A. Jaggar, Feminist Politics and Human Nature (Rowman & Allanheld, 1983); E. Keller, Reflections on Gender and Science (Yale University Press, 1985); Mac-Kinnon, Feminism, Marxism, Method, and the State: An Agenda for Theory, Part 5 this volume; and Feminism, Marxism, Method, and the State: Toward Feminist Jurisprudence, Part 5 this volume; J. Miller, Toward a New Psychology of Women (Beacon, 1976); S. Okin, Women in Western Political Thought (Princeton University Press, 1979). . . .

3. Audre Lorde puts it this way: "By and large within the women's movement today, white women focus upon their oppression as women and ignore differences of race, sexual preference, class and age. There is a pretense to a homogeneity of experience covered by the word [sisterhood] that does not in fact exist." Lorde, Age, Race, Class, and Sex *supra* note 1, at 116. See also b. hooks, Ain't I a Woman: Black Women and Feminism, 194–95 (South End Press, 1981) (white females bring racism to feminism); B. Omolade, Black Women and Feminism, in H. Eisenstein & A. Jardine eds., The Future of Difference 247, 255 (Rutgers University Press, 1985) (black experience needed in feminism for black women to pursue dialogue with white feminists). . . .

4. This poses a special dilemma for feminism, which has celebrated "women's experience" as the touchstone for a new source of authority. If this authority speaks only for the individual, not for the group of women, how can it counter the predominant structures of societal authority? Barbara Johnson describes the dilemma that ensues in discussions of feminist pedagogy: "[I]t would be impossible to deny that female experience has been undervalidated. On the other hand, the moment one assumes one knows what female experience is, one runs the risk of creating another reductive appropriate—an appropriate that consists in the reduction of experiences as self-resistance." B. Johnson, A World of Difference 46 (Johns Hopkins University Press, 1987).

5. See Wasserstrom, Racism, Sexism and Preferential Treatment: An Approach to the Topics, 24 UCLA L. Rev. 581, 581–615 (1977); Thomas, Sexism and Racism, Some Conceptual Differences 90 Ethics 239 (1980).

6. E. Spelman, Inessential Woman: Problems of Exclusion in Feminist Thought (Beacon, 1988)(chapter on Chodorow).

7. N. Fraser & L. Nicholson, Social Criticism without Philosophy: An Encounter Between Feminism and Postmodernism, in A. Cohen & M. Descal, eds., The Institution of Philosophy: A Discipline in Crisis? (Open Court, 1988). Fraser and Nicholson nevertheless conclude that feminism can continue to mean something: a commitment to actual diversity, and a complex, multilayered feminist solidarity. . . .

8. Lorde, Age, Race, Class, and Sex, *supra* note 1, at 119. And, "As a black lesbian feminist comfortable with the many different ingredients of my identity, and a woman committed to racial and sexual freedom from oppression, I find I am constantly being encouraged to pluck out some one aspect of myself and present this as the meaningful whole, eclipsing or denying the other parts of self. But this is a destructive and fragmenting way to live." *Id.*

9. It may be a characteristic of white privilege to deny difference among women because admitting difference would mean overcoming stereotypes and giving up power, not through the mere tokenism of letting some women of color

in but by actually giving up control over the definition of priorities. Audre Lorde attributes this phenomenon to white women's opportunities and temptations to share some of white men's power. Lorde, Age, Race, Class, and Sex, *supra* note 1, at 118. Emphasizing gender rather than other sources of difference and oppression may actually be a tool of social control.

10. Iris Marion Young calls this the risk of assimilation: "[T]he strategy of assimilation aims to bring formerly excluded groups into the mainstream. So assimilation always implies coming in the game after it is already begun, after the rules and standards have already been set, and having to prove oneself according to those rules and standards." Young, Social Movements, Difference and Social Policy, 56 U. Cin. L. Rev. 535 (1987). If self-identity depends on recognition by others with the power to accord recognition, the problem is pervasive. Avoiding participation in elite institutions does not afford escape from prevailing versions of reality that make assigned differences seem actual, inherited categories powerful, and assertions of essences necessary for authoritative knowledge. These are risks for those who want validation, any validation. A challenge, over the long haul, is to choose whose validation you want, for that may be as critical as choosing whom you want to become.

11. 479 U.S. 272 (1987).

12. *Id.* at 289.

13. That this solution will impose costs on employers—costs that will undoubtedly be shifted to nonpregnant workers—should not be denied. But neither should this consequence be misunderstood: the costs of *failing* to accommodate pregnant workers—along with perhaps less calculable costs from underemploying women—are also borne by employers and shifted to individuals, partially adjusted by the social welfare system. To the extent that pregnant women have shouldered the costs of a workplace that has not accommodated them, the legislation requiring accommodation marks a decision not to create new costs but to spread existing costs more widely.

❖ *Race and Essentialism in Feminist Legal Theory*

ANGELA P. HARRIS

. . . SINCE THE beginning of the feminist movement in the United States, black women have been arguing that their experience calls into question the notion of a unitary "women's experience."[1] In the first wave of the feminist movement, black women's[2] realization that the white leaders of the suffrage movement intended to take neither issues of racial oppression nor black women themselves seriously was instrumental in destroying or preventing political alliances between black and white women within the movement. In the second wave, black women are again speaking loudly and persistently, and at many levels our voices have begun to be heard. Feminists have adopted the notion of multiple consciousness as appropriate to describe a world in which people are not oppressed only or primarily on the basis of gender, but on the bases of race, class, sexual orientation, and other categories in inextricable webs. . . .

In feminist legal theory, however, the move away from univocal toward multivocal theories of women's experience and feminism has been slower than in other areas. . . . And in feminist theory, as in the dominant culture, it is mostly white, straight, and socioeconomically privileged people who claim to speak for all us. Not surprisingly, the story they tell about "women," despite its claim to universality, seems to black women to be peculiar to women who are white, straight, and socioeconomically privileged—a phenomenon Adrienne Rich terms "white solipsism."[3] . . .

The notion that there is a monolithic "women's experience" that can be described independent of other facets of experience like race, class, and sexual orientation is one I refer to in this essay as "gender essentialism."[4] A corollary to gender essentialism is "racial essentialism"—the belief that there is a monolithic "Black Experience," or "Chicano Experience." The source of gender and racial essentialism (and all other essentialisms, for the list of categories could be infi-

---

nitely multiplied) is the second voice, the voice that claims to speak for all. The result of essentialism is to reduce the lives of people who experience multiple forms of oppression to additional problems: "racism + sexism = straight black women's experience," or "racism + sexism + homophobia = black lesbian experience." Thus, in an essentialist world, black women's experience will always be forcibly fragmented before being subjected to analysis, as those who are "only interested in race" and those who are "only interested in gender" take their separate slices of our lives. . . .[A]s long as feminists, like theorists in the dominant culture, continue to search for gender and racial essences, black women will never be anything more than a crossroads between two kinds of domination, or at the bottom of a hierarchy of oppressions; we will always be required to choose pieces of ourselves to present as wholeness. . . .

Modified Women and Unmodified Feminism: Black Women in Dominance Theory

Catharine MacKinnon describes her "dominance theory," like the Marxism with which she likes to compare it, as "total": "[T]hey are both theories of the totality, of the whole thing, theories of a fundamental and critical underpinning of the whole they envision."[5] Both her dominance theory (which she identifies as simply "feminism") and Marxism "focus on that which is most one's own, that which most makes one the being the theory addresses, as that which is most taken away by what the theory criticizes. In each theory you are made who you are by that which is taken away from you by the social relations the theory criticizes." In Marxism, the "that" is work; in feminism, it is sexuality.

MacKinnon defines sexuality as "that social process which creates, organizes, expresses, and directs desire, creating the social beings we know as women and men, as their relations create society." Moreover, "the organized expropriation of the sexuality of some for the use of others defines the sex, woman. Heterosexuality is its structure, gender and family its congealed forms, sex roles its qualities generalized to social persona, reproduction a consequence, and control its issue." Dominance theory, the analysis of this organized expropriation, is a theory of power and its unequal distribution. . . .

Despite its power, MacKinnon's dominance theory is flawed by its essentialism. MacKinnon assumes, as does the dominant culture, that there is an essential "woman" beneath the realities of differences between women—that in describing the experiences of "women" issues of race, class, and sexual orientation can therefore be safely ignored, or relegated to footnotes. In her search for what is essential womanhood, however, MacKinnon rediscovers white womanhood and introduces it as universal truth. . . .

MacKinnon's essentialist, "color-blind" approach also distorts the analysis of rape. . . . By ignoring the voices of black female theoreticians of rape, she produces an ahistorical account that fails to capture the experience of black women.

MacKinnon sees sexuality as "a social sphere of male power of which forced sex is paradigmatic." As with beauty standards, black women are victimized by rape just like white women, only more so: "Racism in the United States, by singling out Black men for allegations of rape of white women, has helped obscure the fact that it is men who rape women, disproportionately women of color." In this peculiar fashion MacKinnon simultaneously recognizes and shelves racism, finally reaffirming that the divide between men and women is more fundamental and that women of color are simply "women plus." MacKinnon goes on to develop a powerful analysis of rape as the subordination of women to men, with only one more mention of color: "[R]ape comes to mean a strange (read Black) man knowing a woman does not want sex and going ahead anyway."

This analysis, though rhetorically powerful, is an analysis of what rape means to white women masquerading as a general account; it has nothing to do with the experience of black women. For black women, rape is a far more complex experience, and an experience as deeply rooted in color as in gender.

For example, the paradigm experience of rape for black women has historically involved the white employer in the kitchen or bedroom as much as the strange black man in the bushes. During slavery, the sexual abuse of black women by white men was commonplace. Even after emancipation, the majority of working black women were domestic servants for white families, a job which made them uniquely vulnerable to sexual harassment and rape.

Moreover, as a legal matter, the experience of rape did not even exist for black women. During slavery, the rape of a black woman by any man, white or black, was simply not a crime.[6] Even after the Civil War, rape laws were seldom used to protect black women against either white or black men, since black women were considered promiscuous by nature. In contrast to the partial or at least formal protection white women had against sexual brutalization, black women frequently had no legal protection whatsoever. "Rape," in this sense, was something that only happened to white women; what happened to black women was simply life.

Finally, for black people, male and female, "rape" signified the terrorism of black men by white men, aided and abetted, passively (by silence) or actively (by "crying rape"), by white women. Black women have recognized this aspect of rape since the nineteenth century. For example, social activist Ida B. Wells analyzed rape as an example of the inseparability of race and gender oppression in *Southern Horrors: Lynch Law in All Its Phases*, published in 1892. Wells saw that both the law of rape and Southern miscegenation laws were part of a patriarchal system through which white men maintained their control over the bodies of all black people: "[W]hite men used their ownership of the body of the white female as a terrain on which to lynch the black male."[7] Moreover, Wells argued, though many white women encouraged interracial sexual relationships, white women, protected by the patriarchal idealization of white womanhood, were able to remain silent, unhappily or not, as black men were murdered by mobs. . . .

Nor has this aspect of rape become purely a historical curiosity. Susan Estrich reports that between 1930 and 1967, 89 percent of the men executed for rape in the United States were black;[8] a 1968 study of rape sentencing in Maryland showed that in all 55 cases where the death penalty was imposed the victim had been white, and that between 1960 and 1967, 47 percent of all black men convicted of criminal assaults on black women were immediately released on probation.[9] The case of Joann Little is testimony to the continuing sensitivity of black women to this aspect of rape. As Angela Davis tells the story:

> Brought to trial on murder charges, the young Black woman was accused of killing a white guard in a North Carolina jail where she was the only woman inmate. When Joann Little took the stand, she told how the guard had raped her in her cell and how she had killed him in self-defense with the ice pick he had used to threaten her. Throughout the country, her cause was passionately supported by individuals and organizations in the Black community and within the young women's movement, and her acquittal was hailed as an important victory made possible by this mass campaign. In the immediate aftermath of her acquittal, Ms. Little issued several moving appeals on behalf of a Black man named Delbert Tibbs, who awaited execution in Florida because he had been falsely convicted of raping a white woman.
>
> Many Black women answered Joann Little's appeal to support the cause of Delbert Tibbs. But few white women—and certainly few organized groups within the anti-rape movement—followed her suggestion that they agitate for the freedom of this Black man who had been blatantly victimized by Southern racism.[10]

The rift between white and black women over the issue of rape is highlighted by the contemporary feminist analyses of rape that have explicitly relied on racist ideology to minimize white women's complicity in racial terrorism.

Thus, the experience of rape for black women includes not only a vulnerability to rape and a lack of legal protection radically different from that experienced by white women, but also a unique ambivalence. Black women have simultaneously acknowledged their own victimization and the victimization of black men by a system that has consistently ignored violence against women while perpetrating it against men. The complexity and depth of this experience is not captured, or even acknowledged, by MacKinnon's account.

MacKinnon's essentialist approach recreates the paradigmatic woman in the image of the white woman, in the name of "unmodified feminism." As in the dominant discourse, black women are relegated to the margins, ignored or extolled as "just like us, only more so." But "Black women are not white women with color."[11] Moreover, feminist essentialism represents not just an insult to black women, but a broken promise —the promise to listen to women's stories, the promise of feminist method.

Robin West's "Essential Woman"

While MacKinnon's essentialism is pervasive but covert, Robin West expressly declares her essentialism. . . .

In West's view, women are ontologically distinct from men, because "Women, and *only* women, and *most* women, transcend *physically* the differentiation or individuation of biological self from the rest of human life trumpeted as the norm by the entire Kantian tradition."[12] That is, because only women can bear children, and because women have the social responsibility for raising children, our selves are profoundly different from male selves. "To the considerable degree that our potentiality for motherhood defines ourselves, women's lives are relational, not autonomous. As mothers we nurture the weak and we depend upon the strong. More than do men, we live in an interdependent and hierarchical natural web with others of varying degrees of strength."[13]

This claim about women's essential connectedness to the world becomes the centerpiece of "Jurisprudence and Gender."[14] West begins the article with the question, "What is a human being?"[15] She then asserts that "perhaps the central insight of feminist theory of the last decade has been that wom[e]n are 'essentially connected,' not 'essentially separate,' from the rest of human life, both materially, through pregnancy, intercourse, and breast-feeding, and existentially, through the moral and practical life."[16] For West, this means that "all of our modern legal theory—by which I mean 'liberal legalism' and 'critical legal theory' collectively—is essentially and irretrievably masculine."[17] This is so because modern legal theory relies on the "separation thesis," the claim that human beings are distinct individuals first and form relationships later.

Black women are entirely absent from West's work, in contrast to MacKinnon's; issues of race do not appear even in guilty footnotes. However, just as in MacKinnon's work, the bracketing of issues of race leads to the installation of white women on the throne of essential womanhood.

West's claims are clearly questionable on their face insofar as the experience of some women—"mothers"—is asserted to stand for the experience of all women. As with MacKinnon's theory, West's theory necessitates the stilling of some voices —namely, the voices of women who have rejected their "biological, reproductive role"—in order to privilege others. One might also question the degree to which motherhood, or our potential for it, defines us.[18]

West argues that the biological and social implications of motherhood shape the selfhood of all, or at least most, women. This claim involves at least two assumptions.[19] First, West assumes (as does the liberal social theory she criticizes) that everyone has a deep, unitary "self" that is relatively stable and unchanging. Second, West assumes that this "self" differs significantly between men and women but is the same for all women and for all men despite difference of class, race, and sexual orientation: that is, that this self is deeply and primarily gendered. . . . [T]he notion that the gender difference is primary to an individual's selfhood is one that privileges white women's experience over the experience of black women. . . .

A personal story may also help to illustrate the point. At a 1988 meeting of the West Coast "fem-crits," Pat Cain and Trina Grillo asked all the women present to pick out two or three words to describe who they were. None of the white women mentioned their race; all of the women of color did.

In this society, it is only white people who have the luxury of "having no color"; only white people have been able to imagine that sexism and racism are separate experiences. Far more for black women than for white women, the experience of self is precisely that of being unable to disentangle the web of race and gender—of being enmeshed always in multiple, often contradictory, discourses of sexuality and color. The challenge to black women has been the need to weave the fragments, our many selves, into an integral, though always changing and shifting, whole: a self that is neither "female" nor "black," but both-and. West's insistence that every self is deeply and primarily gendered, then, with its corollary that gender is more important to personal identity than race, is finally another example of white solipsism. By suggesting that gender is more deeply embedded in self than race, her theory privileges the experience of white people over all others, and thus serves to reproduce relations of domination in the larger culture. Like MacKinnon's essential woman, West's essential woman turns out to be white.

The Attractions of Gender Essentialism

. . . I want to briefly sketch some of the attractions of essentialism.

First, as a matter of intellectual convenience, essentialism is easy. Particularly for white feminists—and most of the people doing academic feminist theory in this country at this time are white—essentialism means not having to do as much work, not having to try and learn about the lives of black women, with all the risks and discomfort that that effort entails. Essentialism is also intellectually easy because the dominant culture is essentialist—because it is difficult to find materials on the lives of black women, because there is as yet no academic infrastructure of work by and/or about black women or black feminist theory.

Second, and more important, essentialism represents emotional safety. Especially for women who have relinquished privilege or had it taken away from them in their struggle against gender oppression, the feminist movement comes to be an emotional and spiritual home, a place to feel safe, a place that must be kept harmonious and free of difference. . . .

Third, feminist essentialism offers women not only intellectual and emotional comfort, but the opportunity to play all-too-familiar power games both among themselves and with men. Feminist essentialism provides multiple arenas for power struggle which cross-cut one another in complex ways. The gameswomanship is palpable at any reasonably diverse gathering of feminists with a political agenda. The participants are busy constructing hierarchies of oppression, using their own suffering (and consequent innocence) to win the right to define "women's experience." . . . Eventually, as the group seems ready to splinter into mutually suspicious and self-righteous factions, someone reminds the group that after all, women are women and we are all oppressed by men, and solidarity reappears through the threat of a common enemy. . . .

Finally, as Martha Minow has pointed out, "Cognitively, we need simplifying categories, and the unifying category of 'woman' helps to organize experience, even at the cost of denying some of it."[20] . . .

Beyond Essentialism: Black Women and Feminist Theory . . .

The Abandonment of Innocence

Black women experience not a single inner self (much less one that is essentially gendered), but many selves. This sense of a multiplicitous self is not unique to black women, but black women have expressed this sense in ways that are striking, poignant, and potentially useful to feminist theory. . . .

. . . [B]lack women can bring to feminist theory stories of how it is to have multiple and contradictory selves, selves that contain the oppressor as well as the oppressed.

Strategic Identities and "Difference"

A post-essentialist feminism can benefit not only from the abandonment of the quest for a unitary self, but also from Martha Minow's realization that difference—and therefore identity—is always relational, not inherent. Zora Neale Hurston's work is a good illustration of this notion.

In an essay written for a white audience, "How It Feels to Be Colored Me,"[21] Hurston argues that her color is not an inherent part of her being, but a response to her surroundings. . . .

To be compatible with this conception of the self, feminist theorizing about "women" must similarly be strategic and contingent, focusing on relationships, not essences. One result will be that men will cease to be a faceless Other and reappear as potential allies in political struggle. Another will be that women will be able to acknowledge their differences without threatening feminism itself. In the process, as feminists begin to attack racism and classism and homophobia, feminism will change from being only about "women as women" (modified women need not apply), to being about all kinds of oppression based on seemingly inherent and unalterable characteristics. We need not wait for a unified theory of oppression; that theory can be feminism.

Integrity as Will and Idea

. . . Finally, black women can help the feminist movement move beyond its fascination with essentialism through the recognition that wholeness of the self and commonality with others are asserted (if never completely achieved) through creative action, not realized in shared victimization. Feminist theory at present, especially feminist legal theory, tends to focus on women as passive victims. For example, for MacKinnon, women have been so objectified by men that the miracle is how they are able to exist at all. Women are the victims, the acted-upon, the helpless, until by radical enlightenment they are somehow empowered to act for themselves. Similarly, for West, the "fundamental fact" of women's lives is pain— "the violence, the danger, the boredom, the ennui, the non-productivity, the poverty, the fear, the numbness, the frigidity, the isolation, the low self-esteem, and the pathetic attempts to assimilate."[22]

This story of woman as victim is meant to encourage solidarity by emphasizing women's shared oppression, thus denying or minimizing difference, and to further the notion of an essential woman—she who is victimized. But . . . the notion that women's commonality lies in their shared victimization by men "directly reflects male supremacist thinking. Sexist ideology teaches women that to be female is to be a victim."[23] Moreover, the story of woman as passive victim denies the ability of women to shape their own lives, whether for better or worse. . . .

. . . [A]t another level, the recognition of the role of creativity and will in shaping our lives is liberating, for it allows us to acknowledge and celebrate the creativity and joy with which many women have survived and turned existing relations of domination to their own ends. Works of black literature like *Beloved*, *The Color Purple*, and *Song of Solomon*, among others, do not linger on black women's victimization and misery; though they recognize our pain, they ultimately celebrate our transcendence.

Finally, on a collective level this emphasis on will and creativity reminds us that bridges between women are built, not found. The discovery of shared suffering is a connection more illusory than real; what will truly bring and keep us together is the use of effort and imagination to root out and examine our differences, for only the recognition of women's differences can ultimately bring the feminist movement to strength. . . .

Epilogue: Multiple Consciousness

. . . In order to energize legal theory, we need to subvert it with narratives and stories, accounts of the particular, the different, and the hitherto silenced.

Whether by chance or not, many of the legal theorists telling stories these days are women of color. Mari Matsuda calls for "multiple consciousness as jurisprudential method";[24] Patricia Williams shows the way with her multilayered stories and meditations.[25] These writings are healthy for feminist legal theory as well as legal theory more generally. In acknowledging "the complexity of messages implied in our being,"[26] they begin the task of energizing legal theory with the . . . creative struggle that reflects a multiple consciousness.

Notes

1. For example, in 1851, Sojourner Truth told the audience at the woman's rights convention in Akron, Ohio: "That man over there says women need to be helped into carriages, and lifted over ditches, and to have the best place everywhere. Nobody ever helps me into carriages, or over mud-puddles, or gives me any best place! And ain't I a woman? Look at me! Look at my arm! I have ploughed, and planted, and gathered into barns, and no man could head me! And ain't I a woman? I could work as much and eat as much as a man—when I could get it—and bear the lash as well! And ain't I a woman? I have borne thirteen children, and seen them most all sold off to slavery, and when I cried out with my mother's grief, none but Jesus heard me! And ain't I a woman?" Address by Sojourner Truth (1851), reprinted in B. Loewenberg & R. Bogin eds., Black Women in Nineteenth-Century American Life: Their Words, Their Thoughts, Their Feelings 234, 235 (Pennsylvania State University Press, 1976).

2. . . . I use "black" rather than "Black" because it is my contention in this essay that race and gender issues are inextricably intertwined, and to capitalize "Black" and not "Woman" would imply a privileging of race with which I do not agree.

3. Adrienne Rich defines white solipsism as the tendency to "think, imagine, and speak as if whiteness described the world." A. Rich, Disloyal to Civilization: Feminism, Racism, Gynephobia, in On Lies, Secrets, and Silence 275, 299 (Norton, 1979).

4. Elizabeth Spelman lists five propositions which I consider to be associated with gender essentialism:

1. Women can be talked about "as women."
2. Women are oppressed "as women."
3. Gender can be isolated from other elements of identity that bear on one's social, economic, and political position such as race, class, ethnicity; hence sexism can be isolated from racism, classism, etc.
4. Women's situation can be contrasted to men's.
5. Relations between men and women can be compared to relations between other oppressor/oppressed groups (whites and Blacks, Christians and Jews, rich and poor, etc.), and hence it is possible to compare the situation of women to the situation of Blacks, Jews, the poor, etc.

E. Spelman, Inessential Woman: Problems of Exclusion in Feminist Thought 165 (Beacon, 1988).

5. C. MacKinnon, Desire and Power, in Feminism Unmodified 46, 49 (Harvard University Press, 1987).

6. See Wriggins, Rape, Racism, and the Law, 6 Harv. Women's L.J. 103, 118 (1983).

7. H. Carby, "On the Threshold of Woman's Era": Lynching, Empire and Sexuality in Black Feminist Theory, in H. Gates, Jr. ed., "Race," Writing, and Difference 301, 309 (University of Chicago Press, 1986).

8. S. Estrich, Real Rape 107 n. 2 (Harvard University Press, 1987).

9. Wriggins, Rape, Racism, and the Law, *supra* note 6, at 121 n. 113. According to the study, "the average sentence received by Black men, exclusive of cases involving life imprisonment or death, was 4.2 years if the victim was Black, 16.4 years if the victim was white." *Id.* I do not know whether a white man has ever been sentenced to death for the rape of a black woman, although I could make an educated guess as to the answer.

10. A. Davis, Women, Race and Class 174 (Random House, 1981).

11. B. Omolade, Black Women and Feminism, in H. Eisenstein & A. Jardine eds., The Future of Difference 247, 248 (Rutgers University Press, 1985).

12. West, The Difference in Women's Hedonic Lives: A Phenomenological Critique of Feminist Legal Theory, 3 Wis. Women's L.J. 81 (1987).

13. *Id.* at 141.

14. West, Jurisprudence and Gender, Part I this volume.

15. *Id.* at 75.

16. [Idea expressed *id.* at 78–81, exact citation omitted. *Ed.*]

17. *Id.* at 75.

18. The danger of such a theory is that, like some French feminist scholarship, it threatens to reembrace the old belief, used against women for so long, that anatomy is destiny: "A good deal of French feminist scholarship has been concerned with specifying the nature of the feminine. . . . This principle of femininity is sought in the female body, sometimes understood as the pre-oedipal mother and other times understood naturalistically as a pantheistic principle that requires its own kind of language for expression. In these cases, gender is not constituted, but is considered an essential aspect of bodily life, and we come very near the equation of biology and destiny, that conflation of fact and value, which Beauvoir spent her life trying to refute." J. Butler, Variations on Sex and Gender: Beauvoir, Wittig and Foucault, in S. Benhabib & D. Cornell eds., Feminism as Critique: Essays on the Politics of Gender 128, 140 (University of Minnesota Press, 1987). Curiously, MacKinnon's dominance theory, which claims to be "total," says very little about motherhood at all. See Littleton, Feminist Jurisprudence: The Difference Method Makes (Book Review), 41 Stan. L. Rev. 751, 762 n. 54. (1989).

19. I have taken this analysis from Nancy Fraser and Linda Nicholson's analysis of Nancy Chodorow's work. N. Fraser & L. Nicholson, Social Criticism without Philosophy: An Encounter between Feminism and Postmodernism, in A. Ross ed., Universal Abandon? The Politics of Postmodernism 83, 96 (University of Minnesota Press, 1988). See generally, N. Chodorow, The Reproduction of Mothering: Psychoanalysis and the Sociology of Gender (University of California Press, 1978).

20. Minow, Feminist Reason: Getting It and Losing It, Part 4 herein, at 341. . . .

21. Z. N. Hurston, How It Feels to Be Colored Me, in A. Walker, ed., I Love Myself When I am Laughing . . . And Then Again When I Am Looking Mean and Impressive 152 (Feminist Press, 1979).

22. West, Difference in Women's Hedonic Lives, *supra* note 12, at 143.

23. b. hooks, Feminist Theory: From Margin to Center 45 (South End Press, 1984).

24. Matsuda, When the First Quail Calls: Multiple Consciousness as Jurisprudential Method, 11 Women's Rts. L. Rep. 7 (1989).

25. See, e.g., Williams, Alchemical Notes: Reconstructing Ideals from Deconstructed Rights, Part 5 this volume; Williams, On Being the Object of Property, Part 6 this volume.

26. Williams, Property, Part 6 this volume.

❖ *Feminist Jurisprudence: Grounding the Theories*

PATRICIA A. CAIN

To BE CLASSIFIED as feminist, legal scholarship should be based on women's experience. My particular concern is whether the "women's experience" that informs feminist legal theory excludes lesbian experience. I will briefly discuss what I consider to be the three stages of feminist legal scholarship[1] and will review what impact, if any, lesbian experience has had on the development of each of these stages.

Feminist Legal Scholarship

Stage One: Formal Equality and Reproductive Rights

The period from 1963 to 1966 is generally cited as the beginning of the modern day women's movement, sometimes described as the second wave of feminism. A number of important events occurred during this period. Betty Friedan's book *The Feminine Mystique* was published in 1963. The same year, the Equal Pay Act was enacted. In 1964, Title VII was enacted, prohibiting sex discrimination in employment. Both statutes exhibit a commitment to the principle of equal opportunity. However, early evidence indicated that the Equal Employment Opportunity Commission was less than fully committed to the principle as applied to women. . . . In response, a new national women's activist group was formed in 1966, the National Organization for Women (NOW).

In the beginning, NOW's agenda focused on formal equality in the public arena. The organization avoided issues concerning sexual and reproductive freedom. Some members became concerned when NOW began to consider supporting abortion rights. They split off and formed the Women's Equity Action League (WEAL). NOW adopted a pro-abortion stance shortly thereafter. However, its

---

leaders found the issue of lesbianism to be more problematic.[2] Lesbian feminists who "came out" in the early days of the movement were "disinherited" by their sisters.[3] In the mainstream of the movement, the word "lesbian" was shunned.[4]

In the late 1960s, as the modern women's movement rallied together and began to litigate for women's equality, fewer than 5 percent of all lawyers were women and fewer than 2 percent of all law professors were women. Feminist legal scholarship during this period, to the extent it existed at all, reflected the goals of the concurrent women's movement. Such scholarship tended to focus on equality in the public sphere and to argue that women should be treated the same as men.

Feminists who were concerned with reproductive freedom necessarily had to deal with the ways in which women were different from men. However, much early feminist legal scholarship was written from a viewpoint that implicitly approved the male norm. Specific concern for lesbian issues is missing from this scholarship. To the extent lesbians are no different from heterosexual women, they were, of course, silently included in the fight for equality.[5] But the differences between the experience of lesbians and heterosexual women were irrelevant in the fashioning of feminist legal theory during Stage One.

Stage Two: Women Are Different from Men

Once women began to be treated like men, people began to notice that women really are not like men. Women are most noticeably not like men when they are pregnant. Stage Two theorists began to develop theories of equality that could account for certain differences between women and men. At a minimum, they argued, equality theory should account for the fact that women get pregnant. Lesbians are as biologically different from men as heterosexual women are.[6] Thus, while the focus on difference remained limited to biological differences between women and men, lesbian experience had no special insights to offer.

Some theorists in Stage Two have suggested that women are different from men in ways that go beyond biology. Some cultural feminists, for example, have claimed that the experience of mothering results in social and psychological gender differences. Women, because they give birth and nurture, tend to be more connected and caring than men.

Following the lead of Carol Gilligan, some feminist legal theorists began to focus on ways that women's "different voice" has been ignored by the law. They pointed out that, because the law is masculine, it reflects values of autonomy rather than connection and caring. Then they argued that the law should recognize and protect specifically female values.

Catharine MacKinnon, another Stage Two legal theorist,[7] also has argued that men and women are different, but the difference is that men dominate and women are subordinate. Which came first, dominance or difference, is an unimportant question, in her view. The important thing is to end the dominance. Legal arguments that pose the issue as one of difference between the sexes are not likely to end the dominance. MacKinnon calls for a paradigm shift, away from differences in biology, differences in experience, differences in essence, to the only difference that really matters: the difference in power. Her "inequality" approach to sex discrimination recognizes the imbalance in power between men and women. "Practices which express and reinforce the social inequality of women to men are clear cases of sex-based discrimination. . . . "[8] Sexual harassment is one such practice.

One might expect cultural feminists and dominance theorists who engage in legal scholarship (such as Gilligan and MacKinnon, respectively) to acknowledge the relevance of lesbian experience in their writings. It is particularly surprising to discover the invisible lesbian problem in the work of cultural feminists. In disciplines other than law, feminist theorists working to reclaim women's culture and its values have often focused on lesbian community.[9] But in legal scholarship, discussions of female value focus on "woman as mother."[10]

Robin West's article "Jurisprudence and Gender" is a prime example of the problem. West posits the current (masculine) jurisprudence is based on the concept of human beings as separate from each other and that this "separation thesis" forms the core of both liberal and critical male legal theories. Feminist theory, in contrast, views human beings as primarily connected to one another. Both cultural and radical feminists use this "connection thesis." West begins her article with four examples of women's primary and material experience with connection: (1) pregnancy; (2) heterosexual penetration; (3) menstruation; and (4) breastfeeding. Despite West's awareness of the pressure on all women to be heterosexual, her list of "connection" experiences ignores specifically lesbian experiences of "connection."

Furthermore, West's two categories of feminist thought, cultural and radical, are constructed in such a way as to exclude lesbian feminists. West defines cultural feminists as those who focus on the mother–child connection as the source of women's greater capacity for caring and nurturance. Professor West does not necessarily align herself with these cultural feminists. But I worry that in creating her two categories of feminists (cultural feminists and radical/dominance feminists), she ignores those lesbian feminists who are attempting to develop women's community (connections to other women)[11] and to reclaim feminist value as encompassing both separation and connection.[12]

Dominance theorists also tend to ignore lesbian experience. Catharine MacKinnon, for example, has argued that women are constantly and always subordinated to men. In MacKinnon's view, any special abilities for caring and connection come, not from the positive aspects of motherhood, but from the negative aspects of subordination. Women build webs of connection to survive the subordination. "Women value care because men have valued us according to the care we give them. . . . "[13]

To the claim that lesbian experience is different, that lesbians are not subordinate to men, that their care is not male-directed, MacKinnon appears to have two different responses. Her first response is that exceptions do not matter. MacKinnon's intent is to offer a critique of the structural condition of women as sexual subordinates and not to make existential claims about all women. It does not affect her theory that all women are not always subordinated to men. Thus, for MacKinnon, lesbian experience of non-subordination is simply irrelevant; it denies the claim that lesbian experience is free from male domination.

> Some have argued that lesbian sexuality—meaning here simply women having sex with women, not with men—solves the problem of gender by eliminating men from women's voluntary sexual encounters. Yet women's sexuality remains constructed under conditions of male supremacy; women remain socially defined as women in relation to men; the definition of women as men's inferiors remains sexual even if not heterosexual, whether men are present at the time or not.[14]

I find this passage objectionable for several reasons. My primary objection is that MacKinnon has defined lesbian sexuality to suit her purposes ("simply women having sex with women"—i.e., with nothing else changed except that a woman replaces a man). Although I do not dispute that lesbian couples can sometimes ape their heterosexual counterparts, I am infuriated by MacKinnon's silencing of the rest of lesbian experience. Where is MacKinnon's feminist method? To whom does she choose to listen? Would it not enrich her theory to recognize the reality of non-subordination that some lesbians claim as their experiential reality and ask about its relevance to her underlying theory?[15] And yet, because her theory is premised on a single commonality among women, sexual subordination, MacKinnon fails to see the relevance of the lesbian claim to non-domination, even when it stands—literally—in front of her.[16]

The exclusion of lesbian experience from feminist legal theory is also documented in Clare Dalton's recent summary of feminist legal thought.[17] Dalton describes present aspirations to feminist jurisprudence as falling within two camps: "woman as mother" theories and "woman as sexual subordinate" theories. Neither camp embraces lesbian experience as central to the formation of theory. I suspect Professor Dalton's description is accurate. I can find no major "theory piece" by a legal scholar that focuses on the experience of adult women loving each other as the core experience for building a legal theory premised on caring and connection. And although "woman as sexual subordinate" theorists are more likely to acknowledge the fact of lesbian existence, they focus on a critique of male dominance rather than on lesbian bonding as a positive alternative to male dominance.

Stage Three: Postmodernism

Borrowing from Clare Dalton, I call the third stage of feminist legal theory "postmodernism." Postmodern thought challenges notions such as objectivity and universality. The postmodern "knowing self" is subjective, concrete and particular, constructed through the lived experiences of the subject.

Postmodern feminism is generally associated with French feminists, such as Hélène Cixous, Luce Irigaray, and Julia Kristeva. The influence of Simone de Beauvoir's work on these theorists is evident. Beauvoir's existential analysis of woman as "other" is conceived by postmodern feminists as enabling women to critique the dominant culture. Being "other" allows women to understand "plurality, diversity, and difference."

From a postmodern perspective, feminist theory is inadequate when limited by the perception that there is one essential commonality among all women. Cultural feminists who focus on "woman" solely as "mother" (actual or cultural) do not speak to the full complexity of female experience. Radical feminists, such as MacKinnon, who focus on "woman" solely as "sexual subordinate" also speak limited truths. Good feminist theory ought to reflect the real differences in women's realities, in our lived experiences. These include differences of race, class, age, physical ability, and sexual preference.

Postmodern legal theorists will want to reject the limitations caused by any categorization. Although they will want to listen to the reality of lesbian experience, these theorists will not be inclined to build a grand theory based on the concept of "woman" as "lesbian." In the final part of this essay, I offer some thoughts about the potential relevance of lesbian experience to the postmodern development of feminist legal theory.

The Retelling

I believe that current feminist legal theory is deficient and impoverished because it has not paid sufficient attention to the real life experiences of women who do not speak the "dominant discourse." Elsewhere I have urged that feminist law teaching ought to include "listening to difference" and "making connections."[18] Here I urge the same for feminist legal scholarship.

Most feminist legal theorists, by focusing on sameness and difference, have fallen into either the assimilationist trap (all women are the same as men/all women are the same) or the essentialist trap (all women are different from men in one essential way/all women are different, but what counts is their essential commonality). The only difference between assimilationists and essentialists is that the former ignore the reality of differences whereas the latter say that differences generally do not matter. The two concepts, assimilationism and essentialism, collapse into each other to the extent they treat women as a single class that is essentially the same.

Elizabeth Spelman describes the essentialist's solution to the "differences" problem in feminist theory: "The way to give proper significance to differences among women is to say that such differences simply are less significant than what women have in common. This solution is very neat, for it acknowledges differences among women only enough to bury them."[19] The difficulty arises when an individual essentialist theorist must determine the content of this commonality which is so significant that it trumps differences. When white, straight, economically privileged feminists name the commonality, and ignore differences, the result may be that all women are assimilated into a single class of white, straight, middle-class women.

It is not enough to name the differences of race, class, and sexuality. The differences need to be understood. Much recent feminist legal scholarship includes the perfunctory footnote, dropped the first time the essential category "woman" is mentioned, which acknowledges the differences of race and class, and sometimes of sexual preference. Such politically correct footnotes name the differences, but I see no evidence in the accompanying texts that the differences matter. Scholarship that nominally recognizes differences, but still categorizes "woman" from a single perspective is stuck in the assimilationist/essentialist trap.

I do not mean to ignore the importance of our commonalities. It is valuable to identify the similarities among all women. When we identify what we have in common, we begin to build bridges and connections. Yet if we ignore the differences, we risk distorting those connections, because any connection that fails to recognize differences is not a connection to the *whole* of the other self. A normative principle that honors only what I have in common with each of you fails to respect each of you for the individual woman that you are. To respect you, despite your difference, is an insult. Such respect is not respect for your difference, but only for our sameness. Such respect belittles your difference and says it does not matter. Such "respect" falls into the assimilationist/essentialist trap.

Let me give you an example. A white law professor says to her Black female colleague: "Sometimes I forget that you are Black. Sometimes I think of you as white."[20] The comment is meant as a compliment, but it denies the real life experience of the Black woman to whom it is addressed. It says, ultimately, "what I respect in you is only what you have in common with me."

Now let me give you an example out of lesbian experience. A lesbian college teacher proposes a course entitled "The Outsider in Twentieth-Century American Literature." The course is to include writings of lesbians and gay men, as well as other outsiders, such as persons who have been in mental institutions or prisons. In discussing the potential course, the teacher's (presumably) heterosexual colleagues dismiss the notion that an author's sexuality might be an important aspect of her or his writing, claiming that sexuality is no different from "a thousand other things" that might influence the writer.[21] None of the teacher's colleagues considers "having to live as a 'different' person in a heterosexist culture"[22] as a factor important to one's writing.

Adrienne Rich, a lesbian poet, echoes the same theme in the following story:

Two friends of mine, both artists, wrote me about reading the "Twenty-One Love Poems" with their male lovers, assuring me how "universal" the poems were. I found myself angered, and when I asked myself why, I realized that it was anger at having my work essentially assimilated and stripped of its meaning, "integrated" into heterosexual romance. That kind of "acceptance" of the book seems to me a refusal of its deepest implications. The longing to simplify . . . to assimilate lesbian experience by saying that "relationship" is really all the same, love is always difficult—I see that as a denial, a kind of resistance, a refusal to read and hear what I've actually written, to acknowledge what I am.[23]

There is a commonality between Adrienne Rich and her heterosexual artist friends. They all experience love and relationship. Yet even if some portion of the love experience is universal, the heterosexual world will never understand the gay and lesbian world if we all focus on the commonality, the universal. To claim that lesbians are the same as heterosexual women or that Black women are the same as white women is to fall into the assimilationist/essentialist trap. Such claims deny the reality of our differences among us as women. We must also understand those differences.

I ask those of you . . . who are heterosexual to focus on an important love relationship in your life. This could be a present relationship or a past one, or even the relationship you hope to have. I ask you: how would you feel about this relationship if it had to be kept utterly secret? Would you feel "at one with the world" if a slight mistake in language ("we" instead of "I") could lead to alienation from your friends and family, loss of your job? Would you feel at one with your lover if the only time you could touch or look into each other's eyes was in your own home—with the curtains drawn? What would such self-consciousness do to your relationship?

I use the following exercise [in a feminist legal theory class, *Ed.*] to demonstrate to my students our different points of view. First I ask each student to write down three self-descriptive nouns or adjectives, to name three aspects of her (or his) personal self. When they have finished writing, we go around the room and each student reads the three choices aloud. For my women students, the list almost always includes either the word woman or female. Thus, we share a perception of self as female. The meaning of female may vary, but it is significant that we all view the fact that we are women as one of the three most important facts about ourselves.

As to the rest of the list, there are important differences. For example, no white woman ever mentions race, whereas every woman of color does. Similarly, straight women do not include "heterosexual" as one of the adjectives on their list, whereas lesbians, who are open, always include "lesbian" as one of the words on their lists. The point is, not only are we different from each other in such obvious ways as race and sexuality, but we perceive our differences differently.

The results of my exercise are not surprising. Because of the pervasive influences of sexism, racism, and heterosexism, white, heterosexual women think of gender as something that sets them apart, as something that defines them, whereas neither race nor sexuality seems to matter as much. Yet if neither race nor sexuality matters much to a white, heterosexual woman, how can she begin to understand the ways in which it matters to others who are different from her in these dimensions?

I wonder sometimes whether heterosexual women really understand the role that heterosexuality plays in the maintenance of patriarchy. Indeed, I sometimes wonder whether lesbians really understand. And yet, if feminist legal theory is to provide meaningful guidance for the abolition of patriarchy, feminist theorists must understand heterosexuality as an institution and not merely as the dominant form of sexuality.

Adrienne Rich illuminated the problem years ago in her brilliant critique of heterosexuality:

> [I]t is not enough for feminist thought that specifically lesbian texts exist. Any theory or cultural/political creation that treats lesbian existence as a marginal or less "natural" phenomenon, as mere "sexual preference," or as the mirror image of either heterosexual or male homosexual relations, is profoundly weakened thereby. . . .
>
> . . . Feminist research and theory that contributes to lesbian invisibility or marginality is actually working against the liberation and empowerment of women as a group.[24]

Adrienne Rich encourages us to look at heterosexuality from a new perspective, from the perspective of the "lesbian possibility." The invisibility of lesbian existence, however, removes the lesbian possibility from view. . . .

Connections

The most consistent feminist claim, at least since the publication of Simone de Beauvoir's *The Second Sex*, is that knowledge of reality has been constructed from a male-centered standpoint. From their position as outsider, women have questioned that reality, because women's life experiences differ—often dramatically—from those of men. The most cohesive and challenging critiques of male-centered reality have been made by women from standpoints that are exactly opposite, experientially, from those of men. One such critique is made by cultural feminists from the "woman as mother" standpoint. Another is made by other radical feminists from the "woman as sexual subordinate" standpoint.

The fact that so many women can identify common life experiences that are ignored by the male version of reality makes any critique based on such common experiences compelling and powerful. But theorists ought to resist transforming a critical standpoint into a new all-encompassing version of reality. Indeed, my fear is that what started as a useful critique of one privileged (male) view of reality may become a substitute claim for a different privileged (female) view of reality.

Catharine MacKinnon, for example, critiques the patriarchy from a "woman as sexual subordinate" standpoint. As compelling as her critique is, it should not be viewed as the one and only existential reality for women. And yet MacKinnon herself is so committed to this standpoint that she sometimes seems to claim it as the only reality for women.

MacKinnon's theory is that woman's subordination is universal and constant, but not necessarily inevitable. She cautions against building theory on the basis of Carol Gilligan's discovery of woman's "different voice" because the women Gilligan listened to were all victims of the patriarchy. Thus, MacKinnon is wary of assigning value to their moral voice. As she explains,

> [b]y establishing that women reason differently from men on moral ques-
> tions, [Gilligan] revalues that which has accurately distinguished women
> from men by making it seem as though women's moral reasoning is some-
> how women's, rather than what male supremacy has attributed to women
> for its own use. When difference means dominance as it does with gender,
> for women to affirm differences is to affirm the qualities and characteris-
> tics of powerlessness. . . . To the extent materialism means anything at all,
> it means that what women have been and thought is what they have been
> permitted to be and think. Whatever this is, it is not women's, possessive.[25]

. . . [Lesbian] reality is not irrelevant to feminist theory. . . . [L]esbians who live our private lives removed from the intimate presence of men do indeed experience time free from male domination. When we leave the male-dominated public sphere, we come home to a woman-identified private sphere. That does not mean that *the patriarchy* as an institution does not exist for us or that the patriarchy does not exist during the time that we experience freedom from male domination. It means simply that we experience significant periods of nonsubordination, during which we, as women, are free to develop a sense of self that is our own and not a mere construct of the patriarchy.

Nor do we work at this experience of nonsubordination and creation of authentic self to set ourselves apart from other women. We are not asserting a "proud disidentification from the rest of [our] sex and proud denial of the rest of [our] life."[26] The struggle is to make nonsubordination a reality for all women, and the reality of nonsubordination in some women's lives is relevant to this struggle. The reality of nonsubordination in lesbian lives offers the "lesbian possibility" as a solution.

At the same time, I believe MacKinnon's claim that all women are subordinate to men all the time is a fair claim upon which to critique the male version of reality, because subordination is such a pervasive experience for women. Her claim gives her a valid standpoint for her critique even though it is not experientially true for all women. Similarly, I believe Robin West's claim that all women are "connected" to life is a fair claim upon which to critique the male version of the "separation thesis." But I do not believe that the "connection thesis" is true of all women. Feminist legal theorists must be careful not to confuse "standpoint critiques" with existential reality. And the theorist who has not confused the two must also be careful to prevent her readers from making the confusion.

The problem with current feminist theory is that the more abstract and universal it is, the more it fails to relate to the lived reality of many women. One problem with much feminist legal theory is that it has abstracted and universalized from the experience of heterosexual women. . . .

Why is the lesbian so invisible in feminist legal theory?

Notes

1. These three stages track Clare Dalton's discussion of the development of feminist legal thought in Dalton, Where We Stand: Observations on the Situation of Feminist Legal Thought, Part 1 this volume.

2. B. Friedan, It Changed My Life: Writings on the Women's Movement 159 (Norton, 1976). (At a 1970 national feminist demonstration at which participants were asked to wear lavender lesbian armbands as a symbol of solidarity, Friedan refused. "For me . . . the women's movement . . . had nothing whatsoever to do with lesbianism.")

3. S. Evans, Born for Liberty 294 (Free Press, 1989). See generally N. Myron & C. Bunch eds., Lesbianism and the Women's Movement (Diana Press, 1975).

4. NOW was the organization at the center of the women's movement and although its membership included many active lesbians, the organization itself consciously avoided lesbian issues in the early days. Such homophobic attitudes appear to have been worse on the East Coast than on the West Coast. See D. Martin & P. Lyon, Lesbian Woman 256–76 (Bantam, 1972).

5. Lesbians differed from heterosexual women in one very noticeable respect, however. Lesbians were denied custody of their children because they were deemed unfit mothers. Thus, there is some early separate lesbian-feminist scholarship on custody. See, e.g., Hunter & Polikoff, Custody Rights of Lesbians, 25 Buffalo L. Rev. 691 (1976); Hitchens & Price, Trial Strategy in Lesbian Mother Custody Cases: The Use of Expert Testimony, 9 Golden Gate U.L. Rev. 451 (1978–79).

6. The risk of pregnancy is lower for lesbians, of course. . . . . Thus, accommodation for pregnancy, although relevant for some lesbians, has never been at the top of the lesbian agenda.

7. I include in "Stage Two" all theorists who reject the liberal feminist approach of "Stage One," but do not (yet) embrace postmodernism. (See discussion of Stage Three *infra*.) Because I do embrace postmodernism to the extent it eschews essentialism, universality, and the limits of categorization, I am wary of the categorization I create by placing theorists into what appears to be separate stages of feminist scholarship. I ask the reader to imagine the boundaries as more fluid than my brief identification of the categories/stages suggests.

8. C. MacKinnon, Sexual Harassment of Working Women 174 (Yale University Press, 1979).

9. See generally A. Jaggar, Feminist Politics and Human Nature 249–302 (Rowman & Allanheld, 1983), and sources cited therein. In the field of philosophy, there are works that build ethical theory on women's bonding to other

women. See, e.g., J. Raymond, A Passion for Friends: Toward a Philosophy of Female Affection (Beacon, 1986); S. Hoagland, Lesbian Ethics: Toward New Value (Institute of Lesbian Studies, 1988).

10. Here, I mean mother in the broad social sense as a person who is nurturing and self-sacrificing.

11. See, e.g., M. Daly, Pure Lust: Elemental Feminist Philosophy (Beacon, 1984); M. Daly, Gyn/Ecology: The Metaethics of Radical Feminism (Beacon, 1978).

12. See, e.g., Hoagland, Lesbian Ethics, *supra* note 9.

13. C. MacKinnon, Feminism Unmodified 39 (Harvard University Press, 1987).

14. C. MacKinnon, Toward a Feminist Theory of the State 141–42 (Harvard University Press, 1989).

15. For example, the image of the lesbian in the dominant culture is that of a masculine, often predatory, character, the "butch" of the butch–femme lesbian couple. MacKinnon's references to lesbians often reinforce this stereotype. See, e.g., MacKinnon, Feminist Theory of the State, *supra* note 14, at 119 (lesbian sex does not necessarily transcend the "erotization of dominance and submission"); MacKinnon, Sexual Harassment, *supra* note 8, at 206 (positing a lesbian harasser). I believe MacKinnon does herself (as well as lesbians) a disservice by not acknowledging the reality of co-equal relationships that many lesbians experience. Indeed, the extreme dissonance between traditional male-created concepts of lesbian existence and the reality of much lesbian existence tells us that the patriarchy has constructed lesbianism in a way that supports its norm of enforced heterosexuality. Although MacKinnon recognizes this patriarchal response to lesbianism ("[l]esbians can so violate the sexuality implicit in female gender stereotypes as not to be considered women at all," *id.* at 110), she never reveals an understanding of lesbian existence different from the patriarchal image of the "butch."

16. I mean this statement literally. Mary Dunlap, a lesbian lawyer, was on a panel at the Buffalo Law School with MacKinnon (and others), entitled, "Feminist Discourse, Moral Values and the Law." Responding to MacKinnon's view of "woman," silenced by "man's" foot on her throat, Dunlap rose and said: "I am a woman standing . . . [and] I am not subordinate to any man." MacKinnon failed to acknowledge the potential relevance of Dunlap's life experience as a lesbian to her claim of non-subordination. . . ; see also MacKinnon, Feminism Unmodified, *supra* note 13, at 221, 305–06 n. 6.

17. Dalton, Where We Stand, Part 1 this volume.

18. Cain, Teaching Feminist Legal Theory at Texas: Listening to Difference and Exploring Connections, 38 J. of Legal Educ. 165 (1988). . . .

19. Spelman recognizes the limitations of this solution, concluding, "But it doesn't bury them very effectively." E. Spelman, Inessential Woman: Problems of Exclusion in Feminist Thought 3 (Beacon, 1988).

20. This story comes most recently from Pat Williams, although I have heard it from other persons of color. Remarks by Pat Williams, Critical Legal Studies Conference on Feminism, Pine Manor, Massachusetts (June 1985). I also have white friends who have made similar observations to me about persons of color.

Fran Olsen tells me that in 1960 at a Quaker peace camp, they sang the following song:

> Oh, there'll be no distinction there;
> No, there'll be no distinction there.
> We'll all be white

> In that heavenly light;
> There'll be no distinction there.

Letter from Frances Olsen to Patricia Cain (July 19, 1989).

21. Bulkin, "Kissing/Against the Light": A Look at Lesbian Poetry, in M. Cruikshank ed., Lesbian Studies: Present and Future 40–41 (Feminist Press, 1982).

22. *Id.* (quoting Adrienne Rich).

23. An Interview with Adrienne Rich, quoted in Bulkin, "Kissing/Against the Light," *supra* note 21, at 44–45.

24. Rich, Compulsory Heterosexuality and Lesbian Existence, 5 Signs 631, 632, 647–48 (1980).

25. MacKinnon, Feminist Theory of State, *supra* note 14, at 51.

26. MacKinnon, Feminism Unmodified, *supra* note 13, at 305–06 n. 6.

❖ Race, Racism, and Feminist Legal Theory

MARLEE KLINE

. . . I HAVE TWO major purposes in this essay: first, to draw attention to the diversity of women's experiences of oppression based on gender and race as well as to the implications of this diversity for feminist legal theorizing, and, second, to consider how contemporary feminist legal scholarship is limited by inadequate considerations of race and racism. . . .

. . . Specifically, I will analyze the integrative feminist review of Canadian criminal law by Christine Boyle, Marie-Andree Bertrand, Celine Lacerte-Lamontagne, and Rebecca Shamai; the socialist feminist work of Susan Boyd on child custody law; and the radical feminist work of Catharine MacKinnon. I have chosen these works because of the significance of their contributions to the development of the feminist analysis of law. . . .

These works illustrate three interrelated tendencies in contemporary white feminist legal scholarship: the tendency to overlook racial identity when considering the impact of an issue on women, the tendency to define issues in ways that more significantly address the experiences of white women than the experiences of women of color, and the tendency to oversimplify the sites of women's oppression. . . .

White feminist legal scholars often tend to overlook the racial identity of the women whose experiences we are examining, analyzing or discussing, with the result that the specific experiences of women of color are often rendered invisible in particular analyses. Overlooking racial identity also has the effect of appropriating the pain of specific groups by attributing the particular experiences of women of color to all women, thereby denying the disproportionate impact of an oppressive situation on women of color. The review written by Christine Boyle, Marie-Andree Bertrand, Celine Lacerte-Lamontagne, and Rebecca Shamai on the

---

feminist analysis of criminal law [hereinafter *A Feminist Review*] provides an example of both of these effects.[1]

In general, *A Feminist Review* addresses both the theoretical and practical problems that arise from applying to women a criminal law that has been devised by male legislators to control the anti-social acts committed predominantly by men. More specifically, the authors analyze a number of substantive areas of criminal law which they consider to be of particular interest to women. They discuss, among other things, extending the criminal law to protect women's interests and the constitutional implications of present criminal law and of proposals for reform, especially with regard to the guarantees of equality set out in the Canadian Charter of Rights and Freedoms. In addition, the authors analyze and make specific recommendations concerning substantive offenses significant to women as accused persons (e.g., abortion, infanticide, contempt, and prostitution-related offenses), defenses significant to women as accused persons, and offenses committed against women (e.g., pornography, hate propaganda, and sexual assault). Criminal procedure, evidence, and sentencing are also considered. Underlying their analysis is the fundamental question: "how can the criminal law be used as a weapon against patriarchy, and at the same time be reduced as a weapon of patriarchy?" . . .

The authors make a point of observing that the integrative feminist approach on which they primarily rely in *A Feminist Review* is premised on an understanding of the reality of contemporary women's lives. Throughout *A Feminist Review*, however, they speak of the experiences of women as though the reality of race and racism did not exist. There are only about four references to race in the whole report, and three of these are only general references to criminal law and not discussions of the different ways white women and women of color experience Canadian criminal law. The fourth reference, the only one that mentions the racial identity of the women caught within the criminal justice system, is brief and undeveloped. After noting that three American articles found racial discrimination in the sentencing of young female offenders, and acknowledging that these findings are similarly applicable to First Nations women in Canada, one of the authors observes that:

> Native women offenders are overrepresented in prison and there is a greater proportion of Native women offenders than Native male offenders. They serve long sentences and are not paroled before mandatory parole.[2]

There is no attempt to consider the deeper implications of such an observation for *A Feminist Review*, nor to theorize the interaction between race and gender discrimination in the context of the criminal law.

The absence of any serious attempt to integrate the distinct experiences of First Nations women into the analysis is troubling because of the particular vulnerability of First Nations women within the criminal justice system in Canada. As Carol LaPrairie has recently documented, throughout Canada the female population of provincial correction centers is disproportionately comprised of First Nations women.[3] . . . Furthermore, First Nations women are more likely than other women to be incarcerated for committing violent crimes and defaulting on payment of fines, and they are more often charged with alcohol-related offenses. Those First Nations women who are caught by the criminal process are often very young and many become repeat offenders.

These facts suggest that the experiences of First Nations women would have been directly relevant in *A Feminist Review*, at least in the sections where alcohol-related charges, the defenses of self-defense and provocation, and the impact of fines on women are considered. Examination of racial identity would also have been relevant in the section on judicial interim release. In that section, one author points out that in considering judicial interim release, one of the assessments made by the judge is the "badness" or "dangerousness" of the person, i.e., the threat posed by the person to society if released. In this context, society's perceptions about different women might come into play. Since race affects dominant perceptions of women's "badness" or "goodness," some examination should be made of how women of color are perceived by judges to determine whether there might be discrimination on the basis of societal perceptions.

. . . In her recent article, LaPrairie . . . hypothesizes specific reasons why First Nations women fall into the hands of the criminal justice system.

> First, Native women may retaliate in kind against physically abusive Native men. Secondly, Native women may escape from a violent or otherwise abusive situation at home and migrate to an urban area where discrimination by the larger society, combined with a usually low level of skills and education, may relegate them to the ranks of the unemployed or unemployable. That in turn increases the probability of resorting to alcohol or drug abuse, or to prostitution, all of which increase the probability of conflict with the law. Even without engaging in any of these activities, being in an urban area increases their exposure to police, some of whom may be biased in the way they exercise their discretionary judgment when deciding whether or not to arrest a Native person. Finally, having observed neglectful or abusive treatment of children among role models in her community, or having experienced such treatment herself, the Native woman may be predisposed to treating her children in like manner.[4]

The cycle of poverty, dispossession, alcohol, drugs, and violence that are part of the experiences of many First Nations women, and the consequences of disproportionate contact with the criminal justice system, must be essential parts of any analysis of women and the criminal justice system. . . . Ignoring this differential impact by focusing our analysis on women in general not only submerges the need for important social and legal reforms, but also effectively denies the particular experiences of pain in the lives of First Nations women. . . . It is, I believe, an example of the need for deeper sensitivity on the part of white feminist theorists. . . .

Susan Boyd's work on child custody law provides another example of the tendency of feminist legal scholars to overlook racial identity when considering the impact of a particular issue on women. Her work also illustrates the tendency of feminist legal scholars to focus on problems which more significantly address the experiences of white women than the experiences of women of color. Boyd focuses on the implications of child custody law for women in the context of intra-family custody disputes, with a view toward exploring the assumptions and ideologies that underlie the cases and legislation in this area.[5] Her work is informed by a socialist feminist perspective, and she argues for an "understanding of ideology that attends to the variety and complexity of various ideological discourses and the interplay between them."[6] This approach is particularly helpful in the context of custody law where Boyd demonstrates the oppressive effects on employed women of conflicting and contradictory ideologies concerning the family. She concentrates on contested custody cases between fathers and employed mothers and demonstrates how employed mothers may have difficulty gaining custody of their children because "they fail on the one hand to meet the traditional expectations of the ideology of motherhood, and on the other hand, fail to demonstrate to judges economic self-sufficiency comparable to their husbands as expected by the 'ideology of equality.'"[7]

Boyd's analysis enables us to understand some of the ways in which women are disadvantaged by the courts in child custody cases. However, her analysis is limited in two ways. First, because she overlooks the racial identity of the participants when considering the impact of child custody law on employed women, she fails to examine how distinguishing the impact on Black women from the impact on white women would complicate her analysis of the ideology of motherhood. Second, because she limits her analysis to intra-family child custody issues rather than undertaking a broader analysis of the many ways in which women lose custody of their children, she focuses on a problem that more significantly addresses the experiences of white women than the experiences of women of color. . . .

The ideologies of motherhood on which Boyd relies play out somewhat differently when applied to Black women. In fact, when Boyd refers to "the traditional expectations of stay-at-home motherhood," she is speaking only of the ideology of white motherhood. The traditional ideological division between motherhood and employment that has been applied to white women has not applied in the same way to Black women, who have traditionally been perceived simultaneously as workers and mothers. Ideologies of Black female domesticity and motherhood, then, have not been constructed in the same way as white ideologies of domesticity and motherhood. Under those ideologies, white women's roles are regarded as resting in the private sphere represented by the family. In contrast,

> [i]deologies of black female domesticity and motherhood have been constructed, through their employment (or chattel position) as domestics and surrogate mothers to white families rather than in relation to their own families.[8]

Thus, while the ideology of motherhood that Boyd describes has dictated that white women stay at home, Black women have been regarded as particularly suited for work outside the home, often in someone else's home. For example, West Indian women are encouraged to immigrate to Canada and Britain specifically to take positions as domestic workers, office cleaners, and the like. At the same time, however, the role of Black women as mothers to their own children often goes unrecognized and is sometimes actively ignored and discouraged. This is illustrated by the immigration laws and policies of Britain and Canada that make it very difficult and often impossible for women who enter the country alone in order to work to bring their children over later to join them. Thus, as compared with white women, Black women may be affected in more complex and contradictory ways by the ideological expectations concerning work and motherhood.

The differing ideologies of domesticity, work, and motherhood would likely affect the way that judges decide child custody cases for Black women and white women. While white women are expected to conform to an ideology of motherhood which dictates that mothers should not work outside their homes, Black mothers, who may be presumed from the outset to work, may then be "seen to fail as mothers precisely because of their position as workers."[9] Thus, incorporating the experiences of Black women into discussions of child custody decisions might necessitate a more complex consideration of the ideologies of motherhood and domesticity in Boyd's analysis.

Consideration of the experiences of First Nations women in Canada also complicates Boyd's framing of the custody issue. Boyd conceptualizes the custody issue for employed mothers in terms of private custody battles that arise on the breakdown of a marriage. A dominant concern of First Nations women with regard to child custody, however, is not with private custody battles between themselves and their husbands but with custody battles between themselves and the state. . . .

Examining the impact of child welfare laws and policies on First Nations women would not only extend Boyd's original custody framework; it would further complicate her ideological analysis as well. Expanding the analysis to include child welfare decisions necessitates expanding our concern from the ideology of motherhood to a more general consideration of the dominant ideology of childcare practices. The ideological insights of our analysis will become less specifically gender-oriented and more concerned with the conflict between dominant and subordinate cultures. . . . In other words, Boyd's conception of the ideology of motherhood, considered as the dominant ideology, might provide the backdrop against which to consider questions with respect to the traditional care of First Nations children by extended family members. Such a comparison between actual child-care practices among First Nations peoples and the expectations of the dominant ideology regarding child care practices might also help to explain why First Nations families have generally been considered unfit for fostering or adoption.

The above analysis exposes important gaps in Boyd's work with respect to the experiences of Black women and First Nations women in the context of separation from their children, whether as a result of intra-family custody disputes or coercive removal by the state. The more complex analysis suggested above, however, need not fundamentally challenge Boyd's theoretical premise that an analysis of ideology helps us to understand the impact of child custody law on women. On the contrary, Boyd's existing framework need only be extended in such a way as to include differing ideologies and their impact on Black women and First Nations women, as well as other women of color. . . .

Unlike the two examples already examined, Catharine MacKinnon, in her radical feminist work,[10] includes a number of discussions about the experiences of Black and First Nations women. She does not, however, sufficiently incorporate the perspectives and experiences of women of color into her general theoretical framework. There is a tension in her work between her acknowledgment that intersections between race, gender, and class must be accounted for and the premises and tenets of the theory she develops. While she recognizes the experiences of women of color and makes them visible in her work, she has not, as Carby suggests we must, allowed those experiences to "challenge the use of some of the *central categories* and *assumptions*"[11] of her theory. As a result, her work is illustrative of a tendency of feminist legal scholars to oversimplify the sites of women's oppression.[12]

MacKinnon considers the feminist project to be one of explaining male dominance. For MacKinnon, sexuality—"the gaze that constructs women as objects for male pleasure"[13]—is the "primary social sphere of male power,"[14] the "linchpin of gender inequality."[15] She regards the social differentiation of the sexes as grounded in the eroticization of gender inequality and believes that this division "underlies the totality of social relations"[16] Thus, for her, "feminism is a theory of how the erotization of dominance and submission creates gender, creates woman and man in the social form in which we know them."[17] In particular, MacKinnon identifies sexual objectification as "the primary process of the subjection of women."[18]

In her analysis, MacKinnon focuses on what she considers to be the collective experience of women. . . . MacKinnon recognizes the multiplicity of differences that exist among women: she acknowledges that "all women are not the same."[19] But her concern is to counter the view that differences that exist among women serve "to undercut the meaningfulness or . . . reality of gender."[20] In particular, she believes that recognition of women's differences does not dictate an emphasis on the diversity of women's experiences. Instead, MacKinnon's goal is to "see if women's condition is shared, even when contexts or magnitudes differ,"[21] and this is the particular "approach to race and ethnicity" she attempts. . . . Her aspiration is therefore "to include all women in the term 'women' in some way, without violating the particularity of any woman's experience."[22]

This aspiration is reflected in MacKinnon's acknowledgment that "gender . . . appears partly to comprise the meaning of, as well as bisect, race and class, even as race and class specificities make up, as well as cross-cut, gender."[23] MacKinnon does make an effort in her work to draw attention to the particular experiences of women of color. In *Feminism Unmodified*, for example, there are numerous references to the experiences of Black women and First Nations women, as well as an extended discussion of the implications of a particular case for First Nations women. At the same time, however, race specificities do not appear to have had very much impact on the development of her theoretical arguments. Overall, MacKinnon's work is limited in a number of important ways by her theoretical focus on subsuming all of the many forms of oppression to which women are subjected within a central explanation.

To begin with, while MacKinnon accepts that "[a] general theory of social inequality is prefigured, if inchoately, in [the] connections"[24] between race, class, and gender, she still concentrates her discussions on considering how her own theory of sexuality contributes to analyses of race and class hierarchies. For example, in *Feminism Unmodified*, she states: "Women get their class status through their sexual relations with men of particular classes; perhaps their racial status, also no less real for being vicarious, similarly derives from racial hierarchies among men."[25]

Even where MacKinnon provides an in-depth analysis of the particular experiences of women of color, she does not allow those experiences to challenge the premise of her theory. In her discussion of the implications of Santa Clara Pueblo v. Martinez [436 U.S. 49 (1978)] for First Nations women, she considers a First Nations American tribal rule that denies tribal status to the children of First Nations women who marry men outside the tribe, but not to the children of men who do so, not only as a male supremacist solution to a complex problem concerning the maintenance of First Nations land for First Nations people, but also from the perspective of the members of the tribe who defended the rule before the courts. Her discussion is notable because she confronts the complexity of the issue without trying to reduce the interaction between racism and sexism to a theoretical emphasis on male supremacy and because she emphasizes that First Nations women should define their own meaning of equality. Her discussion of *Santa Clara Pueblo*, however, is an exception, not the rule, for despite these valuable and important insights, MacKinnon still maintains in her theory generally that sexuality is central to women's oppression. Thus, it is not surprising that about half of MacKinnon's examples of the particular experiences of women of color in *Feminism Unmodified* refer to racism only in the context of pornography or rape. The other examples of the particular experiences of Black women and First Nations women are confined to brief comments and footnotes.

A further difficulty lies in the way MacKinnon deals with racism by drawing comparisons between the recognition and operation of racism and sexism in American society. Most problematic are the assumptions which underlie her identification of differences between the two systems of oppression. For example, MacKinnon appears to assume that sexism is more abstruse and insidious than racism. As she states:

> Substantively considered, the situation of women is not really like anything else. . . . Most important, I think it never was a central part of the ideology of racism that the system of chattel slavery of Africans really was designed for their enjoyment and benefit. . . . [F]ew people pretended that the entire system existed because of its basis in love and mutual respect and veneration, and that white supremacy really treated Blacks in many cases better than whites, and that the primary intent and effect of their special status was and is their protection, pleasure, fulfillment, and liberation. Crucially, many have believed, and some actually still do, that Black people were not the equals of whites. But at least since Brown v. Board of Education, few have pretended, much less authoritatively, that the social system, as it was, was equality for them.[26]

MacKinnon further argues that in the United States, racism has been recognized and legally redressed to a degree not yet attained with respect to sexism; for example, she notes that whereas "Black people's movement for equality" has advanced to the point where the group characteristics of Blacks have been generally recognized as "constitutive of the fully human," women's particular qualities have not yet been so recognized.[27] Because MacKinnon obscures the substantial ways in which Blacks and other people of color continue to be oppressed by racism, she loses sight of the important impact of racism in the lives of women of color. As Mariana Valverde has argued in her review of *Feminism Unmodified*, "[t]he constant refrain 'they wouldn't allow that to be done to blacks' betrays a willful disregard for the realities of racism (whatever the legal situation may be). . . ."[28]

Thus, while MacKinnon may purport to have identified the forms of oppression common to all women, the particular forms of oppression experienced by women of color are not always sufficiently visible in her work. Ultimately MacKinnon's insights with regard to the relationship between gender and race only marginally capture the complex and powerful role that racism plays in the lives of women of color.

The core difficulty with MacKinnon's definition of the feminist project, then, lies in the uneasy fit between her emphasis on comprehending the defining commonalities of the group "women" and her insight that race, gender, and class are necessarily interconnected. . . .

First, MacKinnon's premise that women come from a shared social position must be modified: women do not come from a shared social position. We are divided from each other by class, race, and other factors that affect our relative positions in the social hierarchy of our present society. By downplaying this reality, MacKinnon obscures the fact that women who are subject to sexism through and in addition to racism have concerns and priorities for change not only different from, but often in conflict with, those of white women. For example, as Amos and Parmar argue, "[w]hile [debates concerning sexuality] rage virulently amongst white feminists, many Black[29] women have rightly felt that [they] do not have the 'luxury' of engaging in them. . . ."[30] On the contrary, intense societal racism and its consequences have already defined their theoretical and political agendas for them: "Our very position as Black women in a racist society has meant that we have been forced to organize around issues relating to our very survival."[31] Thus, in the lives of women of color, issues in and around sexuality often play a secondary role to the more immediate concerns that arise from racism. Once we recognize this important difference in experience and priority, MacKinnon's focus on the centrality of sexuality to the oppression of women is seriously problematic. Most importantly, in identifying sexual objectification as the primary process of the subjection of women, MacKinnon greatly oversimplifies the sites of women's oppression and submerges priorities and interests not consistent with this theoretical tenet.

Second, the centrality of sexuality in MacKinnon's work might be best understood in light of the power that white women within the feminist movement and academic community have had and continue to have to define the priorities and agenda of feminist practice and theory. According to MacKinnon:

> The centrality of sexuality emerges from . . . feminist practice on diverse issues including abortion, birth control, sterilization abuse, domestic battery, rape, incest, lesbianism, sexual harassment, prostitution, female sexual slavery and pornography. In all these areas, feminist efforts confront and change women's lives concretely and experientially. Taken together, they are producing a feminist political theory centering upon sexuality. . . .[32]

The problem with the link drawn between feminist practice and feminist theory in this passage is that it does not account for the relative position of power that has enabled white women to determine these issues as the most important for feminist organizing and political action in the first place. . . . MacKinnon's assertion that the content of feminist practice supports her insistence on the centrality of sexuality to feminism is tautological. She appears to accept white feminist practice as coincident with feminism rather than challenging the limits of white feminist practice when applied to or used as a basis for explaining the oppression of women of color.

. . . [H]er emphasis on a common site of women's oppression limits her capacity to do that which she aspires to do—to engage in the collective process of explaining women's oppression.

. . . [T]hree reasons advanced by white feminists . . . justify not recognizing fully the racial differences that exist among women or failing to incorporate adequately the implications of such differences into their analyses: the desire to avoid complexity, fear of superficial treatment of difference . . . and strategic concerns about fragmentation.

With respect to the first of these, to recognize fully the implications of the diversity of women's experiences is to confront the complexity of the world in which we live. But the complexity is alarming, and, as Martha Minow has pointed out, "[f]ull acknowledgment of all people's differences threatens to overwhelm us."[33] This fear of complexity is a poor excuse, however, for failing to develop more complete and realistic understandings of women's oppression. . . .

Some feminists are also apprehensive that recognizing the diversity of women's experiences in our theories will merely encourage superficial treatment of our differences. . . . The concern is that the array of [such groups as women, blacks, gays, youth] not only suggests that all characteristics are of equal significance, but also submerges the intersections among different forms of oppression. Thus, . . . women are . . . marginalized in Neo-Marxist political, legal, and social theory. . . .

. . . One way in which feminist scholars might avoid the superficiality of analysis . . . is to be specific about which group's particular experiences we are discussing. However, we cannot allow our desire to avoid engaging in superficial analysis to impede our attempts to work out the implications of women's diverse experiences of oppression.

Lastly, fully confronting the differences that exist among women may appear to fragment and weaken the solidarity and strength of feminists. . . . While these strategic concerns are important, I believe we have little choice but to follow the path of recognizing difference. White, privileged feminists have always maintained and still maintain hegemonic control over feminist discourse. If we now attempt to maintain the appearance of uniformity and universality for strategic reasons at the expense of ignoring our own hegemonic position and the challenges of, among others, women of color, we risk irreparable fragmentation. While we should work toward building solidarity, we cannot pretend union when it does not exist. Rather, we must acknowledge we are divided and develop strategies to overcome our fears and prejudices as well as our position of power in relation to women of color. It is acceptance of the challenge to acknowledge and understand the heterogeneity and complexity of experience and oppression which will ultimately be feminism's strength, not its weakness. . . .

. . . [I]t is imperative that white feminist legal theorists problematize and complicate our analyses by taking into account the real and contradictory differences of interest and power between women that are generated by, and generate, racism. . . .

At the same time, for white feminist legal theorists simply to complicate and thereby strengthen the analysis in our own scholarship will not overcome the fundamental differences in power that exist between women of color and white women in the legal academic world and elsewhere. It is necessary, therefore, that we confront the differences in power that presently exist between women of color and white women and commit ourselves actively to breaking down this hierarchy in academia, in political organizing, and in society at large.

Notes

1. J. Russell ed., A Feminist Review of Criminal Law (Minister of Supply and Services, Canada, 1985).

2. M.-A. Bertrand, Sexism in Sentencing, in *id.*, at 144–45.

3. C. LaPrairie, Native Women and Crime in Canada: A Theoretical Model, in E. Adelberg & C. Currie eds., Too Few to Count: Canadian Women in Conflict with the Law 103 (Press Gang Publisher, 1987). See also LaPrairie, Selected Criminal Justice and Socio-Demographic Data on Native Women, 26 Can. J. of Criminology 161 (1984) (cited in A Feminist Review, *supra* note 1, at 145, 145 n. 29).

4. LaPrairie, Native Women and Crime, *supra* note 3, at 109.

5. See S. Boyd, Child Custody and Working Mothers, in K. Mahoney & S. Martin eds., Equality and Judicial Neutrality 168 (Carswell, 1987); Boyd, Child Custody, Ideologies and Employment, 3 Can. J. Women & Law 41 (1988); S. Boyd, From Gender Specificity to Gender Neutrality? Ideologies in Canadian Child Custody Law, in S. Sevenhuijsen & C. Smart eds., Child Custody and the Politics of Gender (Routledge, 1990).

6. Boyd, From Gender Specificity, *supra* note 5, at 3.

7. Boyd & Sheehy, Feminist Perspectives in Law: Canadian Theory and Method, 2 Can. J. Women & Law 1, 29 (1986) (describing Boyd, Child Custody and Working Mothers, *supra* note 5) (footnote omitted).

8. From Boyd, Gender Specificity, *supra* note 5, at 215.

9. H. Carby, White Women Listen! Black Feminism and the Boundaries of Sisterhood, in Center for Contemporary Cultural Studies, The Empire Strikes Back: Race and Racism in 70's Britain 212, 219 (Hutchinson, 1982) (noting that this notion existed in post–World War II Britain.)

10. In my analysis of MacKinnon's work, I will concentrate on her recent book, C. MacKinnon, Feminism Unmodified: Discourses on Life and Law (Harvard University Press, 1987). I will also consider two of her earlier contributions to feminist theory: MacKinnon, Feminism, Marxism, Method, and the State: An Agenda for Theory, Part 5 this volume; MacKinnon, Feminism, Marxism, Method, and the State: Toward Feminist Jurisprudence, Part 5 this volume.

Although MacKinnon once acknowledged her approach as radical feminist in perspective, she now characterizes it as "feminism unmodified." See generally MacKinnon, Feminism Unmodified, *supra*. . . .

11. Carby, White Women Listen! *supra* note 9, at 213 (emphasis added). . . .

12. Other feminist theorists have also oversimplified the sites of women's oppression by reducing them to a single, gender-related cause, such as patriarchy, see Rifkin, Toward a Theory of Law and Patriarchy, Part 5 this volume; reproduction, see M. O'Brien, The Politics of Reproduction (Routledge & Kegan Paul, 1981); or the sexual division of labor, see N. Hartsock, Money, Sex and Power: Toward a Feminist Historical Materialism (Longman, 1983). Focusing exclusively on any one of these concerns leaves out the daily reality of the struggles and contradictions in many women's lives, as well as the privileges and relative advantages enjoyed by other women.

13. C. MacKinnon, Desire and Power, in MacKinnon, Feminism Unmodified, *supra* note 10, at 53.

14. MacKinnon, Feminism, Marxism, Method, and the State: An Agenda for Theory, Part 5 this volume, at 443.

15. *Id.* at 446.

16. *Id.* at 437. See also MacKinnon, Desire and Power, *supra* note 13, at 49. . . .

17. MacKinnon, Desire and Power, *supra* note 13, at 50. Cf. Mackinnon, Feminism, Marxism, Method, and the State: An Agenda for Theory, Part 5 this volume, at 446 ("Women and men are divided by gender, made into the sexes as we know them, by the social requirement of heterosexuality, which institutionalized male sexual dominance and female sexual submission." [footnote omitted]).

18. MacKinnon, Feminism, Marxism, Method, and the State: An Agenda for Theory, Part 5 this volume, at 448.

19. C. MacKinnon, On Exceptionality: Women as Women in Law, in MacKinnon, Feminism Unmodified, *supra* note 10, at 76. For example, she relies on this fact to demonstrate that the subordinated status of women is socially constructed as opposed to biologically determined. See MacKinnon, Desire and Power, *supra* note 13, at 56.

20. MacKinnon, Desire and Power, *supra* note 13, at 56. . . .

21. MacKinnon, Feminism, Marxism, Method, and the State: An Agenda for Theory, Part 5 this volume, at 451 n. 4.

22. *Id.*

23. C. MacKinnon, Introduction: The Art of the Impossible, in MacKinnon Feminism Unmodified, *supra* note 10, at 2.

24. *Id.,* at 2–3.

25. *Id.* at 2.

26. C. MacKinnon, Francis Biddle's Sister: Pornography, Civil Rights, and Speech, in MacKinnon, Feminism Unmodified, *supra* note 10, at 166–68 (footnote omitted). . . .

27. MacKinnon, Difference and Dominance, Part 3 this volume, at 284.

28. Valverde, Book Review, Can. Woman Studies/Les Cahiers de la Femme 8, no. 4, at 100, 101 (1987) (reviewing C. MacKinnon, Feminism Unmodified).

29. Consistent with the British context in which they were writing, Amos and Parmar use the term "Black" to refer to all women who are subject to systemic barriers on the basis of skin color.

30. Amos & Parmar, Challenging Imperial Feminism, 17 Feminist Rev. 3, 11 (1984). . . .

31. *Id.* at 12. Cf. M. LaChapelle, Beyond Barriers: Native Women and the Women's Movement 257, 261–62, in M. Fitzgerald, C. Guberman & M. Wolfe eds., Still Ain't Satisfied (Women's Press, 1982) (observing that many First Nations women do not have the time and resources to become involved in the women's movement because they must concentrate on sheer survival); Ng, Immigrant Women: The Silent Partners of the Women's Movement in Still Ain't Satisfied 249, 253 (observing that for many immigrant women the overwhelming survival needs of their families on a day-to-day basis make all other issues seem secondary).

32. MacKinnon, Feminism, Marxism, Method, and the State: An Agenda for Theory, Part 5 this volume, at 443.

33. Minow, The Supreme Court, 1986 Term—Foreword: Justice Engendered, Part 3 this volume.

❖ Demarginalizing the Intersection of Race and Sex: A Black Feminist Critique of Antidiscrimination Doctrine, Feminist Theory and Antiracist Politics

KIMBERLE CRENSHAW

ONE OF THE VERY FEW Black women's studies books is entitled *All the Women Are White, All the Blacks Are Men, but Some of Us Are Brave.*[1] I have chosen this title as a point of departure in my efforts to develop a Black feminist criticism because it sets forth a problematic consequence of the tendency to treat race and gender as mutually exclusive categories of experience and analysis.[2] In this essay, I want to examine how this tendency is perpetuated by a single-axis framework that is dominant in antidiscrimination law and that is also reflected in feminist theory and antiracist politics.

I will center Black women in this analysis in order to contrast the multidimensionality of Black women's experience with the single-axis analysis that distorts these experiences. Not only will this juxtaposition reveal how Black women are theoretically erased, it will also illustrate how this framework imports its own theoretical limitations that undermine efforts to broaden feminist and antiracist analyses. With Black women as the starting point, it becomes more apparent how dominant conceptions of discrimination condition us to think about subordination as disadvantage occurring along a single categorical axis. I want to suggest further that this single-axis framework erases Black women in the conceptualization, identification and remediation of race and sex discrimination by limiting inquiry to the experiences of otherwise-privileged members of the group. In other words, in race discrimination cases, discrimination tends to be viewed in terms of sex- or class-privileged Blacks; in sex discrimination cases, the focus is on race- and class-privileged women.

This focus on the most privileged group members marginalizes those who are multiply burdened and obscures claims that cannot be understood as resulting from discrete sources of discrimination. I suggest further that this focus on otherwise-privileged group members creates a distorted analysis of racism and sexism because the operative conceptions of race and sex become grounded in experi-

1989 U. Chi. Legal F. 139.

ences that actually represent only a subset of a much more complex phenomenon. After examining the doctrinal manifestations of this single-axis framework, I will discuss how it contributes to the marginalization of Black women in feminist theory and in antiracist politics. . . .

The Antidiscrimination Framework

The Experience of Intersectionality and the Doctrinal Response

One way to approach the problem of intersectionality is to examine how courts frame and interpret the stories of Black women plaintiffs. . . . To illustrate the difficulties inherent in judicial treatment of intersectionality, I will consider [a] Title VII case . . .: DeGraffenreid v. General Motors.[3] . . .

DeGraffenreid v. General Motors

In *DeGraffenreid*, five Black women brought suit against General Motors, alleging that the employer's seniority system perpetuated the effects of past discrimination against Black women. Evidence adduced at trial revealed that General Motors simply did not hire Black women prior to 1964 and that all of the Black women hired after 1970 lost their jobs in a seniority-based layoff during a subsequent recession. The district court granted summary judgment for the defendant, rejecting the plaintiffs' attempt to bring a suit not on behalf of Blacks or women, but specifically on behalf of Black women. The court stated:

> [P]laintiffs have failed to cite any decisions which have stated that Black women are a special class to be protected from discrimination. The Court's own research has failed to disclose such a decision. The plaintiffs are clearly entitled to a remedy if they have been discriminated against. However, they should not be allowed to combine statutory remedies to create a new "super-remedy" which would give them relief beyond what the drafters of the relevant statutes intended. Thus, this lawsuit must be examined to see if it states a cause of action for race discrimination, sex discrimination, or alternatively either, but not a combination of both.[4]

Although General Motors did not hire Black women prior to 1964, the court noted that "General Motors has hired . . . female employees for a number of years prior to the enactment of the Civil Rights Act of 1964." Because General Motors did hire women—albeit *white women*—during the period that no Black women were hired, there was, in the court's view, no sex discrimination that the seniority system could conceivably have perpetuated.

After refusing to consider the plaintiffs' sex discrimination claim, the court dismissed the race discrimination complaint and recommended its consolidation with another case alleging race discrimination against the same employer. The plaintiffs responded that such consolidation would defeat the purpose of their suit since theirs was not purely a race claim, but an action brought specifically on behalf of Black women alleging race and sex discrimination. The court, however, reasoned:

> The legislative history surrounding Title VII does not indicate that the goal of the statute was to create a new classification of "black women" who would have greater standing than, for example, a black male. The prospect of the creation of new classes of protected minorities, governed only by the mathematical principles of permutation and combination, clearly raises the prospect of opening the hackneyed Pandora's box.[5]

Thus, the court apparently concluded that Congress either did not contemplate that Black women could be discriminated against as "Black women" or did not intend to protect them when such discrimination occurred. The court's refusal in *DeGraffenreid* to acknowledge that Black women encounter combined race and sex discrimination implies that the boundaries of sex and race discrimination doctrine are defined respectively by white women's and Black men's experiences. Under this view, Black women are protected only to the extent that their experiences coincide with those of either of the two groups.[6] Where their experiences are distinct, Black women can expect little protection as long as approaches, such as that in *DeGraffenreid*, which completely obscure problems of intersectionality prevail. . . .

. . . I am suggesting that Black women can experience discrimination in ways that are both similar to and different from those experienced by white women and Black men. Black women sometimes experience discrimination in ways similar to white women's experiences; sometimes they share very similar experiences with Black men. Yet often they experience double discrimination—the combined effects of practices which discriminate on the basis of race, and on the basis of sex. And sometimes, they experience discrimination as Black women—not the sum of race and sex discrimination, but as Black women.

Black women's experiences are much broader than the general categories that discrimination discourse provides. Yet the continued insistence that Black women's demands and needs be filtered through categorical analyses that completely obscure their experiences guarantees that their needs will seldom be addressed.

The Significance of Doctrinal Treatment of Intersectionality

DeGraffenreid [is a] doctrinal manifestation . . . of a common political and theoretical approach to discrimination which operates to marginalize Black women. Unable to grasp the importance of Black women's intersectional experiences, not only courts, but feminist and civil rights thinkers as well have treated Black women in ways that deny both the unique compoundedness of their situation and the centrality of their experiences to the larger classes of women and Blacks.

Black women are regarded either as too much like women or Blacks and the compounded nature of their experience is absorbed into the collective experiences of either group or as too different, in which case Black women's Blackness or femaleness sometimes has placed their needs and perspectives at the margin of the feminist and Black liberationist agendas.

While it could be argued that this failure represents an absence of political will to include Black women, I believe that it reflects an uncritical and disturbing acceptance of dominant ways of thinking about discrimination. Consider first the definition of discrimination that seems to be operative in antidiscrimination law: Discrimination which is wrongful proceeds from the identification of a specific class or category; either a discriminator intentionally identifies this category, or a process is adopted which somehow disadvantages all members of this category. According to the dominant view, a discriminator treats all people within a race or sex category similarly. Any significant experiential or statistical variation within this group suggests either that the group is not being discriminated against or that conflicting interests exist which defeat any attempts to bring a common claim. Consequently, one generally cannot combine these categories. Race and sex, moreover, become significant only when they operate to explicitly *disadvantage* the victims; because the *privileging* of whiteness or maleness is implicit, it is generally not perceived at all.

Underlying this conception of discrimination is a view that the wrong which antidiscrimination law addresses is the use of race or gender factors to interfere with decisions that would otherwise be fair or neutral. This process-based definition is not grounded in a bottom-up commitment to improve the substantive conditions for those who are victimized by the interplay of numerous factors. Instead, the dominant message of antidiscrimination law is that it will regulate only the limited extent to which race or sex interferes with the process of determining outcomes. This narrow objective is facilitated by the top-down strategy of using a singular "but for" analysis to ascertain the effects of race or sex. Because the scope of antidiscrimination law is so limited, sex and race discrimination have come to be defined in terms of the experiences of those who are privileged *but for* their racial or sexual characteristics. Put differently, the paradigm of sex discrimination tends to be based on the experiences of white women; the model of race discrimination tends to be based on the experiences of the most privileged Blacks. Notions of what constitutes race and sex discrimination are, as a result, narrowly tailored to embrace only a small set of circumstances, none of which include discrimination against Black women.

To the extent that this general description is accurate, the following analogy can be useful in describing how Black women are marginalized in the interface between antidiscrimination law and race and gender hierarchies: Imagine a basement which contains all people who are disadvantaged on the basis of race, sex, class, sexual preference, age and/or physical ability. These people are stacked— feet standing on shoulders—with those on the bottom being disadvantaged by the full array of factors, up to the very top, where the heads of all those disadvantaged by a singular factor brush up against the ceiling. Their ceiling is actually the floor above which only those who are *not* disadvantaged in any way reside. In efforts to correct some aspects of domination, those above the ceiling admit from the basement only those who can say that "but for" the ceiling, they too would be in the upper room. A hatch is developed through which those placed immediately below can crawl. Yet this hatch is generally available only to those who—due to the singularity of their burden and their otherwise privileged position relative to those below—are in the position to crawl through. Those who are multiply burdened are generally left below unless they can somehow pull themselves into the groups that are permitted to squeeze through the hatch.

As this analogy translates for Black women, the problem is that they can receive protection only to the extent that their experiences are recognizably similar to those whose experiences tend to be reflected in antidiscrimination doctrine. If Black women cannot conclusively say that "but for" their race or "but for" their gender they would be treated differently, they are not invited to climb through the hatch but told to wait in the unprotected margin until they can be absorbed into the broader, protected categories of race and sex.

Despite the narrow scope of this dominant conception of discrimination and its tendency to marginalize those whose experiences cannot be described within its tightly drawn parameters, this approach has been regarded as the appropriate framework for addressing a range of problems. In much of feminist theory and, to some extent, in antiracist politics, this framework is reflected in the belief that sexism or racism can be meaningfully discussed without paying attention to the lives of those other than the race-, gender- or class-privileged. As a result, both feminist theory and antiracist politics have been organized, in part, around the equation of racism with what happens to the Black middle-class or to Black men, and the equation of sexism with what happens to white women. Looking at historical and contemporary issues in both the feminist and the civil rights communities, one can find ample evidence of how both communities' acceptance of the dominant framework of discrimination has hindered the development of an adequate theory and praxis to address problems of intersectionality. This adoption of a single-issue framework for discrimination not only marginalizes Black women within the very movements that claim them as part of their constituency but it also makes the illusive goal of ending racism and patriarchy even more difficult to attain.

Feminism and Black Women: "Ain't We Women?"

Oddly, despite the relative inability of feminist politics and theory to address Black women substantively, feminist theory and tradition borrow considerably from Black women's history. For example, "Ain't I a Woman" has come to represent a standard refrain in feminist discourse. Yet the lesson of this powerful oratory is not fully appreciated because the context of the delivery is seldom examined. I would like to tell part of the story because it establishes some themes that have characterized feminist treatment of race and illustrates the importance of including Black women's experiences as a rich source for the critique of patriarchy. In 1851, Sojourner Truth declared "Ain't I a Woman?" and challenged the sexist imagery used by male critics to justify the disenfranchisement of women. The scene was a Women's Rights Conference in Akron, Ohio; white male hecklers, invoking stereotypical images of "womanhood," argued that women were too frail and delicate to take on the responsibilities of political activity. When Sojourner Truth rose to speak, many white women urged that she be silenced, fearing that she would divert attention from women's suffrage to emancipation. Truth, once permitted to speak, recounted the horrors of slavery, and its particular impact on Black women:

> Look at my arm! I have ploughed and planted and gathered into barns, and no man could head me—and ain't I a woman? I could work as much and eat as much as a man—when I could get it—and bear the lash as well! And ain't I a woman? I have born thirteen children, and seen most of 'em sold into slavery, and when I cried out with my mother's grief, none but Jesus heard me—and ain't I a woman?[7]

By using her own life to reveal the contradiction between the ideological myths of womanhood and the reality of Black women's experience, Truth's oratory provided a powerful rebuttal to the claim that women were categorically weaker than men. Yet Truth's personal challenge to the coherence of the cult of true womanhood was useful only to the extent that white women were willing to reject the racist attempts to rationalize the contradiction—that because Black women were something less than real women, their experiences had no bearing on true womanhood. Thus, this nineteenth-century Black feminist challenged not only patriarchy, but she also challenged white feminists wishing to embrace Black women's history to relinquish their vestedness in whiteness.

Contemporary white feminists inherit not the legacy of Truth's challenge to patriarchy but, instead, Truth's challenge to their forbearers. Even today, the difficulty that white women have traditionally experienced in sacrificing racial privilege to strengthen feminism renders them susceptible to Truth's critical question. When feminist theory and politics that claim to reflect *women's* experience and *women's* aspirations do not include or speak to Black women, Black women must ask: "Ain't We Women?" If this is so, how can the claims that "women are," "women believe" and "women need" be made when such claims are inapplicable or unresponsive to the needs, interests and experiences of Black women?

The value of feminist theory to Black women is diminished because it evolves from a white racial context that is seldom acknowledged. Not only are women of color in fact overlooked, but their exclusion is reinforced when *white* women speak for and as *women*. The authoritative universal voice—usually white male subjectivity masquerading as non-racial, non-gendered objectivity—is merely transferred to those who, but for gender, share many of the same cultural, economic and social characteristics. When feminist theory attempts to describe women's experiences through analyzing patriarchy, sexuality or separate spheres ideology, it often overlooks the role of race. Feminists thus ignore how their own race functions to mitigate some aspects of sexism and, moreover, how it often privileges them over and contributes to the domination of other women. Consequently, feminist theory remains *white*, and its potential to broaden and deepen its analysis by addressing non-privileged women remains unrealized.

An example of how some feminist theories are narrowly constructed around white women's experiences is found in the separate spheres literature. The critique of how separate spheres ideology shapes and limits women's roles in the home and in public life is a central theme in feminist legal thought. Feminists have attempted to expose and dismantle separate spheres ideology by identifying and criticizing the stereotypes that traditionally have justified the disparate societal roles assigned to men and women. Yet this attempt to debunk ideological justifications for *women's* subordination offers little insight into the domination of *Black* women. Because the experiential base upon which many feminist insights are grounded is white, theoretical statements drawn from them are overgeneralized at best, and often wrong. Statements such as "men and women are taught to see men as independent, capable, powerful; men and women are taught to see women as dependent, limited in abilities, and passive,"[8] are common within this literature. But this "observation" overlooks the anomalies created by crosscurrents of racism and sexism. Black men and women live in a society that creates sex-based norms and expectations which racism operates simultaneously to deny; Black men are not viewed as powerful, nor are Black women seen as passive. An effort to develop an ideological explanation of gender domination in the Black community should proceed from an understanding of how crosscutting forces establish gender norms and how the conditions of Black subordination wholly frustrate access to these norms. Given this understanding, perhaps we can begin to see why Black women have been dogged by the stereotype of the pathological matriarch or why there have been those in the Black liberation movement who aspire to create institutions and to build traditions that are intentionally patriarchal.

Because ideological and descriptive definitions of patriarchy are usually premised upon white female experiences, feminists and others informed by feminist literature may make the mistake of assuming that since the role of Black women in the family and in other Black institutions does not always resemble the familiar manifestations of patriarchy in the white community, Black women are somehow exempt from patriarchal norms. For example, Black women have traditionally worked outside the home in numbers far exceeding the labor participation rate of white women. An analysis of patriarchy that highlights the history of white women's exclusion from the workplace might permit the inference that Black women have not been burdened by this particular gender-based expectation. Yet the very fact that Black women must work conflicts with norms that women should not, often creating personal, emotional and relationship problems in Black women's lives. Thus, Black women are burdened not only because they often have to take on responsibilities that are not traditionally feminine but, moreover, their assumption of these roles is sometimes interpreted within the Black community as either Black women's failure to live up to such norms or as another manifestation of racism's scourge upon the Black community. This is one of the many aspects of intersectionality that cannot be understood through an analysis of patriarchy rooted in white experience. . . .

In sum, sexist expectations . . . and racist assumptions . . . combined to create a distinct set of issues confronting Black women. These issues have seldom been explored in feminist literature nor are they prominent in antiracist politics. . . . This is the paradigmatic political and theoretical dilemma created by the intersection of race and gender: Black women are caught between ideological and political currents that combine first to create and then to bury Black women's experiences.

When and Where I Enter: Integrating an Analysis of Sexism into Black Liberation Politics

Anna Julia Cooper, a nineteenth-century Black feminist, coined a phrase that has been useful in evaluating the need to incorporate an explicit analysis of patriarchy in any effort to address racial domination. Cooper often criticized Black leaders and spokespersons for claiming to speak for the race, but failing to speak for Black women. Referring to one of Martin Delaney's public claims that where he was allowed to enter, the race entered with him, Cooper countered: "Only the Black Woman can say, when and where I enter . . . then and there the whole Negro race enters with me."[9]

Cooper's words bring to mind a personal experience involving two Black men with whom I had formed a study group during our first year of law school. One of our group members, a graduate from Harvard College, often told us stories about a prestigious and exclusive men's club that boasted memberships of several past United States presidents and other influential white males. He was one of its very few Black members. To celebrate completing our first-year exams, our friend invited us to join him at the club for drinks. Anxious to see this fabled place, we approached the large door and grasped the brass door ring to announce our arrival. But our grand entrance was cut short when our friend sheepishly slipped from behind the door and whispered that he had forgotten a very important detail. My companion and I bristled, our training as Black people having taught us to expect yet another barrier to our inclusion; even an informal one-

Black-person quota at the establishment was not unimaginable. The tension broke, however, when we learned that we would not be excluded because of our race, but that I would have to go around to the back door because I was a female. I entertained the idea of making a scene to dramatize the fact that my humiliation as a female was no less painful and my exclusion no more excusable than had we all been sent to the back door because we were Black. But, sensing no general assent to this proposition, and also being of the mind that due to our race a scene would in some way jeopardize all of us, I failed to stand my ground. After all, the club was about to entertain its first Black guests—even though one would have to enter through the back door.[10]

Perhaps this story is not the best example of the Black community's failure to address problems related to Black women's intersectionality seriously. The story would be more apt if Black women, and only Black women, had to go around to the back door of the club and if the restriction came from within, and not from the outside of the Black community. Still this story does reflect a markedly decreased political and emotional vigilance toward barriers to Black women's enjoyment of privileges that have been won on the basis of race but continue to be denied on the basis of sex.

The story also illustrates the ambivalence among Black women about the degree of political and social capital that ought to be expended toward challenging gender barriers, particularly when the challenges might conflict with the antiracism agenda. While there are a number of reasons—including antifeminist ones—why gender has not figured directly in analyses of the subordination of Black Americans, a central reason is that race is still seen by many as the primary oppositional force in Black lives. If one accepts that the social experience of race creates both a primary group identity as well as a shared sense of being under collective assault, some of the reasons that Black feminist theory and politics have not figured prominently in the Black political agenda may be better understood.

The point is not that African Americans are simply involved in a more important struggle. Although some efforts to oppose Black feminism are based on this assumption, a fuller appreciation of the problems of the Black community will reveal that gender subordination does contribute significantly to the destitute conditions of so many African Americans and that it must therefore be addressed. Moreover, the foregoing critique of the single-issue framework renders problematic the claim that the struggle against racism is distinguishable from, much less prioritized over, the struggle against sexism. Yet it is also true that the politics of racial otherness that Black women experience along with Black men prevents Black feminist consciousness from patterning the development of white feminism. For white women, the creation of a consciousness that was distinct from and in opposition to that of white men figured prominently in the development of white feminist politics. Black women, like Black men, live in a community that has been defined and subordinated by color and culture.[11] Although patriarchy clearly operates within the Black community, presenting yet another source of domination to which Black women are vulnerable, the racial context in which Black women find themselves makes the creation of a political consciousness that is oppositional to Black men difficult.

Yet while it is true that the distinct experience of racial otherness militates against the development of an oppositional feminist consciousness, the assertion of racial community sometimes supports defensive priorities that marginalize Black women. Black women's particular interests are thus relegated to the periphery in public policy discussions about the presumed needs of the Black community. The controversy over the movie *The Color Purple* is illustrative. The animating fear behind much of the publicized protest was that by portraying domestic abuse in a Black family, the movie confirmed the negative stereotypes of Black men. The debate over the propriety of presenting such an image on the screen overshadowed the issue of sexism and patriarchy in the Black community. Even though it was sometimes acknowledged that the Black community was not immune from domestic violence and other manifestations of gender subordination, some nevertheless felt that in the absence of positive Black male images in the media, portraying such images merely reinforced racial stereotypes. The struggle against racism seemed to compel the subordination of certain aspects of the Black female experience in order to ensure the security of the larger Black community.

The nature of this debate should sound familiar to anyone who recalls Daniel Moynihan's diagnosis of the ills of Black America.[12] Moynihan's report depicted a deteriorating Black family, foretold the destruction of the Black male householder and lamented the creation of the Black matriarch. His conclusions prompted a massive critique from liberal sociologists and from civil rights leaders.[13] Surprisingly, while many critics characterized the report as racist for its blind use of white cultural norms as the standard for evaluating Black families, few pointed out the sexism apparent in Moynihan's labeling Black women as pathological for their "failure" to live up to a white female standard of motherhood.

The latest versions of a Moynihanesque analysis can be found in the Moyers televised special "The Vanishing Black Family," and, to a lesser extent, in William Julius Wilson's *The Truly Disadvantaged*.[14] In "The Vanishing Black Family," Moyers presented the problem of female-headed households as a problem of irresponsible sexuality, induced in part by government policies that encouraged family breakdown. The theme of the report was that the welfare state reinforced the deterioration of the Black family by rendering the Black male's role obsolete. As the argument goes, because Black men know that someone will take care of their families, they are free to make babies and leave them. A corollary to the Moyers view is that welfare is also dysfunctional because it allows poor women to leave men upon whom they would otherwise be dependent.

Most commentators criticizing the program failed to pose challenges that might have revealed the patriarchal assumptions underlying much of the Moyers report. They instead focused on the dimension of the problem that was clearly recognizable as racist. White feminists were equally culpable. There was little, if any, published response to the Moyers report from the white feminist community. Perhaps feminists were under the mistaken assumption that since the report focused on the Black community, the problems highlighted were racial, not gender based. Whatever the reason, the result was that the ensuing debates over the future direction of welfare and family policy proceeded without significant feminist input. The absence of a strong feminist critique of the Moynihan/Moyers model not only impeded the interests of Black women, but it also compromised the interests of growing numbers of white women heads of household who find it difficult to make ends meet.

William Julius Wilson's *The Truly Disadvantaged* modified much of the moralistic tone of this debate by reframing the issue in terms of a lack of marriageable Black men. According to Wilson, the decline in Black marriages is not attributable to poor motivation, bad work habits or irresponsibility but instead is caused by structural economics which have forced Black unskilled labor out of the workforce. Wilson's approach represents a significant move away from that of Moynihan/Moyers in that he rejects their attempt to center the analysis on the morals of the Black community. Yet, he too considers the proliferation of female-headed households as dysfunctional per se and fails to explain fully why such households are so much in peril. Because he incorporates no analysis of the way the structure of the economy and the workforce subordinates the interests of women, especially childbearing Black women, Wilson's suggested reform begins with finding ways to put Black men back in the family. In Wilson's view, we must change the economic structure with an eye toward providing more Black jobs for Black men. Because he offers no critique of sexism, Wilson fails to consider economic or social reorganization that directly empowers and supports these single Black mothers.

My criticism is not that providing Black men with jobs is undesirable; indeed, this is necessary not only for the Black men themselves, but for an entire community, depressed and subject to a host of sociological and economic ills that accompany massive rates of unemployment. But as long as we assume that the massive social reorganization Wilson calls for is possible, why not think about it in ways that maximize the choices of Black women? A more complete theoretical and political agenda for the Black underclass must take into account the specific and particular concerns of Black women; their families occupy the bottom rung of the economic ladder, and it is only through placing them at the center of the analysis that their needs and the needs of their families will be directly addressed.[15]

Expanding Feminist Theory and Antiracist Politics by Embracing the Intersection

If any real efforts are to be made to free Black people of the constraints and conditions that characterize racial subordination, then theories and strategies purporting to reflect the Black community's needs must include an analysis of sexism and patriarchy. Similarly, feminism must include an analysis of race if it hopes to express the aspirations of non-white women. Neither Black liberationist politics nor feminist theory can ignore the intersectional experiences of those whom the movements claim as their respective constituents. In order to include Black women, both movements must distance themselves from earlier approaches in which experiences are relevant only when they are related to certain clearly identifiable causes (for example, the oppression of Blacks is significant when based on race, of women when based on gender). The praxis of both should be centered on the life chances and life situations of people who should be cared about without regard to the source of their difficulties.

I have stated earlier that the failure to embrace the complexities of compoundedness is not simply a matter of political will, but is also due to the influence of a way of thinking about discrimination which structures politics so that struggles are categorized as singular issues. Moreover, this structure imports a descriptive and normative view of society that reinforces the status quo.

It is somewhat ironic that those concerned with alleviating the ills of racism and sexism should adopt such a top-down approach to discrimination. If their efforts instead began with addressing the needs and problems of those who are most disadvantaged and with restructuring and remaking the world where necessary, then others who are singularly disadvantaged would also benefit. In addition, it seems that placing those who currently are marginalized in the center is the most effective way to resist efforts to compartmentalize experiences and undermine potential collective action.

It is not necessary to believe that a political consensus to focus on the lives of the most disadvantaged will happen tomorrow in order to recenter discrimination discourse at the intersection. It is enough, for now, that such an effort would encourage us to look beneath the prevailing conceptions of discrimination and to challenge the complacency that accompanies belief in the effectiveness of this framework. By so doing, we may develop language which is critical of the dominant view and which provides some basis for unifying activity. The goal of this activity should be to facilitate the inclusion of marginalized groups for whom it can be said: "When they enter, we all enter."

Notes

1. Gloria T. Hull, et al., eds., All The Women Are White, All The Blacks Are Men, but Some of Us Are Brave (Feminist Press, 1982).

2. The most common linguistic manifestation of this analytical dilemma is represented in the conventional usage of the term "Blacks and women." Although it may be true that some people mean to include Black women in either "Blacks" or women," the context in which the term is used actually suggests that often Black women are not considered. . . .

3. [DeGraffenreid was subsequently appealed. The appellate court affirmed the dismissal of Title VII Claims, but reversed dismissal of race discrimination claims and remanded the case. 558 F.2d 480 (8th Cir. 1977). Ed.]

4. *Id.* at 143.

5. *Id.* at 145.

6. I do not mean to imply that all courts that have grappled with this problem have adopted the *DeGraffenreid* approach. Indeed, other courts have concluded that Black women are protected by Title VII. See, for example, Jefferies v. Harris Community Action Ass'n., 615 F.2d 1025 (5th Cir. 1980). I do mean to suggest that the very fact that the Black women's claims are seen as aberrant suggests that sex discrimination doctrine is centered in the experiences of white women. Even those courts that have held that Black women are protected seem to accept that Black women's claims raise issues that the "standard" sex discrimination claims do not. See Shoben, Compound Discrimination: The Interaction of Race and Sex in Employment Discrimination, 55 N.Y.U. L. Rev. 793, 803–04 (1980) (criticizing the *Jefferies* use of a sex-plus analysis to create a subclass of Black women).

7. E. Flexner, Century of Struggle: The Women's Rights Movement in the United States 91 (Belknap Press of Harvard University Press, 1975). See also b. hooks, Ain't I a Woman: Black Women and Feminism 159–60 (South End Press, 1981).

8. Wasserstrom, Racism, Sexism and Preferential Treatment: An Approach to the Topics, 24 UCLA L. Rev. 581, 588 (1977). . . .

9. See A. Cooper, A Voice from the South 31 (Negro Universities Press, 1969; reprint of Aldine Printing House, 1892).

10. In all fairness, I must acknowledge that my companion accompanied me to the back door. I remain uncertain, however, as to whether the gesture was an expression of solidarity or an effort to quiet my anger.

11. For a discussion of how racial ideology creates a polarizing dynamic which subordinates Blacks and privileges whites, see Crenshaw, Race, Reform and Retrenchment: Transformation and Legitimation in Antidiscrimination Law, 101 Harv. L. Rev. 1331, 1371–76 (1988).

12. D. Moynihan, The Negro Family: The Case for National Action (Office of Policy Planning and Research, United States Department of Labor, 1965).

13. See L. Rainwater and W. Yancey, The Moynihan Report and the Politics of Controversy 427–29 (MIT Press, 1967) (containing criticisms of the Moynihan Report . . .).

14. W. Wilson, The Truly Disadvantaged: The Inner City, The Underclass and Public Policy (University of Chicago Press, 1987).

15. Pauli Murray observes that the operation of sexism is at least the partial cause of social problems affecting Black women. See Murray, The Liberation of Black Women, in J. Freeman ed., Women: A Feminist Perspective 351–62 (Mayfield, 1975).

❖ PART 5

Theories of Law

❖ *Introduction*

THE ESSAYS IN Part 5 examine issues in the theory of law. In addition to analyzing various theoretical issues from a feminist perspective, they also explore from this perspective certain principles adhered to by different schools of legal thought. The essays at the beginning of the Part address the role of law in the maintenance of women's subordination.

The concept of patriarchy is central to contemporary feminism. One scholar has remarked: "It is the concept of patriarchy which marks the most distinctive and innovative contribution by feminism to political thought."[1] Although the term is variously defined, patriarchy may be understood as a system of male domination that oppresses women through its social, political, and economic institutions.[2] The notion thus singles out the male sex as the primary agency of women's oppression and expresses the totality of exploitative relations that affect women. The first two essays, by Janet Rifkin and Diane Polan, explore the relationship between law and patriarchy.[3] Catharine MacKinnon in the following two essays introduces an alternative theory about the roots of women's oppression.

Feminists in general disagree about both the definition and the sources of patriarchy. Classic definitions, psychoanalytic and psychocultural, are given by two leading contemporary feminist writers, Juliet Mitchell and Kate Millett respectively. Mitchell, in her *Psychoanalysis and Feminism*,[4] explains patriarchy as the law of the father. According to Mitchell, patriarchy is embodied in kinship systems and etched into the unconscious during the Oedipus complex to produce gendered characteristics. Capitalism sustains this outmoded form of kinship relation, although it offers an opportunity for women to overthrow patriarchy by means of a cultural revolution. An alternative definition of patriarchy is formulated by Kate Millett in *Sexual Politics*.[5] Millett defines patriarchy as men dominating women, with older men dominating younger. For her, patriarchy signifies a cultural learning process in which attitudes are acquired during the socialization process, first by the agency of the family and subsequently by other patriarchal institutions.

In addition to differences in definition, feminist theorists disagree in their characterizations of the source of women's subordination. Two views are especially prominent. Socialist or Marxist feminists locate the source in the economic context, placing the roots of patriarchy in the capitalist system with its sexual division of labor.[6] These views stem from Friedrich Engels's central thesis in *Origin of the Family, Private Property and the State* (1884) that the emergence of patriarchy can be traced to capitalism, in particular the establishment of private property and the emergence of commodities to be used for exchange and profit. In contrast, radical feminists attribute the source of patriarchy to biological roots— male sexuality, which devalues women, specifically the capacity to rape.[7]

The depiction of alternative approaches to the law that derives from the differences between Marxist and radical feminist perspectives is important for historic documentation of the development of feminist legal theory. Marxism long has occupied an important place in feminist thinking. As Eisenstein points out:

> The importance of Marxist analysis to the study of women's oppression is twofold. First it provides a class analysis necessary for the study of power. Second, it provides a method of analysis which is historical and dialectical. Although the dialectic (as method) is most often used by Marxists to study class and class conflict, it can also be used to analyze patriarchal relations governing women's existence and hence women's revolutionary potential.[8]

In recent years, many feminists have turned their attention to the influence of Marxism in examining the role of the welfare state in defining and constraining women's lives. These examinations focus both on the intervention of the state in the economy and the state's role in organizing family life and sexuality.[9]

Yet these contemporary feminist scholars are increasingly skeptical of the classical Marxist view of the state.[10] The central debate is whether the state can be used to advance women's interests or whether it is experienced by women as yet another form of social control.

Radical feminists have also come in for their share of criticism. For example, Alison Jaggar claims that some radical feminists, in their emphasis on the primacy of the body, have developed a deterministic picture of human nature as unchanging.[11] Other critics point to additional shortcomings of radical feminism, such as its defining itself in opposition to male culture and thereby defining that culture as the norm from which to deviate, and as dooming women to a perpetual rebellion and separation that ultimately serves not women but men.[12]

The essays in this Part give an explanation and critique of many philosophical perspectives important to feminist legal theory. At the same time, it is essential to "understand each of these to be a partial and provisional answer to the 'woman question(s),' providing a unique perspective with its own methodological strengths and weaknesses."[13] That is, increasingly feminists are coming to regard these perspectives as merely partial explanations and to reject their monolithic account of causation of women's oppression.

It is important to understand too that the depictions of the differences between Marxist feminism and radical feminism represent a stage in feminist legal theory. The current emphasis on diversity among women, brought into focus in part by the essentialism debate (see Part 4) has shifted the problematic, in part, from issues of women's subordination to men to epistemological issues among women. These epistemological issues are taken up in other Parts in this collection.

Bearing this in mind, the first four essays in this Part examine the two diverse perspectives (Marxist feminism and radical feminism) which have been so important to the development of feminist thought and feminist legal thought. Rifkin, in "Toward a Theory of Law and Patriarchy," attempts to explain how the rise of capitalism profoundly changed the role of women. She finds the answer in law, which made more explicit women's subordination by excluding women from the public world and relegating them to the private world. She typifies law as both a vehicle and a symbol of male authority. She also attempts to explain why legal change does not lead to social reordering. Because of certain attributes of law, she claims, the law masks fundamental social and political questions, thereby suppressing social change.

Polan, in an article also entitled "Toward a Theory of Law and Patriarchy," continues the examination of the role of law and the role of capitalism in the perpetuation of patriarchy. Similar to Rifkin, she points to the limitations of law in the abolition of patriarchy. But Polan's essay is a response, specifically, to the Marxist explanation of legal phenomena as supporting class domination, a view adhered to by those in the school of critical legal theory.[14] Polan, similar to Catharine MacKinnon in the work that follows, is critical of Marxist theory. In this regard, both Polan and MacKinnon belong to a long-standing tradition of feminists who recognize the weaknesses of traditional Marxism's treatment of women. Unlike MacKinnon, however, who proposes an alternative theory, Polan attempts to integrate Marxist and feminist approaches to explain how law has supported and perpetuated patriarchy. Her essay is especially insightful in identifying of the difficulties encountered in such an attempt.

Catharine MacKinnon is one of the foremost feminist legal theorists. She is also one of the most controversial. Her articles and books include explanations of feminist legal theory in general, as well as specific applications of feminist theory to such areas as rape, sexual harassment, pornography, and abortion. Her writing has been especially influential in creating new legal theories, in particular, of sexual harassment and pornography.[15]

MacKinnon presents her general theoretical ideas in two classic introductory essays.[16] Although she shares the perspective of radical feminism, her theory goes beyond a biological explanation for women's domination. True, MacKinnon links dominance with sexuality rather than with economic (class) interests or psychological factors. But she attributes such domination to the social construct of sexuality. She argues that biological differences between the sexes are given meaning by social practices, including the practice of law. For MacKinnon, the key to understanding the meaning of male dominance is the meaning society ascribes to sexuality.

MacKinnon begins her essay "Feminism, Marxism, Method and the State: Toward Feminist Jurisprudence" with the assertion that feminism has no theory of the state. She then proceeds to formulate one. According to MacKinnon, the liberal state coercively and authoritatively constitutes the social order in the interest of men, through its legitimizing norms, relation to society, and substantive policies. It achieves this objective through embodying and ensuring male control over women's sexuality at every level, occasionally cushioning, qualifying, or de jure prohibiting its excesses when necessary to its normalization. The state, through law, institutionalizes male power.

In formulating her theory of the state, MacKinnon ultimately rejects the Marxist approach to feminism[17] as well as the liberal approach to feminism. Her essay "Feminism, Marxism, Method, and the State: An Agenda for Theory" is noteworthy for its discussion of her early views of the similarities and differences between Marxism and feminism. MacKinnon addresses both Marxist criticisms of feminism and feminist criticisms of Marxism. Both enunciate theories of power. Both theories furnish accounts of the manner in which social arrangements of patterned disparity can be internally rational yet unjust. Apart from these similarities, Marxism and feminism pose fundamental questions for each other.

One of the central differences between Marxism and feminism, MacKinnon explains, concerns method. In her explanation she attempts to dispel the perception that feminism lacks a method or a form of systematic analysis. Marxist methodology is dialectical materialism. Feminist method, MacKinnon points outs, is consciousness raising—listening to and believing women's descriptions of their own experiences. This essay elaborates not only on her definition of the distinctive methodology of consciousness raising but also her explanation of the importance of this methodology to the development of feminist theory.

Thus, MacKinnon's work, similar to the preceding essays, questions the roots of women's subordination. In so doing, however, MacKinnon's theory is more far-reaching. She proposes a single unifying theory that explains the manner in which the state maintains and perpetuates women's subordination. Her explanation of women's subordination, in these introductory essays as well as in her subsequent work, has been criticized by numerous legal scholars.[18] Thus she has been criticized for the false "totality" of her theory (i.e., "not every fact related to women's experience neatly and unreservedly supports her thesis of male dominance");[19] her distortion of legal precedents to provide support for the absolutism of her theory;[20] her inadequate attention to the subject of how power should be used once women achieve it;[21] for discovering less a unified theory of women's situation than a unified method of discovery;[22] for emphasizing women's descriptions of subordination and discounting women's descriptions of freedom;[23] for perpetuating a stereotype of women as victims and implying that women are no more than victims;[24] for embracing a deterministic vision of male–female relations.[25] (Criticisms of her essentialism are taken up in Part 4). These criticisms do not detract from the originality and power of her work. Her work continues to occupy a prominent place in the definition and vision of feminist legal theory.

The next two essays (by Margot Stubbs and Mari Matsuda) explore fundamental issues in jurisprudence. The field of jurisprudence explores the nature of law and the functioning of legal institutions. Jurisprudence encompasses various schools of thought that shed light on these theoretical issues. The oldest of these schools of legal theory include, to name a few, natural law, legal positivism, and legal realism. Feminist jurisprudence and critical legal studies are two new additions to the rostrum.

Legal positivism, the subject of the essay by Stubbs, was developed by scholars such as John Austin, Jeremy Bentham, and Hans Kelsen. Primary among the views held by these scholars was that law is a command backed by force. In the positivist tradition, law is a coherent closed system in which results are ordained by rules. Many scholars have critiqued this school of thought. Some opponents, that is, legal realists, have rejected the positivist deductive theory of law in favor of a theory that explores the operation of the law in reality. That is, they offer a perspective opposing the law as doctrine and regard law, instead, as the product of human decision making in which social factors control legal outcomes. The most prominent writers in this tradition include Roscoe Pound, Karl Llewellyn, Jerome Frank, and Oliver Wendell Holmes.

Margot Stubbs, in "Feminism and Legal Positivism," develops a feminist critique of legal positivism. She characterizes legal positivism as a formalistic and apolitical understanding of the law that represents the law as an autonomous, self-contained system uninvolved in the process of production and reproduction of class relationships. After identifying the basic tenets of positivism jurisprudence, Stubbs critiques these tenets from a feminist perspective. Based on an examination of English and Australian precedents (including the functioning of the less formalistic legal body of the New South Wales' equal opportunity tribunal), Stubbs concludes that a feminist theory of law must transcend the conceptual limitations of legal positivism in order to engage the law as an instrument of emancipation.

Stubbs, as well as Mari Matsuda in the essay that follows, examines the underpinnings of our legal system. At the heart of legal positivism is a legal epistemology based on the philosophy of legal liberalism. The origins of the positivist tradition in jurisprudence, as explored by Stubbs, stem from classical liberalism as expressed in the work of Hobbes, Locke, and Hume. Mari Matsuda, "Liberal Jurisprudence and Abstracted Visions of Human Nature," takes up the examination of these fundamental principles in her critique of one of the standard texts in jurisprudence by John Rawls.[26] Rawls's *A Theory of Justice* constitutes a defense of the philosophy of liberalism. In his book Rawls constructs a theory of justice as fairness and posits the development of a utopian social order that protects the individual. In her essay Matsuda critiques Rawls's theory of justice from a feminist perspective. She points out that the foundation of American liberalism on which Rawls's theory rests is nonexistent. She questions the assumptions about human nature on which Rawls's theory is based. Matsuda not only provides a methodological critique, but also suggests an alternative feminist substantive theory of justice. Such a theory of justice would have its own methodology (consciousness raising) for derivation of principles. Moreover, it would envision a feminist utopia far different from a Rawls utopia.

The next three essays (Olsen, Williams, Schneider) explore a central point of contention between feminist legal theory and the body of legal theory known as "critical legal studies" (CLS). This point of contention concerns two different jurisprudential conceptions of rights.

Critical legal studies is a scholarly project of the New Left undertaken by a group of law teachers, lawyers, law students, and social scientists.[27] CLS scholars have developed a critical analysis of the role of legal ideas and institutions in maintaining the status quo. Much CLS theory is closely aligned with neo-Marxist social theory, sharing its emphasis on the role of social alienation in shaping and maintaining social structures. This CLS perspective conceptualizes social hierarchies as the source of alienation in capitalist societies. It critiques the legal system for legitimizing existing hierarchies by linking the concept of freedom to legal concepts that assume the inevitability of existing social structures. Thus, by legitimizing individuals' existential experiences of alienation, and perpetuating collective powerlessness in place of authentic egalitarian social connection, the legal system shapes public consciousness toward passive acquiescence of the status quo.

A parallel CLS perspective critiques "liberalism," the dominant Western capitalist ideology (as distinct from the narrower meaning of "liberal" in liberal/conservative politics), for viewing the world in terms of contradictory values such as reason/desire, freedom/necessity, individualism/ altruism, autonomy/community, and subjectivity/objectivity. This perspective critiques the legal system for reflecting these dichotomies while failing to resolve their fundamental conflicts. Abstract legal concepts premised on contradictions allow courts to move from one result to another without any consistent normative theory; results are rationalized retrospectively. Thus liberal legal concepts cannot transform oppressive social arrangements.[28]

Both CLS perspectives lead to radical critiques of liberalism's ideology of rights as a vehicle for the legal system's maintenance of the status quo. Traditional rights rhetoric stems from declarations, in the U.S. Constitution and other documents, of rights as universal and inalienable in nature, of natural or God-given origin.[29] CLS critiques this concept of abstract rights divorced from a social context, arguing that no right can be universal; specific rights make sense only in specific cultures at specific times.[30] Rights are relative: the recognition of specific rights in a given society is itself what constitutes that society. This relativization of rights means they are inherently unstable, not universal; small changes in social settings can render a rights claim moot.[31] Closely related to this instability critique is the indeterminacy critique: because the language of rights is abstract and formalistic, it is inherently incoherent and manipulable. The "indeterminacy of rights" means that no particular outcome is logically compelled when rights arguments are applied to a given set of facts. Instead, legal decisions often uphold the rights of the privileged, who enjoy superior material and psychological resources for exercising their rights.[32]

In addition to the criticisms of instability and indeterminacy, a third CLS rights critique concerns the reification of rights: liberal rights ideology attributes a false concreteness or frozen character to the abstract legal concepts of rights. While the language of rights attempts to protect the important yet contradictory human needs of independence and community solidarity, the goal of realization of reified general rights is abstracted from those needs. This reification of rights substitutes the value of "exercising a right" (such as the right to free speech) for political issues and goals of social movements, thus compelling their support of the same rights for those with unrelated or even opposite political agendas (such as the free-speech rights of Nazis or pornographers).[33]

Further, the abstract nature of rights reflects the possessive individualism of capitalist society. Conventionally, "individuals are imagined to possess rights in the same way that they possess more tangible kinds of property."[34] Rights-bearing citizens are perceived as separated owners of individual bundles of passive rights, which are mostly negative rights that guarantee freedom from interference. Positive rights (entitlements) receive almost no constitutional protection.[35] In this perception of rights as property, "the assertion of one person's rights is likely to impinge on and diminish the rights of others."[36] Thus, liberalism's rights rhetoric perpetuates social alienation by supporting fears of one other and undermines experiences of connectedness and community.

Finally, CLS critiques rights ideology for its political disutility.[37] The instability, indeterminacy, reification, and individualized nature of rights render them marginally useful in advancing radical social change. Indeed, "crits" argue that rights rhetoric is often affirmatively harmful to such movements, wielded instead in support of existing social hierarchies. Further, even when such movements win rights victories, these victories encourage such movements to substitute rights-consciousness for their self-understanding. In doing so, they allow the state to reinterpret their radical social goals in terms of rights and affirm that social power resides in the state, not the people. Thus their struggle for rights reinforces alienation and powerlessness, and coopts them into maintaining the status quo.[38]

CLS and feminist legal theory share some similarities and many differences.[39] Both strive to expose the hierarchical and decontextualized nature of law. Both have as their objective the elimination of oppression. But the two schools of thought have different points of departure. CLS, a movement composed primarily of white males, starts its analysis from a position of power. Feminist legal theory, espoused mostly by women scholars, views the world as subjects of domination, oppression, and devaluation. CLS seeks to deconstruct the law, whereas feminist legal theory seeks to empower women through the law.[40]

In addition, one fundamental distinction between CLS and feminist legal theory encompasses their different perceptions of rights ideology. The three concluding writers in this Part (Olsen, Williams, and Schneider) take up this debate about the value of rights ideology to feminist theory.

Frances Olsen, "Statutory Rape: A Feminist Critique of Rights Analysis," utilizes the debates between liberals and critical legal scholars over rights analysis and among feminists over sexuality as vehicles for evaluating the relevance of rights critiques to feminist issues. She agrees with the CLS critique of rights as indeterminate. Rights theory does not provide an adequate basis for legal decisions, she claims, because it cannot transcend the fundamental conflict between the right to privacy, which values freedom of action, and the right to protection, which values security: rights analysis cannot indicate which value should prevail in a given case. Further, rights analysis distorts feminist thinking about sexuality, she asserts. The central feminist project of challenging the dominant conception of sexuality is redefined through rights analysis into a divisive line-drawing dispute between the values of social protection (attacked for allowing sexist societal controls) and sexual freedom (attacked for protecting men's freedom to exploit women). Similarly, in the feminist struggle against separate spheres ideology, rights rhetoric cannot solve the conflict between women's right to security, which exposes them to public oppression by the state, and the right to privacy, which leaves women unprotected against private oppression within the private patriarchal family.

Another facet of the rights critique regards rights as an aspect of "bourgeois individualism" that fosters alienation and undermines community. Nevertheless, Olsen argues, individualism is progressive for women, for whom "community" means the unequal and oppressive control of fathers, husbands, sexual harassers, and rapists, for example. Thus Olsen concludes that women's rights to autonomy, which are an expression of their collective political resistance to forced community, should be supported.

Some feminists have gone beyond questioning the value of rights theory to questioning the value of law itself as a means for achieving political gains for women. Since law is fundamentally patriarchal, they argue that articulating women's struggles in the law's terms inevitably reinforces patriarchy. While agreeing that litigation alone cannot achieve the broader economic, social, and cultural changes necessary to achieve feminism's goals, Olsen concludes that feminist gains have been achieved in the legal arena. She points out these gains are attributable to concrete struggles, however, rather than rights analysis.

Patricia Williams contributes a different perspective to the role of rights ideology in legal theory. Williams examines the CLS critique of rights ideology from the perspective of Blacks' struggle for civil rights. Williams's point of departure is that the mostly white elite CLS has failed to make it applicable to those most in need of assistance. Specifically, CLS critiques rights as contradictory, indeterminate, reified, and marginally decisive in social behavior. This negative conception of rights, Williams claims, stems from an understanding of social relationships colored by whites' perception of achievement as a function of committed self-control and self-possession. In contrast, Blacks' understanding of social relationships is dominated by historical patterns of physical and psychic dispossession, to which rights assertions present a positive challenge. Thus, CLS, in ignoring the different degrees to which Blacks and whites experience rights assertions as empowering or disempowering, has ignored the different meanings of rights to different people.

Williams also challenges the CLS critique of rights for its "disutility" in political advancement. The disutility argument assumes that rights analysis keeps one in permanent alienation from relationships and social reform and leads to CLS's advocacy of abandoning rights arguments in favor of needs. Williams points out that, in the experience of Blacks, politically effective action has occurred mainly in connecting with asserting rights. Moreover, she adds, for Blacks, a focus on needs has been a political failure: white institutions never treat Black needs as priorities. In the context of their historical memory of slavery, Blacks regard the prospect of obtaining full rights under the law as a motivational, almost religious, hope. For the historically disempowered, attaining rights has a different meaning: it signifies the due respectful behavior and collective responsibility owed by society.

Finally, Williams argues that CLS's proposal to replace formal rights in favor of an informal system will not lead to improved outcomes. Informal systems similar to formal ones are fueled by irrational fears, hatreds, and taboos, which enforce alienation. Williams concludes that the concept of rights is a powerful symbol of selfhood, visibility, inclusion, empowerment, citizenship, participation, and relationship for Blacks. Rights ideology, therefore, should not be discarded but should be expanded to transcend the limitations of present rights discourse.

Elizabeth Schneider agrees with Williams's critique of the CLS view of the limitations of rights, but for different reasons. Schneider challenges two assumptions inherent in CLS and feminist rights critiques: that rights and politics are static, distinct categories; and that rights are often an obstacle to the political growth of social movements. CLS scholars base their rights critique on the individualistic nature of rights and their reification under liberal legalism. Feminists critique rights as formal and hierarchical, reflecting and reinforcing the patriarchal nature of law. Schneider claims that both CLS and feminist critics share a view of the limits of rights, that is, the ways in which rights discourse can reinforce alienation and passivity and constrict political vision and debate. By failing to see the possibilities of rights discourse (its potential to affirm human values, enhance political growth, and assist in the development of collective identity), their critiques have rigidified rather than challenged liberalism's dichotomies of individual–community and rights–politics.

Schneider emphasizes that these rights critiques suffer from an analysis that separates theory from practice. Schneider's alternative approach is to analyze rights as a dialectical process, perceiving theory and practice as related through the dynamic interrelationship of praxis: theory emerges from practice, then informs and reshapes practice, which in turn reshapes theory. She conceptualizes feminist theory, feminist method, and feminist politics as a dialectical process. Feminist theory emphasizes dialectical process by valuing the dynamic interrelationship between individuals and community. The feminist method of consciousness raising, she argues, is a form of praxis because it transcends the theory–practice dichotomy. Consciousness raising starts with women's concrete personal experiences, integrates their experiences into theory, then relates theory back to concrete experiences for further refinement. Schneider's experiences in women's rights litigation illustrates feminist theory in practice: lawmaking as praxis. Instead of a static abstract concept, a rights claim is a "moment" in an ongoing process of political activity; it flows initially from political analysis, then becomes the basis in turn for more self-reflective political analysis. Thus legal argumentation through litigation expresses the concerns of a social movement and assists in the political development of that movement.

Schneider then applies her analysis to the women's rights movement. The experience of the women's rights movement reveals both the communal possibility of rights and the limits of political strategy focused on rights. Schneider's analysis of the women's rights movement as a dialectical process reveals that rights are developed in the middle, not the end, of political dialogue. She concludes, similar to Williams, that while women's rights claims should not perceived as the total answer, they should not be abandoned. According to Schneider, rights claims, through praxis, are an important part of the ongoing feminist conversation.

The essays in this Part all make substantial contributions to legal theory. Feminist writing has been criticized for deemphasizing theory.[41] Olsen identifies three reasons for this feminist hostility to theory. First, some feminists see theory as a masculine enterprise that has excluded women and encouraged them to blame themselves for not understanding. Second, feminists distinguish between theory and practice, contrasting theory unfavorably with practice as useless and lacking meaning to women's lives. The third objection to theory (in particular, to grand theory) is its oversimplification of experience and suppression of complexity, its tendency toward closure for not admitting further critique.

The essays in this Part challenge that criticism. They provide philosophical answers to troubling questions in legal theory. In this regard they expand the development of feminist legal theory. In addition, given the relationship between feminist legal theory and practice, they make a political contribution. They illustrate the idea that "[t]heory can be a form of practice, a step in a dialectical process aimed at improvement of the lives and status of women."[42]

Notes

1. D. Coole, Women in Political Theory (Wheatsheaf Books, 1988).
2. M. Humm, The Dictionary of Feminist Theory (Ohio State University Press, 1990).

3. For another interesting essay on law and patriarchy, see Boris & Bardaglio, The Transformation of Patriarchy: The Historic Role of the State, in I. Diamond, ed., Families, Politics, and Public Policy 70–93 (Longman, 1983).

4. J. Mitchell, Psychoanalysis and Feminism (Penguin, 1974).

5. K. Millett, Sexual Politics (Doubleday, 1970).

6. See, e.g., H. Hartmann, Capitalism, Patriarchy and Job Segregation by Sex, in M. Blaxall and B. Reagan eds., Women and the Workplace: The Implications of Occupational Segregation (University of Chicago Press, 1976); and H. Hartmann, The Unhappy Marriage of Marxism and Feminism, in P. Sargent ed., Women and Revolution (South End Press, 1981); Z. Eisenstein ed., Capitalist Patriarchy and the Case for Socialist Feminism (Monthly Review Press, 1979). Although Marxist feminism and socialist feminism share some similarities, there are differences between these perspectives as well. For a discussion of these differences, see A. Jaggar, Feminist Politics and Human Nature 207–47, 303–50 (Rowman and Allanheld, 1983), and R. Tong, Feminist Thought: A Comprehensive Introduction 173–93 (Westview Press, 1987).

7. See, e.g., S. Brownmiller, Against Our Will: Men, Women and Rape (Simon & Schuster, 1975); A. Dworkin, Woman Hating (Dutton, 1974); idem, Intercourse (Free Press, 1987); S. Griffin, Woman and Nature (Harper & Row, 1978); idem, Rape: The Power of Consciousness (Harper & Row, 1979).

8. Z. Eisenstein, Developing A Theory of Capitalist Patriarchy and Socialist Feminism, in Z. Eisenstein ed., Capitalist Patriarchy, *supra* note 6, at 6–7.

9. For a review of this literature, see Ackelsberg and Diamond, Gender and Political Life: New Directions in Political Science, in B. Hess and M. Ferree eds., Analyzing Gender: A Handbook of Social Science Research 511–14 (Sage, 1987).

10. See, e.g., T. Skocpol, Bringing the State Back In: Strategies of Analysis in Current Research, in P. Evans et al. eds., Bringing the State Back In 3–37 (Cambridge University Press, 1985).

11. Jaggar, *supra* note 6, at 249–302.

12. J. Cocks, Wordless Emotions: Some Critical Reflections on Radical Feminism, 13 Pol. & Soc'y 27–58 (1984). See also Rosemarie Tong's excellent discussions of the criticisms of radical feminism in her Feminist Thought, *supra* note 6, at 127–38.

13. Tong, Feminist Thought, *supra* note 6, at 1.

14. Several comprehensive introductions to the school of thought known as critical legal studies are available. See, e.g., M. Kelman, A Guide to Critical Legal Studies (Harvard University Press, 1987); A. Hutchinson ed., Critical Legal Studies (Rowman and Littlefield, 1989), as well as the sources cited *infra* this introduction.

15. The identification of two types of sexual harassment (quid pro quo and hostile conditions) in MacKinnon's *Sexual Harassment of Working Women: A Case of Sex Discrimination* (Yale University Press, 1979) became the basis for the legal definition adopted by the Supreme Court in Meritor Savings Bank v. Vinson, 477 U.S. 57 (1986). Her writing on pornography (identifying it as a form of gender discrimination) was influential in the formulation of ordinances in Minneapolis and Indianapolis. The Indianapolis ordinance was subsequently enacted but was declared unconstitutional in American Book Sellers v. Hudnut, 771 F.2d 323 (7th Cir. 1985), *aff'd*, 475 U.S. 1001 (1986).

16. Subsequent writings develop her thought further. See, e.g., C. MacKinnon Feminism Unmodified: Discourses on Life and Law (Harvard University Press,

1987); idem, Toward a Feminist Theory of the State (Harvard University Press, 1989).

17. MacKinnon's rejection of both Marxist feminist and liberal feminist is more clearly elaborated in *Feminism Unmodified*. There she points out that liberal feminism categorizes women as "individuals" and thus obscures gender hierarchy. In contrast, socialist feminism characterizes women as the Marxist category of "workers" and thus obscures gender hierarchy.

18. For some of the many reviews of MacKinnon's work, see, e.g., Bartlett, MacKinnon's Feminism: Power on Whose Terms? 75 Calif. L. Rev. 1559 (1987); Finley, The Nature of Domination and the Nature of Women: Reflections on Feminism Unmodified (Book Review), 82 Nw. U.L. Rev. 352 (1988); Littleton, Feminist Jurisprudence: The Difference Method Makes (Book Review), 41 Stan. L. Rev. 751 (1989); Olsen, Feminist Theory in Grand Style (Book Review), 89 Colum. L. Rev. 1131 (1989); Wildman, Review Essay: The Power of Women, 2 Yale J.L. & Feminism 435 (1990).

19. Bartlett, *supra* note 18, at 1565.

20. *Id.* at 1564.

21. *Id.* at 1565.

22. Littleton, Feminist Jurisprudence, *supra* note 18, at 752.

23. Wildman, Review Essay, *supra* note 18, at 439.

24. Finley, Nature of Domination, *supra* note 18, at 378–80.

25. *Id.* at 364.

26. J. Rawls, A Theory of Justice (Harvard University Press, 1971). For another feminist analysis of Rawls's *A Theory of Justice*, see S. Okin, Justice, Gender and the Family 89–109 (Basic Books, 1989).

27. Gabel & Harris, Building Power and Breaking Images: Critical Legal Theory and the Practice of Law, 11 Rev. Law & Soc. Change 369, 370 n.4 (1982–83).

28. Sparer, Critical Legal Studies Symposium: Fundamental Human Rights, Legal Entitlements, and the Social Struggle: A Friendly Critique of the Legal Studies Movement, 36 Stan. L. Rev. 509, 516 (1984).

29. Lynd, Symposium: A Critique of Rights: Communal Rights, 62 Tex. L. Rev. 1417, 1418 (1984).

30. Sparer, Critical Legal Studies Symposium, *supra* note 28, at 521.

31. Tushnet, Symposium: A Critique of Rights: An Essay on Rights, 62 Tex. L. Rev. 1363, 1364 (1984).

32. *Id.* at 1380.

33. *Id.* at 1382–83.

34. Lynd, Symposium *supra* note 29, at 1419.

35. *Id.*

36. *Id.*

37. Tushnet, *supra* note 31, at 1384.

38. Gabel, Symposium: A Critique of Rights: The Phenomenology of Rights-Consciousness and the Pact of the Withdrawn Selves, 62 Tex. L. Rev. 1563, 1596 (1984).

39. For general discussions of the relations between critical legal studies and feminism, see Menkel-Meadow, Feminist Legal Theory, Critical Legal Studies, and Legal Education or The Fem-Crits Go to Law School, 38 J. Legal Educ. 61 (1988);

Rhode, Feminist Critical Theories, 42 Stan. L. Rev. 617 (1990); and West, Deconstructing the CLS-Fem Split, 2 Wis. Women's L.J. 85 (1986).

40. Menkel-Meadow, Feminist Legal Theory, *supra* note 39, at 61–62.

41. Jaggar, Feminist Politics, *supra* note 6, at 287–90; Olsen, Feminist Theory in Grand Style, *supra* note 18, at 1169.

42. Olsen, Feminist Theory in Grand Style, *supra* note 18, at 1172.

❖ *Toward a Theory of Law and Patriarchy*

Janet Rifkin

Ideology, Law and Power

THE NATURE AND MEANING of patriarchal social order and of patriarchal culture have recently become the subject of intense scholarly questioning. Historians, literary scholars, political theorists, economists, anthropologists, sociologists, psychologists and law teachers have been attempting through their respective disciplines to understand the origin of patriarchy and the perpetuation of a patriarchal social order. By patriarchy, I mean any kind of group organization in which males hold dominant power and determine what part females shall and shall not play, and in which capabilities assigned to women are relegated generally to the mystical and aesthetic and excluded from the practical and political realms, these realms being regarded as separate and mutually exclusive.[1]

Law plays a primary and significant role in social order. The relationship between law and patriarchy, however, needs to be clarified and developed. . . . In this essay, I will examine the . . . origins of patriarchy: how law is a paradigm of maleness; how law and legal ideology under capitalism preserved, transformed and updated pre-existing patriarchal forms to serve the interests of the emerging bourgeoisie; and finally, why legal change does not lead to social reordering.

Law is powerful as both a symbol and a vehicle of male authority. This power is based both on an ideology of law and an ideology of women which is supported by law. One function of ideology is to mystify social reality and to block social change.[2] Law functions as a form of hegemonic ideology.[3] Thus, a court could rule that

> civil law, as well as nature herself, has always recognized a wide difference in the respective spheres and destinies of man and woman. Man is, or should be, woman's protector and defender. The natural and proper timidity and delicacy which belongs to the female sex evidently unfits it for many of the occupations of civil life.[4]

3 Harv. Women's L.J. 83 (1980). Permission granted by Harvard Women's Law Journal. Copyright © 1980 by the President and Fellows of Harvard College.

By the acceptance of this as a statement of reality, law is reinforced as a powerful ideological force of social cohesion and stability.

The ideology of law is also tied to its manifestation as a written set of formulations, principles and regulation. "Freezing ideas and information in words makes it possible to assess more coolly and rigorously the validity of an argument, . . . thus, 'reinforcing a certain kind and measure of [increased] rationality.'"[5] The power of law as ideology is to mask or distort social reality in the name of tradition. Law, in relation to women, is seen as a measured and rational set of beliefs which at the same time asserts a mythological vision which is believed by many to present an accurate statement of the world.

A good example of this phenomenon is found in the suffragist movement of the early twentieth century. "Operating within the male-dominant paradigm, the form, language, and mode of Suffragist protest was set not so much by the objective conditions of female oppression as by their response to the idealizations and mystifications and legalities which rationalized continuance of the *status quo*."[6] Thus, the suffragist, in not challenging the ideology of law which supported an ideology of women, perpetuated mystifications which supported the status quo.

The power of legal ideology is so great that it often becomes hard to differentiate between legal principles and social customs. For example, American women have long worked outside the home in significant numbers. This fact of women's work in the labor market is constantly restricted by specific laws, and is at odds with the basic legal ideology that females should be excluded from the public sphere of work. The legal ideology of these restrictions carries forward the basic message that women are to be at home. The legal ideology of women does not bend to accommodate the economic reality of working women.

In 1908, when a substantial number of American women were working, the United States Supreme Court upheld a maximum hours law which applied to women only, reasoning that "her physical structure and a proper discharge of her maternal functions—having in view not merely her own health, but the well being of the race, justify legislation to protect her from the greed as well as the passion of man."[7] The ideological statement that women should be at home was couched in the context of the capitalist framework of competition for jobs. Economic competition between women and men was recognized, and in the name of protecting women, the hierarchal, male-dominated sex/gender system was reinforced. This reinforcement is supported by the ideological assertion that women are in need of greater protection than men.

The power of law as ideology continues into the present and may be examined in light of massive litigative efforts to change the status of women in contemporary society. The reliance on litigation reflects the belief in law as a source of social change, while ignoring the ideological power of law to mask social reality and block social change. Court battles about "women's issues" are waged and sometimes won with the result that a new body of rights is created and deployed in battle, but the basic sexual hierarchy is not changed. Although the hierarchy may be threatened in that each battle subjects the traditional law and legal ideology to examination and review, the litigation of "rights" never reaches the question of collective social organization.

In the area of the law of abortion, for instance, one sees that while the decisions relating to contraception and abortion have been thought of in terms of the expansion of a woman's right to privacy and reproductive freedom, a challenge asserting a competing claim surfaces after every expression of an apparently broadened claim. Thus, after the decision in Roe v. Wade[8] recognizing a limited constitutional right to abortion, cases were brought alleging that the rights of fathers were violated,[9] arguments were made that the rights of parents would be violated if minors had full rights to choose abortion[10] and laws and restrictions threatened doctors who performed abortions.[11]

Another significant example of this pattern is in the legal war over affirmative action, where there have been numerous lawsuits brought by individuals claiming that granting members of minority groups preference discriminates against members of the majority group. Here the struggle is articulated as a battle between individuals competing for jobs and education. This focus ignores and obscures the more fundamental social and political questions of power which generate these lawsuits.

The crucial point is that these legal battles reflect anger and dissatisfaction which, in reality, potentially threaten the patriarchal hierarchy. The power of law is that by framing the issues as questions of law, claims of right, precedents and problems of constitutional interpretation, the effect is to divert potential public consciousness from an awareness of the deeper roots of the expressed dissatisfaction and anger. The ideology of law serves to mask the real social and political questions underlying these problems of law. At the same time, the paradigm of law which historically has been and continues to be the symbol of male authority is not only unchallenged but reinforced as a legitimate mechanism for resolving social conflict. In the end, patriarchy as a form of power and social order will not be eliminated unless the male power paradigm of law is challenged and transformed. In order to challenge the male paradigm of law, the origin of law as a form of male authority and power must be discovered and examined more thoroughly. . . .

Patriarchy, Law and Capitalism

In *Law and the Rise of Capitalism*, Michael Tigar and Madeline Levy show that the thirteenth century in England and in continental Europe "saw the creation and application of specific rules about contracts, property and procedure which strengthened the power of the rising bourgeoisie."[12] They show that these "rules were fashioned in the context of a legal ideology which identified freedom of action for businessmen with natural law and natural reason."[13]

In their study, however, Tigar and Levy do not examine the emerging law in relation to women. They do not discuss, for example, how the rise of capitalism profoundly changed the nature of work, the family, and the role of women. I maintain that law, which emerged "as a form of rationality appropriate to the social relations generated by the emergence of entrepreneurial capitalism,"[14] retained the pre-existing hierarchy of masculine authority and made more explicit the subordination of women to men by increasingly excluding women from working in trades and relegating them to the private world of the home, which itself also became more and more non-productive.

The feudal world, which was organized for war, was essentially a masculine world. Although laws and custom put wives under the power of their husbands, records indicate, nonetheless, participation by some noble women in social, political and legal activities. Women also demonstrated great productive capacity when society was organized on the basis of family and domestic industry. At the end of the fourteenth century, one-fourth of the cloth woven in York was produced by women.[15] Laws, restrictive in some spheres, there encouraged women's economic participation. The Act of 1363, for example, declared:

> [T]he intent of the king and of his council is that women, that is to say brewers, bakers, carders and spinners, and workers as well of wool as of linen-clothing . . . , and all other that do use and work all handiworks, may freely use and work as they have done before this time.[16]

This attitude began to change, however, during the next century as legal regulations promulgated by various guilds became increasingly restrictive of women's participation. Many of these laws reflected the blatant threat of competition to the male workers. In Bristol in 1461, it was complained that weavers employed their wives, daughters, and maidens "by the which many and divers of the king's liege people, likely men to do the king service in his wars and in the defence of this his land, and sufficiently learned in the said craft, goeth vagrant and unoccupied, and may not have their labour to their living."[17]

Sometimes a guild prohibited employment of women, though generally widows could work in their husband's craft. As late as 1726, the Baker's craft in Aberdeen which was distressed by the competition of women who used their own ovens and sold the produce themselves passed a law which mandated a severe fine to any freeman in the baking trade who allowed a woman to use his oven.[18] Other craft guilds were equally restrictive of women working in trades. Rachel Baxter, for example, was admitted to the tailor's craft provided "that she shall . . . have only the privilege of mantua-making, and no ways make stays, or import the same to sell from any other place . . . and it is hereby declared that thi[*sic*] presents to be no precedent to any woman in tyme coming."[19]

Thus, with the emergence of capitalism and through the power of legal regulation, women were affected in several fundamental ways: individual wages were substituted for family earnings, enabling men to organize themselves in the competition of the labor market without sharing with the women of their families all the benefits derived through their combination; the withdrawal of wage-earners from home life to work upon the premises of the masters and the prevention of the employment of the wage-earner's wife in her husband's occupation, and the rapid increase of wealth which allowed the upper class women to withdraw altogether from business.

Whereas the system of family industry united labor and capital in one person or family group, capitalism brought them into conflict and competition; men and women struggled with each other to secure work and wages. The keystone of the male journeymen's superior economic position in capitalism lay in their ability to restrict their own numbers by promulgating and enforcing laws which specifically limited numbers, imposed long apprenticeship programs and limited the number of apprentices.[20]

The pre-existing patriarchal culture supported historically by kinship bonds and custom was transformed in capitalism through law in the service of new economic interest.

> [C]ustomary and traditional modes of conceptualizing bonds of obligation and duty were of diminishing relevance in bourgeois society, where people experienced a growing and radical separation between public life and private life. . . . [F]amily, and personal dependence begin to dissolve and crumble under the corrosive impact of the single universalist principles of social solidarity underlying capitalist social relations—*exchange*.[21]

The role of law in early capitalism was to help create a climate in which production for exchange could thrive. To accomplish this, law, always a symbol of male authority, fostered competition between women and men and severely limited female participation in the world of market production. Law became a primary and powerful tool of the rising bourgeoisie. Legal regulations were enacted which symbolized a continuation of the male authority of the past and which transformed and updated patriarchal society to serve new capitalistic interests. Laws were used increasingly to restrict women from working in trades, relegating them to the private world of the home. Thus, legal rules helped to create a social order where women were excluded from the public world of production exchange. And these new laws, justified in the name of the natural order, were accepted as an accurate vision of the world. . . .

Conclusion

. . . Law emerges as the symbol of patriarchal authority in varying ways. With the emergence of capitalist society, law became a crucial, substantial and ideological mechanism which updated a pre-existing patriarchal social order to meet the needs of emerging capitalist interests. Through law, women were relegated to the private world of the home and family and excluded from the public world of monetary exchange.

Although the recent litigation efforts to change the role of women in society have resulted in alleviating some oppressive practices, the paradigm of law as a symbol of male authority has not been challenged. Indeed, the reliance on litigative and legitimate strategies has reinforced the belief that the law-paradigm is a legitimate mechanism for resolving conflict and that it is a source of social change. As long as the male-dominant power paradigm of law remains unchallenged, the basic social hierarchy will not change. The struggle for sexual equality can be successful only if it challenges, rather than reifies, the male paradigm of law.

Notes

1. A. Rich, On Lies, Secrets and Silence 78 (Norton, 1979).

2. Kellner, Ideology, Marxism, and Advanced Capitalism, 42 Socialist Rev. 38 (1978).

3. *Id.* at 49–50. "Ideology becomes hegemonic when it is widely accepted as describing 'the way things are,' inducing people to consent to their society and its way of life as natural, good, and just." *Id.*

4. Bradwell v. State, 83 U.S. (16 Wall.) 130, 141 (Bradley, J., concurring).

5. Kellner, Ideology, *supra* note 2, at 45, quoting A. Gouldner, The Dialectic of Ideology and Technology: The Origins, Grammar and Future of Ideology 41 (Seabury Press, 1976).

6. Elshtain, Moral Woman and Immoral Man: A Consideration of the Public–Private Split and Its Political Ramifications, 4 Pol. & Soc'y 453, 469 (1974).

7. Muller v. Oregon, 208 U.S, 412, 422 (1908).

8. 410 U.S. 113 (1973).

9. Planned Parenthood of Cent. Missouri v. Danforth, 428 U.S. 52 (1976); Coe v. Gerstein, 376 F.Supp. 695 (S.D. Fla. 1973), *cert. denied*, 417 U.S. 279 (1974); Doe v. Rampton, 366 F. Supp. 189 (D. Utah), *vacated and remanded*, 410 U.S. 950 (1973); Coe v. General Hosp., No. 1477–71 (D.D.C. 1972); Doe v. Doe, 365 Mass. 556, 314 N.E.2d 128 (1974); Jones v. Smith, 278 So.2d 339 (Fla. Dist. Ct. App. 1973), *cert. denied*, 415 U.S. 958 (1974).

10. Bellotti v. Baird, 332 U.S. 622 (1979); Planned Parenthood of Cent. Missouri v. Danforth, 428 U.S. 52 (1976).

11. Colautti v. Franklin, 439 U.S. 463 (1979); Commonwealth v. Edelin, 359 N.E.2d 4 (Mass. 1976).

12. M. Tigar & M. Levy, Law and the Rise of Capitalism 6 (Monthly Review Press, 1978).

13. *Id.*

14. Fraser, The Legal Theory We Need Now, 37 Socialist Rev. 147, 154 (1978).

15. E. Lipson, 1 The Economic History of England 359. 7th ed. (Monthly Review Press, 1937).

16. *Id.* at 361.

17. *Id.*

18. E. Bain, Merchant and Craft Guilds: A History of the Aberdeen Incorporated Trades 228 (J. & J.P. Edmond & Spark, 1887).

19. *Id.* at 257.

20. A. Clark, Working Life of Women in the Seventeenth Century 298 (Dutton, 1919).

21. Fraser, Legal Theory We Need Now, *supra* note 14, at 154–55 (emphasis in original).

❖ Toward a Theory of Law and Patriarchy

DIANE POLAN

THE GOAL OF this essay is to suggest ways to broaden critical legal theory beyond a Marxist analysis of the ways in which law and legal traditions have supported and/or perpetuated existing economic and social relations and class domination to include a feminist analysis of the role of the law in maintaining male domination, or patriarchy.[1] What is needed is a critical examination of the relationship between law and women's subordination that integrates feminist and Marxist theoretical perspectives.[2] This essay is an attempt to assess the applicability of critical legal theory to the relationship between law and patriarchy, and to suggest the beginnings of a Marxist-feminist approach to law.

To begin with, the essay agrees with the stance of all critical theory that law does not operate neutrally, ahistorically, or independently of the underlying power relationships in society. For the purposes of a *feminist* critical theory, those "underlying power relationships" must be understood as having both a class and a gender dimension. Thus, if critical legal theory is grounded on a belief that the legal system of capitalist society ultimately supports the existing capitalist social order, a feminist critical theory likewise supposes that the legal system of a patriarchal society enforces and maintains a male supremacist social order as well. The questions asked by critical legal theory focus on how the legal system fulfills that role and how the role of the law has changed as capitalism itself has developed and changed. At the least, a feminist critical theory would ask those same questions about the relationship between law and patriarchy. . . . But before proceeding further, it is important to point out and briefly discuss some problems and limitations inherent in this approach.

Problems of Integrating Marxist
and Feminist Approaches to the Law

First, feminist theory is fundamentally different from Marxist theory. While Marxism locates the basis of class oppression in the control of the underlying productive resources of society, there is no analogous feminist explanation of the origin of female oppression. Moreover, capitalism developed at a particular historical moment and adapted the institutions of the law to its own purposes, while patriarchy has been a social institution for a far longer time and antedates modern legal systems. Thus, it probably is correct to say that any legal system that developed in a patriarchal culture, including the Anglo-American legal system, would be, by definition, a patriarchal institution.

Second, given that capitalism is a relatively recent historical development, whereas patriarchy seems always to have been with us, it is a far more difficult task to arrive at one satisfactory explanation of the genesis of patriarchy.[3] But, whatever the explanation of the origin of male supremacy, and regardless of whether patriarchy predated capitalism,[4] it seems clear that by now the capitalist system has so integrated and institutionalized the arguably preexisting subordination of women that modern women's inferior status and powerlessness must be seen as the product of the interaction of two separate systems of domination: capitalism and patriarchy.[5]

In the past decade, a variety of Marxist-feminist approaches and theories have been developed.[6] While they differ significantly, they all share a dissatisfaction with both the failure of classical Marxism to recognize male supremacy as a separate and distinct source of women's oppression, and the failure of liberal feminist analyses to examine the historical relationship between sex oppression and capitalist economic development. Rather than try to discover the origin of male supremacy, Marxist-feminists have focused on the interactions of capitalism and patriarchy in maintaining women's oppression in modern society. In so doing, they have demonstrated that the oppression of women has not remained static over time but has changed historically in a dialectical relationship to changes in economic and social development and related changes in the role of the family.

Third, capitalism and patriarchy do not always operate in analogous ways, which has implications for an understanding of the role of law in relationship to each of these systems. For example, while it is possible to roughly describe and identify a capitalist "ruling class," whose interests are served by certain legal decisions, rules, and arrangements, it is much more problematic to identify an analogous patriarchal "ruling class," whose "interests" the law serves. The fact is that *all men* benefit from laws and legal decisions which disadvantage women or render them legally powerless—for example, laws that exclude husbands from prosecution under criminal rape laws. At the same time, because the law operates in support of *both* patriarchy and capitalism, people stand in different relationships to the legal system by virtue of their sex and class positions. To use a simplified example, a male worker may, at the same time, be oppressed by laws that punish union organization but benefit from laws that exclude women from certain occupations. Similarly, while it is certainly true that all women are subordinated by male supremacist laws, some women—by virtue of their class position—do benefit from the legal system.

Lastly, the law may, in fact, play a much different (and possibly less significant) role in the maintenance of patriarchy than it has in the perpetuation of capitalism. It can be quite persuasively argued that patriarchy has been primarily maintained not by legal means but by nonlegal forces and social institutions, in particular, the family.[7] Nevertheless, at least on the level of ideology, the law may be seen to play a similar role in maintaining exploitative relationships of domination and subordination between both class- and gender-based groups. Patriarchal ideology—ideas about women and their "place" in society—has probably played at least as important a role in the modern subordination of women as capitalist ideology has played in supporting advanced industrial capitalism. Particularly at those historical movements when significant material and technological changes, with the capacity to alter women's social and economic position, have occurred, ideology has been successfully used to maintain women's oppression.

How Does the Law Perpetuate Patriarchy?

Applying a traditional Marxist concept, we might ask whether the legal system maintains patriarchy by operating directly against women, as an "instrument" of patriarchal power. Alternatively, using the neo-Marxist categories of critical legal theory, different questions might be appropriate: If the law has played a direct role in keeping women subordinate, to what extent has that role changed? And is it more accurate to view the law today as playing a more hegemonic role, whose ultimate purpose is to legitimate a status quo in which male supremacy is accepted as natural and unchangeable? A corollary question might be: To what extent has the legal system, as part of an overall hegemonic function, operated independently of, or even in apparent conflict with, the immediate interests of male supremacy?

Prior to the twentieth century, Anglo-American law, legal rules, and judicial decisions gave absolute and clear-cut support to male supremacy. Thus, it is indisputable that our legal system has operated directly to maintain women's subordination.[8] However, this is not a full or sufficient explanation of how the law operates to support patriarchy. Over the past century, the legal system has rejected some of its most blatant sexist notions and expressions without ceasing to reinforce male power and female subordination. For this reason, it is essential to examine and try to understand the less direct and instrumental ways in which the legal system operates to perpetuate male supremacy.

Like capitalism, patriarchy has never operated solely on the level of physical coercion, although it is striking to what extent the subordination of women *has* been maintained through the use or threat of physical force or violence by men. Throughout history, ideas about women, the family, and the relationship between women and the outside world have been effectively used to rationalize inequality and the inferior status of women. Patriarchal ideology has been successful to the extent that it has convinced women that our social, political, and economic subordination and our psychological feelings of inferiority are the result of natural forces rather than exploitative social relations. Although patriarchal ideology has itself undergone changes over time, particularly in response to developments in the capitalist economic system and the labor force needs of particular periods, its overall function—the legitimation of male supremacy—has remained the same.

The ideas about women expressed in American legal decisions have generally tracked prevailing patriarchal ideologies. For example, Supreme Court opinions in the late-nineteenth and early-twentieth centuries reverberated with an ideology that has been described as the "public/private" split. The essence of this ideology was that the world was naturally divided into two parts, or spheres: one, a public sphere, of work and politics, inhabited by men; and the second, a personal or domestic sphere, encompassing home and family life, which was deemed the realm of women. Not surprisingly, these ideas gained currency at a historical moment when the development of capitalism had resulted in the movement of production out of the home and into the factory.[9]

The public/private ideology served at least two distinct and identifiable purposes. One was to convince women, by use of assertions about their natural domesticity and their primary role as childbearers and child rearers, to stay at home and out of the workplace. Equally important was the function that this ideology played as a justification for *actually* barring women from participation in the world outside the home. The manipulation of this ideology within the legal system performed both of these functions.

The legal system has also used the public/private dichotomy in another, more subtle fashion that has further reinforced patriarchy. By placing the operation of law squarely in the public realm and, at least rhetorically, removing itself from the "private realm" of personal life and the family, the legal system created a distinction between a public realm of life, which is a proper arena for legal or social regulation, and another, fundamentally different, personal sphere, which is somehow outside the law's or society's authority to regulate. Thus, the legal system has functioned to legitimate that very distinction by asserting it as a natural, rather than socially imposed, ground for different treatment.

One practical result of the "hands-off" rhetorical stance of the law toward activities within the "private realm of the family" has been to license men's exploitation of women within the family unit. In essence, by purportedly withdrawing itself from regulation of the private sphere, the legal system has lent its actual support to male supremacy by permitting men to completely dominate and control family life. Even today, it is difficult to get courts to intervene in domestic violence situations because of a supposed deference to the "privacy of the family."

Closely related to the law's role as an exponent of particular ideologies that support male supremacy, such as the public/private ideology, is its hegemonic function in support of patriarchy. While the concept of hegemony has thus far been articulated and applied in the context of understanding and explaining the *class* domination of advanced industrial society, it may also be useful to apply this concept in trying to understand how male supremacy is maintained. In respect to patriarchy, a set of ideas could be said to operate hegemonically to the extent it succeeds in convincing women that their inferior political, economic, and social status, as well as their subordination to husbands and fathers within the family unit, is a result of a *natural* division of the world into separate spheres and *natural* differences between male and female personalities that suit women and men for different roles, rather than the result of exploitation and domination.

Laws and court opinions that embody and express these kinds of ideas can play an important part in maintaining patriarchal hegemony. Interestingly, this hegemonic effect has sometimes occurred in the context of legal decisions that appear to actually *improve* women's lives. For example, beginning in the mid-twentieth century, a series of Supreme Court cases struck down restrictions on the use of contraceptives and then abortion as an unconstitutional state interference into people's private sexual lives. In all of these decisions, the Court emphasized the privacy of the family and asserted that sexual relations are part of a private sphere that is outside the state's authority to regulate. Thus, while the outcome of the birth control and abortion cases was beneficial to women by giving at least some women a greater degree of control over their reproduction, these decisions must also be understood as serving a hegemonic function, by legitimating the notion that there are naturally separate private and public spheres of human existence. Since it is the ideological construct of the public/private split that has been used both to exclude women from the public sphere and to devalue the social work women perform in the home, the law can be seen as operating in support of patriarchy when, by asserting that different legal rules govern public and private matters, it legitimizes that distinction as natural rather than as socially imposed.

Finally, the related notion of the "relative autonomy of the law" has been advanced by those arguing in favor of the law's hegemonic role. It is difficult to apply this concept to the historical experience of women (and nonwhites) within the American legal system because our legal system—at least until very recently—has not operated at all "autonomously" of the interests of white or male supremacy. Rather, our laws and judicial interpretations of them have directly enforced both sexism and racism. Although it may be true that the law has operated with the appearance of neutrality and even-handedness toward white men of both the upper and lower classes, there has not been even the *appearance* of fairness or equal treatment in the operation of the American legal system toward blacks and women. As a result, the legal system has in the past had very little legitimacy in the minds of many blacks and women, who have quite correctly viewed it as an instrument or tool of their domination and as an integral aspect of their subordinate status in society.

However, that situation has been changing in some limited ways over the past several decades. With the rise of the feminist and black liberation movements, the legal system has been forced to accommodate some of their demands in order to preserve the threatened legitimacy of the social order. To the extent that the legal system has taken some steps to repudiate its past racism and sexism, some sort of relatively autonomous role for the law in relation to both blacks and women may be developing. If the relative-autonomy concept is valid, one would expect to see greater legitimacy accorded to the legal system by those groups who have been previously excluded from the law's purported justice and equal treatment as well as greater enthusiasm on their part for pressing their demands within the legal arena. The response of the legal system to these demands in turn has a direct effect on social stability: when oppressed individuals and groups believe that they can rely on the legal system to redress their grievances and remedy their subordinate status in society, there is a decreasing likelihood that they will seek more radical solutions to their situation.

Thus, a subtle testimony to the law's success in achieving legitimacy is that women, and other groups who are oppressed and dominated within society, now largely accept the law's categories and its modes of discourse. To the extent that those groups choose to articulate their social criticism and their grievances in the law's limited categories—"equal rights" and "equal opportunities"—and confine their action to litigation and lawmaking rather than struggle in such alternative arenas as the workplace, the family, and in organized religion, they are giving up the battle, because in so doing, they are tacitly approving the underlying social order and thus undermining more radical challenges to the overarching male supremacist and white supremacist structure of society. This suggests that the law, in the very process of reducing its role as a direct instrument of patriarchal power, is effectively maintaining sex oppression in different, more subtle ways. Its success in establishing its own legitimacy among previously excluded and disenfranchised groups allows the law to operate hegemonically, thereby coopting the radical impulse behind the struggle against patriarchy and diverting the energy of the women's liberation movement into a narrow focus on legally articulable claims.

Concluding Thoughts

This analysis does not necessarily mean that the law should be abandoned or ignored in the fight against sexism. Some victories may be won in the courts and legislatures. It is quite clear that the law's own rules and precedents can and have been used to expand women's rights, and sometimes they do deal effective blows to patriarchy. For example, while the Supreme Court's early birth control decisions applied only to the right of married couples to use contraception, the rhetoric and logic of those cases has been successfully used to expand constitutional protection to single women's right to control their own reproduction.[10] As recent abortion decisions make clear, however, the logic of the prior decisions carries only so far: apparently, only women with adequate financial resources have constitutionally protected rights to control their reproduction.[11]

Second, it is important to recognize that legal gains for women depend on a variety of social, economic, and political circumstances, including the relative strength of women's movements and conflicts between patriarchy and the needs of the capitalist economic system. For example, the controversy concerning coverage of pregnancy-related disabilities by employers' insurance programs reflects an underlying tension between the economy's need for women workers and patriarchy's interest in keeping women economically dependent by hindering their participation in the work force. We must therefore try to identify and understand these potential contradictions, as well as the particular historical context of any given legal battle, in order to successfully exploit them for the benefit of women.

Finally, we cannot underestimate the practical limitations we face with any law-oriented strategy. The experience of going to court on a regular basis underscores the pervasive maleness of the legal system: it is a system infused with sexist values. Regardless of the language of a statute, it is individual judges who decide cases. The judiciary remains overwhelmingly male. Judges have grown up in a patriarchal culture; their attitudes are inevitably shaped by their life experiences and by their position as the beneficiaries of male supremacy. . . . Furthermore, even if sexism were formally eliminated from the legal system, and even if half the lawmakers and legal decision makers were women, the legal system would not become a nonsexist institution. The whole structure of law—its hierarchical organization; its combative, adversarial format; and its undeviating bias in favor of rationality over all other values—defines it as a fundamentally patriarchal institution.

Thus, it is not so much that laws must be changed; it is patriarchy that must be changed. Actions taken within the legal system cannot by themselves eliminate patriarchy, which is a pervasive social phenomenon. Because law is one, but only one, locus of male supremacy, legal efforts to end women's subordinate status cannot effectively challenge or cripple patriarchy unless they are undertaken in the context of broader economic, social, and cultural changes.

Notes

1. For my purposes here, "patriarchy" may be defined as a system of social relations in which men as a group have power over women as a group; it is a system that is characterized by relationships of domination and submission, superiority and inferiority, power and powerlessness, based on sex.

2. Unfortunately, there has been no adequate integration of feminist and Marxist theories concerning the relationship between the law and women's op-

pression. The feminist legal scholarship that exists lacks an economic analysis, . . . while Marxist-oriented critical approaches have thus far confined their analyses to social relations within the public sphere, ignoring the private sphere that is so central to women's lives and women's subordination.

3. This problem has been the focus of much writing, debate, and disagreement among feminist theorists. See, e.g., S. Firestone, The Dialectic of Sex (Morrow, 1970); S. Brownmiller, Against Our Will: Men, Women and Rape (Bantam Books, 1975); S. de Beauvoir, The Second Sex (Vintage Books, 1974); G. Rubin, The Traffic in Women: Notes on the Political Economy of Sex, in R. Reiter ed., Toward an Anthropology of Women (Monthly Review Press, 1975).

4. Engels and others have argued that women's subordination is historically related to the development of capitalism, private property, and the property-based family. See F. Engels, The Origin of the Family, Private Property and the State (International Publishers, 1942); E. Reed, Women's Evolution (Pathfinder Press, 1975); K. Gough, The Origin of the Family, in Reiter, Toward an Anthropology of Women, *supra* note 3. Many contemporary feminists disagree. See note 3 *supra*.

5. The term "capitalist patriarchy" has been used to describe and emphasize the "mutually reinforcing dialectical relationships between capitalist class structure and hierarchical sexual structuring" in the modern subordination of women. Z. Eisenstein, Capitalist Patriarchy and the Case for Socialist Feminism (Monthly Review Press, 1979), at 5.

6. See, e.g., J. Mitchell, Women's Estate (Penguin, 1971); A. Oakley, Women's Work (Vintage, 1974); E. Zaretsky, Capitalism, the Family and Personal Life (Harper Colophon, 1976).

7. See, e.g., D. Dinnerstein, The Mermaid and the Minotaur (Harper & Row, 1976); N. Chodorow, The Reproduction of Mothering: Psychoanalysis and the Sociology of Gender (University of California Press, 1978).

8. Examples abound: laws restricted married women's control of property and eliminated their contractual rights: the marital "merger" of husband and wife meant that the wife lost all legal existence; the judiciary upheld state laws that barred women from entering professions; women were denied basic political rights; rape laws excluded husbands from prosecution; etc. . . .

9. See V. Klein, The Feminine Character: History of an Ideology 10 (International Universities Press, 1949); Oakley, Women's Work, *supra* note 6, at 33; Zaretsky, Capitalism, *supra* note 6, at 49.

10. Griswold v. Connecticut, 381 U.S. 381 (1961) (married couples); Eisenstadt v. Baird, 405 U.S. 438 (1972) (single women).

11. Compare Roe v. Wade, 410 U.S. 113 (1973) with Maher v. Roe, 432 U.S. 464 (1977) and Harris v. McRae, 448 U.S. 297 (1980).

Feminism, Marxism, Method, and the State: Toward Feminist Jurisprudence

Catharine A. MacKinnon

FEMINISM HAS NO theory of the state. It has a theory of power: sexuality is gendered as gender is sexualized. Male and female are created through the erotization of dominance and submission. The man/woman difference and the dominance/submission dynamic define each other. This is the social meaning of sex and the distinctively feminist account of gender inequality.[1] Sexual objectification, the central process within this dynamic, is at once epistemological and political.[2] The feminist theory of knowledge is inextricable from the feminist critique of power because the male point of view forces itself upon the world as its way of apprehending it.

The perspective from the male standpoint[3] enforces women's definition, encircles her body, circumlocutes her speech, and describes her life. The male perspective is systemic and hegemonic. The content of the significant "woman" is the content of women's lives. Each sex has its role, but their stakes and power are not equal. If the sexes are unequal, and perspective participates in situation, there is no ungendered reality or ungendered perspective. And they are connected. In this context, objectivity—the nonsituated, universal standpoint, whether claimed or aspired to—is a denial of the existence or potency of sex inequality that tacitly participates in constructing reality from the dominant point of view. Objectivity, as the epistemological stance of which objectification is the social process, creates the reality it apprehends by defining as knowledge the reality it creates through its way of apprehending it. Sexual metaphors for knowing are no coincidence. The solipsism of this approach does not undercut its sincerity, but it is interest that precedes method.

Feminism criticizes this male totality without an account of our capacity to do so or to imagine or realize a more whole truth. Feminism affirms women's point of view by revealing, criticizing, and explaining its impossibility. This is not a dialectical paradox. It is a methodological expression of women's situation, in

From *Signs: Journal of Women in Culture and Society* 1983, Vol. 8, No. 4. © 1983 by The University of Chicago. All rights reserved.

which the struggle for consciousness is a struggle for world: for a sexuality, a history, a culture, a community, a form of power, an experience of the sacred. If women had consciousness or world, sex inequality would be harmless, or all women would be feminist. Yet we have something of both, or there would be no such thing as feminism. Why can women know that this—life as we have known it—is not all, not enough, not ours, not just? Now, why don't all women?

The practice of a politics of all women in the face of its theoretical impossibility is creating a new process of theorizing and a new form of theory. Although feminism emerges from women's particular experience, it is not subjective or partial, for no interior ground and few if any aspects of life are free of male power. Nor is feminism objective, abstract, or universal.[4] It claims no external ground or unsexed sphere of generalization or abstraction beyond male power, nor transcendence of the specificity of each of its manifestations. How is it possible to have an engaged truth that does not simply reiterate its determinations? Disengaged truth only reiterates *its* determinations. Choice of method is choice of determinants—a choice which, for women as such, has been unavailable because of the subordination of women. Feminism does not begin with the premise that it is unpremised. It does not aspire to persuade an unpremised audience because there is no such audience. Its project is to uncover and claim as valid the experience of women, the major content of which is the devalidation of women's experience.

This defines our task not only because male dominance is perhaps the most pervasive and tenacious system of power in history, but because it is metaphysically nearly perfect.[5] Its point of view is the standard for point-of-viewlessness, its particularity the meaning of universality. Its force is exercised as consent, its authority as participation, its supremacy as the paradigm of order, its control as the definition of legitimacy. Feminism claims the voice of women's silence, the sexuality of our eroticized desexualization, the fullness of "lack," the centrality of our marginality and exclusion, the public nature of privacy, the presence of our absence. This approach is more complex than transgression, more transformative than transvaluation, deeper than mirror-imaged resistance, more affirmative than the negation of our negativity. It is neither materialist nor idealist; it is feminist. Neither the transcendence of liberalism nor the determination of materialism works for us. Idealism is too unreal; women's inequality is enforced, so it cannot simply be thought out of existence, certainly not by us. Materialism is too real; women's inequality has never not existed, so women's equality never has. That is, the equality of women to men will not be scientifically provable until it is no longer necessary to do so. Women's situation offers no outside to stand on or gaze at, no inside to escape to, too much urgency to wait, no place else to go, and nothing to use but the twisted tools that have been shoved down our throats. If feminism is revolutionary, this is why.

Feminism has been widely thought to contain tendencies of liberal feminism, radical feminism, and socialist feminism. But just as socialist feminism has often amounted to marxism applied to women, liberal feminism has often amounted to liberalism applied to women. Radical feminism is feminism. Radical feminism—after this, feminism unmodified—is methodologically post-marxist. It moves to resolve the marxist-feminist problematic on the level of method. Because its method emerges from the concrete conditions of all women as a sex, it dissolves the individualist, naturalist, idealist, moralist structure of liberalism, the politics of which science is the epistemology. Where liberal feminism sees sexism primarily as an illusion or myth to be dispelled, an inaccuracy to be corrected, true feminism sees the male point of view as fundamental to the male power to create the world in its own image, the image of its desires, not just as its delusory end product. Feminism distinctively as such comprehends that what counts as truth is produced in the interest of those with power to shape reality, and that this process is as pervasive as it is necessary as it is changeable. Unlike the scientific strain in marxism or the Kantian imperative in liberalism, which in this context share most salient features, feminism neither claims universality nor, failing that, reduces to relativity. It does not seek a generality that subsumes its particulars or an abstract theory or a science of sexism. It rejects the approach of control over nature (including us) analogized to control over society (also including us) which has grounded the "science of society" project as the paradigm for political knowledge since (at least) Descartes. Both liberalism and marxism have been subversive on women's behalf. Neither is enough. To grasp the inadequacies for women of liberalism on one side and marxism on the other is to begin to comprehend the role of the liberal state and liberal legalism within a post-marxist feminism of social transformation.

As feminism has a theory of power but lacks a theory of the state, so marxism has a theory of value which (through the organization of work in production) becomes class analysis, but a problematic theory of the state. Marx did not address the state much more explicitly than he did women. Women were substratum, the state epiphenomenon. Engels, who frontally analyzed both, and together, presumed the subordination of women in every attempt to reveal its roots, just as he presupposed something like the state, or state-like social conditions, in every attempt to expose its origins.[6] Marx tended to use the term "political" narrowly to refer to the state or its laws, criticizing as exclusively political interpretations of the state's organization or behavior which took them as sui generis. Accordingly, until recently, most marxism has tended to consider political that which occurs between classes, that is, to interpret as "the political" instances of the marxist concept of inequality. In this broad sense, the marxist theory of social inequality has been its theory of politics. This has not so much collapsed the state into society (although it goes far in that direction) as conceived the state as determined by the totality of social relations of which the state is one determined and determining part—without specifying which, or how much, is which.

In this context, recent marxist work has tried to grasp the specificity of the institutional state: how it wields class power, or transforms class society, or responds to approach by a left aspiring to rulership or other changes. While liberal theory has seen the state as emanating power, and traditional marxism has seen the state as expressing power constituted elsewhere, recent marxism, much of it structuralist, has tried to analyze state power as specific to the state as a form, yet integral to a determinate social whole understood in class terms. This state is found "relatively autonomous." This means that the state, expressed through its functionaries, has a definite class character, is definitely capitalist or socialist, but also has its own interests which are to some degree independent of those of the ruling class and even of the class structure. The state as such, in this view, has a specific power and interest, termed "the political," such that class power, class interest expressed by and in the state, and state behavior, although inconceivable in isolation from one another, are nevertheless not linearly or causally linked or strictly coextensive. Such work locates "the specificity of the political" in a mediate "region" between the state as its own ground of power (which alone, as in the liberal conception, would set the state above or apart from class) and the state as possessing no special supremacy or priority in terms of power, as in the more orthodox marxist view.

The idea that the state is relatively autonomous, a kind of first among equals of social institutions, has the genius of appearing to take a stand on the issue of reciprocal constitution of state and society while straddling it. Is the state essentially autonomous of class but partly determined by it, or is it essentially determined by class but not exclusively so? Is it relatively constrained within a context of freedom or relatively free within a context of constraint? As to who or what fundamentally moves and shapes the realities and instrumentalities of domination, and where to go to do something about it, what qualifies what is as ambiguous as it is crucial. Whatever it has not accomplished, however, this literature has at least relieved the compulsion to find all law—directly or convolutedly, nakedly or clothed in unconscious or devious rationalia—to be simply bourgeois, without undercutting the notion that it is determinately driven by interest.

A methodologically post-marxist feminism must confront, on our own terms, the issue of the relation between the state and society, within a theory of social determination adequate to the specificity of sex. Lacking even a tacit theory of the state of its own, feminist practice has instead oscillated between a liberal theory of the state on the one hand and a left theory of the state on the other. Both treat law as the mind of society: disembodied reason in liberal theory, reflection of material interest in left theory. In liberal moments the state is accepted on its own term as a neutral arbiter among conflicting interests. The law is actually or potentially principled, meaning predisposed to no substantive outcome, thus available as a tool that is not fatally twisted. Women implicitly become an interest group within pluralism, with specific problems of mobilization and representation, exit and voice, sustaining incremental gains and losses. In left moments, the state becomes a tool of dominance and repression, the law legitimizing ideology, use of the legal system a form of utopian idealism or gradualist reform, each apparent gain deceptive or cooptive, and each loss inevitable.

Applied to women, liberalism has supported state intervention on behalf of women as abstract persons with abstract rights, without scrutinizing the content of these notions in gendered terms. Marxism applied to women is always on the edge of counseling abdication of the state as an arena altogether—and with it those women whom the state does not ignore or who are, as yet, in no position to ignore it. Feminism has so far accepted these constraints upon its alternatives: either the state, as primary tool of women's betterment and status transformation, without analysis (hence strategy) for it as male; or civil society, which for women has more closely resembled a state of nature. The state, with it the law, has been either omnipotent or impotent: everything or nothing.

The feminist posture toward the state has therefore been schizoid on issues central to women's survival: rape, battery, pornography, prostitution, sexual harassment, sex discrimination, abortion, the Equal Rights Amendment, to name a few. Attempts to reform and enforce rape laws, for example, have tended to build on the model of the deviant perpetrator and the violent act, as if the fact that rape is a crime means that the society is against it, so law enforcement would reduce or delegitimize it. Initiatives are accordingly directed toward making the police more sensitive, prosecutors more responsive, judges more receptive, and the law, in words, less sexist. This may be progressive in the liberal or the left senses, but how is it empowering in the feminist sense? Even if it were effective in jailing men who do little different from what nondeviant men do regularly, how would such an approach alter women's rapability? Unconfronted are *why* women are raped and the role of the state in that. Similarly, applying laws against battery to husbands, although it can mean life itself, has largely failed to address, as part of the strategy for state intervention, the conditions that produce men who systematically express themselves violently toward women, women whose resistance is disabled, and the role of the state in this dynamic. Criminal enforcement in these areas, while suggesting that rape and battery are deviant, punishes men for expressing the images of masculinity that means their identity, for which they are otherwise trained, elevated, venerated, and paid. These men must be stopped. But how does that change them or reduce the chances that there will be more like them? Liberal strategies entrust women to the state. Left theory abandons us to the rapists and batterers. The question for feminism is not only whether there is a meaningful difference between the two, but whether either is adequate to the feminist critique of rape and battery as systemic and to the role of the state and the law within that system.

Feminism has descriptions of the state's treatment of the gender difference, but no analysis of the state as gender hierarchy. We need to know. What, in gender terms, are the state's norms of accountability, sources of power, real constituency? Is the state to some degree autonomous of the interests of men or an integral expression of them? Does the state embody and serve male interests in its form, dynamics, relation to society, and specific policies? Is the state constructed upon the subordination of women? If so, how does male power become state power? Can such a state be made to serve the interests of those upon whose powerlessness its power is erected? Would a different relation between state and society, such as may pertain under socialism, make a difference? If not, is masculinity inherent in the state form as such, or is some other form of state, or some other way of governing, distinguishable or imaginable? In the absence of answers to such questions, feminism has been caught between giving more power to the state in each attempt to claim it for women and leaving unchecked power in the society to men. Undisturbed, meanwhile, like the assumption that women generally consent to sex, is the assumption that we consent to this government. The question for feminism, for the first time on its own terms, is: what is this state, from women's point of view?

As a beginning, I propose that the state is male in the feminist sense. The law sees and treats women the way men see and treat women. The liberal state coercively and authoritatively constitutes the social order in the interests of men as a gender, through its legitimizing norms, relation to society, and substantive policies. It achieves this through embodying and ensuring male control over women's sexuality at every level, occasionally cushioning, qualifying, or de jure prohibiting its excesses when necessary to its normalization. Substantively, the way the male point of view frames an experience is the way it is framed by state policy. To the extent possession is the point of sex, rape is sex with a woman who is not yours, unless the act is so as to make her yours. If part of the kick of pornography involves eroticizing the putatively prohibited, obscenity law will putatively prohibit pornography enough to maintain its desirability without ever making it unavailable or truly illegitimate. The same with prostitution. As male is the implicit reference for human, maleness will be the measure of equality in sex discrimination law. To the extent that the point of abortion is to control the reproductive sequelae of intercourse, so as to facilitate male sexual access to women, access to abortion will be controlled by "a man or The Man." Gender, elaborated and sustained by behavioral patterns of application and administration, is maintained as a division of power.

Formally, the state is male in that objectivity is its norm. Objectivity is liberal legalism's conception of itself. It legitimizes itself by reflecting its view of existing society, a society it made and makes by so seeing it, and calling that view, and that relation, practical rationality. If rationality is measured by point-of-viewlessness, what counts as reason will be that which corresponds to the way things are. Practical will mean that which can be done without changing anything. In this framework, the task of legal interpretation becomes "to perfect the state as mirror of the society."[7] Objectivist epistemology is the law of law. It ensures that the law will most reinforce existing distributions of power when it most closely adheres to its own highest ideal of fairness. Like the science it emulates, this epistemological stance can not see the social specificity of reflection as method or its choice to embrace that which it reflects. Such law not only reflects a society in which men rule women; it rules in a male way: "The phallus means everything that sets itself up as a mirror."[8] The rule form, which unites scientific knowledge with state control in its conception of what law is, institutionalizes the objective stance as jurisprudence. A closer look at the substantive law of rape in light of such an argument suggests that the relation between objectification (understood as the primary process of the subordination of women) and the power of the state is the relation between the personal and the political at the level of government. This is not because the state is presumptively the sphere of politics. It is because the state, in part through law, institutionalizes male power. If male power is systemic, it *is* the regime. . . .

[The detailed discussion of rape is omitted here, as it will appear in Volume 2, Feminist Legal Theory: Applications. *Ed.*]

The state's formal norms recapitulate the male point of view on the level of design. In Anglo-American jurisprudence, morals (value judgments) are deemed separable and separated from politics (power contests), and both from adjudication (interpretation). Neutrality, including judicial decision making that is dispassionate, impersonal, disinterested, and precedential, is considered desirable and descriptive. Courts, forums without predisposition among parties and with no interest of their own, reflect society back to itself resolved. Government of laws not men limits partiality with written constraints and tempers force with reasonable rule following. This law aspires to science: to the immanent generalization subsuming the emergent particularity, to prediction and control of social regularities and regulations, preferably codified. The formulaic "tests" of "doctrine" aspire to mechanism, classification to taxonomy. Courts intervene only in properly "factualized" disputes, cognizing social conflicts as if collecting empirical data. But the demarcations between morals and politics, the personality of the judge and the judicial role, bare coercion and the rule of law, tend to merge in women's experience. Relatively seamlessly they promote the dominance of men as a social group through privileging the form of power—the perspective on social life—feminist consciousness reveals as socially male. The separation of form from substance, process from policy, role from theory and practice, echoes and reechoes at each level of the regime its basic norm: objectivity.

Consider a central example. The separation of public from private is as crucial to the liberal state's claim to objectivity as its inseparability is to women's claim to subordination. Legally, it has both formal and substantive dimensions. The state considers formal, not substantive, the allocation of public matters to itself to be treated objectively, of private matters to civil society to be treated subjectively. Substantively, the private is defined as a right to "an inviolable personality,"[9] which is guaranteed by ensuring "autonomy or control over the intimacies of personal identity."[10] It is hermetic. It means that which is inaccessible to, unaccountable to, and unconstructed by anything beyond itself. Intimacy occurs in private; this is supposed to guarantee original symmetry of power. Injuries arise in violating the private sphere, not within and by and because of it. Private means consent can be presumed unless disproven. To contain a systematic inequality contradicts the notion itself. But feminist consciousness has exploded the private. For women, the measure of the intimacy has been the measure of the oppression. To see the personal as political means to see the private as public. On this level, women have no privacy to lose or to guarantee. We are not inviolable. Our sexuality, meaning gender identity, is not only violable, it *is* (hence we are) our violation. Privacy is everything women as women have never been allowed to be or to have; at the same time the private is everything women have been equated with and defined in terms of *men's* ability to have. To confront the fact that we have no privacy is to confront our private degradation as the public order. To fail to recognize this place of the private in women's subordination by seeking protection behind a right to that privacy is thus to be cut off from collective verification and state support in the same act. The very place (home, body), relations (sexual), activities (intercourse and reproduction), and feelings (intimacy, selfhood) that feminism finds central to women's subjection form the core of privacy doctrine. But when women are segregated in private, one at a time, a law of privacy will tend to protect the right of men "to be let alone," to oppress us one at a time. A law of the private, in a state that mirrors such a society, will translate the traditional values of the private sphere into individual women's right to privacy, subordinating women's collective needs to the imperatives of male supremacy. It will keep some men out of the bedrooms of other men.

Liberalism converges with the left at this edge of the feminist critique of male power. Herbert Marcuse speaks of "philosophies which are 'political' in the widest sense—affecting society as a whole, demonstrably transcending the sphere of privacy."[11] This does and does not describe the feminist political: "Women both have and have not had a common world."[12] Isolation in the home and intimate degradation, women share. The private sphere, which confines and separates us, is therefore a political sphere, a common ground of our inequality. In feminist translation, the private is a sphere of battery, marital rape, and women's exploited labor; of the central social institutions whereby women are deprived of (as men are granted) identity, autonomy, control, and self-determination; and of the primary activity through which male supremacy is expressed and enforced. Rather than transcending the private as a predicate to politics, feminism politicizes it. For women, the private necessarily transcends the private. If the most private also most "affects society as a whole," the separation between public and private collapses as anything other than potent ideology. The failure of marxism adequately to address intimacy on the one hand, government on the other, is the same failure as the indistinguishability between marxism and liberalism on questions of sexual politics.

Interpreting further areas of law, a feminist theory of the state will reveal that the idealism of liberalism and the materialism of the left have come to much the same for women. Liberal jurisprudence that the law should reflect society and left jurisprudence that all law does or can do is reflect existing social relations will emerge as two guises of objectivist epistemology. If objectivity is the epistemological stance of which women's sexual objectification is the social process, its imposition the paradigm of power in the male form, then the state will appear most relentless in imposing the male point of view when it comes closest to achieving its highest formal criterion of distanced aperspectivity. When it is most ruthlessly neutral, it will be most male; when it is most sex blind, it will be most blind to the sex of the standard being applied. When it most closely conforms to precedent, to "facts," to legislative intent, it will most closely enforce socially male norms and most thoroughly preclude questioning their content as having a point of view at all. Abstract rights will authoritize the male experience of the world. The liberal view that law is society's text, its rational mind, expresses this in a normative mode; the traditional left view that the state, and with it the law, is superstructural or epiphenomenal expresses this in an empirical mode. Both rationalize male power by presuming that it does not exist, that equality between the sexes (room for marginal corrections conceded) is society's basic norm and fundamental description. Only feminism grasps the extent to which the opposite is true: that antifeminism is as normative as it is empirical. Once masculinity appears as a specific position not just as the way things are, its judgments will be revealed in process and procedure, as well as adjudication and legislation. Perhaps the objectivity of the liberal state has made it appear "autonomous of class." Including, but beyond, the bourgeois in liberal legalism, lies what is male about it. However autonomous of class the liberal state may appear, it is not autonomous of sex. Justice will require change, not reflection—a new jurisprudence, a new relation between life and law.

Notes

1. Much has been made of the distinction between sex and gender. Sex is thought the more biological, gender the more social. The relation of each to sexuality varies. Since I believe sexuality is fundamental to gender and fundamentally social, and that biology is its social meaning in the system of sex inequality, which is a social and political system that does not rest independently on biological differences in any respect, the sex/gender distinction looks like a nature/culture distinction. I use sex and gender relatively interchangeably.

2. This analysis is developed in MacKinnon, "Feminism, Marxism, Method, and the State: An Agenda for Theory," Part 5 herein. . . .

3. Male is a social and political concept, not a biological attribute. As I use it, it has *nothing whatever* to do with inherency, preexistence, nature, inevitability, or body as such. It is more epistemological than ontological, undercutting the distinction itself, given male power to conform being with perspective. . . . The perspective from the male standpoint is not always each man's opinion, although most men adhere to it, nonconsciously and without considering it a point of view, as much because it makes sense of their experience (the male experience) as because it is in their interest. It is rational for them. A few men reject it; they pay. Because

it is the dominant point of view and defines rationality, women are pushed to see reality in its terms, although this denies their vantage point as women in that it contradicts (at least some of) their lived experience. Women who adopt the male standpoint are passing, epistemologically speaking. This is not uncommon and is rewarded. The intractability of maleness as a form of dominance suggests that social constructs, although they flow from human agency, can be less plastic than nature has proven to be. If experience trying to do so is any guide, it may be easier to change biology than society.

4. To stress: the feminist criticism is not that the objective stance fails to be truly objective because it has social content, all the better to exorcize that content in the pursuit of the more truly point-of-viewless viewpoint. The criticism is that objectivity is largely accurate to its/the/a world which world is criticized; and that it becomes more accurate as the power it represents and extends becomes more total. . . .

5. Andrea Dworkin helped me express this.

6. I am criticizing Engels's assumptions about sexuality and women's place and his empiricist method, and suggesting that the two are linked. F. Engels, Origin of the Family, Private Property and the State (International Publishers, 1942).

7. L. Tribe, "Constitution as Point of View," Harvard Law School, Cambridge, Mass., 1982, mimeographed, 13.

8. M. Gagnon, "Body I," in E. Marks & I. de Courtivron eds., New French Feminisms (University of Massachusetts Press, 1980), 180. . . .

9. S. D. Warren & L. D. Brandeis, "The Right to Privacy," Harv. L. Rev. 4 (1890): 193–205.

10. T. Gerety, "Redefining Privacy," Harvard C.R.-C.L. L. Rev. 12, no. 2 (Spring 1977): 236.

11. H. Marcuse, "Repressive Tolerance," in R. Wolff, B. Moore, Jr., & H. Marcuse eds., A Critique of Pure Tolerance 81–117, (Beacon Press, 1965), esp. 91.

12. A. Rich, "Conditions for Work: The Common World of Women," in S. Ruddick & P. Daniels eds., Working It Out: Twenty-three Women Writers, Artists, Scientists, and Scholars Talk about Their Lives and Work xiv–xxiv (Pantheon, 1977), esp. xiv.

[*Editor's note*: MacKinnon renders "marxism" herein in lower case from her desire to place marxism and feminism in equipoise. She capitalizes Blacks in recognition of it as a heritage, an experience, and a cultural personal identity, and similar in many respects to linguistic, tribal, or religious ethnicities that are normally capitalized. Her explanation is found at 7 Signs 515, 516 n. (1982).]

❖ *Feminism, Marxism, Method, and the State: An Agenda for Theory*

CATHARINE A. MACKINNON

SEXUALITY IS TO FEMINISM what work is to marxism: that which is most one's own, yet most taken away. Marxist theory argues that society is fundamentally constructed of the relations people form as they do and make things needed to survive humanly. Work is the social process of shaping and transforming the material and social worlds, creating people as social beings as they create value. It is that activity by which people become who they are. Class is a structure, production its consequence, capital its congealed form, and control its issue.

Implicit in feminist theory is a parallel argument: the molding, direction, and expression of sexuality organizes society into two sexes—women and men—which division underlies the totality of social relations. Sexuality is that social process which creates, organizes, expresses, and directs desire,[1] creating the social beings we know as women and men, as their relations create society. As work is to marxism, sexuality to feminism is socially constructed yet constructing, universal as activity yet historically specific, jointly comprised of matter and mind. As the organized expropriation of the work of some for the benefit of others defines a class—workers—the organized expropriation of the sexuality of some for the use of others defines the sex, woman. Heterosexuality is its structure, gender and family its congealed forms, sex roles its qualities generalized to social persona, reproduction a consequence, and control its issue.

Marxism and feminism are theories of power and its distribution: inequality. They provide accounts of how social arrangements of patterned disparity can be internally rational yet unjust. But their specificity is not incidental. In marxism to be deprived of one's work, in feminism of one's sexuality, defines each one's conception of lack of power per se. They do not mean to exist side by side to ensure that two separate spheres of social life are not overlooked, the interests of two groups are not obscured, or the contributions of two sets of variables are not ignored. They exist to argue, respectively, that the relations in which many work

From *Signs: Journal of Women in Culture and Society* 1982, Vol. 7, No. 3. © 1982 by The University of Chicago. All rights reserved.

and few gain, in which some fuck and others get fucked,[2] are the prime moment of politics.

. . . Can two theories, each of which purports to account for the same thing—power as such—be reconciled? Or, is there a connection between the fact that the few have ruled the many and the fact that those few have been men?

Confronted on equal terms, these theories pose fundamental questions for each other. Is male dominance a creation of capitalism or is capitalism one expression of male dominance? What does it mean for class analysis if one can assert that a social group is defined and exploited through means largely independent of the organization of production, if in forms appropriate to it? What does it mean for a sex-based analysis if one can assert that capitalism would not be materially altered if it were sex integrated or even controlled by women? If the structure and interests served by the socialist state and the capitalist state differ in class terms, are they equally predicated upon sex inequality? To the extent their form and behavior resemble one another, could this be their commonality? Is there a relationship between power of some classes over others and that of all men over all women?

Rather than confront these questions, marxists and feminists have usually either dismissed or, in what amounts to the same thing, subsumed each other. Marxists have criticized feminism as bourgeois in theory and in practice, meaning that it works in the interest of the ruling class. They argue that to analyze society in terms of sex ignores class divisions among women, dividing the proletariat. Feminist demands, it is claimed, could be fully satisfied within capitalism, so their pursuit undercuts and deflects the effort for basic change. Efforts to eliminate barriers to women's personhood—arguments for access to life chances without regard to sex—are seen as liberal and individualistic. Whatever women have in common is considered based in nature, not society; cross-cultural analyses of commonalities in women's social conditions are seen as ahistorical and lacking in cultural specificity. The women's movement's focus upon attitudes and feelings as powerful components of social reality is criticized as idealist; its composition, purportedly of middle-class educated women, is advanced as an explanation for its opportunism.

Feminists charge that marxism is male defined in theory and in practice, meaning that it moves within the world view and in the interest of men. Feminists argue that analyzing society exclusively in class terms ignores the distinctive social experiences of the sexes, obscuring women's unity. . . . Marxist demands, it is claimed, could be (and in part have been) satisfied without altering women's inequality to men. Feminists have often found that working-class movements and the left undervalue women's work and concerns, neglect the role of feelings and attitudes in a focus on institutional and material change, denigrate women in procedure, practice, and everyday life, and in general fail to distinguish themselves from any other ideology or group dominated by male interests. Marxists and feminists thus accuse each other of seeking (what in each one's terms is) reform—

changes that appease and assuage without addressing the grounds of discontent—where (again in each one's terms) a fundamental overthrow is required. The mutual perception, at its most extreme, is not only that the other's analysis is incorrect, but that its success would be a defeat.

Neither set of allegations is groundless. In the feminist view, sex, in analysis and in reality, does divide classes, a fact marxists have been more inclined to deny or ignore than to explain or change. Marxists, similarly, have seen parts of the women's movement function as a special interest group to advance the class-privileged: educated and professional women. To consider this group coextensive with "the women's movement" precludes questioning a definition of coalesced interest and resistance which gives disproportionate visibility to the movement's least broadly based segment. But advocates of women's interests have not always been class conscious; some have exploited class-based arguments for advantage, even when the interests of working-class *women* were thereby obscured.

For example, in 1866, in an act often thought to have inaugurated the first wave of feminism, John Stuart Mill petitioned the English parliament for women's suffrage with the following partial justification: "Under whatever conditions, and within whatever limits, men are admitted to suffrage, there is not a shadow of justification for not admitting women under the same. The majority of women of any class are not likely to differ in political opinion from the majority of men in the same class."[3] Perhaps Mill means that, to the extent class determines opinion, sex is irrevelant. In this sense, the argument is (to some persuasively) narrow. It can also justify limiting the extension of the franchise to women who "belong to" men of the same class that already exercises it, to the further detriment of the excluded underclass, "their" women included.

This kind of reasoning is confined neither to the issue of the vote nor to the nineteenth century. Mill's logic is embedded in a theoretical structure that underlies much contemporary feminist theory and justifies much of the marxist critique. That women should be allowed to engage in politics expressed Mill's concern that the state not restrict individuals' self-government, their freedom to develop talents for their own growth, and their ability to contribute to society for the good of humanity. As an empirical rationalist, he resisted attributing to biology what could be explained as social conditioning. As a utilitarian, he found most sex-based inequalities inaccurate or dubious, inefficient, and therefore unjust. The liberty of women as individuals to achieve the limits of self-development without arbitrary interference extended to women his meritocratic goal of the self-made man, condemning (what has since come to be termed) sexism as an interference with personal initiative and laissez-faire.

The hospitality of such an analysis to marxist concerns is problematic. One might extend Mill's argument to cover class as one more arbitrary, socially conditioned factor that produces inefficient development of talent and unjust distribution of resources among individuals. But although this might be in a sense materialist, it would not be a class analysis. Mill does not even allow for income leveling. Uequal distribution of wealth is exactly what laissez-faire and unregulated personal initiative produces. The individual concept of rights that this theory requires on a juridical level (especially but not only in the economic sphere), a concept which produces the tension between liberty for each and equality among all, pervades liberal feminism, substantiating the criticism that feminism is for the privileged few.

The marxist criticism that feminism focuses upon feelings and attitudes is also based on something real: the centrality of consciousness raising. Consciousness raising is the major technique of analysis, structure of organization, method of practice, and theory of social change of the women's movement. In consciousness raising, often in groups, the impact of male dominance is concretely uncovered and analyzed through the collective speaking of women's experience, from the perspective of that experience. Because marxists tend to conceive of powerlessness, first and last, as concrete and externally imposed, they believe that it must be concretely and externally undone to be changed. Women's powerlessness has been found through consciousness raising to be both internalized and externally imposed, so that, for example, femininity is identity to women as well as desirability to men. The feminist concept of consciousness and its place in social order and change emerge from this practical analytic. What marxism conceives as change in consciousness is not a form of social change in itself. For feminism, it can be, but because women's oppression is not just in the head, feminist *consciousness* is not just in the head either. But the pain, isolation, and thingification of women who have been pampered and pacified into nonpersonhood—women "grown ugly and dangerous from being nobody for so long"[4]—is difficult for the materially deprived to see as a form of oppression, particularly for women whom no man has ever put on a pedestal.

Marxism, similarly, has not just been misunderstood. Marxist theory *has* traditionally attempted to comprehend all meaningful social variance in class terms. In this respect, sex parallels race and nation as an undigested but persistently salient challenge to the exclusivity—or even primacy—of class as social explanation. Marxists typically extend class to cover women, a division and submersion that, to feminism, is inadequate to women's divergent and common experience. In 1912 Rosa Luxemburg, for example, addressed a group of women on the issue of suffrage: "Most of these bourgeois women who act like lionesses in the struggle against 'male prerogatives' would trot like docile lambs in the camp of conservative and clerical reaction if they had the suffrage. Indeed, they would certainly be a good deal more reactionary than the male part of their class. Aside from the few who have taken jobs or professions, the bourgeoisie do not take part in social production. They are nothing but co-consumers of the surplus product their men extort from the proletariat. They are parasites of the social body."[5] Her sympathies lay with "proletarian women" who derive their right to vote from being "productive for society like the men." With a blind spot analogous to Mill's within her own perspective, Luxemburg defends women's suffrage on class grounds, although in both cases the vote would have benefited women without regard to class.

Women as women, across class distinctions and apart from nature, were simply unthinkable to Luxemburg, as to most marxists. Feminist theory asks marxism: What is class for women? Luxemburg, again like Mill in her own context, subliminally recognizes that women derive their class position, with concomitant privileges and restrictions, from their associations with men. For a feminist, this may explain why they do not unite against male dominance, but it does not explain that dominance, which cuts across class lines even as it takes forms peculiar to classes. What distinguishes the bourgeois women from her domestic servant is that the latter is paid (if barely), while the former is kept (if contingently). But is this a difference in social productivity or only in its indices, indices which themselves may be products of women's undervalued status? Luxemburg sees that the bourgeois woman of her time is a "parasite of a parasite" but fails to consider her commonality with the proletarian woman who is a slave of a slave. In the case of bourgeois women, to limit the analysis of women's relationship to capitalism to their relations through men is to see only its vicarious aspect. To fail to do this in the case of proletarian women is to miss its vicarious aspect.

Feminist observations of women's situation in socialist countries, although not conclusive on the contribution of marxist theory to understanding women's situation, have supported the theoretical critique. In the feminist view, these countries have solved many social problems, women's subordination not included. The criticism is not that socialism has not automatically liberated women in the process of transforming production (assuming that this transformation is occurring). Nor is it to diminish the significance of such changes for women: "There is a difference between a society in which sexism is expressed in the form of female infanticide and a society in which sexism takes the form of unequal representation on the Central Committee. And the difference is worth dying for."[6] The criticism is rather that these countries do not make a priority of working for women that distinguishes them from nonsocialist societies. Capitalist countries value women in terms of their "merit" by male standards; in socialist countries women are invisible except in their capacity as "workers," a term that seldom includes women's distinctive work: housework, sexual service, childbearing. The concern of revolutionary leadership for ending women's confinement to traditional roles too often seems limited to making their labor available to the regime, leading feminists to wonder whose interests are served by this version of liberation. Women become as free as men to work outside the home while men remain free from work within it. This also occurs under capitalism. . . .

Where such attitudes and practices come to be criticized, as in Cuba or China, changes appear gradual and precarious, even where the effort looks major. If seizures of state and productive power overturn work relations, they do not overturn sex relations at the same time or in the same way, as a class analysis of sex would (and in some cases did) predict. Neither technology nor socialism, both of which purport to alter women's role at the point of production, have ever yet equalized women's status relative to men. In the feminist view, nothing has. At minimum, a separate effort appears required—an effort that can be shaped by revolutionary regime and work relations—but a separate effort nonetheless. In light of these experiences, women's struggles, whether under capitalist or socialist regimes, appear to feminists to have more in common with each other than with leftist struggles anywhere.

Attempts to create a synthesis between marxism and feminism, termed socialist-feminism, have not recognized the depth of the antagonism or the separate integrity of each theory. These juxtapositions emerge as unconfronted as they started: either feminist or marxist, usually the latter. . . .

Most attempts at synthesis attempt to integrate or explain the appeal of feminism by incorporating issues feminism identifies as central—the family, housework, sexuality, reproduction, socialization, personal life—within an essentially unchanged marxian analysis. According to the persuasion of the marxist, women become a caste, a stratum, a cultural group, a division in civil society, a secondary contradiction, or a nonantagonistic contradiction; women's liberation becomes a precondition, a measure of society's general emancipation, part of the superstructure, or an important aspect of the class struggle. Most commonly, women are reduced to some other category, such as "women workers," which is then treated as coextensive with all women. Or, in what has become near reflex, women become "the family," as if this single form of women's confinement (then divided on class lines, then on racial lines) can be *presumed* the crucible of women's determination. Or, the marxist meaning of reproduction, the iteration of productive relations, is punned into an analysis of biological reproduction, as if women's bodily differences from men must account for their subordination to men; and as if this social analogue to the biological makes women's definition material, therefore based on a division of *labor* after all, therefore real, therefore (potentially) unequal. Sexuality, if noticed at all, is, like "everyday life," analyzed in gender-neutral terms, as if its social meaning can be presumed the same, or coequal, or complementary, for women and men. Although a unified theory of social inequality is presaged in these strategies of subordination, staged progression, and assimilation of women's concerns to left concerns, at most an uneven combination is accomplished. However sympathetically, "the woman question" is always reduced to some other question, instead of being seen as *the* question, calling for analysis on its own terms.

. . . The failure to contain both theories on equal terms derives from the failure to confront each on its own ground: at the level of method. Method shapes each theory's vision of social reality. It identifies its central problem, group, and process, and creates as a consequence its distinctive conception of politics as such. Work and sexuality as concepts, then, derive their meaning and primacy from the *way* each theory approaches, grasps, interprets, and inhabits its world. Clearly, there is a relationship between how and what a theory sees; is there a marxist method without class? a feminist method without sex? Method in this sense organizes the apprehension of truth; it determines what counts as evidence and defines what is taken as verification. Instead of engaging the debate over which came (or comes) first, sex or class, the task for theory is to explore the conflicts and connections between the methods that found it meaningful to analyze social conditions in terms of those categories in the first place.

Feminism has not been perceived as having a method, or even a central argument, with which to contend. It has been perceived not as a systematic analysis but as a loose collection of factors, complaints, and issues which, taken together, describe rather than explain the misfortunes of the female sex. The challenge is to demonstrate that feminism systematically converges upon a central explanation of sex inequality through an approach distinctive to its subject yet applicable to the whole of social life, including class.

Under the rubric of feminism, woman's situation has been explained as a consequence of biology or of reproduction and mothering, social organizations of biology; as caused by the marriage law or, as extensions, by the patriarchal family, becoming society as a "patriarchy"; or as caused by artificial gender roles and their attendant attitudes. Informed by these attempts, but conceiving nature, law, the family, and roles as consequences, not foundations, I think that feminism fundamentally identifies sexuality as the primary social sphere of male power. The centrality of sexuality emerges not from Freudian conceptions but from feminist practice on diverse issues, including abortion, birth control, sterilization abuse, domestic battery, rape, incest, lesbianism, sexual harassment, prostitution, female sexual slavery, and pornography. In all these areas, feminist efforts confront and change women's lives concretely and experientially. Taken together, they are producing a feminist political theory centering upon sexuality: its social determination, daily construction, birth to death expression, and ultimately male control.

Feminist inquiry into these specific issues began with a broad unmasking of the attitudes that legitimize and hide women's status, the ideational envelope that contains woman's body: notions that women desire and provoke rape, that girls' experiences of incest are fantasies, that career women plot and advance by sexual parlays, that prostitutes are lustful, that wife beating expresses the intensity of love. Beneath each of these ideas was revealed bare coercion and broad connections to woman's social definition as a sex. Research on sex roles, pursuing Simone de Beauvoir's insight that "one is not born, one rather becomes a woman,"[7] disclosed an elaborate process: how and what one learns to become one. Gender, cross-culturally, was found to be a learned quality, an acquired characteristic, an assigned status, with qualities that vary independent of biology and an ideology that attributed them to nature. The discovery that the female archetype is the feminine stereotype exposed "woman" as a social construction. Contemporary industrial society's version of her is docile, soft, passive, nurturant, vulnerable, weak, narcissistic, childlike, incompetent, masochistic, and domestic, made for child care, home care, and husband care. Conditioning to these values permeates the upbringing of girls and the images for emulation thrust upon women. Women who resist or fail, including those who never did fit—for example, black and lower-class women who cannot survive if they are soft and weak and incompetent, assertively self-respecting women, women with ambitions of male dimensions—are considered less female, lesser women. Women who comply or succeed are elevated as models, tokenized by success on male terms or portrayed as consenting to their natural place and dismissed as having participated if they complain.

If the literature on sex roles and the investigations of particular issues are read in light of each other, each element of the female *gender* stereotype is revealed as, in fact, *sexual*. Vulnerability means the appearance/reality of easy sexual access; passivity means receptivity and disabled resistance, enforced by trained physical weakness; softness means pregnability by something hard. Incompetence seeks help as vulnerability seeks shelter, inviting the embrace that becomes the invasion, trading exclusive access for protection . . . from the same access. Domesticity nurtures the consequent progeny, proof of potency, and ideally waits at home dressed in Saran Wrap.[8] Woman's infantilization evokes pedophilia; fixation on dismembered body parts (the breast man, the leg man) evokes fetishism; idolization of vapidity, necrophilia. Narcissism ensures that woman identifies with that image of herself that man holds up: "Hold still, we are going to do your portrait, so that you can begin looking like it right away." Masochism means that pleasure in violation becomes her sensuality. Lesbians so violate the sexuality implicit in female gender stereotypes as not to be considered women at all.

Socially, femaleness means femininity, which means attractiveness to men, which means sexual attractiveness, which means sexual availability on male terms. What defines woman as such is what turns men on. Good girls are "attractive," bad girls "provocative." Gender socialization is the process through which women come to identify themselves as sexual beings, as beings that exist for men. It is that process through which women internalize (make their own) a male image of their sexuality *as* their identity as women. It is not just an illusion. Feminist inquiry into women's own experience of sexuality revises prior comprehensions of sexual issues and transforms the concept of sexuality itself—its determinants and its role in society and politics. According to this revision, one "becomes a woman" —acquires and identifies with the status of the female—not so much through physical maturation or inculcation into appropriate role behavior as through the experience of sexuality: a complex unity of physicality, emotionality, identity, and status affirmation. Sex as gender and sex as sexuality are thus defined in terms of each other, but it is sexuality that determines gender, not the other way around. This, the central but never stated insight of Kate Millett's *Sexual Politics*, resolves the duality in the term "sex" itself: what women learn in order to "have sex," in order to "become women"—woman as gender—comes through the experience of, and is a condition for, "having sex"—woman as sexual object for man, the use of women's sexuality by men. Indeed, to the extent sexuality is social, women's sexuality *is* its use, just as our femaleness *is* its alterity.

Many issues that appear sexual from this standpoint have not been seen as such, nor have they been seen as defining a politics. Incest, for example, is commonly seen as a question of distinguishing the real evil, a crime against the family, from girlish seductiveness or fantasy. Contraception and abortion have been framed as matters of reproduction and fought out as proper or improper social constraints on nature. Or they are seen as private, minimizing state intervention into intimate relations. Sexual harassment was a nonissue, then became a problem of distinguishing personal relationships or affectionate flirtation from abuse of position. Lesbianism, when visible, has been either a perversion or not, to be tolerated or not. Pornography has been considered a question of freedom to speak and depict the erotic, as against the obscene or violent. Prostitution has been understood either as mutual lust and degradation or an equal exchange of sexual need for economic need. The issue in rape has been whether the intercourse was provoked/mutually desired, or whether it was forced: was it sex or violence? Across and beneath these issues, sexuality itself has been divided into parallel provinces: traditionally, religion or biology; in modern transformation, morality or psychology. Almost never politics.

In a feminist perspective, the formulation of each issue, in the terms just described, expresses ideologically the same interest that the problem it formulates expresses concretely: the interest from the male point of view. Women experience the sexual events these issues codify as a cohesive whole within which each resonates. The defining theme of that whole is the male pursuit of control over women's sexuality—men not as individuals nor as biological beings, but as a gender group characterized by maleness as socially constructed, of which this pursuit is definitive. For example, women who need abortions see contraception as a struggle not only for control over the biological products of sexual expression but over the social rhythms and mores of sexual intercourse. These norms often appear hostile to women's self-protection even when the technology is at hand. As an instance of such norms, women notice that sexual harassment looks a great deal like ordinary heterosexual initiation under conditions of gender inequality. Few women are in a position to refuse unwanted sexual initiatives. That consent rather than nonmutuality is the line between rape and intercourse further exposes the inequality in normal social expectations. So does the substantial amount of male force allowed in the focus on the woman's resistance, which tends to be disabled by socialization to passivity. If sex is ordinarily accepted as something men do *to* women, the better question would be whether consent is a meaningful concept. Penetration (often by a penis) is also substantially more central to both the legal definition of rape and the male definition of sexual intercourse than it is to women's sexual violation or sexual pleasure. Rape in marriage expresses the male sense of entitlement to access to women they annex; incest extends it. Although most women are raped by men they know, the closer the relation, the less women are allowed to claim it was rape. Pornography becomes difficult to distinguish from art and ads once it is clear that what is degrading to women is compelling to the consumer. Prostitutes sell the unilaterality that pornography advertises. That most of these issues codify behavior that is neither countersystemic nor exceptional is supported by women's experience as victims: these behaviors are either not illegal or are effectively permitted on a large scale. As women's experience blurs the lines between deviance and normalcy, it obliterates the distinction between abuses *of* women and the social definition of what a woman *is*.

These investigations reveal rape, incest, sexual harassment, pornography, and prostitution as not primarily abuses of physical force, violence, authority, or economics. They are abuses of sex. They need not and do not rely for their coerciveness upon forms of enforcement other than the sexual; that those forms of enforcement, at least in this context, are themselves sexualized is closer to the truth. They are not the erotization *of* something else; eroticism *itself* exists in their form. Nor are they perversions of art and morality. They *are* art and morality from the male point of view. They are sexual because they express the relations, values, feelings, norms, and behaviors of the culture's sexuality, in which considering things like rape, pornography, incest, or lesbianism deviant, perverse, or blasphemous is part of their excitement potential.

Sexuality, then, is a form of power. Gender, as socially constructed, embodies it, not the reverse. Women and men are divided by gender, made into the sexes as we know them, by the social requirements of heterosexuality, which institutionalizes male sexual dominance and female sexual submission. If this is true, sexuality is the linchpin of gender inequality.

A woman is a being who identifies and is identified as one whose sexuality exists for someone else, who is socially male. Women's sexuality is the capacity to arouse desire in that someone. If what is sexual about a woman is what the male point of view requires for excitement, have male requirements so usurped its terms as to have become them? Considering women's sexuality in this way forces confrontation with whether there is any such thing. Is women's sexuality its absence? If being *for* another is the whole of women's sexual construction, it can be no more escaped by separatism, men's temporary concrete absence, than eliminated or qualified by permissiveness, which, in this context, looks like women emulating male roles. As Susan Sontag said: "The question is: *what* sexuality are women to be liberated to enjoy? Merely to remove the onus placed upon the sexual expressiveness of women is a hollow victory if the sexuality they become freer to enjoy remains the old one that converts women into objects. . . . This already 'freer' sexuality mostly reflects a spurious idea of freedom: the right of each person, briefly, to exploit and dehumanize someone else. Without a change in the very norms of sexuality, the liberation of women is a meaningless goal. Sex as such is not liberating for women. Neither is more sex."[9] Does removing or revising gender constraints upon sexual expression change or even challenge its norms? This question ultimately is one of social determination in the broadest sense: its mechanism, permeability, specificity, and totality. If women are socially defined such that female sexuality cannot be lived or spoken or felt or even somatically sensed apart from its enforced definition, so that it *is* its own lack, then there is no such thing as a woman as such, there are only walking embodiments of men's projected needs. For feminism, asking whether there is, socially, a female sexuality is the same as asking whether women exist.

Methodologically, the feminist concept of the personal as political is an attempt to answer this question. Relinquishing all instinctual, natural, transcendental, and divine authority, this concept grounds women's sexuality on purely relational terrain, anchoring women's power and accounting for women's discontent in the same world they stand against. The personal as political is not a simile, not a metaphor, and not an analogy. It does not mean that what occurs in personal life is similar to, or comparable with, what occurs in the public arena. . . . It means that women's distinctive experience as women occurs within that sphere that has been socially lived as the personal—private, emotional, interiorized, particular, individuated, intimate—so that what it is to *know* the *politics* of woman's situation is to know women's personal lives.

The substantive principle governing the authentic politics of women's personal lives is persuasive powerlessness to men, expressed and reconstituted daily *as* sexuality. To say that the personal is political means that gender as a division of power is discoverable and verifiable through women's intimate experience of sexual objectification, which is definitive of and synonymous with women's lives as gender female. Thus, to feminism, the personal is epistemologically the political, and its epistemology is its politics. Feminism, on this level, is the theory of women's point of view. . . . Consciousness raising is its quintessential expression. Feminism does not appropriate an existing method—such as scientific method—and apply it to a different sphere of society to reveal its preexisting political aspect. Consciousness raising not only comes to know different things as politics; it necessarily comes to know them in a different way. Women's experience of politics, of life as sex object, gives rise to its own method of appropriating that reality: feminist method.[10] As its own kind of social analysis, within yet outside the male paradigm just as women's lives are, it has a distinctive theory of the *relation* between method and truth, the individual and her social surroundings, the presence and place of the natural and spiritual in culture and society, and social being and causality itself.

Having been objectified as sexual beings while stigmatized as ruled by subjective passions, women reject the distinction between knowing subject and known object—the division between subjective and objective postures—as the means to comprehend social life. Disaffected from objectivity, having been its prey, but excluded from its world through relegation to subjective inwardness, women's interest lies in overthrowing the distinction itself. Proceeding connotatively and analytically at the same time, consciousness raising is at once common sense expression and critical articulation of concepts. Taking situated feelings and common detail (common here meaning both ordinary and shared) as the matter of political analysis, it explores the terrain that is most damaged, most contaminated, yet therefore most women's own, most intimately known, most open to reclamation. . . .

Through consciousness raising, women grasp the collective reality of women's condition from within the perspective of that experience, not from outside it. The claim that a sexual politics exists and is socially fundamental is grounded in the claim of feminism *to* women's perspective, not from it. Its claim to women's perspective *is* its claim to truth. In its account of itself, women's point of view contains a duality analogous to that of the marxist proletariat: determined by the reality the theory explodes, it thereby claims special access to that reality. Feminism does not see its view as subjective, partial, or undetermined but as a critique of the purported generality, disinterestedness, and universality of prior accounts. These have not been half right but have invoked the wrong whole. Feminism not only challenges masculine partiality but questions the universality imperative itself. Aperspectivity is revealed as a strategy of male hegemony.[11]

"Representation of the world," de Beauvoir writes, "like the world itself, is the work of men; they describe it from their own point of view, which they confuse with the absolute truth."[12] The parallel between representation and construction should be sustained: men *create* the world from their own point of view, which then *becomes* the truth to be described. This is a closed system, not anyone's confusion. *Power to create the world from one's point of view is power in its male form.*[13] The male epistemological stance, which corresponds to the world it creates, is objectivity: the ostensibly noninvolved stance, the view from a distance and from no particular perspective, apparently transparent to its reality. It does not comprehend its own perspectivity, does not recognize what it sees as subject like itself, or that the way it apprehends its world is a form of its subjugation and presupposes it. The objectively knowable is object. Woman through male eyes is sex object, that by which man knows himself at once as man and as subject.[14] What is objectively known corresponds to the world and can be verified by pointing to it (as science does) because the world itself is controlled from the same point of view. Combining, like any form of power, legitimation with force, male power extends beneath the representation of reality to its construction: it makes women (as it were) and so verifies (makes true) who women "are" in its view, simultaneously confirming its way of being and its vision of truth. The eroticism that corresponds to this is "the use of things to experience self."[15] As a coerced pornography model put it, "You do it, you do it, and you do it; then you become it."[16] The fetish speaks feminism.

Objectification makes sexuality a material reality of women's lives, not just a psychological, attitudinal, or ideological one.[17] . . . Sexual objectification is the primary process of the subjection of women. It unites act with word, construction with expression, perception with enforcement, myth with reality. Man fucks woman; subject verb object.

The distinction between objectification and alienation is called into question by this analysis. Objectification in marxist materialism is thought to be the foundation of human freedom, the work process whereby a subject becomes embodied in products and relationships. Alienation is the socially contingent distortion of that process, a reification of products and relations which prevents them from being, and being seen as, dependent on human agency. But from the point of view of the object, objectification *is* alienation. For women, there is no distinction between objectification and alienation because women have not authored objectifications, we have been them. Women have been the nature, the matter, the acted upon, to be subdued by the acting subject seeking to embody himself in the social world. Reification is not just an illusion to the reified; it is also their reality. The alienated who can only grasp self as other is no different from the object who can only grasp self as a thing. To be man's other *is* to be his thing. Similarly, the problem of how the object can know herself as such is the same as how the alienated can know its own alienation. This, in turn, poses the problem of feminism's account of women's consciousness. How can women, as created, "thingified in the head,"[18] complicit in the body, see our condition as such?

In order to account for women's consciousness (much less propagate it) feminism must grasp that male power produces the world before it distorts it. Women's acceptance of their condition does not contradict its fundamental unacceptability if women have little choice but to *become* persons who freely choose women's roles. For this reason, the reality of women's oppression is, finally, neither demonstrable nor refutable empirically. Until this is confronted on the level of method, criticism of what exists can be undercut by pointing to the reality to be criticized. Women's bondage, degradation, damage, complicity, and inferiority—together with the possibility of resistance, movement, or exceptions—will operate as barriers to consciousness rather than as means of access to what women need to become conscious of in order to change.

Male power is real; it is just not what it claims to be, namely, the only reality. Male power is a myth that makes itself true. What it is to raise consciousness is to confront male power in this duality: as total on one side and a delusion on the other. In consciousness raising, women learn they have *learned* that men are everything, women their negation, but that the sexes are equal. The content of the message is revealed true and false at the same time; in fact, each part reflects the other transvalued. If "men are all, women their negation" is taken as social criticism rather than simple description, it becomes clear for the first time that women *are* men's equals, everywhere in chains. Their chains become visible, their inferiority—their inequality—a product of subjection and a mode of its enforcement. Reciprocally, the moment it is seen that this—life as we know it—is not equality, that the sexes are not socially equal, womanhood can no longer be defined in terms of lack of maleness, as negativity. For the first time, the question of what a woman *is* seeks its ground in and of a world understood as neither of its making nor in its image, and finds, within a critical embrace of woman's fractured and alien image, that world women have made and a vision of its wholeness. Feminism has unmasked maleness as a form of power that is both omnipotent and nonexistent, an unreal thing with very real consequences. . . .

Feminism is the first theory to emerge from those whose interest it affirms. Its method recapitulates as theory the reality it seeks to capture. As marxist method is dialectical materialism, feminist method is consciousness raising: the collective critical reconstitution of the meaning of women's social experience, as women live through it. Marxism and feminism on this level posit a different relation between thought and thing, both in terms of the relationship of the analysis itself to the social life it captures and in terms of the participation of thought in the social life it analyzes. To the extent that materialism is scientific it posits and refers to a reality outside thought which it considers to have an objective—that is, truly nonsocially perspectival—content. Consciousness raising, by contrast, inquires into an intrinsically social situation, into that mixture of thought and materiality which is women's sexuality in the most generic sense. It approaches its world through a process that shares its determination: women's consciousness, not as individual or subjective ideas, but as collective social being. This method stands inside its own determinations in order to uncover them, just as it criticizes them in order to value them on its own terms—in order to *have* its own terms at all. Feminism turns theory itself—the pursuit of a true analysis of social life—into the pursuit of consciousness and turns an analysis of inequality into a critical embrace of its own determinants. The process is transformative as well as perspective, since thought and thing are inextricable and reciprocally constituting of women's oppression, just as the state as coercion and the state as legitimizing ideology are indistinguishable, and for the same reasons. The pursuit of consciousness becomes a form of political practice. Consciousness raising has revealed gender relations to be a collective fact, no more simply personal than class relations. This implies that class relations may also be personal, no less so for being at the same time collective. The failure of marxism to realize this may connect the failure of workers in advanced capitalist nations to organize in the socialist sense with the failure of left revolutions to liberate women in the feminist sense.

Feminism stands in relation to marxism as marxism does to classical political economy: its final conclusion and ultimate critique. Compared with marxism, the place of thought and things in method and reality are reversed in a seizure of power that penetrates subject with object and theory with practice. In a dual motion, feminism turns marxism inside out and on its head.

To answer an old question—how is value created and distributed?—Marx needed to create an entirely new account of the social world. To answer an equally old question, or to question an equally old reality—what explains the inequality of women to men? or, how does desire become domination? or, what is male power?—feminism revolutionizes politics.

Notes

1. "Desire" is selected as a term parallel to "value" in marxist theory to refer to that substance felt to be primordial or aboriginal but posited by the theory as social and contingent. . . .

2. I know no nondegraded English verb for the activity of sexual expression that would allow a construction parallel to, for example, "I am working," a phrase that could apply to nearly any activity. This fact of language may reflect and contribute to the process of obscuring sexuality's pervasiveness in social life. Nor is there *any* active verb meaning "to act sexually" that specifically envisions a woman's action. If language constructs as well as expresses the social world, these words support heterosexual values.

3. J. S. Mill, "The Subjection of Women," in A. Rossi ed., Essays on Sex Equality (University of Chicago Press, 1970), 184–85.

4. Toni Cade (now Bambara) thus describes a desperate Black woman who has too many children and too little means to care for them or herself in "The Pill: Genocide or Liberation?" in T. Cade ed., The Black Woman: An Anthology (Mentor, New American Library, 1970), 168. By using her phrase in altered context, I do not want to distort her meaning but to extend it. Throughout this essay, I have tried to see if women's condition is shared, even when contexts or magnitudes differ. (Thus, it is very different to be "nobody" as a Black woman than as a white lady, but neither is "somebody" by male standards.) This is the approach to race and ethnicity attempted throughout. I aspire to include all women in the term "women" in some way, without violating the particularity of any woman's experience. Whenever this fails, the statement is simply wrong and will have to be qualified or the aspiration (or the theory) abandoned.

5. R. Luxemburg, "Women's Suffrage and Class Struggle," in D. Howard ed., Selected Political Writings (Monthly Review Press, 1971), pp. 219–20. . . .

6. B. Ehrenreich, "What Is Socialist Feminism?" Win (June 3, 1976), reprinted in Working Papers on Socialism and Feminism (New American Movement, n.d.). . . .

7. S. de Beauvoir, The Second Sex (Knopf, 1970), 249.

8. M. Morgan, The Total Woman (Fleming H. Revell, 1973). "Total Woman" makes blasphemous sexuality into a home art, redomesticating what prostitutes have marketed as forbidden.

9. S. Sontag, "The Third World of Women," *Partisan Review* 40, no. 2 (1973): 180–206, esp. 188.

10. . . . [S]ee S. Bartky, "Toward a Phenomenology of Feminist Consciousness," in M. Vetterling-Braggin et al. eds., Feminism and Philosophy (Littlefield, Adams, 1977). Susan Griffin reflects/creates the process: "We do not rush to speech. We allow ourselves to be moved. We do not attempt objectivity. . . . We said we had experienced this ourselves. I felt so much for her then, she said, with her head cradled in my lap, she said, I knew what to do. We said we were moved to see her go through what we had gone through. We said this gave us some knowledge" (Woman and Nature: The Roaring Inside Her [Harper & Row, 1978], 197). Assertions such as "our politics begin with our feelings" have emerged from the practice of consciousness raising. Somewhere between mirror-reflexive determination and transcendence of determinants, "feelings" are seen as both access to

truth—at times a bit phenomenologically transparent—and an artifact of politics. There is both suspicion of feelings and affirmation of their health. They become simultaneously an inner expression of outer lies and a less contaminated resource for verification. See San Francisco Redstockings, "Our Politics Begin with Our Feelings," in B. Roszak & T. Roszak eds., Masculine/Feminine: Readings in Sexual Mythology and the Liberation of Women (Harper & Row, 1969).

11. Feminist scholars are beginning to criticize objectivity from different disciplinary standpoints, although not as frontally as here, nor in its connection with objectification. J. Sherman & E. Beck eds., The Prism of Sex: Essays in the Sociology of Knowledge (University of Wisconsin Press, 1979); M. Eichler, The Double Standard: A Feminist Critique of Feminist Social Science (St. Martin's Press, 1980); E. Keller, "Gender and Science," Psychoanalysis and Contemporary Thought 1, no. 3 (1978): 409–33. A. Rich, "Toward a Woman-centered University," in F. Howe ed., Woman and the Power to Change (McGraw-Hill, 1975).

12. de Beauvoir, Second Sex, *supra* note 7.

13. This does not mean all men *have* male power equally. American Black men, for instance, have substantially less of it. . . . Although historically receiving more attention, race and nation are otherwise analogous to sex in the place they occupy for, and the challenge they pose to, marxist theory. If the real basis of history and activity is class and class conflict, what other than "false consciousness," is one to make of the historical force of sexism, racism, and nationalism? Similarly, positing a supra-class unit with true meaning, such as "Black people," is analytically parallel to positing a supra-class (and supra-racial) unit "women." Treating race, nation, and sex as lesser included problems has been the major response of marxist theory to such challenges. Any relationship *between* sex and race tends to be left entirely out of account, since they are considered parallel "strata.". . .

14. This suggests a way in which marxism and feminism may be reciprocally illuminating, without, for the moment, confronting the deep divisions between them. Marxism comprehends the *object* world's *social* existence: how objects are constituted, embedded in social life, infused with meaning, created in systematic and structural relation. Feminism comprehends the *social* world's *object* existence: how women are created in the image of, and as, things. The object world's social existence varies with the structure of production. Suppose that wherever the sexes are unequal, women are objects, but what it means to be an object varies with the productive relations that create objects as social. Thus, under primitive exchange systems, women are exchange objects. Under capitalism, women appear as commodities. That is, women's sexuality as object for men is valued as objects are under capitalism, namely as commodities. Under true communism, women would be collective sex objects. If women have universally been sex objects, it is also true that matter as the acted-upon in social life has a history. If women have always been things, it is also true that things have not always had the same meaning. Of course, this does not explain sex inequality. It merely observes, once that inequality exists, the way its dynamics may interact with the social organization of production. Sexual objectification may also have a separate history, with its own periods, forms, structures, technology, and potentially, revolutions.

15. A. Dworkin, Pornography: Men Possessing Women (Putnam, 1981), 124. . . .

16. L. Lovelace, Ordeal (Citadel Press, 1980). The same may be true for class. See R. Sennett & J. Cobb, The Hidden Injuries of Class (Knopf, 1972). Marxism teaches that exploitation/degradation somehow necessarily produces resistance/revolution. Women's experience with sexual exploitation/degradation teaches that it also produces grateful complicity in exchange for survival and self-loathing to the point of the extinction of self, respect for which makes resistance conceivable. The problem here is not to explain why women acquiesce in their condition but why they ever do anything but.

17. The critique of sexual objectification first became visibly explicit in the American women's movement with the disruption of the Miss America Pageant in September 1968. R. Morgan, "Women Disrupt the Miss America Pageant," Rat (September 1978), reprinted in Going Too Far: The Personal Chronicle of a Feminist (Random House, 1977), 62–67. . . .

Marxist attempts to deal with sexual objectification have not connected the issue with the politics of aesthetics or with subordination. . . . Resentment of white beauty standards is prominent in Black feminism. Beauty standards incapable of achievement by any woman seems to fulfill a dual function. They keep women buying products (to the profit of capitalism) and competing for men (to be affirmed by the standard that matters). That is, they make women feel ugly and inadequate so we need men and money to defend against rejection/self-revulsion. . . .

18. S. Rowbotham, Women's Liberation and the New Politics, Spokesman Pamphlet No. 17 (Falling Wall Press, 1971), 17.

❖ *Feminism and Legal Positivism*

Margot Stubbs

. . . The purpose of this paper is . . . to illustrate how the conceptual framework of legal positivism (a doctrine that constitutes the methodological infrastructure of western legal discourse) has very effectively constrained the development of a feminist critique of law. . . .

. . . [T]he point of this paper is not to overview the literature on legal positivism, or focus on variations on its basic themes from Bentham through to Austin and Hart, for this has been more than adequately addressed. . . . Rather, this paper has a more fundamental purpose, and that is to extract the basic definition or understanding of what law is which is implicit in positivist jurisprudence, and to examine, from a feminist perspective, the conceptual and political imperatives that flow from it. This paper postulates that the development of a theory of law which is properly feminist in character must necessarily transcend positivism's claim to trans-historicity and universality, and should articulate the functional and ideological role of legal positivism in the reproduction of the sex and economic class relations of capitalist society. . . .

The key reason why it has been so observably difficult to develop a feminist critique of law relates directly to the conceptual limitations of the *definition* of law provided in the legal-positivist tradition. A feminist critique of law cannot be expressed within a framework that is predicated on the autonomy of the law—that is, one based on an understanding of law as a neutral and independent structure that is supposedly uninvolved as an institution in the repression of women. The corollary of this approach is that women's problems with the law are thus only problems with particular legal rules or, at the most, particular areas of the law. A feminist critique of law must reject this view of the legal systems, and should be predicated on an understanding of law as *praxis*—that is, as Klare defines the term, as being a form of "practice" through which the social order is defined.[1] As will be illustrated, a feminist analysis of the law must clearly reject the central

---

3 Aust. J. Law & Soc'y 63 (1986).

tenet of legal positivism—that is, that law is external to the question of class—for such a position by definition renders it impossible to develop a political critique of the legal system. A feminist critique of law, in other words, must recognize and transcend the "mind-forged manacles"[2] of positivist jurisprudence, for this, it is contended, is the first and necessary step in developing a politically meaningful line of inquiry into the relation between law and the subordination of women. It is absolutely crucial that feminists unravel the role the law plays in maintaining and reproducing the sex and economic divisions in our society, for capitalism has a class structure that is innately patriarchal.[3]

These themes will be illustrated by showing the threat to the political interests of the dominant class that are posed by any attempt to "transform" this legal process—that is, to make it more receptive to the claims of the sexually and politically disadvantaged in society—by reference to an examination of the structure and function of the New South Wales Equal Opportunity Tribunal.

To start with: what is legal positivism? . . . H.L.A. Hart succinctly outlines a set of five propositions.[4] . . . [F]irstly, that all laws are the command of human beings, (that is, emanating from a sovereign); secondly, the contention that there is no necessary connection between law and morals—that is, law as it is and law as it should be; thirdly, the analysis of legal concepts should be distinguished from historical inquiry into the causes and origins of law, and should be separated from sociological inquiry into the relationship between law and other social phenomena; fourthly, positivism contends that the legal system is a closed, logical system, in which correct legal decisions can be deduced by logical means from pre-determined legal rules, without reference to social aims, policies or moral standards; and finally, that moral judgments are unable to be established or defended—as can statements of fact—by rational argument, evidence or proof.

As Hart's summary adverts to it, legal positivism is concerned with abstract notions of sovereignty, hierarchy and command as the intrinsic condition of the law. It defines law simply as a set of rules carried from "sovereign" to "subject," that is processed through a legal system that is held out to be primarily administrative in character. Legal positivism presents us with a model of the legal process: the courts, the styles of consciousness with which lawyers perceive and resolve problems, the way in which they interact between client and system, and the role of the judiciary, which is supposedly separate from politics, and which is presented as intrinsically neutral and value-free.

Feminist legal inquiry to date has generally been expressed within this conceptual tradition, as it has focused primarily on the function of the law at those points where it directly intersects the social experience of women. For example, there have been extensive feminist critiques of the law relating to rape, abortion, criminal and family law and so forth, but there has been comparatively little attention directed to the broader question as to how the very *structure* of the legal order in contemporary capitalist society—its structural qualities of formality, generality and autonomy— serve to reinforce and reproduce existing sex and economic class relationships.

Feminist inquiry should appreciate that the distinguishing attributes of the western legal order—its "generality, uniformity, publicity and coercion"[5]—perform an express political function in the reproduction of class relationships, and ideologically find their expression in a particular legal philosophy—legal positivism—that animates and legitimates capitalist society. Positivism in law is structurally connected to a deeper set of presuppositions about society that are expressed under the rubric of "liberalism." Liberal philosophy embraces legal positivism in the way it presents the legal system as a neutral, independent and apolitical mechanism for resolving social tension. This presentation of law is given its political expression in the notion of the "Rule of Law"—that is, the legal doctrine that all people are equal under the law and can expect from it a neutral and unbiased determination of their rights. The "Rule of Law," in fact, is widely accepted as the linchpin of individual liberty and justice in liberal-democratic society. Indeed, the very legitimacy of the modern state hinges on this "reification" of the law—that is, in obscuring the role the law as an institution plays in the reconstitution of class relationships. In fact, far from recognizing the role the law plays in the process of institutional repression, liberal philosophy presents it as perhaps the only bulwark standing against it. . . .

Thus, the very conceptual framework of liberalism—its definition of "rights," "justice" and "freedom"—is ultimately grounded in law and is given expression through the legal system. Hence, the need to justify and to legitimate the operation of law (and thereby the political propriety of people's subjugation to it)—must logically stand at the heart of the liberal philosophical project. It is essential to the legitimacy of the capitalist state that "law" has the ideological veneer of being "autonomous from society . . . a neutral and unchanging state apparatus."[6]

Legal positivism provides a definition of law that clearly complements the understanding of society implicit in liberal philosophy—that is, that society is an artificial aggregation of freely contracting, autonomous individuals. As Gabel notes,

> at the heart of this positivist model, we find precisely this atomistic view; a normative theory insists on the radical liberty of the individual (positivism's subjectivity of values), a legal epistemology that separates fact from value (the formal rule) and a rationalization of practice which accords legal validity only to rule-dictated outcomes.[7]

It stands to reason that positivism in law should thus be subjected to the same criticisms that have been directed at liberalism—namely that it provides us with a largely artificial understanding of the way modern society works. Legal positivism, however, has not been subjected to as incisive or developed a criticism as has liberal philosophy. . . .

Legal positivism presents us with a highly formalistic and apolitical understanding of the law. The legal system as defined in this tradition is not part of "the problem" and "reforming the law" has, even from a feminist perspective, become almost synonymous with changing the content of particular rules or areas of the law. This of course has an important place in feminist political strategy, but if we are to understand the way in which the legal system reinforces the class oppression of women, we must look beyond the largely artificial way law is defined in the positivist tradition. Feminist legal inquiry needs, in short, a different starting point if it is to understand the specific way in which law mediates class relations, specifically the class relations of sex. From a feminist perspective, "the law" must be understood NOT as autonomous from society, but as being a form of practice through which existing sex and economic class relations are reproduced. This involvement can be described in shorthand by approaching the legal system as a form of "praxis"—henceforth to be understood as connoting human activity through which people define or change their world. Thus an acceptance of the understanding of the law presented in mainstream Western jurisprudence (as defined by the "science of legal positivism") limits the development of a political critique of law as it presents the law as an autonomous, self-contained system, fueled by its own logic, which is supposedly uninvolved in the processes of class production and reproduction, simply to the positivist "constituting conventions which set the boundaries among particular interests so that the interests will not destroy each other."[8] The consequence of legal positivism is, in short, to set up a theoretical schism between law and other social phenomena, conceptually separating it from the capitalist whole of which it is, in reality, a fundamental part. Legal positivism developed at the same historical conjuncture as liberal philosophy, and we must appreciate that it serves the same ideological function—and that is, taking some license with Poulantzas, "to hide the real contradictions, [and] reconstitute at an imaginary level a relatively coherent discourse which serves as the horizon of agents' experience."[9] Indeed, it is not overstating the case to argue that the veneer of legal positivism is the cornerstone of legitimacy in the capitalist social order, which is unable to countenance even the suggestion that "the Courts" or "the Judiciary" are anything other than autonomous and "politically neutral" arbiters of social tension.

The rejection of the schema of law provided by liberal positivism, however, does not propel us into a crude Marxist instrumentalism—that is, the approach that conceptualizes "the law" as simply an instrument of social control of the bourgeoisie. In its own way, this is as artificial an understanding of the function of the law as is found in liberal legalism, as it is also predicated on a concept or understanding of "law" that has a strong epistemologically positivist flavor, as still presented in terms of "rules" or "commands." Indeed, pluralist and vulgar Marxist analyses both posit law as an "instrument"—the two views differing simply on the empirical point of *whose* interest it expresses—in the former, that of a (generally democratically elected sovereign) and in the latter, the naked class interests of the bourgeoisie. These approaches are both inadequate as they allow no dynamism to the structure of the *legal system* in the production and reproduction of class relations—as Balbus notes, that is, for the way in which "this form [of law] articulates the overall requirements of the capitalist system in which these social actors function."[10]

As suggested, a feminist analysis of law must address the significance of the *form* of law in regulating the oppression of women in capitalist society. That is, a necessary element of any feminist critique of law must be the examination of the way in which the structural characteristics of the western legal system—its formality, its generality, its autonomy and its professionalism—function to mediate social tension in the political interest of capital, an interest that we have seen is necessarily predicated upon the political, sexual and economic subordination of women.

Our critique of law—a feminist critique of law—needs to be developed within a theory of social reproduction; it is only by transcending the positivist conceptual framework of both liberal legalism and Marxist instrumentalism that we can make the conjunction between "the woman question" and "the law"—and thus articulate the crucial role the law plays in the production (and, importantly, the *reproduction*) of the iniquitous class relationships of capitalist society.

Beyond Positivism—Law and Social Reproduction

This essay proposes to offer a way to approach the fundamental connections between patriarchy and law by showing how our legal system presents us with a dispute resolution process that has (ideological claims to neutrality and impartiality aside) the express political function of mediating social tension in the political interests of the dominant classes—that is, serves to define and reconstitute, sex and economic class relations in the interests of capital.

The feminist strategy of "deconstructing" what Klare terms "liberal legalism" requires us to address, *inter alia*, those structural attributes such as the principle of formal legal equality (what Weber refers to as the "generality" and "universality" of legalism), the significance of the professionalization of the law and its hierarchical court structure, and the nature and function of "legal method." A feminist sociology of law should illustrate how these characteristics of legalism frustrate the use of the law as an instrument of social change—a vehicle that women can employ in the interests of their political emancipation—as in concert they preclude the "qualitatively different interests and social origins of individuals from entering into the calculus of political exchange."[11] These structural characteristics of legalism collapse together to constitute a form of practice through which the social order of capitalism—a social order predicated at heart on the subordination of women—is reconstituted across time. The following section will show how the Western legal order serves to perpetuate and maintain patriarchal domination under what is essentially an ideological facade of formal justice, procedural equity, neutrality and judicial impartiality—to illustrate, in short, that "law-making" for women in capitalist societies is characteristically a "mode of *domination* rather than freedom."[12]

"Legalism" is committed to generality and universality in its application of the law. That is to say, it applies abstract legal principles without distinction or qualification to those people within its jurisdiction. In bourgeois legal philosophy, "justice" is identified with legal equality, which is conceived of as "the pure formal principle of legal impartiality."[13] This "equal treatment of all citizens before the law"—in Dicey's terms, the "equal subjection of all classes to the ordinary law of the land"[14]—underpins the Rule of Law doctrine and is ideologically central to the legitimacy of the modern state.

Legalism, in short, is predicated on a *formal* equality of all persons; an insistence that is, in *substance*, quite anti-democratic. As Thomas Platt outlines, it insists on treating unlike cases alike, notionalizing a legal relationship in *form* that invariably does not exist in fact.[15] Transposed upon a system of marked and systemic social inequality, a system predicated upon the social and economic subordination of women, the universality and generality of the law serve to "confer on the propertied classes a sort of factual autonomy"[16]—a characteristic that is advantageous to those agents with economic and social advantage—and, in both areas, women are structurally disadvantaged as a class relative to men.

That is, apart from its ideological role in the legitimation of the modern state, the principle of "formal legal equality" functions to "*de-politicize*" the dispute before the court, by filling litigants with what Marx calls an "unreal universality."[17] That is to say, it serves to divest people of their real, individual life, of those "political" attributes such as *sex*, social class, race and educational status which, in all likelihood were the very factors underpinning the dispute in the first place. It is contended that Marx's critique of politics in "On the Jewish Question" is equally pertinent to the function of the law in contemporary capitalist society. Paraphrasing Marx,

> The *law* abolishes, after its own function, the distinctions established by *sex*, birth, social rank, education, occupation, when it decrees that *sex*, birth, social rank, education, occupation are non-political distinctions; when it proclaims, without regard to these distinctions, that every member of a society is an equal partner at *law*, and treats all the elements arising out of the real life of the nation from the standpoint of *the formal equality of the law*. But *the law*, none the less, allows *sex*, private property, education, occupation, to act after their own fashion and *to manifest their particular nature*. Far from abolishing these effective distinctions, *the law only exists so far as they are presupposed*; [emphasis added] it is conscious of being innately political and manifests its universality only in opposition to these elements [Author's note: changes to the original text are *italicized*.][18]

Thus, far from ensuring social equality, legalism's insistence on the principle of formal equality before the law serves to perpetuate social *in*equality. Platt illustrates how certain forms of *actual equality* are necessary conditions for the realization of *legal equality*—and shows that if some important conditions of living are unequal, legal equality—implying a principle of *impartiality*, becomes a form of *maintaining* and *preserving* actual class inequalities. Indeed, "it is precisely this abstract character [that] constitutes the decisive merit of formal justice to those who wield economic power."[19] Women, as that class located strategically (and, in the logic of the capitalist formation, necessarily) the furthest from all loci of economic, social or political power in contemporary Western society, are placed at a considerable structural disadvantage by the principle of formal legal equality. This principle is (to draw again on Marx) "a phenomenal form which makes the actual relations invisible and, indeed, shows the direct opposite of that relation"[20] and as such is one of the "key mystifications of the capitalist mode of production" as it underpins "its illusions as to liberty"[21] The *political function* of formal legal equality is thus to "de-politicize" the dispute: to exclude, from the calculus of legal exchange, those political variables, such as the sex, race, class and education of the litigants, that are properly causally related to the matter before the court.

Apart from being both "general" and "universal," legalism is strikingly "autonomous"—a characteristic Unger in *Law in Modern Society* holds to have four key dimensions. Unger holds Law to be *institutionally* autonomous when its rules are applied by highly specialized judicial institutions—"Courts"—the specific task of which is adjudication. It is *methodologically* autonomous when it employs a mode of justifying its acts—that is, its decision of cases—that differ from the kinds of justification used in other disciplines or practices (i.e., the formalism of judicial reasoning). The law is *substantively* autonomous when the rules it has to apply are unable to be evaluated on any criteria extrinsic to the legal system; that is to say, the political origins, significance and ramifications of the rules are supposedly beyond the purview of the court. Finally, legalism is *occupationally* autonomous, having a specialized group "defined by its activities, prerogatives and training, that manipulates the rules, staffs the institutions, and engages in the practice of legal argument."[22]

This characteristic "autonomy" of the Western legal order can be dissected to illustrate its political function in the reproduction of existing class structures across time. Weber illustrates how the emergence of a "distinct" legal profession—what he terms a "status group"—was the necessary condition for the emergence of "logical formal rationality" in a legal system,[23] as it required the development of "unique skills, roles and modes of thought (if it were to be able) to create and maintain universal rules."[24] The "alienation" of the law, in short, requires the development of a professional class to mediate access to it. . . . As is convincingly illustrated by Griffiths,[25] the articulation and implementation of the law is controlled by the values and morality of the class that is constituted to run it, and is thus in substance bourgeois. The moral themes and social perceptions of this class pervade, with little exception, women's attempts to employ the law in their political interests.[26] This fact constitutes yet another structural disadvantage to any woman who may aspire to use "the law" to invoke, or to protect, her civil rights, for these "rights" will be both defined, determined, and articulated, primarily by a class that has a vested interest in maintaining the social relations of capitalist production, relations which are predicated at heart on the subordination of women. . . . The class profile of the legal profession and the existence (as we shall later see) of a certain discretionary latitude in judicial reasoning collapse together to fuse a patriarchal bias into "the law" at every level: and accordingly, the processes by which this class homogeneity of the profession is *maintained* should be of concern to a feminist critique of law. . . .

The structural characteristic that Unger describes under the rubric of "methodological autonomy" refers to that specific mode of discourse that is associated with the decision-making process in legalism. The particular and specialized methodology employed in "the law"—in the courts, by lawyers, and in legal academia—is more generally referred to as legal "formalism" and, as Wallace and Fiocco illustrate, it serves to control cognition by employing devices such as specialized legal logic, hierarchical and procedural rules, dichotomous definitions, and an entrenched analytical focus on appellate court decisions. That is to say, formalism is based upon

> a pattern of evaluation of law and legal institutions which is contoured heavily by these cognitive controls which principally measure the internal consistency of rules and their sources to the exclusion of their substantive content and social effect.[27]

Legal formalism underpins the judicial decision-making process in Australian courts and has a strong ideological significance as it *purportedly* separates the reasoning process from the personal/political/moral caprices or persuasions of the judges themselves and ties it to an external legal standard. Indeed, as Kirby[28] notes, legalism's greatest proponent of this "strict logic and high technique," Sir Owen Dixon, declared that

> It is taken for granted that the decision of the Court will be "correct" or "incorrect," "right" or "wrong" as it conforms with ascertained legal principles and applies them according to a standard of reasoning which is not personal to the judges themselves. *But it is basal.* The Court would feel that the function it performed had lost its meaning and purpose if there were no external (*that is "legal"*) standard of correctness. [Emphasis in original.] [29]

However, as we shall see, this legal methodology *fails* to constrain judicial creativity, and certainly does not ensure the "neutrality" of the decision-making process. Indeed, as Horwitz observes,

> the paramount condition for legal formalism to flourish in a society is for the powerful groups in that society to have a great interest in disguising and suppressing the inevitable political and redistributive functions of law.[30]

The legal method employed by the judges is governed by the doctrine of *stare decisis* (precedent) and the rules of statutory interpretation, the bench in both cases purportedly guided by "neutral principles of interpretation in relation to abstract legal concepts.[31] Professor Mossman well illustrates this point in her analysis of the *French* and "Person cases," showing how the courts will generally avail themselves of the opportunity (particularly in politically contentious cases) to disavow their consideration of the political and social ramifications of the matter before them. [Mossman's essay is included in Part 6. *Ed.*]

The historical experience of feminists' attempts to engage the law as an instrument of social and political emancipation well illustrates that the foundations of legal formalism, its axiomatic principles of methodological neutrality and judicial impartiality are, in substance, a facade. This *his*tory has been well documented by feminist legal scholars such as Sachs and Wilson, Scutt and Mossman.[32] . . . [A]n overview of this literature and some key cases will serve to illustrate . . . that these purportedly neutral principles of judicial interpretation mask what is, in reality, a certain discretionary latitude on the part of the judiciary . . .—and thus serves to ensure that the articulation of "the law" is underpinned by a value matrix that is innately bourgeois. That is, it aims to show, as Stone cogently argued in his classic *Legal Systems and Lawyers' Reasoning* the system of precedent is based on what he terms "a legal category of indeterminate or concealed multiple reference—the *'ratio decidendi'* of the case"—that confers a *de facto* discretion on the judges in choosing between, in distinguishing, qualifying or rejecting authorities and in delimiting the scope of statutes.[33]

Stone's charge that the "logical form" is often fallacious and that the (purported) exclusion of judicial consideration of "social needs, social policies and personal evaluation by the Courts" is correspondingly illusory[34] is also highlighted with particular clarity in what are generally referred to as the "person cases." What these articles need to address in more detail, however, is the political *function* of legal method in the process of social reproduction, and the way it relates to other structural attributes of liberal legalism in law's overall political project of maintaining sexual and economic subordination.

In . . . [a] series of cases, the British and Australian judiciary wrestled for decades with the problem as to whether women, at law, were entitled to be regarded as "persons." As Scutt[35] outlines, these cases were related to the right of women to be classified as "persons" for the purpose of standing for various public offices (including Parliament, local councils, and juries) and to take up other civil rights.

In the first of these cases, Jex-Blake v. Senatus of the University of Edinburgh ([1973] 11M 747), seven women were denied permission to "attend instruction" in medicine at the University of St. Andrews in Scotland, in spite of the fact that the University regulations provided that "persons" were so entitled . . . .

. . . Scutt notes how the definition of "person" as it is commonly understood— for example, as defined in the Oxford Dictionary, as being "an individual human being . . . of or belonging to the genus homo as opposed to animals, machines or mere objects"—was implicitly *rejected* by the judges in this case.[36] Indeed, their decision flies in the face of even the broadest application of the canons of statutory interpretation . . . which provided that

> in all acts, words purporting the masculine gender shall be deemed and taken to include females, . . . unless the contrary . . . is expressly provided. [Acts Interpretation Act § (1850)]

In spite of this clear and express statutory provision, their Lordships were nevertheless able to determine that "the Law" could still recognize the difference of sex and for the purpose of excluding women from the University on the grounds that they were not "persons." That this decision turned expressly upon what Stone terms "the social policies . . . and personal evaluation of the Court" rather than an adherence to an external standard of legal logic[37] is well illustrated in the decision of Lord Neave, who based his decision on the

> . . . belief, widely entertained, that there is a great difference in the mental constitution of the two sexes, just as there is in their physical conformation. The powers and susceptibilities of women are as noble as those of men; but they are thought to be different, and, in particular, it is considered that they have not the same power of intense labour that men are endowed with. If this be so, it must form a serious objection to uniting them under the same course of academic study. I confess that, to some extent, I share this view, and would regret to see our young females subjected to the severe and incessant work which my own observation and experience have taught me to consider as indispensable to any high attainment in learning. A disregard of such an inequality would be fatal to any scheme of public instruction, for, as it is certain that the general mass of any army cannot move more rapidly than its slowest and weakest portion, so a general course of study must be toned and tempered down to suit the average of all classes of students for whom it is intended; and the average will always be lowered by the existence of any considerable numbers who cannot keep pace with the rest.[38]

> Add to this the special acquirements and accomplishments at which women must aim, but from which men may easily remain exempt. Much time must, or ought to be, given by women to the acquisition of a knowledge of household affairs and family duties, as well as to those ornamental parts of education which tend so much to social refinement and domestic happiness, and the study necessary for mastering these must always form a serious distraction from severer pursuits, while there is little doubt that, in public estimation, the want of these feminine arts and attractions in a woman would be ill supplied by such branches of knowledge as a University could bestow.[39]

The judicial discretion in delimiting the scope of statutes and distinguishing, qualifying and rejecting authorities is clearly presented in the ratio of another of the "person" cases, Chorlton v. Lings ([1868] LR 4CP 374). In this case, a woman *prima facie* satisfied all the statutory requirements of the Representation of the People Act of 1867, which specified that "every man shall, in and after the year 1868, be entitled to be registered as a voter."

The applicant's counsel argued that on a straightforward application of section 5 of the Acts Interpretation Act (1850), his client was entitled to have her name upon the voting register. It is to be recalled that the Acts Interpretation Act provided that it applied to all subsequent legislation unless the legislation in question expressly excluded it. The legislation before the court in this case—the Representation of the People Act—had no exemption clause.

Nevertheless, the Court was again able to justify a decision contrary to the straightforward and clear intention of the statute. In an exercise in flawed syllogistic logic, the Court held that

> it was not necessary that express words exclude (the Acts Interpretation Act) because the subject matter of (the Representation of the People Act) makes it quite clear that women are not to be taken as being covered by virtue of the word "man" being used; on the contrary, because man is used women were thereby expressly excluded.[40]

The selectivity and judicial latitude inherent in the doctrine of precedent is reflected with particular clarity in this case. Scutt, for example, illustrates how counsel for the applicant presented extensive research and case authorities documenting women's participation in various public offices and professions across English history.[41]

Nevertheless, Chief Justice Bovill was able to hold that these authorities were "of little account" (despite being *directly* on the point in issue!!!); and he distinguished them simply on the basis that they were "not mentioned in some [law] reports"[42] and thus attached little weight to them. It is contended that the case well illustrates Stone's contention that

> the massiveness of the areas for judicial choice at any particular time, *including that between following or distinguishing an earlier case*, is a function not only of the accumulation of past decisions, not only of changes in the environment, but also of new insights and perspectives both on old problems and on new problems . . . (and that) . . . *in many cases, the only authoritative guides . . . usually consist of alternatives amongst which, by the system of stare decisis itself, they have in any case an inescapable duty to choose*. . . . And which alternative is chosen from the versions of the material facts (or the ratio of the precedent case) made or left available by the authoritative materials, will reflect the assessments thus made.[43] [Emphasis in original.]

It is difficult to distill any clear procedural logic in the process by which the judiciary determined these cases. They were chosen as they illustrate clearly the selective use of precedent and the discretionary characterization of statutes that in *practice* underpins the interpretive function of the judges—and because, as Mossman's analysis of later cases illustrates, they set the tone for most subsequent feminist engagements with the law. These cases stand as stark testimony to Lord Reid's observation in *Essays XXV* that "notwithstanding all the apparatus of authority, the judge nearly always has some degree of choice." It is in this "latitude"—what Stone refers to as "the leeways of choice"[44]—that legalism structurally incorporates a value input from the class that has been constituted to administer the legal system—a value input, an interpretive perspective that is almost invariably conservative. That is, in these "leeways" the class position and moral world view of the judicial class becomes *structurally* significant—for capital creates along class (and sex) lines an underlying code through which people interpret their world and evaluate the behavior of those with whom they interact. The interpretation of matters before the Court is thus articulated from the perspective of the world view of the bourgeoisie—that (invariably) middle-class male judge, to whom the subordination of women is inscribed in the grand logical design of life—as was so clearly presented in Lord Neave's misogynistic dictum in *Jex-Blake*. To deify, as did Dixon, the "strict logic and high procedure" of formalism as providing an "*external* standard of correctness"—that purportedly ensures the neutrality and impartiality of legal method—is to worship a false god—for as Stone notes, there is no such thing as "ineluctable legal logic," but in reality legal method collapsed into "a composite of the relations between legal propositions, of observation of facts and consequences, and of value judgments about the acceptability of these consequences, is what finally comes to bear upon the alternatives with which the rule of *stare decisis* confronts the courts."[45] Although it is true that the subjugation to a system of rules sets a very general framework which limits the *overt* or naked exercise of discretion of the individual law-maker/adjudicator who occupied a central position in legal forms past, it serves to replace it with a more insidious and class-based value bias that is cloaked by the all-pervasive ideology of neutrality and impartiality. That is, as Mossman notes, the "nature of decision-making requires choices of the judges that they cannot make without taking into account other factors; and it seems, moreover, that judges may be influenced, often implicitly, by their own life experiences in making such choices."[46]

As Wallace and Fiocco note, the other key characteristic of legal formalism is its analytical focus on "the internal consistency of the rules and their sources to the exclusion of their substantive content and social effect."[47] It relies upon binding, fixed and determinate rules, that pre-exist the dispute and serve to determine the relationship between the parties to it before the matter even comes before the court, employing what Tribe terms an essentially static (as well as instrumental) model of law and policy in which

[1] The state is deemed to have a certain policy or not

[2] the policy of the state is deemed to be expressed solely by its positive body of enacted law; and

[3] a state's policies are then applied or not applied in a particular fact situation.[48]

The notorious uncorroborated evidence rule of the common law provides a clear example of how the law structures the relationship between the parties before the dispute presents itself for resolution, and illustrates the innate conservatism of a dispute resolution process that expressly (in the interests of "justice"?) excludes any consideration by the Court of the moral or ethical basis—or, indeed, the contemporary social relevance of—the rules that it is applying. Although statutorily amended in some jurisdictions in recent years (for example, New South Wales) the general principle of corroboration at common law is that an accused person is able to be convicted solely on the testimony of a single, reliable witness. At common law, this general prescription is qualified by two key exceptions: the jury in a criminal trial must be warned against convicting an accused person on the uncorroborated evidence of a child, and a similar warning must be issued in the case of a conviction on the uncorroborated testimony of a complainant in trials of sexual offenses. . . . [U]nderpinning this . . . has been the assumption that the accusation of the offense may have been made "owing to sexual neurosis, jealousy, fantasy, spite, or a girl's refusal to admit that she consented to an act of which she is now ashamed."[49]

Such a claim has no empirical foundation. . . . Nevertheless, no such aspersion—implying that women *qua* women are "irrational and quixotic"[50]—is cast in parallel on the credibility of the testimony of male victims of common and violent assaults.

Clearly, the procedural requirements of such a judicial warning serves to define the relationship between the parties before the matter presents itself for resolution. That is, the female witness is branded (with complete disregard to the particular qualities of reliability and credibility that she may as an individual possess) as inherently unreliable and childlike—that is, as *intrinsically* unable to be relied upon under oath—in the direction that the judge is obliged to give the jury. The innate *conservatism* of such fixed-rule determinations cannot be overstated. The conduct of the trial is unfairly tilted in the favor of the accused by what is in effect an extremely misogynistic prescription that colors the credibility of the victim's evidence and which she has *no legal right to challenge*. As we shall see, such fixed-rule provisions are antithetical to a legal technique that seeks to incorporate evolving visions of law and society (including changes in the political status of women) into legal principle—because it defines these rules as "outside" the calculus of legal exchange, and, as such, is a method of resolving disputes that is appropriate only to a legal system that aspires to remain "frozen in time."[51] The political function of these fixed-rule determinations of positivism is "to surely deprive the polity of new arguments, and of new data, from which a new moral consensus might emerge."[52]

The structural attributes of legalism—the generality and universality of the law, its alienation and professionalization, its specific methodology, and its fixed-rule determinations—serve to frustrate the use of the law as an instrument for social emancipation as in concert they effectively "preclude the qualitatively different interests and social origins of individuals from entering into the calculus of legal exchange"[53] and, further, cloak the intrinsically bourgeois-patriarchal interpretive perspective of the Court with the ideological facade of neutrality and judicial impartiality. That is, "legalism" is innately conservative in that it provides a dispute-resolution framework that *refuses* to recognize the political factors that causally underpin any dispute that comes before it.

Feminism and Legal Formalism: An Examination of the Function of the Equal Opportunity Tribunal in New South Wales

The political function of this form of law—its role in the reproduction of the class relations of capitalist society—is highlighted by an examination of the structure and function of the New South Wales Equal Opportunity Tribunal—which has attempted to make the legal process more receptive to the claims of the sexually disadvantaged in society. The Tribunal has attempted to move away from the constraints of judicial formalism in endeavoring to provide a more substantive consideration of the real social issues it was attempting to address than was available within the evidential and procedural constraints of the general law. The Tribunal was constituted under the Anti-Discrimination Act 1977 (NSW), Part VIIIA. By virtue of sections 107 and 108, the Tribunal was relieved of the burden of adhering strictly to the procedural rules of evidence and pleading, is able to inform itself of any matter it sees fit, and is directed to act in accord with "good conscience, equity, and the substantial merits of the case" (that is, adhering to the principles of natural justice) without recourse to technicalities or legal form. It would appear *prima facie* that such a forum would be better equipped to address tensions in social relations in the real, political context in which they arise. It offers the potential, in other words, to give some voice to women—to that class that is located strategically, and in the logic of capital accumulation, necessarily, the furthest away from all loci of power in our society. Unfettered by the formalist constraints of the legalist tradition, the Tribunal *has* been more able than the Court to address the question of justice in the real social context in which it arises between the parties. . . .

By sacrificing strict legalism, the Equal Opportunity Tribunal has actually managed (albeit tortuously, and generally at great personal cost to the plaintiff[54]) to achieve something that approaches "social" justice. It hardly comes as a surprise that its successes have engendered such a strident exhortation of competitive capitalist ideology and demands for a return to strict formalism—for it is clear that the closer we get to the heart of capitalist domination, the more raw a politico-legal nerve we trigger. This explains the almost invariable tradition of appeal from Tribunal decisions (using the most ingenious of legal argument, particularly jurisdictional, to ground the appeal within section 118)—to attempt to re-cast the problem in the Supreme Court, where the formality and generality of the law can be invoked to preclude the qualitatively different interests and characteristics of the parties that the Tribunal was able to take cognizance of.

The existence of this right of appeal has served to force a legalistic flavor on Tribunal decisions—the *Anti-Discrimination Board Annual Report* 1983/1984 noting that "it is apparent *(from the conduct of parties to complaints)* that they are becoming more aware of the encroachment of legalism into this field."

Thus, if exercised (and indeed, in potential effect), the right of appeal serves to re-formalize the process of dispute resolution, stultify legal creativity,[55] places an almost unmanageable financial burden on the weaker party (usually the complainant—illustrating once again the class invisibility of formalism) and serves to re-introduce that element of judicial conservatism into what we earlier saw to be the "leeways" of judicial interpretation.

Despite such constraints, however, the Tribunal mechanism nevertheless offers the potential to relax the formality, generality and autonomy of the law, and thus to permit the introduction of the qualitatively different interests and social origins of women into the calculus of legal exchange—effectively, thus, "politicizing" the law.

The reaction expressed in the following (representative) letter to the *Sydney Morning Herald* as part of the conservative hysteria surrounding the *Jane Hill* case (Jane Hill v. The Water Resources Commission, [1985] EOC 92 127) provides a clear functional example of how the formality, generality and autonomy of the law contributes to the maintenance of existing socioproductive relations—showing the threat to entrenched interests proffered by a form of law that is, to paraphrase Unger "crack'd open to politics."[56]

DISCRIMINATION

Sir: If ever there was an event which demonstrated the dangers of introducing the law into the area of human relations, it must surely be the Jane Hill case (*Herald*, May 11).

In finding for Ms. Hill and penalising her employers, the Anti-Discrimination Tribunal, aided by the Premier, has ensured that justice has not only not been done, but it can't even be seen to have been done.

Apart from a relatively small pecuniary gain by Ms. Hill, it is difficult to see any benefits at all which have come from this extraordinary decision. Ms. Hill will find it impossible to work in a normal work situation without being subjected to considerable suspicion and comment by her workmates.

The people found by the tribunal as being Ms. Hill's tormentors have been left in a curious situation, having been named by the tribunal as the perpetrators of most unsavoury acts upon their victim, but being denied, by the Premier, the opportunity to state their case in a proper court of law.

Last but not least, the taxpayers of NSW have been collectively fined $35,000 for sexually harassing a person unknown to virtually all of them.

The precedents set by the Jane Hill case are frightening in their implications. It is obvious that the legislation which created the tribunal could well exacerbate the situation which it sets out to remedy.[57]

The author's view that "the law" should not be introduced into the arena of human relations presupposes that the ordering of human relations, and the perceptions of self and society thereby engendered, are NOT articulated to the productive base of society. The social relations of capitalism are fundamentalized on the appropriation of the labor of women, the attendant ideological commodification of women that this entails and their necessarily limited public autonomy. The author's position becomes clear; what he is in fact saying is that the interests of this class cannot be permitted substantive legal expression—a view that is perfectly logical if your definition of the logic is the logic of capital accumulation. Any development in legal form that allows the substantive (as opposed to the ideological value of token) recognition of these interests must be "frightening in their implications" for the author and those "fellows" of his ilk—the members of those classes possessing the real social and financial autonomy in the capitalist social formation. The rationale underlying his exhortation to re-formalize the dispute—to present it in what he terms a "proper" court of law—thus becomes comprehensible. "Proper," as defined in the *Concise Oxford Dictionary*, means "relating exclusively or distinctively to"—and the unspoken point of reference in the author's use of the term are those interests that we have seen are reinforced by legalism. Further, his comments that the Tribunal decision was one wherein "justice" was not done, and was not seen to be done—has an acid irony to it—inverting the concept of justice by tying it to its formal expression in legalism rather than articulating it to the real social matrix in which disputes between the parties are played out.

Therefore the relationship between "women" and "the law" can only properly be understood by approaching the legal system as a form of "praxis"—that is, as a form of practice that has the express political function of mediating social tension in the interest of capital. There is a certain paradox involved in feminists' attempts to invoke "the law" in the interests of their political emancipation; for as we have seen (its ideological claims to political neutrality and judicial impartiality aside), the methodological and structural characteristics of legalism are functionally related to both reinforcing and reproducing the dynamics predicated at heart on the political, economic and sexual subordination of women.

This essay has examined some of the structural barriers in legalism that militate against its use as an instrument of social reform. Women must *prima facie* contend with the principle of formal legal equality when attempting to resolve grievances through the legal system. By divesting the dispute of its "political" character—that is, by filling complainant and respondent with an "artificial political equivalence" before the Court—the law relieves itself of having to consider the structural inequities underpinning the matter before it. By refusing (in the perverse interpretation of "*justice*") to recognize variables such as sex, class, private property, occupation and education as causally and evidentially significant, "the law" accords them a *de facto* autonomy and in real terms permits them to continue to "act after their own fashion, and to manifest their particular nature."[58] Legalism's insistence on formal equality serves to perpetuate sexual *in*equality—as it "precludes the qualitatively different interests and social origins of *women* from entering into the calculus of political exchange."[59] Formal legal equality—ideologically central to legalism's claim to justice and legitimacy—translates in practical terms to a form of maintaining and preserving sex and economic class relationships, constituting, in short, what Balbus terms "the political expression of bourgeois class interests."[60] This feature of legalism renders it inherently difficult for "the law" to accommodate legislation that is predicated on the recognition of *structural* inequality. . . .

The individualist themes of the liberal legalist tradition render it difficult for it to conceptualize, and give legal expression to, the concept of structural group disadvantage—such as sex (or, for that matter, race, class, etc.)—which at heart is the raison d'être of anti-discrimination legislation.

The alienation of the law—"its control by experts socialised in elite institutions and distanced from the lived reality of everyday life in capitalist societies"[61]—constitutes yet another impediment to feminists' attempts to engage the law in either the declaration or protection of civil rights for women. The quintessentially middle-class homogeneity of the legal profession serves to ensure that the moral themes and social perceptions of this class pervade women's attempts to employ the law in their political interest—the political interests of the bourgeoisie are necessarily patriarchal. Even at the most basic of levels, the class values of the profession structure feminist engagement with the law by controlling their very *access* to it. For example, the *NSW Task Force on Domestic Violence*[62] reported that women were fortunate (!) if they were able to locate a solicitor who believed their account of their assault and was prepared to constructively assist them in employing even what limited remedies were available to ameliorate their situation.

Having overcome the hurdle of access, women then have to deal with the fact that the "rights" they are petitioning the Court to recognize will be both defined and articulated by the judiciary—the "most professional" of the professional caste constituted to run the legal system—who have themselves a vested class interest in maintaining the social relations of capitalist production. We have earlier seen how the "legal method" employed by the Courts falls far short of its claim to provide an external standard of legal "correctness," an "ineluctable legal logic,"[63] which supposedly ensures neutrality and impartiality in the application of the law—claims which ideologically mask what is in reality an interpretive latitude on the part of the bench. Through the discretion outlined in legal reasoning—the "leeways of choice"—legalism is able to incorporate a value input from that class that is constituted to administer the system, and thus has an interpretive bias that reflects the world view of the bourgeoisie.

"Patriarchy" is thus incorporated into the very *fabric* of the law by the collapsing together of the class character of the legal profession and the interpretive discretion inhering in "legal reasoning"—a bias that has been effectively obscured by the ideological veneer of neutrality and judicial impartiality.

Legalism provides an essentially static and innately conservative model of dispute resolution in its resolute commitment to binding, pre-determined rules, which pre-exist the dispute and which serve to define the relationship between the parties before the matter even presents itself before the Court. Such prescriptions (that is, as considered, the uncorroborated evidence rule)—are antithetical to a legal process that aims to incorporate evolving social mores into the law as it places these prescriptions outside the calculus of legal exchange, and serves, as Tribe observes, to deny the litigant (that is, the woman rape victim) any explanation of the state's assumptions about her reliability and credibility. Indeed, Tribe further argues that such a method for dealing with social tension is inconsistent with anything but "an unacceptably atomistic, anomic and anticommunal conception of social life"[64]—a conception that is given its practical expression in the social relations of capitalist production. The "fixed-rule determinism" of legalism serves to render it more difficult for women to successfully employ the law in the resolution of their political grievances as the conduct of the trial can be tilted against them before the matter is even given a hearing.

Finally, we saw the hierarchical structure of the Court system plays a key role in constraining any grass-roots pressures for a more substantive expression of justice through the legal system. If the lower courts exercise too much latitude with the rules of evidence and procedure—that is, if they take too broad (or even "political") a cognizance of the case before them—the decision will be held to be flawed at law and will be re-cast on appeal to a "higher" court where the formality and generality of the law can be invoked in the name of "justice" and the legalistic self-coherency of "the law" reinforced.

The law constitutes the sole basis of legitimate domination and normative order in Western capitalist societies—and to it, and to it alone, is entrusted the ultimate responsibility for mediating social tension. "Legalism" *purports* to perform this task (in the grand positivist tradition) neutrally and impartially—allegedly serving to merely "constitute conventions which set the boundaries between particular interest so that they do not destroy each other."[65] This definition of the *function* of the law—of ideological centrality to the legitimacy of the capitalist state—is *not*, as we have seen, vindicated in practice. Beneath this facade, we have found *in fact* a dispute resolution process that is intimately involved in reinforcing and reproducing the sex and economic class relations of capitalism. It provides a mechanism for resolving social tension that confers a *de facto* advantage to entrenched social, sexual and economic interests. It provides an interpretive perspective that reflects the (patriarchal) world view of the bourgeoisie, and its reliance on fixed and determinate rules, which pre-exist the dispute, serves an innately conservative function as they determine the relationship between the parties before the matter presents itself for adjudication and further provides a legal technique that is unable to incorporate evolving social mores into legal principle at a responsive and democratic level, that is, the function of this legal system is to stifle, or at least filter into insignificance, any claims for social justice made upon it by women. Although it is true, as Thompson[66] notes, that the ideological function of the law requires that it occasionally give substantive effect to its claims to equity and justice (which the women's movement has, it is acknowledged, had past cause to be thankful for), its *general* function is to structurally frustrate the attainment of sexual liberation through the legal process.

These structural features collapse together to constitute a form of practice through which the social order of capitalism is reproduced across time; serving to maintain and perpetuate and, indeed, legitimate patriarchal domination under its veneer of formal justice, procedural equity, neutrality and judicial impartiality. Expressed within such a framework, it is hardly surprising that feminist litigators have not, as observed by Rifkin, "challenged the fundamental patriarchal social order"[67] in spite of the fact that the practice of law now includes experienced and talented feminist litigators and academics. Rather than reflect some sex-typed lack of legal ability, feminist difficulties in engaging the law in the struggle against patriarchy are attributable to the structure of liberal legalism—a *form* of law which for women (to borrow a term used by Connell in another context) effectively constitutes a "praxis trap"—that is, it is "a situation in which people (i.e., feminist litigators and academics) do things for good reasons and skillfully, in situations that turn out to make their original purpose *difficult* to achieve."[68] Feminists will continue to find the pursuit of "justice" (as we understand the term) within the parameters of legalism to be a chimera—always promised, never realized—for we are attempting to employ in our interests a legal framework that has the express political function of perpetuating the powerlessness of women, and which institutionally reinforces the patriarchal logic of capital accumulation.

The purpose of this essay has been to suggest a framework within which the fundamental connections between culture, patriarchy and law can be constructively addressed. It is contended that the lacunae in feminist scholarship in relation to law seriously impairs the feminist political project: for, as we have seen, "the law" plays a key institutional role in both reinforcing and reproducing the class subordination of women to men. I have argued that it [is] simply incorrect to "dismiss" the law from feminist scholastic and strategic inquiry as some "inert" mechanism for giving effect to "male" interests; it is, rather, an organic social relation that is actively involved in mediating and controlling the tensions engendered in a class-structured society. "The law" is intimately involved in structuring every aspect of women's lives; it stands at the very center of the "arena of social struggle" and is of fundamental significance to the very legitimacy of the capitalist state and, by implication, the legitimacy of sexual subordination. I believe that a reorientation of the "feminist" approach to law is long overdue: for as it is politically central to patriarchal domination, we simply cannot afford to keep it at the penumbra of our political project. Our task, as I perceive it, is to "crack open" law to politics: to reject the conceptual framework of positivist jurisprudence, and to approach the law as a form of praxis, for only then can we unveil its particular function in the process of reproducing the exploitative sexual and economic class structures of capitalist society.

Notes

1. Klare, Law-Making as Praxis, 40 Telos 123, 128 (1979).

2. D. Hay, Authority and the Criminal Law, in Albion's Fatal Tree: Crime and Society in Eighteenth-Century England 48–49 (Allen Lane, 1975).

3. Although an analysis of this inter-relationship is beyond the scope of this article, it is a nexus that is of *fundamental* importance in developing a feminist critique of law. It is well addressed, *inter alia*, in R. Connell, Which Way Is Up? 33–49 (Allen and Unwin, 1983); I. Hartmann, Capitalism, Patriarchy and Job Segregation by Sex, in M. Blaxall & B. Reagan eds., Women and the Workplace: The Implications of Occupational Segregation (University of Chicago Press, 1976); P. Connolly, Last Hired, First Fired: Women and the Canadian Workforce (Women's Press, 1979).

4. Hart, Positivism and the Separation of Morals, 71 Harv. L. Rev. 601–02 (1958).

5. R. Unger, Law in Modern Society: Toward a Criticism of Social Theory 72–73 (Free Press, 1976).

6. S. Picciotto, The Theory of the State, Class Struggle and the Rule of Law, in Capitalism and the Rule of Law: From Deviancy Theory to Marxism (Academic Press, 1979).

7. Gabel, Taking Rights Seriously (Book Review), 91 Harv. L. Rev. 302, 304 (1977).

8. R. Unger, Knowledge and Politics 72 (Free Press, 1975).

9. N. Poulantzas, Political Power and Social Classes 207 (New Left Books, 1978).

10. Balbus, Legal Form and Commodity Form: An Essay on the Relative Autonomy of the Law, 11 Law & Soc'y Rev. 571 (1977).

11. Balbus, Legal Form and Commodity Form, *supra* note 10, at 576.

12. Klare, Law-Making as Praxis, *supra* note 1, at 132.

13. W. Lang, Marxism, Liberalism and Justice, in A. Tay & E. Kamenka eds., Justice 135 (Arnold, 1979).

14. A. Dicey, Introduction to the Study of the Constitution 20, 202–03, 9th ed. (St. Martin's 1959).

15. Platt, Equality: Actual and Legal, 6 J. Soc. Phil. 14 (1975).

16. M. Rheinstein ed., Max Weber on Law in Economy and Society 699 (Harvard University Press, 1954).

17. K. Marx, On the Jewish Question, in The Marx-Engels Reader 30 (Norton, 1972).

18. K. Marx, Capital 33 (Progress Publishers, 1978). See also Klare, Law-Making as Praxis, *supra* note 1, at 132.

19. Pheinstein, Max. Weber on Law in Economy and Society, *supra* note 16, at 228–29.

20. K. Marx, Capital 505 (Progress Publishers, 1978).

21. *Id.* at 506.

22. Unger, Law in Modern Society, *supra* note 5, at 52–53.

23. Trubek, Max Weber on Law and the Rise of Capitalism, 1972 Wis. L. Rev. 720, 737.

24. *Id.* at 739ff.

25. J. Griffiths, The Politics of the Judiciary (Fontana Press, 1985).

26. Thus, misogynism is incorporated into the very fabric of the law by the collapsing together of the class nature of the legal profession (particularly the judiciary) and the interpretive discretion that . . . Stone (*inter alia*) has shown is a structural characteristic of formalism. J. Stone, Legal Systems and Lawyers' Reasoning (Maitland, 1964). Examples abound in every jurisdiction in which women come into contact with the law. For example:

Mr. Justice Slynn: "It does not seem to me that the appellant is a criminal in the sense in which that word is frequently used in these courts. Clearly, he is a man who, on the night in question, allowed his enthusiasm for sex to overcome his usual behaviour." (Unreported decision. Old Bailey, April 1976)

Button v. Button: "The wife does not get a share in the House simply because she cleans the walls or works in the garden. . . . Those are the sorts of things a wife does without altering title to, or interest in, the property." (1968 I All ER 1064.CA)

Peake v. Automotive Products Ltd: "It would be very wrong, to my mind, if [the EEO] statute were thought to do away with chivalry and courtesy which we expect mankind to give to womankind." ([1978] 2 All ER 106 per Lord Denning MR)

R. v. El Vino: "I must acknowledge at the outset that it appears to me trivial and banal even when topped up with legalistic froth. In light of the history those claims [of discrimination] are in my view artificial and pretentious; but the industrial Tribunal thought otherwise and their only concern appears to have been as to how great a sum they could award to this excessively outraged victim of sex discrimination." ([Rept NCCL Rights for Women Publication] Ct. of Appeal, 24 July 1981 per Lord Shaw)

27. Wallace & Fiocco, Recent Criticisms of Formalism in Legal Theory and Legal Education, 7 Adelaide L. Rev. 309 (1980–81).

28. M. Kirby, Reform the Law: Essays on the Reversal of the Australian Legal System 37 (Oxford University Press, 1983).

29. *Id.*

30. Wallace & Fiocco, Recent Criticisms of Formalism, *supra* note 27, at 310 (citing M. Horwitz, The Transformation of American Law 1790–1860 [Harvard University Press, 1977]).

31. See Mossman, Feminism and Legal Method, Part 6 this volume.

32. A. Sachs & J. Wilson, Sexism and the Law: A Study of Male Beliefs and Judicial Bias (Martin Robertson, 1978); Scutt, Sexism in Legal Language, 59 Australian L.J. 163 (1985); Mossman, Feminism and Legal Method, Part 6 this volume.

33. Stone, Legal Systems, *supra* note 26, at 235ff.

34. *Id.* at 241.

35. Scutt, Sexism in Legal Language, *supra* note 32, at 167.

36. *Id.* at 164.

37. Stone, Legal Systems, *supra* note 26, at 241.

38. Sachs & Wilson, Sexism and the Law, *supra* note 32, at 18.

39. Scutt, Sexism in Legal Language, *supra* note 32, at 165.

40. Chorlton v. Lings (1868) LR 4 CP 374, 392.

41. Scutt, Sexism in Legal Language, *supra* note 32, at 170–71.

42. Chorlton v. Lings (1868) LR 4 CP 374.

43. Stone, Legal Systems, *supra* note 26, at 282, 283.

44. *Id.* at 274ff.

45. *Id.* at 284.

46. Mossman, Feminism and Legal Method, Part 6 this volume.

47. Wallace & Fiocco, Recent Criticisms of Formalism, *supra* note 27, at 309.

48. Tribe, Structural Due Process, 10 Harv. C.R.-C.L. L. Rev. 269, 290 (1975).

49. M. Aronson, N. Reaburn, & M. Weinberg, Litigation: Evidence and Procedure 606 (Butterworths, 1982).

50. P. Pattullo, Judging Women 21 (NAAC Publication, 1983).

51. Tribe, Structural Due Process, *supra* note 48, at 307.

52. *Id.*

53. Balbus, Legal Form and Commodity Form, *supra* note 10, at 576.

54. Thornton, Board's First Decision 4 *LSB* 180 (1979).

55. Trubek, On Law and the Rise of Capitalism, *supra* note 23, at 749–50.

56. Unger, The Critical Legal Studies Movement, 96 Harv. L. Rev. 561, 563 (1983).

57. *Sydney Morning Herald*, June 7, 1985.

58. Marx, On the Jewish Question, *supra* note 17, at 30.

59. Balbus, Legal Form and Commodity Form, *supra* note 10, at 576.

60. I. Balbus, The Dialectics of Legal Repression 7 (Russell Sage Foundation, 1973).

61. Klare, Law-Making as Praxis, *supra* note 1, at 132.

62. NSW Task Force on Domestic Violence 1903–1972, 2nd ed. (NSW Government Printer, 1981).

63. Stone, Legal Systems, *supra* note 26, at 282.

64. Tribe, Structural Due Process, *supra* note 48, at 311.

65. Unger, Knowledge and Politics, *supra* note 8, at 72.

66. E. Thompson, Whigs and Hunters: Origins of the Black Acts 257–67 (Penguin, 1977).

67. Rifkin, Toward a Theory of Law and Patriarchy, Part 5 herein.

68. Connell, Which Way Is Up? *supra* note 3, at 156.

❖ *Liberal Jurisprudence and Abstracted Visions of Human Nature: A Feminist Critique of Rawls' Theory of Justice*

Mari J. Matsuda

This essay presents the thesis, derived from feminist theory, that Rawls' "theory of justice"[1] fails because of its central choice of abstraction as a method of inquiry. Abstraction as a methodology encompasses the belief that visions of social life can be constructed without reference to the concrete realities of social life. The choice of abstraction is a key move that allows Rawls to ignore powerful alternative constructions, and gives his theory an attractive internal logic. This internal logic, or "moral geometry," is then tested against intuitive impressions of what goes on in the concrete world. The choice of abstraction as a starting place, however, makes any meaningful reality check impossible.

To test this thesis, this essay reviews the most abstract component of Rawls' theory, the [concept of] original position. The decision to abstract all but a select body of knowledge out of the original position strengthens the internal logic of the theory and ultimately reveals it as one that must be accepted on faith alone. I reach this conclusion by considering the assumptions about human nature that are built into the original position, and the equally plausible counterassumptions that are abstracted out.

Because Rawls offers no reason for his choices from among equally valid assumptions, it is impossible to embark upon the journey through his elaborate moral geometry without taking an *a priori* leap of faith. Thus . . . the Theory of Justice . . . fails to convince the unconvinced that it is a theory of justice preferable to intuitively attractive alternatives.

The primary tenet of feminist theory, that the personal is the political, and the primary method of feminist inquiry, consciousness raising, are the sources of this critique. This essay will [review] the primary elements of Rawls' theory and feminist theory. It will next note the assumptions about human nature inherent in Rawls' theory, and will then suggest equally plausible counterassumptions derived from feminist thought.

16 N. Mex. L. Rev. 613 (1986).

Rawls' Defense of Liberalism:
An Introduction to the Methodology of Abstraction in *A Theory of Justice*

Rawls' neo-Kantian defense of liberalism is one of the most widely read [in] Anglo-American jurisprudence. . . . The social order defended by the theory is an improved version of American liberal democracy. In Rawls' world, which he modestly does not designate a utopia, the rights of the individual to personal autonomy and political recognition are paramount. In a significant critique of pure utilitarianism, and perhaps unintentionally, of the existing American social order, Rawls' theory also suggests the need for full recognition of the equality principle, going so far as to suggest modified redistribution of wealth to the least advantaged in order to rectify inherent inequalities. . . .

The central abstraction in the theory is called the original position. Imagine, Rawls suggests, a group of people deciding what kind of political structure they would like to live under. Rawls places these people in an imaginary spot behind what he calls the "veil of ignorance." Behind the veil, these people do not know who they will be when they emerge in the real world. They do not know whether they will be rich or poor, male or female, black or white, talented or untalented, swift or slow. Not knowing their future status, Rawls argues, these people will decide upon two principles—the liberty principle and the difference principle—for development of a political order that will allow maximum pursuit of each individual's chosen life plan.

The liberty principle encompasses basic civil liberties, such as individual freedom and political recognition. The difference principle adopts equality as a primary goal, with the proviso that distributional decisions should aid, or at least not make worse, the condition of the least advantaged members of society. . . .

The use of the original position and the veil of ignorance are classically abstract theory-building devices reminiscent of other well-known philosophical abstractions. . . . The use of veil imagery is itself interesting. In much of veil imagery—the bridal veil, the Muslim veil—it is women-as-object behind the veil. Women, representing in patriarchal discourse intuition, emotion, sexuality, nurturing and the antithesis of reason, would disrupt the cool theory-building Rawls proposes. Behind Rawls' veil, woman-thinking, the terrifying Other, is abstracted out.[2]

Rawls gives explicit priority to abstraction, following the Kantian tradition. . . . The following section discusses a feminist critique of abstraction and develops some alternative conceptions of human nature derived from feminist thought.

Feminist Ideas about Abstraction, Theory-Building, and Justice

[F]eminist theory, as rich and diverse as it is, is characterized by some basic tenets. First is the charge of androcentrism in mainstream scholarship—the charge that traditional scholarly discourse largely ignores the lives and voices of women.[3] Second is the charge of dualism. Dualism is the oppositional understanding of intuition, experience, and emotion as the inferior antitheses of logic, reason, and science, coupled with a tendency to equate women with the former grouping and men with the latter.[4] A related dualism places men in the public domain—politics, law, paid work—and women in the private—home, absence of law, unpaid work. From these critiques of mainstream scholarship, feminists have derived two insights. The first is that the personal is political.[5] By this it is meant that what happens in the daily lives of real people has political content in the same way as does what we normally think of as politics—the structure of economic systems and governments. That is, who makes breakfast, who gets a paycheck, who gets whistled at in the street—all the experiences of daily life are a part of the distribution of wealth and power in society. The second insight is that consciousness raising—collective focus on the particularities of real-life experience—is essential to truth-seeking. . . .[6]

. . . An important element of [feminist theory] is the rejection of existing abstractions that constrain our vision. Abstraction is a key methodology in mainstream jurisprudence, inviting feminist critique. Abstraction as a methodology is criticized by feminist scholars because abstraction is the first step down the road of androcentric ignorance. The refusal to acknowledge context—to acknowledge the actual lives of human beings affected by a particular abstract principle—has meant time and again that women's well-grounded, experiential knowledge is subordinated to someone else's false abstract presumptions.

Legal history is rife with examples. The abstract principle that women as the weaker sex belong in a separate sphere, protected and cared for by men, supported the rule preventing married women from owning property. In their life experience, however, many women went uncared for, and were required to provide for themselves through their own resources. Women's experiential reality confronted the male-created abstraction of women's privileged sphere, and eventually women succeeded in altering the abstraction.[7]

Similarly, women who are currently told that strict enforcement of the legal guarantee of equal pay for equal work has created an abstract condition called "equality" look at their own experience as underpaid workers, and then redefine "equality" as equal pay for work of equal value.[8] This is not to suggest that the abstraction of "equality" lacks instrumental value to feminists. Rather, for women, the pursuit of equal rights as an abstract goal was developed around the struggle for tangible manifestations of equality in their daily lives: the vote, the ownership of property, and pay equity.[9] This connection to the concrete has made women particularly conscious of the ever looming paradoxes and abuses inherent in the equality principle.

Time and again women have found that their own experiences are more valuable truth-seeking tools than the abstractions of others. Many women report feelings of craziness when their own experience fails to comport with the dominant theory of what they should feel. The way out of this craziness is talk with other women about women's experiences. This talk, or consciousness raising, has taught women several things. First, that they are not crazy—or at least not alone in their craziness. Second, that consciousness raising is a useful method for theory-building. Third, that conversation with empathetic peers is a good in and of itself—that is, it has spiritual and humane value. And finally, it has taught distrust of theory built without the foundation of contextual understanding.

A critique of Rawls' theory of justice that is informed by feminist distrust of abstraction does not pick apart the foundation of American liberalism. Rather, it points out that the foundation is not there. The Theory of Justice rests on ideology, on air, on faith. For those disenchanted with the prospects for enriched human life under dominant legal ideology, there remains solid ground upon which to build a new theory of justice.

In addition to providing a methodological critique of abstraction, feminism suggests an alternative substantive theory of justice. What is the feminist conception of the good and of the right? Feminism is a theory-in-progress, collectively formed. It would be somewhat unfeminist for one woman to write a book called *The Feminist Theory of Justice*. Anthologies and coauthored books are more characteristic of feminist statements, and are themselves a form representing the feminist idea of collective effort.[10] In response to Rawls' admirable effort, a few feminist alternatives are worth consideration.

Feminism differs from intuitionism in that it does suggest a methodology—consciousness raising—for derivation of first principles. Through the shared experience of women's lives and through concrete struggle against patriarchy—including, historically, the struggle for formal equality, for reproductive freedom, and against violence against women—feminists are deriving a conception of the good. Within feminist theory, the particulars of that good are the subject of lively debate, while the general is becoming a matter of consensus.

The feminist utopia looks something like this: it is a place without hierarchy, where children are nourished and told they are special, where gardens grow wheat and roses too, where the desire to excel at the expense of another is thought odd, where love is possible, and where the ordinary tragedies of human life are cushioned by the care and concern of others.

This admittedly sentimental utopian vision is presented here for comparison with the just world suggested by Rawls. Rawls' theory is not teleological. He focuses on procedural principles for allowing maximum individual pursuit of individual ends. He would neither endorse nor oppose the feminist utopia, attempting instead to avoid preliminary debate over right and good.

Rawls argues that it is impossible to convince the unconvinced without limiting the sphere of assumptions and possibilities, at least preliminarily. If we just look at the world and argue, he seems to say, we will never convince. I would respond as a feminist that there is no other way. To argue at the level of abstraction proves nothing and clouds our vision. What we really need to do is to move forward through Rawls' veil of ignorance, losing knowledge of existing abstractions. We need to return to concrete realities, to look at our world, rethink possibilities, and fight it out on this side of the veil, however indelicate that may be. By ignoring alternative visions of human nature, and by limiting the sphere of the possible, Rawls creates a gridlock in which escape from liberalism is impossible, and dreams of the seashore futile.

Assumptions about Human Nature Abstracted into the Original Position

[A]ssumptions about human nature . . . lock us into Rawls' grid. . . . Rawls assumes self-interest and mutual disinterest. In the original position, no one knows what advantages they will have or what plan they will have for their life. They do know, however, that they will want to maximize their advantages and carry out their plan. They know that in general they will not be concerned with the relative disadvantage of others. . . . They know that there will be scarcity of goods and advantages. They know that they will prefer larger shares of these. They know that conflict is inherent in social life and that cooperation is preferable only to the extent that cooperation is mutually rewarding. Rawls is not always explicit about all of these facts, but they are implicitly a part of the unchanging state of human affairs that Rawls accepts as factual.

Rawls also presumes a serious world in which people are constrained to justice. They need to know what's in it for them. He speaks of duties, obligations, shame—dismal words suggesting a noncelebratory outlook on life.[11] People are happy, he says, when they are carrying out their life plans. One of the most important of primary goods is self-respect—a sense of worth and of power to pursue one's own ends. Associative ties, cooperation, and family are means to this same individual end.

Persons in the original position, viewing the world of human possibilities as Rawls does, and knowing nothing of their own place in that world, would quite likely choose the two principles of justice as fairness. In a world where everyone looks after themselves, and where mutual concern is merely an extension of self-interest, people are wise to place primary value on liberty. Liberty is less important in a context of trust and love, but this is the context Rawls accepts as a fact admissible in the original position. "Nothing would be gained," he states, "by attributing benevolence to the parties in the original position." . . . [12]

Feminist theory suggests alternative conceptions. . . . Feminist theory suggests that we can achieve identity of interest on the real-life side of the veil. In that world, people would not be moved solely by self-interest, but also by feelings of love, intimacy, and care for others. They would be in a perpetual state of mutual concern. Rawls begins to consider this possibility when he discusses families and social unions, but his dominant idea is that it is personally advantageous for individuals to join social unions. Feminist experience suggests there is something beyond personal advantage—a collectivist way of thinking that presumes it natural, joyful, and easy to care for others. There is an element of self-interest in this proposition, but it is not a dismal struggle for individual advantage within the merely convenient context of social union that Rawls proposes.

Another counterassumption is that this may not be a world of an endless mad grab for limited goods. First, it may be possible for all of us to achieve happiness by deciding we don't want the goods anymore. The desire for wealth and property may be the product of false consciousness and consumerist, patriarchal traditions. The desire for power and achievement may be a product of never learning to rejoice at the excellence of others; of never learning to play for the sake of playing rather than winning. Second, the scarcity of goods may be an illusion. Science and technology, good fortune and good weather, cooperation and creativity, may change the availability of most of the goods we covet.

This leaves the problem of distribution of such Rawlsian goods as self-respect and excellences, or natural talents and assets. The whole concept of self-respect presumes that others will try to interfere with our plans. Self-respect is defined by Rawls as being left alone to pursue one's own ends. Again, this is a nonsensical concept unless one presumes that individualism is the only possible creed of human conduct. Similarly, excellences are the subject of envy only if it is presumed that we can't rejoice at the gifts of others, and that they won't rejoice in the use of their gifts to help us without some *quid pro quo*.

This leads to another counterassumption, one that challenges Rawls' stern view of what feels good. Achievement, carrying out a plan, excellence feel good to him. Feminist thought, derived through consciousness raising, considers the possibility that humor, modesty, conversation, spontaneity, laziness, and enjoying the talents and differences of others also feel good. Because Rawls imposes a limited view of what feels good upon the deliberators in the original position, they adopt a limited formula for redistribution. This ignores the possibility that we can take collective pleasure in knowing that there is some rare and fine advantage that only a few can have, and that we can all celebrate when those few are chosen. . . .

Conclusion

There are many hopeful counterpremises that Rawls ignores, and the method of abstraction allows him to do this. Rawls might characterize the counterassumptions suggested here as alternative conceptions of the good that will be considered in the abstract in the original position. That response is not good enough. It doesn't explain why the presumptions of self-interest and mutual disinterest are not abstracted out, but taken as given, while the possibility of collectivism is just another possibility that saints may choose on the real-life side of the veil.

Rawls' technique may have value, but it is unfair to achieve consensus by fiat. What we really have to do is to leave the original position, and argue on the common ground of this planet earth. We have to consider the possibility that we can all choose to be saints and that we can set up institutions that allow us to do this. Once we have explored the real-life potential of humankind in a concrete context, it may then be valuable to go back behind the veil and rework the theory with a set of general facts about human nature that are more fairly derived. I suspect, however, that once we have the answers on this side of the veil, we won't need to resort to abstraction. The proof will lie in the lives we will live.

This essay has criticized in particular Rawls' quickness to use abstraction. This is not to suggest that theory and abstraction are without value. The suggestion made here is a more modest one. Theory has value, as long as we remember that real people create theory and that real people live their lives in worlds affected by theory. Half of those people are women, and their experiences can teach us something about justice. . . .

This essay is an attempt to engage in traditional jurisprudential discourse with a female voice. Unlike the fields of history and literary criticism, mainstream jurisprudence has not yet experienced the nudge of feminism. While in other academic realms feminist criticism has evolved into multi-layered schools, genres, and stages, feminist jurisprudence remains nascent.[13] This essay is typical of first-stage criticism in that it attempts to deconstruct a standard text, suggesting only the possibility of gynocentric reconstruction. . . .[14]

. . . Implicit in this critique of Rawls is the belief that the enterprise of jurisprudence is worthwhile, and that feminists will gain from careful consideration of mainstream texts. This essay is one small effort in that direction, in anticipation of a great flowering of feminist jurisprudence in the coming years.

There is, as Rawls suggests, a place called Justice, and it will take many voices to get there.

Notes

1. J. Rawls, A Theory of Justice (Harvard University Press, 1971).

2. Simone de Beauvoir developed the theory of "women as other" in The Second Sex (Knopf, 1953).

3. Gerda Lerner credits the historian Mary Beard for first arguing that mainstream historiography focuses on men's history—war, politics, business—and omits the experience of women. G. Lerner, The Majority Finds Its Past, Placing Women in History xxii (Oxford University Press 1979). Lerner's book in itself defies the androcentric tradition, asking the questions, "What were women doing? How were they doing it? What was their own understanding of their place in the world?" Id. at xxv, and "What would the past be like if women were placed at the center of inquiry? What would the past be like if man were regarded as woman's 'other'?" Id. at xxxi.

4. As Myra Jehlen stated: "Feminist thinking is really rethinking, an examination of the way certain assumptions about women and the female character

enter into the fundamental assumptions that organize all our thinking. For instance, assumptions such as the one that makes intuition and reason opposite terms parallel to female and male may have axiomatic force in our culture, but they are precisely what feminists need to question—or be reduced to checking the arithmetic, when the issue lies in the calculus." Jehlen, Archimedes and the Paradox of Feminist Criticism, in N. Keohane et al. eds., Feminist Theory, A Critique of Ideology 189 (University of Chicago Press, 1982). See also Vickers, Memoirs of an Ontological Exile: Methodological Rebellion of Feminist Research, in A. Miles & G. Finn eds., Feminism in Canada: From Pressure to Politics 30 (Black Rose Books, 1982) ("The rationalist tradition, within which our scholarly disciplines can be placed, derives its rationale from a presumption that the liberated man can transcend his passions, his prejudices, and even his death, through an elevation of his reason and a suppression of his nonreason. As we will see, the elevation of this premise into canons of method has helped men hide key aspects of human life. It is against such canons and such hiding that the key methodological rebellions of feminist research are directed."); Olsen, The Family and the Market, 96 Harv. L. Rev. 1497, 1575–77 (1983); F. Olsen, The Sex of Law, in D. Kairys ed., The Politics of Law: A Progressive Critique, 2nd ed. (Pantheon, 1990).

5. This is really a restatement of the decontextualization critique, that is, the criticism of any method of inquiry that avoids consideration of real life context and experience. See, e.g., Vickers, Memoirs of an Ontological Exile, *supra* note 4, at 34.

6. Consciousness raising is the deliberate sharing of personal experiences in dialogue with others in order to better understand the human condition. The history of consciousness raising and its centrality to the women's movement is discussed in C. Hymowitz & M. Weissman, A History of Women in America 351-55 (Bantam 1978); and in Lerner, Majority Finds Its Past, *supra* note 3. Lerner states that consciousness raising groups "become a community, a substitute family. It provides a noncompetitive, supportive environment of like-minded sisters. Many see it in a model for the good society of the future, which would conceivably include enlightened men. It is interesting that feminists have unwittingly revitalized the mode of cooperation by which American women have traditionally lightened their burdens and improved their lives, from quilting bees to literary societies and cooperative child-care centers." *Id.* at 43.

7. See M. Matsuda, The West and the Legal Status of Women: Explanations of Frontier Feminism, in D. Langum ed., Law in the West (Sunflower University Press, 1985) (discussing the role of feminist activists in altering the legal status of women in the nineteenth-century western United States). The separate sphere ideology, replayed as the public–private distinction, remains problematic for women. Feminist theorists continue to tackle this abstraction. See, e.g., Olsen, Family and Market, *supra* note 4, at 1497, 1501; Powers, Sex Segregation and the Ambivalent Directions of Sex Discrimination, 1979 Wis. L. Rev. 55, 70–87.

8. See, e.g., A. Cook, Comparable Worth: The Problem and States' Approach to Wage Equity (Industrial Relations Center, University of Hawaii, 1983); Feldberg, Comparable Worth: Toward Theory and Practice in the United States, 10 Signs 311 (1984).

9. I would suggest that it is no accident that feminist legal scholarship continues to focus primarily on specific issues such as rape, battering, child support,

employment, and criminal defense of female offenders. Feminist scholars have, of necessity, found themselves on the front line of real-life struggle.

10. See, e.g., E. Bulkin, M. Pratt & B. Smith, Yours in Struggle, Three Feminist Perspectives on Anti-Semitism and Racism (Long Haul Press, 1984); E. Abel ed., Writing and Sexual Difference (University of Chicago Press 1982) (thirteen authors and four respondents); The Signs Reader, Women, Gender, and Scholarship (1983) (fourteen authors); Feminist Theory, A Critique of Ideology, *supra* note 4 (1982) (fourteen authors).

11. Carol Gilligan recognizes the morality of obligation as part of female consciousness, but her description of obligation differs from Rawls'. Rawls' concept of duty implies constraint and forced conformity. Gilligan, in contrast, suggests that doing for others is part of a female sense of self-worth. C. Gilligan, In A Different Voice 64–105 (Havard University Press, 1982). . . .

12. Rawls, Theory of Justice, *supra* note 1, at 191.

13. First-stage, compensatory feminist historiography, for example, focused on the role of notable women in the events already identified as significant by male-dominated scholarship. Second-stage feminist historiography focused on previously unnoticed events and processes that formed the center of women's lives. For a history of feminist historiography, see Lerner, Majority Finds Its Past, *supra* note 3, at 65–67, suggesting questions and problems regarding Black women in history. Similarly, in literary criticism, earlier feminist work pointed out the sexist stereotypes and absences in dominant, male literature. Second-stage criticism focused instead on the works of women writers, searching for uniquely female language, structure, and sign. Elaine Showalter identifies four models of feminist literary criticism—biological, linguistic, psychoanalytic, and cultural— each with a body of supporting scholarship. See E. Showalter, Feminist Criticism in the Wilderness in Writing and Sexual Difference (Pantheon, 1982). Feminist literary criticism has, in fact, evolved to the point of supporting a critique of the critique. See, e.g., Jehlen, Archimedes and the Paradox of Feminist Criticism, *supra* note 4. Jehlen's argument that "the problem, if we as feminists want to address our whole culture is to deal with what we do not like but recognize as nonetheless, valuable, serious, good," is in part the justification for this essay addressing Rawls.

14. For a good example of much needed first-stage feminist legal criticism, see Frug, Re-reading Contracts: A Feminist Analysis of a Contracts Case Book, 34 Am. U. L. Rev. 1065 (1985). This article is, in part, inspired by Frug's example.

Statutory Rape: A Feminist Critique of Rights Analysis

FRANCES OLSEN

A MAN ACCUSED of raping his wife may feel that his privacy rights are being violated; a woman may feel that she is sexually exploited by pornography even if it is viewed privately. The right to privacy and the right to protection exist in fundamental conflict—a conflict that illustrates the contradiction between freedom of action and security that recurs throughout our legal system.[1] Privacy assures the freedom to pursue one's own interests; protection assures that others will not harm us. We want both security and freedom, but seem to have to choose between them. Our historical experience with censorship warns us to be wary of state protection; our experience with domestic violence warns us to be wary of privacy. An individual may be just as oppressed by the state's failure to protect him as by the state's restraint of his freedom for the sake of protecting another. Every difficult legal or political decision can be justified as either protecting freedom or protecting security and attacked as either undermining security or undermining freedom.

This conflict between freedom and security implicates two important and related controversies—the debate between liberals and critical legal scholars over rights analysis and the debate among feminists over sexuality. The central problem of the rights debate is that many social reforms appear to be based on rights, yet every theory of rights that has been proposed can be shown to be internally inconsistent or incoherent.[2] The central problem of the sexuality debate is that women are oppressed by moralistic controls society places on women's sexual expression, yet women are also oppressed by violence and sexual aggression that society allows in the name of sexual freedom.

Rights theory does not indicate which of the two values—freedom or security—the decisionmaker should choose in a given case. Because it cannot transcend this fundamental conflict of values, rights theory does not offer an adequate basis for legal decisions.[3]

---

63 Texas L. Rev. 387 (1984).

Moreover, thinking in terms of rights encourages a partial and inadequate analysis of sexuality. Just as rights theory conceptualizes a society composed of self-interested individuals whose conflicting interests are mediated by the state, it conceptualizes the problem of sexuality as a question of where social controls should end and sexual freedom should begin. Libertines and moralists alike tend to think of sexuality as a natural, presocial drive that is permitted or repressed by society; they disagree only over where to draw the line between freedom and social control. At one extreme, social control is limited to requiring consent of the participants; the realm of sexual freedom should extend to all consensual sexual activity. At the other extreme, freedom is limited to procreational sex within marriage; social control should restrict sexuality outside this realm.

The important issue, however, is not where to draw such a line, but the substance and meaning that we give to sexuality. Unfortunately, feminists who set out to discuss sexuality find their arguments trivialized into a line-drawing debate. Some feminists focus on the sexist nature of social control and assert that in practice it means social control of women. Other feminists focus on the sexist nature of sexual freedom and point out that freedom means freedom for men to exploit women. But the fundamental issue addressed by both sides—the nature of sexuality and our ability to reconstruct it—is ultimately redefined through rights analysis as a question about the location of the boundary between sexual freedom and social control. In this way, feminists who are or should be engaged in a joint or parallel project of challenging the dominant definition of sexuality come to perceive themselves as opposing one another. Feminists on one side of the debate accuse those on the other side of being anti-sex, and the other side accuses those on the first of contributing to their own oppression through "false consciousness." Another set of polemical charges is that the feminists on one side are overly preoccupied with violence and sexual domination and those on the other are defending male supremacy at the expense of women.

This essay focuses primarily upon the rights debate, but it also necessarily implicates the debate about sexuality. It . . . examine[s] rights analysis and evaluate[s] [its] relevance . . . to women's struggles. . . .

Feminism and Women's Rights

The claim that women have rights may be descriptive, hortatory, or analytic. As description, it expresses a set of established social practices that are fairly decent for women. The claim may also refer to legal procedures that will activate certain government institutions on behalf of women.

As exhortation, the statement that women have rights is an assertion about the kind of society we want to live in, the kind of relations among people we wish to foster, and the kind of behavior that is to be praised or blamed. The assertion that women have rights is a moral claim about how human beings should act toward one another. On a personal level, to claim a right is to assert one's self-worth, to affirm one's moral value and entitlement. It is a way for a woman to make a claim about herself and her role in the world. This claim has a positive emotional content that should not be trivialized; it would be difficult and unprofitable to drain the word "right" of its emotive value.

As an analytic tool, the concept that women have rights seems powerful but in practice it turns out not to be helpful; it cannot answer any difficult questions. Women's right to freedom of action conflicts with their right to security; their right to substantive equality conflicts with their right to formal equality.[4] Only by ignoring at least half the rights that could be asserted can rights rhetoric even appear to solve concrete problems. This conflict between rights becomes even more apparent if we consider men's rights to freedom and security. If we recognize these multiple rights claims and try to "balance" the conflicting rights or to choose between them, we wind up talking politically about how we want to live our lives, not abstractly about rights.

In the following subparts, I consider a variety of rights arguments used by feminists. . . .

Women's Rights in and beyond Their "Separate Sphere"

During much of the last century, struggles for women's rights centered on women's exclusion from public and political life. Feminists and their allies challenged laws denying women the vote, barring them from numerous occupations and trades, and all but forcing them to remain in the home—their "separate sphere." These challenges have been largely successful, although as late as 1961, the Supreme Court allowed states to use predominantly male juries so that women could stay home with their domestic chores.[5] The critique of rights is largely irrelevant to these early rights claims. No one argues that women's right to vote is incoherent. The feminists worked together to achieve concrete political gains. They used rights claims as exhortation and description, not as analytic tools.

Early feminists also struggled against the patriarchal family. Laws granted men considerable power over their wives and all too often left women subject to their husbands' unfettered oppression; women could not count on legal protection in the home. According to some scholars, the courts' refusal to monitor a husband's treatment of his wife carried an ideological message: all the important affairs of life were regulated by law; the domestic sphere was not regulated by the law and was not important.[6]

The long-asserted judicial reluctance to intrude into family life finds expression today in the "right to privacy." State regulation of the family raises complex problems similar to those raised by state regulation of other "private" matters, such as sexuality. Here the critique of rights is relevant. The freedom promised by the right to privacy runs up against women's right to security in the home, and rights rhetoric cannot decide the conflict. Any effort to protect women from private oppression by their husbands may expose them to public oppression by the state; any effort to keep the state out of our personal lives will leave us subject to private domination.

The Right of Women to Autonomy

One rights critique—the one that is least convincing to feminists—debunks rights as an aspect of "bourgeois individualism" and complains that the rhetoric of rights undermines community by picturing people as separated owners of their respective bundles of rights. Proponents of this critique assert that the concept of "rights" grows out of and feeds our fear of one another, that it fosters alienation instead of autonomy, and that it does not contribute to a society in which we will be able to share life as a common creation.[7]

To the extent that family life and the treatment of women in general has remained "feudal" long after the success of the bourgeois revolutions,[8] individualism can seem progressive. The denial to women of the "bourgeois rights" granted to men does not help to create good community. For many years women were forced into unequal and oppressive "community" under the control first of their fathers and then of their husbands. Nor is forced community just a problem of the past for women. Men force community upon women when they make sexual advances to coworkers and subordinates or pester women strangers with unwelcomed conversations. A rapist may believe he is seeking community with his victim, especially if she is his wife or social friend. The male members of an organization may be attempting to force community when they object or try to prevent the female members from meeting by themselves. When a woman is still struggling for "a room of her own,"[9] she is unlikely to complain that rights isolate her.

Thus, rights for women, including "individualistic" and "alienating" rights, may be necessary and should be supported. Here it is important to make some clear distinctions. The women's "rights" that we should support are an expression of the social practice of allowing women to resist forced community. The "bourgeois individualism" critique of rights is mistaken to the extent that it opposes this social practice. The critique is correct to the extent that it accepts the social practice but criticizes a particular understanding of its underlying basis. The distinction is important; the social practice that allows women to resist forced community is itself the result of collective political activity. Women may be politically demobilized if they come to believe that their "rights" protect them and forget that in this context "rights" simply describes a social practice. Women should have the right to autonomy, but must remember that they can secure the right only through continuous collective political activity.

The Right of Women to Formal Equality

The political struggle over the equal rights amendment has focused attention on the right of women to formal equality. The amendment would subject sexual classifications to the same "strict scrutiny" to which courts subject racial classifications. Some feminists are skeptical about the effectiveness of strict scrutiny, however, because its application has not ended racism or significantly reduced the subordination of non-whites. The critique of rights supports this skeptical attitude.

In the absence of an equal rights amendment, most courts subject sexual classifications to "middle-tier" scrutiny. Under this standard, courts examine sexual classifications to determine whether they bear a "substantial" relationship to an "important" state purpose. Ann Freedman characterizes this procedure as an elaborate charade by the Supreme Court to avoid appearing "political."[10] She criticizes even those Justices who consistently oppose sexist laws for implying that only irrational classifications are harmful and for failing to articulate a theory that identifies with specificity the "harmful consequences of sexism." She describes the "analysis" by which the Justices manipulate this "middle tier" means–end test. First, they declare illegitimate the real goal of legislation, such as the maintenance of traditional sex roles or, in the case of statutory rape laws, the protection of female chastity. The state then must invent a new, "acceptable" purpose, which the Court will consider to be legitimate and important. If the Court wishes to invalidate a certain statute, it simply asserts that the means (i.e., sexual classification) do not bear a sufficiently "substantial" relation to that purpose. If the Court wishes to uphold the statute, it asserts that the classification is permissible because it is based on a "real difference" between the sexes that does bear a substantial relationship to the statute's purpose. The "real sex differences" approach has drawn considerable criticism from feminists.

1. Critique of "Real Sex Differences." Feminists complain that the Supreme Court's approach to sexual classifications articulates an ideology that attempts to justify differential treatment of men and women. Although recent cases reject the gross generalizations made in many earlier cases about the proper role for women, the Court continues to allow unequal treatment in other cases, particularly those involving pregnancy. In this way the Court appears to be concerned with equality, but allows discrimination to continue by finding "real" differences that prevent women from being similarly situated to men. Thus, the Court perpetuates the inferior status of women while attempting to reconcile them to that status by "holding out the promise of liberation."[11] The Court uses the language of equality to legitimate the continuing unequal treatment of men and women.

Feminists argue that this doctrine wrongly denies women formal equality; the Court defines the concept of "real sex differences" so broadly that it is meaningless as an analytic concept.[12] Moreover, many decisions based on the doctrine of "real sex differences" confuse the relationship between biological sex differences and cultural arrangements and mistakenly treat a variety of culturally determined differences between men and women as natural and immutable.

   2. *Critique of Pseudo-Neutrality.*   Feminists also contend that current equal protection doctrine denies women formal equality by upholding rules that are "pseudo-neutral." Nadine Taub, for example, has argued that "rules formulated in a male-dominated society reflect male needs, male concerns, and male experience."[13] An example of such pseudo-neutrality is a state employees' insurance plan that covers all male medical conditions, but excludes pregnancy and other female medical conditions.[14] Some feminists propose replacing these male-oriented pseudo-neutral rules with "truly neutral rules" that will serve "neutral" interests and apply equally to everyone.[15]

The Right of Women to Substantive Equality

   A few feminists have recognized that formal equality can perpetuate inequality in actual practice and have begun to search for ways in which women can achieve substantive equality. This effort has produced sharp disagreements among feminists, which I explore below. It is important to understand that these disagreements are part of a debate *within* rights analysis; they are particular manifestations of the classical liberal debate between equality of opportunity and equality of result.

   1. *"Differences" versus "Inequalities."*   Catharine MacKinnon recently presented a powerful argument in favor of substantive rather than merely formal equality for women. In *Sexual Harassment of Working Women*[16] she proffers an "inequalities" approach to sex discrimination as an alternative to the more conventional approach, which she refers to as the "differences" approach. The "differences" doctrine, the dominant perspective of the Supreme Court, focuses on the relationship between a gender-based classification and the state's purpose for making the classification. Here, the issue of sex inequality is the accuracy of the classifications.

   The "inequalities" approach, by contrast, explicitly inquires whether a particular classification tends to facilitate and reinforce the subordination of women to men. Under this approach, sex discrimination is wrong not because it is irrational or arbitrary, but because it creates and maintains a sexual hierarchy that systematically disadvantages women. The "inequalities" doctrine criticizes the search for "neutral principles"[17] and recognizes that "the best way to preserve a concretely unequal status quo may be the rigorous application of a neutral standard."[18] Here, the issue of sex inequality is male dominance; sex equality means an end to it.

   2. *"Equal Treatment" versus "Special Treatment."*   Nadine Taub interprets MacKinnon's "inequalities" analysis as an argument in favor of special treatment and presents the classic—though I believe flawed—argument in favor of equal treatment. Taub warns that MacKinnon's "inequalities" analysis is likely to deteriorate into a new form of "detrimental protectionism."[19] To Taub and others, "neu-

trality" is crucial. Indeed, even applying a heightened level of scrutiny to discrimination against women—the "middle-tier" approach—Taub considers dangerous. She argues that the use of MacKinnon's "inequalities" analysis, even as a "short-run tool," is very risky. The male-dominated court system too often will fail to recognize women as disadvantaged. Thus, women's best chance for equality is to advocate "truly neutral" standards applicable to everyone. Any legislation that grants special benefits for women provides doctrinal support for imposing special detriments upon them also. As Wendy Williams argues, "[W]e can't have it both ways, [and] we need to think carefully about which way we want to have it."[20]

Feminists on the other side of the debate disagree. They point out that ending the subordination of women is hardly special protection. The idea that conflict should be resolved by a system of neutral rules was itself formulated in a male-dominated society and reflects male needs, male concerns, and male experience.[21] If, as Taub argues, a male-dominated legal system cannot be trusted to apply an "inequalities" approach, what reason is there to believe that it can be trusted to apply the "differences" approach? These feminists further argue that the equal treatment analysis is based on the disempowering concept that the best way for feminists to get what they want is to set up ground rules and then pretend to ignore the results. They contend that this approach is alienated and misguided. They point to the continued oppression of women as evidence of its failure.

Both sides in the debate tend to assume that "equal treatment" is a more coherent and meaningful concept than it really is. Those who claim that feminists cannot have it "both ways" fail to recognize the male supremacy built into the "neutral" rights doctrine. The crucial issue is how "both ways" is defined. One could argue, for example, that antifeminists have long had it "both ways." During the heyday of legal formalism, courts nullified popular legislation [e.g., minimum wage laws for women. *Ed.*] for interfering with liberty of contract and threatening property rights, but never hesitated to transfer a woman's property to her husband by fiat and against her will.[22] Courts that understood equality to mean that employers and employees were "equal contracting partners" with a vested right to enter into exploitative contracts never felt forced by logic to treat married women as equal contracting partners—or even as capable of forming a contract. More important than the debate between equal treatment and special treatment are the questions about what counts as equal treatment and what kind of special treatment women would receive.

The debate between special treatment and equal treatment becomes more interesting when it is expressed in overtly political terms. Proponents of equal treatment argue that any form of special protection can divide women—from one another, as well as from men. For example, provisions for special pregnancy leaves might shift attention away from the general inadequacy of sick-leave policies and focus it on the unfairness of protecting one class of worker and not others.

These concerns raise complicated questions of political strategy. Protective legislation limited to one group might or might not divide people and divert attention, depending on the historical and political context within which the legislation is enacted and enforced.[23] There is no simple way to determine *a priori* whether a partial reform that protects one class will advance or retard the general reform effort. The abstract legal concepts that most equal treatment advocates think important do not help us decide whether to support a particular reform. The choice between equal treatment and special treatment is meaningful—if at all—only on a case-by-case basis.

Feminist Embrace of the Critique of Rights:
Law as a Male Norm

Some feminists question the value not only of rights theory, but of law itself in achieving concrete political gains for women. They criticize the fundamental premises underlying liberal thought and challenge the structural framework of conventional legal practice—referred to disparagingly as "liberal legalism."[24] They argue that law is fundamentally patriarchal,[25] that objectivity and neutrality are male norms, and that resolution of conflict through appeal to legal rights is a limited, masculine approach.[26]

These feminists suggest that if women articulate their grievances in terms of equal rights and confine their struggles to litigation and lobbying, they are "giving up the battle" for broader reform, which can occur only "in the context of broader economic, social, and cultural change."[27] Some argue that litigation "cannot lead to social changes, because in upholding and relying on the paradigm of law, the paradigm of patriarchy is upheld and reinforced."[28] To eliminate patriarchy, "the male power paradigm of law [must be] . . . challenged and transformed."[29]

These criticisms are very useful, although I do not entirely agree with them. As I argue elsewhere, law is not fundamentally patriarchal, however much some men may try to claim law as their own.[30] Objectivity and neutrality are—on an ideological level—"male norms," but law is not objective or neutral. Liberal legalists cannot make law objective and neutral any more than they can really settle conflicts by appealing to legal rights. Law is a complex social practice and some feminist gains have been and will continue to be achieved in the legal arena. Although these gains are often characterized as achieving rights for women, they result from concrete struggles, not from rights analysis. . . .

[Discussion of rights analysis as applied to the example of statutory rape is omitted here. *Ed.*]

Notes

1. See Kennedy, The Structure of Blackstone's Commentaries, 28 Buff. L. Rev. 205, 211–13 (1979); Singer, The Legal Rights Debate in Analytical Jurispru-

dence from Bentham to Hohfeld, 1982 Wis. L. Rev. 930, 975. Oliver Wendell Holmes identified the same conflict when he argued that the right to compete in the economic arena (freedom of action) was in direct, systemic conflict with the right to property (security). See Holmes, Privilege, Malice, and Intent, 8 Harv. L. Rev. 1, 6 (1984).

Of course, not all exercises of freedom undermine the security of others, but most of the exercises of freedom that people seek to restrict do threaten someone else's security. Similarly, most efforts by the state to protect the security of one person or group interfere with the freedom of another. . . .

2. See, e.g., Tushnet, An Essay on Rights, 62 Texas L. Rev. 1363, 1375–82 (1984). It could be argued that rights analysis has a consistency in that people with power have rights and those without do not. For example, some feminists argue that the conflict between rights as security and rights as freedom is made less sharp by privileging men—giving them both freedom and security while depriving women of both. Men can be secure from women and free to exploit women as long as women do not have rights. As description, this may be all too true, but it does not affect the critique of rights as an analytic tool nor does it argue in favor of conceptualizing social struggles in terms of rights.

3. The recognition that rights theory does not provide an objective, apolitical basis for decisionmaking has led critical legal scholars to characterize rights analysis as "ambiguous and internally contradictory," Klare, Labor Law as Ideology: Toward a New Historiography of Collective Bargaining Law, 4 Indus. Rel. L.J. 450, 478 (1981), "wholly indeterminate"; Dalton, Book Review, 6 Harv. Women's L.J. 229, 235 (1983); and "incoherent," Kennedy, Critical Labor Law Theory: A Comment, 4 Indus. Rel. L.J. 503, 506 (1981). . . .

The critique of rights has generated a flurry of objections, ranging from charges of nihilism, see Fiss, Objectivity and Interpretation, 34 Stan. L. Rev. 739, 740–41 1982); Levinson, Book Review, 96 Harv. L. Rev. 1466, 1470 (1983), to warnings that the critique promotes totalitarianism, see Sparer, Fundamental Human Rights, Legal Entitlements, and the Social Struggle: A Friendly Critique of the Critical Legal Studies Movement, 36 Stan. L. Rev. 509 (1984). The critique is said to be nihilistic for denying that law has a "discernible content independent of the [particular] moral and political desires of those who purport to make decisions in the name of the law." Levinson, Book Review, *supra*, at 1470. Furthermore, some critics argue that the critique frustrates efforts to construct positive programs of reform or social transformation. See *id.* at 1469; see also Kennedy, Critical Labor Law Theory, *supra* note 3, at 505 (supporting the critique, but noting that it "cannot tell us what to do next"). Finally, some contend that the project of protecting human rights transcends our present liberal society. See, e.g., Lynd, Government Without Rights: The Labor Law Vision of Archibald Cox, 4 Indus. Rel. L.J. 483, 494 (1981). Guarantees of human freedom will be needed in any society. See Sparer, Fundamental Human Rights, *supra*, at 534–35.

Although the rights debate has continued for several years, surprisingly little has been written on it from a feminist perspective. . . .

4. By "formal equality" I mean equality in the abstract, legal sense; by "substantive equality" I mean equality in fact. . . .

5. Hoyt v. Florida, 368 U.S. 57 (1961). . . .

6. See Taub & Schneider, Perspectives on Women's Subordination and the Role of Law, Part 1 this volume, at 13. The insulation of the women's sphere

conveys an important message: "In our society law is for business and other important things. The fact that the law in general has so little bearing on women's day-to-day concerns reflects and underscores their insignificance." [Citation is omitted here; originally cited in D. Kairys ed,. The Politics of Law, 2nd ed. (1990), at 156. *Ed.*]

. . . . The history of laissez-faire policies toward domestic life is considerably more complex than this description suggests. . . . Laws have regulated family life, directly and indirectly, for centuries. See Olsen, The Family and the Market: A Study of Ideology and Legal Reform, 96 Harv. L. Rev. 1497, 1501–07 (1983).

7. See generally Gabel, The Phenomenology of Rights-Consciousness and the Pact of the Withdrawn Selves, 62 Tex. L. Rev. 1563 (1984) (presenting a more complex and less flawed "bourgeois individualism" critique of rights).

8. See Olsen, Family and Market, *supra* note 6, at 1516–20; Olsen, The Politics of Family Law, 2 Law & Ineq. J. 1, 6–7 (1984). The assertion of rights for women began as an internal critique of the theory and practice of classical liberalism. The "rights of man" established in the bourgeois revolutions of the 18th and 19th centuries have come only slowly through struggle, actually to mean the rights of men *and* women.

9. Virginia Woolf used this phrase as a metaphor for autonomy. Woolf suggested that in order to write, a woman must have "a room of her own"—an identity of her own, not merely physical space to herself. V. Woolf, A Room of One's Own (Harcourt, Brace, 1929).

10. Freedman, Sex Equality, Sex Differences, and the Supreme Court, 92 Yale L.J. 913, 951 (1983).

11. Taub & Schneider, Part 1 this volume, at 19 (quoting Freeman, Legitimizing Racial Discrimination through Antidiscrimination Law: A Critical Review of Supreme Court Doctrine), 62 Minn. L. Rev. 1049, 1052 (1978).

12. See Freedman, Sex Equality, Sex Differences, *supra* note 10, at 944–45.

13. Taub, Book Review, 80 Colum. L. Rev. 1686, 1694 (1980).

14. See, e.g., Geduldig v. Aiello, 417 U.S. 484 (1974). . . .

15. See Taub, Book Review, *supra* note 13, at 1689.

16. C. MacKinnon, Sexual Harassment of Working Women (Yale University Press, 1979). MacKinnon's argument could also be interpreted as more than just an argument for substantive equality, but as a complete departure from rights analysis.

17. This term was popularized by Wechsler in his article Toward Neutral Principles of Constitutional Law, 73 Harv. L. Rev. 1 (1959).

18. MacKinnon, Sexual Harassment, *supra* note 16, at 127.

19. Taub, Book Review, *supra* note 13, at 1691.

20. Williams, The Equality Crisis: Some Reflections on Culture, Courts, and Feminism, 8 Women's Rts. L. Rep. 175, 196 (1982).

21. See MacKinnon, Feminism, Marxism, Method and the State: Toward Feminist Jurisprudence, Part 5 herein.

22. At common law, a woman's property was transferred to her husband upon their marriage. This was changed by statutes ("married women's property acts"), not by case law. In fact, some courts invalidated reform statutes when they were first passed. See L. Friedman, A History of American Law 184–86 (Simon & Schuster, 1973).

23. See Petchesky, Reproductive Freedom: Beyond A Woman's Right to Choose, in C. Stimpson & E. Person eds., Women: Sex and Sexuality 92, 112–13 (University of Chicago Press, 1980).

24. Karl Klare defines "liberal legalism" as "the particular historical incarnation of legalism . . . which characteristically serves as the institutional and philosophical foundation of the legitimacy of the legal order in capitalist societies. Its essential features are the commitment to general 'democratically' promulgated rules, the equal treatment of all citizens before the law, and the radical separation of morals, politics and personality from judicial action. . . ." Klare, Law-Making as Praxis, Telos, Summer 1979, at 123, 132 n.28.

25. . . . Polan, Toward a Theory of Law and Patriarchy in The Politics of Law, Part 5 herein, at 421; see Rifkin, Toward a Theory of Law and Patriarchy, Part 5 herein.

26. See MacKinnon, Toward Feminist Jurisprudence, Part 5 herein. Law "not only reflects a society in which men rule women; it rules in a male way." *Id.* at 432.
. . .

Liberal legalism is incomplete, based only upon the experiences of men. The weaknesses of liberal legalism are weaknesses that might be expected to inhere in any system devised by men in a bifurcated and sexist society. See F. Olsen, The Sex of Law in D. Kairys ed., The Politics of Law, 2nd ed. (Pantheon, 1990). . . .

27. Polan, Toward a Theory of Law and Patriarchy, Part 5 this volume, at 425.

28. Rifkin, Toward a Theory of Law and Patriarchy, Part 5 this volume. [Citation is omitted here; originally cited at 3 Harv. Women's L.J. 83, 88 (1980). *Ed.*]

29. *Id.* at 414.

30. See Olsen, Sex of Law, *supra* note 26.

❖ *Alchemical Notes: Reconstructing Ideals from Deconstructed Rights*

Patricia J. Williams

A Bit of CLS Mythology: The Brass Ring and the Deep Blue Sea

The Meta-Story

ONCE UPON A TIME, there was a society of priests who built a Celestial City whose gates were secured by Word-Combination locks. The priests were masters of the Word, and, within the City, ascending levels of power and treasure became accessible to those who could learn ascendingly intricate levels of Word Magic. At the very top level, the priests became gods; and because they then had nothing left to seek, they engaged in games with which to pass the long hours of eternity. In particular, they liked to ride their strong, sure-footed steeds, around and around the perimeter of heaven: now jumping word-hurdles, now playing polo with the concepts of the moon and of the stars, now reaching up to touch that pinnacle, that fragment, that splinter of Refined Understanding which was called Superstanding, the brass ring of their merry-go-round.

In time, some of the priests-turned-gods tired of this sport, denounced it as meaningless. They donned the garb of pilgrims, seekers once more, and passed beyond the gates of the Celestial City. In this recursive passage, they acquired the knowledge of Undoing Words.

Beyond the walls of the City lay a Deep Blue Sea. The priests built themselves small boats and set sail, determined to explore the uncharted courses, the open vistas of this new and undefined domain. They wandered for many years in this manner, until at last they reached a place that was half-a-circumference away from the Celestial City. From this point, the City appeared as a mere shimmering illusion; and the priests knew that at last they had reached a place which was

---

Beyond the Power of Words. They let down their anchors, the plumb lines of their reality, and experienced godhood once more.

The Story

Under the Celestial City, dying mortals called out their rage and suffering, battered by a steady rain of sharp hooves whose thundering, sound-drowning path described the wheel of their misfortune.

At the bottom of the Deep Blue Sea, drowning mortals reached silently and desperately for drifting anchors dangling from short chains far, far overhead, which they thought were life-lines meant for them.

I wrote "The Brass Ring and The Deep Blue Sea" in response to a friend who asked me what Critical Legal Studies was *really* all about; the Meta-Story was my impressionistic attempt to explain. Then my friend asked me if there weren't lots of blacks and minorities, organizers and grass-roots types in an organization so diametrically removed from tradition. Her question immediately called to mind my first days on my first job out of law school. . . . I walked through the halls of Los Angeles Criminal and Civil Courthouses, from assigned courtroom to assigned courtroom. The walls of every hall were lined with waiting defendants and families of defendants, almost all poor, Hispanic and/or black. As I passed, they stretched out their arms and asked me for my card; they asked me if I were a lawyer, they called me "sister" and "counselor." The power of that memory is fused with my concern about the disproportionately low grass-roots membership in or input to CLS. CLS wields significant power in shaping legal strategies which affect—literally from on high—the poor and oppressed. . . .

In my experience, most non-corporate clients looked to lawyers almost as gods. They were frightened, pleading, dependent (and resentful of their dependence), trusting only for the specific purpose of getting help (because they had no choice) and distrustful in a global sense (again, because they most often had no choice). Subservience is one way I have heard the phenomenon described . . ., but actually I think it's something much worse. . . .

[W]hat I saw in the eyes of those who reached out to me in the hallways of the courthouse was a profoundly accurate sense of helplessness—a knowledge that without a sympathetically effective lawyer (whether judge, prosecutor or defense attorney) they would be lining those halls and those of the lockup for a long time to come. I probably got more than my fair share of outstretched arms because I was one of the few people of color in the system at that time. . . . CLS has . . . failed to make [itself] applicable to those in this society who need its powerful assistance most. . . .

[I]n CLS, I have sometimes been left with the sense that lawyers and clients engaged in the pursuit of "rights" are viewed as foolish, "falsely conscious," benighted, or misled.[1] Such an attitude . . . [may] keep CLS reaching in the wrong direction, locked in refutation of formalist legal scholarship.

The present essay is an attempt to detail my discomfort with that part of CLS which rejects rights-based theory, particularly that part of the debate and critique which applies to the black struggle for civil rights. There are many good reasons for abandoning a system of rights which is premised on inequality and helplessness; yet despite the acknowledged and compelling force of such reasons, most blacks have not turned away from the pursuit of rights even if what CLS scholars say about rights—that they are contradictory, indeterminate, reified and marginally decisive in social behavior[2]—is so. I think this has happened because the so-called governing narrative, or metalanguage, about the significance of rights is quite different for whites and blacks. For most whites, including the mostly white elite of CLS, social relationships are colored by viewing achievement as the function of committed self-control, of self-possession. For blacks, including black lawyers, academics and clients, on the other hand, relationships are frequently dominated by historical patterns of physical and psychic *dis*possession. In a semantic, as well as a substantive sense, then, I think that CLS has ignored the degree to which rights-assertion and the benefits of rights have helped blacks, other minorities and the poor.

I by no means want to idealize the importance of rights in a legal system in which rights are so often selectively invoked to draw boundaries, to isolate, and to limit. At the same time, it is very hard to watch the idealistic or symbolic importance of rights being diminished with reference to the disenfranchised, who experience and express their disempowerment as nothing more or less than the denial of rights.[3] It is my belief that blacks and whites do differ in the degree to which rights-assertion is experienced as empowering or disempowering. The expression of these differing experiences creates a discourse boundary, reflecting complex and often contradictory societal understandings.[4] The remainder of this essay attempts to show how that opposition arises. . . .

A Tale with Two Stories

Mini-Story (In Which Peter Gabel and I Set Out to Teach Contracts in the Same Boat While Rowing in Phenomenological Opposition)

Some time ago, Peter Gabel[5] and I taught a contracts class together . . . . Inevitably, I suppose, we got into a discussion of trust and distrust as factors in bargain relations. It turned out that Peter had handed over a $900 deposit, in cash, with no lease, no exchange of keys and no receipt, to strangers with whom he had no ties other than a few moments of pleasant conversation. Peter said that he didn't need to sign a lease because it imposed too much formality. The handshake and the good vibes were for him indicators of trust more binding than a distancing form contract.

I, meanwhile, had friends who found me an apartment in a building they owned. In *my* rush to show good faith and trustworthiness, I signed a detailed, lengthily negotiated, finely printed lease firmly establishing me as the ideal arm's-length transactor.

. . . We both wanted to establish enduring relationships with the people in whose houses we would be living; we both wanted to enhance trust of ourselves and to allow whatever closeness, whatever friendship, was possible. This similarity of desire, however, could not reconcile our very different relations to the word of law. Peter, for example, appeared to be extremely self-conscious of his power potential (either real or imagistic) as a white or male or lawyer authority figure. . . . The logical ways of establishing some measure of trust between strangers were for him an avoidance of conventional expressions of power and a preference for informal processes generally.[6]

I, on the other hand, was raised to be acutely conscious of the likelihood that, no matter what degree of professional or professor I became, people would greet and dismiss my black femaleness as unreliable, untrustworthy, hostile, angry, powerless, irrational and probably destitute. . . . Therefore it is helpful for me, even essential for me, to clarify boundary; to show that I can speak the language of lease is my way of enhancing trust of me in my business affairs. . . . I grew up in a neighborhood where landlords would not sign leases with their poor, black tenants, and *demanded* that rent be paid in cash; although superficially resembling Peter's transaction, such "informality" in most white-on-black situations signals distrust, not trust. Unlike Peter, I am still engaged in a struggle to set up transactions at arm's length, as legitimately commercial, and to portray myself as a bargainer of separate worth, distinct power, sufficient *rights* to manipulate commerce, rather than to be manipulated as the object of commerce.

Peter, I speculate, would say that a lease or any other formal mechanism would introduce distrust into his relationships and that he would suffer alienation, leading to the commodification of his being and the degradation of his person to property. In contrast, the lack of a formal relation to the other would leave me estranged. It would risk a figurative isolation from that creative commerce by which I may be recognized as whole, with which I may feed and clothe and shelter myself, by which I may be seen as equal—even if I am stranger. For me, stranger–stranger relations are better than stranger–chattel.

Meta-Mini-Story (In Which I Reflect upon My Experiences with Peter, Climb to Celestial Heights While Juggling the Vocabulary of Rights Discourse, and Simultaneously Undo Not a Few Word-Combination Locks)

The unifying theme of Peter's and my experiences . . . is that one's sense of empowerment defines one's relation to the law, in terms of trust–distrust, formality–informality, or rights–no rights (or "needs"). In saying this I am acknowledging and affirming points central to CLS literature: that rights may be unstable[7] and indeterminate.[8] Despite this recognition, however, and despite a mutual struggle to reconcile freedom with alienation, and solidarity with oppression, Peter and I found the expression of our social disillusionment lodged on opposite sides of the rights/needs dichotomy.

On a semantic level, Peter's language of circumstantially defined need—of informality, of solidarity, of overcoming distance—sounded dangerously like the language of oppression to someone like me who was looking for freedom through the establishment of identity, the *form*-ation of an autonomous social self. To Peter, I am sure, my insistence on the protective distance which rights provide seemed abstract and alienated.

Similarly, while the goals of CLS and of the direct victims of racism may be very much the same, what is too often missing from CLS works is the acknowledgment that our experiences of the same circumstances may be very, very different; the same symbol may mean different things to each of us. . . .

While rights may not be ends in themselves, it remains that rights rhetoric has been and continues to be an effective form of discourse for blacks. The vocabulary of rights speaks to an establishment that values the guise of stability, and from whom social change for the better must come (whether it is given, taken or smuggled). . . .

What is needed, therefore, is not the abandonment of rights language for all purposes, but an attempt to become multilingual in the semantics of each others' rights-valuation. . . .

[O]ne of the most troubling positions advanced by some in CLS is that of rights' actual disutility in political advancement. That position seems to discount entirely the voice and the experiences of blacks in this country, for whom politically effective action has occurred mainly in connection with asserting or extending rights.

The CLS disutility argument is premised on the assumption that rights' rigid systematizing may keep one at a permanent distance from situations which could profit from closeness and informality. . . . Furthermore, any marginal utility to be derived from rights discourse is perceived as being gained at the expense of larger issues; rights are pitted against, rather than asserted on behalf of, the agencies of social reform. This reasoning underlies much of the rationale for CLS' abandonment of rights discourse, and for its preference for informality—for restyling, for example, arguments about rights to shelter for the homeless into arguments about the "needs" of the homeless.

However, such statements about the relative utility of "needs" over "rights" discourse overlook that blacks have been describing their needs for generations. They overlook a long history of legislation *against* the self-described needs of black people, the legacy of which remains powerful today. . . .

For blacks, describing needs has been a dismal failure as political activity. It has succeeded only as a literary achievement. The history of our need is certainly moving enough to have been called poetry, oratory and epic entertainment—but it has never been treated by white institutions as a statement of political priority. . . .

It may be different when someone white is describing need. . . . [W]hite statements of black needs suddenly acquire the sort of stark statistical authority which lawmakers can listen to and politicians hear. But from blacks, stark statistical statements of need are heard as "strident." . . .

For blacks, therefore, the battle is not deconstructing rights, in a world of no rights; nor of constructing statements of need, in a world of abundantly apparent need. Rather, the goal is to find a political mechanism that can confront the *denial* of need. The argument that rights are disutile, even harmful, trivializes this aspect of black experience specifically, as well as that of any person or group whose genuine vulnerability has been protected by that measure of actual entitlement which rights provide.

For many white CLSers, the word "rights" seems to be overlaid with capitalist connotations of oppression, universalized alienation of the self, and excessive power of an external and distancing sort. . . .

For most blacks, on the other hand . . ., the experience of rights-assertion has been one of both solidarity and freedom, of empowerment of an *in*ternal and very personal sort; it has been a process of finding the self.

These differences in experience between blacks and whites are not, I think, solely attributable to such divisions as positive/negative, bourgeois/proletariat; given our history, they are differences rooted firmly in race, and in the unconsciousness of racism. It is only in acknowledging this difference, however, that one can fully appreciate the underlying common ground of the radical left and the historically oppressed: the desire to heal a profound existential disillusionment. Wholesale rejection of rights does not allow for the expression of such essential difference. . . . For the historically disempowered, the conferring of rights is symbolic of all the denied aspects of humanity: rights imply a respect which places one within the referential range of self and others, which elevates one's status from human body to social being. For blacks, then, the attainment of rights signifies the due, the respectful behavior, the collective responsibility properly owed by a society to one of its own.

Mega-Story (In Which, by Virtue of My Own Mortality, I Am Dragged from a Great Height in Order to Examine the Roots of My Existence)

Another way of describing the dissonance between blacks and CLS is in terms of the degree of moral utopianism[9] with which blacks regard rights. I remember, for example, going to a family funeral in Georgia, where, in the heat of summer and the small church, fans with pictures of Martin Luther King, Jr. on them were passed out—as they still are in many black churches around the country. This icon of King is a testament to the almost sacred attachment to the transformative promise of a black-conceived notion of rights, which exists, perhaps, somewhat apart from the day-to-day reality of their legal enforcement, but which gives rise to their power as a politically animating, socially cohesive force.

For blacks, the prospect of attaining full rights under the law has always been a fiercely motivational, almost religious, source of hope. It is an oversimplification to describe that hope as merely a "compensation for . . . feelings of loss," rights being a way to "conceal those feelings. . . ."[10] Black "loss" is not of the sort that can be "compensated" for or "concealed" by rights-assertion. It must be remembered that from the *experiential perspective of blacks*, there was and is no such thing as "slave law."[11] The legal system did not provide blacks with structured expectations, promises or reasonable reliances of any sort. If one views "rights" as emanating from either that body of "legal" history or from that of modern bourgeois legal structures,[12] then of course rights would mean nothing because blacks have had virtually nothing under either. And if one envisions "rights" as economic advantages over others, one might well conclude that "because this sense of illegitimacy [of incomplete social relation] is always threatening to erupt into awareness, there is a need for 'the law.'"[13] Where, however, one's experience is rooted not just in a "sense" of illegitimacy but in *being* illegitimate, in being raped, and in the fear of being murdered, then the black adherence to a scheme of negative rights—to the self, to the sanctity of one's personal boundaries—makes sense.

The individual and unifying cultural memory of black people is the helplessness, the uncontrollability of living under slavery. . . . Thus, when I decided to go to law school, my mother told me that "the Millers were lawyers so you have it in your blood." Now the Millers were the slaveholders of my maternal grandmother's clan. The Millers were also my great-great-grandparents and great-aunts and who knows what else. My great-great-grandfather Austin Miller, a thirty-five-year-old lawyer, bought my eleven-year-old great-great-grandmother, Sophie, and her parents (being "family Negroes," the previous owner sold them as a matched set). By the time she was twelve, Austin Miller had made Sophie the mother of a child, my great-grandmother Mary. . . .

The problem, as I have come to see it, is not really one of choice of rhetoric, of formal over informal, of structure and certainty over context, of right over need. Rather, it is a problem of appropriately choosing signs within any system of rhetoric. From the object-property's point of view (e.g., that of my great-great-grandmother . . .) [Williams's elaboration of her great-great grandmother as an object of property is included in her essay in Part 6. *Ed*.] the rhetoric of certainty (of rights, formal rules and fixed entitlements) has been enforced *at best as though* it were the rhetoric of context (of fluidity, informal rules, and unpredictability). Yet the fullness of context, the trust which enhances the use of more fluid systems, is lost in the lawless influence of cultural insensitivity. So while it appears to jurisdictionally recognized and invested parties that rights designate outcomes with a clarity akin to wisdom, to the object-property, the effect is one of existing in a morass of unbounded irresponsibility.

But this failure of rights discourse, much noted in CLS scholarship, does not necessarily mean that informal systems will lead to better outcomes.[14] Some structures are the direct products of people and social forces who wanted them that way.[15] If one assumes, as blacks must, not that the larger world wants to overcome alienation, but that many heartily embrace it, driven not just by fear but by hatred and taboo, then one is compelled to recognize the degree to which informal systems as well as formal systems are run by unconscious and/or irrational forces. . . .

This underscores my sense of the importance of rights: rights are to law what conscious commitments are to the psyche. This country's worst historical moments have not been attributable to rights-*assertion*, but to a failure of rights-*commitment*. From this perspective, the problem with rights discourse is not that the discourse is itself constricting, but that it exists in a constricted referential universe. The body of private laws epitomized by contract, including slave contracts, for example, is problematic not only because it endows certain parties with rights, but because it denies the object of contract any rights at all. . . .

I am . . . not one of those who believes that the future and well-being of blacks lie solely with ourselves. Although I don't always yet trust this imagery of dependence, I think it is the reality, and necessity, if balanced coexistence is to occur. Blacks cannot be alone in this recognition, however. Whites, too, must learn to appreciate the communion of blacks in more than body, as more than the perpetually neotenized, mothering non-mother. . . .

Whites must confer upon blacks their recognition of black need and black identity, for is not "what we have in common precisely what is given to each of us as something exclusively his?"[16]

To say that blacks never fully believed in rights is true; yet it is also true that blacks believed in them so much and so hard that we gave them life where there was none before. We held on to them, put the hope of them into our wombs, and mothered them—not just the notion of them. We nurtured rights and gave rights life. And this was not the dry process of reification, from which life is drained and reality fades as the cement of conceptual determinism hardens round—but its opposite. This was the resurrection of life . . . the parthenogenesis of unfertilized hope.

The making of something out of nothing took immense alchemical fire: the fusion of a whole nation and the kindling of several generations. The illusion became real for only a very few of us; it is still elusive and illusory for most. But if it took this long to breathe life into a form whose shape had already been forged by society and which is therefore idealistically if not ideologically accessible, imagine how long would be the struggle without even that sense of definition, without the power of that familiar vision. What hope would there be if the assignment were to pour hope into a timeless, formless futurism? The desperate psychological and physical oppression suffered by black people in this society makes such a prospect either unrealistic (i.e., experienced as unattainable) or other-worldly (as in the false hopes held out by many religions of the oppressed).

It is true that the constitutional foreground of "rights" was shaped by whites, parceled out to blacks in pieces, ordained in small favors, as random insulting gratuities. Perhaps the predominance of that imbalance obscures the fact that the recursive insistence of those rights is also defined by black desire for them, desire not fueled by the sop of minor enforcement of major statutory schemes like the Civil Rights Act, but by knowledge of, and generations of existing in, a world without any meaningful boundaries. And "without boundary" for blacks has meant not untrammeled vistas of possibility, but the crushing weight of totalistic—bodily and spiritual—*intrusion*. "Rights" feels so new in the mouths of most black people. It is still so deliciously empowering to say. It is a sign for and a gift of selfhood that is very hard to contemplate reconstructing (deconstruction is too awful to think about!) at this point in history. It is the magic wand of visibility and invisibility, of inclusion and exclusion, of power and no-power. The concept of rights, both positive and negative, is the marker of our citizenship, our participatoriness, our relation to other.

In many mythologies, the mask of the sorcerer is also the source of power. To unmask the sorcerer is to depower. So CLS' unmasking rights mythology in liberal America is to reveal the source of much powerlessness masquerading as strength. It reveals a universalism of need and oppression among whites as well as blacks.

In those ancient mythologies, however, unmasking the sorcerer was only part of the job. It was impossible to destroy the mask without destroying the balance of things, without destroying empowerment itself. Therefore, the mask had to be donned by the acquiring shaman, and put to good ends. As rulers range from despotic to benign, as anarchy can become syndicalism, so the power mask in the right hands can transform itself from burden into blessing.

The task for CLS, therefore, is not to discard rights, but to see through or past them so that they reflect a larger definition of privacy, and of property: so that privacy is turned from exclusion based on *self*-regard, into regard for another's fragile, mysterious autonomy; and so that property regains its ancient connotation of being a reflection of that part of the self which by virtue of its very externalization is universal. The task is to expand private property rights into a conception of civil rights, into the right to expect civility from others.

In discarding rights altogether, one discards a symbol too deeply enmeshed in the psyche of the oppressed to lose without trauma and much resistance. Instead, society must *give* them away. . . . Give to all of society's objects and untouchables the rights of privacy, integrity and self-assertion; give them distance and respect. . . .

Notes

1. See, e.g., Gabel & Kennedy, Roll Over Beethoven, 36 Stan. L. Rev. 1 *passim* (1984).

2. See Trubek, Where the Action Is: Critical Legal Studies and Empiricism, 36 Stan L. Rev. 575, 578 (1984).

3. See D. Bell, Race, Racism and American Law, 2d ed. (Little Brown, 1980); Bell, The Supreme Court, 1984 Term—Foreword: The Civil Rights Chronicles, 99 Harv. L. Rev. 4 (1985); Bell, *Bakke*, Minority Admissions, and the Usual Price of Racial Remedies, 67 Cal. L. Rev. 3 (1979); Edley, Affirmative Action and the Rights Rhetoric Trap, 3 Harv. Blackletter J. 9 (1986).

4. In another context, such a discourse boundary has been described as follows: "[T]he women's movement has raised a fundamental question concerning everyone in complex systems: how communication is possible, how to communicate with 'another' without denying the difference by power relations. Beyond the demand for equality, beyond the inclusion in the field of masculine rights, women are yet speaking of the right to difference and to 'otherness.' That is why they sometimes choose silence, because it is difficult to find words other than those of the dominant language." Melucci, The Symbolic Challenge of Contemporary Movements, 52 Soc. Res. 789, 811 (1985).

5. Peter Gabel was one of the first to bring critical theory to legal analysis; as such he is considered one of the "founders" of Critical Legal Studies.

6. See generally Delgado, Dunn, Brown, Lee, & Hubbert, Fairness and Formality: Minimizing the Risk of Prejudice in Alternative Dispute Resolution, 1985 Wis. L. Rev. 1359.

7. "Can anyone seriously think that it helps either in changing society or in understanding how society changes to discuss whether [someone is] exercising rights protected by the First Amendment? It matters only whether they engaged in politically effective action." Tushnet, An Essay on Rights, 62 Tex. L. Rev. 1363, 1370–71 (1984); see also D. Kairys ed., The Politics of Law: A Progressive Critique (Pantheon, 1982); Frug, The Ideology of Bureaucracy in American Law, 97 Harv. L. Rev. 1276 (1984); Gabel, Reification in Legal Reasoning, 3 Res. Law & Soc. 25 (1980); Gabel & Harris, Building Power and Breaking Images: Critical Legal Theory and the Practice of Law, 11 N.Y.U. Rev. L. & Soc. Change 369 (1982–83); Kennedy, The Structure of Blackstone's Commentaries, 28 Buff. L. Rev. 205 (1979); Kennedy, Form and Substance in Private Law Adjudication, 89 Harv. L. Rev. 1685 (1976).

8. See Tushnet, Essay on Rights, *supra* note 7, at 1375; see also Gordon, Historicism in Legal Scholarship, 90 Yale L.J. 1017 (1981); Trubek, Where the Action Is, *supra* note 2; Unger, The Critical Legal Studies Movement, 96 Harv. L. Rev. 561 (1983).

9. "Every social system contains a certain amount of moral and totalizing expectations toward happiness, justice, truth, and so on. These claims do not have social attributions, do not involve specific social interests or practical-historical projects. They live on the borders of great religions or great cultural and political waves, in the form of small sects, heretical cults, theological circles. The great collective processes offer a channel to express this moral utopianism, which otherwise would survive in marginal enclaves." Melucci, Challenge of Contemporary Movements, *supra* note 4, at 803.

10. Gabel, Reification in Legal Reasoning, *supra* note 7, at 28.

11. M. Tushnet, The American Law of Slavery 37–42 (Princeton University Press, 1981). Tushnet's analysis is premised, in part, on an understanding of the law of slaveholders as creating a system of enforceable expectations and limited rights for slaves.

12. *Id.*

13. Gabel, Reification in Legal Reasoning, *supra* note 7, at 29.

14. See R. Abel ed., The Contradictions of Informal Justice, 1 Politics of Informal Justice: The American Experience 267 (Academic Press, 1982); Delgado et al., Fairness and Formality, *supra* note 6.

15. "There are two explanations for the unconscious nature of our racially discriminatory beliefs and ideas. First, Freudian theory states that the human mind defends itself against the discomfort of guilt by denying or refusing to recognize those ideas, wishes, and beliefs that conflict with what the individual has learned is good or right. . . .

"Second, the theory of cognitive psychology states that the culture—including, for example, the media and an individual's parents, peers, and authority figures—transmits certain beliefs and preferences. Because these beliefs are so much a part of the culture, they are not experienced as explicit lessons. Instead, they seem part of the individual's rational ordering of her perceptions of the world." Lawrence, The Id, the Ego, and Equal Protection: Reckoning with Unconscious Racism, 39 Stan. L. Rev. 317, 322–23 (1987) (citations omitted).

16. I. Calvino, Mr. Palomar 14 (W. Weaver trans., Harcourt, Brace, 1983).

❖ *The Dialectic of Rights and Politics: Perspectives from the Women's Movement*

Elizabeth M. Schneider

THE NATURE OF legal rights has long been a subject of interest to legal scholars and activists.[1] Recently, dialogue on the issue has intensified, provoked by numerous critiques of liberal rights, particularly by Critical Legal Studies (CLS) scholars. These recent critiques have tended to view rights claims and rights consciousness as distinct from and frequently opposed to politics, and as an obstacle to the political growth and development of social movement groups.

This essay joins this dialogue on rights with a different voice. Recent critiques of rights have looked at rights and politics as static categories, and focused primarily on the way in which rights claims and rights consciousness mask and obscure important political choices and values. In this essay, I develop a dialectical perspective on rights. Central to this perspective is an understanding of the dynamic interrelationship of rights and politics, as well as the dual and contradictory potential of rights discourse[2] to blunt and advance political movement. . . .

The Debate on Rights

The idea that legal rights have some intrinsic value is widespread in our culture. A rights claim can make a statement of entitlement that is universal and categorical. This entitlement can be seen as negative because it protects against intrusion by the state (a right to privacy), or the same right can be seen as affirmative because it enables an individual to do something (a right to choose whether to bear a child). Thus, a rights claim can define the boundaries of state power and the entitlement to do something, and, by extension, provide an affirmative vision of human society. Rights claims reflect a normative theory of the person, but a normative theory can see the rights-bearing individual as isolated or it can see the

From Schneider, The Dialectics of Rights and Politics: Perspectives from the Women's Movement, 61 N.Y.U. L. Rev. 589 (1986).

individual as part of a larger social network. Recently, legal scholars, in particular CLS and feminist scholars, have debated the meanings of rights claims and have questioned the significance of legal argumentation focused on rights.

CLS scholars question whether rights claims and rights discourse can facilitate social reconstruction. The CLS critique has several interrelated themes which flow from a more general critique of liberalism. CLS scholars argue that liberalism is premised on dichotomies, such as individual and community or self and other, that divide the world into two mutually exclusive spheres. Rights claims only perpetuate these dichotomies, which, to CLS scholars, limit legal thinking and inhibit necessary social change. CLS scholars base their critique of rights on the inherently individualistic nature of rights under legal liberalism, the "reification" of rights generally, and the indeterminate nature of rights claims.

CLS scholars argue that rights are "permeated by the possessive individualism of capitalist society."[3] Because rights "belong" to individuals—rights rhetoric portrays individuals as "separated owners of their respective bundle of rights[4]—they are necessarily individualistic." This notion of ownership delimits the boundaries of state authority from that of individual autonomy, the self from other. Rights discourse tends to overemphasize the separation of the individual from the group, and thereby inhibits an individual's awareness of her connection to and mutual dependence upon others.

CLS scholars also see rights discourse as taking on a "thing-like" quality—a fixed and external meaning—that "freezes and falsifies" rich and complex social experience.[5] This "attribution of a thing-like or fixed character to socially constructed phenomena," called reification, "is an essential aspect of alienated consciousness, leading people to accept existing social orders as the inevitable 'facts of life.'"[6] This process thus gives people a sense of "substitute connection" and an illusory sense of community that disables any real connection. Finally, these scholars see rights claims as indeterminate because argumentation based on rights does not solve the problem of how to resolve conflicts between rights and cannot transform social relations.

CLS scholars criticize the use of rights claims by social movement groups on related grounds.[7] They argue that the use of rights discourse by a social movement group and the consequent reliance on rights can keep people passive and dependent upon the state because it is the state which grants them their rights. Individuals are only allowed to act—to "exercise their rights"—to the degree to which the state permits. Legal strategies based on rights discourse, then, tend to weaken the power of a popular movement by allowing the state to define the movement's goals. Rights discourse obscures real political choice and determination. Further, it fosters social antagonisms by magnifying disagreement within and conflicts between groups over rights. From a strategic perspective, then, reliance on rights by social movements can be politically debilitating.

Nevertheless, at least one prominent CLS scholar sees rights claims as potentially important and useful. To this end, Duncan Kennedy urges the "transformation of rights rhetoric."

> [T]he critique of rights as liberal philosophy does not imply that the left should abandon rights rhetoric as a tool of political organizing or legal argument. Embedded in the rights notion is a liberating accomplishment of our culture: the affirmation of free human subjectivity against the constraints of group life, along with the paradoxical countervision of a group life that creates and nurtures individuals capable of freedom. We need to work at the slow transformation of rights rhetoric, at dereifying it, rather than simply junking it.[8]

Some feminist critiques of rights see rights claims as formal and hierarchical—premised on a view of law as patriarchal.[9] From this perspective, law generally, and rights particularly, reflect a male viewpoint characterized by objectivity, distance, and abstraction. As Catharine MacKinnon, a leading exponent of this position writes, "Abstract rights will authoritize the male experience of the world."[10] However, these critics do not argue that rights claims should be given up completely either.

Some legal writers see similarities between the CLS critique of rights based on "liberal legalism" and the feminist critique based on "patriarchy." Both liberal legalism and patriarchy rely upon the same set of dichotomies. Further, the critiques usefully emphasize the indeterminacy of rights, and the ways in which rights discourse can reinforce alienation and passivity. Both critiques highlight the ways in which rights discourse can become divorced from political struggle. They appropriately warn us of the dangers social movements and lawyers encounter when relying on rights to effect social change.

But both critiques are incomplete. They do not take account of the complex, and I suggest dialectical, relationship between the assertion of rights and political struggle in social movement practice. They see only the limits of rights, and fail to appreciate the dual possibilities of rights discourse. Admittedly, rights discourse can reinforce alienation and individualism, and can constrict political vision and debate. But, at the same time, it can help to affirm human values, enhance political growth, and assist in the development of collective identity.

By failing to see that both possibilities exist simultaneously, these critiques have rigidified, rather than challenged, the classic dichotomies of liberal thought —law and politics, individual and community, and ultimately, rights and politics. Radical social theory, such as CLS and feminist scholarship, must explore the dialectical dimensions of each dichotomy, not reinforce the sense that the dichotomies are frozen and static. Radical social theory must explain how these dichotomies can be transcended. . . .

Dialectics and Praxis as Methodology:
The Examples of Feminist Theory
and Feminist Legal Practice

My perspective on rights is grounded in a view of the dialectical nature of consciousness and social change and a view that theory and practice must be understood as interrelated. . . .

The concept of dialectics has shaped much of contemporary social theory and has developed different meanings and uses. Most significantly here, it stands for the idea of the process, connection, and opposition of dualities, and for subsequent change and transcendence. . . . At any given "moment," ideas may appear to be connected or in opposition because connection or opposition exists in only one stage of a larger process. The dialectical process is not a mechanical confrontation of an opposite from outside, but an organic emergence and development of opposition and change from within the "moment" or idea itself.

The critiques of rights that I have described suffer from an analysis that divorces theory from practice. Rights are analyzed in the abstract, viewed as static—as a form of legal theory separate from social practice—and then criticized for being formal and abstract. My approach to rights views theory and practice as dialectically related, and I look to the philosophical concept of praxis to describe this process. The fundamental aspect of praxis is the active role of consciousness and subjectivity in shaping both legal theory and practice, and the dynamic interrelationship that results.[11] As Karl Klare has explained, lawmaking can be a form of praxis; it can be constitutive, creative, and an expression of "the embeddedness of action-in-belief and belief-in-action."[12] For purposes of this essay, my focus on praxis impels me to explore how rights claims can flow from and express the political and moral aspirations of a social movement group, how rights claims are experienced or perceived in social movement practice, and how rights discourse impacts on social movement practice generally. . . .

. . . Over the last several years, feminist theoretical work in a range of disciplines has made important contributions to the development of social and political theory. This work emphasizes dialectical change and the relationship between theory and practice, thereby enriching social perspectives on law and understandings of rights. At the same time, my experience with feminist legal practice gives me a concrete understanding of the dialectical nature of rights discourse—of the way in which rights claims can not only constrain, but also can creatively express political vision, and the way in which rights claims can be understood as a form of praxis.

Feminist Theory

Feminist theory is characterized by an emphasis on dialectical process[13] and the interrelationship of theory and practice. Feminist theory emphasizes the value of direct and personal experience as the place that theory should begin, as embodied in the phrase "the personal is political." This phrase reflects the view that the realm of personal experience, the "private" which has always been trivialized, particularly for women, is an appropriate and important subject of public inquiry, and that the "private" and "public" worlds are inextricably linked. The notion of consciousness-raising as feminist method flows from this insight. In consciousness-raising groups, learning starts with the individual and personal (the private), moves to the general and social (the public), and then reflects back on itself with .heightened consciousness through this shared group process. Consciousness-raising as feminist method is a form of praxis because it transcends the theory and practice dichotomy. Consciousness-raising groups start with personal and concrete experience, integrate this experience into theory, and then, in effect, reshape theory based upon experience and experience based upon theory. Theory expresses and grows out of experience but it also relates back to that experience for further refinement, validation, or modification.

The idea of consciousness-raising as a method of analysis suggests an approach to social change which recognizes dynamic tension, reflection, and sharing as essential aspects of growth. . . .

Feminist theory thus reveals the social dimension of individual experience and the individual dimension of social experience. . . . In particular, it values the dynamic interrelationship of the individual and community. . . .

The fact that this process begins with the self, and then connects to the larger world of women, is important. For feminists, theory is not "out there," but rather is based on the concrete, daily, and "trivial" experiences of individuals, and so emerges from the shared experience of women talking. Because feminist theory grows out of direct experience and consciousness actively asserting itself, feminist theory emphasizes context and the importance of identifying experience and claiming it for one's own.

Feminist theory involves a particular methodology, but it also has a substantive viewpoint and political orientation. Recognizing the links between individual change and social change means understanding the importance of political *activity*, not just theory. Theory emerges from practice and practice then informs and reshapes theory. . . .

Feminist Legal Practice: Feminist Theory in Practice

While feminist theory has shaped my view of the relationship between theory and practice, much of my perspective on the use of rights has understandably been shaped by my own experience. . . . As a college student in the 1960s, active in civil rights and other political work, and studying political science and social theory, I saw many instances of lawyers from the civil rights movement using the law to advance group political efforts. . . .

First as a law student and then as a lawyer, I was privileged to work at the Center for Constitutional Rights. Center lawyers had a long history of using the law to affect social change and to change the law to reflect the experience of those previously excluded by the law. In the early 1970s, women lawyers on the Center's staff began to work on women's rights issues. . . .

Of the many cases on which I worked at the Center, one, State v. Wanrow,[14] stands out for me because it so clearly demonstrates that legal argumentation which is tied to and expresses the concerns of a social movement can assist in the political development of that movement. In *Wanrow*, a jury convicted Yvonne Wanrow, a Native American woman, of second-degree murder for shooting and killing a white man named William Wesler, who she believed had tried to molest one of her children. Wesler had entered her babysitter's home uninvited when Wanrow and her children were there. Wanrow, who had a cast on her leg and was using crutches at the time, claimed that, based on her perceptions of the danger created by Wesler, she had acted in self-defense. The trial court, however, instructed the jury to consider only the circumstances "at or immediately before the killing" when evaluating the gravity of the danger the defendant faced, even though Wanrow claimed that she had information which led her to believe that Wesler had a history of child molestation and had previously tried to molest one of her children. The trial court also instructed the jury to apply the equal force standard, whereby the person claiming self-defense can only respond with force equal to that which the assailant uses. Wesler had not been carrying a gun.

Center lawyers became involved in the case on appeal to the Washington Supreme Court. Reading the trial manuscript, we realized that the judge's instructions prevented the jury from considering Yvonne Wanrow's state of mind, as shaped by her experiences and perspective as a Native American woman, when she confronted this man. . . .

We developed the legal argument for women's "equal right to trial," which challenged sex-bias in the law of self-defense, based upon our knowledge of the particular problems women who killed men faced in the criminal justice system: the prevalence of homicides committed by women in circumstances of male physical abuse or sexual assault; the different circumstances in which men and women killed; myths and misconceptions in the criminal justice system concerning women who kill as "crazy"; the problems of domestic violence, physical abuse, and sexual abuse of women and children; the physical and psychological barriers that prevented women from feeling capable of defending themselves; and stereotypes of women as unreasonable. If the jury did not understand Yvonne Wanrow's experience and the way in which it shaped her conduct, it could not find her conduct to have been reasonable and therefore an appropriate act of self-defense. Since the jury would not be able to consider this defense plausible, Wanrow could not be treated fairly.

On appeal, Wanrow's conviction was reversed. A plurality of the court voted to reverse on the ground that the trial court's instructions violated Washington law in three ways. First, the instruction that limited the jury's consideration to the circumstances "at or immediately before the killing" misconstrued Washington law. Properly construed, state law allowed the jury to consider Wanrow's knowledge of the deceased's reputation, prior aggressive behavior, and all other prior circumstances, even if that knowledge were acquired long before the killing. Second, the instruction concerning equal force misstated state law and denied Wanrow equal protection:

> The impression created—that a 5'4" woman with a cast on her leg and using a crutch must, under the law, somehow repel an assault by a 6'2" intoxicated man without employing weapons in her defense, unless the jury finds her determination of the degree of danger to be objectively reasonable—constitutes a separate and distinct misstatement of the law and, in the context of this case, violates the respondent's right to equal protection of the law.[15]

Third, the trial court's instructions failed to direct the jury to consider the reasonableness of Wanrow's act *from Wanrow's perspective*, or, in other words, "seeing what [s]he sees and knowing what [s]he knows." The Washington Supreme Court affirmed a standard of self-defense based on the individual defendant's perception, as required by Washington state law, and underscored the need for this standard by recognizing the existence of sex-bias in the law of self-defense generally.

> The respondent was entitled to have the jury consider her actions in the light of her own perceptions of the situation, including those perceptions which were the product of our nation's "long and unfortunate history of sex-discrimination.". . . Until such time as the effects of that history are eradicated, care must be taken to assure that our self-defense instructions afford women the right to have their conduct judged in light of the individual physical handicaps which are the product of sex discrimination. To fail to do so is to deny the right of the individual woman involved to trial by the same rules which are applicable to male defendants.[16]

Thus the political insights into sex-bias in self-defense that could help explain Yvonne Wanrow's situation arose out of legal formulation and argumentation. But the legal argument concerning the "equal right to trial" grew out of a political analysis of sex discrimination that the legal team shared, discussed, and applied to the particular case. The legal argumentation brought together diverse strands of feminist analysis and theory concerning sex-biased treatment of women in the criminal justice system.

This legal argumentation reflected a perspective which feminist activists and lawyers were beginning to express and share. Feminist writers were beginning to explore these issues as well. Further, aspects of this argument were asserted at the same time in other courts in different cases. The rights formulation reflected the political analysis and activity of women's groups concerned with violence against women, the treatment of women within the criminal justice system, and the work of defense committees organizing around particular women defendant's cases. It was a formulation which made sense to many women on an experiential level.

In this sense, the legal formulation grew out of political analysis, but it also . . . moved the political work to a different level. It raised the political question of what a women's perspective might be and what equal treatment would look like. It focused further legal work on the disparate hurdles that limited women defendants' choice of defense—particularly the various ways in which women's experiences were excluded from the courtroom—and laid the foundation for political and legal strategies to remedy the problems created by this exclusion.

. . . Many courts have now accepted the view that there is sex-bias in the law of self-defense. Still, the ongoing legal work in this area teaches us new lessons. . . . [For example,] [c]ourts which have applied the insight reflected in the equal trial argument have unwittingly recreated the very sex stereotypes of female incapacity that women's self-defense work was intended to overcome. But these new dilemmas of feminist theory can also help to clarify issues, sharpen debate, and deepen insight into these matters.

Wanrow exemplifies the way in which the legal formulation of rights emerging from political analysis and practice can be expressive. It demonstrates the way a rights claim initially flows from political analysis and then becomes the basis for a more self-reflective political analysis. The rights formulation is part of an ongoing process of politics. The rights claim is a "moment" in that process in which the political vision emerges from within the claim of rights.

The Center's work in *Wanrow,* as in many other cases, was an example of feminist theory in practice—of what lawmaking as praxis is like. The legal theory emerged from political experience; the legal theory in turn served to refine and sharpen political insights and to clarify tensions in the political struggle; the political struggle was reassessed in light of the legal theory; and finally, experience reshaped the legal theory. In short, the rights claims grew out of politics and then turned into politics. This experience of praxis, then, provides a framework for my analysis of rights and politics.

Toward a Dialectical Understanding of Rights and Politics

The dialectical methodology detailed in the previous section suggests that rights discourse and politics can be understood as interconnected, even though they may appear at times to be in opposition. . . .

As suggested earlier, recent rights critics have viewed the experience of rights discourse and rights assertion in a static and rigid way. They have accepted the opposition of rights and politics and the reification of rights generally. A dialectical perspective, however, sees rights and politics as part of a more dynamic, complex, and larger process characterized by the possibility that rights discourse can simultaneously advance and obscure political growth and vision. A dialectical view of rights develops the expressive, transformative, and problematic aspects of rights. . . . Rights discourse can be an alienated and artificial language that constructs political debate, but it can also be a means to articulate new values and political vision. The way in which a social movement group uses the rights claim and places it in a broader context affects the ability of rights discourse to aid political struggle. Rights discourse and rights claim, when emerging from and organically linked to political struggle, can help to develop political consciousness which can play a useful role in the development of a social behavior.

Rights discourse can express human and communal values; it can be a way for individuals to develop a sense of self and for a group to develop a collective identity. Rights discourse can also have a dimension that emphasizes the interdependence of autonomy and community. It can play an important role in giving individuals a sense of self-definition, in connecting the individual to a larger group and community, and in defining the goals of a political struggle, particularly during the early development of a social movement.

My effort to detail the . . . affirmative dimensions of rights discourse owes much to the many rights theorists who are engaged in similar efforts to reimagine rights. . . .

Communal Rights

Although it has been argued that rights are inherently individualistic because individuals "possess" them, rights need not be perceived that way. Staughton Lynd, for example, has developed the idea of rights as "communal," infused with the values of community, compassion, and solidarity.[17] Although he focuses on some rights as particularly communal, he argues in favor of fighting for the communal content of as many rights as possible and challenging the zero-sum perspective on rights generally. He looks to the historical context in which a right develops as a primary force shaping the particular collective aspect of the right. . . . For example, Lynd's view of the right to engage in collective bargaining activity under section 7 of the National Labor Relations Act as a paradigmatic communal right is based on his perception of this right as "derived from the actual character of working-class solidarity and accordingly a right that foreshadows a society in which group life and individual self-realization mutually reinforce each other."[18] Lynd's understanding of the collective aspect of rights has several dimensions. He maintains that a right developed in the context of a social movement struggle may have a collective cast to it. Further, the exercise of rights by an individual can expand the ability of the larger group to exercise their rights generally. Finally, Lynd suggests that the concept of the inalienability of rights—that an individual cannot give up a right because it belongs to the group—is premised on an underlying assumption based on the communal aspect of rights. Lynd's analysis, then, provides a framework to challenge the notion that rights claims must be articulated and perceived exclusively as the property of rights-bearing individuals.

Individual Selfhood and Collective Identity

Another aspect of a dialectical view of rights is the role that rights discourse can play for individual self-development and collective identity. Carol Gilligan's work in charting differences between male and female moral and psychological development provides a basis for exploring this issue. She suggests that these differences can shape the way that individuals experience rights. . . .

Gilligan posits that the developmental challenges of maturity are different for men and women. Men, whose lives have emphasized separateness, must ultimately learn care and connection. Women, whose lives have emphasized connection to and caretaking for others, must ultimately learn to value and care for themselves. Mature moral and psychological development for both sexes would seek to synthesize moral perspectives based on both rights and responsibilities.

For this reason, Gilligan suggests that the assertion of rights can play a particularly important role in women's moral development. She suggests that women's articulation of rights challenges women's sense of self and transforms women's experience of selflessness. "[T]he essential notion of rights [is] that the interests of the self can be considered legitimate. In this sense, the concept of rights changes women's conceptions of self, allowing them to see themselves as stronger and to consider directly their own needs."[19]. . .

Gilligan outlines a process of moral development for women that moves from an emphasis on selflessness and care for others, to a recognition of self and autonomy, and then to a self-reflective understanding of the way in which self and other are interconnected. She suggests that assertion of rights, particularly women's rights, can play a crucial role in the transformation of women's sense of self. Public assertion of women's legal rights reverberates in the consciousness of individual women. . . . [Further,] assertion of women's rights can provide women with a sense of collective identity, a sense that self and other are connected. . . .

Gilligan's suggestion that the psychological experience and social function of rights assertion may perform different developmental tasks for men and women may be overboard in its link to gender. But the sense of self-definition and collective identification that Gilligan details is, nevertheless, an important aspect of rights claims. . . .

Interdependent Rights

Gilligan implies that the gender-linked oppositions of rights and care-based morality can be transcended in a dialectical fashion in a third stage of development in which men and women see the importance and interconnection of rights and responsibilities. . . . [T]his third stage of development will be based upon the synthesis of male and female voices—those of rights and responsibilities. . . . She suggests that if you include both voices, you will transform the very nature of the conversation; the discourse is no longer either simply about justice or simply about caring; rather it is about bringing them together to transform the domain. Although feminist scholars have questioned whether this third stage is really transformative, Gilligan's vision of rights articulated in this different voice has stimulated attempts by legal scholars to reimage rights and to conceive of them as "interdependent."

For example, in a number of recent articles Martha Minow has sought an understanding of rights that resolves the tension between autonomy and caretaking.[20] . . . Minow attempts to redefine the substance of purportedly individualistic rights by positing a right to connection, by developing the interconnection of rights and responsibilities, and by suggesting that rights claims can focus on the social and economic preconditions for rights.

William Simon's recent article on welfare rights which contrasts the New Deal social work jurisprudence of welfare rights with the contemporary New Property conception of rights, suggests a similar perspective that he calls "regenerative."[21] Simon sees the New Property conception of rights as reincarnating classical legalist views of rights based on the protection of individual independence and self-sufficiency from the collective power of the state. In contrast, he suggests that rights in New Deal social work jurisprudence differed from the classical model because they challenged this distinction between the individual and the community and reflected a norm of interdependence. Rights were used as part of a dialectical process of political development, and a means of education . . . a means by which people on welfare come to understand and articulate their goals and a way for the individual claimant to get involved in political activity. . . .

Kenneth Karst's effort to reconstruct constitutional law as a "jurisprudence of interdependence" is similarly premised on Gilligan's work.[22] . . . [H]e seeks to infuse rights talk . . . to take greater account of the morality of care. . . . The notions of interdependent rights that these various theorists have envisioned are efforts to redefine the substance of rights claims and the process of rights assertion so as to modify and transform the individualistic dimension of rights. . . .

Rights as Conversation

The theoretical efforts discussed above focused on the way that rights connected to political struggle can be part of an ongoing conversation and can have a character, content, and meaning that is more communal because they reflect the very political struggle from which they emerged. This political context might affect both the process by which rights are articulated as well as the content of the rights themselves: what the rights mean to individuals and members of the group who claim them at a particular time, and how they are understood and experienced at that time. However, even if rights discourse is understood as part of a process of political education and mobilization, how do we ensure that the articulation of rights claims will truly assist in that larger process? How can we be sure that if rights discourse starts the conversation of politics, the conversation will ever move beyond rights? We must take seriously Peter Gabel's caution that rights can substitute the illusion of community for a more authentic and genuine sense of community.[23] A preoccupation with or excessive focus on rights consciousnss can reinforce alienation or powerlessness and weaken the power of popular movements. In and of themseles, rights claims are not a basis for building a sustained political movement, nor can rights claims perform the task of social reconstruction. Still, their importance should not be underestimated. Articulation of political insight in rights terms *can* be an important vehicle for political growth, and can help develop a sense of collective identity. . . .

Women's Rights and Feminist Struggle

Recent experience with claims of legal rights for women suggests the importance of understanding the relationship between rights and political struggle from a dialectical perspective. This experience demonstrates the richly textured process by which a social movement group articulates political demands through a rights claim and the way in which that claim affects the development of the group. Most significantly, the experience of the women's rights movement simultaneously reveals the communal possibilities of rights and underscores the limits of political strategy focused on rights. This part briefly examines . . . areas of women's rights work which highlight this experience. . . .

Historically, the feminist movement in this country has focused on notions of rights. In 1848, the women's rights convention at Seneca Falls issued a Declaration of Sentiments and passed resolutions which set forth a platform on women's rights. The first wave of feminism in the nineteenth century sought to enhance women's access to political and economic opportunity by challenging laws that denied women the right to vote and barred them from various occupations. For example, the struggle to win passage of the Nineteenth Amendment emphasized the importance for women of the right to vote. Rights claims grew out of early feminists' political analyses which saw women's exclusion from public and political life as central to their continued subordination.

Spurred by the explosion of feminist consciousness in the 1960s, women's rights have been claimed in a variety of contexts, focusing primarily on issues of equality—the right to equal treatment and the right to reproductive choice. . . . Claims of rights and use of the language of rights have affected both public discourse and individual consciousness, and suggest the possibilities and limits of rights discourse.

Rights Claims and Discourse in the Women's Movement

Over the last twenty years, claims for women's rights have increasingly been used to articulate political demand for equality and for change in gender roles. A claim of right can make a political statement and transmit a powerful message concerning "the kind of society we want to live in, the kind of relations among people we wish to foster, and the kind of behavior that is to be praised or blamed. [It] is a moral claim about how human beings should act toward one another."[24] As we have already seen, on an individual level, a claim of right can be an assertion of one's self-worth and an affirmation of one's moral value and entitlement. . . .

The women's rights movement has had an important affirming and individuating effect on women's consciousness. The articulation of women's rights provides a sense of self and distinction for individual women, while at the same time giving women an important sense of collective identity. Through this articulation, women's voices and concerns are heard in a public forum and afforded a legal vehicle for expression.

But rights claims do not only define women's individual and collective experience, they also actively shape public discourse. Claims of equal rights and reproductive choice, for example, empowered women. Women as a class had not previously been included within the reach of the Fourteenth Amendment. Women's concerns now rose to the level of constitutional (serious, grown-up) concerns. By claiming rights, women asserted their intention to be taken seriously in society. This "liberal" assertion of rights gave women the "audacity to compare" themselves with men.[25] Women could now claim that they were *entitled* to the equal protection of the law, not just *permitted* to seek it. Women's interests, previously relegated to the private sphere, and therefore outside the public protection of the law, now received the protection of the Constitution. The claims reinforced on a powerful ideological level that the "personal is political" and changed previously private concerns into public ones that needed to be dealt with by the society at large.

The public nature of rights assertion is especially significant because of the private nature of discrimination against women. The locus of women's subordination is frequently the private and individual sphere—the home and family—and is thus perceived as isolated and experienced in isolation. Women also tend to see individual fault rather than to identify a systemic pattern of social discrimination. Thus, public claims of legal rights do more than simply put women's sense of self into the personal moral equation. The assertion of rights claims and use of rights discourse help women to overcome this sense of privatization and of personal blame which has perpetuated women's subordination. Rights claims and rights discourse have thus had a self-defining aspect as well as a collective dimension because the inner experience of the right ties the individual and her particular experiences to the larger experiences of women as a class. Rights claims assert women's selfhood collectively, thereby giving women a sense of group identity and pride; they make manifest the fact that women can act and claim their place in history.

Formulations of women's rights emerged from the women's movement itself, from the experiences of women, and from feminist theory. This integration of experience and theory reflected in rights claims was heightened by the fact that at the same time notions of women's rights were articulated, the number of women in the legal profession was increasing dramatically. Many of the women lawyers who have focused on women's rights work entered law school because of the women's movement or were drawn into the women's movement during law school. . . . This made the experience of lawyering in these cases particularly intense and powerful. It undoubtedly shaped the way in which women lawyers perceived legal problems, the insights that women litigators brought to sex-discrimination cases, and the strategies that women litigators developed to handle these cases. . . .

Perhaps for this reason, women's rights litigation has involved several important aspects . . . : the use of experience and intuition as starting point and guide, the creative use of both political and social contexts, and the exploration of the the human impact and context of the case in concrete terms. Much women's rights litigation has implemented a strategy which uses amicus curiae briefs to present their broader perspectives to ensure that women's voices are heard in court. In this way, women's rights litigation has frequently expanded the possibilities of creative political envisioning through the use of rights discourse.

It is sometimes difficult to remember how visionary the notion of equality from a woman's perspective is—how much it really challenges. Recent critiques of rights have suggested that rights rhetoric inevitably abstracts and distances, but women's rights litigation has concretized women's experience and emphasized women's specificity and particularity. Women's rights litigation began the process of shaping the law of equality to reflect a women's perspective. Women's rights discourse linked the specific experience of women with the universal claim of rights. This is, in and of itself, a radical and transforming notion.

In addition, the advocacy process itself has had a significant effect in mobilizing women for political action. For women who have historically been excluded from public life and political action, activity in the public sphere helps to transcend the public and private dichotomy. It also helps women learn skills that are necessary to organize and mobilize political support. In this sense, the struggle for rights has enabled women to become politically active and to gain power.

At the same time, the women's movement's experience with rights suffers from some of the problems discussed by rights critics. First, in some sense the idea of equal rights, although radical in conception, has not captured the scope and depth of the feminist program. Women's rights have been, in a sense, "too little" for the women's movement, although perhaps "too much" for society. Feminists understand that genuine equality for women will not be achieved simply by winning rights in court. Rather, equality requires social reconstruction of gender roles within the workplace and the family. Rights claims, however, do not effectively challenge existing social structures. Reflecting on the reproductive rights experience, Rosalind Petchesky wrote:

> [T]he concept of "rights," [is,] in general, a concept that is inherently static and abstracted from social conditions. Rights are by definition claims staked within a given order of things. They are demands for access for oneself, or for "no admittance" to others; but they do not challenge the social structure, the social relations of production and reproduction. The claim for "abortion rights" seeks access to a necessary service, but by itself it fails to address the social relations and sexual divisions around which responsibility for pregnancy and children is assigned. In real-life struggles, this limitation exacts a price, for it lets men and society neatly off the hook.[26]

Second, the articulation of a right can, despite a movement's best efforts, put the focus of immediately political struggle on winning the right in court. Thus, even if one is concerned with and understands the need for social reconstruction, it is hard to sustain an understanding of short-term goals at the same time. The concreteness and immediacy of legal struggle tends to subsume the more diffuse role of political organizing and education. Thus, while there has been a positive attitude toward the use of legal rights in court as an aspect of law reform work, the problems with rights have caused the women's movement to view the use of rights with some ambivalence.

Third, since women's rights formulations oblige the state to act, serious questions about the appropriate role of the state in the context of women's rights have emerged. Women's rights litigators argue that by fighting for women's rights in the courts they do not exclusively rely on the state. However, feminist skepticism over the ability of the state to help women understandably heightens concern over feminist law reform efforts both in the courts and the legislatures.

Finally, despite some substantive gains in the legal treatment of women, rights claims generally have had only limited success in the courts. . . . For example, even though women's rights to reproductive choice have improved, access to those rights for poor women and especially poor women of color has not been adequately protected. More generally, even with concrete legal gains, it is not clear how the lives of most women, particularly poor women and women of color, have changed. . . .

Yet in some areas of women's rights, there have been important victories for individual women, for women as a class, and for the development of substantive legal doctrine. Public consciousness of sex discrimination in the law, for example, has increased. Looking at the gains and losses together, I believe that the strug-

gles around legal rights have moved the women's movement forward and reinforced a sense of collective experience for the moment. . . .

A Dialectical Perspective Reconsidered

What does an examination of the practice and experience of the women's rights
movement reveal about rights? Does it suggest that a dialectical approach to the
relationship between rights and politics is appropriate? I want to draw some implications for theory from the women's movement's experience with rights. . . .

The women's movement's experience with rights shows how rights emerge
from political struggle. The legal formulation of the rights grew out of and reflected feminist experience and vision and culminated in a political demand for
power. The articulation of feminist theory in practice in turn heightened feminist
consciousness of theoretical dilemmas and at the same time advanced feminist
theoretical development. This experience, reflecting the dynamic interrelationship of theory and practice, mirrored the experience of the women's movement in
general.

This analysis of the women's rights movement, shaped by an understanding of
praxis, reveals a conception of both the process through which rights are formulated as well as the content of the rights themselves. The process has been "regenerative" as rights were developed in the "middle," not at the "end," of political
dialogue. Rights were the product of consciousness-raising and were often articulated by both political activists and lawyers translating and explaining their own
experience. Further, rights asserted in the context of the women's movement enabled women to develop an individual and collective identity as women and to
understand the connection between individual and community. The articulation
of rights, then, has been a means of projecting, reflecting, and building upon a
burgeoning sense of community developing within the women's movement.

The content of these rights contained both individual and communal dimensions. A particular right did not simply benefit a particular woman, but rather
benefited women as a class. . . .

Indeed, the content of women's rights claims suggests Karst's jurisprudence of
interdependence. . . . Feminist litigation has reflected many of the aspects which
Karst discusses—creativity, experience, intuition, and the use of a broader political and social context. Perhaps the ladder of rights can, in some contexts, be
reshaped by the web of connection. Perhaps rights, in some contexts, can truly be
interdependent or at least can have interdependent dimensions.

The use of rights and legal struggle by the women's movement started the
"conversation" about women's role in society. Assertion of equal rights, reproductive rights, rights to be free from sexual harassment and battering assisted political organizing and education at least early in the women's movement. Rights discourse encouraged the articulation of feminist vision and furthered the process of

political assertion. In this sense, legal formulations of these rights laid the basis for the further articulation of women's demands. By challenging notions of equality, for example, women sought to enter the world of public citizenship. But the persistence of separate spheres of work and family divided along gender-based lines, and the tenacity of female responsibility for child rearing emerged as limitations to that world. Nonetheless this language of equality was a necessary prerequisite for the development of the different visions and strategies that the legal formulation of this problem, the debate over equal/special treatment of pregnancy, has eventually revealed.

The articulation of rights claims energized the women's movement and started the conversation. But once a right is articulated, or even won, the issues change. How will the right be applied? How will it be enforced? Women's rights have been necessary for the political development of women, particularly because they combat the privatization of women's oppression. However, rights, although they must vigorously be fought for, cannot perform the task of social reconstruction. The present economic crisis for women in this country underscores the need for a radical redefinition of social and economic responsibility and a restructuring of work and family which would transform the lives of women, particularly the many women who live in poverty. Rights, even rights which are interdependent, can only begin to help people organize themselves and identify with larger groups.

Even if one agrees that rights claims can be interdependent and that the rights claims in the women's movement have had this character, an important question remains: does the experience of rights change according to gender, culture, class, or race? Are rights asserted by a particular group at a particular time *in fact* more interdependent, or are they just perceived that way? Is the content of an interdependent right more collective than a traditional right?[27]

The experience of rights in the women's movement supports the need for a perspective on rights and politics grounded in a dialectical sensibility, a view that allows us to acknowledge both the univeral, affirming, expressive, and creative aspects of rights claims and at the same time maintain a critical impulse toward rights. We must hold on to and not seek to deny the contradictions between the possibilities and the limits of rights claim and discourse. In the women's movement, a wide range of feminist activists and commentators have participated in a broad critique of rights analysis, both on theoretical and practical levels. A common theme of these critiques has been the need to strengthen legal challenges for equal rights while at the same time not limiting our vision to a narrow conception of rights. We need to continue to strive for a political strategy that expresses a politics and vision of social reconstruction sensitive to women's real concerns. Legal strategy must be developed in the context of political strategy. It should attack formal doctrinal barriers which inhibit the recognition of the interconnectedness of women's oppression and look at the particular factual context of discrimination in shaping legal responses.

A struggle for rights can be both a vehicle of politics and an affirmation of who we are and what we seek. Rights can be what we make of them and how we use them. The experience of rights assertion in the women's movement can move us forward to a self-reflective recognition of the importance and the limitations of political and legal strategy that utilizes rights.

Notes

1. See, e.g., R. Dworkin, Taking Rights Seriously (Harvard University Press, 1977); S. Scheingold, The Politics of Rights (Yale University Press, 1974). Frank Michelman has suggested that the range of theoretical justifications advanced in support of rights indicates that "[h]owever articulated, defended, or accounted for, the sense of legal rights as claims whose realization has intrinsic value can fairly be called rampant in our culture and traditions." Michelman, The Supreme Court and Litigation Access Fees: The Right to Protect One's Own Rights (pt. 1), 1973 Duke L.J. 1153, 1177.

2. I intend the term rights discourse to encompass both rights claims and rights consciousness.

3. Lynd, Communal Rights, 62 Tex. L. Rev. 1417, 1418 (1984); see also Gabel, The Phenomenology of Rights-Consciousness and the Pact of the Withdrawn Selves, 62 Tex. L. Rev. 1563, 1577 (1984) (explaining how our self-identity is based, in large part, on individualistic nature of rights).

4. Olsen, Statutory Rape: A Feminist Critique of Rights Analysis, Part 5 herein, at 488.

5. Gabel & Kennedy, Roll Over Beethoven, 36 Stan. L. Rev. 1, 3–6 (1984); see also Gabel, Phenomenology of Rights-Consciousness, *supra* note 3, at 1582 (discussing how we give a "false concreteness" to legal concepts and rights); Tushnet, An Essay on Rights, 62 Tex. L. Rev. 1363, 1382 (1984) (discussing how we conceptualize rights as real based upon our experiences in exercise of those rights).

6. Gabel & Harris, Building Power and Breaking Images: Critical Legal Theory and the Practice of Law, 11 N.Y.U. Rev. L. & Soc. Change 369, 373 n.10 (1982–83).

7. See Gabel, Phenomenology of Rights-Consciousness, *supra* note 3, at 1573; Tushnet, Essay on Rights, *supra* note 5, at 1384.

8. Kennedy, Critical Labor Law Theory: A Comment, 4 Indus. Rel. L. J. 503, 506 (1980–81); see also Gabel & Harris, Building Power, *supra* note 6, at 376 n.13 (many lawyers on left support use of rights rhetoric to aid effective political organizing).

9. See MacKinnon, Feminism, Marxism, Method and the State: Toward Feminist Jurisprudence, Part 5 herein; Olsen, Statutory Rape: A Feminist Critique of Rights Analysis, Part 5 herein; Polan, Toward a Theory of Law and Patriarchy, Part 5 herein; Rifkin, Toward a Theory of Law and Patriarchy, Part 5 herein.

10. MacKinnon, Toward Feminist Jurisprudence, Part 5 herein, at 435.

11. See R. Bernstein, Praxis and Action 42–43 (University of Pennsylvania Press, 1971). Praxis describes "a unity of theory and action." Sparer, Fundamental Human Rights, Legal Entitlements, and the Social Struggle: A Friendly Critique

of the Critical Legal Studies Movement, 36 Stan. L. Rev. 509, 553 (1984) (footnote omitted). It is used in this essay as it was used in Sparer's "as a shorthand term for the theory-practice-social change relationship." *Id.* at 553 n.10. Karl Klare uses the term praxis in the broadest sense—"any social-world producing activity." Klare, Law-Making as Praxis, 40 Telos 123, 124 n.5 (1979).

12. Klare, Law-Making as Praxis, *supra* note 11, at 124 n.5.

13. The notion of a dialectical process is a critical aspect of feminist theory. The term dialectical and the concept of dialectic are frequently used by feminist theorists in a wide range of contexts. See, e.g., S. de Beauvoir, The Second Sex xvi–xxi (Knopf, 1952) (discussing dialectical relationship between one and other, master and slave); K. Ferguson, The Feminist Case Against Bureaucracy 197 (Temple University Press, 1984) (writing that "[a] community that recognizes the dialectical need for connectedness within freedom and for diversity within solidarity would strive to nurture the capacity for reflexive redefinition of self"); C. Gilligan, In a Different Voice 174 (Harvard University Press, 1982) (discussing the "dialectic of human development"); A. Jaggar, Feminist Politics and Human Nature 12 (Rowman and Allanheld, 1983)(discussing "the on-going and dialectical process of feminist theorizing"); E. Marks & I. de Courtivron eds., New French Feminisms: An Anthology xi–xii (Schocken, 1981)(writing that recent French feminists "take from . . . dialectics those modes of thinking that allow them to make the most connections between the oppression of women and other aspects of their culture"); Feminist Discourse, Moral Values and the Law—A Conversation, 34 Buff. L. Rev. 11, 57, 86 (1985) (comment by C. Menkel-Meadow) (discussing process of development within women's movement as "part of a much larger dialectical process where we begin with a reform, be it liberal, radical, or in some cases even conservative, and some of us unite behind it while others do not").

14. 88 Wash. 2d 221, 559 P. 2d 548 (1977). Nancy Stearns and I were co-counsel in *Wanrow* on appeal. For a fuller discussion of *Wanrow*, see Schneider, Equal Rights to Trial for Women: Sex Bias in the Law of Self-Defense, 15 Harv. C.R.-C.L. L. Rev. 623, 641–42 (1980); Schneider & Jordan, Representation of Women Who Defend Themselves in Response to Physical or Sexual Assault, 4 Women's Rts. L. Rep. 149, 156–58 (1978). . . .

15. *Wanrow*, 88 Wash. 2d at 240, 559 P. 2d at 558–59.

16. *Id.* at 240–41, 559 P. 2d at 559 (citation omitted).

17. Lynd, Communal Rights, *supra* note 3, at 1419 . . .

18. *Id.* at 1430.

19. Gilligan, In a Different Voice, *supra* note 13, at 149.

20. See Minow, Book Review, 13 Reviews in American History 240 (1985); Minow, Book Review, 98 Harv. L. Rev. 1084 (1985); Minow, Book Review, 53 Harv. Educ. Rev. 444 (1983).

21. Simon, The Invention and Reinvention of Welfare Rights, 44 Md. L. Rev. 1, 16 (1985).

22. See Karst, Women's Constitution, 1984 Duke L.J. 447, 461.

23. See Gabel, Phenomenology of Rights-Consciousness, *supra* note 3, at 1577.

24. Olsen, Statutory Rape: A Feminist Critique of Rights Analysis, Part 5 herein, at 485–86.

25. MacKinnon, Excerpts from MacKinnon/Schlafly Debate, 1 Law & Ineq. J. 341, 342 (1983). . . .

26. R. Petchesky, Abortion and Woman's Choice: The State, Sexuality, and Reproductive Freedom 7 (Northeastern University Press, 1984) (footnote omitted). Similarly, Isabel Marcus has questioned, in conversation with me, whether the language of rights is inherently too constraining. Does rights formulation make it hard for us to think beyond the language of rights and get to the task of social reconstruction? For one answer, see Olsen, Statutory Rape: A Feminist Critique of Rights Analysis, Part 5 herein [citation omitted here; originally cited at 63 Tex. L. Rev. 387, 429 n. 199. *Ed.*] ("rights . . . are devices used by feminists to deny what we really want while getting what we want indirectly"). Sylvia Law has articulated a similar feminist reaction to rights. She believes that rights can permit access to male experience but cannot do the job of social reconstruction. For example, rights, particularly those won through litigation efforts, might actually perpetuate the interrelated problems that exacerbate women's subordination, such as primary responsibility for childrearing. See Law, Rethinking Sex and the Constitution, 132 U. Pa. L. Rev. 955, 995–97 (1984). . . .

27. Important questions lurking beneath the source of this essay are whether women's experience of rights might be more interdependent than men's experience, and whether the content of rights asserted by the women's movement has been more collective. Gilligan now claims that the dichotomy of rights and care is not linked by gender; her recent work underscores that she is talking about a "different voice," not a female voice. Gilligan, Feminist Discourse, *supra* note 13, at 47. This suggests that an understanding of the dialectical relatedness of the ladder of rights and web of connection is not particular to women—it may be an aspect of an individual's or a group's experience of rights more generally.

On the other hand, some feminist theorists have argued that Gilligan's description of weblike rights is particular to women because women have a sense of self based more on connection with others than separation. See Ferguson, Feminist Case Against Bureaucracy, *supra* note 13, at 161. [S]ince women's sense of self is more closely intertwined with a sense of other, women's experience of rights may have less of an exclusively individual and more of a collective dimension. Does this suggest that women's experience of a sense of self-assertion through rights claims has a more dialectical aspect and communal dimension than men's experience? If, as Gilligan suggests, empathy, compassion, and the ability to integrate diverse needs rather than balance opposing claims are more common to women, how does this affect women's experience of legal rights?

Of course it is arguable that rights are not transformative—that even rights infused by values of the web will not be different. . . . Perhaps a more realistic and limited view of rights claims for women is that rights can only help women to assert themselves and see self and other as separate and individuated, but cannot do more. Perhaps weblike rights simply judgment that is more tolerant and less absolute.

As feminists, we want the possibilities of inclusion without the problems of self-sacrifice. We want to inform rights with feminist concerns of care and connection and use rights to protect women from too much caring. *Id.* at 171. With rights as a buffer, women's experience will not be "distorted by subordination or rendered partial by a too-great fear of loss." *Id.* at 197.

❖ PART 6

Feminist Legal Methods

❖ *Introduction*

FEMINIST METHOD signifies the manner in which feminist scholars attempt to answer the epistemological question "how do we know what we know?" (epistemology being the theory of knowledge). Feminist research methods have been the subject of interest in many academic disciplines, including anthropology, history, literature, metaphysics, sociology, and philosophy.[1] Until recently, however, little has been written about feminist methodology in the law.[2]

Feminist methodology in law owes much to the study of feminist methodology in the social sciences. Early feminist works critiqued sociological methods and their underlying assumptions.[3] So much sociological literature on feminist methodology existed that a decade ago, social scientists were able to compile a bibliography on feminist methodology.[4] From this bibliography, feminist scholars subsequently synthesized five epistemological principles.[5] These basic principles, which are equally descriptive of feminist methodology in law, include (1) the necessity of continuously and reflexively attending to the significance of gender and gender asymmetry as a basic feature of all social life, including the conduct of research; (2) the centrality of consciousness raising as a specific methodological tool and a general orientation or "way of seeing"; (3) the need to challenge the norm of objectivity that assumes that the subject and object of research can be separated from one another and that personal and/or grounded experiences are unscientific; (4) concern for the ethical implications of feminist research and recognition of the exploitation of women as objects of knowledge; and (5) emphasis on the empowerment of women and transformation of patriarchal social institutions through research.[6]

A point of departure of early feminist sociological research was the lack of relevance of traditional scientific methodology to research on issues concerning women. Sociologist Joyce Nielsen cites two illustrative studies: Freeman's study of the emergence of the women's movement and Oakley's study of the transition to motherhood.[7] Both studies challenged the traditional subject–object distance thought to be a prerequisite for objective and scientific research. These researchers demonstrated that successful research strategies depend on intense personal involvement and friendship with the subjects. This lack of relevance of traditional methods is also a theme in the writing of feminist legal scholars.

Feminist theory does not have a single methodology; several methods may be labeled "feminist methods." These methods have several characteristics. Feminist methodology has been characterized as eclectic, discouraging artificial separations of related ideas and promoting cross-disciplinary thinking that furthers its animating values.[8] Feminist research also has been described as contextual, inclusive, experiential, involved, socially relevant, multimethodological, complete but not necessarily replicable, open to the environment, and inclusive of emotions and events as experienced.[9]

Feminist social scientists, similar to feminist legal theorists, utilize methodologies that have been labeled distinctively although not uniquely feminine. In the social sciences these methods include such qualitative techniques as oral history, experiential analysis, case history, and participant observation. Social scientists argue that these qualitative techniques, which involve a closeness to the subject under study, better reflect the nature of women's experience than do more quantifiable methods.[10] Feminist legal theorists have also developed their own methodologies. Among the feminist legal methodologies are consciousness raising, storytelling, and asking the woman question. Katharine Bartlett, in her essay in this Part, explains these methodologies in more detail.

Feminist methods in general, both in law and sociology, constitute part of a larger intellectual movement that represents a shift away from long-standing methodological principles and traditions. The feminist approach to research methods rejects the positivist-empirical tradition in science. This tradition (influenced by Enlightenment beliefs and such scholars as Descartes and Kant) is based on the "scientific method" characterizing such disciplines as astronomy, biology, chemistry, and physics. It consists of an emphasis on empirical evidence, experimentation, verification, and the use of deductive logic. It is based on the fundamental assumption that through observation and measurement by an objective researcher, we can obtain reliable information about reality.

Feminist theory is part of a movement that challenges this tradition and its underlying assumptions. Feminist methods reject the scientific method and challenge the idea of a subject–object relationship that is objective and detached. In this respect, feminist research in law, as in the social sciences generally, is indebted to two traditions of thought in the social sciences: the interpretive (or hermeneutic) and the critical.[11]

The sociologist Max Weber inspired the development of the interpretive tradition. He incorporated the problem of "understanding" in his sociological approach, calling his perspective "interpretive" or "understanding" sociology.[12] Weber rejected the assumption of objectivity, claiming that it is impossible to study social phenomena without recognizing that the researcher is a human agent who attaches meaning to actions. Weber believed that although true objectivity was impossible, social scientists should strive to remain value free and not to let their biases influence their perceptions.

The phenomenologist Alfred Schutz further developed the interpretive method in the social sciences. Similar to Weber, he accepted the underlying assumption in the subjectivity of the observer. But Schutz suggested that the researcher must conduct research by suspending subjectivity. The researcher must set aside personal beliefs in order to assume the attitude of the disinterested observer. The works of Weber and Schutz provide a theoretical foundation for the development of the qualitative tradition in sociology, especially the research strategy of participant observation.[13] Much of feminist research in sociology is conducted in this research tradition and is premised on the notion of the inevitable subjectivity of research.

Another important school of thought in the social sciences that has influenced the development of feminist methods in law is critical theory, also referred to as the Frankfurt school. The Frankfurt school emerged in Germany during the 1920s and 1930s and included such members as Horkheimer, Adorno, Marcuse, and Habermas, who contributed to elaborating a critical theory of society. These scholars were concerned with the way in which social interests, conflicts, and contradictions were produced and reproduced in systems of domination.[14] Adherents to this tradition also reject the idea of an objective, neutral, disinterested perspective. They add the insight that knowledge is socially constructed; the individual's understanding of reality is influenced by both social and historical context.

Similar to the interpretive tradition, critical theorists also reject the positivist scientific model for social inquiry. The critical theoretical and interpretative traditions may be differentiated, however:

> Criticism in this tradition means more than a negative judgement; it refers to the more positive act of detecting and unmasking, or exposing, existing forms of beliefs that restrict or limit human freedom. Thus it differs from the hermeneutic tradition in its purpose. To adopt Habermas's trichotomous identification of the cognitive interests that generate the different research/knowledge traditions considered here, we can say that the positivists' goal is to predict and control, the hermeneutics' is to understand, and the critical theorists' approach is to emancipate—that is, to uncover aspects of society, especially ideologies, that maintain the status quo by restricting or limiting different groups' access to the means of gaining knowledge."[15]

Another tradition that has offered many insights to feminism and to feminist legal theory is postmodernism.[16] As Flax writes:

> As a type of postmodern philosophy, feminist theory reveals and contributes to the growing uncertainty within Western intellectual circles about the appropriate grounding and methods for explaining and/or interpreting human experience. Contemporary feminists join other postmodern philosophers in raising important metatheoretical questions about the possible nature and status of theorizing itself. . . .[17]

The term "postmodernism" is often used interchangeably with "poststructuralism" to describe the work of several influential French theorists, including Lacan, Derrida, Foucault, and Kristeva. Postmodern discourses, of which feminism is one, are termed "deconstructive"; that is, they seek to expose the social construction of beliefs concerning truth, knowledge, power, the self, and language that serve to legitimize existing structures of dominance in contemporary Western culture.[18] One basic postmodern tenet rejects humanism's concept of a self-contained, authentic human self, or "subject," with intentions, attributes, and consciousness separable from social reality.[19] From the postmodern position, as Bartlett explains in her essay in this Part, the subject itself is a social construct; the product of multiple social, historical, and cultural discourses beyond individual control.[20]

A correlative postmodern tenet rejects the possibility of a universal truth about reality; no perspective on the world can escape partiality, as each observer is situated in a particular sociopolitical historical context.[21] Thus, postmodernism removes the grounding from all systems of power or truth that claim legitimacy from external authorities.[22] According to postmodernism, no neutral process of reason or science can reveal reliable universal truths. Instead, knowledge is the result of ideological or cultural invention. Nor is there an objective language of knowledge: "rational" discourse is not neutral but rather a social construct through which certain "truths"—those which perpetuate power hierarchies—are maintained.[23]

Thus, among the contributions of postmodernism to feminist method is the understanding of the subject as a cultural product and of social discourse as an operation of power that leads to a new understanding about the construction of gender. A major postmodernist project seeks to deconstruct binary oppositions in language, law, and other institutions. Poststructuralism has been a vantage point from which feminist legal theorists have criticized the sameness–difference debate we saw in Part 4. From the postmodern perspective, all assertions of essential gender differences (whether patriarchy's negative classifications or cultural feminism's positive models) merely re-create these constructions and thereby sustain existing discourses of power. Further, and this is the significance of postmodernism for feminist legal methods, postmodernism's challenge to external, objective truths offers feminism the critical insight that law itself and the criteria for legal legitimacy are social constructs, not universal givens.[24] This insight lends new meaning to the feminist project of exposing the mechanisms of sexist oppression. Feminist theorists echo postmodernist discourses as they begin to deconstruct universalist notions of reason, knowledge, and self and reveal the hierarchical gender arrangements concealed beneath their neutral facades.[25]

The existence and nature of a distinctively feminist method is another of the many controversial debates within feminism. The debate has now reached the legal arena. Many issues emerge in a discussion of feminist methods; several of these are examined by the authors in this Part, including (1) is there an identifiable feminist approach to research? (2) what does this approach consist of? (3) how is this approach similar to and different from other ways of knowing? (4) what does feminist methodology contribute to the development of feminist theory, specifically, and to the discipline of law in general?

Some aspects of legal methods have been explored previously in this volume. For example, MacKinnon defined and discussed the importance of the method of consciousness raising for feminist theory. The relationship between method and theory also has been explored elsewhere in this volume (see Part 5). For example, MacKinnon, again, suggested that method makes a positive contribution to theory by organizing the apprehension of truth, determining what counts as evidence and defining what is taken as verification. The task for theory, she noted, is to explore the conflicts and connections between methods. And Elizabeth Schneider, in her essay in Part 5, highlighted the dialectical process between method and theory.

The essays in this Part are all concerned with various aspects of feminist methods. Mary Jane Mossman, "Feminism and Legal Method: The Difference It Makes," highlights the fact that legal method is not objective, neutral, and detached. She points out that although legal method is characterized by the opportunity for choice as to which precedents are relevant and which approach to statutory interpretation is preferred, the application of legal method is heavily influenced by social and historical context. In this regard, Mossman echoes a theme familiar to many postmodern feminist theorists who emphasize a concern for the context of the individual's perspective.

Mossman explores the relationship between feminism and legal method by identifying features of legal method in the context of two early twentieth-century cases in which women sought to be admitted to the professions in Canada. The first case involved the judicial denial of the application of Mabel French to practice law in New Brunswick in 1905. Mossman notes that the legal reasoning used to deny French's application seems inconsistent with recognized principles of legal method: a reliance on evidence, the use of precedents, and a rational conclusion supported by evidence and legal principles. Instead, she notes that the reasoning derives from the cultural and professional milieu in which the judges lived. By contrast, this judicial approach changed by the time of the "Persons" case in 1928 that permitted women entrance to public office. Mossman attributes this change to a difference in general attitudes toward women. By way of explanation, she emphasizes the existence of judicial choice in the application of precedents, choices that are not neutral but normative. In this regard, Mossman echoes a criticism of several other authors in this collection concerning the "myth of neutrality" of the law. Her essay highlights the relevance of this myth, specifically in regard to legal method.

Katherine Bartlett, in "Feminist Legal Methods," identifies and examines various methods, which include asking the woman question, feminist practical reasoning, and consciousness raising. These methods all reveal aspects that traditional legal methods ignore. Bartlett then addresses the epistemological implications of these feminist legal methods by exploring the nature of their claims to truth. Specifically, she evaluates three theories of knowledge in feminist legal writing—rational empiricism, standpoint epistemology, and postmodernism—to determine if they can generate the insights necessary to challenge existing structures of power and to reconstruct better structures.

In conclusion, Bartlett introduces a fourth approach, "positionality," which she believes provides advantages. According to Bartlett, positionality recognizes that truth is partial and provisional. It requires that other perspectives be sought and examined. It imposes obligations both to consider values that have emerged from methods of feminism and to be open to other perspectives. Instead of being a strategy that seeks to reconcile competing interests, it seeks to reconcile the existence of experience-based claims of truth with the need to question and improve these claims. Bartlett proposes positionality as a foundation for further knowledge.

Bartlett's essay is significant not only for its definition of feminist methods but also because it highlights the nature of their importance to theory and practice. As she emphasizes, by improving feminist methods, we improve feminists' ability to be engaged in the critical transformative practice of feminism. Such an improved effort will enhance the possibility of the attainment of feminist goals.

Lucinda Finley, "Breaking the Silence in Law: The Dilemma of the Gendered Nature of Legal Reasoning," examines the relationship between language, power, and the law. Her essay might be placed in the tradition of the poststructuralists who explore issues of language, knowledge and power. Finley begins by challenging the notion that law is an "objective" or "neutral" discourse. She suggests that the so-called objectivity and neutrality of the law represent the manner in which patriarchy valorizes male perspectives and experiences. She claims that the legal system, as well as legal reasoning and language, have been framed on the basis of life experiences typical to empowered males. This does not signify that the law ignores women; rather, man's understanding of women is reflected in the law.

Finley illustrates her point with numerous examples. Rape law contains man's definition of sex; labor law uses a gendered meaning of work; tort law defines injuries and measures compensation in male terms. The language of law, she adds, is a gendered language of dichotomies, oppositions and conflict. The law's approach to reproductive freedom provides an illustrative example: it characterizes the issue as one of opposing rights amid a situation of conflict.

Finley proposes a solution to the problem of the gendered nature of legal structure and discourse. She disapproves of the strategy of French feminists of creating a new language. Similarly, she rejects the idea of abandoning attempts to change the law. Instead, she proposes for feminists "a critical engagement with the nature of language"—that they try to bring more of women's perspectives, experiences, and voices into law to empower women and help legitimate their experiences. She concludes that feminist methodology must expand the traditional forms of legal discourse in order to reflect women's voices and experiences more accurately.

In her criticism of feminism, Finley's essay shares many similarities with the views of Robin West in Part I of this volume. Whereas West focuses philosophically on the law's reasoning structure, however, Finley expands the focus to explore applications of legal reasoning to various substantive areas of law. Finley also broadens the issue by suggesting solutions to the problem that she and West, among other feminist theorists, name and criticize.

The final two essays—Marie Ashe, "Zig-zag Stitching and the Seamless Web," and Patricia Williams, "On Being the Object of Property"—are examples of what Mari Matsuda terms "multiple consciousness as jurisprudential method." Matsuda, in an essay on legal method,[26] argues for the utilization of a new jurisprudential method. She proposes utilization of the multiple consciousness of outsiders (feminists and people of color) as method. Multiple consciousness as jurisprudential method stems from a deliberate choice to view the world from the standpoint of the oppressed, with all the concrete details and emotions of life under patriarchy and racial hierarchy. It criticizes the abstraction of dominant discourse, which permits legal theorists to discuss concepts such as liberty, property, and legal rights with no connection to their impact on people's real lives. The duality of multiple consciousness allows both abstraction and the details of specific knowledge to inform jurisprudence. It challenges dominant discourse's abstract concept of neutrality. By focusing on the immediate needs of outsider communities, multiple consciousness yields proposals for affirmative, nonneutral legal measures that challenge domination. Through multiple consciousness, Matsuda urges, a new and improved progressive jurisprudence will emerge.

The final two essays in this Part are also two preeminent examples of feminist narrative scholarship. Storytelling is a feminist methodology in the law that has also appeared in critical race scholarship. Narrative scholarship in general has been the focus of considerable attention in the legal literature[27] and the target of considerable criticism.[28]

Narrative scholarship has made several contributions to legal scholarship. It is extremely innovative in highlighting problems often ignored by traditional scholars. It is characterized by certain features, some of which are distinct from the use of narratives in critical race scholarship. According to a recent study by Kathryn Abrams, feminist narrative differs from critical race narratives in several ways, including its corporeality, violation of privacy-related taboos, nonlinearity, and rejection of abstract argumentation.[29] Feminist narratives examine personal experiences such as domestic violence, rape, reproduction, and childbirth and focus on aspects that typically invite discomfort or denial. They often include highly subjective accounts of body sensations. Feminist narratives start from a few premises: "a preference for particularity of description, a belief that describing events or activities 'from the inside'—that is, from the perspective of a person going through them—conveys a unique vividness of detail that can be instructive to decisionmakers."[30] These features are evident in the essays by Ashe and by Williams.

Ashe's "Zig-zag Stiching and the Seamless Web" explores the legal regulation of reproduction. Ashe's account is replete with her emotional reactions to legal cases dealing with aspects of reproductive control. Ashe's technique helps the reader understand that one's perspective about legal issues, such as the regulation of reproduction, is inevitably influenced by personal experiences such as child-birth, miscarriage, and death. Her technique helps the reader to understand the full extent of legal regulation over women's lives—not merely in extraordinary lifesaving medical procedures but even in "normal" hospitalized births. Only through jarring the reader from a posture of distance and neutrality, that is, by getting the reader to feel what the author feels, does Ashe enable the reader to gain a new perspective on reality. Ashe's work vividly makes the point that the law has been formulated on the basis of life experiences typical of white males without taking into account the experiences of women. From this vantage point, Ashe calls for legal reforms based on an empathic perspective. According to Ashe, the law must take into account the experiences of those it regulates.

Patricia Williams's essay also uses narrative as a means of focusing attention on long-ignored aspects of legal reality. Williams's focus is on what it feels like to be regulated, that is, the object of property. By the use of third-person narratives, she recounts stories of family members: an adolescent slave mother (Williams' great-great-greatgrandmother) and a cousin who was given away because of her dark skin color by a lighter-skinned mother (Williams's mother's cousin). She jux-taposes the account of the adolescent slave mother who was forced to part with her child with that of a contemporary surrogate mother. Through the creation of empathy, she vividly conveys the sense of powerlessness imposed by law over the dispossessed as a result of a contract regulating "property." Similar to Ashe, Wil-liams's accounts jar the reader from a stance of neutrality and force an identifica-tion with the objects whom the law regulates. In this manner, Williams's essay, as well as Ashe's, formulates a better vantage point from which to contemplate legal reforms—one of the goals of feminist legal theory.

Feminist methodology in law is a field in the process of becoming. To date, work is just beginning on theorizing about feminist methods in law. One hopes that such theorizing will continue and aid the development of the epistemological foundation of the discipline and that such work will contribute thereby to the transformation through research of the patriarchal nature of society and its insti-tutions.

Notes

1. See generally J. McCarl Nielsen ed., Feminist Research Methods: Exem-plary Readings in the Social Sciences (Westview Press, 1990); S. Harding &

M. Hintikka eds., Discovering Reality: Feminist Perspectives on Epistemology, Metaphysics, Methodology and Philosophy of Science (D. Reidel, 1983); Unger, Sex as a Social Reality: Field and Laboratory Research, 5 Psyc. Women Q. 645 (1981); J. Sherman and E. Beck eds., The Prism of Sex: Essays in the Sociology of Knowledge (University of Wisconsin Press, 1979).

2. Witness, for example, the following observation: "Specifically, I propose that there has been an absence—or an aborted development—in American feminist thought of the kind of epistemological inquiry which might define the soundness and legitimacy of the critical base upon which feminism poises itself." Ashe, Mind's Opportunity: Birthing a Poststructuralist Feminist Jurisprudence, 38 Syracuse L. Rev. 1129, 1150 (1987).

3. See, e.g., Bernard, My Four Revolutions: An Autobiographical History of the ASA, 78 Am. J. Soc. 773 (1973); Smith, Women's Perspective as a Radical Critique of Sociology, 44 Soc. Inquiry 7 (1974); M. Millman & R. Kanter, Editorial Introduction, in M. Millman & R. Kanter eds., Another Voice (Anchor Books, 1975).

4. Reinharz, Bombyk, & Wright, Methodological Issues in Feminist Research: A Bibliography of Literature in Women's Studies, Sociology and Psychology, 6 Women's Stud. Int. 437 (1983).

5. Cook & Fonow, Knowledge and Women's Interests: Issues of Epistemology and Methodology in Feminist Sociological Research, 56 Soc. Inquiry 2 (1986).

6. *Id.* at 5.

7. J. Freeman, The Politics of Women's Liberation (David McKay, 1975); A. Oakley, Interviewing Women: A Contradiction in Terms, in H. Roberts ed., Doing Feminist Research 30–61 (Routledge & Kegan Paul, 1981), cited in Nielsen, Feminist Research Methods, *supra* note 1, at 5–6.

8. Sherwin, Philosophical Methodology and Feminist Methodology: Are They Compatible?, in L. Code, S. Mullett & C. Overall eds., Feminist Perspectives: Philsophical Essays on Methods and Morals 13, 20 (University of Toronto Press, 1988).

9. Nielsen, Feminist Research Methods, *supra* note 1, at 6.

10. S. Reinharz, Experiential Analysis: A Contribution to Feminist Research, in G. Gowles and R. Klein eds., Theories of Women's Studies 162–91 (Routledge & Kegan Paul, 1983).

11. Nielsen makes this point in regard to the social sciences in her introduction to her collection of essays. See Nielsen, Feminist Research Methods, *supra* note 1, at 7–10.

12. H. Gerth & C. Mills, From Max Weber: Essays in Sociology 56 (Oxford University Press, 1958).

13. See generally B. Glaser & A. Strauss, The Discovery of Grounded Theory: Strategies for Qualitative Research (Aldine, 1967).

14. See generally Held, Frankfurt School, in T. Bottomore ed., A Dictionary of Marxist Thought 182–88 (Harvard University Press, 1983).

15. Nielsen, Feminist Research Methods, *supra* note 1, at 9. On the differences between the traditions, see generally R. Bernstein, Beyond Objectivism and Relativism: Science, Hermeneutics, and Praxis (University of Pennsylvania Press, 1983).

16. See generally L. Nicholson ed., Feminism/Postmodernism (Routledge, 1990), R. Tong, Feminist Thought: A Comprehensive Introduction (Westview

Press, 1989), esp. chap. 8, "Postmodern Feminism," 217–33, and the articles in the symposium at 62 U. Colo. L. Rev. 455–598 (1991).

17. Flax, Postmodernism and Gender Relations in Feminist Theory, 12 Signs 621, 624 (1987).

18. *Id.*

19. Alcoff, Cultural Feminism versus Poststructuralism: The Identity Crisis in Feminist Theory, 13 Signs 405, 415 (1988).

20. Bartlett, Feminist Legal Methods, Part 6 herein.

21. Hawkesworth, Knowers, Knowing, Known: Feminist Theory and Claims of Truth, 14 Signs 533, 536 (1989).

22. Bartlett, Feminist Legal Methods, Part 6 herein.

23. Ashe, Mind's Opportunity: Birthing a Poststructuralist Feminist Jurisprudence, 38 Syracuse L. Rev. 1129, 1158 (1987).

24. Bartlett, Feminist Legal Methods, Part 6 herein.

25. Flax, Postmodernism, *supra* note 17, at 626.

26. Matsuda, When the First Quail Calls: Multiple Consciousness as Jurisprudential Method, 11 Women's Rt. L. Rep. 7 (1989).

27. See, e.g., the symposia on legal storytelling in 87 Mich. L. Rev. 2073 (1989), and the debate about the use of race narratives in Kennedy, Racial Critiques of Legal Academia, 102 Harv. L. Rev. 1745 (1989) and Delgado, When a Story Is Just a Story: Does Voice Really Matter? 76 Va. L. Rev. 95 (1990). See generally Abrams, Hearing the Call of Stories, 79 Calif. L. Rev. 971 (1991).

28. Abrams, Hearing the Call, *supra* note 27, at 977–80. Abrams identifies various objections to narrative scholarship as a legal methodology, including (1) the lack of normative legal content; (2) the lack of reliability through its rejection of neutrality; and (3) the lack of generalizability, which militates against this scholarship as the basis for legal change.

29. *Id.* at 974 n.10.

30. *Id.* at 982.

Feminism and Legal Method: The Difference It Makes

MARY JANE MOSSMAN

. . . To WHAT EXTENT can feminist theory impact, if at all, on the structure of legal inquiry? . . .

Feminism's quest for an understanding of the nature of men and women demands a reassessment of the structure of our inquiry. Not only are the answers subject to scrutiny, but also the way in which we search for them. In challenging the validity of "facts," the possibility of "neutrality" and the equity of the "conclusions" which result from such analysis, the feminist perspective directs its attention to our "ways of knowing" about men and women as well as to our efforts to seek greater equality for women. Such a quest, moreover, may require new methods of inquiry. . . .

. . . Traditionally, legal method has operated within a highly structured framework which offers little opportunity for fundamental questioning about the *process* of defining the issues, selecting relevant principles, and excluding irrelevant ideas. In this context, decision-making takes place according to a form which usually "sees" present questions according to patterns established in the past, and in a context in which ongoing consistency in ideas may be valued more often than their future vitality.

To explore this relationship between feminism and legal method, I decided to try to identify the features of legal method in practice, and to do so in the context of "women's rights" cases, in which the claims being asserted might be expected to reflect feminist ideas and objectives. . . .

Women, Difference and Legal Method

A few years before the nineteenth century drew to a close, Clara Brett Martin was admitted to the practice of law in Ontario; she was the first woman to become a lawyer in the British Commonwealth.[1] Her petition for admission was initially

---

3 Aust. J. Law & Soc'y 30 (1986).

denied by the Law Society because there were no precedents for admitting women to the practice of law. However, in 1892 a legislative amendment was passed permitting women to practice as solicitors; three years later, another legislative amendment similarly permitted women to practice as barristers.[2] . . .

Because of admission arrangements in Ontario, the Law Society of Upper Canada, rather than the superior court, reviewed Clara Brett Martin's entitlement to admission as a lawyer. By contrast, a court in the Province of New Brunswick reviewed Mabel French's[3] admission to legal practice in 1905. When her application was presented to the court, the judges denied it unanimously, stating there were no precedents for the admission of women as lawyers. In the next year, however, after the enactment of a legislative amendment, Mabel French was admitted to legal practice in New Brunswick.[4] The same pattern (judicial denial of the application followed by legislative amendment) occurred again some years later when she applied for admission by transfer to the legal profession in British Columbia, and in a number of the other Canadian provinces when women applied to be admitted to practice as lawyers.

In contrast to cases in which women sought to enter the legal profession and were denied admission by the courts, the *Persons* case[5] provided that the Governor General "shall . . . summon qualified Persons to the Senate." . . . Even though the language of the section was gender-neutral, no woman in Canada had ever been summoned to become a senator.

The Supreme Court of Canada in 1928 . . . concluded that women were not "persons" and therefore were not eligible to become Senators. On appeal to the Privy Council the next year, the decision was reversed. Ironically, it was in the Privy Council, and not in the indigenous courts of Canada, that the claim of "equal rights of women" to participate in public life was successful.

The decisions in these cases offer an interesting historical picture of legal process in the cultural milieu of the early twentieth century. In the cases about the admission of women to the legal profession, judges accepted the idea that there was a difference between men and women, a difference which "explained" and "justified" the exclusion of women from the legal profession. However, the Privy Council's decision in the *Persons* case completely discounted any such difference in relation to the participation of women in public life.

Why were there differing approaches to these claims: was it the nature of the claims, the type of court in which the claims were presented, or the time and context of the decisions? More significantly, what can we learn from the reasoning in these cases about the nature of legal method, especially in the context of challenges to deeply held beliefs, vested interests, and the status quo? In other words, what do these cases suggest about the potential impact of feminism on legal method?

The Idea of Difference

Mabel French's case in New Brunswick provides a good illustration of judicial decision-making regarding women in law. . . . The court decided that women were not eligible for admission to legal practice. The argument proceeded on a number of different levels. For example, Mr. Justice Tuck was concerned about the long-term implications of a decision allowing women to become lawyers. . . . Mr. Justice Tuck [explained]:

> If I dare to express my own views I would say that I have no sympathy with the opinion that women should in all branches of life come in competition with men. Better let them attend to their own legitimate business.[6]

It seems likely that he would have agreed with the views expressed by Mr. Justice Barker in the case. Relying on the decision of the United States Supreme Court in Bradwell v. Illinois in 1873,[7] Mr. Justice Barker adopted as his own the "separate spheres" doctrine enunciated there. . . .

The language of the *Bradwell* decision expressed very clearly an unqualified acceptance of the idea of difference between men and women, a difference which was social as well as biological. It is significant, however, that no evidence was offered for the assertions about the "timidity and delicacy" of women in general; no authorities were cited for the existence of "divine law" . . . , and no studies were examined in support of the conclusion that the domestic sphere belonged "properly" to women (and vice versa). . . .

The legal reasoning used by Mr. Justice Barker does not seem consistent with the recognized principles of legal method: the reliance on relevant and persuasive evidence to determine facts, the use of legal precedents to provide a framework for analysis and a rational conclusion supported by both evidence and legal principles. Yet, if Mr. Justice Barker's ideas are not the product of legal method, what is their source?

The answer, of course, seems to be that the ideas he expressed were those prevailing in the cultural and professional milieu in which he lived. The ideas of mainstream religion, for example, emphasized the differences between men and women. Moreover, even when women and men were regarded as equal in the eyes of God (in the ideas of reformers such as Calvin, for example), women were still treated as subordinate to men, their subordination reflecting:

> . . . the divinely created social order by which God has ordained the rule of some and the subjugation of others: rulers over subjects, masters over servants, husbands over wives, parents over children.[8]

The idea of a divinely created "social office" in the religious tradition, which required women and men to perform quite different social roles, was reinforced by secular ideas in philosophy in which the role of the family defined women's roles. . . .[9] Even John Stuart Mill, who was well known for his progressive views about the rights of women, considered that equal rights to education, political life, and the professions could be granted only to single women who did not have family responsibilities. . . .

It is significant in Mabel French's case . . . that the court uncritically accepted ideas from the mainstreams of religion, philosophy, and science as if they were factual rather than conceptual. Moreover, in accepting those ideas and making them an essential part of his decision, Mr. Justice Barker provided an explicit and very significant reinforcement of the idea of gender-based difference. In this way, the particular decision to deny Mabel French's claim to practice law had an impact which was felt well beyond the instant case. Thereafter, in the law, as well as in other intellectual traditions, there was established a recognized and "legitimate" difference between women and men.[10]

Two other points must also be mentioned. It is significant to an assessment of legal method that the ideas about the role of women, first expressed in [*Bradwell*], were adopted unquestioningly over thirty years later in French's case in 1905. That the court apparently did not question the appropriateness of applying a precedent from an earlier generation, and from a foreign jurisdiction, seems remarkable. . . .

The *Bradwell* decision also relied in part on the inability of married women to enter into contracts because of the common law disability that was still in existence in 1873. Mr. Justice Barker might have commented on the fact that married women's property legislation, both in Canada and in the United States, had erased most of the disabilities in 1905. This fact would have provided an additional reason for distinguishing rather than following *Bradwell*. . . .

More fundamentally, the ideas accepted in *Bradwell* and restated in *French* were quite inconsistent, and probably known to be so by the judges, with the reality of "women's work" outside the home at the turn of the century. In Canada, as well as in Great Britain:

> Very few of the women whom the judges knew, whether they were litigants, or cleaners of the courtroom, or servants in the home, actually corresponded in any way to the judicial representation. At the time when judges were speaking, more than a million unmarried women alone were employed in industry, while a further three quarters of a million were in domestic service. . . . For the great majority of Victorian women, as for the great majority of Victorian men, life was characterized by drudgery and poverty rather than by refinement and decorum.[11]

Despite this reality, Mr. Justice Barker reiterated without criticism or qualification the authoritative statement from *Bradwell*:

> The paramount destiny and mission of women are to fulfill the noble and benign offices of wife and mother. This is the law of the Creator. And the rules of civil society must be adapted to the general constitution of things. . . .[12]

The conflict between the judicial description of all women, and the known conditions in which at least some of them lived at that time, suggests a further element of legal method: its abstraction from the "real" lives of women. Indeed, what seems evident is a willingness to use the ideas of (male) theologians, philosophers and scientists as the basis of "reality" in preference to the facts of life in the lives of actual women.

The judicial approach evident in *French* changed significantly, however, by the time of the *Persons* case. There is little mention in that case of gender-based difference in the analysis of either the Supreme Court of Canada or the Privy Council. . . .

Nothing in the judgments of the Supreme Court of Canada reflects the rhetoric and ideas expressed by Mr. Justice Barker in Mabel French's case. Indeed, by contrast, Lord Sankey commenced his opinion in the Privy Council by stating:

> The exclusion of women from all public offices is a relic of days more barbarous than ours, but it must be remembered that the necessity of the times often forced on man customs which in later years were not necessary.[13]

His words suggested a clear signal that, although the treatment of women in the past may have been understandable in the context of those times, the world had changed.

In the *Persons* case, the quote above is the only reference to the difference between men and women. The contrast between the reliance on gender-based difference as incontrovertible fact in *French* at the turn of the century, and the virtual absence of such ideas in the *Persons* case in the late 1920s, is highly insignificant. It offers an explanation for the differing outcomes in the two cases: when difference was emphasized in *French*, women were excluded from membership in the legal profession; when it was discounted as in the *Persons* case, women were included with men in the opportunities to participate in public life.

This approach to the case . . . suggests that the dictates of legal methods were not strictly followed by the judges in their decision-making process. In addition, it is necessary to assess the legal method actually described by the judges in the cases. The contrast between what they said they were doing and what they actually did also offers some important insights into legal method. . . .

The Principles of Legal Method

The stated reasons in these cases were consistent with well-established principles of legal method. The principles can be analyzed in terms of three aspects: (1) the characterization of the issues; (2) the choice of legal precedent to decide the validity of the women's claims; and (3) the process of statutory interpretation, especially in determining the effect of statutes to alter common law principles. Both the principles themselves and their application to these specific claims are important for an understanding of the potential impact of feminism on legal method.

Characterizing the Issue

In both the *French* case and the *Persons* case, the judges consistently characterized the legal issues as narrowly as possible, eschewing their "political" or "social" significance, and explaining that the court was interested only in the law. . . .

Clearly evident in these judicial statements is a felt need to distance the court from the "political" or moral issue, and a desire to be guided only by neutral principles of interpretation in relation to abstract legal concepts. The justices' confidence in the principles of legal method as a means of deciding the issue, even confined so narrowly, is also evident. . . .

Just as clearly, the women claimants never intended to bring to the court a "neutral" legal issue for determination; they petitioned the court to achieve their objectives, and their goals were evidently "political" ones. Yet the court expressed the views of judicial process as neutral interpretation. More significantly, the court's power to define the "real issues" carried with it an absence of responsibility on the part of the male judges for any negative outcome. It was the law, rather than the male person interpreting it, which was responsible. The result of the characterization process, therefore, is to reinforce the law's detachment and neutrality rather than its involvement and responsibility; and to extend these characteristics beyond law itself to judges and lawyers involved as well.

Yet, it is difficult to accommodate this characterization of detachment and neutrality with the opinions expressed, especially in *French*, about the roles of women. The ideas about gender-based differences expressed forcefully by Mr. Justice Barker in that case appear very close to an expression about the "desirability" of women lawyers and are not merely dispassionate and neutral in their application of legal precedents. Thus, at least in *French*, there is an inconsistency between the legal method declared by the judges to be appropriate, and the legal method actually adopted in their decision-making. In this context, the idea of detachment and neutrality both masks and legitimates their personal views about women's "proper" sphere.

Using Precedents in the Common Law Tradition

The existence of women's common law disability was regularly cited in both these cases as the reason for denying the claimant's admittance to the legal profession and participation in public life. . . .

At the end of the nineteenth century, of course, women (especially married women) suffered disabilities at common law in a number of respects: married women were denied the right to hold interests in property until the married women's property statutes,[14] and all women were denied the right to vote until the twentieth century. Courts regularly asserted that, because of women's common law disabilities, there were no precedents for admitting women to the legal profession or to full participation in public life. . . .

From a broader perspective, moreover, this difficulty epitomizes the negative effects of the doctrine of precedent on newly emerging claims to legal rights. If a precedent is required in order to uphold a claim, only existing claims will receive legal recognition. The doctrine of precedent thus becomes a powerful tool for maintaining the status quo and for rationalizing the denial of new claims. Seen in this light, the law itself is an essential means of protecting the status quo, notwith-standing the challenge of feminist ideas.

However, if this conclusion is correct, how can the Privy Council's decision be understood? It was a decision which did not utilize the doctrine of precedent as had its predecessors. After canvassing the precedents, Lord Sankey stated:

> The fact that no woman had served or has claimed to serve such an office is not of great weight when it is remembered that custom would have prevented the claim being made or the point being contested. Customs are apt to develop into traditions which are stronger than law and remain un-challenged long after the reason for them has disappeared. The appeal of history therefore in this particular matter is not conclusive.[15]

Obviously, the Privy Council in the *Persons* case was less concerned with the absence of precedent in their decision-making than the judges in *French*. Is the Privy Council's approach simply an early example of a court of highest jurisdiction deciding not to be bound by precedent in certain cases, or is there some other explanation?

One suggestion is that the decision of the Privy Council in 1929 simply reflected the spirit of the times in relation to the role of women. Much had indeed changed since Clara Brett Martin and Mabel French had sought admission to the legal profession at the turn of the century. As was noted earlier, there had been legislation enabling married women to enter into contracts and to hold interests in property even before the end of the nineteenth century. In the early part of the twentieth century, moreover, women had participated actively in World War I; and they had attained suffrage in many jurisdictions after the war. . . .

At the same time, if this explanation is accepted, it is difficult to account for the differences in perspective of the judges of the Supreme Court of Canada in 1928 from those in the Privy Council in 1929. . . . What, then, is the explanation for these differing perspectives of the justices and the different outcomes that resulted in the two courts?

In terms of the legal method described by the judges, of course, there is no answer to this question. Neither the judgments in the Supreme Court of Canada nor Lord Sankey's opinion in the Privy Council expressly consider at all the realities of women's experiences of the time, and they specifically do not consider the realities of experience for the actual women claimants in the *Persons* case. Thus, even if the judges' perspectives on women's place were different in the two courts, there is virtually nothing in their judgments expressly reflecting them. For this reason, it is impossible to demonstrate that Lord Sankey's differing perspective was the reason for the different outcome in the Privy Council. At the same time, however, it is hard to find any other convincing explanation.

What does seem clear is the existence of judicial choice in the application of precedents. In the process of choosing earlier cases and deciding that they are binding precedents, the judges were making choices about the aspects of the cases which were "relevant" and "similar," choices which were not neutral but normative. In suggesting that the earlier decisions (relied on by the Supreme Court of Canada as binding precedents) were not determinative, Lord Sankey was declaring that the precedents should not be regarded as exactly the same as the situation before the court in the *Persons* case. In this way, Lord Sankey's decision demonstrates the availability of choice in the selection of facts, in the categorization of principles and in the determination of relevance. At the same time, his opinion completely obscures the process and standards which guided the choice he actually made. To the myth of "neutrality," therefore, Lord Sankey adds the "mystery" of choice.

Interpreting Statutes and Parliament's Intent

The interpretation of the law relating to women's claims was complicated by the need for judges to construe statutes as well as take account of the common law principles. In some earlier cases, for example, women had challenged their exclusion from statutory rights when statutory language referred only to "men." Such claims were based on earlier legislation in England which provided that "words importing the masculine gender should be deemed and taken to include females, unless the contrary was clearly expressed." . . .

Even in the statutes which used gender-neutral language, however, there were problems of statutory interpretation in cases which challenged male exclusivity. The legislation reviewed in the *Persons* case, as well as in the cases of both Clara Brett Martin and Mabel French, used the word "person" in describing the qualifications for appointment to the Senate and admission to legal practice, respectively. . . .

The Canadian judges uniformly interpreted the word "person" in a way that seemed most consistent with their time and experiences. For them, it was radical indeed to think of a woman in public office or in the legal profession, and their interpretation of the statutory language reflected their own understanding of what Parliament might have "intended," had Parliament considered the matter explicitly. . . .

Once again, however, the opinion of the Privy Council is different. After reviewing at some length the legislative provisions of the B.N.A. Act, Lord Sankey stated:

> The word "person" . . . may include members of both sexes, and to those who ask why the word should include females, the obvious answer is why should it not? In these circumstances the burden is upon those who deny that the word includes women to make out their case.[16]

No precedent was cited to support this presumption in favor of the most extensive meaning of the statutory language, even though it expressly contradicted the principles of statutory interpretation adopted in the decision of the Supreme Court of Canada.

In the end, just as the Privy Council decision was puzzling in relation to the effect of legal precedents about women's common law disabilities, it is also difficult to reconcile Lord Sankey's conclusions about the interpretation of the statute to the principles and precedents accepted in the Supreme Court of Canada. Clearly, the Privy Council departed from the Supreme Court's approach to legal method in reaching its conclusion to admit the women's claims. It is less clear how we should identify Lord Sankey's reasons for doing so.

In this context, what conclusion is appropriate in discerning feminism's potential for perspective transforming in the context of legal method?

Feminism and Legal Method

The analyses of these cases illustrates quite well the structure of inquiry identified as legal method. First of all, legal method defines its own boundaries. Questions which are inside the defined boundaries can be addressed, but those outside the boundaries are not "legal" issues, regardless of their importance to "politics" or "morals," etc. Thus, the question of women becoming lawyers or senators was simply a matter of interpreting the law; it did not require any consideration of utility or benefit to the women themselves or to society in general. The purpose and the result of the boundary-defining exercise are to confer "neutrality" on the law and on its decision-makers. In so doing, the process also relieves both the law and its decision-makers of accountability for unjust or just decisions. . . .

More sinister than this boundary-defining exercise is the potential for judicial attitudes to be expressed, and to be used in decision-making (either explicitly or implicitly), when there is no "objective" evidence to support them. Because of the myth of neutrality which surrounds the process, such attitudes may acquire legitimacy in a way that strengthens and reinforces ideas in "politics" and "morals" which were supposedly outside the law's boundary. After the decision in *French*, for example, women were different as a matter of law, and not just in the minds of people like Mr. Justice Barker. . . .

Second, legal method defines "relevance" and accordingly excludes some ideas while admitting others. Some facts, such as inherent gender-based traits, were regarded as relevant in *French*, for example, while in both *French* and the *Persons* case the actual conditions in which women lived their lives were not relevant at all. Clearly relevant in both cases, however, were earlier decisions about similar circumstances from which the judges could abstract principles of general application. That all of the earlier cases had been decided by men, who were interpreting legislation drafted when women had no voting rights, was completely irrelevant to the decision-making . . . even though the cases represented direct and significant challenges to the continuation of gender-exclusive roles. . . . The irony of solemn judicial reliance on precedents that excluded women, in the context of significant efforts by women to change the course of history, underlines the significant role of legal method in preserving the status quo.

Finally, the case analyses demonstrate the opportunity for choice in legal method: choice as to which precedents are relevant and which approach to statutory interpretation is preferred; and choice as to whether the ideas of the mainstream or those of the margins are appropriate. The existence of choice in legal method offered some possibility of positive outcomes in the women's rights cases. . . . Lord Sankey's opinion in the Privy Council is an example of choice in legal method which is as remarkable for its common sense as it is for its distinctiveness in legal method. Because Lord Sankey obscured the reasons for his choice, however, he also preserved the power and mystery of legal method. . . .

That legal method is structured in such a way that it is impervious to a feminist perspective is a sobering conclusion. Within the women's movement, it has important consequences for the design of strategies to achieve legal equality. It suggests, for example, the general futility of court action for achieving significant change in women's rights, even though litigation of women's claims may be useful to monitor interpretation by courts or to focus attention on legal problems. . . .

Such a critique exposes the structural barriers within the law that prevent [a woman's] voice from being heard. It also suggests the importance of law in reinforcing patriarchal norms, and implicitly denies the possibility that feminism can transform the perspective of legal method, at least in the absence of changes in women's real political power.

Taking this conclusion seriously, as I think we must, leads to some significant conclusions. . . . It is simply not enough just to introduce women's experience into the curriculum or to examine the feminist approach to legal issues, although both of these activities are important. There is no solution . . . to confront the reality that gender and power are inextricably linked in the legal method we use in our work, our discourse, and our study, especially because there is so much resistance in legal method itself to ideas that challenge the status quo. Honestly confronting the barriers of our conceptual framework may at least permit us to begin to ask more searching and important questions. . . .

Notes

1. Martin was admitted to practice in 1897 as a barrister and solicitor. For an excellent account of her efforts to become a lawyer, see Backhouse, "To Open the Way for Others of My Sex"; Clara Brett Martin's Career as Canada's First Woman Lawyer, 1 Can. J. Women & Law 1 (1985).

2. . . . See 55 V. ch. 32, § 1 (1892) (admission of women as solicitors); 58 V. ch. 27, § 1 (1985) (admission as barristers-at-law); and S.O. 1970, ch. 19 (admission of persons). . . .

3. In re French, 37 N.B.R. [New Brunswick Reports] 359 (1905).

4. 6 Ed. VII chap. 5 (1906). Some of the story of French's attempts to gain admission appears in A. Watts, History of the Legal Profession in British Columbia 1869–1984, 133–35 (Law Society of British Columbia, 1984). . . .

5. Reference re Meaning of the Word "Persons" in § 24 of the B.N.A. Act, S.C.R. [Supreme Court Reports] 276 (1928); Edwards v. A.G. for Canada, A.C. 124 (1930).

6. In re French, 37 N.B.R. [New Brunswick Reports] 359, at 361–62.

7. 16 Wall. 130 (1872).

8. See R. Reuther, Sexism and God-Talk: Toward a Feminist Theology 98 (Beacon, 1983). . . .

9. See S. Okin, Women in Western Political Thought (Princeton University Press, 1979).

10. This point is important in relation to arguments about the legitimating force of the law. See, for example, K. O'Donovan, Before and After: The Impact of Feminism on the Academic Discipline of Law in D. Spender ed., Men's Studies Modified: The Impact of Feminism on the Academic Disciplines (Pergamon, 1981), chap. 1.

11. A. Sachs and J. Wilson, Sexism and the Law (Martin Robertson, 1978), at 54. See also S. Mann Trofimenkoff and A. Prentice, The Neglected Majority: Essays in Canadian History (McClelland & Stewart, 1977).

12. In re French, 37 N.B.R. [New Brunswick Reports], at 366.

13. Edwards v. A.G., *supra* note 5, at 128.

14. There are several monographs analyzing the process of matrimonial property reform on both sides of the Atlantic in the latter half of the nineteenth century; for example, see L. Holcombe, Wives and Property: Reform of the Married Women's Property Law in Nineteenth-Century England (University of Toronto Press, 1983); N. Basch, In the Eyes of the Law: Women, Marriage and Property in Nineteenth-Century New York (Cornell University Press, 1982); and E. Griffith, In Her Own Right: The Life of Elizabeth Cady Stanton (Oxford University Press, 1984).

15. Edwards v. A.G., *supra* note 5, at 134.

16. *Id.* at 138.

❖ *Feminist Legal Methods*

Katharine T. Bartlett

In what sense can legal methods be "feminist"? Are there specific methods that feminist lawyers share? If so, what are these methods, why are they used, and what significance do they have to feminist practice? Put another way, what do feminists mean when they say they are doing law,[1] and what do they mean when, having done law, they claim to be "right"?

Feminists have developed extensive critiques of law and proposals for legal reform. Feminists have had much less to say, however, about what the "doing" of law should entail and what truth status to give to the legal claims that follow. These methodological issues matter because methods shape one's view of the possibilities for legal practice and reform. Method "organizes the apprehension of truth; it determines what counts as evidence and defines what is taken as verification."[2] Feminists cannot ignore method, because if they seek to challenge existing structures of power with the same methods that have defined what counts within those structures, they may instead "recreate the illegitimate power structures [that they are] trying to identify and undermine."[3]

Method matters also because without an understanding of feminist methods, feminist claims in the law will not be perceived as legitimate. . . . Feminists have tended to focus on defending their various substantive positions or political agendas. . . . Greater attention to issues of method may help to anchor these defenses, to explain why feminist agendas often appear so radical (or not radical enough), and even to establish some common ground among feminists.

As feminists articulate their methods, they can become more aware of the nature of what they do, and thus do it better. . . .

Feminist Doing in Law

When feminists "do law," they do what other lawyers do: they examine the facts of a legal issue or dispute, they identify the essential features of those facts, they

---

103 Harv. L. Rev. 829 (1990).

determine what legal principles should guide the resolution of the dispute, and they apply those principles to the facts. . . . [F]eminists . . . use a full range of methods of legal reasoning—deduction, induction, analogy, and use of hypotheticals, policy, and other general principles.

In addition to these conventional methods of doing law, however, feminists use other methods. . . .

Asking the Woman Question

A question becomes a method when it is regularly asked. Feminists across many disciplines regularly ask a question . . . known as "the woman question,"[4] which is designed to identify the gender implications of rules and practices which might otherwise appear to be neutral or objective. . . .

. . . In law, asking the woman question means examining how the law fails to take into account the experiences and values that seem more typical of women than of men, for whatever reason, or how existing legal standards and concepts might disadvantage women. The question assumes that some features of the law may be not only nonneutral in a general sense, but also "male" in a specific sense. The purpose of the woman question is to expose those features and how they operate, and to suggest how they might be corrected.

Women have long been asking the woman question in law. The legal impediments associated with being a woman were, early on, so blatant that the question was not so much whether women were left out, but whether the omission was justified by women's different roles and characteristics. American women such as Elizabeth Cady Stanton and Abigail Adams may seem today all too modest and tentative in their demands for improvements in women's legal status. Yet while social stereotypes and limited expectations for women may have blinded women activists in the eighteenth and nineteenth centuries, their demands for the vote, for the right of married women to make contracts and own property, for other marriage reforms, and for birth control challenged legal rules and social practices that, to others in their day, constituted the God-given plan for the human race.

Within the judicial system, Myra Bradwell was one of the first to ask the woman question when she asked why the privileges and immunities of citizenship did not include, for married women in Illinois, eligibility for a state license to practice law.[5] The opinion of the United States Supreme Court in *Bradwell*'s case evaded the gender issue, but Justice Bradley in his concurring opinion set forth the "separate spheres" legal ideology underlying the Illinois law. . . . Women, and sometimes employers, continued to press the woman question in challenges to sex-based maximum work-hour legislation, other occupation restrictions, voting limitations, and jury-exemption rules. The ideology, however, proved extremely resilient.

Not until the 1970s did the woman question begin to yield different answers about the appropriateness of the role of women assumed by law. The shift began in 1971 with the Supreme Court's ruling on a challenge by Sally Reed to an Idaho statute that gave males preference over females in appointments as estate administrators.[6] Although the Court in *Reed* did not address the separate spheres ideology directly, it rejected arguments of the state that "men [are] as a rule more conversant with business affairs than . . . women,"[7] to find the statutory preference arbitrary and thus in violation of the equal protection clause. This decision was followed by a series of other successful challenges by women arguing that beneath the protective umbrella of the separate spheres ideology lay assumptions that disadvantage women in material significant ways.

Although the United States Supreme Court has come to condemn explicitly the separate spheres ideology when revealed by gross, stereotypical distinctions, the Court majority has been less sensitive to the effects of more subtle sex-based classifications that affect opportunities for and social views about women. The Court ignored, for example, the implications for women of a male-only draft registration system in reserving combat as a male-only activity.[8] Similarly, in upholding a statutory rape law that made underage sex a crime of males and not of females, the Court overlooked the way in which assumptions about male sexual aggression and female sexual passivity construct sexuality in limiting and dangerous ways.[9]

Pregnancy has been a special problem. . . . Although feminists have split over whether women have more to lose than to gain from singling out pregnancy for different, some would say "favored," treatment, they agree on the critical question: what are the consequences for women of specific rules or practices?

Feminists today ask the woman question in many areas of law. They ask the woman question in rape cases when they ask why the defense of consent focuses on the perspective of the defendant and what he "reasonably" thought the woman wanted, rather than the perspective of the woman and the intentions she "reasonably" thought she conveyed to the defendant. Women ask the woman question when they ask . . . why the conflict between work and family responsibilities in women's lives is seen as a private matter for women to resolve within the family rather than a public matter involving restructuring of the workplace. . . . Asking the woman question reveals the ways in which political choice and institutional arrangement contribute to women's subordination. Without the woman question, differences associated with women are taken for granted and, unexamined, may serve as justification for laws that disadvantage women. The woman question reveals how the position of women reflects the organization of society rather than the inherent characteristics of women. As many feminists have pointed out, difference is located in relationships and social institutions—the workplace, the family, clubs, sports, childrearing patterns, and so on—not in women themselves. In exposing the hidden effects of laws that do not explicitly discriminate on the basis of sex, the woman question helps to demonstrate how social structures embody norms that implicitly render women different and thereby subordinate.

Once adopted as a method, asking the woman question is a method of critique as integral to legal analysis as determining the precedential value of a case, stating the facts, or applying law to facts. "Doing law" as a feminist means looking beneath the surface of law to identify the gender implications of rules and the assumptions underlying them and insisting upon applications of rules that do not perpetuate women's subordination. It means recognizing that the woman question always has potential relevance and that "tight" legal analysis never assumes gender neutrality. . . .

Feminist Practical Reasoning

Some feminists have claimed that women approach the reasoning process differently than men do. In particular, they say that women are more sensitive to situation and context, that they resist universal principles and generalizations, especially those that do not fit their own experiences, and that they believe that "the practicalities of everyday life" should not be neglected for the sake of abstract justice. Whether these claims can be empirically sustained, this reasoning process has taken on normative significance for feminists, many of whom have argued that individualized factfinding is often superior to the application of bright-line rules, and that reasoning from context allows a greater respect for difference and for the perspectives of the powerless. . . .

As a form of legal reasoning, practical reasoning has many meanings invoked in many contexts for many different purposes. I present a version of practical reasoning in this section that I call "feminist practical reasoning." This version combines some aspects of a classic Aristotelian model of practical deliberation with a feminist focus on identifying and taking into account the perspectives of the excluded. . . .

Feminist practical reasoning builds upon the traditional mode of practical reasoning by bringing to it the critical concerns and values reflected in other feminist methods, including the woman question. The classical exposition of practical reasoning takes for granted the legitimacy of the community whose norms it expresses, and for that reason tends to be fundamentally conservative. Feminist practical reasoning challenges the legitimacy of the norms of those who claim to speak, through rules, for the community. No form of legal reasoning can be free, of course, from the past or from community norms, because law is always situated in a context of practices and values. Feminist practical reasoning differs from other forms of legal reasoning, however, in the strength of its commitment to the notion that there is not one, but many overlapping communities to which one might look for "reason." Feminists consider the concept of community problematic,[10] because they have demonstrated that law has tended to reflect existing structures of power. Carrying over their concern for inclusionism from the method of asking the woman question, feminists insist that no one community is legitimately privileged to speak for all others. Thus, feminist methods reject the monolithic community often assumed in male accounts of practical reasoning, and seek to identify perspectives not represented in the dominant culture from which reason should proceed.

Feminist practical reasoning, however, is not the polar opposite of a "male" deductive model of legal reasoning. The deductive model assumes that for any set of acts, fixed, preexisting legal rules compel a single, correct result. [V]irtually no one, male or female, now defends the strictly deductive approach to legal reasoning. Contextualized reasoning is also not . . . the polar opposite of a "male" model of abstract thinking. All major forms of legal reasoning encompass processes of both contextualization and abstraction. . . .

. . . [F]eminist methods require the process of abstraction, that is, the separation of the significant from the insignificant. Concrete facts have significance only if they represent some generalizable aspect of the case. Generalizations identify what matters and draw connections to other cases. . . . For feminists, practical reasoning and asking the woman question may make more facts relevant or "essential" to the resolution of a legal case than would more nonfeminist legal analysis. . . .

Similarly, the feminist method of practical reasoning is not the polar opposite of "male" rationality. The process of finding commonalities, differences, and connections in practical reasoning is a rational process. To be sure, feminist practical reasoning gives rationality new meanings. Feminist rationality acknowledges greater diversity in human experiences and the value of taking into account competing or inconsistent claims. It openly reveals its positional partiality by stating explicitly which moral and political choices underlie that partiality, and recognizes its own implications for the distribution and exercise of power.[11] Feminist rationality also strives to integrate emotive and intellectual elements and to open up the possibilities of new situations rather than limit them with prescribed categories of analysis. Within these revised meanings, however, feminist method is and must be understandable. It strives to make more sense of human experience, not less, and is to be judged upon its capacity to do so.

Applying the Method. Although feminist practical reasoning could apply to a wide range of legal problems, it has its clearest implications where it reveals insights about gender exclusion within existing legal rules and principles. . . .

[One] example is the 1981 New Jersey Supreme Court case, State v. Smith.[12] In rejecting the defendant's marital-exemption defense in a criminal prosecution for rape, the court engaged in a multi-layered process of reasoning; it examined the history of the exemption, the strength and evolution of the common law authority, the various justifications offered by the state for the exemption, the surrounding social and legal context in which the defendant asserted the defense, and the particular actions of the defendant in this case that gave rise to the prosecution. . . .

The *Smith* case . . . illustrates how practical reasoning respects, but does not blindly adhere to, legal precedent. In contrast to courts that have followed more formalistic approaches, the *Smith* court saw itself as an active participant in the formulation of legal authority. Without ignoring the importance to law of consistency and tradition, the court took an approach sensitive to the human factors that a more mechanical application of precedent might ignore.

Although the *Smith* case illustrates some of the attributes of a highly contextual, pragmatic approach to decisionmaking, feminist practical reasoning would pursue some elements further than the court did. For example, feminist practical reasoning would more explicitly identify the perspective of the woman whose interest a marital rape exemption entirely subordinates to that of her estranged husband. This recognition would help to demonstrate how a rule may ratify gender-based structures of power, and thus provide the court stronger grounds for finding the exemption inapplicable to the *Smith* facts. On the other hand, feminist practical reasoning would also require more explicit recognition of the interests that supported the exemption and that the court too summarily dismissed. For example, the court rejected without discussion the state's interest in the reconciliation of separated spouses that the marital rape exemption was intended in part to serve. It also failed to address the state's concern about the evidentiary problems raised in marital rape cases. The facts of the *Smith* case illustrate the weakness of these state interests. A more forthright analysis of them would have given a fuller picture of the issues, as well as guidance for other courts to which these factors may seem more significant.

A fuller, practical-reasoning approach would also have given greater attention to the "due process" notice interests of the defendant who, when he acted, may have thought his actions were legal. Despite the heinous nature of the defendant's actions in this case, practical reasoning requires the examination of all perspectives, including those that a court might ultimately reject. The *Smith* court examined some relevant factors in its due process analysis, such as whether the court's ruling would be unexpected, the relationship between the exemption and the rule to which the exemption applied, and the type of crime. It failed, however, to examine the role social conditioning plays in acculturating men to expect, and demand, sex. Such a examination, repeated in other cases, may help to identify the real problems society has to face in rape reform, and to challenge more deeply both male and female expectations about sex.

Feminist Practical Reasoning: Method or Substance? The *Smith* case raises further questions about the relationship between feminist method and substance. . . .

Whether the relationship between feminist practical reasoning and legal substance is a "proper" one depends upon some crucial assumptions about legal decisionmaking. If one assumes that methods can and should screen out political and moral factors from legal decisionmaking, practical reasoning is not an appropriate mode of legal analysis. . . .

On the other hand, if one assumes that one neither can nor should eliminate political and moral factors from legal decisiomaking, then one would hope to make these factors more visible. . . .

Feminists, not surprisingly, favor the second set of assumptions over the first. Feminists' substantive analyses of legal decisionmaking have revealed to them that so-called neutral means of deciding cases tend to mask, not eliminate, political and social considerations from legal decisionmaking. Feminists have found that neutral rules and procedures tend to drive underground the ideologies of the decisionmaker, and that these ideologies do not serve women's interests well. Disadvantaged by hidden bias, feminists see the value of modes of legal reasoning that expose and open up debate concerning the underlying political and moral considerations. By forcing articulation and understanding of those considerations, practical reasoning forces justification of results based upon what interests are actually at stake.

The "substance" of feminist practical reasoning consists of an alertness to certain forms of injustice that otherwise go unnoticed and unaddressed. Feminists turn to contextualized methods of reasoning to allow greater understanding and exposure of that injustice. Reasoning from context can change perceptions about the world, which may then further expand the contexts within which such reasoning seems appropriate, which in turn may lead to still further changes in perceptions. The expansion of existing boundaries of relevance based upon changed perceptions of the world is familiar to the process of legal reform. The shift from Plessy v. Ferguson[13] to Brown v. Board of Education,[14] for example, rested upon the expansion of the "legally relevant" in race discrimination cases to include the actual experiences of black Americans and the inferiority implicit in segregation. Much of the judicial reform that has been beneficial to women, as well, has come about through expanding the lens of legal relevance to encompass the missing perspectives of women and to accommodate perceptions about the nature and role of women. Feminist practical reasoning compels continued expansion of such perceptions.

Consciousness-Raising

Another feminist method for expanding perceptions is consciousness-raising.[15] Consciousness-raising is an interactive and collaborative process of articulating one's experiences and making meaning of them with others who also articulate their experiences. As Leslie Bender writes, "Feminist consciousness-raising creates knowledge by exploring common experiences and patterns that emerge from shared tellings of life events. What were experienced as personal hurts individually suffered reveal themselves as a collective experience of oppression."[16]

Consciousness-raising is a method of trial and error. When revealing an experience to others, a participant in consciousness-raising does not know whether others will recognize it. The process values risk-taking and vulnerability over caution and detachment. Honesty is valued above consistency, teamwork over self-sufficiency, and personal narrative over abstract analysis. The goal is individual and collective empowerment, not personal attack or conquest.

Elizabeth Schneider emphasizes the centrality of consciousness-raising to the dialectical relationship of theory and practice. . . . The interplay between experience and theory "reveals the social dimension of individual experience and the individual dimension of social experience" and hence the political nature of personal experience.[17]

Consciousness-raising operates as feminist method not only in small personal growth groups, but also on a more public, institutional level, through "bearing witness to evidences of patriarchy as they occur, through unremitting dialogues with and challenges to the patriarchs, and through the popular media, the arts, politics, lobbying, and even litigation."[18] Women use consciousness-raising when they publicly share their experiences as victims of marital rape, pornography, sexual harassment on the job, street hassling, and other forms of oppression and exclusion, in order to help change public perceptions about the meaning to women of events widely thought to be harmless or flattering.

Consciousness-raising has consequences, further, for laws and institutional decisionmaking more generally. Several feminists have translated the insights of feminist consciousness-raising into their normative accounts of legal process and legal decisionmaking. Carrie Menkel-Meadow, for example, has speculated that as the number of women lawyers increases, women's more interactive approaches to decisionmaking will improve legal process.[19] Similarly, Judith Resnik has argued that feminist judging will involve more collaborative decisionmaking among judges.[20] Such changes would have important implications for the possibilities for lawyering and judging as matters of collective engagement rather than the individual exercise of judgment and power.

The primary significance of consciousness-raising, however, is as meta-method. Consciousness-raising provides a substructure for other feminist methods—including the woman question and feminist practical reasoning—by enabling feminists to draw insights and perceptions from their own experiences and those of other women and to use these insights to challenge dominant versions of social reality.

Consciousness-raising has done more than help feminists develop and affirm counter-hegemonic perceptions of their experiences. As consciousness-raising has matured as method, disagreements among feminists about the meaning of certain experiences have proliferated. Feminists disagree, for example, about whether women can voluntarily choose heterosexuality, or motherhood; or about whether feminists have more to gain or lose from restrictions against pornography, surrogate motherhood, or about whether women should be subject to a military draft. They disagree about each other's roles in an oppressive society: some feminists accuse others of complicity in the oppression of women.[21] Feminists disagree even about the method of consciousness-raising; some women worry that it sometimes operates to pressure women into translating their experiences into positions that are politically, rather than experientially, correct.[22]

These disagreements raise questions beyond those of which specific methods are appropriate to feminist practice. Like the woman question and practical reasoning, consciousness-raising challenges the concept of knowledge. It presupposes that what I thought I knew may not, in fact, be "right." How, then, will we know when we *have* got it "right"? Or, backing up one step, what does it mean to *be* right? And what attitude should I have about that which I claim to know? The next section will focus on these questions.

Feminist Knowing in Law

A point—perhaps *the* point—of legal methods is to reach answers that are legally defensible or in some sense "right." . . .

In this section, I explore several feminist explanations for what it means to be "right" in law . . . [looking at] . . . a range of positions that have emerged from within feminist theory. . . . I evaluate each position from the same pragmatic viewpoint reflected in the feminist methods I have described: how can that position help feminists, using feminist methods, to generate the kind of insights, values, and self-knowledge that feminism needs to maintain its critical challenge to existing structures of power and to reconstruct new, and better, structures in their place? . . .

The Rational/Empirical Position

Feminists across many disciplines have engaged in considerable efforts to show how, by the standards of their own disciplines, to improve accepted methodologies. These efforts have led to the unraveling of descriptions of women as morally inferior, psychologically unstable, and historically insignificant—descriptions these disciplines long accepted as authoritative and unquestionable.

Similarly, feminists in law attempt to use the tools of law, on its own terms, to improve law. Using the methods [previously discussed], feminists often challenge assumptions about women that underlie numerous laws and demonstrate how laws based upon these assumptions are not rational and neutral, but rather irrational and discriminatory. When engaged in these challenges, feminists operate from a rational/empirical position that assumes that the law is not objective, but that identifying and correcting its mistaken assumptions can make it more objective.

When feminists challenged employment rules that denied disability benefits to pregnant women, for example, they used empirical and rational arguments about the similarity between pregnancy and other disabilities. . . . Each side of the debate defended a different concept of equality, but the underlying argument focused upon which is the most rational, empirically sound, and legally supportable interpretation of equality.

In other areas of the law, feminists have also operated from within this rational/empirical stance. . . . [For example, some feminists] argue that particular reforms in child custody law would more rationally meet the law's express purpose of protecting the best interests of the child. Some feminists favor the tender-years doctrine or the maternal-preference rule, on the ground that women are likely to be the actual caretakers of children. . . . Still other feminists advocate a primary caretaker presumption on the empirical ground that a child's primary caretaker is most likely to be the parent in whose custody the child's best interest lies. . . . Finally, some feminists favor rules that promote joint custody, based upon empirical claims about which rules best serve the interests of children and women.

All of these arguments from the rational/empirical stance share the premise that knowledge is accessible and, when obtained, can make law more rational. . . . The relevant empirical questions are often very difficult ones. . . . The rational/empirical position presumes, however, that answers to such questions can be improved—that there is a "right" answer to get—and that once gotten, that answer can improve the law.

Some feminists charge that improving the empirical basis of law or its rationality is mere "reformism" that cannot reach the deeper gendered nature of law.[23] This charge unfortunately undervalues the enormous transformation in thinking about women that the empirical challenge to law, in which all feminists have participated, has brought about. Feminist rational/empiricism has begun to expose the deeply flawed factual assumptions about women that have pervaded many disciplines, and has changed, in profound ways, the perception of women in this society. Few, if any, feminists, however, operate entirely within the rational/empirical stance, because it tends to limit attention to matters of factual rather than normative accuracy, and thus fails to take account of the social construction of reality through which factual or rational propositions mask normative constructions. Empirical and rational arguments challenge existing assumptions about reality and, in particular, the inaccurate reality conveyed by stereotypes about women. But if reality is not representational or objective and not above politics, the method of correcting inaccuracies ultimately cannot provide a basis for understanding and reconstructing that reality. The rational/empirical assumption that principles such as objectivity and neutrality can question empirical assumptions within law fails to recognize that knowability is itself a debatable issue. I explore positions that challenge, rather than presuppose, knowability in the following sections.

Standpoint Epistemology

The problem of knowability in feminist thought arises from the observation that what women know has been determined—perhaps overdetermined[24]—by male culture. Some of the feminists most concerned about the problem of overdetermination have adopted a "standpoint epistemology"[25] to provide the grounding upon which feminists can claim that their own legal methods, legal reasoning, and proposals for substantive legal reform are "right."

Feminist standpoint epistemology identifies woman's status as that of victim, and then privileges that status by claiming that it gives access to understanding about oppression that others cannot have. . . .

Feminists have located the foundation of women's subordination in different aspects of women's experiences. Feminist post-Marxists find this foundation in women's activities in production, both domestic and in the marketplace; others emphasize women's positions in the sexual hierarchy, in women's bodies, or in women's responses to the pain and fear of male violence. . . .

Standpoint epistemology has contributed a great deal to feminist understandings of the importance of our respective positioning within society to the "knowl-edge" we have. Feminist standpoint epistemologies question "the assumption that the social identity of the observer is irrelevant to the 'goodness' of the results of research," and reverse the priority of a distanced, "objective" standpoint in favor of one of experience and engagement.[26]

Despite the valuable insights offered by feminist standpoint epistemology, however, it does not offer an adequate account of feminist knowing. First, in isolating gender as a source of oppression, feminist legal thinkers tend to concen-trate on the identification of woman's true identity beneath the oppression and thereby essentialize her characteristics. Catharine MacKinnon, for example, in ex-posing what she finds to be the total system of male hegemony, repeatedly speaks of "women's point of view," of "woman's voice," of empowering women "on our own terms," of what women "really want," and of standards that are "not ours." Ruth Colker sees the discovery of women's "authentic self" as a difficult job given the social constructions imposed upon women, but nonetheless, like MacKinnon, insists upon it as a central goal of feminism. Robin West, too, assumes that woman has a "true nature" upon which to base a feminist jurisprudence.

Although the essentialist positions taken by these feminists often have strategic or rhetorical value, these positions obscure the importance of differences among women and the fact that factors other than gender victimize women. . . .

In addition to imposing too broad a view of gender, standpoint epistemologists also tend to presuppose too narrow a view of privilege. . . . Although victims know something about victimization that non-victims do not, victims do not have exclu-sive access to truth about oppression. The positions of others—co-victims, passive by-standers, even the victimizers—yield perspectives of special knowledge that those who seek to end oppression must understand.

Standpoint epistemology's claim that women have special access to knowledge also does not account for why all women, including those who are similarly situ-ated, do not share the same interpretations of those situations. . . .

A final difficulty with standpoint epistemology is the adversarial we/they poli-tics it engenders. Identification from the standpoint of victims seems to require enemies, wrongdoers, victimizers. Those identified as victims ("we") stand in stark contrast to others ("they"), whose claim to superior knowledge becomes not only false but suspect in some deeper sense: conspiratorial, evil-minded, criminal. . . . Men are . . . evil, corrupt, irredeemable. They conspire to protect male advantage and to perpetuate the subordination of women. Even women must choose sides, and those who chose badly are condemned.

This adversarial position hinders feminist practice. It impedes understanding by would-be friends of feminism and paralyzes potential sympathizers. Even more seriously, it misstates the problem that women face, which is not that men act "freely" and women do not, but that both men and women, in different but inter-related ways, are confined by gender. The mystifying ideologies of gender con-struction control men, too, however much they may also benefit from them. . . .

In short, gender reform must entail not so much the conquest of the now-all-powerful enemy male, as the transformation of those ideologies that maintain the current relationships of subordination and oppression.

Postmodernism

The postmodern or poststructural critique of foundationalism resolves the problem of knowability in a quite different way.[27] While standpoint epistemology relocates the source of knowledge from the oppressor to the oppressed, the postmodern critique of foundationalism questions the possibility of knowledge, including knowledge about categories of people such as women. This critique rejects essentialist thinking as it insists that the subject, including the female subject, has no core identity but rather is constituted through multiple structures and discourses that in various ways overlap, intersect, and contradict each other. Although these structures and discourses "overdetermine" woman and thereby produce "the subject's experience of differentiated identity and . . . autonomy,"[28] the postmodern view posits that the realities experienced by the subject are not in any way transcendent or representational, but rather particular and fluctuating, constituted within a complex set of social contexts. Within this position, being human, or female, is strictly a matter of social, historical, and cultural construction.

Postmodern critiques have challenged the binary oppositions in language, law, and other socially constituting systems, oppositions which privilege one presence—male, rationality, objectivity—and marginalize its opposite—female, irrationality, subjectivity. Postmodernism removes the grounding from these oppositions and from all other systems of power or truth that claim legitimacy on the basis of external foundations or authorities. In so doing, it removes external grounding from any particular agenda for social reform. In the words of Nancy Fraser and Linda Nicholson, postmodern social criticism "floats free of any universalist theoretical ground. No longer anchored philosophically, the very shape or character of social criticism changes; it becomes more pragmatic, ad hoc, contextual, and local."[29] There are no external, overarching systems of legitimation; "[t]here are no special tribunals set apart from the sites where inquiry is practiced." Instead, practices develop their own constitutive norms, which are "plural, local, and immanent."[30]

The postmodern critique of foundationalism has made its way into legal discourse through the critical legal studies movement. The feminists associated with this movement have stressed both the indeterminacy of law and the extent to which law, despite its claim to neutrality and objectivity, masks particular hierarchies and distributions of power. These feminists have engaged in deconstructive projects that have revealed the hidden gender bias of a wide range of laws and legal assumptions.[31] Basic to these projects has been the critical insight that not only law itself, but also the criteria for legal validity and legitimacy, are social constructs rather than universal givens.[32]

Although the postmodern critique of foundationalism has had considerable influence on feminist legal theory, some feminists have cautioned that this critique poses a threat not only to existing power structures, but to feminist politics as well.[33] To the extent that feminist politics turns on a particular story of woman's oppression, a theory of knowledge that denies that an independent, determinate reality exists would seem to deny the basis of that politics. Without a notion of objectivity, feminists have difficulty claiming that their emergence from male hegemony is less artificial and constructed than that which they have cast off, or that their truths are more firmly grounded than those whose accounts of being women vary widely from their own. Thus, as Deborah Rhode observes, feminists influenced by postmodernism are "left in the awkward position of maintaining that gender oppression exists while challenging [their] capacity to document it."[34]

Feminists need a stance toward knowledge that takes into account the contingency of knowledge claims while allowing for a concept of truth or objectivity that can sustain an agenda for meaningful reform. The postmodern critique of foundationalism is persuasive to many feminists, whose experiences affirm that rules and principles asserted as universal truths reflect particular, contingent realities that reinforce their subordination. At the same time, however, feminists must be able to insist that they have identified unacceptable forms of oppression and that they have a better account of the world free from such oppression. Feminists, according to Linda Alcoff, "need to have their accusations of misogyny validated rather than rendered 'undecidable.'"[35] In addition, they must build from the postmodern critique about "how meanings and bodies get made," Donna Haraway writes, "not in order to deny meanings and bodies, but in order to build meanings and bodies that have a chance for life."[36]

To focus attention on this project of rebuilding, feminists need a theory of knowledge that affirms and directs the construction of new meanings. Feminists must be able to both deconstruct *and construct* knowledge. In the next section, I develop positionality as a stance toward knowledge from which feminists may trust and act upon their knowledges, but still must acknowledge and seek to improve their social groundings.

Positionality

Positionality is a stance from which a number of apparently inconsistent feminist "truths" make sense. The positional stance acknowledges the existence of empirical truths, values, and knowledge, and also their contingency. It thereby provides a basis for feminist commitment and political action, but views these commitments as provisional and subject to further critical evaluation and revision.

Like standpoint epistemology, positionality retains a concept of knowledge based upon experience. Experience interacts with an individual's current perceptions to reveal new understandings and to help that individual, with others, make sense of those perceptions. Thus, from women's position of exclusion, women have come to "know" certain things about exclusion: its subtlety; its masking by "objective" rules and constructs; its pervasiveness; its pain; and the need to change it. These understandings make difficult issues decidable and answers non-arbitrary.

Like the postmodern position, however, positionality rejects the perfectibility, externality, or objectivity of truth. Instead, the positional knower conceives of truth as situated and partial. Truth is situated in that it emerges from particular involvements and relationships. These relationships, not some essential or innate characteristics of the individual, define the individual's perspective and provide the location for meaning, identity, and political commitment. Thus, as discussed above, the meaning of pregnancy derives not just from its biological characteristics, but from the social place it occupies—how workplace structures, domestic arrangements, tort systems, high schools, prisons, and other societal institutions construct its meaning.

Truth is partial in that the individual perspectives that yield and judge truth are necessarily incomplete. No individual can understand except from some limited perspective. Thus, for example, a man experiences pornography as a man with a particular upbringing, set of relationships, race, social class, and sexual preference, and so on, which affect what "truths" he perceives about pornography. A woman experiences pregnancy as a woman with a particular upbringing, race, social class, set of relationships, sexual preference, and so on, which affect what "truths" she perceives about pregnancy. As a result, there will always be "knowers" who have access to knowledge that other individuals do not have, and no one's truth can be deemed total or final.

Because knowledge arises within social contexts and in multiple forms, the key to increasing knowledge lies in the effort to extend one's limited perspective. . . . My perspective gives me a source of special knowledge, but a limited knowledge that I can improve by the effort to step beyond it, to understand other perspectives, and to expand my sources of identity.[37] To be sure, I cannot transcend my perspective; by definition, whatever perspective I currently have limits my view. But I can improve my perspective by stretching my imagination to identify and understand the perspectives of others.

Positionality's requirement that other perspectives be sought out and examined checks the characteristic tendency of all individuals—including feminists—to want to stamp their own point of view upon the world. This requirement does not allow certain feminist positions to be set aside as immune from critical examination.[38] When feminists oppose restrictive abortion laws, for example, positionality compels the effort to understand those whose views about the sanctity of potential human life are offended by assertion of women's unlimited right to choose abortion. When feminists debate the legal alternative of joint custody at divorce, positionality compels appreciation of the desire by some fathers to be responsible, co-equal parents. And (can it get worse?) when feminists urge drastic reform of rape laws, positionality compels consideration of the position of men whose social conditioning leads them to interpret the actions of some women as "inviting" rather than discouraging sexual encounter.

Although I must consider other points of view from the positional stance, I need not accept their truths as my own. Positionality is not a strategy of process and compromise that seeks to reconcile all competing interests. Rather, it imposes a twin obligation to make commitments based on the current truths and values that have emerged from methods of feminism, and to be open to previously unseen perspectives that might come to alter these commitments. . . . Positionality, however, sets an ideal of self-critical commitment whereby I act, but consider the truths upon which I act subject to further refinement, amendment, and correction.

Some "truths" will emerge from the ongoing process of critical reexamination in a form that seems increasingly fixed or final. . . . For feminists, the commitment to ending gender-based oppression has become one of these "permanent truths." The problem is the human inclination to make this list of "truths" too long, to be too uncritical of its contents, and to defend it too harshly and dogmatically.

Positionality reconciles the existence of reliable, experience-based grounds for assertions of truth upon which politics should be based, with the need to question and improve these grounds. The understanding of truth as "real," in the sense of produced by the actual experiences of individuals in their concrete social relationships, permits the appreciation of plural truths. By the same token, if truth is understood as partial and contingent, each individual or group can approach its own truths with a more honest, self-critical attitude about the value and potential relevance of other truths.

The ideal presented by the positionality stance makes clear that current disagreements within society at large and among feminists—disagreements about abortion, child custody, pornography, the military, pregnancy, and motherhood, and the like—reflect value conflicts basic to the terms of social existence. If resolvable at all, these conflicts will not be settled by reference to external or pre-social standards of truth. From the positional stance, any resolutions that emerge are the products of human struggles about what social realities are better than others. Realities are deemed better not by comparison to some external, "discovered" moral truths or "essential" human characteristics, but by internal truths that make the most sense of experienced, social existence. Thus, social truths will emerge from social relationships and what, after critical examination, they tell social beings about what they want themselves, and their social world, to be. . . .

In this way, feminist positionality resists attempts at classification either as essentialist on the one hand, or relativistic on the other. . . . Positionality is both nonrelative and nonarbitrary. It assumes some means of distinguishing between better and worse understanding; truth claims are significant or "valid" for those who experience that validity. But positionality puts no stock in fixed, discoverable foundations. If there is any such thing as ultimate or objective truth, I can never, in my own lifetime, be absolutely sure that I have discovered it. I can know important and non-arbitrary truths, but these are necessarily mediated through human experiences and relationships. There can be no universal, final, or objective truth; there can be only "partial, locatable, critical knowledges,"[39] no aperspectivity—only improved perspectives. . . .

A stance of positionality can reconcile the apparent contradiction within feminist thought between the need to recognize the diversity of people's lives and the value in trying to transcend that diversity. Feminists, like those associated with the critical legal studies movement, understand that when those with power pretend that their interests are natural, objective, and inevitable, they suppress and ignore other diverse perspectives. This understanding compels feminists to make constant efforts to test the extent to which they, also, unwittingly project their experiences upon others. To understand human diversity, however, is also to understand human commonality. From the positional stance, I can attain self-knowledge through the effort to identify not only what is different, but also what I have in common with those who have other perspectives. This effort, indeed, becomes a "foundation" for further knowledge. . . .

Because of its linkage between knowledge and seeking out other perspectives, positionality provides the best foothold from which feminists may insist upon both the diversity of others' experiences, and their mutual relatedness and common humanity with others. This dual focus seeks knowledge of individual and community, apart and as necessarily interdependent. As others have noted, much of the recent scholarship that attempts to revive ideals of republicanism and the public virtue has given inadequate attention to the problem of whose interests are represented and whose are excluded by expressions of the "common" or "public" interest.[40] Positionality locates the source of community in its diversity and affirms Frank Michelman's conclusions about human commonality: "The human universal becomes difference itself. Difference is what we most fundamentally have in common."[41]

All three of the methods discussed in this essay affirm, and are enhanced by, the stance of positionality. In asking the woman question, feminists situate themselves in the perspectives of women affected in various ways and to various extents by legal rules and ideologies that purport to be neutral and objective. The process of challenging these rules and ideologies, deliberately, from particular, self-conscious perspectives, assumes that the process of revealing and correcting various forms of oppression is never-ending. Feminist practical reasoning, likewise, exposes and helps to limit the damage that universalizing rules and assumptions can do; universalizations will always be present, but contextualized reasoning will help to identify those currently useful and eliminate the others. Consciousness-raising links that process of reasoning to the concrete experiences associated with growth from one set of moral and political insights to another. Positional understanding enhances alertness to the special problems of oppressive orthodoxies in consciousness-raising, and the insights developed through collaborative interaction should remain open to challenge, and not be held hostage to the unfortunate tendency in all social structures to assume that some insights are too politically "correct" to question.

Positional understanding requires efforts both to establish good law and to keep in place, and renew, the means for deconstructing and improving that law. In addition to focusing on existing conditions, feminist methods must be elastic enough to open up and make visible new forms of oppression and bias. Reasoning from context and consciousness-raising are self-renewing methods that may enable continual new discoveries. Through critical practice, new methods should also evolve that will lead to new questions, improved partial insights, better law, and still further critical methods.

Conclusion: Feminist Methods as Ends

I have argued that feminist methods are means to feminist ends: that asking the woman question, feminist practical reasoning, and consciousness-raising are methods that arise from and sustain feminist practice. Having established the feminist stance of positionality, I now want to expand my claim to argue that feminist methods are also ends in themselves. Central to the concept of positionality is the assumption that although partial objectivity is possible, it is transitional, and therefore must be continually subject to the effort to reappraise, deconstruct, and transform. That effort, and the hope that must underlie it, constitute the optimistic version of feminism to which I adhere. Under this version, human flourishing means being engaged in the world through the kinds of critical yet constructive feminist methods I have described. These methods can give feminists a way of doing law that expresses who they are and who they wish to become.

This is, I contend, a goal central to feminism: to be engaged, with others, in a critical, transformative process of seeking further partial knowledges from one's admittedly limited habitat. This goal is the grounding of feminism, a grounding that combines the search for further understandings and sustained criticism toward those understandings. Feminist doing is, in this sense, feminist knowing. And vice versa.

Notes

1. [T]his essay is primarily about "doing law" in the limited sense encompassed by the professional activities of practicing lawyers, lawmakers, law professors, and judges.
2. MacKinnon, Feminism, Marxism, Method, and the State: An Agenda for Theory, Part 5 this volume, at 443.

3. Singer, Should Lawyers Care About Philosophy? (Book Review), 1989 Duke L.J. 1752.

4. See, e.g., Gould, The Woman Question: Philosophy of Liberation and the Liberation of Philosophy, in C. Gould & M. Wartofsky eds., Women and Philosophy: Toward A Theory of Liberation 5 (Putnam, 1976) (discussing the woman question in philosophy); Hawkesworth, Feminist Rhetoric: Discourses on the Male Monopoly of Thought, 16 Pol. Theory 444, 452–56 (1988) (examining the treatment of the woman question in political theory). The first use of the term "woman question" of which I am aware is in S. de Beauvoir, The Second Sex xxvi (Knopf, 1957).

5. See Bradwell v. Illinois, 83 U.S. (16 Wall.) 130 (1873). For a detailed historical analysis of the *Bradwell* case, see Olsen, From False Paternalism to False Equality: Judicial Assaults on Feminist Community, Illinois 1869–1895, 84 Mich. L. Rev. 1518 (1986).

6. See Reed v. Reed, 404 U.S. 71 (1971).

7. Brief for Appellee at 12, *Reed* (No. 70-4). . . .

8. See W. Williams, The Equality Crisis: Some Reflections on Culture, Courts and Feminism, 7 Women's Rts L. Rep. 175, 181–90 (1982) (criticizing Rostker v. Goldberg, 453 U.S. 57 (1981)). . . .

9. See *id.* (criticizing Michael M. v. Superior Ct. 450 U.S. 464 (1981)). . . .; Olsen, Statutory Rape: A Feminist Critique of Rights Analysis, Part 5 this volume.

10. See Abrams, Law's Republicanism, 97 Yale L.J. 1591, 1606–07 (1988) (noting that "localities have a disturbing history of intolerance toward non-conforming groups"); Sullivan, Rainbow Republicanism, 97 Yale L.J. 1713, 1721 (1988) (criticizing the failure of "republicanism" to nurture private associations through which "deviance, diversity, and dissent" are possible).

11. Haraway, Situated Knowledges: The Science Question in Feminism and the Privilege of Partial Perspective, 14 Feminist Stud. 575, 590 (1988); Minow, The Supreme Court, 1986 Term—Foreword: Justice Engendered, Part 3 this volume. See also Flax, Postmodernism and Gender Relations in Feminist Theory, 12 Signs 621, 633 (1987) (describing the need to be sensitive to interconnections between knowledge and power); Minow & Spelman, Passion for Justice, 10 Cardozo L. Rev. 37, 57–60 (1988) (calling for "a direct human gaze between those exercising power and those governed by it"); Gabel & Harris, Building Power and Breaking Images: Critical Theory and the Practice of Law, 11 N.Y.U. Rev. L. & Soc. Change 369, 375 (1982–83) (suggesting a focus on "counter-hegemonic" law practice that draws attention to issues of power distribution).

12. 85 N.J. 193, 426 A.2d 38 (1981).

13. 163 U.S. 537 (1896).

14. 347 U.S. 483 (1954).

15. Catharine MacKinnon sees consciousness-raising as the method of feminism. . . . MacKinnon, Agenda for Theory, Part 5 this volume. Many feminist legal thinkers have emphasized the importance of consciousness-raising to feminist practice and method. . . . For historical perspectives on consciousness-raising in the American women's movement, see C. Hymowitz & M. Weissman, A History of Women in America 351–55 (Bantam, 1978); and G. Lerner, The Majority Finds Its Past: Placing Women in History 42–44 (Oxford University Press, 1979).

16. Bender, A Lawyer's Primer on Feminist Theory and Tort, Part 1 this volume; (citations omitted); see also Z. Eisenstein, Feminism and Sexual Equality: Crisis in Liberal America 150–57 (Monthly Review Press, 1984) (stressing the importance of building feminist consciousness out of sex-class consciousness); T. de Lauretis, Alice Doesn't: Feminism, Semiotics, Cinema 185 (Indiana University Press, 1984) (describing consciousness-raising as "the collective articulation of one's experience of sexuality and gender—which has produced, and continues to elaborate, a radically new mode of understanding the subject's relation to social-historical reality"); J. Mitchell, Woman's Estate 61 (Penguin Books, 1971) (maintaining that through consciousness-raising, women proclaim the painful and transform it into the political).

17. See Schneider, The Dialectic of Rights and Politics: Perspectives from the Women's Movement, Part 5 this volume, at 511. Hence the feminist phrase: "The personal is the political." MacKinnon's explanation of this phrase is perhaps the best: "It means that women's distinctive experience as women occurs within that sphere that has been socially lived as the personal—private, emotional, interiorized, particular, individual, intimate—so that what it is to *know* the *politics* of woman's situation is to know women's personal lives," MacKinnon, Agenda for Theory, Part 5 this volume, at 447.

18. Bender, A Lawyer's Primer on Feminist Theory and Tort, Part 1 this volume [citation omitted here; originally cited at 38 J. Legal Ed. 3, 9–10 (1988). *Ed.*]. . . .

19. See Menkel-Meadow, Portia in a Different Voice: Speculations on a Woman's Lawyering Process, 1 Berkeley Women's L.J. 39, 55–58 (1985).

20. Resnik, On the Bias: Feminist Reconsiderations of the Aspirations for Our Judges, 61 S. Cal. L. Rev. 1877 (1988). . . .

21. See C. MacKinnon, Feminism Unmodified 198–205 (Harvard University Press, 1987) (accusing women who defend first amendment values against restrictions on pornography of collaboration).

22. See Colker, Feminism, Sexuality and Self: A Preliminary Inquiry into the Politics of Authenticity (Book Review), 68 B.U. L. Rev. 217, 253–54 (1988) (noting that consciousness-raising may influence women to adopt "inauthentic" expressions of themselves).

23. Christine Littleton and Catharine MacKinnon, for example, associate rational/empirical efforts to open up more opportunities for women with "assimilationism" or "liberal feminism," which, in retaining its focus on individualism, provides no basis from which to challenge the way in which women's individuality has been determined by men rather than freely chosen, or to validate any of the choices that individuals make. See Littleton, Feminist Jurisprudence: The Difference Method Makes (Book Review), 41 Stan. L. Rev. 751, 754–63 (1989); MacKinnon, Feminism Unmodified, *supra* note 21, at 137.

24. Cf. Alcoff, Cultural Feminism Versus Post-Structuralism: The Identity Crisis in Feminist Theory, 13 Signs 405, 416 (1988) (describing Derrida's and Foucault's view that "we are overdetermined . . . by a social discourse and/or cultural practice"); Mitchell, Women's Estate, *supra* note 16, at 99–122. Juliet Mitchell defines overdetermination as "a complex notion of 'multiple causation' in which the numerous factors can reinforce, overlap, cancel each other out, or contradict one another." J. Mitchell, Psychoanalysis and Feminism 309 n.12 (Penguin, 1974). . . .

25. Sandra Harding finds the roots of the standpoint approach in Hegel's analysis of the relationship between master and slave, which was elaborated by Engels, Marx, and Lukacs, and extended to feminist theory by Jane Flax, Hilary Rose, Nancy Hartsock, and Dorothy Smith. See S. Harding, The Science Question in Feminism 26 (Cornell University Press, 1986).

26. *Id.* at 162.

27. Postmodernism and poststructuralism are often used interchangeably, although each term has a somewhat unique genealogy. Postmodernism, originally used to describe a movement in art and architecture, has been used by Jean-Francois Lyotard and Fredric Jameson to describe the general character of the present age. For Lyotard, whose concern is primarily epistemological, the postmodern condition has resulted from the collapse of faith in the traditional "Grand Narratives" that have legitimated knowledge since the Enlightenment. See J. Lyotard, The Postmodern Condition: A Report on Knowledge 37–41, 51, 60 (G. Bennington & B. Massumi trans., University of Minnesota Press, 1984). For Jameson, who focuses mainly on changes in the cultural realm, postmodernism characterizes the "cultural dominant" of the "logic of late capitalism." Jameson, Postmodernism, or the Cultural Logic of Late Capitalism, 146 New Left Rev. 53, 55 (1984). Poststructuralism refers to a series of regional analyses that have undermined notions of foundationalism and of a unified self-transparent subject. As a movement that has undermined the ideals and the project of the Enlightenment, poststructuralism has contributed to the general condition of postmodernism. . . .

In this essay, I use the terms postmodernism and poststructuralism more or less interchangeably. . . .

28. Coombe, Room for Manoeuver: Toward a Theory of Practice in Critical Legal Studies, 14 Law & Soc. Inquiry 69, 85 (1989).

29. Fraser & Nicholson, Social Criticism Without Philosophy: An Encounter Between Feminism and Postmodernism, in A. Ross ed., Universal Abandon? The Politics of Postmodernism 85 (University of Minnesota Press, 1988).

30. *Id.* at 87.

31. See, e.g., Dalton, An Essay in the Deconstruction of Contract Doctrine, 94 Yale L.J. 997 (1985); Olsen, The Family and the Market: A Study of Ideology and Legal Reform, 96 Harv. L. Rev. 1487 (1983); Bender, A Lawyer's Primer on Feminist Theory and Tort, Part 1 this volume.

32. Although feminist legal theory has taken seriously the postmodern critique of foundationalism, it has yet to make much sense or use of the postmodern critique of the subject. Marie Ashe has argued that the poststructural subject, defined as "a being that is maintained only through interactive exchanges within a social order," Ashe, Mind's Opportunity: Birthing a Poststructuralist Feminist Jurisprudence, 38 Syracuse L. Rev. 1129, 1165 (1987), "appears utterly at odds with the notions of individual autonomy and personhood valued as fundamental in the liberal legal tradition." *Id.* at 1151. The direction in which Ashe urges feminist jurisprudence should move, however, appears to turn on the existence of certain "real" experiences on the part of women who are pregnant and bear children, which are at odds, she suggests, with the reality assumed by law. In universalizing these experiences and speaking of the "inner discourses of mothers," Ashe seems to abandon the poststructural view. See Ashe, Law-Language of Maternity: Discourse Holding Nature in Contempt, 22 New Eng. L. Rev. 521, 527 (1988).

Drucilla Cornell has hinted at a concept of gender differentiation drawn from poststructural theory that might prove fruitful for feminist legal practice. Building on the importance of the excluded "Other" in the construction of woman, she suggests that "what we are as subjects [can never be] fully captured by gender categories," that an interrelational intersubjectivity is more than the sum of its parts, and that immanent in the gender system is "more than this" which has the potential for freeing us from the false choice between universality and absolute difference. See Cornell & Thurschwell, Feminism, Negativity, Intersubjectivity, in S. Benhabib & D. Cornell eds., Feminism as Critique 143, 161–62 (University of Minnesota Press, 1987). . . .

33. See, e.g., Bordo, Feminism, Postmodernism, and Gender-Scepticism, in L. Nicholson ed., Feminism/Post-Modernism 133 (Routledge, 1990); Fraser & Nicholson, Social Criticism, *supra* note 29, at 83; Poovey, Feminism and Deconstruction, 14 Feminist Stud. 51 (1988). . . .

34. D. Rhode, Feminist Critical Theories, 42 Stan L. Rev. 617, 620 (1990).

35. Alcoff, Cultural Feminism, *supra* note 24, at 419.

36. Haraway, Situated Knowledges, *supra* note 11, at 580.

37. Neither postmodernism nor standpoint epistemology fosters or even makes possible this attitude. The privilege that standpoint epistemology grants to a particular perspective leaves little reason to look beyond that perspective for further truth. Postmodernism, by denying any meaningful basis for making qualitative judgments between perspectives, leaves no reason to stretch beyond one's current perspective in order to improve it.

38. The absence of a self-critical account is the principal difficulty I have with Christine Littleton's presentation of feminist method (interpreting Catharine MacKinnon) as that of believing women's accounts of sexual use and abuse by men. See Littleton, Feminist Jurisprudence, *supra* note 23, at 764–65. Neither Littleton nor MacKinnon brings into their discussions of feminist method the necessity for feminists to be critical of themselves or of other women. . . . Although feminists want to give full voice to women whose accounts of their experiences have for so long been ignored or devalued, feminists cannot assume that women's accounts will always be truthful or valid, or for that matter that men's accounts will always be untruthful or invalid.

39. Haraway, Situated Knowledges, *supra* note 11, at 584.

40. See, e.g., Bell & Bansal, The Republican Revival and Racial Politics, 97 Yale L.J. 1609 (1988); Young, Impartiality and the Civic Public: Some Implications of Feminist Critiques of Moral and Political Theory, in Benhabib & Cornell eds., Feminism as Critique, *supra* note 32, at 66.

41. Michelman, The Supreme Court, 1985 Term—Foreword: Traces of Self-Government, 100 Harv. L. Rev. 4, 32 (1986). Michelman incorporates points made by Drucilla Cornell and Martha Minow. . . .

❖ *Breaking Women's Silence in Law: The Dilemma of the Gendered Nature of Legal Reasoning*

Lucinda M. Finley

Language matters. Law matters. Legal language matters.

I make these three statements not to offer a clever syllogism, but to bluntly put the central thesis of this essay: it is an imperative task for feminist jurisprudence and for feminist lawyers—for anyone concerned about what the impact of law has been, and will be, on the realization and meanings of justice, equality, security, and autonomy for women—to turn critical attention to the nature of legal reasoning and the language by which it is expressed. . . .

The Gendered Nature of Legal Language Is What Makes It Powerful and Limited

Why Law Is a Gendered (Male) Language

Throughout the history of Anglo-American jurisprudence, the primary linguists of law have almost exclusively been men—white, educated, economically privileged men. Men have shaped it, they have defined it, they have interpreted it and given it meaning consistent with their understandings of the world and of people "other" than them. As the men of law have defined law in their own image, law has excluded or marginalized the voices and meanings of these "others". . . . Law, along with all the other accepted academic disciplines, has exalted one form of reasoning and called only this form "reason." Because the men of law have had the societal power not to have to worry too much about the competing terms and understandings of "others," they have been insulated from challenges to their language and have thus come to see it as natural, inevitable, complete, objective, and neutral.[1]

Volume 64, Issue 5, *The Notre Dame Law Review* (1989). Reprinted with permission. © by *Notre Dame Law Review*, University of Notre Dame. The publisher bears responsibility for any errors which have occurred in reprinting or editing.

Thus, legal language and reasoning is gendered, and that gender matches the male gender of its linguistic architects. . . .[2]

The claim that legal language and reasoning is male gendered is partly empirical and historical. The legal system and its reasoning structure and language have been framed on the basis of life experiences typical to empowered white males. Law's reasoning structure shares a great deal with the assumptions of the liberal intellectual and philosophical tradition, which historically has been framed by men. The reasoning structure of law is thus congruent with the patterns of socialization, experience, and values of a particular group of privileged, educated men. Rationality, abstraction, a preference for statistical and empirical proofs over experiential or anecdotal evidence, and a conflict model of social life corresponds to how these men have been socialized and educated to think, live, and work.

My claim that legal reasoning and language are patriarchal also has a normative component, in the sense that male-based perspectives, images, and experiences are often taken to be the norms in law. Privileged white men are the norm for equality law; they are the norm for assessing the reasonable person in tort law; the way men would react is the norm for self-defense law; and the male worker is the prototype for labor law.

. . . [L]egal language is a male language because it is principally informed by men's experiences and because it derives from the powerful social situation of men, relative to women. Universal and objective thinking is male language because intellectually, economically, and politically privileged men have had the power to ignore other perspectives and thus to come to think of their situation as the norm, their reality as reality, and their views as objective. Disempowered, marginalized groups are far less likely to mistake their situation, experience, and views as universal. Male reasoning is dualistic and polarized thinking because men have been able, thanks to women, to organize their lives in a way that enables them not to have to see such things as work and family as mutually defining. Men have acted on their fears of women and nature to try to split nature off from culture, body from mind, passion from reason, and reproduction from production. Men have had the power to privilege—to assign greater value to—the side of the dichotomies that they associate with themselves. Conflict-oriented thinking, seeing matters as involving conflicts of interests or rights, as contrasted to relational thinking, is male because this way of expressing things is the primary orientation of more men than women. . . .[3]

The claim that law is patriarchal does not mean that women have not been addressed or comprehended by law. Women have obviously been the subjects or contemplated targets of many laws. But it is men's understanding of women, women's nature, women's capacities, and women's experiences—women refracted through the male eye—rather than women's own definitions, that has informed law. . . .

One notable example of a male judicial perspective characterizing women as men see them is the often-flayed U.S. Supreme Court decision in Bradwell v.

Illinois,[4] in which Justice Bradley exalted the delicate timidity and biologically bounded condition of women to conclude that women were unfit for the rude world of law practice. Another example is the decision in Geduldig v. Aiello,[5] in which the Court cordoned off the female experience of pregnancy and called this experience unique, voluntary, and unrelated in any way to the workplace.

The legal definition of rape provides another example of the male judicial perspective. It is the male's view of whether the woman consented that is determinative of consent; it is men's view of what constitutes force against men and forms of resistance by men in situations other than rape that defines whether force has been used against a woman and a woman has resisted; it is men's definition of sex—penetration of the vagina by the penis—rather than women's experience of sexualized violation and violation that defines the crime. . . .

The Power and Limitations of Male Legal Language

Analysis of the way the law structures thought and talk about social problems is necessary to understand how the law can limit our understandings of the nature of problems and can confine our visions for changes. . . . [A] male-gendered way of thinking about social problems is to speak in terms of objectivity, of universal abstractions, of dichotomy, and of conflict. These are essentially the ways law talks about social problems.

Modern Anglo-American law talks about social problems within the individualistic framework of patriarchal Western liberalism, a theory that itself has been challenged by feminists as resting on a fundamentally male world view.[6] This framework sees humans as self-interested, fundamentally set apart from other people, and threatened by interactions with others.[7] To control the threat of those who would dominate you or gain at your expense, you must strive to gain power over them. This power can easily become domination because the point of its exercise is to protect yourself by molding another to your will.

As part of this individualistic framework, law is conceptualized as a rule-bound system for adjudicating the competing rights of self-interested, autonomous, essentially equal individuals capable of making unconstrained choices. Because of the law's individualistic focus, it sees one of the central problems that it must address to be enforcing the agreements made by free autonomous individuals, as well as enforcing a few social norms to keep the battle of human life from getting out of hand. It envisions another central task to be eliminating obvious constraints on individual choice and opportunity. The constraints are thought to emanate primarily from the state or from the bad motivations of other individuals. An individualistic focus on choice does not perceive constraints as coming from history, from the operation of power and domination, from socialization, or from class, race, and gender. A final key task for individualistic liberal law is to keep the state from making irrational distinctions between people, because such distinctions can frustrate individual autonomy. It is not an appropriate task to alter structures and institutions, to help the disempowered overcome subordination, to eliminate fear and pain that may result from encounters masquerading as "freely chosen," to value nurturing connections,[8] or to promote care and compassion for other people.

To keep its operation fair in appearance, which it must if people are to trust resorting to the legal method for resolving competing claims, the law strives for rules that are universal, objective, and neutral. The language of individuality and neutrality keeps law from talking about values, structures, and institutions, and about how they construct knowledge, choice, and apparent possibilities for conducting the world. Also submerged is a critical awareness of systematic, systemic, or institutional power and domination. There are few ways to express within the language of law and legal reasoning the complex relationship between power, gender, and knowledge. Yet in order for feminists to use the law to help effectuate change, we must be able to talk about the connection between power and knowledge. This connection must be acknowledged in order to demystify the "neutrality" of the law, to make the law comprehend that women's definitions have been excluded and marginalized, and to show that the language of neutrality itself is one of the devices for this silencing.

The language of neutrality and objectivity can silence the voices of those who did not participate in its creation because it takes a distanced, decontextualized stance. Within this language and reasoning system, alternative voices to the one labeled objective are suspect as biased. An explicit acknowledgment of history and the multiplicity of experiences—which might help explode the perception of objectivity—is discouraged. To talk openly about the interaction between historical events, political change, and legal change is to violate neutral principles, such as adherence to precedent—and precedents themselves are rarely talked about as products of historical and social contingencies. For example, in the recent U.S. Supreme Court decision declaring a municipal affirmative action plan unconstitutional, City of Richmond v. Croson,[9] the majority talks in the language of neutrality, of color-blindness, and of blind justice—and it is the more classically legal voice. The dissent, which cries out in anguish about the lessons of history, power, and domination, is open to the accusation that it speaks in the language of politics and passions, not law.

In legal language, experience and perspective are translated as bias, as something that makes the achievement of neutrality more difficult. Having no experience with or prior knowledge of something is equated with perfect neutrality. This way of thinking is evident in jury selection. A woman who has been raped would almost certainly be excluded as a juror in a rape trial—it is assumed that her lived experience of rape makes her unable to judge it objectively. Legal language cannot imagine that her experience might give her a nuanced, critical understanding capable of challenging the male-constructed vision of the crime. Yet a person with no experience of rape, either as victim, perpetrator, or solacer/supporter of victim, is deemed objective, even though it may be just a lack of experience that leaves that person prone to accept the biased myths about women's behavior that surround this crime.

Because it is embedded in a patriarchal framework that equates abstraction and universalization from only one group's experiences as neutrality, legal reasoning views male experiences and perspectives as the universal norm around which terms and entire areas of the law are defined. . . .

Many doctrinal areas of the law are also fundamentally structured around men's perspectives and experiences. The field of labor law uses a gendered meaning of work—as that which is done for wages outside your own home—as its focus. Thus, any talk about reforming labor law, or regulating work, will always leave unspoken, and thus unaffected, much of what women do, even women who also "work" in the legal conventional sense. Legal intervention in work—or the perception that no intervention is needed—assumes that workers are men with wives at home who tend to the necessities of life. It is only in this framework that we can even think of work and family as separate and conflicting spheres.

Tort law defines injuries and measures compensation primarily in relation to what keeps people out of work and what their work is worth. It is in this framework that noneconomic damages, such as pain and suffering or compensation for emotional injuries, which are often crucial founts of recovery for women, are deemed suspect and expendable. . . . All of this suggests that for feminist law reformers, even using the terms "equality," "work," "injury," "damages," "market," and "contract" can involve buying into, and leaving unquestioned, the male frames of reference. It also leaves unspoken, and unrecognized, the kinds of work women do, or the kinds of injuries women suffer.

The language of law is also a language of dichotomies, oppositions, and conflict. No doubt this is partly attributable to the fact that law so frequently is invoked in situations of conflict—it is called on to resolve disputes, to respond to problems that are deemed to arise out of conflicting interests. . . .

The conflict aspect of legal language—the way it talks about situations and social problems as matters of conflicting rights or interests—fosters polarized understandings of issues and limits the ability to understand the other side. It also squeezes out of view other ways of seeing things, nonoppositional possibilities for dealing with social problems. Since a language of conflict means that one side has to be preferred, there will always be winners and losers. In a polarized language of hierarchical dualisms set within a patriarchal system, it will often be women, and their concerns, that will lose, be devalued, or be overlooked in the race to set priorities and choose sides. . . .

[A]nother problematic instance of the language of conflicting rights is the law's approach to issues of women's reproductive freedom. These issues are being framed by the law as conflicts between maternal rights, such as the right to privacy and to control one's body, and fetal rights, such as the right to life, or the right to be born in a sound and healthy state. They are also framed as conflicts between maternal rights and paternal rights, such as the man's interest in reproductive autonomy. To talk about human reproduction as a situation of conflict is a very troublesome way to understand this crucial human event in which the well-being, needs, and futures of all participants in the event, including other family members, are inextricably, sensitively connected. Just because everything that happens to one participant can affect the other does not mean they are in conflict. It suggests, rather, that they are symbiotically linked. The fetus is not there and cannot exist without the mother. An action taken for the sake of the mother that may, in a doctor's but not the mother's view, seem to pose a risk to the fetus, such as her decision to forego a caesarean birth, or to take medication while pregnant, may actually be necessary (although perhaps also still presenting a risk of harm) for the fetus because without an emotionally and physically healthy mother there cannot be a sustained fetus or child. . . .

If we stop talking about reproductive issues as issues of opposing interests, but discuss them as matters where the interests of all are always linked, for better or worse, then there is much less risk that one person in the equation—the woman—will drop out of the discussion. Yet that is what often happens in dualistic, win–lose conflict-talk. As one commentator has said, "respect for the fetus is purchased at the cost of denying the value of women."[10] . . . Legal discourse is frequently guided by the male-based medical perspective, which, when matched with the earning process of win–lose legal discourse, pushes the mother further into the recesses of invisibility. Dawn Johnsen offers an insightful analysis of how this process works: "[b]y separating the interests of the fetus from those of the pregnant woman, and then examining, often post hoc, the effect on the fetus of isolated decisions made by the woman on a daily basis during pregnancy, the state is likely to exaggerate the potential risks to the fetus and undervalue the costs of the loss of autonomy suffered by the woman."[11] A chilling example of the process of obliterating the woman occurred in a case in which a court ordered a caesarean section performed on a woman over her religious objections. The mother virtually disappeared from the text, and certainly her autonomy was of little concern to the court, as the judge wrote that all that stood between the fetus and "its independent existence, was, put simply, a doctor's scalpel."[12] The court did not even say an incision in "the mother." Just "a scalpel"—the mother was not mentioned as a person who would be cut by that scalpel, who would have to undergo risky surgery. She was not mentioned as someone whose health and existence were necessary to the child's life; she was no more than an obstacle to the fetus' life. . . .

The legal approach to the problem of pornography as if it presented a conflict between women's and men's interests in not being objectified and degraded, and the societal interest in free speech, is another example of unproductive conflict-talk which limits our understanding of a problem and of women's experiences. . . . Talking about the pornography issue as presenting an inherent conflict with free speech, and thus simply a matter of balancing the weights of the respective interests, leaves the meaning and scope to be given to "speech" undiscussed. The conflict-talk also leaves the framework of free speech law unexamined. Yet the terms of that framework define moral harm to the consumers of pornography, and not physical harm to the people who are used to make it or are victimized by it, as the appropriate focus of legal concern. . . .

The dichotomous, polarized, either/or framework of legal language also makes it a reductionist language—one that does not easily embrace complexity or nuance. Something either must be one way or another. It cannot be a complicated mix of factors and still be legally digestible. . . .

. . . The law has a hard time hearing, or believing, other languages. That is part of its power. One of the other languages that the law does not easily hear is that associated with the emotions, with expression of bursting human passion and aspirations. Law is a language firmly committed to the "reason" side of the reason/emotion dichotomy. Indeed, the law distrusts injuries deemed emotional in character; it suspects them as fraudulent, as feigned, as not important. The inability to hear the voice of emotion, to respond to thinking from the emotions, is one of the limitations of the legal voice. There are some things that just cannot be said by using the legal voice. Its terms depoliticize, decharge, and dampen. Rage, pain, elation, the aching, thirsting, hungering for freedom on one's own terms, love and its joys and terrors, fear, utter frustration at being contained and constrained by legal language—all are diffused by legal language. . . .

Examples of the "fit" problem can be found throughout law. How can we fit a woman's experience of living in a world of violent pornography into obscenity doctrine, which is focused on moral harm to consumers of pornography? How can women fit the reality of pregnancy into equality doctrine without getting hung up on the horns of the sameness–difference dilemma? How can women fit the difference between a wanted and an unwanted pregnancy into the doctrinal rhetoric of privacy and "choice"? This rhetoric presumes a sort of isolated autonomy alien to the reality of a pregnant woman. How can women fit the psychological and economic realities of being a battered woman into criminal law, which puts the word "domestic" before "violence"? This choice of terminology reduces the focus on the debilitating effects of violence and increases attention to the fact that the setting is the home, an environment in which we are all supposedly free to come and go as we "choose." How can women fit the way incest victims repress what has happened to them until the memory is released by some triggering event in adulthood with the narrow temporal requirements of statute of limitations law? How can women fit the fact that this crime, and others of sexualized violence against women, so often happens behind closed doors with no "objective witnesses," into the proof requirements of evidentiary law? . . .

Legal language frames the issues, it defines the terms in which speech in the legal world must occur, it tells us how we should understand a problem and which explanations are acceptable and which are not. Since this language has been crafted primarily by white men, the way it frames issues, the way it defines problems, and the speakers and speech it credits, do not readily include women. Legal language commands: abstract a situation from historical, social, and political context; be "objective" and avoid the lens of nonmale experience; invoke universal principles such as "equality" and "free choice"; speak with the voice of dispassionate reason; be simple, direct, and certain; avoid the complexity of varying, interacting perspectives, and overlapping multi-textured explanations; and most of all, tell it and see it "like a man"—put it in terms that relate to men and to which men can relate.

Feminist theory, on the other hand, which is not derived from looking first to law, but rather to the multiple experiences and voices of women as the frame of reference, tells us to look at things in their historical, social, and political context, including power and gender; distrust abstractions and universal rules, because "objectivity" is really perspectived and abstractions just hide the biases; question everything, especially the norms or assumptions implicit in received doctrine, question the content and try to redefine the boundaries; distrust attributions of essential difference and acknowledge that experiences of both men and women are multiple, diverse, overlapping and thus difference itself may not be a relevant legal criterion; break down hierarchies of race, gender, or power; embrace diversity, complexity, and contradiction—give up on the need to tell "one true story" because it is too likely that that story will be the story of the dominant group; listen to the voice of "emotion" as well as the voice of reason and learn to value and legitimate what has been denigrated as "mere emotion."[13]

Dealing with the Dilemma of Legal Language

So, what's a woman do? Give up on law, on legal language entirely? Disengage from the legal arena of the struggle? Neither of these strategies is really an available option. . . . Because law is such a powerful, authoritative language, one that insists that to be heard you try to speak its language, we cannot pursue the strategy suggested by theorists from other disciplines such as the French feminists, of devising a new woman's language that rejects "phallologocentric" discourse.[14]

Nor can we abandon caring whether law hears us. Whether or not activists for women look to law as one means for pursuing change, the law will still operate on and affect women's situations. Law will be present through direct regulation, through nonintervention when intervention is needed, and through helping to keep something invisible when visibility and validation are needed.[15] Law will continue to reflect and shape prevailing social and individual understandings of problems, and thus will continue to play a role in silencing and discrediting women.

Since law inevitably will be one of the important discourses affecting the status of women, we must engage it. We must pursue trying to bring more of women's experiences, perspectives, and voices into law in order to empower women and help legitimate these experiences. But this is not as easy as it sounds, because there is no "one truth" of women's experiences, and women's own understandings of their experiences are themselves affected by legal categorization. . . .

There have been examples of promising word changes and consequent meaning changes in legal discourse. Consider the now widespread use of the term "sexual harassment," for what used to be considered a tort of invading individual dignity or sensibilities; the term "battering" for domestic violence. But even these language changes get confined by the legal frameworks into which they are placed. . . .

It is not my purpose to offer a simple, neat, for all times solution to the dilemma of legal language. Indeed, to even think that is possible would be contradictory to my message—it would be a capitulation to the legal ways of thinking that I seek to destablize in order to expand. But I am not without solutions to the dilemma of the gendered nature of legal reasoning. . . . [C]ritical awareness of the dilemma is itself important. . . . This leads to self-conscious strategic thinking about the philosophical and political implications of the meanings and programs we do endorse. Critical thinking about norms and what they leave unexamined opens up conversations about altering the norms and thus the vision of the problem. This leads to thinking about new ways of reasoning and talking. It leads to offering new definitions of existing terms; definitions justified by explorations of context and the experiences of previously excluded voices. Or, it leads to thinking about offering wholly new terms.

In addition to critical engagement with the nature of legal language, another promising strategy is to sow the mutant seeds that do exist within legal reasoning. . . . Because legal reasoning can be sensitive to context, we can work to expand the context that it deems relevant. By pulling the contextual threads of legal language, we can work toward making law more comfortable with diversity and complexity, less wedded to the felt need for universalizing, reductive principles.

The law's oft-proclaimed values of equity and fairness can also work as mutating agents. The equity side of law counsels taking individual variations and needs into account. Arguments about when this should be done in order to achieve fairness must proceed with reference to context, to differing perspectives, and to differing power positions. The more we can find openings to argue from the perspective of those often overlooked by legal language, such as the people upon whom the legal power is being exercised, or those disempowered or silenced or rendered invisible by the traditional discourse, the more the opportunities to use the engine of fairness and equity to expand the comprehension of legal language.

Notes

1. The critique of objectivity and neutrality as not what they claim to be but as partial, male-biased perspectives is a standard and crucial part of current feminist theory that has moved beyond being merely reformist to challenging the

foundations of disciplines. I have developed it elsewhere; see Finley, Transcending Equality Theory: A Way Out of the Maternity and the Workplace Debates, Part 2 this volume; and Finley, Choice and Freedom: Elusive Issue in the Search for Gender Justice, 96 Yale L.J. 914 (1987). In feminist legal theory, its best-known expositor, and one of the first to promote it, is Catharine MacKinnon. . . . For examples from other disciplines, see C. Gilligan, In a Different Voice: Psychological Theory and Women's Development (Harvard University Press 1982); S. Harding, The Science Question in Feminism (Cornell University Press 1986); A. Jaggar, Feminist Politics and Human Nature (Rowman and Allanheld 1983).

2. Some linguistic theorists have posited, compellingly I believe, that all language, as we currently know it, is male. . . . Consequently, some feminist theorists say that in order to escape patriarchy, women need to create a new language all their own, emanating from their bodies/embodied selves. See, e.g., M. Daly, GYN/Ecology, The Meta-Ethics of Radical Feminism (Beacon, 1978). Consider also French feminist theorists such as Luce Irigaray and Julia Kristeva. See I. de Courtivron & E. Marks eds., New French Feminisms: An Anthology (Schocken, 1981).

3. This is why Gilligan calls the rights-based ethic the male voice, and the care-based ethic the female voice. She, too, disclaims biological determinism. See Gilligan, In a Different Voice, *supra* note 1.

4. 83 U.S. 442 (1873).

5. 417 U.S. 484 (1973).

6. See, e.g., Jaggar, Feminist Politics, *supra* note 1.

7. See Harding, Science Question, *supra* note 1, at 171. See also N. Hartsock, Money, Sex and Power: Toward a Feminist Historical Materialism (Longman, 1983); Jaggar, Feminist Politics, *supra* note 1.

8. Tort law, for example, reluctantly and rarely allows recovery for emotional distress caused when a loved one is injured.

9. 488 U.S. 469 (1989).

10. Farrel-Smith, Rights-Conflict, Pregnancy and Abortion, in C. Gould ed., Beyond Domination: New Perspectives on Women and Philosophy 27 (Rowman and Allanheld, 1983).

11. Johnsen, The Creation of Fetal Rights: Conflicts with Women's Constitutional Rights to Liberty, Privacy and Equal Protection, 95 Yale L.J. 599, 613 (1986).

12. In the Matter of Madyun Fetus, 114 Daily Washington L. Rep. 2233, 2240 (D.C. Super. Ct. July 26, 1986).

13. For examples of work that seeks to value the voice of caring [in addition to Gilligan], see N. Noddings, Caring—A Feminine Approach to Ethics and Moral Education (University of California Press, 1984); S. Ruddick, Maternal Thinking: Toward a Politics of Peace (Beacon, 1989); Bender, A Lawyer's Primer on Feminist Theory and Tort, Part 1 this volume; and Tronto, Beyond Gender Difference to a Theory of Care, 12 Signs 644 (1987).

The elements of feminist theory I have laid out in this paragraph are themselves not universal characteristics of a unified, universal feminist theory. They are the elements of where I am at in my feminist thinking about law, drawn from many sources. Some of my more post-modernist, post-structuralist claims will be particularly controversial, but I have found feminist works from this intellectual movement most helpful to my thinking about the nature of law and how we can work to change its meanings. See, e.g., Harding, Science Question, *supra* note 7; Flax, Postmodernism and Gender Relations in Feminist Theory, 12 Signs 621 (1987); Scott, Deconstructing Equality Versus Difference: Or, the Uses of Post-structuralist Theory for Feminism, 14 Feminist Stud. 33 (1988).

14. For examples of the French feminist theory, see L. Irigaray, This Sex Which Is Not One (C. Porter trans., Cornell University Press, 1985), and Speculum of the Other Woman (G. Gill trans., Cornell University Press, 1985); Cixous, Laugh of the Medusa, in de Courtivron & Marks eds., New French Feminisms, *supra* note 2. Note that one of the French feminist language theorists, Julia Kristeva, proposes critical engagement with the existing language as a way to change it. . . .

15. For a discussion of these three ways in which law intervenes, even when it is not seeming to do so, see K. O'Donovan, Sexual Divisions in Law 11–19 (Weidenfeld & Nicolson, 1985); see also Olsen, The Myth of State Intervention in the Family, 18 U. Mich. J.L. Ref. 835 (1985).

❖ Zig-zag Stitching and the Seamless Web: Thoughts on "Reproduction" and the Law

MARIE ASHE

WHENEVER I READ law relating to women and motherhood, I find myself sickened. When I read Roe v. Wade[1] I am filled with anger; when I read the *Baby M*[2] trial court decision, I am enraged. . . . Feelings of humiliation, of indignation, of desperation, horror, of rage. Reading *A.C.*,[3] I feel something close to despair.

Often, in the last several weeks, I have set aside my notes and readings concerning motherhood and law. I leave them with a sense of hopelessness. Often I have picked up some needlework—sewing, embroidery, needlepoint, knitting—seeking respite from the feelings that overwhelm me, restoration. The rhythm of my fingers becomes a rhythm of my inner being, a peace in my breast. A dropped stitch. A gentle flutter. A minor interruption of rhythm and pattern. I pick it up easily, drawing it into the larger design. I exist in a silent space. Untroubled.

Law reaches every silent space. It invades the secrecy of women's wombs. It breaks every silence, uttering itself. Law-language, juris-diction. It defines. It commands. It forces.

Law as the seamless web we believe and die in. I cannot think of a single case involving legal regulation of motherhood without thinking of all. They constitute an interconnected network of variegated threads. Abortion. "Surrogacy." Supervision of women's pregnancies. Exclusion of pregnant women from the workplace. Termination of the parental rights of indigent or battered women. Enforcement of the "relinquishments" for adoption executed by confused and vulnerable women. Forced Caesarean sections. Policings of home births. Following the thread which is any one, I find it intertwined with each of the others. When I loosen a single thread, it tightens the others. Each knotted and entangled in fabrications of legal doctrine; each attached to notions of neutrality and generality.

Work on the seamless web. Writing of women, of mothers, of language and law. Rather different from passing threads through my fingers, working them into subtle or dazzling color. More like the impossible task of the miller's daugh-

---

13 Nova L. Rev. 355 (1989).

ter.[4] Except not merely to spin into golden thread a room full of straw. Beyond that, to work the threads into some recognizable shape, some better fit.

We have been weaving forever. And, apparently forever, our work has been assigned and defined by others. The work of victims: *She knows not what the curse may be/And so she weaveth steadily/ And little other care has she/The Lady of Shalott.* Work lacking inherent value: That of Penelope. Work of unfounded pride: That of Arachne. Ancillary work: That of Ariadne. Work of destruction: That of Medea.[5] Regulation and definition have always already assessed our work and our nature. . . .

During each of the past thirty-five winters, I have—depending on the size of that winter's bed—either folded at its foot or spread over its width a counterpane worked by my maternal grandmother.[6] I never met my grandmother. She lived all her life in the West of Ireland and has been dead more than half my lifetime. . . .

I remember the first winter when her coverlet came to me. I was, at that time of lesser sophistication, dubious about its color: a mingling of yarrow and goldenrod. Its warmth was extraordinary. Its great weight, its heaviness: transformative. Sleeping beneath it I am not merely warmed, but flattened, altered, changed in my being: I winter below the frost line.

This year I have found its yarns frayed and worn in several places. I have begun to wonder whether I will be able to repair it. I would like to give to my own daughter my grandmother's work, this text inscribing her touch and her bodily being, blessed by her eyes, recording the rhythm of breath and heartbeat, the scent of her lap.

Does the strongest of stitching come from our bodies? The mother of Snow White stained her sewing with blood. What if we wrote with words from the deepest parts of our bodies, our selves. Hélène Cixous and Luce Irigaray recommend, and simulate, writing with milk and with blood.[7] Which makes for a different *écriture*. A writing inscribing lineaments of female bodies. Marked by our varying rhythms and cycles. Our stitches will seldom be straight.

Zig-zag stitchings and zig-zag thought. Useful (as in buttonholing) for definition; (as in edging seams) for strength; (as in embroidery) for beauty.

It has seemed to me that the major attributes of legal discourse concerning women and mothers are these: it originates in men; it defines women with certainty; it attempts to mask the operations of power; it silences other discourse.[8] I take as given: Law that silences any discourse is without warrant.

Primigravida

My first birthing happened eighteen years ago. I was a *primigravida*. I had read all I could find concerning pregnancy. I was therefore able, upon hearing myself referred to as a "*prima*," on the morning of October 31, 1970, at Newton-Wellesley Hospital, to recognize that what was meant was "*primigravida*," a woman for the first time gravid, heavy and ripe with child. I was, however surprised to find myself so-called by someone I had not expected to meet. The doctor whom I had come to consider "my obstetrician" made no appearance that Saturday morning. I arrived at the hospital at 6:30 A.M., at which time a labor room nurse called my doctor's office and reached the physician, unfamiliar to me, who arrived at 6:50. He examined me briefly and went to the phone at the nurses' station fifteen feet from my bed. It was 7:00. I'm not sure I'll be able to make it by 9:00, he said. I'm stuck here with a *prima*. It may be awhile.

I had never given birth before (I was a *prima*). I had no idea how long the process would take. I knew he was in a hurry. I knew that the "*prima*" reference was relevant to his weekend plans, that "*primas*" often take longer in labor than "*multis*."

At 7:10 I felt a change. The grinding and tearing pain abated. The nurse shouted to someone, She's ten centimeters dilated. The doctor left the nursing area. I felt a sensation of incredible pressure, without pain, and a headiness. The nurse wheeled my labor room bed through a short hallway, through the double doors of the delivery room. She positioned it alongside a narrow table. Climb across, she said. I felt utter astonishment. She spoke matter-of-factly. Did it happen that other women were able, at this stage of their labors, to climb with agility from one table to another? I don't think I can do it alone, I told her. She helped me across.

The table was extremely narrow and hard. It was like lying on an ironing board. She lifted up silver stirrups for my heels, and drew loose white cotton stockings over my legs, over my thighs. There were other people in the delivery room then. I was unable to recognize them; they were robed in green, masked and gloved.

I recognized the doctor's voice as he spoke to the nurses. Push whenever you feel the urge, the nurse said to me. I felt the urge, and I pushed. Can I raise myself up on my elbows, I asked them. That won't work on this table, the nurse said. Just push again, now, it won't be long. I pushed again and uttered a long, low moan, lasting the duration of the push. There's no need for that kind of noise, he said. I felt humiliation and fury. Damn it, he said, she's not pushing hard enough. Get me a forceps.

I pushed again, my back and shoulders against the table. I liked its resistance to me. I felt you slip down. Stop, stop, he said. Stop pushing now, I have to numb you for the episiotomy. I tried not to push. He had a hypodermic needle between my knees and pricked it into my vagina. It hurt. I need to push, I told them. I could feel you like a ball of fire between my thighs. I reached down to touch my own flesh, to comfort myself, to slow your passage slightly, to let you out easily. Keep your hand away from there, he said. That's a sterile area. I needed to push again. He slit my vagina. Then he backed off. You slipped out gently. (You were so beautiful.) I cried and I laughed. I could not take my eyes off you, Anna. It was 7:30 A.M.

A.C. was a *prima*, too, it appears. Primigravid and, in the court's words, *in extremis*. She was dying.

I think that when people are dying they call up in imagination the times of their childhood, times of having felt nurtured. I imagine that at my own death I will be less a "mother" than I am at this moment, and much more nearly a "child." My good friend Jennifer died of cancer at age thirty-four, leaving her two young daughters. On the day of her death I visited her. She did not recognize me. Her mother was with her, and when Jennifer spoke at all, she spoke, in fragments, of her childhood. She did not speak, at that dying time, of further sacrifices that she might make for her daughters, for whom she had sacrificed much in her life.

As my father died, slowly, last year, I found, each time I visited him, that his thoughts and preoccupations turned, progressively, to earlier and earlier times of his life. He cared not so much about the experiences of yesterday as about the experiences of eighty years ago.

As A.C. submitted to the pain of her dying, as she passed through that deep and solitary inner experience of body and soul, she was offered by medicine and law—not comfort but additional trial by torment. The representatives of medicine and law found it impossible to tolerate the mysterious unboundaried commingling which constituted the being of Angie Carder. What nature and her own strong desire and intent joined together, they set asunder. Finding insufficient her sharing the strength of every dying breath with her child-to-be, they violently wrenched from Angie Carder that not-ready-to-be-born being who died almost immediately thereafter. A forced abortion. The abortling passed from blissful water, through bloody fire, through hostile air. To earth with the flesh of her mother.

For Angie Carder, *primigravida*, maternity was mandatory, at the time when she was most incapable of it, at the time when she herself most needed mothering, the time of her being, "*in extremis.*" No representative of law and medicine mothered Angie Carder. Her own mother's intercession on behalf of Angie was ignored by medicine and law. Angie's own mother and Angie. The abortling and Angie. Each forcibly separated from the other. Angie's dying body cut, bled, stitched and scarred. Marked by the mutilation of a *rite de passage.* Followed by final passage. Newspaper accounts reported that Angie and the aborted being were reunited at their funeral. *Pietà manqué.* And the grandmother grieving. Pietà within pietà? Not precisely.

Did the judges understand these things? Should they have known? Could they have known? Is it a mystery in its very essence? An Eleusinian mystery? Is there something we ought to have said, or ought to begin to say, to alter legal understanding of women: our bodies, our selves. . . .

"Mortal Decisions"

The "ordinary" medico-legal regulations of pregnancy and birthing (restricting time, place, and manner of conducting pregnancy and of giving birth) are so pervasive that we often fail to recognize them as in fact regulations—particular cultural variants, perhaps, of a general and universal regulation of female sexuality and female personhood. The "extraordinary" regulations that have recently become apparent in abortion regulation as well as in requirements—including major surgery—imposed upon pregnant women by courts, are in fact not different in kind from the "ordinary" regulations. Nonetheless, the suddenness of their introduction or the inadequacies of the theoretical structures within which they have been discussed have disclosed their problematic nature.

The rhetoric surrounding both discussion of abortion and discussion of recently intensified regulation of pregnancy in the name of "fetal" protection has tended to polarize into divisions about the relative "rights" that should attach, respectively, to women and to "fetal life." There has often seemed no common structure within which proponents and opponents of various regulatory schemes might speak meaningfully and understandingly with one another, with respect for our different experiences.

One of the most striking features of "pro-life" rhetoric is its recognition of abortion as a deathly act—the extinguishment of some form of human life—and its exposure of underlying experiences of horror—generally transmuted into self-recrimination and moral certitude—in the reports that pro-life women produce in recounting their abortion experiences. I have been struck, correspondingly, by the absence from most "pro-choice" rhetoric of a discourse of death as well as of discourses of horror or guilt. Pro-life advocates have accurately recognized in pro-choice discourse a practice of abstraction that tends to obliterate or to erase the realities of bloodiness and violence attached to abortion. Women who consciously experience abortion become familiar with those realities and respond variously to them; women whose anaesthetized experiences of abortion distance us from awareness of the bloody violence of abortion sometimes discover in post-abortion experiences reminders of the death-dealing power that is exercised in abortion. Both kinds of recognition—that occurring during the course of abortion and that arising later—may evoke a range of differing responses in different women.

Abortion is not merely a "moral" but also a "mortal" decision. The failure of pro-choice discourse to so recognize it—to acknowledge the violence intrinsic to abortion—has constructed impediments to our speaking truly and deeply—and more variously—of what abortion means to us. It has discouraged our discoveries—beneath rhetoric and sloganeering, and beneath the obfuscation of medico-legal discourse—of the reality of common bodily experience underlying the various interpretations of different women.

The same failures of discourse have affected discussions of the proper legal treatment of pregnancy in general. The *A.C.* court properly characterized the judgment to be made in that case as a "mortal decision." In that characterization, it hints at the questions that lie at the heart of all "reproduction"-related matters presented as legal issues: Who will be permitted to exercise the power of extinguishing certain forms of human life? May women be entrusted to exercise such power? Ought the choice of mortality by women—or the willing assumption of certain risks of death be tolerated by law?

I ask myself: What does it mean to put to death, intentionally, a living thing?

Sheltered, like most urban people, from the realities of death-dealing that underlie daily life, I have seldom consciously accomplished the death of another being whom I have recognized as "like" me, seldom executed clearly "mortal" decisions. In the summer of 1983, during one of my pregnancies, our dog, Flash, gave birth to a litter of pups. A Monday in July. A midwestern summer afternoon. Brilliant, glaring sunlight. Oppressive heat. I watch Flash dig a deep trench alongside the foundation of our house, in the afternoon sun. She works with a kind of determined ferocity. I observe her with interest, coming, gradually, to recognize in her frenzy a preparation for her imminent birthing.

I take some soft towels and newspapers into the garage to make a nest for her, hopeful that she will come into that cool, dark place which, to me, seems more comfortable that the place she has selected. I call her into the garage and pet her. I close the door so that she won't go outside again. I leave her, to take a nap.

My son comes into my room in excitement. He sits on the edge of my bed. Flash has seven puppies, he tells me, but I think there's something wrong with one of them. . . . It's not moving. In my weariness, I am not eager to go down to the dog. I tell David that I'll come soon. I rest a bit longer and then go downstairs. David meets me in the kitchen. There are eleven now, he tells me. I groan silently and go out to see Flash.

She lies on the toweling. Her eyes slightly glazed. I count eleven pups: two appear lifeless; nine squirm about. I sit on a bench and watch her deliver three more, lick them off, chew on and swallow their sacs. She looks exhausted.

I pick up the lifeless pups and wrap them in paper toweling. Put them into a shoe box. I find Flash's water bowl, fill it up, bring it to her. She drinks, lying still in her sodden nest. Using the backyard hose I fill up an old laundry tub. I then select five pups and carry them one at a time, to the tub. I drop each one into the water.

I am inexperienced at death-dealing. I don't want to watch the pups drown. I don't want my children to watch them. I drag the tub to the side of the house. I cover it with a metal lid. Cowardly, then, I leave them.

Later, in early evening, I return to uncover the tub. I lift each pup, in fascinated horror, out of the tub. I wrap each in paper towels. I am too tired and too sick to bury them. I place them, in a plastic bag, in the trash can, to be carried away in the morning.

I have never felt a continuing guilt, a profound regret, a deep misgiving about that "mortal decision." But it has remained in my memory—a grave act. I have not forgotten the weight of these small, wet, stiffened forms in my hands.

Is what I did there "right" or "wrong"? It is neither. It is only what I have done. Another women might have done differently. Even performing what appeared an identical act, she might have done differently. The farm woman drowning kittens as a matter of course may have an experience different from mine. Another woman might have felt unable to intervene in any way to cause the deaths of the helpless pups. In acting decisively I spent little or no time in reflection. What I did was what seemed to me proper, if somewhat unpleasant.

For those of us living in cities, even the care of our animals is ordinarily so medicalized—so delegated to medical practice that in our closest contact with animal life we are generally removed from the more immediate contact with animal death that has characterized human experience in other times and places. We are seldom required to confront very directly—by our own agency or observation—the choices that present themselves to us because of the limitations of life, because of the reality of death underlying all life and encroaching upon it. We formulate moral theory in places removed from the physical realities of our death-dealing decisions. Because of our distance from those physical realities we often fail to feel—in our flesh and bones—the shudder of horror that ordinarily arises at witnessing sudden, willfully accomplished transitions from the state of individual existence to a state of undifferentiation.

Anthropologists and ethnologists report the existence of an area defined as "sacred" surrounding the intentional dealing of death—the sacrifice of animal or of human life. I wonder whether those accounts have some relevance for our understanding of the processes underlying present formulations of abortion law—Roe v. Wade as well as more restrictive state statutory schemes—and the formulations expressed in *A.C.* Certainly, the medicalization of our "reproductive" processes has significantly distanced most of us—including legislators and judges—from the immediacy of the female bodily experiences of pregnancy, birth, and abortion. That distancing has obscured the horror and fear that—ethnologists theorize—arises universally in the face of female violence and that seeks to control and regulate women's "mortal decisions" for the reason that such decisions remind us of our frailties: our dependence upon the flesh and minds of our mothers; the finitude of our bodily lives; the constant imminence of a death that may swallow us up.[9] Is it possible to speak of experiences of abortion and other "mortal decisions" in a different discourse, outside the language of law and of medicine?

Many writers have theorized about the powerful ambivalences about death which, displaced against maternal bodies, have motivated the pan-cultural subordination of women through regulation of the broad range of our activity currently subsumed under the term "reproduction." They have noted, as a most striking attribute of discourse regulating women's activity, its unfounded confidence about the nature of "woman" and of motherhood—a confidence that purports to justify its own exercise of power.[10] Such ambivalence about maternal bodies resides in women as well as in men. Barbara Johnson,[11] in a dense and powerful discussion of the rhetoric of abortion expressed in women's poetry, has found evidence that not only medical technologists but pregnant women ourselves seem unable to speak of abortion in voices free of identification with the "fetus." She finds in the pronomic usages embodied in those texts evidence not only of the non-binary nature of the pregnancy experience but also of the reality of a recollective identification with the experience of pre-natality, of "fetal" being.

Such rhetorical and psychological analyses point to the difficulty of speaking of abortion in ways that adequately utter its subjective realities, its meanings for our personhoods. They invite deeper exploration. It seems to me that the departure point for such exploration must be women's own accounts of our experiences, uttered with a commitment of faithfulness to the truths of female bodies suppressed in the dominant discourse. To the degree that women produce such writings, we may avoid the abstraction that has characterized and limited the work of certain cautious and sensitive male commentators presently writing about female "reproductive" experiences. To the degree that we avoid essentialism we will recognize the undesirability of *any* regulation of abortion.

If the purpose of contemporary feminist critique is to expose and explore profound and powerful ambivalences—most strongly expressed in the medico-legal discourse of women—it will succeed, however temporarily, only to the degree that its own discourse departs from or ruptures through the dominant rhetoric, expressing a different knowledge. Thus, women's critiques of the prevailing discourse must be marked by a tentativeness, a newness, a preciseness, an insistent refusal to venture into abstraction unconnected to the common experiences of very different women, and a firm rejection of simplistic and violent categorizations. Our alternative discourse must be capable of responding persuasively to the question by which we must judge not only medico-legal but every discursive account of women: How do you know what you claim to know?

I have experienced a number of spontaneous abortions—miscarriages—and one intentional abortion. Of the latter experience, I am able to say with certainty that its physical and emotional aftermaths have been far more severely negative than I had been led by any medical practitioner to expect. Of the actual surgical procedure I can say virtually nothing. I was anaesthetized during the procedure, which took place quite early in my pregnancy, and therefore had no real awareness of what was done to my body. Like a woman anaesthetized in childbirth, I experience a gap between the physical trauma to my body and my waking consciousness thereof.

In the miscarriages that I have sustained, my experience has been quite other. In those situations, I have always been very much aware—and, in all those cases, distressed by—my changing body. In all those cases I have wished that the pregnancies would continue, and have grieved their endings as losses. . . .

What I have known of abortion led me, for a long time, to generalize, to think, with Gwendolyn Brooks, that "Abortions do not let you forget. You remember the babies you got that you did not get."[12] It led me, in overgeneralization, to believe that the choice of abortion is always a difficult and troubled moral decision. However, in recent years I have come to recognize that even that generalization may be without foundation. That *my* experience is not the experience of every woman. That grief is not necessarily the prevailing emotion attached to abortion.

I have become familiar with accounts of my friends—and of other women—that express the enormous relief they have felt at bringing body into harmony with mind through abortion, at restoring their bodies to the unitary, non-pregnant states that conformed with the definitions of selfhood articulated by those women at the times when they chose abortion. Such accounts have begun to be offered to courts making abortion decisions. . . .[13] For some women, abortion is nothing other than a relief, it appears, while for others it becomes nothing other than a kind of dying—suicidal if not murderous.[14]

Different constructions of bodily experience. Different stitchings of web. When I hear varying narratives and when I recognize the various truths in different accounts, I ask whether *any* legal regulation of "reproduction" can avoid a perpetration of violence upon women. I wonder if there is any possibility of "equality" where regulation rests upon essentialist notions of gender and sexuality.

A.C. Again

Theorists sometimes identified as "cultural feminists" have often proposed that female experience gives rise to an ethic of "caring" that differs from the dominant ethic of "rights" constructed out of the profound alienation of men from their mothers' bodies. Other feminist writers have critiqued the "caring" emphasis as merely a variant on rhetorics that operate to justify traditional self-victimization of women.[15] I ask: What ethic relating to "reproduction" ought to be reflected in law?

In reading of *A.C.* and of Angie Carder, I have found one clear expression marked by the attributes that, I suggested above, will characterize powerful deconstructive and reconstructive feminist critique—attributes of clarity, newness, faithfulness to bodily experience, rejection of abstraction, and refusal to be reduced or simplified to facilitate categorization. That expression comes closer to uttering what I find a persuasive feminist ethic than any other voice I have heard in discussion of *A.C.* and related cases. It is the voice of Angie Carder's mother, Nettie Stoner.

Nettie Stoner, at the time of the *A.C.* hearing, was a woman who had already known much physical suffering. She had lost both her legs in an accident that had occurred nine years before. That loss had enabled her understanding of her daughter Angie's experience of amputation two years later, incident to treatment of her cancer. So intimately did Nettie Stoner understand her daughter's experience that she recognized the recurrence of Angie's cancer during pregnancy, before that recurrence had been recognized by her diagnostic physicians. Likewise, she felt certain that the "fetus" would not survive, as a healthy child, the court-ordered surgery performed upon Angie Carder.

Nettie Stoner testified at the hearing before the trial court that ordered her daughter's submission to caesarean section. The following is an account of the testimony she gave in response to questioning by the court-appointed "lawyer for the 'fetus.'" It is testimony that arises out of maternal knowledge—a particular, local knowledge—that expresses an ethic characterized not by the sentimentality expected of and tolerated in mothers, but by a cold-eyed, unflinching strength, a clear recognition of the impossibility of finally avoiding death:

When it was time for the court to hear from Nettie, everyone leaned forward a bit to hear about Angie. "She wanted to live long enough to hold that baby," Nettie began. "She did not want me to have to take care of that baby. She told me that. She wanted to live to hold that baby."

Mishkin: "This is terribly difficult for you, I know, and I'm sorry to have to ask you some questions, but I think it's important at least to get some sense of how you, as a family, would be able to cope if there were a live baby to come out of this. Do you have, for example, is there medical insurance? Is there any way that you have or are you totally stranded?"

Nettie: "Nobody. Nobody would insure a baby. Nobody would insure my daughter. Nobody."

Mishkin: "So there is no family insurance that would cover the baby's care?

Nettie: "No. That doesn't even enter into it. I don't care about the money. It's just that I know there will be something wrong with this baby. I can't handle it. I've handled [Angie] and myself."

Mishkin: "I understand."

Nettie: "Nobody else can love a child like that and I know what it would be. No."

Mishkin: "Would you—would you even have the resources to handle a healthy baby?"

Nettie: "No."

Mishkin: "If the baby was not compromised?"

Nettie: "Not really. Rick, her husband, they have only been married eight months. I mean, he hasn't even had her long enough. How is he going to cope with a baby? They don't have any family, just Rick and his mom. It's me and I'm in a wheelchair. I can't put that burden on us anymore. Angela is the only one that wanted that baby to love. She said she wanted something of her very own."

Mishkin: "Would you consider placing the baby for adoption?"

Nettie: "Never. Never."

Mishkin: "What would you do if the baby survived?"

Nettie: "Who wants it?"

At this point, Mishkin recalls, some of the people in the room seemed shocked at Nettie's bluntness. "I'm sure it was out of stress," Mishkin says. She pushed on.

Mishkin: "I guess I'm asking you a terribly difficult question, but I'm trying to determine. . . .

Nettie: "I would take care of the baby. I would never put it up for adoption. I would do the best I could, but we don't want it. Angela wanted that baby. It was her baby. Let the baby die with her."

> *Rick* [Angie's husband]: "Please."
> *Nettie:* "It's hers."
> *Mishkin:* "I have no further questions."[16]

Nettie Stoner's voice speaks of honoring life by honoring death. It accepts ambivalence. In discourse that "some" might find "shocking," that others dismiss as arising "out of stress," she honors a truth of maternity. Nettie Stoner speaks of both the limitations and the enormous power of mother-love. She expresses the truths that "fetal life" depends utterly upon the life and will of a pregnant woman; that sometimes "fetal" death and maternal death—human deaths are the best life has to offer; and that "Death is the mother of beauty."[17] I hear in Nettie Stoner's words the enduring and insistent assertion that legally endorsed violations of women's bodies in the name of "life"—hateful legal constructs that impose "love" and "self-sacrifice" upon women as our duties—are perverse. That in its alienation from nature law works harms far more destructive than the deaths that arise out of nature or out of the natural limitations of women.

These words spoken by Nettie Stoner from her wheelchair echo with power, with passion, with honest love. I honor her "mortal decision."

When will her thought, her decision, find expression in law that explicitly lets women be—in our limitations and in our differences, law that leaves us alone?

The self-accounts of mothers and of all women—pregnant, birthing, aborting, suffering violations, or growing in power—constitute utterances closer to the reality of women's experiences than does any formulation of law or of medicine. While our generalizations and extrapolations from those experiences may be in conflict, when we attend to one another we discover truths that, rising out of our natural and acculturated bodies, do not conflict. How to work those yarns into the fabric of a law that calls itself "humanist?" . . .

I want a law that will let us be women. That, recognizing the violence inherent in every regulation of female "reproduction," defines an area of non-regulation, within which we will make, each of us, our own "mortal decisions."

There is a kind of embroidery called cut-work. It is executed by the careful placement of smooth satin stitch and the excision of fabric within the area outlined by that stitching. The cut-work opens up spaces within the fabric. Openness itself constitutes, then, both part of the fabric and non-part. It requires both needle and scissors. Construction and deconstruction. Within and against patterns of sameness, it inscribes difference.

Notes

1. Roe v. Wade, 410 U.S. 113, *reh'g denied*, 410 U.S. 959 (1973).
2. In re Baby M, 109 N.J. 396, 537 A.2d 1227 (1988), *reversing in part* 217 N.J. Super. 313, 525 A.2d 1128 (1987).

3. [In re A.C. involved Angela Carder, a pregnant woman who was terminally ill. When she was twenty-six weeks pregnant, Angela had a recurrence of the cancer which she had experienced as an adolescent. At the initiative of a hospital administrator, a trial court judge ordered a cesarean in the interests of the fetus—despite the objections of Angela's family, husband, and physicians. Following the surgery, the infant lived two hours; Angela died two days later. Several years after her death, an appellate court reversed the decision. *Ed.*] In re A.C., 533 A.2d 611 (D.C. 1987), *vacated and reh'g granted*, 539 A.2d 203 (1988); *reversed and remanded*, 573 A.2d 1235 (D.C.App. 1990).

4. J. Grimm, The Complete Grimm's Fairy Tales (Pantheon, 1972).

5. A. Tennyson, The Lady of Shalott, in The Complete Works of Alfred Lord Tennyson (1983). For accounts of Penelope, Arachne, Ariadne and Medea, see R. Graves, The Greek Myths (Penguin, 1960).

6. Julia O'Donnell Cahill (1882–1966).

7. H. Cixous (with Catherine Clement), The Newly Born Woman (University of Minnesota Press, 1985); L. Irigaray, Speculum of the Other Woman (Cornell University Press, 1985) and This Sex Which Is Not One (Cornell University Press, 1985).

8. For a most powerful discussion of these features of Western tradition and its figuration of the "Other" as feminine, see A. Jardine, Gynesis: Configurations of Women and Modernity (Cornell University Press, 1985).

9. See Semiotics of Biblical Abomination, in J. Kristeva, Powers of Horror: An Essay on Abjection (Columbia University Press, 1982).

10. *Id.* See also D. Dinnerstein, The Mermaid and the Minotaur: Sexual Arrangements and Human Malaise (Harper & Row, 1976); and N. Chodorow, The Reproduction of Mothering: Psychoanalysis of the Sociology of Gender (University of California Press, 1978).

11. B. Johnson, Apostrophe, Animation and Abortion, in A World of Difference (Johns Hopkins University Press, 1987).

12. G. Brooks, the mother, in Selected Poems (Harper & Row, 1963).

13. Amicus Brief for the National Abortion Rights Action League et al., Thornburgh v. American College of Obstetricians and Gynecologists, Nos. 84-498 and 84-1379. . . . For the Supreme Court opinion, see 476 U.S. 747 (1986).

14. See A. Rich, Of Woman Born 272–74 (Norton, 1976).

15. See Feminist Discourse, Moral Values and the Law: A Conversation, 34 Buff. L. Rev. 11 (1985).

16. The preceding account of the hearing testimony is borrowed directly from D. Remnick, "Whose Life Is It Anyway?" Washington Post Magazine, February 21, 1988, at 18, 20.

17. Sunday Morning, in W. Stevens, The Collected Poems of Wallace Stevens (Vintage, 1982).

❖ *On Being the Object of Property*

PATRICIA J. WILLIAMS

On Being Invisible

Reflections

FOR SOME TIME I have been writing about my great-great-grandmother. I have considered the significance of her history and that of slavery from a variety of viewpoints on a variety of occasions: in every speech, in every conversation, even in my commercial transactions class. I have talked so much about her that I finally had to ask myself what it was I was looking for. . . .

I decided that my search was based in the utility of such a quest, not mere indulgence, but a recapturing of that which had escaped historical scrutiny, which had been overlooked and underseen. I, like so many blacks, have been trying to pin myself down in history, place myself in the stream of time as significant, evolved, present in the past, continuing into the future. To be without documentation is too sustaining, too spontaneously ahistorical, too dangerously malleable in the hands of those who would rewrite not merely the past but my future as well. So I have been picking through the ruins for my roots.

What I know of my mother's side of the family begins with my great-great-grandmother. Her name was Sophie and she lived in Tennessee. In 1850, she was about twelve years old. I know that she was purchased when she was eleven by a white lawyer named Austin Miller and was immediately impregnated by him. She gave birth to my great-grandmother Mary, who was taken away from her to be raised as a house servant. I know nothing more of Sophie (she was, after all, a black single mother—in today's terms—suffering the anonymity of yet another statistical teenage pregnancy). While I don't remember what I was told about Austin Miller before I decided to go to law school, I do remember that just before my first day of class, my mother said, in a voice full of secretive reassurance, "The Millers were lawyers, so you have it in your blood."

From *Signs: Journal of Women in Culture and Society* 1988, vol. 14, no. 1. © 1988 by The University of Chicago. All rights reserved.

When my mother told me that I had nothing to fear in law school, that law was "in my blood," she meant it in a very complex sense. First and foremost, she meant it defiantly; she meant that no one should make me feel inferior because someone else's father was a judge. She wanted me to reclaim that part of my heritage from which I had been disinherited, and she wanted me to use it as a source of strength and self-confidence. At the same time, she was asking me to claim a part of myself that was the dispossessor of another part of myself; she was asking me to deny that disenfranchised little black girl of myself that felt powerless, vulnerable, and, moreover, rightly felt so.

In somewhat the same vein, Mother was asking me not to look to her as a role model. She was devaluing that part of herself that was not Harvard and refocusing my vision to that part of herself that was hard-edged, proficient, and Western. She hid the lonely, black, defiled-female part of herself and pushed me forward as the projection of a competent self, a cool rather than despairing self, a masculine rather than a feminine self.

I took this secret of my blood into the Harvard milieu with both the pride and the shame with which my mother had passed it along to me. . . .

Reclaiming that from which one has been disinherited is a good thing. Self-possession in the full sense of that expression is the companion to self-knowledge. Yet claiming for myself a heritage the weft of whose genesis is my own disinheritance is a profoundly troubling paradox.

Images

A friend of mine practices law in rural Florida. His office is in Belle Glade, an extremely depressed area where the sugar industry reigns supreme, where blacks live pretty much as they did in slavery times. . . . They are penniless and illiterate and have both a high birth rate and a high death rate.

My friend told me about a client of his, a fifteen-year-old young woman pregnant with her third child, who came seeking advice because her mother had advised a hysterectomy—not even a tubal ligation—as a means of birth control. The young woman's mother, in turn, had been advised of the propriety of such a course in her own case by a white doctor some years before. Listening to this, I was reminded of a case I worked on when I was working for the Western Center on Law and Poverty about eight years ago. Ten black Hispanic women had been sterilized by the University of Southern California–Los Angeles County General Medical Center, allegedly without proper consent, and in most instances without even their knowledge.[1] Most of them found out what had been done to them upon inquiry, after a much-publicized news story in which an intern charged that the chief of obstetrics at the hospital pursued a policy of recommending caesarean delivery and simultaneous sterilization for any pregnant woman with three or more children and on welfare. In the course of researching the appeal in that case, I remember learning that one-quarter of all Navajo women of childbearing age—literally all those of childbearing age ever admitted to a hospital—have been sterilized.

As I reflected on all this, I realized that one of the things passed on from slavery, which continues in the oppression of people of color, is a belief structure rooted in a concept of black (or brown, or red) anti-will, the antithetical embodiment of pure will. We live in a society in which the closest equivalent of nobility is the display of unremittingly controlled will-fulness. To be perceived as unremittingly will-less is to be imbued with an almost lethal trait.

Many scholars have explained this phenomenon in terms of total and infantilizing interdependency of dominant and oppressed.[2] Consider, for example, Mark Tushnet's distinction between slave law's totalistic view of personality and the bourgeois "pure will" theory of personality: "Social relations in slave society rest upon the interaction of owner with slave; the owner, having total dominion over the slave. In contrast, bourgeois social relations rest upon the paradigmatic instance of market relations, the purchase by a capitalist of a worker's labor power; that transaction implicates only a part of the worker's personality. Slave relations are total, engaging the master and slave in exchanges in which each must take account of the entire range of belief, feeling, and interest embodied by the other; bourgeois social relations are partial, requiring only that participants in a market evaluate their general productive characteristics without regard to aspects of personality unrelated to production."[3]

Although such an analysis is not objectionable in some general sense, the description of master–slave relations as "total" is, to me, quite troubling. Such a choice of words reflects and accepts—at a very subtle level, perhaps—a historical rationalization that whites had to, could do, and did do everything for these simple, above-animal subhumans. It is a choice of vocabulary that fails to acknowledge blacks as having needs beyond those that even the most "humane" or "sentimental" white slavemaster could provide.[4] In trying to describe the provisional aspect of slave law, I would choose words that revealed its structure as rooted in a concept of, again, black anti-will, the polar opposite of pure will. I would characterize the treatment of blacks by whites in whites' law as defining blacks as those who had no will. I would characterize that treatment not as total interdependency, but as a relation in which partializing judgments, employing partializing standards of humanity, impose generalized inadequacy on a race: if pure will or total control equals the perfect white person, then impure will and total lack of control equals the perfect black man or woman. Therefore, to define slave law as comprehending a "total" view of personality implicitly accepts that the provision of food, shelter, and clothing (again assuming the very best of circumstances) is the whole requirement of humanity. It assumes also either that psychic care was provided by slave owners (as though a slave or an owned psyche could ever be reconciled with mental health) or that psyche is not a significant part of a whole human.

Market theory indeed focuses attention away from the full range of human potential in its pursuit of a divinely willed, invisibly handed economic actor. Master—slave relations, however, focused attention away from the full range of black human potential in a somewhat different way: it pursued a vision of blacks as simple-minded, strong-bodied economic actants.[5] Thus, while blacks had an indisputable generative force in the marketplace, their presence could not be called activity; they had no active role in the market. To say, therefore, that "market relations disregard the peculiarities of individuals, whereas slave relations rest on the mutual recognition of the humanity of master and slave"[6] (no matter how dialectical or abstracted a definition of humanity one adopts) is to posit an [inaccuracy]. . . . In the context of slavery this . . . mistakes whites' overzealous and oppressive obsession with projected specific peculiarities of blacks for actual holistic regard for the individual. It overlooks the fact that most definitions of humanity require something beyond mere biological sustenance, some healthy measure of autonomy beyond that of which slavery could institutionally or otherwise conceive. Furthermore, it overlooks the fact that both slave and bourgeois systems regarded certain attributes as important and disregarded certain others. . . . The experiential blinders of market actor and slave are focused in different directions, yet the partializing ideologies of each makes the act of not seeing an unconscious, alienating component of seeing. Restoring a unified social vision will, I think, require broader and more scattered resolutions than the simple symmetry of ideological bipolarity.

Thus, it is important to undo whatever words obscure the fact that slave law was at least as fragmenting and fragmented as the bourgeois worldview—in a way that has persisted to this day, cutting across all ideological boundaries. As "pure will" signifies the whole bourgeois personality in the bourgeois worldview, so wisdom, control, and aesthetic beauty signify the whole white personality in slave law. The former and the latter, the slavemaster and the burgermeister, are not so very different when expressed in those terms. The reconciling difference is that in slave law the emphasis is really on the inverse rationale: that irrationality, lack of control, and ugliness signify the whole slave personality. "Total" interdependence is at best a polite way of rationalizing such personality splintering. . . . I would just call it schizophrenic, with all the baggage that that connotes. That is what sounds right to me. Truly total relationships (as opposed to totalitarianism) call up images of whole people dependent on whole people; an interdependence that is both providing and laissez-faire at the same time. Neither the historical inheritance of slave law nor so-called bourgeois law meets that definition.

None of this, perhaps, is particularly new. Nevertheless, as precedent to anything I do as a lawyer, the greatest challenge is to allow the full truth of partializing social constructions to be felt for their overwhelming reality—reality that otherwise I might rationally try to avoid facing. In my search for roots, I must assume, not just as history but as an ongoing psychological force, that, in the eyes of white culture, irrationality, lack of control, and ugliness signify not just the whole slave personality, not just the whole black personality, but me. . . .

On Ardor

The Child

One Saturday afternoon not long ago, I sat among a litter of family photographs telling a South African friend about Marjorie, my godmother and my mother's cousin. She was given away by her light-skinned mother when she was only six. She was given to my grandmother and my great-aunts to be raised among her darker-skinned cousins, for Marjorie was very dark indeed. Her mother left the family to "pass," to marry a white man—Uncle Frederick, we called him with trepidatious presumption yet without his ever knowing of our existence—an heir to a meat-packing fortune. When Uncle Frederick died thirty years later and the fortune was lost, Marjorie's mother rejoined the race, as the royalty of resentful fascination—Lady Bountiful, my sister called her—to regale us with tales of gracious upper-class living.

My friend said that my story reminded him of a case in which a swarthy, crisp-haired child was born, in Durban, to white parents. The Afrikaner government quickly intervened, removed the child from its birth home, and placed it to be raised with a "more suitable," browner family.

When my friend and I had shared these stories, we grew embarrassed somehow, and our conversation trickled away into a discussion of laissez-faire economics and governmental interventionism. Our words became a clear line, a railroad upon which all other ideas and events were tied down and sacrificed.

The Market

As a teacher of commercial transactions, one of the things that has always impressed me most about the law of contract is a certain deadening power it exercises by reducing the parties to the passive. It constrains the lively involvement of its signatories by positioning enforcement in such a way that parties find themselves in a passive relationship to a document: it is the contract that governs, that "does" everything, that absorbs all responsibility and deflects all other recourse.

Contract law reduces life to fairy tale. The four corners of the agreement become parent. Performance is the equivalent of obedience to the parent. Obedience is dutifully passive. Passivity is valued as good contract-socialized behavior; activity is caged in retrospective hypotheses about states of mind at the magic moment of contracting. Individuals are judged by the contract unfolding rather than by the actors acting autonomously. Nonperformance is disobedience; disobedience is active; activity becomes evil in contrast to the childlike passivity of contract conformity.

One of the most powerful examples of all this is the case of Mary Beth Whitehead, mother of Sara—of so-called Baby M. Ms. Whitehead became a vividly original actor *after* the creation of her contract with William Stern; unfortunately for her, there can be no greater civil sin. It was in this upside-down context, in the picaresque unboundedness of breachor, that her energetic grief became hysteria and her passionate creativity was funneled, whorled, and reconstructed as highly impermissible. Mary Beth Whitehead thus emerged as the evil stepsister who deserved nothing.

Some time ago, Charles Reich visited a class of mine.[7] He discussed with my students a proposal for a new form of bargain by which emotional "items"—such as praise, flattery, acting happy or sad—might be contracted for explicitly. One student, not alone in her sentiment, said, "Oh, but then you'll just feel obligated." Only the week before, however (when we were discussing the contract which posited that Ms. Whitehead "will not form or attempt to form a parent–child relationship with any child or children"), this same student had insisted that Ms. Whitehead must give up her child, because she had *said* she would: "She was obligated!" I was confounded by the degree to which what the student took to be self-evident, inalienable gut reactions could be governed by illusions of passive conventionality and form.

It was that incident, moreover, that gave me insight into how Judge Harvey Sorkow, of New Jersey Superior Court, could conclude that the contract that purported to terminate Ms. Whitehead's parental rights was "not illusory."[8]

(As background, I should say that I think that, within the framework of contract law itself, the agreement between Ms. Whitehead and Mr. Stern was clearly illusory.[9] On the one hand, Judge Sorkow's opinion said that Ms. Whitehead was seeking to avoid her *obligations*. In other words, giving up her child became an actual obligation. On the other hand, according to the logic of the judge, this was a service contract, not really a sale of a child; therefore delivering the child to the Sterns was an "obligation" for which there was no consideration, for which Mr. Stern was not paying her.)

Judge Sorkow's finding the contract "not illusory" is suggestive not just of the doctrine by that name, but of illusion in general, and delusion, and the righteousness with which social constructions are conceived, acted on, and delivered up into the realm of the real as "right," while all else is devoured from memory as "wrong." From this perspective, the rhetorical tricks by which Sara Whitehead became Melissa Stern seem very like the heavy-worded legalities by which my great-great-grandmother was pacified and parted from her child. In both situations, the real mother had no say, no power; her powerlessness was imposed by state law that made her and her child helpless in relation to the father. My great-great-grandmother's powerlessness came about as the result of a contract to which she was not a party; Mary Beth Whitehead's powerlessness came about as a result of a contract that she signed at a discrete point of time—yet which, over time, enslaved her. The contract-reality in both instances was no less than magic: it was illusion transformed into not-illusion. Furthermore, it masterfully disguised the brutality of enforced arrangements in which these women's autonomy, of flesh and their blood, were locked away in word vaults, without room to reconsider—*ever*.

In the months since Judge Sorkow's opinion, I have reflected on the similarities of fortune between my own social positioning and that of Sara Melissa Stern Whitehead. I have come to realize that an important part of the complex magic that Judge Sorkow wrote into his opinion was a supposition that it is "natural" for people to want children "like" themselves. What this reasoning raised for me was an issue of what, exactly, constituted this "likeness"? (What would have happened, for example, if Ms. Whitehead had turned out to have been the "passed" descendant of my "failed" godmother Marjorie's mother? What if the child she bore had turned out to be recessively and visibly black? Would the sperm of Mr. Stern have been so powerful as to make this child "his" with the exclusivity that Judge Sorkow originally assigned?) What constitutes, moreover, the collective understanding of "un-likeness"?

These questions turn, perhaps, on not-so-subtle images of which mothers should be bearing which children. Is there not something unseemly, in our society, about the spectacle of a white woman mothering a black child? A white woman giving totally to a black child; a black child totally and demandingly dependent for everything, for sustenance itself, from a white woman. The image of a white woman suckling a black child; the image of a black child sucking for its life from the bosom of a white woman. The utter interdependence of such an image; the selflessness, the merging it implies; the giving up of boundary; the encompassing of other within self; the unbounded generosity, the interconnectedness of such an image. Such a picture says that there is no difference; it places the hope of continuous generation, of immortality of the white self in a little black face.

When Judge Sorkow declared that it was only to be expected that parents would want to breed children "like" themselves, he simultaneously created a legal right to the same. With the creation of such a "right," he encased the children conforming to "likeliness" in protective custody, far from whole ranges of taboo. Taboo about touch and smell and intimacy and boundary. Taboo about ardor, possession, license, equivocation, equanimity, indifference, intolerance, rancor, dispossession, innocence, exile, and candor. . . . Taboos that amount to death. Death and sacredness, the valuing of body, of self, of other, of remains. The handling lovingly in life, as in life; the question of the intimacy versus the dispassion of death.

In effect, these taboos describe boundaries of valuation. Whether something is inside or outside the marketplace of rights has always been a way of valuing it.

When a valued object is located outside the market, it is generally understood to be too "priceless" to be accommodated by ordinary exchange relationships; when, in contrast, the prize is located within the marketplace, all objects outside become "valueless." Traditionally, the Mona Lisa and human life have been the sorts of subjects removed from the fungibility of commodification, as "priceless." Thus when black people were bought and sold as slaves, they were placed beyond the bounds of humanity. And thus, in the twistedness of our brave new world, when blacks have been thrust out of the market and it is white children who are bought and sold, black babies have become "worthless" currency to adoption agents— "surplus" in the salvage heaps of Harlem hospitals. . . .

Notes

1. Madrigal v. Quilligan, U.S. Court of Appeals, 9th Circuit, Docket no. 78-3187, October 1979.

2. See generally S. Elkins, Slavery (Grosset & Dunlap, 1963); K. Stampp, The Peculiar Institution (Vintage, 1956); W. Jordan, White over Black (Penguin Books, 1968).

3. M. Tushnet, The American Law of Slavery 6 (Princeton University Press, 1981) . . . . [M]y intention [is not] to impugn the body of his research, most of which I greatly admire. The choice of this passage for analysis has more to do with . . . the fact that he is one of the few legal writers to attempt, in the context of slavery, a juxtaposition of political theory with psychoanalytic theories of personality; and the fact that he is perceived to be of the political left, which simplifies my analysis in terms of its presumption of sympathy, i.e., that the constructions of thought revealed are socially derived and unconscious rather than idiosyncratic and intentional.

4. In another passage, Tushnet observes: "The court thus demonstrated its appreciation of the ties of sentiment that slavery could generate between master and slave and simultaneously denied that those ties were relevant in the law." *Id.* at 67. What is noteworthy about the reference to "sentiment" is that it assumes that the fact that emotions could grow up between slave and master is itself worth remarking: slightly surprising, slightly commendable for the court to note (i.e., in its "appreciation")—although "simultaneously" with, and presumably in contradistinction to, the court's inability to take official cognizance of the fact. Yet, if one really looks at the ties that bound master and slave, one has to flesh out the description of master–slave with the ties of father–son, father–daughter, half–sister, uncle, aunt, cousin, and a variety of de facto foster relationships. And if one starts to see those ties as more often than not intimate family ties, then the terminology "appreciation of . . . sentiment . . . between master and slave" becomes a horrifying mockery of any true sense of family sentiment, which is utterly, utterly lacking. The court's "appreciation," from this enhanced perspective, sounds blindly cruel, sarcastic at best. And to observe that courts suffused in such "appreciation" could simultaneously deny its legal relevance seems not only a truism; it misses the point entirely.

5. "Actants have a kind of phonemic, rather than a phonetic role: they operate on the level of function, rather than content. That is, an actant may embody itself in a particular character (termed an acteur) or it may reside in the function of more than one character in respect of their common role in the story's underlying "oppositional" structure. In short, the deep structure of the narrative generates and defines its actants at a level beyond that of the story's surface content." T. Hawkes, Structuralism and Semiotics 89 (University of California Press, 1977).

6. Tushnet, American Law of Slavery, *supra* note 3 at 69.

7. Charles Reich is author of *The Greening of America* (Random House, 1970) and professor of law at the University of San Francisco Law School.

8. See generally In the Matter of Baby "M," A Pseudonym for an Actual Person, 217 N.J. Super. 313, 525 A.2d 1128 (Ch. Div. 1987), *aff'd in part, rev'd in part, remanded*, 109 N.J. 396, 537 A.2d 1227 (1988). The trial court decision was appealed, and on February 3, 1988, the New Jersey Supreme Court ruled that surrogate contracts were illegal and against public policy. In addition to the contract issue, however, the appellate court decided the custody issue in favor of the Sterns but granted visitation rights to Mary Beth Whitehead.

9. "An illusory promise is an expression cloaked in promissory terms, but which, upon closer examination, reveals that the promisor has committed himself not at all." J. Calamari & J. Perillo, Contracts, 3rd ed. 288 (West, 1987).

TABLE OF CASES

INDEX

❖ CONTRIBUTORS

MARIE ASHE is Roscoe P. Posten Professor of Law, West Virginia University College of Law.

KATHARINE T. BARTLETT is Professor of Law, Duke University School of Law.

MARY E. BECKER is Professor of Law, University of Chicago Law School.

LESLIE BENDER is Professor of Law, Syracuse University College of Law.

PATRICIA A. CAIN is Professor of Law, University of Iowa College of Law.

RUTH COLKER is Professor of Law, Tulane University School of Law.

PATRICIA N. COONEY is an attorney in private practice in Berkeley, California.

KIMBERLE CRENSHAW is Acting Professor, University of California, Los Angeles, School of Law.

CLARE DALTON is Professor of Law, Northeastern University School of Law.

LUCINDA M. FINLEY is Professor of Law, State University of New York at Buffalo School of Law.

ANGELA P. HARRIS is Acting Professor, Boalt Hall School of Law, University of California, Berkeley.

HERMA HILL KAY is Jennings Professor of Law and Dean, Boalt Hall School of Law, University of California, Berkeley.

MARLEE KLINE is Assistant Professor, University of British Columbia, Faculty of Law.

LINDA J. KRIEGER is Lecturer, Stanford Law School.

CHRISTINE A. LITTLETON is Professor of Law, University of California, Los Angeles, School of Law.

CATHARINE A. MACKINNON is Professor of Law, University of Michigan Law School.

DIANA MAJURY is Assistant Professor, Faculty of Law, University of Western Ontario, London, Ontario.

MARI J. MATSUDA is Associate Professor of Law, University of Hawaii, William S. Richardson School of Law.

MARTHA MINOW is Professor of Law, Harvard University Law School.

MARY JANE MOSSMAN is Professor of Law, Osgoode Hall Law School, York University, Canada.

FRANCES OLSEN is Professor of Law, University of California, Los Angeles, School of Law.

DIANE POLAN is a practicing attorney with the firm of Williams and Wise in New Haven, Connecticut.

HON. RICHARD A. POSNER is Judge, United States Court of Appeals for the Seventh Circuit, and Senior Lecturer, University of Chicago Law School.

JANET RIFKIN is Professor of Legal Studies, University of Massachusetts at Amherst.

ANN C. SCALES is Professor of Law, University of New Mexico School of Law.

ELIZABETH M. SCHNEIDER is Professor of Law, Brooklyn Law School.

MARGOT STUBBS is Professor of Law, University of Wollongong, New South Wales, Australia.

NADINE TAUB is Professor and S. I. Newhouse Scholar, Rutgers, The State University of New Jersey, S. I. Newhouse Center for Law and Justice, Newark.

ROBIN WEST is Professor of Law, University of Maryland School of Law.

PATRICIA J. WILLIAMS is Professor of Law, University of Wisconsin Law School.

WENDY W. WILLIAMS is Professor of Law and Associate Dean, Georgetown University Law Center.

HEATHER RUTH WISHIK is Visiting Associate Professor, Dartmouth College Department of Government.